FOURTH EDITION

The Mind and Heart
of the Negotiator

Leigh L. Thompson

Kellogg School of Management
Northwestern University

Prentice Hall
Upper Saddle River, New Jersey 07458

Library of Congress Cataloging-in-Publication Data

Thompson, Leigh L.
　The mind and heart of the negotiator / Leigh L. Thompson. — 4th ed.
　　p. cm.
　Includes index.
　ISBN-13: 978-0-13-174227-7
　ISBN-10: 0-13-174227-2
　1. Negotiation in business.　2. Negotiation.　I. Title.
　HD58.6.T478 2009
　658.4'052—dc22

　　　　　　　　　　　　　　　　　2008032483

Acquisitions Editor: Jennifer M. Collins
Editorial Director: Sally Yagan
Product Development Manager: Ashley Santora
Editorial Assistant: Elizabeth Davis
Editorial Project Manager: Claudia Fernandes
Director of Marketing: Patrice Lumumba Jones
Marketing Manager: Nikki Jones
Marketing Assistant: Ian Gold
Permissions Project Manager: Charles Morris
Associate Managing Editor: Suzanne DeWorken
Production Project Manager: Ann Pulido
Operations Specialist: Carol O'Rourke
Creative Director: Jayne Conte
Cover Designer: Alissa Treible
Cover Illustration/Photo: Robert Weeks
Composition: Aptara®, Inc.
Full-Service Project Management: Ravi Bhatt/Aptara®, Inc.
Printer/Binder: STP/RRD/Harrisonburg
Typeface: 10/12 Times Ten Roman

Credits and acknowledgments borrowed from other sources and reproduced, with permission, in this textbook appear on appropriate page within text.

Pearson Education Ltd., London
Pearson Education Singapore, Pte. Ltd
Pearson Education, Canada, Inc.
Pearson Education—Japan
Pearson Education Australia PTY, Limited

Pearson Education North Asia, Ltd., Hong Kong
Pearson Educación de Mexico, S.A. de C.V.
Pearson Education Malaysia, Pte. Ltd
Pearson Education Upper Saddle River, New Jersey

Prentice Hall
is an imprint of

www.pearsonhighered.com

10 9 8 7 6 5 4 3 2 1
ISBN-13: 978-0-13-174227-7
ISBN-10:　0-13-174227-2

To the loves of my life:
Bob, Sam, Ray, and Anna

Brief Contents

Contents

Note: Every effort has been made to provide accurate and current Internet information in this book. However, the Internet and information posted on it are constantly changing, so it is inevitable that some of the Internet addresses listed in this textbook will change.

Preface

This book is dedicated to negotiators who want to improve their ability to negotiate—whether in multimillion-dollar business deals or personal interactions. It is possible for most people to dramatically improve their ability to negotiate. You can improve your monetary returns and feel better about yourself and the people with whom you deal. This book contains an integration of theory, scientific research, and practical examples. Moreover, the practical examples—selected from hundreds of real-world negotiations involving people from several companies—illustrate effective, as well as ineffective, negotiation skills.

Here is what you can expect when you read this book:

- *Illustrative case studies and real-life negotiations.* I include multiple examples and actual cases of negotiating in managerial and executive contexts. Each chapter opens with a case study or actual business situation (from business, government, community, and personal life). Furthermore, many of the points in the chapters are supplemented with illustrations and examples drawn from actual negotiations, both contemporary and historical. I do not use these examples to *prove* a theory; rather, I use them to *illustrate* how many of the concepts in the book are borne out in real-world situations.
- *Skills-based approach.* I provide practical take-away points for the manager and the executive. A good example is Chapter 4 on integrative negotiation. A series of hands-on principles that have been proven to increase the value of negotiated deals are provided. Moreover, several students and clients have written, indicating how they utilized the tools in their actual business negotiations. Those examples are also included.
- *Self-insight.* I include several ways that negotiators can test their own intuition and approach. For example, Chapter 5, gives negotiators an opportunity to assess their "instinctive" bargaining style and provides suggestions for how to further develop their bargaining repertoire. Moreover, Chapter 10 provides a deep look at cultural differences in negotiation so that the negotiator can better understand his or her own cultural style and that of others.
- *Sophisticated bargaining skills.* The second and third sections of the book deal with complex, yet commonly occurring negotiating situations, such as negotiating with agents, mediation and arbitration, negotiating via e-mail and conference calls, negotiating with competitor companies, and, of course, negotiating cross-culturally.

I took the task of revising *The Mind and Heart of the Negotiator* very seriously. Every chapter has a new opening section that illustrates a real-world negotiation and no fewer than 90 examples from the business world have been added since the last edition. Also, I cited the groundbreaking results of more than a hundred new scientific articles on negotiation. I benefit greatly from the advice, comments, and critiques given to me by my students and colleagues, and I hope their advice keeps coming so that I am able to improve upon the book even further.

The research and ideas in this book come from an invaluable set of scholars in the fields of social psychology, organizational behavior, sociology, negotiation, and cognitive psychology. My research, thinking, and writing have been inspired in important ways by the following people: Wendi Adair, Cameron Anderson, Linda Babcock, Chris Bauman, Max

Bazerman, Kristin Behfar, Terry Boles, Jeanne Brett, Susan Brodt, Karen Cates, Hoon-Seok Choi, Susan Crotty, Jeanne Egmon, Gary Fine, Craig Fox, Adam Galinsky, Wendi Gardner, Dedre Gentner, Robert Gibbons, Kevin Gibson, James Gillespie, Rich Gonzalez, Deborah Gruenfeld, Reid Hastie, Andy Hoffman, Elizabeth Howard, Peter Kim, Shirli Kopelman, Rod Kramer, Laura Kray, Terri Kurtzburg, Geoffrey Leonardelli, John Levine, Allan Lind, George Loewenstein, Jeff Loewenstein, Deepak Malhotra, Beta Mannix, Kathleen McGinn, Vicki Medvec, Tanya Menon, Dave Messick, Terry Mitchell, Don Moore, Michael Morris, Keith Murnighan, Janice Nadler, Maggie Neale, Kathy Phillips, Robin Pinkley, Ashleigh Rosette, Nancy Rothbard, Marwan Sinaceur, Harris Sondak, Roderick Swaab, Tom Tyler, Leaf Van Boven, Kimberly Wade-Benzoni, Laurie Weingart, and Judith White. Throughout the text of *The Mind and Heart of the Negotiator*, I use the pronoun "we" because so much of my thinking has been influenced and shaped by this set of eminent scholars.

The revision of this book would not have been possible without the dedication, organization, and editorial skills of Silva Kurtisa, Melissa Martin, and Kristin Dolick who created the layout, organized hundreds of drafts, mastered the figures, and researched many case studies for this book.

In this book, I talk about the "power of the situation" and how strongly the environment shapes our behavior. The Kellogg School of Management is one of the most supportive, dynamic environments I have ever had the pleasure to be a part of. In particular, Dean Dipak Jain and the Dean of Research, Kathleen Hagerty, have strongly supported research as well as teaching, and intellectual leadership as well as pedagogical leadership. I am particularly indebted to my wonderful visionary colleague, Jeanne Brett, who created the Dispute Resolution Research Center (DRRC) at Kellogg in 1986, and to the Hewlett Foundation for their generous support of the DRRC.

This book is very much a team effort of the people I have mentioned here, whose talents are diverse, broad, and extraordinarily impressive. I am deeply indebted to my colleagues and my students, and I feel grateful that they have touched my life and this book.

Overview

This book is divided into three major sections. The first section deals with the essentials of negotiation—the key principles and groundwork for effective negotiation. Chapter 2 leads the manager through effective preparation strategies for negotiation. Chapter 3 discusses distributive negotiation skills, or how to optimally allocate resources in ways that are favorable to one's self—a process called "slicing the pie." Chapter 4 is probably the most important chapter in the book; it focuses on "win-win" negotiation or, more formally, integrative negotiation. This creative part of negotiation involves expanding the pie of resources in ways that provide more gains to go around.

The second section of the book deals with advanced and expert negotiation skills. Chapter 5 focuses on assessing and developing your negotiation style. This chapter invites readers to honestly appraise their own negotiation style in terms of three dimensions: motivation, approach, and emotion. The negotiator can accurately assess his or her own style and its limitations and learn to assess the styles adopted by other negotiators. Chapter 6 focuses on establishing trust and building a relationship. This chapter examines business and personal relationships and how trust is developed, broken, and repaired. Chapter 7 discusses power, persuasion, and influence tactics. This chapter looks at the topic of persuasion and influence as it occurs across the bargaining table and also deals with the important issue of ethics in negotiation. In Chapter 8, the focus is on problem solving and creativity. This chapter provides strategies for learning how to think out of the box and provides techniques for using creativity and imagination in negotiation.

The third section deals with special scenarios in negotiation. Chapter 9 examines the complexities of negotiating with multiple parties, such as conflicting incentives, coalitions, voting rules, and how to leverage one's own bargaining position when negotiating with multiple parties. Chapter 10 focuses on cross-cultural negotiation, which addresses the key cultural values and negotiation norms across a variety of nationalities, along with some advice for cross-cultural negotiations. Chapter 11 deals with dilemmas, or situations in which negotiators make choices in a mixed-motive context, where cooperation involves building trust with the other party and competition involves an attempt to increase one's own share of resources. This chapter examines the nature of social dilemmas and how to negotiate successfully within various types of dilemmas. Chapter 12 focuses on information technology and its impact on negotiation and uses a place-time model of social interaction to examine the challenges and opportunities of negotiation as it occurs in the technological age.

Four appendices provide a variety of additional material: Appendix 1 invites readers to examine the rationality of their negotiation beliefs and preferences; Appendix 2 provides a short course on lie detection and nonverbal communication; Appendix 3 reviews the essentials of third-party intervention; and Appendix 4 provides tips and a worksheet for negotiating a job offer.

Part I: Essentials of Negotiation

CHAPTER 1

Negotiation: The Mind and The Heart

In early 2008, Microsoft Corporation offered $31 a share to buy Yahoo Inc., beginning what would become a long and bitter battle at the negotiation table. Microsoft's goal: to become a formidable competitor in the world of Internet search-related advertising against Google, the market leader. Yahoo quickly turned down Microsoft's first offer, saying the bid was much too low. Disagreements over price continued, and after months of negotiations, Microsoft withdrew its offer from the table, saying it had "moved on." The inability to reach an agreement caused concern and anger among Yahoo shareholders and led to an aggressive move by billionaire investor Carl Icahn: he bought a stake in Yahoo, in hopes of naming an entirely new Board of Directors that would be willing to accept Microsoft's offer. According to Icahn, Yahoo's directors "acted irrationally and lost the faith of shareholders." Seeking an alternative to the Microsoft buyout, Yahoo began talks with Google to discuss the possibility of delivering Google ads next to Yahoo search results. Microsoft took the threat seriously and just weeks after withdrawing its bid, was in talks with Yahoo yet again. This time the talks did not revolve around a full takeover, but rather around the possibility of a collaboration between the two companies on Internet advertising. Microsoft hoped a deal would hinder Yahoo's potential deal with Google.[1] However, weeks later Yahoo announced that its negotiations with Microsoft were in fact over and that the company had struck the deal with Google. The new deal failed to sit well with much of Yahoo's top management, and within a week, five top executives as well as several senior engineers announced their intention to leave the company. Microsoft, who had publicly admitted that much of the reason they sought to acquire Yahoo was for its group of talented engineers, saw an opportunity. The company took out a full-page ad in the San Jose Mercury News, whose distribution area includes the Yahoo headquarters, to recruit Internet search specialists.[2]

---

[1]Sorkin, A. R. & Lohr, S. (2008, May 19). Pursuing Yahoo again, Microsoft shows need for a franchise. *New York Times*, p. A1.
[2]Helft, M. (2008, June 20). At Yahoo, the exodus continues. *New York Times*, p. A1.

Negotiations like the one between Microsoft and Yahoo often involve a complex mix of strategy, signaling, and personality. Whereas most of us are not negotiating giant corporate deals, one thing that business scholars and businesspeople are in complete agreement on is that everyone negotiates nearly every day. *Getting to Yes* begins by stating, "Like it or not, you are a negotiator. . . . Everyone negotiates something every day" (p. xvii).[3] Similarly, Lax and Sebenius, in *The Manager as Negotiator,* state that "Negotiating is a way of life for managers . . . when managers deal with their superiors, boards of directors, even legislators" (p. 1).[4] G. Richard Shell, who wrote *Bargaining for Advantage,* asserts, "All of us negotiate many times a day" (p. 6).[5] Herb Cohen, author of *You Can Negotiate Anything,* dramatically suggests that "your world is a giant negotiation table" (p. 15).[6] Perhaps these statements indicate why a recent business article on negotiation warned, "However much you think negotiation is part of your life, you're underestimating" (p. 76).[7] *Negotiation is your key communication and influence tool* inside and outside the company. Anytime you cannot achieve your objectives (whether it be a company merger or a dinner date) without the cooperation of others, you are negotiating. We provide dramatic (and disturbing) evidence in this chapter that most people do not live up to their negotiating potential. The good news is that you can do something about it.

The sole purpose of this book is to improve your ability to negotiate in the contexts that matter most to you. We present this information through an integration of scientific studies of negotiation and real business cases. And, in case you are wondering, it is not all common sense. Science drives the best practices covered in this book. We focus on business negotiations, and understanding business negotiations helps people to be more effective negotiators in their personal lives.[8]

In this book, we focus on three major negotiation skills: (a) creating value, (b) claiming value, and (c) building trust. By the end of this book, you will have a mind-set that will allow you to know what to do and say in virtually every negotiation situation. Moreover, the fact that you have a mind-set (also called a *mental model*)[9] will mean that you can prepare effectively for negotiations and enjoy the peace of mind that comes from having a game plan. Things may not always go according to plan, but your mental model will allow you to update effectively and most important, to learn from your experiences.

NEGOTIATION: DEFINITION AND SCOPE

Negotiation is an interpersonal decision making process necessary whenever we cannot achieve our objectives single-handedly. Negotiations include not only the one-on-one business meeting but also multiparty, multicompany, and multimillion-dollar deals. Whether simple or complex, negotiations boil down to people, communication, and influence. Even the most complex of business deals can be analyzed as a system of one-on-one relationships.

---

[3]Fisher, R., & Ury, W. (1981). *Getting to yes.* Boston: Houghton Mifflin.
[4]Lax, D. A., & Sebenius, J. K. (1986). *The manager as negotiator.* New York: Free Press.
[5]Shell, G. R. (1999). *Bargaining for advantage: Negotiation strategies for reasonable people.* New York: Viking.
[6]Cohen, H. (1980). *You can negotiate anything.* Secaucus, NJ: Lyle Stuart.
[7]Walker, R. (2003, August). Take it or leave it: The only guide to negotiating you will ever need. *Inc., 25*(8) 75–82.
[8]Gentner, D., Loewenstein, J., & Thompson, L. (2003). Learning and transfer: A general role for analogical encoding. *Journal of Educational Psychology, 95*(2), 393–408.
[9]van Boven, L., & Thompson, L. (2003). A look into the mind of the negotiator: Mental models in negotiation. *Group Processes & Intergroup Relations, 6*(4), 387–404.

People negotiate in their personal life (e.g., with their spouses, children, school-teachers, neighbors), as well as in their business life. Thus, the scope of negotiation ranges from one on one to highly complex multiparty and multinational deals. In the business world, people negotiate at multiple levels and contexts: within departmental or business units, between departments, between companies, and even across industries. For this reason, managers must understand enough about negotiations to be effective negotiating within, between, up, and across all of these organizational environments.

NEGOTIATION AS A CORE MANAGEMENT COMPETENCY

Negotiation skills are increasingly important for managers. Key reasons for the importance of negotiation skills include (a) the dynamic nature of business, (b) interdependence, (c) competition, (d) the information age, and (e) globalization.

Dynamic Nature of Business

Mobility and flexibility are the dictates of the new world of work. Most people do not stay in the same job that they take upon graduating from college or receiving their MBA degree. Members of Generation Y will change jobs, on average, every two years.[10] The dynamic, changing nature of business means that people must negotiate and renegotiate their existence in organizations throughout the duration of their careers. The advent of decentralized business structures and the absence of hierarchical decision making provide opportunities for managers, but they also pose some daunting challenges. People must continually create possibilities, integrate their interests with others, and recognize the inevitability of competition both within and between companies. Managers must be in a near-constant mode of negotiating opportunities. Negotiation comes into play when people participate in important meetings, get new assignments, head a team, participate in a reorganization process, and set priorities for their work unit. Negotiation should be second nature to the business manager, but often it is not.

Interdependence

The increasing interdependence of people within organizations, both laterally and hierarchically, implies that people need to know how to integrate their interests and work across business units and functional areas. For example, after the merger of Adobe and Macromedia, many Macromedia employees worried that their company's distinctive culture would disappear. In an attempt to instill some of that culture in the new company, several ex-Macromedia employees were rewarded with key positions. Then, suddenly the tables turned: Macromedia was taking over, and it was the Adobe employees who were nervous.[11] The increasing degree of specialization and expertise in the business world implies that people are more and more dependent on others. However, others do not always have similar incentive structures, so managers must know how to promote their own interests while simultaneously creating joint value for their organizations. This task requires negotiation.

---

[10]Trunk, P. (2007, June 30). The world of generation Y. *Los Angeles Daily News.*
[11]Lacy, S. (2006, February 13). A flashy new Adobe. *Business Week, 3971,* 52.

Competition

Business is increasingly competitive. In the first three months of 2008, 8,713 businesses filed for bankruptcy, the highest quarterly bankruptcy level since 2005.[12] Such volatility means that companies must be experts in competitive environments. Managers not only need to function as advocates for their products and services, but they also must recognize the competition that is inevitable between companies and, in some cases, between units within a given company. Understanding how to navigate this competitive environment is essential for successful negotiation.

Information Age

The information age also provides special opportunities and challenges for the manager as negotiator. The information age has created a culture of 24/7 availability. With technology that makes it possible to communicate with people anywhere in the world, managers are expected to negotiate at a moment's notice. Computer technology, for example, extends a company's obligations and capacity to add value to its customers. For example, Scott McNealy, chairman and ex-CEO of Sun Microsystems Inc., checks his email every 15 to 20 minutes, beginning at 6:00 a.m., even if it means he has to walk behind the bleachers during his son's soccer games. McNealy's father, who was a senior executive for American Motors, once said that he didn't spend more time with his kids because he was "responsible for 10,000 people at work, and that their lives would be disrupted if he didn't make the right decisions." McNealy used the same philosophy in his own work.[13]

Globalization

Most managers must effectively cross cultural boundaries to do their jobs. Setting aside obvious language and currency issues, globalization presents challenges in terms of different norms of communication. For example, the alliance between Upjohn, a U.S. pharmaceutical company, and the Swedish business Pharmacia was threatened when it became obvious that the cultures of the two companies were clashing. The Americans could not understand why the Swedes went on vacation for the whole month of August, and the Swedes could not understand why the Americans did not allow alcohol to be served at lunch. Over time, small disagreements grew into more serious ones.[14] Managers need to develop negotiation skills that can be successfully employed with people of different nationalities, backgrounds, and styles of communication. Consequently, negotiators who have developed a bargaining style that works only within a narrow subset of the business world will suffer unless they can broaden their negotiation skills to effectively work with different people across functional units, industries, and cultures.[15] It is a challenge to develop negotiation skills general enough to be used across different contexts, groups, and continents but specialized enough to provide meaningful behavioral strategies in a given situation.

---

[12]Private equity firms reinvent themselves in challenging credit environment: Inbound M&A activity recovering and getting stronger. (2008, June 23). *PR Newsire.*
[13]Anders, G. (2007, November 7). Business: For CEOs, off-duty isn't an option. *The Wall Street Journal,* p. A2.
[14]Witzel, M. (2006, November 10). The power of difference. Collaboration often entails working with companies across national and cultural borders. *Financial Times,* p.13.
[15]Bazerman, M. H., & Neale, M.A. (1992). *Negotiating rationally.* New York: Free Press.

MOST PEOPLE ARE INEFFECTIVE NEGOTIATORS

On the question of whether people are effective negotiators, managers and scholars often disagree. Many people regard themselves to be effective at negotiation. These same people believe most of their colleagues are distinctly ineffective at the negotiation table. However, our performance speaks louder than our self-proclaimed prowess. Most people often fall extremely short of their potential at the negotiation table, judging from their performance on realistic business negotiation simulations.[16] Numerous business executives describe their negotiations as win-win only to discover that they left hundreds of thousands of dollars on the table. Fewer than 4% of managers reach win-win outcomes when put to the test;[17] and the incidence of outright lose-lose outcomes is 20%.[18] Even on issues on which negotiators are in perfect agreement, they fail to realize it 50% of the time.[19] Moreover, we make the point several times throughout this book that effective negotiation is not just about money—it is equally about relationships and trust.

NEGOTIATION SANDTRAPS

In our research, we have observed and documented four major shortcomings in negotiation:

1. *Leaving money on the table*   (also known as "lose-lose" negotiation) occurs when negotiators fail to recognize and exploit win-win potential.
2. *Settling for too little*   (also known as "the winner's curse") occurs when negotiators make too-large concessions, resulting in a too-small share of the bargaining pie.
3. *Walking away from the table*   occurs when negotiators reject terms offered by the other party that are demonstrably better than any other option available to them. (Sometimes this shortcoming is traceable to hubris or pride; other times, it results from gross miscalculation.)
4. *Settling for terms that are worse than the alternative*   (also known as the "agreement bias") occurs when negotiators feel obligated to reach agreement even when the settlement terms are not as good as their other alternatives.

This book teaches you how to avoid these errors, create value in negotiation, get your share of the bargaining pie, reach agreement when it is profitable to do so, and quickly recognize when agreement is not a viable option in a negotiation.

---

[16]Neale, M. A., & Bazerman, M. H. (1991). *Cognition and rationality in negotiation.* New York: Free Press; Thompson, L., & Hrebec, D. (1996). Lose-lose agreements in interdependent decision making. *Psychological Bulletin, 120*(3), 396–409; Loewenstein, J., Thompson, L., & Gentner, D. (2003). Analogical learning in negotiation teams: Comparing cases promotes learning and transfer. *Academy of Management Learning and Education, 2*(2), 119–127.

[17]Nadler, J., Thompson, L., & van Boven, L. (2003). Learning negotiation skills: Four models of knowledge creation and transfer. *Management Science, 49*(4), 529–540.

[18]Thompson & Hrebec, "Lose-lose agreements."

[19]Ibid.

WHY PEOPLE ARE INEFFECTIVE NEGOTIATORS

The dramatic instances of lose-lose outcomes, the winner's curse, walking away from the table, and the agreement bias raise the question of why people are not more effective at the bargaining table. Because negotiation is so important for personal and business success, it is rather surprising that most people do not negotiate very well. Stated starkly: It just does not make sense that people would be so poor at something that is so important for their personal and business life. The reason is not due to a lack of motivation or intelligence on the part of negotiators. The problem is rooted in four fundamental problems: egocentrism, confirmatory information processing, satisficing, and self-reinforcing incompetence.

Egocentrism

Egocentrism is the tendency for people to view their experiences in a way that is flattering or fulfilling for themselves. Two-thirds of MBA students rank their decision making abilities as above average.[20] Egocentrism and the suspension of reality certainly influenced executives at Citigroup and J.P. Morgan Chase & Co. to manipulate cash flows at Enron.[21] The belief that they could mislead Enron shareholders and minimize perceived risk of being accused of deception was likely fueled by unwarranted beliefs about their role. Egocentrism also played a role in the American Airlines negotiations in April 2003 in which bankruptcy was narrowly avoided. American said it had to have $1.8 billion in annual cuts from all employee groups as part of a $4 billion effort to restructure the company. The airline was losing $5 million a day. The three major groups involved—pilots union, professional flight attendants, and the ground workers of the transport workers union—all believed they deserved more than that to which they believed others were entitled.[22]

Confirmation Bias

Confirmation bias is the tendency of people to see what they want to see when appraising their own performance. The confirmation bias leads individuals to selectively seek information that confirms what they believe is true. Whereas the confirmation bias may seem perfectly harmless, it results in a myopic view of reality and can hinder learning.

Satisficing

A third reason why people often fall short in negotiation is the human tendency to satisfice.[23] According to Nobel Laureate Herb Simon, **satisficing** is the opposite of **optimizing**. In a negotiation situation, it is important to optimize one's strategies by setting high aspirations and attempting to achieve as much as possible; in contrast,

---

[20]Diekmann, K., & Galinsky, A. (2006). Overconfident, underprepared: Why you may not be ready to negotiate. *Negotiation, 7,* 6–9.
[21]Thornton, E., & France, M. (2003, August 11). For Enron's bankers, a "get out of jail free" card. *Business Week, 3845,* 29.
[22]Torbenson, E. (2003, April 3). American pilots agree to plan to avoid bankruptcy. *Dallas Morning News.*
[23]Simon, H. (1955). A behavioral model of rational choice. *Quarterly Journal of Economics, 69,* 99–118.

when people satisfice, they settle for something less than they could otherwise have. Over the long run, satisficing (or the acceptance of mediocrity) can be detrimental to both individuals and companies, especially when a variety of effective negotiation strategies and skills can be cheaply employed to dramatically increase profit. (We discuss these strategies in detail in the next three chapters.)

Self-Reinforcing Incompetence

To achieve and maintain effectiveness in the business world, people must have insight into their limitations. The same is true for negotiation. However, most people are "blissfully unaware of their own incompetence."[24] Moreover, it creates a cycle in which the lack of skill deprives them not only of the ability to produce correct responses but also of the expertise necessary to surmise that they are not producing them. As a case in point, Dunning and colleagues examined the question of whether students taking a test had insight into their performance. The students were grouped into quartiles based on their performance.[25] The lowest-performing quartile greatly overestimated their performance on the test. Even though they were actually in the 12th percentile, they estimated themselves to be in the 60th percentile. This example is not an isolated case, according to Dunning. People overestimate their percentile ranking relative to others by as much as 40 to 50 points. A study of CEOs' merger and acquisition decisions revealed that CEOs develop overconfidence through a self-attribution bias when making deals. CEOs overly attribute their influence when deals are successful. This leads CEOs to make more deals that are not successful.[26] A better business plan would involve judging each deal on its own merits, rather than simply using the past to justify the present decision. Moreover, the problem cannot be attributed to a lack of incentives. The overestimation pattern even appears after people are promised significant financial rewards for accurate assessments of their performance.[27]

Related to the principle of self-reinforcing incompetence is the fact that people are reluctant to change their behavior and experiment with new courses of action because of the risks associated with experimentation. In short, the fear of losing keeps people from experimenting with change. Negotiators instead rationalize their behavior in a self-perpetuating fashion. The fear of making mistakes may result in a manager's inability to improve his or her negotiation skills. In this book, we remove the risk of experimentation by providing several exercises and clear demonstrations of how changing one's behavior can lead to better results in negotiation. We invite managers to be active learners in terms of understanding their own values when it comes to negotiation.

[24]Dunning, D., Johnson, K., Ehrlinger, J., & Kruger, J. (2003). Why people fail to recognize their own incompetence. *Current Directions in Psychological Science, 12*(3), 83–87.
[25]Kruger, J., & Dunning, D. (1999). Unskilled and unaware of it: How difficulties in recognizing one's own incompetence lead to inflated self-assessments. *Journal of Personality and Social Psychology, 77,* 1121–1134.
[26]Billet, M. T., & Qian, Y. (2008). Are overconfident CEOs born or made? Evidence of self-attribution bias from frequent acquirers. *Management of Science, 54*(6), 1037–1051.
[27]Ehrlinger, J., Johnson, K., Banner, M., Dunning, D., & Kruger, D. (2008). Why the unskilled are unaware: Further explorations of (absent) self-insight among the incompetent. *Organizational Behavior and Human Decision Processes, 106*(1), 92–121.

DEBUNKING NEGOTIATION MYTHS

When we delve into managers' theories and beliefs about negotiation, we are often startled to find that they operate with faulty beliefs. Before we start on our journey toward developing a more effective negotiation strategy, we need to dispel several faulty assumptions and myths about negotiation. These myths hamper people's ability to learn effective negotiation skills and, in some cases, reinforce poor negotiation skills. In this section, we expose six of the most prevalent myths about negotiation behavior.

Myth 1: Negotiations Are Fixed-Sum

Probably the most common myth is that most negotiations are fixed-sum, or fixed-pie, in nature, such that whatever is good for one person must ipso facto be bad for the other party. The truth is that most negotiations are not purely fixed-sum; in fact, most negotiations are variable-sum in nature, meaning that if parties work together, they can create more joint value than if they are purely combative. However, effective negotiators also realize that they cannot be purely trusting because any value that is created must ultimately be claimed by someone at the table. Our approach to negotiation is based on Walton and McKersie's conceptualization that negotiation is a mixed-motive enterprise, such that parties have incentives to cooperate as well as compete.[28]

Myth 2: You Need to Be Either Tough or Soft

The fixed-sum myth gives rise to a myopic view of the strategic choices that negotiators have. Most negotiators believe they must choose between either behaving in a tough (and sometimes punitive fashion) or being "reasonable" to the point of soft and concessionary. We disagree. The truly effective negotiator is neither tough as nails nor soft as pudding but, rather, principled.[29] Effective negotiators follow an "enlightened" view of negotiation and correctly recognize that to achieve their own outcomes they must work effectively with the other party (and hence, cooperate) but must also leverage their own power and strengths.

Myth 3: Good Negotiators Are Born

A pervasive belief is that effective negotiation skills are something that people are born with, not something that can be readily learned. This notion is false because most excellent negotiators are self-made. In fact, naturally gifted negotiators are rare. We tend to hear their stories, but we must remember that their stories are *selective,* meaning that it is always possible for someone to have a lucky day or a fortunate experience. This myth is often perpetuated by the tendency of people to judge negotiation skills by their car-dealership experiences. Purchasing a car is certainly an important and common type of negotiation, but it is not the best context by which to judge your negotiation skills. The most important negotiations are those that we engage in every day with our colleagues, supervisors, coworkers, and business associates. These relationships provide a much better index of one's effectiveness in negotiation. In short, effective negotiation requires practice and feedback. The problem is that most of us do not get

---

[28]Walton, R. E., & McKersie, R. B. (1965). *A behavioral theory of labor relations.* New York: McGraw-Hill.
[29]Bazerman & Neale, *Negotiating rationally;* Fisher & Ury, *Getting to yes.*

an opportunity to develop effective negotiation skills in a disciplined fashion; rather, most of us learn by doing. Experience is helpful but not sufficient.

Myth 4: Experience Is a Great Teacher

It is only partly true that experience can improve negotiation skills; in fact, experience in the absence of feedback is largely ineffective in improving negotiation skills.[30] Natural experience as an effective teacher has three strikes against it. First, in the absence of feedback, it is nearly impossible to improve performance. For example, can you imagine trying to learn mathematics without ever doing homework or taking tests? Without diagnostic feedback, it is very difficult to learn from experience.

The second problem is that our memories tend to be selective, meaning that people are more likely to remember their successes and forget their failures or shortcomings. This tendency is, of course, comforting to our ego, but it does not improve our ability to negotiate.

In addition, experience improves our confidence, but not necessarily our accuracy. People with more experience grow more confident, but the accuracy of their judgment and the effectiveness of their behavior do not increase in a commensurate fashion. Overconfidence can be dangerous because it may lead people to take unwise risks.

Myth 5: Good Negotiators Take Risks

A pervasive myth is that effective negotiation necessitates taking risks and gambles. In negotiation, this approach may mean saying things like "This is my final offer" or "Take it or leave it" or using threats and bluffs. This is what we call a "tough" style of negotiation. Tough negotiators are rarely effective; however, we tend to be impressed by the tough negotiator. In this book, we teach negotiators how to evaluate risk, how to determine the appropriate time to make a final offer, and, more important, how to make excellent decisions in the face of the uncertainty of negotiation.

Myth 6: Good Negotiators Rely on Intuition

An interesting exercise is to ask managers and anyone else who negotiates to describe their approach to negotiating. Many seasoned negotiators believe that their negotiation style involves a lot of "gut feeling," or intuition. We believe that intuition does not serve people well. Effective negotiation involves deliberate thought and preparation and is quite systematic. The goal of this book is to help managers effectively prepare for negotiation, become more self-aware of their own strengths and shortcomings, and develop strategies that are **proactive** (i.e., they anticipate the reactions of their opponent) rather than **reactive** (i.e., they are dependent upon the actions and reactions of their opponent). Thus, excellent negotiators do not rely on intuition; rather, they are deliberate planners. As a general rule, don't rely on your intuition unless you are an expert.

---

[30]Loewenstein, Thompson, & Gentner, "Analogical learning in negotiation"; Nadler, Thompson, & van Boven, "Learning negotiation skills"; Thompson, L., & DeHarpport, T. (1994). Social judgment, feedback, and interpersonal learning in negotiation. *Organizational Behavior and Human Decision Processes, 58*(3), 327–345; Thompson, L., Loewenstein, J., & Gentner, D. (2000). Avoiding missed opportunities in managerial life: Analogical training more powerful than case-based training. *Organizational Behavior and Human Decision Processes, 82*(1), 60–75.

LEARNING OBJECTIVES

This book promises three things: First (and most important), reading this book will *improve your ability to negotiate successfully.* You and your company will be richer, and you will experience fewer sleepless nights because you will have a solid framework and excellent toolbox for successful negotiation. However, in making this promise, we must also issue a warning: Successful negotiation skills do not come through passive learning. Rather, you will need to actively challenge yourself. We can think of no better way to engage in this challenge than to supplement this book with classroom experiences in negotiation in which managers can test their negotiation skills, receive timely feedback, and repeatedly refine their negotiation strategies. Moreover, within the classroom, data suggest that students who take the course for a grade will be more effective than students who take the course pass-fail.[31]

Second, we provide you with a *general strategy for successful negotiation.* Take a look at the table of contents. Notice the distinct absence of chapter titles such as "Negotiating in the Pharmaceutical Industry" or "Real Estate Negotiations" or "High-Tech Negotiations." We don't believe that negotiations in the pharmaceutical world require a fundamentally different set of skills from negotiations in the insurance industry or the software industry. Rather, we believe that negotiation skills are transferable across situations. In making this statement, we do not mean to imply that all negotiation situations are identical. This assumption is patently false because negotiation situations differ dramatically across cultures and industries. However, certain key negotiation principles are essential in all these different contexts. The skills in this book are effective across a wide range of situations, ranging from complex, multiparty, multicultural deals to one-on-one personal exchanges.

In addition, this book offers *an enlightened model of negotiation.* Being a successful negotiator does not depend on your opponent's lack of familiarity with a book such as this one or lack of training in negotiation. In fact, it would be ideal for you if your key clients and customers knew about these strategies. This approach follows what we call a *fraternal twin model,* which assumes that the other person you are negotiating with is every bit as motivated, intelligent, and prepared as you are. Thus, the negotiating strategies and techniques outlined in this book do not rely on "outsmarting" or tricking the other party; rather, they teach you to focus on simultaneously expanding the pie of resources and ensuring the resources are allocated in a manner that is favorable to you.

In summary, our model of learning is based on a three-phase cycle: experiential learning, feedback, and learning new strategies and skills.

THE MIND AND HEART

Across the sections of this book, we focus on the *mind* of the negotiator as it involves the development of deliberate, rational, and thoughtful strategies for negotiation. We also focus on the *heart* of the negotiator, because ultimately we care about relationships

---

[31]Craver, C. (1998). The impact of a pass/fail option on negotiation course performance. *Journal of Legal Education, 48*(2), 176–186.

and trust. We base all our teachings and best practices on scientific research in the areas of economics and psychology, reflecting the idea that the bottom line *and* our relationships are both important.[32] The scandals that surfaced in the corporate world in 2001 fueled a backlash against the business world. These salient incidents rekindled negative perceptions of businesspeople—and MBAs in particular: "[The] emphasis on analysis has produced a generation of MBAs who are critters with lopsided brains, icy hearts, and shrunken souls" (p. 39).[33] Such an assessment provides all the more reason to put the focus on the heart and relationships in business.

[32]Bazerman, M. H., Curhan, J. R., Moore, D. A., & Valley, K. L. (2000). Negotiation. *Annual Review of Psychology, 51,* 279–314.
[33]Leavitt, H. (1989). Educating our MBAs: On teaching what we haven't taught. *California Management Review, 31*(3), 38–50.

CHAPTER

Preparation: What to Do Before Negotiation

Jessica Morrison, an advertising copy writer for Drugstore.com in Seattle, thought she was underpaid. After 5 years at the company and several promotions, her title was associate editor, despite the fact that she had the same duties as a copywriter (a more illustrious title). Suspecting her $42,000 per year salary was significantly lower than the salary of someone else with her duties, she decided to do some research. She looked online, searching sites that compared her pay with others holding a similar job title. She discovered just what she expected: Someone with her experience should be making $50,000 to $60,000 a year. So she decided to talk to her manager. "I was a little nervous going in, but I had done my research." She didn't just receive the title she wanted; her boss also gave her a raise within the pay range she suggested. "If I had gone in without the information, the conversation would have been, 'I feel like I am not making enough money.'"[1]

As the opening example in this chapter illustrates, preparation is the key to successful negotiation. The work that you do prior to negotiation pays off substantially when you finally find yourself seated at the table. The 80–20 rule applies to negotiation: About 80% of your effort should go toward preparation; 20% should be the actual work involved in the negotiation. Most people clearly realize that preparation is important, yet they do not prepare in an effective fashion. Faulty preparation is not due to lack of motivation; rather, it has its roots in negotiators' faulty perceptions about negotiation.

We noted in Chapter 1 that most negotiators view negotiation as a **fixed-pie** enterprise. Most negotiators (about 80% of them) operate under this perception.[2] Negotiators who have fixed-pie perceptions usually adopt one of three mind-sets when preparing for negotiation:

1. They resign themselves to capitulating to the other side (also known as *soft bargaining*).
2. They prepare themselves for an attack (also known as *hard bargaining*).
3. They *compromise* in an attempt to reach a midpoint between their opposing desires (often regarded to be a win-win negotiation, when in fact, it is not).

---

[1]Darlin, D. (2007, March 3). Using web to get boss to pay more. *New York Times*, p. C1.
[2]Thompson, L., & Hastie, R. (1990). Social perception in negotiation. *Organizational Behavior and Human Decision Processes, 47*(1), 98–123.

Depending on what the other party decides to do in the negotiation, fixed-pie perceptions can either lead to a battle of wills (e.g., if both parties are in attack mode), mutual compromise (e.g., if both parties are soft), or a combination of attack and capitulation. The common assumption among all three approaches is that concessions are necessary by one or both parties to reach an agreement. The fixed-pie perception is almost *always* wrong; thus, choosing between capitulation, attack, and compromise is not an effective approach to negotiation.

A more accurate model of negotiation is a mixed-motive decision making enterprise. As a **mixed-motive enterprise**, negotiation involves both cooperation and competition. In this chapter, we review the essentials of effective preparation, whether it be with a next-door neighbor, a corporate executive officer, or someone from a different culture. Effective preparation encompasses three general abilities:

1. Self-assessment
2. Assessment of the other party
3. Assessment of the situation

We systematically review each of these abilities and the skills they require. For each, we pose questions that a negotiator should ask himself or herself when preparing for negotiation.

SELF-ASSESSMENT

The most important questions a negotiator needs to ask of himself or herself at the outset of negotiation are "What do I want?" and "What are my alternatives?" By far, the first question is the more intuitive and easier of the two to answer. Even so, many people do not think carefully about what they want before entering negotiations. The second question defines a negotiator's power in the negotiation and influences the ultimate outcome of the negotiation. We now take up these questions in more detail.

What Do I Want?

In any negotiation scenario, a negotiator needs to determine what constitutes an ideal outcome. This ideal is known as a **target** or **aspiration** (sometimes called a **target point** or **aspiration point**). Identifying a target or aspiration may sound straightforward enough, but three major problems often arise at this point:

1. The **underaspiring negotiator** sets his or her target or aspirations too low. The underaspiring negotiator opens the negotiation by requesting something that is immediately granted, resulting in a regrettable state of affairs known as the **winner's curse**.[3] The winner's curse occurs when a negotiator makes an offer that is immediately accepted by the other party. Consider what happened to Joseph Bachelder who was representing a grocery executive in critical negotiations. Bachelder demanded that his client—the grocer—get a 4.9% stake in the business. The words had barely left his mouth when the company's controlling shareholder jubilantly agreed. Says Bachelder, "I just died. I knew right away that I had underbid.

---

[3]Akerlof, G. (1970). The market for lemons: Quality uncertainty and the market mechanism. *Quarterly Journal of Economics, 84,* 488–500; Neale, M. A., & Bazerman, M. H. (1991). *Cognition and rationality in negotiation.* New York: Free Press.

We could have had more if I had just asked for it."[4] The immediate acceptance of one's offer by an opponent signals that a negotiator did not ask for enough. Another example is that of an army sergeant returning from a tour of duty in the Gulf War. Recently engaged, the sergeant wanted to bring back a beautiful gold necklace for his bride-to-be. When he entered the jewelry store in Saudi Arabia, he knew enough not to offer full price for the gold necklace, so he offered exactly half of the marked price. At that moment, the shopkeeper offered to also include the matching earrings and bracelet! The sergeant's key mistake: His initial offer was too generous because he had not adequately prepared. The winner's curse is nearly impossible to remedy: In a series of experiments, negotiators were given different parameters, full feedback, and several counterexamples in an attempt to counteract the winner's curse, but none was effective in eliminating the faulty behavior.[5]

2. The **overaspiring negotiator** or **positional negotiator** is too "tough"; he or she sets the target point too high and refuses to make any concessions. Take the case of Will Vinton, who received no fewer than three termination offers from Phil Knight of Nike. One of the offers totaled two years' salary as severance and $180,000 for his company stock. Vinton rejected all the offers and ended up with only $50,000.[6] The other problem with positional bargaining is that it reinforces egocentrism. Indeed, people quickly develop ownership of the arguments and positions they make, and these positions become part of people's own self-concept, making any opposition an ego threat.[7] Ego-defensive behavior triggers competitive communication, retaliatory behavior, negative perceptions of the counterparty, and attitude polarization.

3. The **grass-is-greener negotiator** does not know what he or she really wants—only that he or she wants what the other party does not want to give—and does not want what the other party is willing to offer. This type of negotiation behavior is also known as **reactive devaluation**.[8] For example, in a survey of opinions regarding possible arms reductions by the United States and the Soviet Union, respondents were asked to evaluate the terms of a nuclear disarmament proposal, a proposal that was either allegedly taken by the United States, Soviet Union, or a neutral third party.[9] In all cases, the proposal was identical; however, reactions to it depended upon who allegedly initiated it. The terms were seen as unfavorable to the United States when the Soviets were the initiators, even though the same terms appeared moderately favorable when attributed to a neutral third party and quite favorable when attributed to the United States.[10]

What Is My Alternative to Reaching Agreement in This Situation?

A negotiator needs to determine his or her best alternative to a negotiated agreement. This step is so important that it merits into an acronym: **BATNA** (**B**est **A**lternative **T**o

---

[4]Anders, G. (2003, June 25). Upping the ante: As some decry lavish CEO pay, Joe Bachelder makes it happen, *Wall Street Journal,* p. A1.

[5]Grosskopf, B., Bereby-Meyer, Y., & Bazerman, M. (2007). On the robustness of the winner's curse phenomenon. *Theory and Decision, 63*(4), 398–418.

[6]Manning, J., & Turnquist, K. (2003, May 25). Squabble in 'Toon Town. *Oregonian,* p. A1.

[7]DeDreu, C., & Knippenberg, D. (2005). The possessive self as a barrier to conflict resolution: Effects of mere ownership, process accountability, and self-concept clarity on competitive cognitions and behavior. *Journal of Personality and Social Psychology, 89*(3), 345–357.

[8]Ross, L., & Stillinger, C. (1991). Barriers to conflict resolution. *Negotiation Journal, 7*(4), 389–404; Curhan, J. R., Neale, M. A., Ross, L., & Rosencranz-Engelmann, J. (in press). Relational accommodation in negotiation: Effects of egalitarianism and gender on economic efficiency and relational capital. *Organizational Behavior and Human Decision Processes.*

[9]Ross & Stillinger, "Barriers to conflict resolution."

[10]Oskamp, S. (1965). Attitudes toward U.S. and Russian actions: A double standard. *Psychological Reports, 16,* 43–46.

a **N**egotiated **A**greement).[11] A BATNA determines the point at which a negotiator is prepared to walk away from the negotiation table. In practice, it means that negotiators should be willing to accept any set of terms that is superior to their BATNA and reject outcomes that are worse than their BATNA. Surprising as it may seem, negotiators often fail on both counts.

BATNAs and Reality

Despite its simple appeal, the BATNA concept is something that is consistently difficult to convey to most negotiators. When we ask managers to tell us about their BATNA, we usually hear a sermon about how much they deserve. A BATNA is not something that a negotiator wishes for; rather, it is determined by objective reality. In short, if the world does not recognize how great you are, then you do not have a desirable BATNA. A common problem we have seen in our training of MBA students and executives is that negotiators are reluctant to recognize their real BATNAs, and they fall prey to wishful thinking and unrealistic optimism.

Your BATNA is Not Static

Your BATNA—once properly identified—is not static or steady state. Rather, it is *dynamic,* meaning that at any point in time it is either improving or deteriorating as a result of market forces and a variety of other activity. Thus, we don't suggest negotiators simply identify their BATNAs. Once their BATNAs are identified, negotiators should constantly attempt to improve them. One strategy for improving BATNAs is to follow Bazerman and Neale's "falling in love" rule, which applies to most negotiation situations.[12] According to this rule, negotiators should not fall in love with one house, one job, or one set of circumstances, but instead they should try to identify two or three options of interest. For example, Del Monte strategically kept its options open in 2002 when its own board had an offer to sell the company in an all-cash deal. At the same time, H. J. Heinz chairman William R. Johnson offered to give Del Monte a few businesses that would double its size. For two months, Del Monte kept negotiations open with two competing parties offering dramatically different outcomes. They did so to be able to leverage their bargaining position. Del Monte's board wisely directed its chairman, Richard G. Wolford, to keep his options open, which eventually resulted in a better deal for the company.[13] By following this strategy, the negotiator has a readily available set of alternatives that represent viable options should the current alternative come at too high a price or be eliminated. The "falling in love" rule is difficult to follow because most people set their sights on one target job, house, or set of terms and exclude all others. Many negotiators are reluctant to recognize their BATNAs and get them confused with their aspiration point. Another problem associated with the failure to properly identify one's BATNA is that it can be influenced and manipulated by the other party during the course of negotiation.

Do Not Let the Other Party Manipulate Your BATNA

You should constantly improve your BATNA. However, the other party has an incentive to minimize the quality of your BATNA and, thus, will be motivated to provide

---

[11]Fisher, R., & Ury, W. (1981). *Getting to yes.* Boston: Houghton Mifflin.
[12]Bazerman, M. H., & Neale, M. A. (1992). *Negotiating rationally.* New York: Free Press.
[13]Lindeman, T. (2002, August 29). Del Monte weighed being bought as it worked on buying Heinz units. *Pittsburgh Post-Gazette,* p. C11.

negative information vis-à-vis your BATNA. If you have not properly prepared, you might be particularly influenced by such persuasive appeals. However, your BATNA should *not* change as a result of the other party's persuasion techniques. Your BATNA should only change as a result of objective facts and evidence. Negotiators are most likely to fall prey to the counterparty's manipulation attempts when they have not adequately prepared for the negotiation.

In a negotiation, the person who stands to gain most by changing our mind should be the *least* persuasive. Thus, it is important to develop a BATNA before commencing negotiations and to stick to it during the course of negotiations. It is helpful to write your BATNA in ink on a piece of paper and put it in your pocket before negotiating. If you feel tempted to settle for less than your BATNA, it may be a good time to pull out the paper, call a halt to the negotiation process, and engage in an objective reassessment.

Determine Your Reservation Point

Once the negotiator has identified her BATNA, she is in an excellent position to determine her reservation point. The **reservation point** is not determined by what the negotiator wishes and hopes for but, rather, by what her BATNA represents. Consider the example of an MBA student negotiating her employment terms. Let's imagine that the MBA student has a $90,000 job offer from company A, plus some stock options, moving expenses, and a signing bonus. The student is interested in getting an offer from company B. Thus, company A is her BATNA. The question the student should ask herself is, "What does company B need to offer me so that I feel it is as attractive as the offer made by company A?" The answer to this question represents her reservation point, which includes all things relevant to the job offer: not only salary, stock options, moving expenses, and signing bonus but also quality of life and feelings about the city to which she will move. A reservation point, then, is a *quantification* of a negotiator's BATNA with respect to other alternatives.

Many negotiators fail to assess their reservation point when they prepare for negotiation. This failure is a serious strategic error because the negotiator's reservation point has the most direct influence on his or her final outcome. In particular, when three types of information—market price, reservation price, and aspiration—were made available to negotiators, only reservation prices drove final outcomes.[14]

Failure to assess reservation points can lead to two unfortunate outcomes. In some instances, negotiators may agree to an outcome that is worse than their BATNA. In our example, the student could agree to a set of employment terms at company B that are actually worse for her than what company A is offering. A second problem is that negotiators may often reject an offer that is better than their BATNA. For example, the MBA student may reject an offer from company B that is actually more attractive than the offer from company A. Although this example may seem implausible, the incidence of agreeing to something worse than one's BATNA and rejecting an offer better than one's BATNA is quite high. To avoid both of these errors, we suggest that the negotiator follow the steps outlined in Exhibit 2-1.

---

[14]Blount-White, S., Valley, K., Bazerman, M., Neale, M., & Peck, S. (1994). Alternative models of price behavior in dyadic negotiations: Market prices, reservation prices, and negotiator aspirations. *Organizational Behavior and Human Decision Processes, 57*(3), 430–447.

EXHIBIT 2-1 Developing a Reservation Point

Step 1:   **Brainstorm Your Alternatives.** Imagine that you want to sell your house. You have already determined your target point—in this case, $275,000. That is the easy part. The real question is, "What is the lowest offer you will accept for your home?" This step involves thinking about what you will do in the event that you do not get an offer of $275,000 for your house. Perhaps you may reduce the list price by $10,000 (or more), perhaps you may stay in the house, or you may consider renting. You should consider as many alternatives as possible. The only restriction is that the alternatives must be feasible—that is, realistic. This requirement involves research on your part.

Step 2:   **Evaluate Each Alternative.** In this step, you should order the various alternatives identified in step 1 in terms of their relative attractiveness, or value, to you. If an alternative has an uncertain outcome, such as reducing the list price, you should determine the probability a buyer will make an offer at that price. For example, suppose that you reduce the list price to $265,000. You assess the probability of a buyer making an offer of $265,000 for your house to be 70%, based on recent home sale prices in the area. Your reservation price is based on research, not hope. The best, most valuable, alternative should be selected to represent your BATNA.

Step 3:   **Attempt to Improve Your BATNA.** Your bargaining position can be strengthened substantially to the extent that you have an attractive, viable BATNA. Unfortunately, this step is the one that many negotiators fail to develop fully. To improve your BATNA in this case, you might contact a rental company and develop your rental options, or you may make some improvements that have high return on investment (e.g., new paint). Of course, your most attractive BATNA is to have an offer in hand on your house.

Step 4:   **Determine Your Reservation Price.** Once you have determined your most attractive BATNA, it is then time to identify your reservation price—the least amount of money you would accept for your home at the present time. Once again, it is *not* advisable to make a guess. Your assessment *must* be based on facts. For example, you assess the probability of getting an offer on your house of $265,000 (or higher) to be 60%, based upon recent home sales in your area. Suppose that you assess the probability that you will get an offer of $250,000 or higher to be 95%, based upon recent sales activity in your area. You think there is a 5% chance that you will not get an offer of $250,000 and will rent your house. You can use this information to assess your expected probabilities of selling your house:

Reduce the price of your home to $265,000
$$P_{\text{sale}} = 60\%$$
Reduce the price of your home to $250,000
$$P_{\text{sale}} = 35\%$$
Rent the house
$$P_{\text{rent}} = 5\%$$

The probabilities represent the chances that you think your house will sell at a particular price or will have to be rented. Thus, you think that if the list price of your house is reduced to $265,000, it is 60% likely that you will receive an offer of that amount within 6 weeks. If you reduce the price of your home to $250,000, you are 95% certain that you will get an offer. (Note that we write this probability as 35% because it includes the 60% probability of receiving an offer of $265,000.) Finally,

(continued)

EXHIBIT 2-1 Developing a Reservation Point (*continued*)

you think you have only a 5% chance of getting an offer of $250,000 or more in the next 6 weeks and that you will have to rent your house—a value you assess to be worth only $100,000 to you at the present time.

Note that in our calculation, the probabilities always sum to exactly 100%, meaning we have considered all possible events occurring. No alternative is left to chance.

An overall value for each of these "risky" alternatives is assessed by multiplying the value of each option by its probability of occurrence:

Value of reducing price to $265,000
= $265,000 × 0.6 = $159,000
Value of reducing price to $250,000
= $250,000 × 0.35 = $87,500
Value of renting the house
= $100,000 × 0.05 = $5,500

As a final step, we add all the values of the alternatives to arrive at an overall evaluation:

= 0.6($265,000) + 0.35($250,000) + 0.05($100,000)
= $159,000 + $87,500 + $5,000 = $251,500

This value is your reservation price. It means that you would never settle for anything less than $251,500 in the next 6 weeks[*]. It also means that if a buyer were to make you an offer right now of $251,000, you would seriously consider it because it is very close to your reservation price. Obviously, you want to get a lot more than $251,500, but you are prepared to go as low as this amount at the present time.

The offers you receive in the next 6 weeks can change your reservation point. Suppose a buyer offers to pay $260,000 for the house next week. It would be your reservation point by which to evaluate all subsequent offers.

---

[*]After 6 weeks, you may reduce the price of your home to $250,000.

Be Aware of Focal Points

Negotiators who make the mistake of not developing a reservation point before they negotiate often focus on an arbitrary value that masquerades as a reservation price. Such arbitrary points are focal points. **Focal points** are salient numbers, figures, or values that appear to be valid but have no basis in fact—your roommate's job offer, for example. A good example of the arbitrariness of focal points is provided by an investigation in which people were asked for the last four digits of their Social Security number.[15] They were then asked whether the number of physicians in Manhattan was larger or smaller than the number formed by those last four digits. Finally, they were asked to estimate how many physicians are located in Manhattan. Despite the fact that it was obvious to everyone that Social Security digits are random and, therefore, could not possibly be related to the number of doctors in Manhattan, a strong correlation

---

[15]Lovallo, D., & Kahneman, D. (2003). Delusions of success: How optimism undermines executives' decisions. *Harvard Business Review, 81*(7), 56–63.

emerged between the digits and people's estimates. It would seem absurd to base judgments on random digits, but people did.

Beware of Sunk Costs

Sunk costs are just what they sound like—money you have invested that is, for all practical purposes, gone. Economic theory asserts that only future costs and benefits should affect decisions. However, people have a hard time forgetting the past, and they often try to recoup sunk costs. This mind-set can lead to trouble. One type of sunk cost is the purchase price that home sellers paid for their house. Simply stated, at some point in the past a person purchased a house for a certain price. That price, by economic standards, is a sunk cost and should, for all practical purposes, be irrelevant to the negotiation the seller has with a buyer today. However, most people are affected by the past. Sellers and buyers in a simulated real estate negotiation were given the same Multiple Listing Service (MLS) sheet describing a house. However, negotiators were given different information about their previous purchase price.[16] Buyers offered significantly higher amounts for a condominium with larger sunk costs, indicating that the seller's sunk costs influenced the buyer's behavior. Moreover, sellers' BATNAs were significantly lower when they had low, as opposed to high, sunk costs. Final settlements were significantly lower in the low (as opposed to high) sunk cost situations. When preparing for negotiations, negotiators must be aware that sunk costs will not only influence their own behavior but the behavior of the counterparty.

Do Not Confuse Your Target Point with Your Reservation Point

Negotiators often make the mistake of using their target point as their reservation point. This can result in one of two undesirable outcomes. The negotiator who lacks a well-formed reservation point runs the risk of agreeing to a settlement that is worse than what he or she could do by following another course of action. In another case, the negotiator may walk away from a potentially profitable deal. For example, many home sellers reject early offers on their homes that are superior to their reservation point, only to be forced to accept an offer of less value at some later point in time. In 2003, auto parts maker Dana Corp. rejected an offer of $2.7 billion from rival ArvinMeritor Inc. Three years later, in 2006, the company filed for bankruptcy. Prior to the filing, Dana shares traded for about $1 each, far lower than the $18 per share offered by ArvinMeritor.[17]

Identify the Issues in the Negotiation

Many negotiators make the mistake of identifying only a single issue to negotiate. Usually, this issue is money (e.g., sales price or salary, etc.). It is a grave mistake to focus on a single issue in a negotiation because, in reality, more issues are at stake in most negotiation situations. The problem is that they remain "hidden" unless negotiators do the

---

[16]Diekmann, K. A., Tenbrunsel, A. E., Shah, P. P., Schroth, H. A., & Bazerman, M. H. (1996). The descriptive and prescriptive use of previous purchase price in negotiations. *Organizational Behavior and Human Decision Processes, 66*(2), 179–191.

[17]Whiteman, Lou. (2006, March 6). Dana bites the dust. *The Daily Deal.*

work of unbundling them. By identifying other issues, negotiators can add value to negotiations. For example, in the purchase of a car, issues such as payment terms, cash up front, loan agreement, or warranty are all potentially negotiable. Negotiators should take time to brainstorm how a single-issue negotiation may be segmented into multiple issues or they should attempt to add issues.[18]

Identify the Alternatives for Each Issue

Once the negotiator has identified the issues to be negotiated, it is a good idea to identify several alternatives within each issue. For example, in a negotiation for a new car, payment terms might include percentage paid up front or percentage of interest on a loan; a loaner agreement might involve how many months or years the option to buy is available. Negotiators can formalize the issues and alternatives by creating a matrix in which the issues are located along the columns and the alternatives specified along the rows.

Identify Equivalent Multi-issue Proposals

The next step of preparation is to determine a variety of different combinations of the issues that all achieve the target or aspiration point. For example, an MBA student in a job interview might identify salary, signing bonus, and vacation days as key issues. The student might then take the step of identifying highly attractive packages that she could present as opening offers in the negotiation; for example, a starting salary of $90,000, three weeks of vacation per year, and a signing bonus of $10,000 might be subjectively equivalent to a starting salary of $100,000, 10 days of vacation per year, and a signing bonus of $12,000. By identifying multiple-issue packages, negotiators expand their options. *The most important aspect of identifying packages of offers is that the packages should all be of equivalent value or attractiveness to oneself.* This requires that negotiators ask themselves some important questions about what they value and what is attractive to them. (As a first step, consult Appendix 1, which helps prepare a negotiator to identify packages of equivalent value by testing the negotiator's rationality.)

We strongly discourage negotiators from stating a range (e.g., a salary range). By stating a range, the negotiator gives up important bargaining ground and moves too close to his or her BATNA. We call it a *premature concession.* By stating a range ("I would be interested in a salary between $90,000 and $100,000"), a negotiator has already made a concession (implicitly agreeing to a salary of $90,000). Ideally, a negotiator should identify as many possible packages of a given value before making a concession in his or her target point. Another benefit of identifying packages of offers is that the negotiator does not give the counterparty the impression that he or she is a *positional negotiator* (a person who determines a set of terms desired in a negotiation, presents those terms, and refuses to budge on any dimension of any issue).[19] By identifying multiple issues and multiple alternatives within each issue, a negotiator is more likely to achieve his or her target.

---

[18]Lax, D. A., & Sebenius, J. K. (1986). *The manager as negotiator.* New York: Free Press.
[19]Fisher, R., Ury, W., & Patton, B. (1991). *Getting to yes* (2nd ed.). New York: Penguin.

Assess Your Risk Propensity

Negotiations always involve risk. The key question is not necessarily how to minimize risk; rather, the key is to understand how risk affects decision making. As an exercise, suppose you are offered a choice between the following two options:

> Option A: Receiving a cashier's check for $5,000
> Option B: Playing a game that offers a 50% chance of winning a $10,000 cashier's check and a 50% chance of winning nothing

When presented with a choice between a sure thing and a gamble of equivalent value, most people choose option A, the sure thing. Note that the expected value of each choice is $5,000, which would mean that negotiators should be indifferent (or risk-neutral) between the two. However, the strong preference for option A over B reflects a fundamental principle of negotiator behavior: **risk-aversion**.

Now, imagine yourself facing the following unenviable choice:

> Option C: Paying $5,000 for an unexpected expense
> Option D: Playing a game that offers a 50% chance of paying nothing and a 50% chance of paying $10,000

Most people find it difficult to choose between options C and D because both choices are undesirable. However, when forced to make a decision, the majority of negotiators choose option D, even though the expected value of C and D is exactly the same: $5,000. Option D represents the "risky" alternative. The dominant choice of D over C reflects a fundamental principle of human psychology: risk-seeking behavior in the face of loss.

Whereas most people are risk-seeking when it comes to losses, they are risk-averse when it comes to gains. A **reference point** defines what a person considers to be a gain or a loss. Thus, rather than weighing a course of action by its impact on total wealth, people generally "frame" outcomes as either "gains" or "losses" relative to some arbitrary reference point.[20]

What are the implications for negotiation? Negotiators should consider the differential impact of three sources of risk in any negotiation: strategic risk, BATNA risk, and contractual risk.[21]

Strategic Risk

Strategic risk refers to the riskiness of the tactics that negotiators use at the bargaining table. Negotiators often choose between extremely cooperative tactics (such as information sharing and brainstorming) and, at the other extreme, competitive tactics (such as threats and demands). Consider the risk that AOL's David Colburn took when negotiating with Microsoft to get the AOL icon on the Microsoft Windows start page—valuable real estate on the computer desktop because it gave AOL access to untold millions of Microsoft customers who might sign up for the online service.[22] It would mean that AOL would not have to send free disks to get people to sign up because the software would already be installed on the computer. During the negotiation, Colburn threatened to use

---

[20]Kahneman, D., & Tversky, A. (1979). Prospect theory: An analysis of decision under risk. *Econometrica, 47,* 263–291.

[21]Bottom, W. P. (1998). Negotiator risk: Sources of uncertainty and the impact of reference points on negotiated agreements. *Organizational Behavior and Human Decision Processes, 76*(2), 89–112.

[22]Klein, A. (2003, June 15). Lord of the flies. *Washington Post,* p. W06.

the browser of Microsoft's archenemy—Netscape—if Microsoft did not agree to put the AOL icon on the Windows start page. Microsoft agreed. Consider also the risk taken by Sotheby's when selling the Mark Rothko painting *White Center*. Sotheby's promised owner David Rockefeller that the painting would sell for at least $46 million. (The previous record for a Rothko painting was just $22 million, and Sotheby's would have to pay the difference if the painting didn't sell for the record price it promised.) But Sotheby's knew that the potential payoff would be enormous. It would not only receive a commission from the buyer but also would get a cut of 20% of every dollar over the $46 million price. When auction time came, an anonymous bidder bought the 1950 abstract painting for $72.8 million, granting Sotheby's an estimated take of $11.6 million.[23]

Negotiators who have recently experienced a string of failures are more likely to adopt a "loss frame" and feel less "in control" in a negotiation; conversely, negotiators who have experienced a recent string of successes feel greater control.[24] Consequently, loss-framed negotiators are reluctant to reveal information that could be used to exploit them; instead, they prefer to manage risk by delaying outcomes.

BATNA Risk

Whereas the negotiator can and should be fairly sure that he or she can exercise his or her BATNA in the event that the present negotiation does not result in agreement, most negotiation situations involve an element of risk. In actual practice, many people's BATNAs are uncertain because potential alternatives arrive sequentially. For example, consider a student who has several interviews scheduled over the next 10 weeks but no actual offers. The student's BATNA is an estimate about the likelihood of actually receiving an offer. Consider this example of a car dealer's uncertain BATNA: "A car dealer who decides not to make the one last concession needed to close a deal is rarely doing so because an alternative buyer in the next room is waiting to buy the same car at a higher price. The seller must make a conjecture about the likelihood that a more attractive offer will be made in the near future. Rejecting an offer entails a risk that the car will remain on the lot indefinitely, costing the dealer money, with no better offer forthcoming" (p. 94).[25]

Under most circumstances, we might expect negotiators who are in a "gain frame" to be more risk-averse (and therefore, more concessionary) than negotiators who hold a "loss frame" (who might hold out). This gain-loss basis can be a potential problem in negotiation because negotiators can be "framed." To see how, consider the following example: Negotiators who are instructed to "minimize their losses" make fewer concessions, reach fewer agreements, and perceive settlements to be less fair compared to those who are told to "maximize their gains."[26] In short, the negotiators

---

[23]Palmer, C. (2007, June 11). The art of the art deal. *Business Week, 4038,* 65.
[24]Kray, L., Paddock, L., & Galinksy, A. (2004). Historical framing: How a consideration of past successes and failures affects integrative negotiations. Unpublished manuscript, University of California.
[25]Bottom, "Negotiator risk."
[26]Bazerman, M. H., Magliozzi, T., & Neale, M. A. (1985). Integrative bargaining in a competitive market. *Organizational Behavior and Human Decision Processes, 35*(3), 294–313; Neale, M. A., & Northcraft, G. (1986). Experts, amateurs, and refrigerators: Comparing expert and amateur negotiators in a novel task. *Organizational Behavior and Human Decision Processes, 38,* 305–317; Neale, M. A., Huber, V. L., & Northcraft, G. (1987). The framing of negotiations: Contextual versus task frames. *Organizational Behavior and Human Decision Processes, 39*(2), 228–241; Neale, M. A., & Bazerman, M. H. (1991). *Cognition and rationality in negotiation.* New York: Free Press.

who are told to "minimize their losses" adopt more risky bargaining strategies (just as the majority of people choose option D over C in our previous example), preferring to hold out for a better, but more risky, settlement. In contrast, those who are told to "maximize their gains" are more inclined to accept the sure thing (just as most people choose option A over option B in our example). Negotiators who view the glass as "half full" are more inclined to reach agreement, whereas negotiators who view the glass as "half empty" are more likely to use threats and exercise their BATNAs. If one negotiator has a negative frame and the other has a positive frame, the negotiator with the negative frame reaps a greater share of the resources.[27] Thus, a negotiator must be aware of the important psychological impact his or her reference point can have on his or her own behavior. Negotiators should carefully examine their reference points and be wary when their opponents attempt to manipulate those reference points.

A negotiator's BATNA acts as an important reference point from which other outcomes are evaluated. Outcomes and alternatives that fall short of one's BATNA are viewed as losses; outcomes that exceed a negotiator's reservation point or BATNA are viewed as gains. The more risk-averse the negotiator, the more likely it is that she or he will make greater concessions.[28] Thus, given BATNAs of equal expected value, the more risk-averse negotiator will be in a weaker bargaining position.[29] Making a concession is the best way to avoid taking a risk.

Contractual Risk

Contractual risk refers to the risk associated with the willingness of the other party to honor its terms.[30] For example, signing a peace treaty with one's adversaries may lead to genuine peace, or it may lead to a military disadvantage if the other side fails to honor the agreement. One example of contractual risk comes from the business world: The Mitsubishi Estate Company provided a dramatic example of the risk of erroneous estimates in negotiation.[31] In October 1989, Mitsubishi agreed to pay the Rockefeller family trust $846 million in exchange for a controlling interest in the Rockefeller Group, Inc., which owns Rockefeller Center. Unfortunately, Mitsubishi, along with many others, failed to foresee the collapse of the New York real estate market, which dramatically lowered the value of the acquisition. In May 1995, the Mitsubishi Estate Company was forced to seek bankruptcy protection primarily in an attempt to stem the $600 million in losses it had incurred on the investment.[32] Clearly, the Mitsubishi negotiators expected a much better payoff when they signed the original agreement to acquire control of the property.

How does such contractual risk affect negotiator behavior? Under contractual risk, negotiators with negative frames (risk-seeking) are more likely to reach integrative

---

[27]Bottom, W. P., & Studt, A. (1993). Framing effects and the distributive aspect of integrative bargaining. *Organizational Behavior and Human Decision Processes, 56*(3), 459–474.

[28]Neale, M. A., & Bazerman, M. H. (1985). The effects of framing and negotiator overconfidence on bargainer behavior. *Academy of Management Journal, 28,* 34–49.

[29]Crawford, V. P., & Sobel, J. (1982). Strategic information transmission. *Econometrica, 50,* 1431–1451.

[30]Bottom, "Negotiator risk."

[31]Bottom, W. P. (1996). Negotiating risks: Sources of uncertainty and the impact of reference points on concession-making and settlements. Unpublished manuscript, Washington University, St. Louis, MO.

[32]Pacelle, M., & Lipin, S. (1995, May 12). Japanese owner seeks court protection for Manhattan's Rockefeller Center. *Wall Street Journal,* p. A3; Pacelle, M. (1995, June 9). Japan's U.S. property deals: A poor report card. *Wall Street Journal,* p. B1.

agreements than those with positive frames (risk-averse). The reason is that attaining a high aspiration entails some creative risk. Thus, if integrative negotiation outcomes involve "sure things," positive frames are more effective; however, if the integrative outcomes require negotiators to "roll the dice," negative frames are more effective. In a series of studies involving contractual risk, negotiators with a "loss frame" are more cooperative and more likely to settle than those with a "gain frame."[33] Further, "loss frame" negotiators create more integrative agreements.

Endowment Effects

The value or utility we associate with a certain object or outcome should not be influenced by irrelevant factors, such as who owns the object. Simply stated, the value of the object should be about the same, whether we are a buyer or a seller. (*Note:* Buyers and sellers might want to adopt different *bargaining positions* for the object, but their *private valuations* for the object should not differ as a consequence of who has possession of it.) However, negotiators' **reference points** may lead buyers and sellers to have different valuations for objects. Someone who possesses an object has a reference point that reflects his or her current endowment. When someone who owns an object considers selling it, he or she may view the situation as a loss. The difference between what sellers demand and what buyers are willing to pay is a manifestation of loss-aversion, coupled with the rapid adaptation of the reference point. Therefore, sellers demand more than buyers are willing to pay.

One example comes from a class of MBA students who were "endowed" with coffee mugs worth $6, as charged by the university bookstore.[34] The students who were not given a coffee mug were told they had the opportunity to buy a mug from a student who owned one, if the student who owned the mug valued it less. The buyers' willingness to pay for the mug and the sellers' willingness to sell the mug were inferred from a series of choices (e.g., "receive $9.75" versus "receive mug," "receive $9.50 versus a mug," etc.). Basic rationality predicts that about half of the buyers will value the mug more than the seller and therefore trade will occur; similarly, about half of the sellers will value the mug more than the buyer and trade will not occur. The reference point effect, however, predicts that because of the loss-aversion behavior engendered by the seller's loss frame, trade will occur less than expected. Indeed, although 11 trades were expected, on average, only 4 took place. Sellers demanded in excess of $8 to part with their mugs; prospective buyers were only willing to pay list price.[35]

If sellers are risk-seeking by virtue of their endowment, how can it be that horses, cars, furniture, companies, and land are bought and sold every day? The endowment effect operates only when the seller regards himself or herself to be the owner of the object. If a seller expects to sell goods for a profit and views the goods as currency (for example, when MBA students are endowed with tokens rather than coffee mugs), the endowment effect does not occur.

---

[33]Bottom, "Negotiator risk."
[34]Kahneman, D., Knetsch, J. L., & Thaler, R. H. (1990). Experimental tests of the endowment effect and the Coase theorem. *Journal of Political Economy, 98*(6), 1325–1348.
[35]Kahneman, Knetsch, & Thaler, "Experimental tests."

Am I Going to Regret This?

People evaluate reality by comparing it to its salient alternatives.[36] Sometimes we feel we made the "right" decision when we think about alternatives. Other times, we are filled with regret. What determines whether we feel we did the right thing (e.g., took the right job, married the right person) or we feel regret? An important component in determining whether a person experiences regret is counterfactual thinking.[37] **Counterfactual thinking**, or thinking about what might have been but did not occur, may be a reference point for the psychological evaluation of actual outcomes. In negotiation, immediate acceptance of a first offer by the counterparty often means a better outcome for the proposing negotiator; however, the outcome is distinctly less satisfying.[38] One of the benefits of having a first offer accepted is that it can affect preparation positively. Negotiators whose first offer is accepted by the counterparty are more likely to prepare longer for a subsequent negotiation; it also makes negotiators reluctant to make the first offer again.[39]

Consider feelings of regret experienced by athletes in the Olympic games.[40] Although silver medalists should feel happier than bronze medalists because their performance is objectively superior, counterfactual reasoning might produce greater feelings of regret and disappointment in silver medalists than in bronze. Specifically, the bronze medalist's reference point is that of not placing at all, so winning a medal represents a gain. In contrast, the silver medalist views himself or herself as having just missed the gold. With the gold medal as the referent, the silver medalist feels a loss. Indeed, videotapes of medalists' reactions (with the audio portion turned off) reveal that bronze medalists are perceived to be happier than silver medalists.[41] Further, silver medalists report experiencing greater feelings of regret than do bronze medalists.

Violations of the Sure Thing Principle

Imagine you face a decision between going to graduate school X on the East Coast or graduate school Y on the West Coast. You must make your decision before you find out whether your start-up company has received funding from a venture capitalist. In the event you get the funding, the East Coast provides access to many more of your potential customers. In the event that funding does not come through, by going to the East Coast you would be closer to your family, who could help you with finances. This sounds pretty straightforward so far: School X is your dominant choice no matter what the venture capitalist does. In other words, you have chosen school X regardless of whether you get funding. Making a decision between X and Y should not be hard—or should it?

---

[36]Kahneman, D., & Miller, D. (1986). Norm theory: Comparing reality to its alternatives. *Psychological Review, 93,* 136–153.

[37]Gilovich, T., & Medvec, V. H. (1994). The temporal pattern to the experience of regret. *Journal of Personality and Social Psychology, 67*(3), 357–365.

[38]Galinsky, A., Seiden, V., Kim, P. H., & Medvec, V. H. (2002). The dissatisfaction of having your first offer accepted: The role of counterfactual thinking in negotiations. *Personality and Social Psychology Bulletin, 28*(2), 271–283.

[39]Ibid.

[40]Medvec, V. H., Madey, S. F., & Gilovich, T. (1995). When less is more: Counterfactual thinking and satisfaction among Olympic medalists. *Journal of Personality and Social Psychology, 69*(4), 603–610.

[41]Ibid.

When faced with uncertainty about some event occurring (such as whether your company will be funded), people are often reluctant to make decisions and will even pay money to delay decisions until the uncertain event is known. This is paradoxical because no matter what happens, people choose to do the same thing.[42] Consider a situation in which a student has just taken a tough and exhausting qualifying examination.[43] The student has the option of buying a very attractive 5-day Hawaiian vacation package. The results of the exam will not be available for a week, but the student must decide whether to buy the vacation package now. Alternatively, she can pay a nonrefundable fee to retain the right to buy the vacation package at the same price on the day after the exam results are posted. When presented with these three choices, most respondents (61%) choose to pay a nonrefundable fee to delay the decision. Two other versions of the scenario are then presented to different groups of participants. In one version, the student passed the exam, and in the other version, the student failed. In both of these situations, respondents overwhelmingly preferred to go on the vacation. Thus, even though we decide to go on the vacation no matter what the results of the exam, we are willing to pay money to delay making this decision.

This behavior violates one of the basic axioms of the rational theory of decision making under uncertainty: the **sure thing principle**.[44] According to the sure thing principle, if an alternative X is preferred to Y in the condition that some event, A, occurs, and if X is also preferred to Y in the condition that some event, A, does not occur, then X should be preferred to Y, even when it is not known whether A will occur.

Why would people pay a fee to a consultant or intermediary to delay the decision when they would make the same choice either way? Violations of the sure thing principle are rooted in the *reasons* people use to make their decisions. In the Hawaii example, people have different reasons for going to Hawaii for each possible event. If they pass the exam, the vacation is a celebration or reward; if they fail the exam, the vacation is an opportunity to recuperate. When the decision maker does not know whether he or she has passed the exam, he or she may lack a clear reason for going to Hawaii. In the presence of uncertainty, people may be reluctant to think through the implications of each outcome and, as a result, they violate the sure thing principle.

Do I Have an Appropriate Level of Confidence?

How accurate are people in judgments of probability? How do they make assessments of likelihood, especially when full, objective information is unavailable? Judgments of likelihood for certain types of events are often more optimistic than is warranted. The **overconfidence effect** refers to unwarranted levels of confidence in people's judgment of their abilities and the likelihood of positive events and underestimates of the likelihood of negative events. For example, in negotiations involving third-party dispute resolution, negotiators on each side believe the neutral third party will adjudicate in their

---

[42]Tversky, A., & Shafir, E. (1992). The disjunction effect in choice under uncertainty. *Psychological Science, 3*(5), 305–309.
[43]Shafir, E. (1994). Uncertainty and the difficulty of thinking through disjunctions. *Cognition, 50,* 403–430.
[44]Savage, L. J. (1954). *The foundations of statistics.* New York: Wiley.

favor.[45] Obviously, a decision favoring both parties cannot happen. Similarly, in final-offer arbitration, wherein parties each submit their final bid to a third party who then makes a binding decision between the two proposals, negotiators consistently overestimate the probability that the neutral arbitrator will choose their own offer.[46] Obviously, the probability is only 50% that a final offer will be accepted; nevertheless, both parties' estimates typically sum to a number greater than 100%. When we find ourselves to be highly confident of a particular outcome occurring (whether it be our opponent caving in to us, a senior manager supporting our decision, etc.), it is important to examine why. On the other hand, overconfidence about the value of the other party's BATNA might serve the negotiator well. Negotiators who are optimistically biased (i.e., they think their counterpart will concede more than he or she really can) have a distinct bargaining advantage.[47]

SIZING UP THE OTHER PARTY

Once the negotiator has prepared for evaluating what he or she wants in a negotiation situation, it is time to think about the other party (or parties).

Who Are the Other Parties?

It is always important to identify the players in a negotiation. A **party** is a person (or group of people with common interests) who acts in accord with his or her preferences. Parties are readily identified when they are physically present, but often the most important parties are not present at the negotiation table. Such parties are known as the **hidden table**.[48] When more parties are involved in the negotiations, the situation becomes a team or multiparty negotiation, and the dynamics change considerably. A variety of issues crop up as more parties enter the bargaining room. For example, with more than two parties, coalitions may develop, and teams of negotiators may form. Team and multiparty negotiations are so important that we devote an entire chapter to them in this book (Chapter 9). Sometimes, it is obvious who the other parties are, and they have a legitimate place at the table. However, in other situations, the other parties may not be obvious at all, and their legitimacy at the table may be questionable.

---

[45]Farber, H. S., & Bazerman, M. H. (1986). The general basis of arbitrator behavior: An empirical analysis of conventional and final offer arbitration. *Econometrica, 54,* 1503–1528; Farber, H. S., & Bazerman, M. H. (1989). Divergent expectations as a cause of disagreement in bargaining: Evidence from a comparison of arbitration schemes. *Quarterly Journal of Economics, 104,* 99–120; Farber, H. S. (1981). Splitting the difference in interest arbitration. *Industrial and Labor Relations Review, 35,* 70–77.

[46]Neale, M. A., & Bazerman, M. H. (1983). The role of perspective taking ability in negotiating under different forms of arbitration. *Industrial and Labor Relations Review, 36,* 378–388; Bazerman, M. H., & Neale, M. A. (1982). Improving negotiation effectiveness under final offer arbitration: The role of selection and training. *Journal of Applied Psychology, 67*(5), 543–548.

[47]Bottom, W. P., & Paese, P. W. (1999). Judgment accuracy and the asymmetric cost of errors in distributive bargaining. *Group Decision and Negotiation, 8,* 349–364.

[48]Friedman, R. (1992). The culture of mediation: Private understandings in the context of public conflict. In D. Kolb and J. Bartunek (Eds.), *Hidden conflict: Uncovering behind-the-scenes disputes* (pp. 143–164). Beverly Hills, CA: Sage.

Are the Parties Monolithic?[49]

Monolithic refers to whether parties on the same side of the table are in agreement with one another concerning their interests in the negotiation. Although it would make sense for parties on the same side to be of one voice, often they are not. Frequently, the parties are composed of people who are on the same side but have differing values, beliefs, and preferences.

Counterparties' Interests and Position

A negotiator should do as much research and homework as possible to determine the counterparties' interests in the negotiation. For example, of the multiple issues identified, which issues are most important to the other party? What alternatives are most preferable to the other party? For example, Rich Gee was well into negotiations with a potential employer when he asked for a flexible travel schedule, one that would limit the number of business trips required of him. The surprised interviewer asked why. Although what was most important for Mr. Gee was more time at home with his wife and kids, he knew he needed to support his request by considering the employer's interests. He outlined several ways in which cutting travel could save time and money for the company. In his interview, he suggested teleconferencing with clients and meeting vendors at a halfway point, thereby eliminating the need to stay overnight. Impressed by Mr. Gee's ideas, the interviewer offered him the job.[50]

Counterparties' BATNAs

Probably the most important piece of information a negotiator can have in a negotiation is the BATNA of the other party. Unfortunately, unless you are negotiating with an extremely naïve negotiator, it is unlikely the counterparty will reveal his or her BATNA. However, a negotiator should do research about the other party's BATNA. Most negotiators severely under-research their counterparty's BATNA. For example, when purchasing cars, most people have access to a wealth of information about dealers' costs; however, they do not access this information prior to negotiating with car salespersons. This lack of information, of course, limits their ability to effectively negotiate. Similarly, many people do not adequately utilize real estate agents when purchasing houses. Real estate agents can provide a wealth of valuable information about the nature of the market and the history of a house that is for sale—all of which can be valuable when trying to determine the counterparty's BATNA. The other party's aspiration point will be quite clear; however, the negotiator who determines only the other party's aspiration point and not the BATNA is in a severely disadvantageous negotiation position because the counterparty's aspiration may act as an anchor in the negotiation process.

---

[49] This question is raised by Raiffa (1982) in his seminal book *The art and science of negotiation,* Cambridge, MA: Belknap.

[50] Schellenbarger, S. (2007, July 12). The job less traveled: Workers seek relief from business trips. *Wall Street Journal,* p. B5.

EXHIBIT 2-2   Job Negotiation

When Rob Kwong finished his business degree, he had a difficult time finding a job. He was aware of a suitable salary for someone with his degree and posted his resume on various employment Web sites. He landed a few interviews and even received a couple of job offers, but when the employers failed to meet his pay expectations, he turned them down. He was becoming increasingly desperate when he received an offer for $7,000 less than what he thought he should be paid. Seeing no other prospects on the horizon, though, he took the job without negotiating the pay. According to Mr. Kwong, "I took it because I just really needed a job."

However, according to a survey of 875 hiring managers by *CareerBuilder.com*, the majority of employers (about 60 percent) say they consider salary to be negotiable; 30 percent say their first offer is final; but 10 percent say it depends on the candidate and do not rule out the possibility of negotiating salary. Meanwhile, a study done by the Society for Human Resource Management found that four of five corporate recruiters said they were willing to negotiate compensation.

Source: Ransom, D. (2006, August 22). Starting career? Strategy helps land good pay. *Wall Street Journal,* p. D2; Loeb, M. (2006, September 3). It pays to negotiate your salary. *Pittsburgh Post Gazette,* p. D3.

SITUATION ASSESSMENT

Some negotiations differ radically from others. Assess the following *before* negotiating.[51]

Is the Negotiation One Shot, Long Term, or Repetitive?[52]

In a **one-shot negotiation,** a transaction occurs, and no future ramifications accrue to the parties. Most negotiation situations are not one-shot situations in which the parties involved come together only at one point in time to conduct business. One of the few situations that has been identified as a truly one-shot negotiation is the interaction that occurs between customers and wait staff at interstate roadside diners—neither party will likely ever see one another again. (Incidentally, economists are baffled as to why diners leave tips—because tipping is usually a mechanism used in long-term relationships.)

Even if the parties to negotiation change over time, negotiators' reputations precede them to the table. Because most people negotiate in the context of social networks, most negotiations are **long term** in nature because reputation information is carried through those social networks. Repetitive negotiations are situations in which negotiators must renegotiate terms on some regular basis (e.g., unions and their management). In long-term and **repetitive negotiations**, negotiators must consider how their relationship evolves and how trust is maintained over time. Probably the most important long-term relationship is the employment negotiation. Because people want to negotiate economically attractive deals but not sour long-term relationships, job negotiations are generally regarded to be uncomfortable (see Exhibit 2-2). This topic is so important that we devote an entire chapter to trust and relationships (Chapter 6) and a separate appendix on negotiating a job offer.

---

[51]Raiffa, *The art and science of negotiation.*
[52]Ibid.

Do the Negotiations Involve Scarce Resources, Ideologies, or Both?

The two major types of conflict are consensus conflict and scarce resource competition.[53] **Consensus conflict** occurs when one person's opinions, ideas, or beliefs are incompatible with those of another, and the two seek to reach an agreement of opinion. For example, jurors' beliefs may differ about whether a defendant is innocent or guilty; two managers may disagree about whether someone has project management skills; two people may argue over whether gun ownership should be controlled. Consensus conflict is about ideology and fundamental beliefs and, as you might imagine, is difficult to resolve because it involves values and morals. Indeed negotiating over "values" is more difficult than negotiating over "interests," and people are less likely to reach integrative agreements when values are at stake.[54]

Scarce resource competition exists when people vie for limited resources. For example, when business partners are in conflict concerning how to divide responsibilities and profits, each may feel he or she deserves more than the other feels is appropriate.

Many conflict situations involve not only scarce resources but ideologies. People who are in conflict about interests (e.g., money and resources) are more likely to make value-added trade-offs and reach win-win outcomes than are people in conflict about values or beliefs.[55] For example, the Israeli-Palestinian conflict involves the allocation of land (a scarce resource) but stems from fundamentally different religious beliefs and ideologies. When negotiations involve such "sacred issues," more impasses, lower joint profits, and more negative perceptions of the counterparty result; however, this is only true when both parties believe they have attractive BATNAs.[56]

Is the Negotiation One of Necessity or Opportunity?

In many cases, we must negotiate; in other situations, negotiations are more of a luxury or opportunity. As an example, consider a couple selling their home because they have been transferred to a different location. They must negotiate a contract on the residence. Even if they have an attractive BATNA, they eventually must negotiate with someone to achieve their needs. In contrast, a person who is interested in enhancing her salary and benefits might want to improve her employment situation. No pressing need to negotiate exists; rather, negotiation is initiated for opportunistic reasons. Consider how the CEO of United, Jim Goodwin, avoided a negotiation of *necessity* (negotiation with his pilot unions) and instead focused on a negotiation of *opportunity* (a

---

[53]Aubert, V. (1963). Competition and dissensus: Two types of conflict and conflict resolution. *Conflict Resolution, 7,* 26–42; Druckman, D., & Zechmeister, K. (1973). Conflict of interest and value dissensus: Propositions on the sociology of conflict. *Human Relations, 26,* 449–466; Kelley, H. H., & Thibaut, J. (1969). Group problem solving. In G. Lindzey & E. Aronson (Eds.), *Handbook of social psychology* (pp. 1–101). Reading, MA: Addison-Wesley; Thompson, L., & Gonzalez, R. (1997). Environmental disputes: Competition for scarce resources and clashing of values. In M. Bazerman, D. Messick, A. Tenbrunsel, & K. Wade-Benzoni (Eds.), *Environment, ethics, and behavior* (pp. 75–104). San Francisco: New Lexington Press.
[54]Harinck, F., & DeDreu, C. (2004). Negotiating interests or values and reaching integrative agreements: The importance of time pressure and temporary impasses. *European Journal of Social Psychology, 34,* 595–611.
[55]Harinck, F., De Dreu, C. K. W., & Van Vianen, A. E. M. (2000). The impact of conflict issues on fixed-pie perceptions, problem-solving, and integrative outcomes in negotiation. *Organizational Behavior and Human Decision Processes, 81*(2), 329–358.
[56]Tenbrunsel, A., Wade-Benzoni, K., Medvec, V., Thompson, L., & Bazerman, M. (2007). The reality and myth of sacred issues in ideologically-based negotiations. Manuscript under editorial review, *Negotiation and Conflict Management Research.*

possible acquisition of US Airways). The problem for Goodwin was that his failure to focus on the negotiation of necessity led to serious problems.[57]

Many people avoid negotiations of opportunity because they feel they lack skills. Indeed, having confidence in oneself as a negotiator is important for success.[58] Some people are comfortable with negotiations, to the point that they are always involved in them.

Is the Negotiation an Exchange or Dispute Situation?

In a typical negotiation, parties come together to exchange resources. In a classic example, a buyer sees greater value in a seller's goods than the seller wants for them, and an exchange takes place (money is paid for goods or services). In other situations, negotiations take place because a claim has been made by one party and has been rejected by the other party. This is a **dispute**.[59] For example, consider the dispute that involved Michael Capellas, the CEO of WorldCom (renamed MCI), whose rivals allegedly avoided hundreds of millions of dollars in fees over a decade by disguising long-distance calls as local calls or as calls originated by its long-distance competitor, AT&T.[60] The difference between exchanges and disputes concerns the alternatives to mutual settlement. In an exchange situation, parties simply resort to their BATNAs; in a dispute, negotiators often go to court.

Are Linkage Effects Present?[61]

Linkage effects refer to the fact that some negotiations affect other negotiations. One example is in the case of law and setting precedent. Resolutions in one situation have implications for other situations. For example, when the Teamsters union negotiated with the corporate parent of Jewel supermarkets in 2003, company management feared that if the Teamsters won a strong contract, it would serve as a template for unions at its other stores around the country.[62] Albertsons, for example, had more than 400 labor contracts. Often direct linkages will occur when a multinational firm has operations in several countries and a decision made in one country carries over to other countries. Sometimes, indirect linkage effects occur, such as when a decision made at the negotiation table affects some interest group in a fashion that no one anticipates fully. A key reason why mergers are often unsuccessful is that companies do not think about linkage effects with current employees. In most merger scenarios, employees of the purchased company are given little information about the turn of events until well after the deal is settled. Rumors fly about what's going on, and employees are left in limbo, bitter about changes, and worried about their jobs and colleagues. Human resource specialists should be involved in the negotiation process to make the linkages for the employees smoother.

---

[57]Griffin, G., & Leib, J. (2003, June 9). Flying on fumes: A costly pilots contract, the dot-com meltdown and a failed merger put United in a tailspin and sent executives scrambling to recover. *Denver Post,* p. A01.

[58]Sullivan, B. A., O'Connor, K. M., & Burris, E. (2003). How negotiation-related self-efficacy affects tactics and outcomes. Paper presented at the Academy of Management Annual Meeting, Seattle, WA.

[59]Ury, W. L., Brett, J. M., & Goldberg, S. B. (1988). *Getting disputes resolved: Designing systems to cut the costs of conflict.* San Francisco: Jossey-Bass.

[60]Rosenbush, S., & Haddad C. (2003, August 11). MCI is under a new cloud, but it can weather the storm. *BusinessWeek, 3845,* 31.

[61]Raiffa, *The art and science of negotiation.*

[62]Manor, R. (2003, August 13). Jewel, union hammer out tentative 4-year deal. *Chicago Tribune,* p. 3.

Is Agreement Required?[63]

In many negotiation situations, reaching agreement is a matter of preference. For example, in a salary negotiation a person might be willing to decline an offer from one company and either stay with the current company, start his or her own company, or delay negotiations indefinitely. However, in other situations, reaching agreement is not just the only course of action—it is required. For example, on August 17, 1981, when more than 85% of the 17,500 air traffic controllers went on strike for better working conditions and improved wages, President Ronald Reagan told the controllers to return to work or the government would assume the striking controllers had quit. By the end of that week, more than 5,000 Professional Air Traffic Controllers Organization (PATCO) members received dismissal notices from the FAA. Reagan stated that Congress had passed a law in 1947 forbidding strikes by government employees, including a nonstrike oath that each air controller must sign upon hiring. Another example: The Taylor Law bars public employees from striking. This legislation affected the negotiations between New York governor George Pataki and the 14 bargaining units representing 190,000 state employees. Negotiations can be automatically extended under the Taylor Law if no new agreement is reached at the time of expiration.[64]

Is It Legal to Negotiate?

In the United States, it is illegal to negotiate the sale of human organs. In September 1999, the online auction house eBay had to retract a seller's posted auction for a human kidney.[65] The bidding went up to $5.7 million before eBay called off the auction. However, in the Philippines, it is legal to sell kidneys, despite ongoing debate about the issue (see Exhibit 2-3).

Sometimes, no specific laws govern what can or cannot be negotiated; rather, individuals rely on strong cultural norms that are highly situation specific. For example, most people in the United States do not negotiate the price of fruit at major grocery

---

EXHIBIT 2-3   Is It Legal to Negotiate?

Consider the desperation that must have led Romeo Roga, age thirty-six, of the Philippines to do what he did. Roga's one-year-old son was sick with measles, and Roga needed cash to pay medical bills. He earned $1.25 a day carrying sacks of rice at the harbor—not enough to support his family of five children. Roga's stepfather told him he could earn $2,125 by selling his kidney. Said Roga, "I was forced to do it. It was a matter of survival." The Roman Catholic Church denounces the business as unethical and exploitative. However, kidney patients are usually willing to pay any price just to live. Doctors are seeking a middle ground, with the objective of preventing people from commercializing organ donation. Roga's kidney did not get him much. His son died, and the money has since run out. He tires easily with only one kidney. Says Roga, "At least I've helped someone."

Source: Based on Baguioro, L. (1999, November 1). Kidneys for sale. *Newsweek,* p. 50.

---

[63]Raiffa, *The art and science of negotiation.*
[64]Grondahl, P. (2003, March 2). Different worlds, same side of bargaining table. *Times Union-Albany,* p. B1.
[65]Harmon, A. (1999, September 3). Auction for a kidney pops up on eBay's site. *New York Times,* p. A13.

stores, but they do it freely in farmer's markets, such as the Pike Place Market in Seattle, Washington. But farmer's markets are not the only place to haggle. For example, Bill Meyer rarely pays full price for anything. In grocery stores, he tries to get bargains on food that is going to spoil if it is not sold. In thrift stores, he gathers up a pile of stuff and offers a single price for it. At pizza parlors, he asks for pizzas that have not been picked up and gets them for $3 each.[66] Most home electronic stores will negotiate, as will stores that sell large, durable goods. And when it comes to college financial aid packages, families often have more options than they realize and may be able to negotiate larger aid awards for their children. Colleges will usually balk at the idea of "negotiations" but will take another look if they see compelling reasons to do so. Colleges don't want every parent asking for more money, but about 60% of the time, when parents inquire and are prepared, they get more money.[67]

Is Ratification Required?[68]

Ratification refers to whether a party to the negotiation table must have any contract approved by some other body or group. For example, a corporate recruiter may need to have the salary and employment packages offered to recruits ratified by the company's human resources group or the CEO. In some circumstances, negotiators may tell the other side that ratification is required when it is not.

Are Time Constraints or Other Time-Related Costs Involved?[69]

Virtually all negotiations have some time-related costs. Although the negotiator who desperately needs an agreement, or for whom the passage of time is extremely costly, is likely to be at a disadvantage, more time pressure is not necessarily bad.[70] It is important to distinguish *final deadlines* from *time-related costs*.[71] Two negotiators may face radically different time-related costs, but a deadline for one is a deadline for the other. The shortest final deadline is the only one that counts, and if they don't have a deal by that point, the two negotiators must exercise their BATNAs.

Time Pressure and Deadlines

A final deadline is a fixed point in time that ends the negotiations. The rate of concessions made by negotiators increases as negotiators approach final deadlines.[72] According to Moore, negotiators believe that final deadlines (i.e., time pressure) are a strategic weakness, so they avoid revealing their deadlines for fear their "weakness" will be exploited by the counterparty.[73] However, because deadlines restrict the length of the negotiation for all parties, they place all parties under pressure. One person's

---

[66]Trappen, M. (1996, April 30). Shopping on a shoestring: How to haggle. *Oregonian,* p. D01.
[67]Kim, J. (2003, April 22). Negotiating a sweeter college aid deal. *Dow Jones Newswires.*
[68]Raiffa, *The art and science of negotiation.*
[69]Ibid.
[70]Stuhlmacher, A. F., Gillespie, T. L., & Champagne, M. V. (1998). The impact of time pressure in negotiation: A meta-analysis. *International Journal of Conflict Management, 9*(2), 97–116.
[71]Moore, D. A. (2004). The unexpected benefits of final deadlines in negotiation. *Journal of Experimental Social Psychology, 40,* 121–127.
[72]Lim, S. G., & Murnighan, J. K. (1994). Phases, deadlines, and the bargaining process. *Organizational Behavior and Human Decision Processes, 58,* 153–171.
[73]Moore, "The unexpected benefits."

EXHIBIT 2-4   Strategic Deadline Pressure

AOL used its knowledge of time pressure and deadlines in a strategic fashion. Its strategy of creating an "insane deadline" would always begin with a delicate courtship and that would end in up with an ultimatum that would cause leave the client to acquiesce. AOL would begin negotiations as a "slow waltz" between AOL and a prospective client, involving wooing and talk about how great the client's business was, how great it would be if the two sides worked together, how wonderful it would be if the client bought ads on AOL. Naturally, AOL wouldn't mention it was going through precisely the same process with multiple partners. Weeks would go by and then AOL would suddenly demand immediate action. Abruptly, deal makers would draw up a contract, slam it on the table, and order the prospective client to sign it within 24 hours, or else AOL would take the offer to another party, which happened to be waiting to hear from AOL. What's more, the contracts would always be of mammoth size—impossible to penetrate within the time constraints. Moreover, AOL executives forced deal makers of other companies to sit around for hours in a so-called waiting game, just to signal to them that they were not important.

Source: Based on Klein, A. (2003, June 15). Lord of the flies. *Washington Post,* p. W06.

final deadline is also the other's final deadline.[74] For example, consider how Adam Chesnoff revealed his deadline when in negotiations with Haim Saban.[75] When time ran out on the negotiations, Chesnoff came back with his own deadline: his wedding date. "If we can't get [the deal] done by Friday, you won't have a problem with Haim or me, you'll have to deal with my fiancée, which is a much more difficult conversation." However, when negotiators keep their deadlines secret, the result is that they rush to get a deal before the deadline, whereas their opponents, who expect longer negotiations, concede at a more leisurely pace.[76] (For another example of strategic use of deadlines at AOL, see Exhibit 2-4.)

The reason why negotiators so often incorrectly predict the consequences of final deadlines in negotiation has to do with the more general psychological tendency to focus egocentrically on the self when making comparisons or predictions.[77] Negotiators focus on the deadline's effect on themselves more than its effect on their negotiating partners. The same tendency leads people to predict they will be above average on simple tasks and below average on difficult tasks.[78]

Time-Related Costs

Setting a final deadline on the negotiations can be helpful, especially if the passage of time is particularly costly to you.[79] This strategy was used successfully to reach an

[74]Roth A. E., Murnighan, J. K., & Schoumaker, F. (1988). The deadline effect in bargaining: Some experimental evidence. *American Economic Review, 78*(4), 806–823.

[75]Goldfarb, J. (2003, August 11). Tough deadline helps Saban's right-hand man ink deal. *Reuters.*

[76]Moore, "The unexpected benefits."

[77]Moore, D. A., & Kim, T. G. (2003). Myopic social prediction and the solo comparison effect. *Journal of Personality and Social Psychology, 85*(6), 1121–1135.

[78]Kruger, J. (1999). Lake Wobegon be gone! The "below-average effect" and the egocentric nature of comparative ability judgments. *Journal of Personality and Social Psychology, 77,* 221–232; Windschitl, P. D., Kruger, J., & Simms, E. N. (2003). The influence of egocentrism and focalism on people's optimism in competitions: When what affects us equally affects me more. *Journal of Personality and Social Psychology, 85*(3), 389–408.

[79]Moore, "The unexpected benefits."

agreement in the National Basketball Association strike of 1998 to 1999. The owners set a final deadline and threatened to walk out if they could not come to agreement with the players by January 5, 1999. The two sides came to agreement on January 4 on terms that dramatically favored the owners.

Time Horizon

Another time-related question concerns what Okhuysen and colleagues refer to as the **time horizon**—the amount of time between the negotiation and the consequences or realization of negotiated agreements.[80] Greater temporal distance increases the incidence of profitable win-win behavior, including negotiators' preference for multi-issue (as opposed to single-issue proposals), and value-added trade-off.[81] As a general principle, the longer the temporal distance between the act of negotiation and the consequences of negotiated agreements, the better the agreement.[82] The reason is that parties are less contentious since the realization is in the distance. Moreover, this time benefit is particularly pronounced in the cases where negotiations concern "burdens" as opposed to "benefits," because time gives people opportunity to discount the effects of burdens.

Are Contracts Official or Unofficial?

Many negotiation situations, such as the purchase of a house or a job offer, involve official contracts that legally obligate parties to follow through with stated promises. However, in several negotiation situations of equal or greater importance, negotiations are conducted through a handshake or other forms of informal agreements. Considerable cultural variation surrounds the terms of what social symbols constitute agreement (handshakes versus taking tea together), as well as which situations are treated officially or unofficially. Awkwardness can result when one party approaches the situation from a formal stance and the other treats it informally. Consider the negotiations between city commissioners and firefighters in Florida.[83] Pension fund increases were part of a handshake and verbal agreement. However, when it came to the actual signing, the commissioners refused to ratify the concessions to which they had previously agreed. Obviously, ill will can result when implicit contracts are broken. (We take up the topic of broken trust in Chapter 6.)

Where Do the Negotiations Take Place?

Common wisdom holds that it is to one's advantage to negotiate on one's own turf, as opposed to that of the other side. So important is this perception that great preparation and expense are undertaken to find neutral ground for important negotiations. For example, for the summit between former president Ronald Reagan and Soviet leader Mikhail Gorbachev, the site was carefully selected. The two met at the Chateau Fleur d'Eau in Geneva, Switzerland. Similarly, the multiparty Irish talks were stalled in 1991 when conflict broke out concerning where the next set of talks would be held. The

---

[80]Okhuysen, G., Galinsky, A., & Uptigrove, T. (2003). Saving the worst for last: The effect of time horizon on the efficiency of negotiating benefits and burdens. *Organizational Behavior and Human Decision Processes, 91*(2), 269–279.

[81]Henderson, M., Trope, Y., & Carnevale, P. (2006). Negotiation from a near and distant time perspective. *Journal of Personality and Social Psychology, 91*(4), 712–729.

[82]Okhuysen, Galinsky, & Uptigrove, "Saving the worst for last."

[83]Holland, J. (2003, July 3). Hollywood, Fla., backs off pension fund deal for firefighters. *South Florida Sun-Sentinel.*

Unionists, who agreed to talk directly to Irish government ministers about the future of Northern Ireland, were anxious to avoid any impression of going "cap in hand" to Dublin and, therefore, wanted the talks held in London, the capital to which they were determined to remain connected. In contrast, the Social Democratic and Labor Party, which represented the majority of Catholic moderates in the province, preferred that the talks be held in Dublin, the capital to which they felt a strong allegiance.[84] Similarly, in 2008 Walt Disney Co. and union members working at the company's hotel resorts spent months trying to agree on a location to hold contract negotiations. Negotiations had previously been held on Disney turf and union members wanted to keep it that way, believing it allowed the workers to have a voice in the negotiations. However, Disney officials feared that holding talks at one of the hotels would be disruptive to guests and suggested a neutral location. Union members were "insulted" by the suggestion, assuming the location was chosen by Disney for its lack of parking and limited access, keeping workers from "being part of the process."[85]

Are Negotiations Public or Private?[86]

In many areas, the negotiation dance takes place in the public eye. In other negotiation situations, negotiations occur privately. For example, Kelman's work with the Israeli–Palestinian negotiations occurred under strict privacy.[87] As Kelman noted, privacy was instrumental for progress between parties:

> The discussions are completely private and confidential. There is no audience, no publicity, and no record, and one of the central ground rules specifies that statements made in the course of a workshop cannot be cited with attribution outside the workshop setting. These and other features of the workshop are designed to enable and encourage workshop participants to engage in a type of communication that is usually not available to parties involved in an intense conflict relationship. (p. 214)

In contrast, one of the unique aspects of sports negotiations is that they take place in a fishbowl atmosphere, with fans and the media observing every move at the bargaining table.[88] This kind of attention can lead to a media circus, with owners and players projecting their opinions on issues and events:

> The dickering back and forth makes for entertaining theater, but is a hindrance to the rational settlement of differences. It is customary, therefore, for both owners and players to be advised by their leaders to hold their tongues. NBA owners were made subject to fines of $1 million by the league for popping off in the media. (p. 7)

---

[84]Lewthwaite, G. (1991, May 7). Northern Ireland talks deadlock over location. *Baltimore Sun,* p. 5A.
[85]McKibben, D. (2008, February 8). Disney and union not talking. *Los Angeles Times,* p. B1.
[86]Raiffa, *The art and science of negotiation.*
[87]Kelman, H. C. (1991). Coalitions across conflict lines: The interplay of conflicts within and between the Israeli and Palestinian communities. Working paper series (no. 91–9), Harvard University, Center for International Affairs.
[88]Staudohar, P. D. (1999). Labor relations in basketball: The lockout of 1998–99. *Monthly Labor Review, 122*(4), 3–9.

Is Third-Party Intervention a Possibility?[89]

In many negotiation situations, third-party intervention is commonplace (and even expected). Most commonly, third-party intervention takes the form of mediation or arbitration. However, in other areas, third-party intervention is unheard of. The mere presence of third parties may escalate the tension in negotiation situations, if the initial parties egocentrically believe that third parties will favor their own position. In other situations, it is less common (and perhaps a sign of personal failure) to involve third parties. (Third-party intervention is so important that we devote Appendix 3 to it in this book).

What Conventions Guide the Process of Negotiation (Such as Who Makes the First Offer)?

In many negotiations, people have complete freedom of process. However, in other negotiations, strong conventions and norms dictate how the process of negotiation unfolds. For example, when people buy or sell houses in the United States, the first offer is typically made by a prospective buyer and all offers are formalized in writing. However, marked differences characterize the process across the country, with some home negotiations being conducted via spoken word and some via official contract.

Do Negotiations Involve More Than One Offer?

In some situations, it is typical to go back and forth several times before a mutually agreeable deal is struck. In other situations, this type of dealing is considered unacceptable. In the real estate world, for example, buyers and sellers expect to negotiate. These same people, however, would not dream of negotiating in an upscale department store.

As another example, many employers now expect that job candidates will attempt to negotiate what is initially offered to them, but extending the haggling is not acceptable for many. Consider what happened to Jay Kaplan, real estate entrepreneur.[90] He had traveled through the southeastern United States for eight consecutive days and met with five different owners, trying to purchase apartment buildings and shopping centers. Each meeting was a marathon session, with offers and counteroffers, lasting until dawn before an agreement was made. By the eighth day, with one meeting left, Kaplan was tired and decided to use a single-offer strategy. After asking for some aspirin and putting on his most exhausted face, Kaplan said to the other party, "You're asking $4.3 million for your property. I want to buy it for $3.7 million. Let's save ourselves the trouble of a long negotiation. I'm going to make you only one offer. It will be my best shot, and it will be a fair one. If you're a reasonable man, I'm sure you'll accept it." The strategy backfired. Kaplan then offered the other party $4.025 million, and the other party rejected it. They haggled for four hours until they agreed on $4.275. The opponent later told Kaplan there was no way he was going to accept the first offer made—no matter what it was.

---

[89]Raiffa, *The art and science of negotiation.*
[90]Kaplan, J. (1994, January 9). Single-offer tactic can be costly. *Arizona Republic,* p. E6.

Do Negotiators Communicate Explicitly or Tacitly?

In a typical buyer–seller negotiation or employment negotiation, negotiators communicate explicitly with one another. However, in other situations, communication is not explicit but tacit, and people communicate through their actions. This issue is so important that we devote an entire chapter to it (Chapter 11, in a discussion of social dilemmas).

Is There a Power Differential Between Parties?

Technically, negotiation occurs between people who are interdependent, meaning the actions of one party affect those of the other party, and vice versa. If one person has complete authority over another and is not affected by the actions of others, then negotiation cannot occur. However, it is often the case that low-power people can affect the outcomes of high-power others. For example, a CEO has more power than a middle-level manager in the company, but the manager can undoubtedly affect the welfare of the company and the CEO. The presence or absence of a power differential between negotiating parties can strongly affect the nature of negotiations. This topic is so important that we devote an entire chapter to power and influence in this book (Chapter 7).

Is Precedent Important?

In many negotiation situations, precedent is important, not only in anchoring negotiations on a particular point of reference but also in defining the range of alternatives. Often the major argument negotiators must confront when attempting to negotiate for themselves is the other party's agreement that he or she must follow precedent. In a sense, the negotiator fears that making a decision in one case will set him or her up for future negotiations. Of course, most precedents allow for a great deal of interpretation on the part of the precedent follower and the person attempting to challenge the precedent. Oftentimes, negotiators will invoke precedent as a way of cutting off negotiations.

CONCLUSION

Effective preparation places the negotiator at a strategic advantage at the bargaining table. We outlined three general areas of preparation: the self, the other party, and the context or situation. In terms of personal preparation, the negotiator who has identified a personal BATNA and set a reservation price and a target point is in a much better position to achieve the desired objectives. The negotiator who has prepared for negotiation knows when to walk away and how much is reasonable to concede. The negotiator who has adequately researched the counterparty's BATNA and interests is less likely to be tricked or confused by the other party. We outlined several issues the negotiator should consider prior to commencing negotiations. A summary preparation form is presented in Exhibit 2-5. We suggest the negotiator use it when preparing for negotiations. The next two chapters focus on pie-slicing and pie-expanding strategies in negotiations.

EXHIBIT 2-5   Preparation Worksheet for Negotiations

Self-Assessment	Assessment of the Other Party	Assessment of the Situation
• What do I want? (Set a target point) • What is my alternative to reaching agreement? (Identify your BATNA) • What is my reservation point? (See Exhibit 2-1) • What focal points could influence me? • What are my "sunk costs"? • Have I ensured that my target point is not influenced by my reservation point? • What are the issues in the negotiation? • What are the alternatives for the issues? • Have I identified equivalent multi-issue offers? • Have I assessed my risk propensity?	• Who are the other parties? • Are there parties who are likely to not be at the table? • Are the parties monolithic? • What issues are relevant to the other party? • What are the other party's interests? • What are the other party's alternatives for each issue? • What are the other party's positions? • What is the other negotiator's BATNA?	• Is the negotiation one shot, long term, or repetitive? • Do the negotiations involve scarce resources, conflict of ideologies, or both? • Is the negotiation of necessity or opportunity? • Is the negotiation an exchange or dispute situation? • Are there linkage effects? • Is agreement required? • Is it legal to negotiate? • Is ratification required? • Are there time constraints or other time-related costs? • Are contracts official or unofficial? • Where do negotiations take place? • Are negotiations public or private? • Is third-party intervention a possibility? • What conventions guide the process of negotiation? • Do negotiations involve more than one offer by each party? • Do negotiators communicate explicitly or tacitly? • Is there a power differential among parties? • Is precedent important?

CHAPTER 3

Distributive Negotiation: Slicing the Pie

In 2004, Joanna Track launched Sweetspot.ca, a Toronto-based online lifestyle guide. In early 2006, Louise Clements, vice president of digital properties for Rogers Media, approached Track about a minority stake in Sweetspot. Track spent several subsequent weeks in a boardroom negotiating with Rogers executives. Track said of the negotiations, "By nature, I tend not to ask for a lot, but this taught me that you have to ask to get. There's a game involved." A key component of the deal was the offer of promotional placements for Sweetspot on Rogers's Web sites and in its women's magazines through ads and contests, upping the company's exposure. The agreement stated that Track may still include any products she wants in her newsletters, fire and hire at her discretion, and work from home. She has to get Rogers's approval, however, to make a large purchase, take on a new investor, or start a new business under the Sweetspot banner. Track also has to provide monthly profit-and-loss statements to Rogers. At the same time, the deal allowed her to receive more capital from Rogers if Sweetspot exceeded its performance target. The relationship proved to be a success. On the 3-year anniversary of the deal, in July 2009, Rogers will have the option to buy out Track. "This is my baby," she says. "Will I allow it to be morphed into something else? Not while I'm here. But as a businessperson, I would say, 'Never say never.'"[1]

In the deal just described, negotiators distributed scarce resources (money, controlling power, options, etc.) between each other. In this chapter, we focus on how negotiators can best achieve their outcomes—economic (e.g., money and resources) as well as social (e.g., preserving relationships and building trust). We also provide several examples of how these strategies are used in actual business negotiations. In this chapter, we address the question of how best to claim resources. This chapter discusses who should make the first offer, how to respond to an offer made by the other party, the amount of concessions to make, and how to handle an aggressive negotiator.

The entire process of making an opening offer and then reaching a mutually agreeable settlement is known as the **negotiation dance**.[2] Unfortunately, most of us have

---

[1]Mourtada, R. (2008, March 13). Rogers & me. *Globe and Mail Update*, p. 28.
[2]Raiffa, H. (1982). *The art and science of negotiation.* Cambridge, MA: Belknap.

never taken dance lessons or know what to do once we find ourselves on the dance floor. Should we lead? Should we follow? A few hard-and-fast rules of thumb apply, but the negotiator must make many choices that are not so clear-cut. We wrestle with these issues in this chapter.

Although this chapter deals with slicing the pie, it is important to realize that most negotiations involve a win-win aspect (*expanding* the pie), which we discuss in detail in the next chapter. However, even in win-win negotiations, the pie of resources created by negotiators eventually has to be sliced.

THE BARGAINING ZONE AND THE NEGOTIATION DANCE

You analyzed the negotiation situation as best you can. You thought about your target point and your BATNA in a realistic fashion, developed a reservation point, and used all available information to assess the counterparty's BATNA. Now it is time for face-to-face negotiation. Typically, negotiators' target points do not overlap: The seller wants more than the buyer is willing to pay. However, it is often (but not always) the case that negotiators' reservation points *do* overlap, meaning that the most the buyer is willing to pay is more than the least the seller is willing tos accept. Under such circumstances, mutual settlement is profitable for both parties. *However, the challenge of negotiation is to reach a settlement that is most favorable to oneself and does not give up too much of the bargaining zone.* The **bargaining zone**, or **zone of possible agreements (ZOPA)**, is the range between negotiators' reservation points.[3] The final settlement of a negotiation will fall somewhere above the seller's reservation point and below the buyer's reservation point.[4] The bargaining zone can be either positive or negative (see Exhibits 3-1A and 3-1B).

EXHIBIT 3-1A   Positive Bargaining Zone

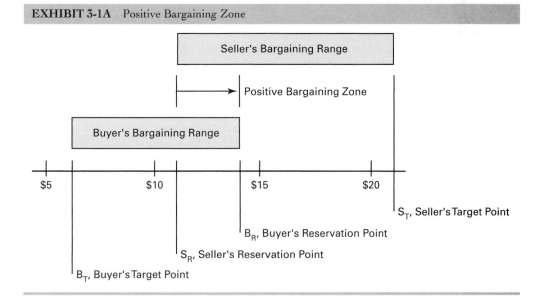

EXHIBIT 3-1B Negative Bargaining Zone

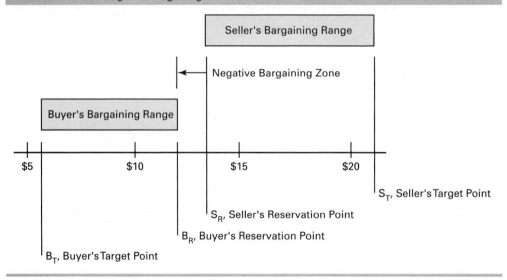

In a positive bargaining zone, negotiators' reservation points overlap, such that the most the buyer is willing to pay is greater than the least the seller will accept. This overlap means that mutual agreement is better than resorting to BATNAs. Consider the bargaining zone in Exhibit 3-1A. The seller's reservation point is $11; the buyer's reservation point is $14. The most the buyer is willing to pay is $3 greater than the very least the seller is willing to accept. The bargaining zone is between $11 and $14, or $3. If the negotiators reach agreement, the settlement will be somewhere between $11 and $14. If the parties fail to reach agreement in this situation, the outcome is an impasse and is **suboptimal** because negotiators leave money on the table and are worse off by not reaching agreement than reaching agreement.

In some cases, the bargaining zone may be nonexistent or even negative. However, the negotiators may not realize it and may spend fruitless hours trying to reach an agreement. This situation can be costly for negotiators; during the time in which they are negotiating, their opportunities may be worsening (i.e., negotiators have time-related costs; see Chapter 2). For example, consider the bargaining zone in Exhibit 3-1B, in which the seller's reservation point is $14 and the buyer's reservation point is $12. The most the buyer is willing to pay is $2 less than the seller is willing to accept at a minimum. This **negative bargaining zone** indicates that there is no positive overlap between the parties' reservation points. In this situation, negotiators should exercise their best alternatives to agreement. Because negotiations are costly to prolong, it is in both parties' interests to determine whether a positive bargaining zone is possible. If not, the parties should not waste time negotiating; instead, they should pursue other alternatives. Consider, for example, the contract negotiations between Gucci and designer Tom Ford. After PPR (the French conglomerate that owns Gucci) bought the Yves Saint Laurent label, Tom Ford started lengthy negotiations for managerial independence and control of both Gucci and YSL. Yves Saint Laurent was critical of Ford, and PPR did not wish to give up management control and appoint a new designer at YSL.

Contract talks dragged on for months. Ultimately, it was realized that a positive bargaining zone did not exist. Tom Ford left the company to pursue other alternatives.[5]

Bargaining Surplus

Mutual settlement is possible when parties' reservation points overlap and impossible when parties' reservation points do not overlap. **Bargaining surplus** is the amount of overlap between parties' reservation points. It is a measure of the size of the bargaining zone (what we refer to in this chapter as "the pie"). The bargaining surplus is a measure of the value that a negotiated agreement offers to both parties over the value of not reaching settlement. Sometimes the surplus is very large; other times it is very small. Skilled negotiators know how to reach agreements even when the bargaining zone is small.

Negotiator's Surplus

Negotiated outcomes will fall somewhere in the bargaining zone. But what determines *where* in this range the settlement will occur? Obviously, each negotiator would like the settlement to be as close to the other party's reservation point as possible, thereby maximizing his or her slice of the pie. In our example in Exhibit 3-1A, the seller would prefer to sell close to $14; the buyer would prefer to buy close to $11. *The best possible economic outcome for the negotiator is one that just meets the counterparty's reservation point, thereby inducing the other party to agree, but allows the focal negotiator to reap as much gain as possible.* This outcome provides the focal negotiator with the greatest possible share of the resources to be divided. In other words, one person gets all or most of the pie.

   The positive difference between the settlement outcome and the negotiator's reservation point is the **negotiator's surplus** (see Exhibit 3-2). The total surplus of the two negotiators adds up to the size of the ZOPA or bargaining surplus. Obviously, negotiators want to maximize their surplus in negotiations; surplus represents resources in excess of what is possible for negotiators to attain in the absence of negotiated agreement.

EXHIBIT 3-2   Bargaining Range and Surplus

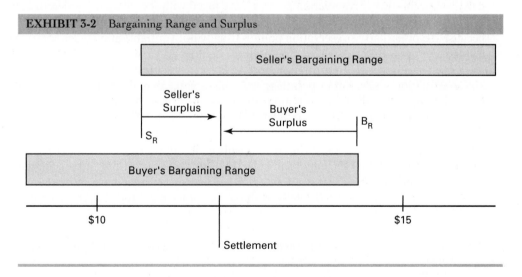

[5]Thomas, D. (2007, July 2–9). Everything a man wants. *Newsweek International.*

The fact that negotiated settlements fall somewhere in the ZOPA and that each negotiator tries to maximize his or her share of the bargaining surplus illustrates the **mixed-motive** nature of negotiation: Negotiators are motivated to *cooperate* with the other party to ensure that settlement is reached in the case of a positive bargaining zone, but they are motivated to *compete* with one another to claim as much of the bargaining surplus as they can.

PIE-SLICING STRATEGIES

The most frequently asked question about negotiation is, "How can I achieve most of the bargaining surplus for myself?" For example, if you are a potential home buyer and you discern that the seller's reservation point is $251,000, that is an ideal offer to make, assuming that your reservation point is much higher. However, the ability to claim bargaining surplus is easier said than done. How do you get information about the other party's reservation point? Most negotiators will not reveal their reservation point, but it may emerge unintentionally. Raiffa cites a humorous story wherein one party opens with a direct request for information about his opponent's reservation price:[6]

> "Tell me the bare minimum you would accept from us, and I'll see if I can throw in something extra." The opponent, not to be taken in, quips, "Why don't you tell us the very maximum that you are willing to pay, and we'll see if we can shave off a bit?"

This quip illustrates the essence of negotiation: How do people make sure they reach agreement if the ZOPA is positive but simultaneously claim as much of the pie as possible?

Another problem emerges as well. Even if someone reveals her reservation point, the other party has no way to verify that the first party is telling the truth. Indeed, the most commonly used phrase in any negotiation is "That's my bottom line." When the counterparty tells us his or her reservation point, we are faced with the dilemma of determining whether the information is valid or not. The negotiator is always at an information deficit because the other party's reservation point is usually not verifiable (it includes subjective factors) whereas a BATNA is based on objective factors and can therefore be verifiable.

Given that "private" information about reservation points is inherently unverifiable, negotiation seems rather pointless. After all, if you can never tell if the other person is telling the truth, then communication would be seen as fruitless (economists refer to such discussions as "cheap talk"[7]). However cheap talk does, in fact, matter.[8]

Some conditions allow negotiators to be more *confident* about the counterparty's reservation point. For example, a car buyer openly invites the dealer to call the competitor as a way of verifying that the buyer can indeed get the same car for less money. Similarly, if a person says something that is not in his or her interest, we may have more reason to believe it. For example, if a seller tells us she does not have another buyer and is under

[6]Raiffa, *The art and science of negotiation,* p. 40.
[7]Croson, R., Boles, T., & Murnighan, J. K. (2003). Cheap talk in bargaining experiments: Lying and threats in ultimatum games. *Journal of Economic Behavior & Organization, 51*(2), 143–159.
[8]Bazerman, M. H., Gibbons, R., Thompson, L., & Valley, K. L. (1998). Can negotiators outperform game theory? In J. Halpern & R. Stern (Eds.), *Debating rationality: Nonrational aspects of organizational decision making* (pp. 78–98). Ithaca, NY: ILR Press.

pressure to sell, we might believe her because this statement is not in her interest. This factor leads to an important cautionary note: It is not necessarily in your best interest to misrepresent your reservation point because you risk the possibility of disagreement. For example, imagine that you are trying to sell your Ipod because you have been given a nicer model as a gift. You would be willing to accept $50 for the used model (your reservation point, based upon a pawnbroker's offer), but you would ideally like to get $100 (your target point). You place an ad, and a potential buyer calls offering to pay $60. If you tell the caller that you have an offer of $70 (when in fact, you do not), you risk the possibility that the potential buyer will not accept because he or she might have a better BATNA.[9]

With regard to slicing the pie, negotiators should be willing to settle for outcomes that exceed their reservation point and reject offers that are worse than their reservation point. However, people frequently settle for outcomes worse than their BATNA (the agreement bias) and often reject offers that are better than their BATNA (hubris). For example, most strikes are eventually settled on terms that could have been reached earlier, without parties incurring the costs that the strike imposes.[10] The key question is why such irrational behavior occurs. The problem can usually be traced to either cognitive or emotional biases. We will elaborate on some of these biases later in this chapter.

If negotiators follow 10 basic strategies, they can substantially increase the probability they will obtain a favorable slice of the pie. Although these strategies don't come with guarantees, they are the best advice we can offer for enhancing one's ability to garner more resources for oneself.

Strategy 1: Assess Your BATNA and Improve It

Many negotiators do not think about their BATNA prior to entering negotiation. Even those who think about their BATNA often do not attempt to improve it. For most negotiators, BATNAs involve some uncertainty (see Chapter 2). However, uncertainty is not a good excuse for failure to assess one's BATNA. *Nothing can help a negotiator get a bigger slice of the pie than having a great BATNA.*

The risk a negotiator takes from not accurately assessing his or her BATNA prior to negotiation is that the negotiator will be unduly influenced by the counterparty. Consequently, negotiators should spend a considerable amount of time attempting to improve upon their BATNA before entering into a negotiation (remember the "falling in love" principle from Chapter 2).

Strategy 2: Determine Your Reservation Point, But Do Not Reveal It

Do not reveal your BATNA or your reservation price during the course of negotiation, even in the friendliest of situations. If you do, the other party will simply offer you your reservation price and you will not have any surplus for yourself. Further, your threats to "hold out" won't work because the counterparty will know that, rationally, you are

---

[9]Farrell, J., & Gibbons, R. (1989). Cheap talk can matter in bargaining. *Journal of Economic Theory, 48,* 221–237.

[10]Keenan, J., & Wilson, R. B. (1993). Bargaining with private information. *Journal of Economic Literature, 31*(1), 45–104; Roth, A. E. (1993). Bargaining experiments. In J. Kagel & A. E. Roth (Eds.), *Handbook of experimental economics.* Princeton, NJ: Princeton University Press.

better off accepting her offer. In only two circumstances do we think it is appropriate to truthfully reveal your reservation price.

> **Situation #1:** You have exhausted your time to negotiate and are about to walk out without a deal and you sense that the bargaining zone may be very small or perhaps negative. Prior to stepping on the plane or leaving the meeting, you might reveal your reservation price.
>
> **Situation #2:** You have a great BATNA and, consequently, an aggressive reservation price, and you would be happy if the counterparty matched or barely exceeded your reservation point. In this sense, negotiators "signal" their BATNA. For example, consider how Stephen Wolf of US Airways signaled his BATNA in negotiations with United Airlines (which was interested in acquiring US Airways). Wolf's opening offer was $88 per share. When United called the price unreasonable because the stock was trading below $30 a share, Wolf signaled that United's archrival—American—might be interested. Consequently, United agreed to pay $60 per share—a price that some United advisers considered to be $10 to $15 too high.[11]

Consider how another company, AOL, signaled its BATNA. One tactic involved an AOL deal maker pitching a deal to a prospective dot-com client. The AOL rep's PowerPoint presentation would include the logo of the client's rival—as if AOL had accidentally mixed up some of the slides from another presentation. The AOL rep would then feign embarrassment and apologize. However, the slip was completely intentional and meant to signal to the dot-com that AOL had a BATNA.[12]

Many negotiators reveal their true reservation price if they trust and like the other party or desire a long-term relationship. However, we think this is ill advised. There are many other ways to demonstrate trust and build a relationship, short of revealing your BATNA. Revealing information about a BATNA or reservation point is not a pie-expanding strategy; it is a pie-slicing strategy, and as a pie-slicing strategy it has the effect of reducing a negotiator's power in a negotiation.

Many negotiators, after studying the rationality of BATNAs and reservation prices, conclude that strategic misrepresentation of their reservation price might be advantageous. We do not believe that negotiators should lie about their BATNA or reservation price during negotiation. Lying is unethical (see Chapter 7) and can backfire strategically. If you lie about your reservation price, you effectively reduce the size of the bargaining zone because the bargaining zone is defined as the overlap of each party's reservation price. A positive but small bargaining zone may be transformed into a negative bargaining zone, and you may reach an impasse because your lie falsely indicated a negative bargaining zone. It is difficult to save face in such a situation because you risk appearing foolish if you retract your demand.

Strategy 3: Research the Other Party's BATNA and Estimate the Reservation Point

Negotiators often fail to sufficiently research the counterparty's BATNA. This reduces their power. Negotiators can use a variety of tactics to garner information that may reveal something about the counterparty's alternatives.

Be careful when the other party discloses, however. When the counterparty discloses his or her BATNA at the outset of the negotiation, negotiators actually make

---

[11]Griffin, G., & Leib, J. (2003, June 9). Flying on fumes: A costly pilots contract, the dot-com meltdown and a failed merger put United in a tailspin and sent executives scrambling to recover. *Denver Post*, p. A01.
[12]Klein, A. (2003, June 15). Lord of the flies. *Washington Post*, p. W06.

less demanding offers, disclose more truthful information, and settle for less profit than when the counterparty does not disclose a BATNA.[13]

Strategy 4: Set High Aspirations (Be Realistic but Optimistic)

Your aspiration, or target point, defines the upper limit on what you can get in a negotiation. Because you will usually never get more than your first offer, your first offer represents an important **anchor point** in the negotiation. As a case in point, consider how United Airlines captain Rick Dubinsky, known for his toughness, began by dropping an anchor in his negotiations with CEO of United, Jim Goodwin, in January 2000. Using a pad of paper on Goodwin's desk, Dubinsky drew two lines, one about an inch above the other. The bottom line, Dubinsky explained, was the current pilots' pay. The top was where Dubinsky expected it to go. Then, Dubinsky drew a delta sign indicating the difference between the two and wrote the number 21. "You are going to settle at 21%. That's the number, Jim. You are going to go there easy or you are going to go there hard, but you are going to go there."[14]

According to Raiffa, the final outcome of any negotiation is usually the midpoint between the first two offers that fall within the bargaining zone.[15] For this reason, it does not make sense to make unrealistic offers because they do not fall within the true bargaining zone. We use the first offer made by each party as a measure of his or her aspirations.[16] Aspirations or target points determine the "final demands" made by negotiators, more so than do BATNAs.[17] Negotiators who set high aspirations end up with more of the pie than those who set lower aspirations. And negotiators whose aspirations exceed those of the counterparty get more of the bargaining zone.[18] For example, negotiators who have unattractive reservation points and high aspirations actually demand more from their opponents than do negotiators with attractive BATNAs and low aspirations. Thus, it pays to set your aspirations high during a negotiation.

However, this generalization does not mean asking for the outrageous. If you ask for something outrageous, you run a risk of souring the relationship. This is known as the **chilling effect**. Strategically, make your first offer slightly lower than the other party's reservation point, and then you can bargain up to their reservation point. Most people are not going to immediately accept your first offer, but they ultimately might accept an offer that is equivalent to their reservation point.

Setting specific, challenging, and difficult goals results in greater profit than does setting easy or nonspecific goals.[19] Nonspecific or easy goals lead to compromise

---

[13]Paese, P. W., & Gilin, D. A. (2000). When an adversary is caught telling the truth: Reciprocal cooperation versus self-interest in distributive bargaining. *Personality and Social Psychology Bulletin, 26*(1), 79–90.

[14]Griffin & Leib, "Flying on fumes," p. 11.

[15]Raiffa, *The art and science of negotiation.*

[16]Kray, L., Thompson, L., & Galinsky, A. (2001). Battle of the sexes: Gender stereotype confirmation and reactance in negotiations. *Journal of Personality and Social Psychology, 80*(6), 942–958.

[17]Thompson, L. (1995). The impact of minimum goals and aspirations on judgments of success in negotiations. *Group Decision Making and Negotiation, 4,* 513–524.

[18]Chen, Y., Mannix, E., & Okumura, T. (2003). The importance of who you meet: Effects of self- versus other-concerns among negotiators in the United States, the People's Republic of China, and Japan. *Journal of Experimental Social Psychology, 39,* 1–15.

[19]Huber, V., & Neale, M. A. (1986). Effects of cognitive heuristics and goals on negotiator performance and subsequent goal setting. *Organizational Behavior and Human Decision Processes, 40,* 342–365; Huber, V., & Neale, M. A. (1987). Effects of self- and competitor goals on performance in an interdependent bargaining task. *Journal of Applied Psychology, 72,* 197–203; Northcraft, G. B., Neale, M. A., & Earley, C. P. (1994). The joint effects of goal-setting and expertise on negotiator performance. *Human Performance, 7,* 257–272; Thompson, "The impact of minimum goals."

agreements, which are suboptimal. High aspirations exert a self-regulating effect on negotiation behavior. Negotiators who are assigned easy goals tend to set harder new goals; however, in spite of adjustments, their new goals are significantly easier than the goals chosen by the difficult-goal negotiators. Thus, it is to a negotiator's advantage to set a high, somewhat difficult aspiration point early in the negotiation.

Moreover, the mindset that a negotiator adopts influences success, above and beyond their actual economic position. For example, when a negotiator focuses on his or her target point during negotiation, this increases the value of the outcome he or she ultimately receives.[20] Similarly, negotiators who focus on "ideals" rather than "oughts" do better in terms of slicing the pie.[21] Negotiators who focus on their accomplishments, hopes, and aspirations claim more resources than negotiators who focus on avoiding negative outcomes, holding constant their actual economic positions.[22] However, negotiators who focus on ideals do not *feel* as satisfied as negotiators who focus on their reservation point or BATNA. Thus, focusing on your targets will lead to an attractive outcome, but it may not feel satisfying. In contrast, focusing on reservation points leads people to *do* worse but *feel* better. Gut feeling or intuition can be misleading. How, then, can successful but unhappy negotiators feel better? If negotiators think about their BATNA after the negotiation, they feel better.[23]

The **winner's curse** occurs when the negotiator's first offer is immediately accepted by the counterparty. Immediate acceptance signals that the negotiator did not set his or her aspirations high enough. Furthermore, we caution negotiators to avoid a strategy known as boulwarism. **Boulwarism** is named after Lemuel Boulware, former CEO of General Electric, who believed in making one's first offer one's final offer. This strategy is not very effective and often engenders hostility from the counterparty.

Another piece of advice: Do not become "anchored" by your reservation point. Stated simply: Do not let your reservation point drive your aspiration point; the two should be separate. Many negotiators who have learned to assess their BATNA and set an appropriate reservation point fail to think about their aspiration or target point. Consequently, the reservation point acts as a psychological anchor for their aspiration point and, in most cases, people make insufficient adjustments—they do not set their target high enough. We discourage negotiators from using any kind of multiplier of their reservation point to determine their target because no logical reason supports doing so.

Strategy 5: Make the First Offer (If You Are Prepared)

Folklore dictates that negotiators should let the counterparty make the first offer. "The experts say it's better to let your adversary make the opening offer."[24] However, there

---

[20]Galinsky, A., Mussweiler, T., & Medvec, V. H. (2002). Disconnecting outcomes and evaluations: The role of negotiator focus. *Journal of Personality and Social Psychology, 83*(5), 1131–1140; Thompson, "The impact of minimum goals."

[21]Galinsky, A., & Mussweiler, T. (2001). First offers as anchors: The role of perspective-taking and negotiator focus. *Journal of Personality and Social Psychology, 81*(4), 657–669.

[22]Galinsky, A. D., Leonardelli, G. J., Okhuysen, G., & Mussweiler, T. (2005). Regulatory focus at the bargaining table: Promoting distributive and integrative success. *Personality and Social Psychology Bulletin, 31*(8), 1087-1098.

[23]Galinsky, Mussweiler, & Medvec, "Disconnecting outcomes and evaluations."

[24]Walker, R. (2003, August 1). Take it or leave it: The only guide to negotiating you will ever need. *Inc.,* 5(8), 74–83.

is no scientific support for this advice. The party who makes the first offer obtains a better final outcome.[25] Why? First offers act as an anchor point and correlate at least .85 with final outcomes.[26]

Negotiators need to think about a number of factors when making an opening offer. First and foremost, an opening offer should not give away too much of the bargaining zone. Second, many people worry they will "insult" the other party if they open too high (if they are selling) or too low (if they are buying). However, the fear of insulting the other party and souring the negotiations is more apparent than real. Managers tell us when they are faced with an extreme opening offer from the other party, they are not insulted; instead, they prepare to make concessions.

The first offer that falls within the bargaining zone acts as a powerful anchor point in negotiation. Recall the example of people's Social Security numbers affecting estimates of the number of physicians in Manhattan. That was a case of insufficient adjustment from an arbitrary anchor. Making the first offer protects negotiators from falling prey to a similar anchoring effect when they hear the counterparty's offer. Ideally, a negotiator's first offer acts as an anchor for the counterparty's counteroffer.

Your first offer should not be a range. Employers often ask prospective employees to state a range in salary negotiations. Do not fall victim to this bargaining ploy. By stating a range, you give up precious bargaining surplus. The counterparty will consider the lower end of the range as your target and negotiate down from there. A far better strategy is to respond to the counterparty's request for a range by making several offers that are all equally satisfying to you.

One more thing about making the first offer: If you have made an offer, then you should expect to receive some sort of counteroffer or response. Once you put an offer on the table, be patient. It is time for the counterparty to respond. In certain situations, patience and silence can be important negotiation tools. Do not interpret silence on the other person's part as a rejection of your offer. Many negotiators make what we call **premature concessions**—they make more than one concession in a row before the other party responds or counteroffers. Always wait for a response before making a further concession. For example, Lewis Kravitz, an Atlanta executive coach and former outplacement counselor, advises patience and knowing when not to speak in the heat of negotiations. In one instance, he was coaching a young man who had just been fired by his team. The young man felt desperate and told Kravitz he was willing to take a $2,000 pay cut and accept $28,000 for his next job. Kravitz told the man to be quiet at the bargaining table and let the prospective employer make the first offer. At the man's next job interview, the employer offered him $32,000, stunning the overjoyed job seeker into momentary silence. The employer interpreted the silence as dissatisfaction and upped the offer to $34,000 on the spot.[27]

Strategy 6: Immediately Reanchor if the Other Party Opens First

If the counterparty makes an offer, then the ball is in your court, and it is wise to make a counteroffer in a timely fashion. For example, in Pixar's on-again-off-again negotiation

[25]Galinsky & Mussweiler, "First offers as anchors."
[26]Ibid.
[27]Lancaster, H. (1998, January 27). You have to negotiate for everything in life, so get good at it. *Wall Street Journal*, p. B1.

with Disney, Pixar had to wait months for Disney to come back with a counterproposal. John Lasseter from Pixar stated, "It was just crazy. It would have been easier just to walk away." Pixar had already started talking to other studios, but the situation changed when Disney's board replaced Michael Eisner with Bob Iger, who promptly made a counteroffer that was accepted and thus Disney could announce acquisition of Pixar.[28] Counteroffers do two things. First, they diminish the prominence of the counterparty's initial offer as an anchor point in the negotiation. Second, they signal your willingness to negotiate. It is essential that you plan your opening offer before hearing the other party's opening—otherwise you risk being anchored by the other party's offer. In one investigation, some negotiators who received an offer from the other party were coached to focus on information that was inconsistent with that offer; others were not given such coaching.[29] The result? *Thinking* about the opponent's BATNA or reservation price or even one's own target point completely negates the powerful anchoring impact that the other party's first offer might have on you. Above all, do not adjust your BATNA based upon the counterparty's offer, and do not adjust your target. It is extremely important not to be "anchored" by the counterparty's offer. An effective counteroffer moves the focus away from the other party's offer as a reference point.

Strategy 7: Plan Your Concessions

Concessions are the reductions that a negotiator makes during the course of a negotiation. First offers are "openers." It is rare (but not impossible) for a first offer to be accepted. If a first offer is immediately accepted by the other party, negotiators are likely to engage in counterfactual thoughts about how they could have done better (e.g., "What could have been different?") and therefore will be less satisfied than negotiators whose first offers are not immediately accepted.[30] Most negotiators expect to make concessions during negotiation. (One exception is the bargaining style known as **boulwarism**, presented previously.)

Negotiators need to consider three things when formulating counteroffers and concessions: (1) the **pattern of concessions**, (2) the **magnitude of concessions**, and (3) the **timing of concessions**.

Pattern of Concessions

Unilateral concessions are concessions made by one party; in contrast, **bilateral concessions** are concessions made by both sides. Consider unilateral concessions made during negotiations for the University of Michigan's school-naming rights. Alumni donate millions of dollars to their business schools, hoping the school will be named after them. Stephen Ross, a property developer, made the first offer of $50 million to the business school's dean. The dean did not accept. Ross then made an immediate concession by doubling his offer to $100 million and received the naming rights.[31] The haunting question is whether he could have offered less and still received the naming rights. Negotiators who make fewer and smaller concessions maximize their slice of the pie,

[28]Schlender, B. (2006, May 29). Pixar's magic man. *Fortune, 153*(10), 139–146.
[29]Galinsky & Mussweiler, "First offers as anchors."
[30]Galinsky, A., Seiden, V., Kim, P. H., & Medvec, V. H. (2002). The dissatisfaction of having your first offer accepted: The role of counterfactual thinking in negotiations. *Personality and Social Psychology Bulletin, 28*(2), 271–283.
[31]News from the schools. Name games. (2007, January 23). *Economist.com.* Retrieved June 23, 2008, from http://www.economist.com/business/globalexecutive/displaystory.cfm?story_id=8546482

compared to those who make larger and more frequent concessions.[32] It is an almost universal norm that concessions take place in a quid pro quo fashion, meaning that negotiators expect a back-and-forth exchange of concessions between parties. People expect others to respond to concessions by making concessions in kind. However, negotiators should not offer more than a single concession at a time to the counterparty. Wait for a concession from the counterparty before making further concessions. An exception would be a situation in which you feel that the counterparty's offer is truly near his or her reservation point.

Magnitude of Concessions

Even though negotiators may make concessions in a back-and-forth method, this exchange does not say anything about the degree of concessions made by each party. Thus, a second consideration when making concessions is to determine how much to concede. The usual measure of a concession is the amount reduced or added (depending upon whether one is a seller or buyer) from one's previous offer. It is unwise to make consistently greater concessions than the counterparty.

The **graduated reduction in tension (GRIT) model** is a method in which parties avoid escalating conflict in order to reach mutual settlement within the bargaining zone. [33] The GRIT model, based on the reciprocity principle, calls for one party to make a concession and invites the other party to reciprocate by making a concession. The concession offered by the first party is significant, but not so much that the offering party is tremendously disadvantaged if the counterparty fails to reciprocate.

Hilty and Carnevale examined the degree of concessions made by negotiators over different points in the negotiation process (e.g., early on versus later). [34] They compared black-hat/white-hat (BH/WH) negotiators with white-hat/black-hat (WH/BH) negotiators. BH/WH negotiators began with a tough stance, made few early concessions, and later made larger concessions. WH/BH negotiators did the opposite: They began with generous concessions and then became tough and unyielding. The BH/WH concession strategy proved to be more effective than the WH/BH strategy in eliciting concessions from the counterparty. Why? The BH-turns-WH sets up a favorable contrast for the receiver. The person who has been dealing with the BH feels relieved to now be dealing with the WH.

Timing of Concessions

The timing of concessions refers to whether they are immediate, gradual, or delayed.[35] In an analysis of buyer-seller negotiations, sellers who made immediate concessions received the most negative reaction from the buyer—who showed least satisfaction and evaluated the object of sale most negatively. In contrast, when the seller made gradual concessions, the buyer's reaction was most positive, with high satisfaction.

---

[32]Siegel, S., & Fouraker, L. E. (1960). *Bargaining and group decision making.* New York: McGraw-Hill; Yukl, G. A. (1974). Effects of the opponent's initial offer, concession magnitude and concession frequency on bargaining behavior. *Journal of Personality and Social Psychology, 30*(3), 323–335.

[33]Osgood, C. E. (1962). *An alternative to war or surrender.* Urbana: University of Illinois Press.

[34]Hilty, J., & Carnevale, P. J. (1993). Black-hat/white-hat strategy in bilateral negotiation. *Organizational Behavior and Human Decision Processes, 55*(3), 444–469.

[35]Kwon, S., & Weingart, L. R. (2004). Unilateral concessions from the other party: Concession behavior, attributions, and negotiation judgments. *Journal of Applied Psychology, 89*(2), 263–278.

Strategy 8: Support Your Offers with Facts

The way in which an offer is presented affects the course of negotiations. Ideally, present a rationale that is objective and invites the counterparty to buy into your rationale. If your proposals are labeled as "fair," "even splits," or "compromises," they carry more impact. The importance of providing a rationale cannot be overestimated. Oftentimes, people simply want to hear that you have a rationale and don't even bother to assess the details of it. For example, Marilyn Machlowitz, a New York executive-search consultant, claims that during frequent case-by-case negotiations for reduced-travel deals sought by new hires, the potential employees are quicker to put family issues on the table. When interviewed for a foundation job that involved 40% travel, an executive candidate responded, "That's impossible. You're asking me not to be a father to my child."[36]

Sometimes, the rationale does not even need to make sense to be effective. Langer, Blank, and Chanowitz examined how often people were successful in terms of negotiating to cut in line at a photocopy machine.[37] Those who did not provide a rationale were the least successful (60%); those who presented a logical rationale were the most successful (94%). Interestingly, those who presented a meaningless rationale (e.g., "I have to cut in line because I need to make copies") were remarkably successful (93%). The next section of this chapter takes up the topic of fairness in detail.

Strategy 9: Appeal to Norms of Fairness

Most negotiators view themselves as fair. The ideal pie-slicing strategy is to determine which norms of fairness would be appropriate for the situation and then to use those norms to argue for your own target point. Fairness is subjective and therefore egocentric, meaning that a variety of norms of fairness exist and that negotiators usually focus on norms of fairness that serve their own interests.[38] Fairness is an arbitrary concept that can be used as a bargaining strategy; the negotiator should simultaneously be prepared to counterargue when the counterparty presents a fairness argument that does not serve his or her own interests. Consider the following example: Under Italian law, any antiquities found on Italian soil belong to the state. Arguments have taken place about many lost treasures, such as the "Getty bronze," a 3rd-century B.C. statue that was found by Italian fishermen and brought to the United States to be placed in the J. Paul Getty Museum in Los Angeles. The Getty Museum insisted it was found in international waters and was therefore acquired in good faith. When Italy filed a suit, the Italian court sided with the Americans. Italy then appealed to norms of fairness by pleading to five American museums to return all antiquities. By doing so, Italy regained almost 70 of their finest treasures, now on display in Rome.[39]

---

[36]Schellenbarger, S. (2007, July 12). The job less traveled: Workers seek relief from business trips. *Wall Street Journal*, p. B5.

[37]Langer, E., Blank, A., & Chanowitz, B. (1978). The mindlessness of ostensibly thoughtful action: The role of placebic information in interpersonal interaction. *Journal of Personality and Social Psychology, 36*, 635–642.

[38]Loewenstein, G. F., Thompson, L., & Bazerman, M. H. (1989). Social utility and decision making in interpersonal contexts. *Journal of Personality and Social Psychology, 57*(3), 426–441.

[39]Europe: Coming home; Italian art treasures. (2008, January 26). *The Economist, 386*(8564), 42.

Strategy 10: Do Not Fall for the "Even Split" Ploy

A common technique is the **even split** between whatever two offers are currently on the negotiation table. In many negotiation situations, such as in car and house buying, negotiators' offers do not overlap. Inevitably, one person has the bright idea of "splitting the difference." The concept of the even split has an appealing, almost altruistic flavor to it. To many of us, it seems unreasonable to refuse to compromise or meet the other person halfway. So what is the problem with even splits? The problem is that they are *based on values arrived at arbitrarily.* Consider a car-buying situation. Suppose you initially offered $33,000 for the car, then $34,000, and finally, $34,500. Suppose the salesperson initially requested $35,200, then reduced it to $35,000, and then to $34,600. The salesperson then suggests you split the difference at $34,550, arguing that an even split of the difference would be "fair." However, the pattern of offers up until that point was not "equal" in any sense. You made concessions of $1,500; the salesperson made concessions of $600. Further, even concessions that were of equal magnitude do not guarantee that the middle value is a "fair" value. It behooves a negotiator to begin with a high starting value and make small concessions. Often, the person who suggests the even split is in an advantageous position. Before accepting or proposing an even split, make sure the anchors are favorable to you.

THE MOST COMMONLY ASKED QUESTIONS

Should I Reveal My Reservation Point?

Revealing your reservation point is generally not a good strategy unless your reservation point is especially good and you suspect the bargaining zone is small. If you reveal your reservation price, be prepared for the other party to offer you your reservation price—but not more.

The most valuable piece of information you can have about the counterparty is his or her reservation point. This knowledge allows you to make the counterparty an offer that barely exceeds his or her reservation point and to claim the entire bargaining surplus for yourself. However, you should assume the counterparty is as smart as you are and therefore not likely to reveal his or her reservation point. By the same token, if you reveal your reservation point, little would stop the counterparty from claiming all of the bargaining surplus.

Some negotiators reveal their reservation point to demonstrate that they are bargaining in good faith and trust the other party. These negotiators rely on the counterparty's goodwill and trust their opponent not to take advantage of this information. Rather than revealing your reservation price, other, more effective ways can be used to build trust. For example, you could show a genuine concern for the needs and interests of the other party. The purpose of negotiation is to maximize your surplus, so why create a conflict of interest by "trusting" the other party with your reservation point?

Should I Lie About My Reservation Point?

If negotiators do well for themselves by not revealing their reservation point, perhaps they might do even better by lying, misrepresenting, or exaggerating their reservation point. Lying is not a good idea for three important reasons.

First, lying is unethical. Lewicki and Stark identified five types of behavior that some consider to be unethical in negotiations, including traditional competitive bargaining (e.g., exaggerating an initial offer or demand); attacking an opponent's network (e.g., attempting to get your opponent fired or threatening to make him or her look foolish); misrepresentation and lying (e.g., denying the validity of information your opponent has that weakens your negotiating position even though the information is valid); misuse of information (e.g., inappropriate information gathering); and false promises (e.g., offering to make future concessions that you know you won't follow through on; guaranteeing your constituency will uphold the settlement, even though you know they won't).[40]

Our examination of egocentrism and lying in tight social networks revealed that even though 40% of people believed that others in the network lied over a 10-week period, these same people admitted lying only about 22% of the time. Perhaps these egocentric perceptions drive the lawsuits that often occur in negotiations. For example, Textron was accused by its union of lying during labor negotiations.[41] Digital Equipment Corporation was accused of lying during pretrial negotiations,[42] and Woolworth was accused of misrepresenting the amount of asbestos in a building during the negotiation of a lease.[43] We are much more likely to see others as deceptive than we are to admit deceiving others. The message: Don't take chances!

Second, lying does not make sense strategically. Lying about your reservation point reduces the size of the bargaining zone. It means that negotiations in which the negotiator would prefer to reach an agreement will sometimes end in an impasse. Negotiators who lie about their reservation point often find it difficult to save face. The most common lie in negotiation is "This is my final offer." It is embarrassing to continue negotiating after making such a statement. Do not back yourself into a corner.

Third, lying hurts your reputation. People in the business community develop reputations that quickly spread via electronic mail, telephone, and word of mouth. Once you have the reputation of a tough negotiator, people behave more competitively with you, making it more difficult for you to claim resources. "Deceptive cheap talk" that is discovered by the other party negatively impacts a negotiator's outcomes.[44] People who discover that they have been deceived seek retribution, even though doing so may be costly to themselves. Experienced negotiators are able to extract more of the pie for themselves, but not when they have reputations for being "distributive."[45] So, avoid being labeled as a negotiator who is more bark than bite and who misrepresents himself at the negotiation table. Misrepresenting your reservation price is a poor substitute for preparation and developing strategy.

---

[40]Lewicki, R. J., & Stark, N. (1996). What's ethically appropriate in negotiations: An empirical examination of bargaining tactics. *Social Justice Research, 9*(1), 69–95.
[41]*Textron v. United Automobile,* 118 S. Ct. 1626 (1998).
[42]*Digital v. Desktop Direct,* 114 S. Ct. 1992, 1995 (1994).
[43]*Century 21 Inc. v. F. W. Woolworth Co.,* 181 A. D. 2D 620 (NY 1992). All three examples in this paragraph were reported in Schweitzer, M., & Croson, R. (1999). Curtailing deception: The impact of direct questions on lies and omissions. *International Journal of Conflict Management, 10,* 225–248.
[44]Croson, Boles, & Murnighan, "Cheap talk in bargaining experiments."
[45]Tinsley, C. H., O'Connor, K. M., & Sullivan, B. A. (2002). Tough guys finish last: The perils of a distributive reputation. *Organizational Behavior and Human Decision Processes, 88,* 621–642.

Should I Try to Manipulate the Counterparty's Reservation Point?

Assuming that the counterparty is reasonably intelligent, motivated, and informed (like you), he or she is not likely to fall prey to this transparent negotiation ploy. Such attempts may actually backfire, entrenching the counterparty more steadfastly in his or her position. Furthermore, you want to avoid other negotiators' attempts to turn the tables on you with similar influence tactics. You probably would not fall for it, so why should they?

Some negotiators are inclined to use scare tactics, such as "If you do not sell your house to us, there will not be another buyer" or "You'll regret not buying this company from me in 10 years when I am a billionaire." An alliance of financial firms planning to acquire the Sallie Mae corporation told the company that legislation passed in 2007 in the U.S. House of Representatives could hurt their business and scuttle the proposed $25 billion deal. The buyers used the warning as a negotiation tactic to get a better price for the company.[46] However, scare tactics are not likely to be effective. Rather, they are likely to backfire or engender ill will.

Should I Make a "Final Offer" or Commit to a Position?

In general, taking such a stance is not an effective negotiation strategy because you lose the ability to be flexible. The phrase "This is my final offer" has much more effective impact when said later in a negotiation. Making an irrevocable commitment, such as a "final offer," really should be done only when you mean it and you feel comfortable walking away from the bargaining table. Of course, you should only walk away from the bargaining table if your BATNA is more attractive than the counterparty's offer. Intimidating the other party is risky. It is difficult to make "binding" commitments that are credible. Consider the threat that New foundland and Labrador Premier Danny Williams made to Exxon Mobil. Williams was negotiating the multi-billion-dollar Hebron offshore oil deal that would live or die on his terms. Williams based his position on the importance of an adequate deal to Newfoundlanders, committed to it and challenged oil companies, "Well, fine. Go somewhere else. We'll still have our oil." In 2007, Exxon Mobil and Chevron gave in and agreed to Williams's terms.[47] In this situation, the threat worked. However, in other situations threats don't work.

SAVING FACE

"Face," or dignity, in a negotiation has been called "one of an individual's most sacred possessions."[48] **Face** is the value a person places on his or her public image, reputation, and status vis-à-vis other people in the negotiation. Direct threats to face in a negotiation include making ultimatums, criticisms, challenges, and insults. Often, the mere presence of an audience can make "saving face" of paramount importance for a negotiator. When a person's face is threatened in a negotiation, it can tip the balance of his or her behavior away from cooperation toward competition, resulting in impasses and lose-lose outcomes.

People differ in terms of how sensitive they are to losing face. A negotiator's face threat sensitivity (FTS) is the likelihood of having a negative reaction to a face

---

[46]Heath, T., & Paley, A. R. (2007, July 12). Sallie Mae deal thrown into question; buyers balk at subsidy cut, but some call it posturing. *Washington Post,* p. D01.
[47]Campbell, C. (2007, September 10–17). How to win, in a fight with Big Oil. *Maclean's: Toronto, 120*(35/36), 62.
[48]Deutsch, M. (1961). The face of bargaining. *Operations Research, 9,* 886–897.

threat.[49] People with high FTS have a lower threshold for detecting and responding to face threats. Their emotional responses range from anger or frustration to a feeling of betrayal or sadness. In turn, they may not trust the other party and refuse to share information. We measured negotiators' FTS and the impact it had on their behavior and the quality of their negotiated outcomes.[50] Negotiators were asked how easily their feelings get hurt, the extent to which they are "thin-skinned" and "don't respond well to criticism." In buyer-seller negotiations, fewer win-win agreements were reached when the seller had high FTS. Moreover, in employment negotiations, job candidates were less likely to make win-win deals if they had high FTS.

The best way to help the other party save face is not to let on, in any way, that you think he or she has lost face and not to put him or her in a take-it-or-leave-it spot. You can take several steps whenever the other person seems to be staking out an irrevocable stance, such as labeling an offer as "final."

First, you may not want to acknowledge statements made by the other party in the heat of conflict. Instead of saying "So, if this is your final offer, I guess things are over," you might say "Let me consider your offer and get back to you." By not acknowledging the finality of an offer, you provide the other party with an "out" to resume negotiations later. For example, during the 1985 Geneva Summit meeting, a tense moment occurred when Mikhail Gorbachev of the Soviet Union glumly declared (after hours of negotiating with U.S. president Ronald Reagan), "It looks as if we've reached an impasse."[51] Instead of acknowledging this comment, Reagan quickly suggested that they take a break and proposed taking a walk outside. This suggestion proved to be a critical move in allowing Gorbachev to come back to the table. Said Gorbachev, "Fresh air may bring fresh ideas." Reagan replied, "Maybe we'll find the two go together."[52]

In other situations, you may have to help the other party by finding a face-saving strategy, perhaps achieved by relabeling some of the terms of the negotiation. An excellent example of face saving occurred in the General Motors–Canadian UAW strike talks. The Canadian union had insisted on a wage increase; GM wanted to institute a profit-sharing scheme but keep wages at a minimum, especially because of GM's fear of a slippery slope. A solution was devised such that wages were kept at a minimum but workers were given an incentive-based increase.[53]

THE POWER OF FAIRNESS

Fairness concerns pervade aspects of social life from corporate policy to sibling squabbles.[54] Next is an "everything you have always wanted to know about fairness" course for the negotiator who is concerned with pie slicing.

[49]Tynan, R. O. (2005). The effects of threat sensitivity and face giving on dyadic psychological safety and upward communication. *Journal of Applied Social Psychology. 35*(2), 223-247.

[50]White, J. B., Tynan, R., Galinsky, A. D., & Thompson, L. L. (2004). Face threat sensitivity in negotiation: Roadblock to agreement and joint gain. *Organizational Behavior and Human Decision Processes, 94,* 102–124.

[51]Thomas, E. (1985, December 2). Fencing at the fireside summit: With candor and civility, Reagan and Gorbachev grapple for answers to the arms-race riddle. *Time,* 22.

[52]Ibid.

[53]Gunnarsson, S., & Collison, R. (Directors/Producers). (1985). *Final offer.* Montreal: National Film Board of Canada.

[54]Deutsch, M. (1985). *Distributive justice: A social-psychological perspective.* New Haven, CT: Yale University

Multiple Methods of Fair Division

Fairness comes in many forms and types. Most often, negotiators use one of three fairness principles when it comes to slicing the pie: equality, equity, and need: [55]

1. ***Equality rule,*** or *blind justice,* prescribes equal shares for all. Outcomes are distributed without regard to inputs, and everyone benefits (or suffers) equally. The U.S. education system and legal systems are examples of equality justice: Everyone receives equal entitlement.

2. ***Equity rule,*** or *proportionality of contributions principle,* prescribes that distribution should be proportional to a person's contribution. The free market system in the United States is an example of the equity principle. In many universities, students bid for classes; those who bid more points have greater entitlement to a seat in the course.

3. ***Needs-based rule,*** or *welfare-based allocation,* states that benefits should be proportional to need. The social welfare system in the United States is based on need. In many universities, financial aid is based on need.

Situation-Specific Rules of Fairness

Different fairness rules apply in different situations.[56] For example, most of us believe that our court/penal justice system should be equality-based: Everyone should have the right to an equal and fair trial regardless of income or need (equality principle). In contrast, most believe that academic grades should be assigned on the basis of an equity-based rule: Students who contribute more should be rewarded with higher marks (equity principle). Similarly, most people agree that disabled persons are entitled to parking spaces and easy access to buildings (needs principle). However, sometimes fierce debates arise (e.g., affirmative action, with some arguing it is important for people who have been historically disadvantaged to have equal access and others arguing for pure equity-based, or merit-only, rules).

The goals involved in a negotiation situation often dictate which fairness rule is employed.[57] For example, if our goal is to minimize waste, then a needs-based or social welfare policy is most appropriate.[58] If our goal is to maintain or enhance harmony and group solidarity, equality-based rules are most effective.[59] If our goal is to enhance productivity and performance, equity-based allocation is most effective.[60]

Similarly, a negotiator's relationship to the other party strongly influences the choice of fairness rules. When negotiators share similar attitudes and beliefs, when they

---

[55]Ibid.

[56]Schwinger, T. (1980). Just allocations of goods: Decisions among three principles. In G. Mikula (Ed.), *Justice and social interaction: Experimental and theoretical contributions from psychological research* (pp. 95–125). New York: Springer-Verlag.

[57]Mikula, G. (1980). On the role of justice in allocation decisions. In G. Mikula (Ed.), *Justice and social interaction: Experimental and theoretical contributions from psychological research* (pp. 127–166). New York: Springer-Verlag.

[58]Berkowitz, L. (1972). Social norms, feelings and other factors affecting helping behavior and altruism. In L. Berkowitz (Ed.), *Advances in experimental social psychology: Vol. 6* (pp. 63–108). New York: Academic Press.

[59]Leventhal, H. (1976). The distribution of rewards and resources in groups and organizations. In L. Berkowitz & E. Walster (Eds.), *Advances in experimental social psychology: Vol. 9* (pp. 92–133). New York: Academic Press.

[60]Deutsch, M. (1953). The effects of cooperation and competition upon group processes. In D. Cartwright & A. Zander (Eds.), *Group dynamics* (pp. 319–353). Evanston, IL: Row, Peterson.

are physically close to one another, or when it is likely they will engage in future interaction, they prefer equality rules. When the allocation is public (others know what choices are made), equality is used; when allocation is private, equity is preferred. Friends tend to use equality, whereas nonfriends or acquaintances use equity. [61] Further, people in relationships with others do not consistently employ one rule of fairness but, rather, use different fairness rules for specific incidences that occur within relationships. For example, when people in relationships are asked to describe a recent incident from their own relationship that illustrates a particular justice principle (equity, equality, or need), needs-based fairness is related to incidents involving nurturing and personal development, whereas equity and equality-based fairness are related to situations involving the allocation of responsibilities. [62] In general, equality-based pie-slicing strategies are associated with more positive feelings about the decision, the situation, and one's partner.

Fairness rules also depend on whether people are dealing with rewards versus costs (recall our discussion about the framing effect in Chapter 2). Equality is often used to allocate benefits, but equity is more commonly used to allocate burdens. [63] For example, in one investigation, people were involved in a two-party negotiation concerning a joint project. [64] In the benefit-sharing condition, negotiators were told that their joint project produced a total earning of 3,000 GL (a hypothetical monetary unit) and their task was to reach an agreement about how to divide this amount with their partner. Participants were told they had personally incurred a cost of 1,350 GL for this project and their final profile would be determined by subtracting 1,350 from the negotiated agreement amount. In the cost-sharing condition, the situation was exactly the same, except participants were told they had personally invested 1,650 GL. Thus, the bargaining situation was identical in both situations, with the exception of the personal investment. Obviously, an equal split of 3,000 GL would mean 1,500 GL apiece, which would result in a gain in the benefit condition and a loss in the cost condition. Negotiators were more demanding and tougher when bargaining how to share costs than benefits. Furthermore, fewer equal-split decisions were reached in the cost condition.

The selection of fairness rules is also influenced by extenuating circumstances. Consider, for example, a physically handicapped person who attains an advanced degree. A person who overcomes external constraints is more highly valued than a person who does not face constraints but contributes the same amount. When a situation is complex, involving multiple inputs in different dimensions, people are more likely to use the equality rule. Thus, groups often split dinner bills equally rather than compute each person's share. This approach can lead to a problem, however. Group members

[61] Austin, W. (1980). Friendship and fairness: Effects of type of relationship and task performance on choice of distribution rules. *Personality and Social Psychology Bulletin, 6,* 402–408.

[62] Steil, J. M., & Makowski, D. G. (1989). Equity, equality, and need: A study of the patterns and outcomes associated with their use in intimate relationships. *Social Justice Research, 3,* 121–137.

[63] Sondak, H., Neale, M. A., & Pinkley, R. (1995). The negotiated allocation of benefits and burdens: The impact of outcome valence, contribution and relationship. *Organizational Behavior and Human Decision Processes, 64*(3), 249–260.

[64] Ohtsubo, Y., & Kameda, T. (1998). The function of equality heuristic in distributive bargaining: Negotiated allocation of costs and benefits in a demand revelation context. *Journal of Experimental Social Psychology, 34,* 90–108.

aware of the pervasive use of equality may actually spend more individually. No group member wants to pay for more than he or she gets; if people cannot control the consumption of others, they consume more. Of course, when everyone thinks this way, the costs escalate, leading to irrational group behavior (a topic we discuss in Chapter 11 on social dilemmas).

Different fairness rules are a potential source of conflict and inconsistency.[65] For example, people who are allocating resources choose different rules of fairness than do people who are on the receiving end. Allocators often distribute resources equally, even if they have different preferences. In contrast, recipients who have been inequitably, but advantageously treated justify their shares—even when they would not have awarded themselves the resources they received.[66]

Social Comparison

Social comparison is an inevitable fact of life in organizations and relationships. Even if we do not desire to compare ourselves with others, we inevitably hear about someone's higher salary, larger office, special opportunities, or grander budget. Social situations are constant reminders of how others (strangers, acquaintances, and friends) compare with us in terms of fortune, fame, and happiness. How do we react to social comparisons? Are we happy for other people—do we bask in their glory when they achieve successes—or are we threatened and angry?

When does performance of another individual enhance our personal self-evaluation, and when does it threaten our self-worth? When we compare ourselves to one another, we consider the relevance of the comparison to our self-concept. People have beliefs and values that reflect their central dimensions of the self. Some dimensions are highly self-relevant; others are irrelevant. It all depends on how a person defines himself or herself. The performance of other people can affect our self-evaluation, especially when we are psychologically close to them. When we observe someone who is close to us performing extremely well in an area that we highly identify with, our self-evaluation is threatened. Such "upward" comparisons can lead to envy, frustration, anger, and even sabotage. Upon hearing that a member of one's cohort made some extremely timely investments in companies that have paid off multifold and is now a multimillionaire, people who pride themselves on their financial wizardry probably feel threatened. The fact that our colleague excels in an area that we pride ourselves on rubs salt in the wounds of the psyche. When another person outperforms us on a behavior that is irrelevant to our self-definition, the better her or his performance and the closer our relationship, the more we take pride in his or her success.

When it comes to pay and compensation, people are more concerned about how much they are paid relative to other people than about the absolute level of their pay (see Exhibit 3-3 for an example of social comparison).[67]

---

[65]Deutsch, *Distributive justice.*

[66]Diekmann, K. A., Samuels, S. M., Ross, L., & Bazerman, M. H. (1997). Self-interest and fairness in problems of resource allocation. *Journal of Personality and Social Psychology, 72*(5), 1061–1074.

[67]Adams, S. (1965). Inequity in social exchange. In L. Berkowitz (Ed.), *Advances in experimental social psychology: Vol. 2* (pp. 267–299). New York: Academic Press; Blau, P. M. (1964). *Exchange and power in social life.* New York: Wiley; Deutsch, *Distributive justice;* Homans, G. C. (1961). *Social behavior: Its elementary forms.* New York: Harcourt, Brace, Jovanovich; Walster, E., Berscheid, E., & Walster, G. W. (1973). New directions in equity research. *Journal of Personality and Social Psychology, 25,* 151–176.

EXHIBIT 3-3   Self-Interest Versus Social Comparison

Imagine that you are being recruited for a position in firm A. Your colleague, Jay, of similar background and skill, is also being recruited by firm A. Firm A has made you and Jay the following salary offers:

Your salary: $75,000
Jay's salary: $95,000

Your other option is to take a position at firm B, which has made you an offer. Firm B has also made your colleague, Ines, an offer:

Your salary: $72,000
Ines's salary: $72,000

Which job offer do you take, firm A's or firm B's? If you follow the principles of rational judgment outlined in Appendix 1, you will take firm A's offer—it pays more money. However, if you are like most people, you prefer firm B's offer because you do not like feeling you are being treated unfairly.

Source: Bazerman, M. H., Loewenstein, G., & White, S. (1992). Reversals of preference in allocating decisions: Judging an alternative versus choosing among alternatives. *Administrative Science Quarterly, 37,* 220–240. Used by permission of Administrative Science Quarterly.

With whom do people compare themselves? Three social comparison targets may be distinguished: upward comparison, downward comparison, and comparison with similar others.

1. *Upward comparison*   occurs when people compare themselves to someone who is better off, more accomplished, or higher in status. The young entrepreneur starting his own software company may compare himself to Bill Gates. Oftentimes, people compare themselves upward for inspiration and motivation.

2. *Downward comparison*   occurs when people compare themselves to someone who is less fortunate, able, accomplished, or lower in status. For example, when a young manager's marketing campaign proves to be a complete flop, she may compare herself to a colleague whose decisions led to the loss of hundreds of thousands of dollars. Downward comparison often makes people feel better about their own state.

3. *Comparison with similar others*   occurs when people choose someone of similar background, skill, and ability with whom to compare themselves. Comparison with similar others is useful when people desire to have accurate appraisals of their abilities.

What drives the choice of the comparison to others? A number of goals and motives may drive social comparison, including the following:

1. *Self-improvement:*   People compare themselves with others who can serve as models of success.[68] For example, a beginning chess player may compare his or her skill level with a grand master. Upward comparison provides inspiration, insight, and challenge, but it can also lead to feelings of discouragement and incompetence.

---

[68]Taylor, S. E., & Lobel, M. (1989). Social comparison activity under threat: Downward evaluation and upward contacts. *Psychological Bulletin, 96,* 569–575.

2. ***Self-enhancement:***   The desire to maintain or enhance a positive view of oneself may lead people to bias information in self-serving ways. Rather than seek truth, people seek comparisons that show them in a favorable light. People make downward comparisons with others who are less fortunate, less successful, and so forth.[69]

3. ***Accurate self-evaluation:***   The desire for truthful knowledge about oneself (even if the outcome is not favorable).

The Equity Principle

When it comes to relationships and slicing the pie, people make judgments about what is fair based on what they are investing in the relationship and what they are getting out of it. Inputs are investments in a relationship that usually entail costs. For example, the person who manages the finances and pays the bills in a relationship incurs time and energy costs. An output is something that a person receives from a relationship. The person who does not pay the bills enjoys the benefits of a financial service. Outputs, or outcomes, may be positive or negative. In many cases, A's input is B's outcome, and B's input is A's outcome. For example, a company pays (input) an employee (outcome) who gives time and expertise (input) to further the company's goals (outcome). Consider the negotiations between the Writers Guild of America (WGA) and its employers. Employers wanted to extend the WGA's existing contract that pays writers residuals based on reuse of their works. However, the writers were frustrated with their compensation and rejected the employers' proposal. The writers created a "Contract Bulletin" that included eight charts emphasizing rising financial profitability at media companies: Growth was evident in almost every single measure of economic performance, including gross revenues in every segment, excellent operating profits, and rising share prices for all six major entertainment companies. In short, the writers argued that their "inputs" were worth more than what the employers gave them.[70]

Equity exists in a relationship if each person's outcomes are proportional to his or her inputs. Equity, therefore, refers to equivalence of the outcome/input ratio of parties; inequity exists when the ratio of outcomes to inputs is unequal. Equity exists when the profits (rewards minus costs) of two actors are equal.[71] However, complications arise if two people have different views of what constitutes a legitimate investment, cost, or reward and how they rank each one. For example, consider salaries paid to players in the National Basketball Association (NBA). With the starting players taking the greatest salaries (capped at a fixed amount), little is left over to pay the last three or four players on a 12-person team roster. The minimum salary of $385,277 might seem extraordinarily high to the average person, but in the context of the team, with an average salary of $7.3 million and a star salary of $29.5 million per year to the Miami Heat's Shaquille O'Neal in 2005, it reflects a sizeable disparity.[72] (See Exhibit 3-4 for the pay differential in Chicago Bears' players.)

---

[69]Wills, T. A. (1981). Downward comparison principles in social psychology. *Psychological Bulletin, 90,* 245–271.

[70]Hiberd, J., & Krukowski, A. (2007, July 16). WGA salvo kicks off contract talks. *Television Week, 26*(29), 3–4.

[71]Homans, *Social behavior.*

[72]HoopsHype.com salaries. (2002–2007). Retrieved June 23, 2008, from http://www.hoopshype.com/salaries.htm

EXHIBIT 3-4 Pay Differential, NFL, Chicago Bears

Player	Base Salary	Sign Bonus	Other Bonus	Total Salary	Cap Value
Adams, Anthony	$ 750,000	$ 750,000	$ 300,000	$ 1,800,000	$ 1,237,500
Adams, Daniel 'Blue'	$ 0	$ 0	$ 0	$ 420,000	$ 0
Anderson, Mark	$ 360,000	$ 156,550	$ 4,680	$ 364,680	$ 403,817
Archuleta, Adam	$ 595,000	$ 500,000	$ 4,503,600	$ 5,098,600	$ 5,098,600
Ayanbadejo, Brendon	$ 595,000	$ 0	$ 4,320	$ 599,320	$ 599,320
Bazuin, Dan	$ 285,000	$ 764,000	$ 421,000	$ 1,049,000	$ 476,000
Beekman, Josh	$ 285,000	$ 392,500	$ 0	$ 677,500	$ 383,125
Benson, Cedric	$ 620,000	$ 4,000,000	$ 1,734,680	$ 624,680	$ 3,133,680
Berrian, Bernard	$ 850,000	$ 672,000	$ 4,680	$ 854,680	$ 1,022,680
Bradley, Mark	$ 435,000	$ 1,550,000	$ 4,800	$ 439,800	$ 899,800
Briggs, Lance	$ 7,206,000	$ 0	$ 0	$ 7,206,000	$ 7,206,000
Brown, Alex	$ 595,000	$ 5,500,000	$ 503,600	$ 1,098,600	$ 2,012,695
Brown, Mike	$ 2,440,000	$ 4,000,000	$ 50,000	$ 2,490,000	$ 3,156,666
Brown, Ruben	$ 1,000,000	$ 1,000,000	$ 204,320	$ 2,204,320	$ 2,204,320
Busing, John	$ 0	$ 0	$ 0	$ 254,118	$ 0
Clark, Desmond	$ 1,225,000	$ 1,000,000	$ 281,720	$ 1,506,720	$ 1,673,386
Davis, Rashied	$ 435,000	$ 0	$ 4,800	$ 439,800	$ 439,800
Dorsey, De De	$ 0	$ 0	$ 0	$ 296,471	$ 0
Dvoracek, Dusty	$ 360,000	$ 754,500	$ 4,680	$ 364,680	$ 553,305
Garay, Antonio	$ 510,000	$ 0	$ 0	$ 480,000	$ 480,000
Garza, Roberto	$ 691,250	$ 0	$ 79,800	$ 771,050	$ 1,516,050
Gattis, Josh	$ 0	$ 0	$ 0	$ 217,941	$ 0
Gilmore, John	$ 595,000	$ 400,000	$ 75,000	$ 670,000	$ 870,000
Gould, Robbie	$ 435,000	$ 0	$ 4,560	$ 439,560	$ 439,560
Graham, Corey	$ 285,000	$ 149,500	$ 0	$ 434,500	$ 322,375
Griese, Brian	$ 1,250,000	$ 0	$ 1,350,000	$ 1,600,000	$ 2,500,000
Grossman, Rex	$ 2,035,000	$ 2,050,000	$ 1,004,800	$ 2,039,800	$ 2,492,300
Harris, Tommie	$ 765,000	$ 2,100,000	$ 1,324,200	$ 1,989,200	$ 2,650,450
Hass, Mike	$ 285,000	$ 0	$ 4,800	$ 289,800	$ 289,800
Hester, Devin	$ 360,000	$ 0	$ 105,420	$ 1,271,820	$ 666,820
Hill, Quadtrine	$ 285,000	$ 0	$ 0	$ 190,000	$ 190,000
Hillenmeyer, Hunter	$ 950,000	$ 0	$ 550,000	$ 1,500,000	$ 1,500,000
Idonije, Israel	$ 1,300,000	$ 1,600,000	$ 503,720	$ 1,803,720	$ 2,203,720
Jimoh, Ade	$ 0	$ 0	$ 0	$ 490,000	$ 0
Jones, Dhani	$ 0	$ 0	$ 0	$ 525,000	$ 0
Kreutz, Olin	$ 3,450,000	$ 0	$ 50,000	$ 3,500,000	$ 5,666,670
Mannelly, Patrick	$ 720,000	$ 560,000	$ 4,680	$ 724,680	$ 836,680
Manning, Danieal	$ 360,000	$ 820,000	$ 559,080	$ 784,080	$ 709,080
Manning, Ricky	$ 1,065,000	$ 0	$ 2,300,000	$ 2,165,000	$ 3,365,000
Maynard, Brad	$ 875,000	$ 900,000	$ 31,720	$ 906,720	$ 1,236,720
McBride, Trumaine	$ 285,000	$ 55,250	$ 0	$ 340,250	$ 298,812
McClover, Darrell	$ 435,000	$ 75,000	$ 4,800	$ 514,800	$ 477,300
McGowan, Brandon	$ 435,000	$ 0	$ 4,800	$ 439,800	$ 439,800

(continued)

McKie, Jason	$ 595,000	$ 1,000,000	$ 50,000	$ 645,000	$ 845,000
Metcalf, Terrence	$ 825,000	$ 3,283,333	$ 4,680	$ 829,680	$ 1,486,346
Miller, Fred	$ 3,000,000	$ 6,000,000	$ 604,560	$ 3,504,560	$ 4,704,560
Muhammad, Muhsin	$ 1,915,000	$ 0	$ 4,080	$ 1,919,080	$ 3,119,080
Ogunleye, Adewale	$ 3,900,000	$ 10,000,000	$ 4,200	$ 3,904,200	$ 5,563,055
Okwo, Michael	$ 285,000	$ 617,500	$ 0	$ 807,500	$ 344,375
Olsen, Greg	$ 285,000	$ 250,000	$ 1,498,718	$ 1,255,000	$ 1,055,000
Orton, Kyle	$ 435,000	$ 458,000	$ 4,320	$ 439,320	$ 553,820
Payne, Kevin	$ 285,000	$ 150,000	$ 0	$ 435,000	$ 322,500
Peterson, Adrian (Ga. Southern)	$ 595,000	$ 0	$ 222,500	$ 620,000	$ 817,500
Polite, Lousaka	$ 435,000	$ 0	$ 0	$ 435,000	$ 435,000
Runnels, J.D.	$ 360,000	$ 85,000	$ 4,680	$ 209,680	$ 230,930
St. Clair, John	$ 750,000	$ 750,000	$ 25,000	$ 775,000	$ 1,025,000
Tait, John	$ 4,450,000	$ 0	$ 50,000	$ 4,500,000	$ 5,000,000
Tillman, Charles	$ 1,045,000	$ 8,500,000	$ 2,559,720	$ 12,104,720	$ 5,432,386

Source: USA Today salaries databases. Retrieved on September 3, 2007. Reprinted by permission of USA Today, from http://content.usatoday.com/sports/football/nfl/salaries/teamdetail.aspx?team=5&year=2007&loc=interstitialskip

Equity exists when a person perceives equality between the ratio of his or her own outcomes (O) to inputs (I) and the ratio of the other person's outcomes to inputs, where a and b represent two people:[73]

$$\frac{O_a}{I_a} = \frac{O_b}{I_b}$$

However, this equity formula is less applicable to situations in which inputs and outcomes might be either positive or negative. The basic equity formula may be reconstructed as follows:

$$\frac{O_a - I_a}{|I_a|^{ka}} = \frac{O_b - I_b}{|I_b|^{kb}}$$

This formula proposes that equity prevails when the disparity between person a's outcomes and inputs and person b's outcomes and inputs are equivalently proportional to the absolute value of each of their inputs. The numerator is "profit," and the denominator adjusts for positive or negative signs of input. Each k takes on the value of either $+1$ or -1, depending on the valence of participants' inputs and gains (outcomes $-$ inputs).

Restoring Equity

Suppose that you were hired by company X last year with an annual salary of $85,000. You felt happy about your salary until you learned that your colleague at the same company, whom you regard to be of equivalent skill and background, is paid $5,000 more per year. How do you deal with this inequity? When people find themselves in an inequitable relationship, they become distressed; the greater the

---

[73]Adams, "Inequity in social exchange," p. 37.

perceived inequity, the more distressed people feel. Distress drives people to attempt to restore equity.

People who believe they are underpaid feel dissatisfied and seek to restore equity.[74] For example, underpaid workers lower their level of effort and productivity to restore equity,[75] and in some cases they leave organizations characterized by inequity to join an organization in which wages are more fairly distributed, even if they are less highly paid in absolute terms.[76] Consider what happened when two vice presidents of a major *Fortune* 100 company were promoted to senior vice president at about the same time in the late 1990s.[77] Both of them moved into new offices, but one of them suspected an inequity. He pulled out blueprints and measured the square footage of each office. His suspicions were confirmed when it turned out the other guy's office was bigger than his by a few feet. A former employee said, "He blew a gasket." Walls were moved, and his office was reconfigured to make it as large as his counterpart's.

People use the following six means to eliminate the tension arising from inequity:[78]

1. ***Alter the inputs.***   (The senior VP could work less hard, take on fewer projects, take more days off, etc.)
2. ***Alter the outcomes.***   (The senior VP could make his office bigger—which he did.)
3. ***Cognitively distort inputs or outcomes.***   (The senior VP could minimize the importance of his contributions and maximize the perceived value of his office—for example, by deciding that his office was quieter than that of his counterpart.)
4. ***Leave the situation.***   (The senior VP could quit his job.)
5. ***Cognitively distort either the inputs or the outcomes of an exchange partner.***   (The senior VP may view the other VP as contributing more, or perhaps regard the big office to be less attractive than it actually is.)
6. ***Change the object of comparison.***   (The senior VP may stop comparing himself to the other senior VP and start comparing himself to someone else in the company.)

The use of the first two strategies depends on whether the person has been over- or underrewarded. Overrewarded individuals can increase their inputs or decrease their outcomes to restore equal ratios, whereas underrewarded people must decrease their inputs or increase their outcomes. For example, people work harder if they think they are overpaid. Conversely, people may cheat or steal if they are underpaid.[79]

Given the various methods of restoring equity, what determines which method will be used? People engage in a cost-benefit analysis and choose the method that maximizes positive outcomes. Usually, this method minimizes the necessity of increasing any of one's own inputs that are difficult or costly to change and also minimizes the necessity of real changes or cognitive changes in inputs/outcomes that are central to self-concept. Simply put, it is often easier to rationalize a situation than to do something about it. Further, this type of change minimizes the necessity of leaving the situation or

---

[74]Walster, Berscheid, & Walster, "New directions in equity research."

[75]Greenberg, J. (1988). Equity and workplace status: A field experiment. *Journal of Applied Psychology, 73,* 606–613.

[76]Schmitt, D., & Marwell, G. (1972). Withdrawal and reward reallocation in response to inequity. *Journal of Experimental Social Psychology, 8,* 207–221.

[77]Klein, "Lord of the flies."

[78]Adams, "Inequity in social exchange."

[79]Greenberg, J. (1990). Employee theft as a reaction to underpayment inequity: The hidden cost of pay cuts. *Journal of Applied Psychology, 75,* 561–568.

EXHIBIT 3-5   Distributed Versus Concentrated Unfairness

Within an organizational setting, many acts of unfair or unjust behavior may occur. For example, a person of color may be passed over for a promotion. A woman with managerial skills may be relegated to administrative and secretarial tasks. How do employees react to injustice in the organization? Consider two hypothetical companies: A and B. In each company, the overall incidence of unfair behavior is identical. In company A, the unfair incidences (i.e., percentage of total acts) are targeted toward a single individual—a black female. In company B, the unfair incidences are spread among three individuals—a black female, a Hispanic male, and an older, handicapped white male. The fact that the incidences are concentrated on a single individual or spread out over many organizational members should be irrelevant, if the overall incidence of unfairness in each organization is the same. In practice, however, these situations are viewed quite differently.

In a simulated organization, each of three employees was victimized in one out of three interactions with a manager. In another company, one of the three employees was victimized in all three out of three interactions with a manager; the two other employees were treated fairly. Thus, in both companies, the incidence of unfairness was identical. However, groups' overall judgment of the unfairness of the manager was greater when the injustice was spread across members than when it was concentrated on one individual. Most disconcertingly, targets of discrimination were marginalized by other group members. Blaming-the-victim effects may be more rampant when individuals are the sole targets of discrimination—ironically, when they need the most support.

Source: Lind, E. A., Kray, L., & Thompson, L. (1996). Adversity in organizations: Reactions to Injustice. Paper presented at the Psychology of Adversity Conference, Amherst, MA.

changing the object of social comparison once it has stabilized. Thus, we are not likely to ask for a salary cut if we think we are overpaid, but we are more inclined to regard the work we do as more demanding. (See Exhibit 3-5 for an examination of factors that can cause to reactions to inequity.)

The equity drive is so strong that people who are denied the opportunity to restore equity will derogate others, thereby restoring **psychological equity**. If distortion must occur, people focus on the other person's inputs or outcomes before distorting their own, especially if such distortion threatens their self-esteem. Leaving the situation and changing the object of comparison involves the highest costs because they disrupt the status quo and violate justice beliefs.

Procedural Justice

In addition to their slice of the pie, people are concerned with the way resources are distributed.[80] People evaluate not only the fairness of outcomes but also the fairness of the procedures by which those outcomes are determined. People's evaluations of the fairness of procedures determine their satisfaction and willingness to comply

---

[80]Thibaut, J., & Walker, L. (1975). *Procedural justice: A psychological analysis.* Hillsdale, NJ: Erlbaum; Thibaut, J., & Walker, L. (1978). A theory of procedure. *California Law Review, 60,* 541–566; Leventhal, "The distribution of rewards and resources"; Leventhal, H. (1980). What should be done with equity theory? New approaches to the study of fairness in social exchange. In K. Gergen, M. Greenberg, & R. Willis (Eds.), *Social exchange: Advances in theory and research* (pp. 27–55). New York: Plenum Press.

with outcomes. For example, managers who educate employees (i.e., explain to them why change is occurring, such as in the case of a merger) find that it increases employee commitment to the change.[81] Employees who believe they have been mistreated are more likely to exit and exhibit work withdrawal.[82] The process of explaining decisions in a change context helps employees adapt to the change, whereas the lack of an explanation is often regarded by employees as unfair, generating resentment toward management and toward the decision.[83] An investigation of 183 employees of seven private-sector organizations, each of whom had just completed a relocation, revealed that perceived fairness was higher when justification was provided in the case of unfavorable change.[84] In 2007, the baseball commissioner's office asked umpires to sign authorizations for background checks. The World Umpires Association reacted to this by instructing its members not to sign the forms but promised to allow background checks if Major League Baseball (MLB) added an additional umpire to each postseason crew. No agreement was reached because MLB didn't see the offer as fair and was "offended by the effort to trade economics against integrity."[85]

Fairness in Relationships

Consider the following situation: You and a college friend developed a potentially revolutionary (and profitable) idea for a new kind of water ski.[86] You spent about half a year in your dorm basement developing a prototype of the new invention. Your friend had the original idea; you developed the design and materials and assembled the prototype. The two of you talk to a patent lawyer about getting a patent, and the lawyer tells you a patent is pending on a similar product but the company will offer you $3,000 for one of the innovative features of your design. You and your friend gladly accept. What division of the $3,000 between you and your friend would you find to be most satisfying?

People's preferences for several possible distributions of the money for themselves and the other person were assessed.[87] People's utility functions were *social* rather than *individual,* meaning that individual satisfaction was strongly influenced by the payoffs received by the other, as well as the payoffs received by the self (see Exhibit 3-6). Social utility functions were tent shaped. The most satisfying outcome was equal shares for the self and other ($1,500 apiece). Discrepancies between payoffs to the self versus the other led to lower satisfaction. However, social utility functions were lopsided in that advantageous inequity (self receives more than other) was preferable to disadvantageous inequity (other receives more than self). Further, the relationship people had with the other party mattered: In positive or neutral relationships, people preferred

[81]Kotter, J., & Schlesinger, L. (1979). Choosing strategies for change. *Harvard Business Review, 57*(2), 106–114.
[82]Boswell, W., & Olson-Buchanan, J. (2004). Experiencing mistreatment at work: The role of grievance filing, nature of mistreatment and employee withdrawal. *Academy of Management Journal, 47*(1), 129–139.
[83]Daly, J. P., & Geyer, P. D. (1994). The role of fairness in implementing large-scale change: Employee evaluations of process and outcome in seven facility relocations. *Journal of Organizational Behavior, 15,* 623–638.
[84]Daly, J. P. (1995). Explaining changes to employees: The influence of justifications and change outcomes on employees' fairness judgments. *Journal of Applied Behavioral Science, 31*(4), 415–428.
[85]Schwarz, A. (2007, August 7). Baseball wants to look at umpires finances. *New York Times,* p. D2.
[86]Loewenstein, Thompson, & Bazerman, "Social utility and decision making."
[87]Ibid.

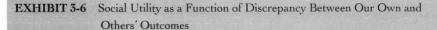

EXHIBIT 3-6   Social Utility as a Function of Discrepancy Between Our Own and
Others' Outcomes

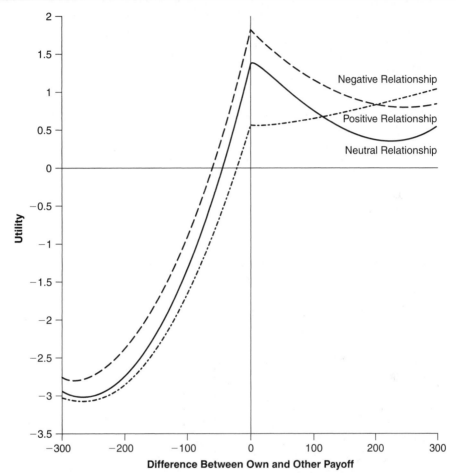

Source: Loewenstein, G. F., Thompson, L., & Bazerman, M. H. (1989). Social utility and decision making in interpersonal contexts. *Journal of Personality and Social Psychology, 57*(3), 426–441.

equality; in negative relationships, people preferred advantageous inequity. (See Exhibit 3-7 for an examination of different types of profiles.)

People will reject outcomes that entail one person receiving more than others and settle for a settlement of lower joint value but equal-appearing shares.[88] This arrangement is especially true when resources are "lumpy" (i.e., hard to divide into pieces), such as an Oriental rug.[89]

[88]McClelland, G., & Rohrbaugh, J. (1978). Who accepts the Pareto axiom? The role of utility and equity in arbitration decisions. *Behavioral Science, 23,* 446–456.
[89]Messick, D. M. (1993). Equality as a decision heuristic. In B. A. Mellers & J. Baron (Eds.), *Psychological perspectives on justice* (pp. 11–31). New York: Cambridge University Press.

EXHIBIT 3-7 Profiles of Pie Slicers

Have you ever wondered whether most people are truly interested in other people or are only concerned about their own profit? To examine this question, MBA students were given several hypothetical scenarios, such as the situation involving the ski invention, and asked what division of resources (and, in some cases, costs) they preferred. Further, people made responses for different kinds of relationships: friendly ones, antagonistic ones, and neutral ones. Three types of people were identified:

- *Loyalists*   prefer to split resources equally, except in antagonistic relationships (27%).

- *Saints*   prefer to split resources equally no matter whether relationships are positive, neutral, or negative (24%).

- *Ruthless competitors*   prefer to have more resources than the other party, regardless of relationship (36%).

Source: Loewenstein, G. F., Thompson, L., & Bazerman, M. H. (1989). Social utility and decision making in interpersonal contexts. *Journal of Personality and Social Psychology, 57*(3), 426–441.

Egocentrism

Consider a group of three people who go out for dinner. One person orders a bottle of expensive wine, an appetizer, and a pricey main course. Another abstains from drinking and orders an inexpensive side dish. The third orders a moderately priced meal. Then the bill arrives. The wine drinker immediately suggests that the group split the bill into thirds, explaining that this approach is the simplest. The teetotaler winces and suggests that the group ask the waiter to bring three separate bills. The third group member argues that, because he is a student, the two others should cover the bill, and he invites the two over to his house the next week for pizza. This example illustrates that any situation can have as many interpretations of fairness as it has parties involved. Two people may both truly want a fair settlement, but they may have distinctly different and equally justifiable ideas about what is fair. Consider, for example, "fairness opinions" that underpin mergers and acquisitions. Some are written by independent firms unconnected to the deal, but the majority aren't.[90] Banks can rack up millions of dollars in fees by acting simultaneously as agents and appraisers, presumably fueled by self-serving interests.

Why are people self-serving? People want or prefer more than what they regard as fair (basic hedonism). In short, our preferences are more primary, or immediate, than our social concerns. People are more in touch with their own preferences than with the concerns of others. We have immediate access to our preferences; fairness is a secondary judgment. For this reason, fairness judgments are likely to be tainted by preferences. Because preferences are primary and immediate, they often color a person's evaluation of fairness in a self-serving fashion. In a sense, our preferences act as a self-serving primer on our judgments of fairness.

---

[90]Henry, D. (2003, November 24). A fair deal—but for whom? *BusinessWeek, 3859,* 108–109.

EXHIBIT 3-8   Egocentric Interpretations of Fairness

For piecemeal work, you worked for 7 hours and were paid $25, while another person worked for 10 hours. How much do you think the other person should get paid? If you are like most people, you believe the other person should get paid more for doing more work—about $30.29 on average. It is hardly a self-serving response. Now, let's turn this question on its head: The other person worked for 7 hours and was paid $25. You worked for 10 hours. What is a fair wage for you to be paid? The average response is $35.24. The difference between $35.24 and $30.29 is about $5, which illustrates the phenomenon of egocentric bias: People pay themselves substantially more than they are willing to pay others for doing the same task.

Source: Messick, D. M., & Sentis, K. P. (1979). Fairness and preference. *Journal of Experimental Social Psychology, 15*(4), 418–434.

Allocating more money to ourselves (see Exhibit 3-8) is only one way that people show egocentric bias. Egocentric judgments of fairness also emerge in other ways. For example, people select fairness rules in a self-serving fashion: When people make minimal contributions, they often prefer equality rather than equity; however, when people's contributions are substantial, they opt for equity rather than equality.[91] Even if people agree to use the same fairness rule, they think it is fair for them to get more than others in a similar situation because they think they would have contributed more.[92]

Another way people can engage in egocentric evaluation is to selectively weight different aspects of the exchange situation in a way that favors themselves. Consider a situation in which participants are told how many hours they worked on a task of assembling questionnaires, as well as how many questionnaires they completed. The key dimensions are hours worked and productivity. Participants are then asked to indicate what they believe is fair payment for their work. Those who worked long hours but did not complete many questionnaires emphasize the importance of hours; in contrast, those who worked short hours but completed many questionnaires emphasize quantity completed. Thus, people emphasize the dimension that favors themselves.[93]

Appeals to equality can also be self-serving.[94] At a superficial level, equality is simple. Employing equality as a division rule in practice, however, is complex because of the multiple dimensions on which equality may be established.[95] Furthermore, equality is not consistently applied. For example, when the outcome is evenly divisible by the number in the group, people will use equality more than when even division is not possible.[96] The problem with egocentric judgment is that it makes negotiations more difficult to resolve. (See Exhibit 3-9 for an example.)

---

[91]van Avermaet, E. (1974). *Equity: A theoretical and experimental analysis.* Unpublished doctoral dissertation, University of California, Santa Barbara.
[92]Messick, D. M., & Rutte, C. G. (1992). The provision of public goods by experts: The Groningen study. In W. B. G. Liebrand, D. M. Messick, & H. A. M. Wilke (Eds.), *Social dilemmas: Theoretical issues and research findings* (pp. 101–109). Oxford, England: Pergamon Press.
[93]van Avermaet, *Equity.*
[94]Messick, D. M. (1993). Equality as a decision heuristic. In B. A. Mellers & J. Baron (Eds.), *Psychological perspectives on justice* (pp. 11–31). New York: Cambridge University Press.
[95]Harris, R. J., & Joyce, M. (1980). What's fair? It depends on how you ask the question. *Journal of Personality and Social Psychology, 38,* 165–170.
[96]Allison, S. T., & Messick, D. M. (1990). Social decision heuristics in the use of shared resources. *Journal of Behavioral Decision Making, 3*(3), 195–204.

> **EXHIBIT 3-9** Fairness and Strikes
>
> The likelihood and length of strikes may be directly predicted by the difference in perceived fair wages between management and union. In other words, if management and union have widely differing perceptions of what constitutes a fair settlement, a strike is more likely. Even more disconcertingly, providing each party (management and labor) with additional unbiased information concerning the dispute has the effect of exaggerating each party's perceptions of fair settlement outcomes and excluding parties in their positions. It is a good example of how more information is not always better in negotiations.
>
> *Source:* Thompson, L., & Loewenstein, G. F. (1992). Egocentric interpretations of fairness and negotiation. *Organizational Behavior and Human Decision Processes, 51,* 176–197. Reprinted by permission of Elsevier via RightsLink.

The preceding examples suggest that people immediately seize upon any opportunity to favor themselves. However, in many situations, people would ultimately be better off by not having egocentric views. Consider arbitration situations: People's predictions of judges' behavior are biased in a manner that favors their own side. Efforts to de-bias litigants meet with virtually no success. Informing parties of the potential bias or providing them with information about the counterparty's point of view does little to assuage biased perceptions of fairness, suggesting that egocentric biases are deeply ingrained.[97]

People really do care about fairness but usually do not realize that they are behaving in a self-interested fashion. Egocentric judgments of responsibility and fairness are attributable to ways in which people process information. Several cognitive mechanisms allow the development of egocentric judgments:

- *Selective encoding and memory.* Our own thoughts distract us from thinking about the contributions of others. We rehearse our own actions and fit them into our own cognitive schemas, which facilitates retention and subsequent retrieval. If encoding mechanisms lead to self-serving judgments of fairness, then a person who learns of the facts before knowing which side of a dispute he or she is on should not be egocentric. However, the egocentric effect still emerges even when the direction of self-interest occurs subsequent to the processing of information, suggesting that encoding is not the sole mechanism producing egocentric judgment.

- *Differential retrieval.* When making judgments of responsibility, people ask themselves "How much did I contribute?" and they attempt to retrieve specific instances.[98] Because it is cognitively easier to retrieve instances involving oneself, a positive correlation exists between recall and responsibility attributions.[99] Not surprisingly, when people are asked to think about how much others contributed to a joint task, egocentrism decreases.[100] However, after considering others' contributions to joint tasks, people report less enjoyment and lower satisfaction.

---

[97]Babcock, L., Loewenstein, G., Issacharoff, S., & Camerer, C. (1995). Biased judgments of fairness in bargaining. *The American Economic Review, 85*(5), 1337–1343.

[98]Ross, M., & Sicoly, F. (1979). Egocentric biases in availability attribution. *Journal of Personality and Social Psychology, 8,* 322–336.

[99]Kahneman, D., & Tversky, A. (1982). On the study of statistical intuitions. *Cognition, 11*(2), 123–141.

[100]Caruso, E., Epley, N., & Bazerman, M. (2006). The costs and benefits of undoing egocentric responsibility assessments in groups. *Journal of Personality and Social Psychology, 91*(5), 857–871.

- ***Informational disparity.***   People often are not privy to the contributions made by others, which suggests that information, not goals, mediates the self-serving effect. Even when information is constant but goals are manipulated, self-serving effects emerge,[101] suggesting that information itself is not solely responsible for the egocentric effect.[102]

Most situations are ambiguous enough that people can construe them in a fashion that favors their own interests. One unfortunate consequence is that people develop different perceptions of fairness even when they are presented with the same evidence. Consider a strike situation in which people are provided with background information on a hypothetical teachers union and board of education. The background material is constructed so that some facts favor the teachers and other facts favor the board of education. On balance, the facts are equal. In one condition, both disputants are presented with extensive, identical background information concerning the dispute. In another condition, disputants are presented with abbreviated, much less extensive background information. Those who have extensive information are more likely to go on strikes that last longer and are more costly to both parties, compared to disputants who do not have extensive information, even though the information is identical for both sides.[103] Information, even when shared among parties, creates ambiguity and provides fertile ground for unchecked self-interest to operate.

Reducing egocentrism is not easy. In general, leading people to consider other members' contributions to a joint task reduces self-centered judgments.[104] However, this can backfire by activating egoistic theories of people's behavior and claiming more in subsequent situations.[105]

WISE PIE-SLICING

The distribution of resources (pie-slicing) is an unavoidable and inevitable aspect of negotiation. What principles should we live by when slicing the pie? Messick suggests the following guidelines: consistency, simplicity, effectiveness, and justifiability.[106] We add consensus, generality, and satisfaction.[107]

Consistency

One of the hallmarks of a good pie-slicing heuristic is consistency or invariance across settings, time, and respect to the enforcer of the procedure. For example, most of us would be outraged if those managers up for performance review did better if the

---

[101]Thompson, L., & Loewenstein, G. F. (1992). Egocentric interpretations of fairness and negotiation. *Organizational Behavior and Human Decision Processes, 51,* 176–197.

[102]Camerer, C., & Loewenstein, G. (1993). Information, fairness, and efficiency in bargaining. In B. A. Mellers & J. Baron (Eds.), *Psychological perspectives on justice* (pp. 155–181). Boston: Cambridge University Press.

[103]Thompson & Loewenstein, "Egocentric interpretations."

[104]Caruso, Epley, & Bazerman. "The costs and benefits of undoing egocentric responsibility"; Epley, E., Caruso, E., & Bazerman, M. (2006). When perspective taking increases taking: Egoism in social interaction. *Journal of Personality and Social Psychology, 91*(5), 872–889.

[105]Epley, Caruso, & Bazerman, "When perspective taking increases taking."

[106]Messick, "Equality as a decision heuristic".

[107]Levine, J., & Thompson, L. (1996). Conflict in groups. In E. T. Higgins & A. Kruglanski (Eds.), *Social psychology: Handbook of basic principles* (pp. 745–776). New York: Guilford.

meeting was scheduled in the morning rather than the afternoon. This example represents a clear bias of the interviewer. Fairness procedures are often inconsistent because of heuristic decision making. Heuristic judgment processes are necessary when normative decision procedures are absent or when their application would be inefficient. Unfortunately, people are typically unaware of the powerful contextual factors that affect their judgments of fairness.

Simplicity

Pie-slicing procedures should be clearly understood by the individuals who employ them and those who are affected by them. Group members should be able to explain the procedure used to allocate resources. This allows the procedure to be implemented with full understanding and the outcomes of the procedure to be evaluated against a clear criterion.

Effectiveness

Pie-slicing policies should produce a choice, meaning that the allocation procedure should yield a clear decision. If the procedure does not produce such a decision, then conflict may erupt among group members who try to identify and implement a decision post hoc.

Justifiability

Pie-slicing procedures should be justifiable to other parties. A fairness rule may be consistent, simple, and effective, but if it cannot be justified it is not likely to be successful. For example, suppose that a manager of an airline company decides that raises will be based upon hair color: Blondes get big raises, brunettes do not. This policy is consistent, simple, and effective but hardly justifiable.

Consensus

Group members should agree upon the method of allocation. Effective pie-slicing procedures are often internalized by group members, and norms act as strong guidelines for behavior and decision making in groups. Because social justice procedures often outlive current group members, new members are frequently indoctrinated with procedures that the group found useful in the past.[108]

Generalizability

The pie-slicing procedure should be applicable to a wide variety of situations. Procedures and norms develop when intragroup conflict is expected, enduring, or recurrent, and effective policy therefore specifies outcome distribution across situations.

Satisfaction

To increase the likelihood that negotiators will follow through with their agreements, the pie-slicing procedure should be satisfying to all. Susan Lyne, President and CEO of

---

[108]Bettenhausen, K., & Murnighan, J. K. (1985). The emergence of norms in competitive decision-making groups. *Administrative Science Quarterly, 30,* 350–372; Levine, J., & Moreland, R. L. (1994). Group socialization: Theory and research. In I. W. Stroebe & M. Hewstone (Eds.), *The European review of social psychology: Vol. 5* (pp. 305–336). Chichester, England: Wiley.

Martha Stewart Living Omnimedia stated, "Always leave a little something on the table. A total win for one side in any negotiation is just wrong because it's almost always a pyrrhic victory. You end up with bad partnerships. And we have long careers, and it is very likely you're going to be meeting the same people at some point down the line, so it's important to make sure that nobody feels like they have been either embarrassed or beaten in a negotiation. I think you only get the best partnership if both people feel good about the terms."[109]

CONCLUSION

When it comes to slicing the pie, the most valuable information is a negotiator's best alternative to reaching agreement (BATNA). Nothing can substitute for the power of a strong BATNA. Negotiators can enhance their ability to garner a favorable slice of the pie by engaging in the following strategies: determine their BATNA prior to negotiations and attempt to improve upon it; determine your reservation point; research the other party's BATNA; set high aspirations; make the first offer; immediately re-anchor if the other party opens with an "outrageous" offer, plan your concessions; support your offers with facts; appeal to norms of fairness; and do not fall for the "even split" ploy. Negotiators should not reveal their reservation price (unless it is very attractive) and never lie about their BATNA. A negotiator who is well versed in the psychology of fairness is at a pie-slicing advantage in negotiation.

---

[109]7 leaders on life lessons. (2005, November 14). *Newsweek International, 146(20)*, 52.

CHAPTER

Win-Win Negotiation: Expanding the Pie

When NBC Universal invested $415 million in Paxson Communications, the strategy was to take a minority interest in Paxson, while waiting for the Federal Communications Commission (FCC) to lift its cap on station ownership. Because the FCC limits the number of stations one company can own, adding Paxson's 60 stations put NBC well over the limit. NBC began to grow frustrated with its investment in Paxson. When NBC bought Spanish-language network Telemundo in 2001, it guaranteed it would never have enough room to add the Paxson stations and further strained its partnership with Paxson. The relationship grew more complicated. Serious negotiations began in August 2004 when the two sides came to the table with a list of 150 issues. NBC pushed for a management change, but removing chairman Lowell Paxson, who controlled 60% of the voting shares in the company, proved difficult. The two sides finally reached an agreement that guaranteed a price for Mr. Paxson's shares, as well as protection for public shareholders. Brandon Burgess was appointed the new chief executive of Paxson and the new deal satisfied the FCC cap on station ownership by calling for NBC to find a controlling partner for the company within 18 months. Deals were set in place for cable coverage throughout the country, and with the growth of digital technology, the stations had the capacity to increase their channel offerings significantly. According to Randel Falco of NBC, "This is absolutely the best outcome for everybody—for the shareholders, for NBC and for the Paxson employees. This gives Paxson a bright future."[1]

Even the most contentious negotiations contain potential for win-win agreements. However, win-win negotiation techniques are not necessarily intuitive. Many people who regard themselves to be win-win negotiators often leave money on the table without even realizing it. This chapter outlines strategies for realizing all the potential from negotiation situations.

---

[1]Carter, B. (2005, November 8). Deal brings an end to NBC-Paxson feud. *New York Times,* p. C7.

WHAT IS WIN-WIN NEGOTIATION?

Many negotiators proudly describe their negotiations as win-win. However, closer inspection usually reveals that money was squandered, resources were wasted, and potential joint gain went untapped. Negotiators' minds and hearts were in the right places, but they did not achieve an integrative agreement that fully leveraged parties' interests. Most people erroneously equate win-win negotiations with fair division of resources. Obviously, allocating resources is always necessary in negotiation, but win-win means something entirely different. Win-win is *not:*

- *Compromise:*   Compromise refers to reaching a middle ground between negotiators' positions. Win-win negotiation does not pertain to how the pie is divided (Chapter 3) but, rather, to how the pie is *enlarged* by negotiators. Negotiators may compromise, yet leave money on the table.
- *Even split:*   Even splits, like compromises, refer to how the bargaining zone is divided among the negotiators. For example, two sisters who quarrel over an orange and ultimately decide to cut it in half have reached an even split. However, if they fail to realize that one sister wants all the juice and the other wants all of the rind, it is painfully clear that the even split is not win-win.[2]
- *Satisfaction:*   Satisfaction is no guarantee that money and resources have not been wasted; in fact, many "happy" negotiators do not expand the pie.[3]
- *Building a relationship:*   Building a relationship and establishing trust comprise an important aspect of negotiation. However, people with a genuine interest in the other party may think creatively and craft win-win deals. In fact, people who would seem to have the most interest in building a relationship with the other party (for example, husbands and wives, dating couples, and long-term partners) often fail to reach integrative agreements.[4]

Win-win negotiation *really* means that all creative opportunities are leveraged and no resources are left on the table. We call these outcomes **integrative negotiations**.

TELLTALE SIGNS OF WIN-WIN POTENTIAL

Integrative potential exists in just about every negotiation situation. However, people often fail to see it because they do not believe that win-win is possible. The following are questions for negotiators to ask when assessing the potential of a negotiation situation.

Does the Negotiation Contain More Than One Issue?

Most negotiations begin as single-issue negotiations. By definition, single-issue negotiations are not win-win because whatever one party gains, the other party loses. However, it is usually possible to identify more than one issue. The probability that negotiators will

[2]Follett, M. (1994). In P. Graham (Ed.), *Mary Parker Follett: Prophet of management—A celebration of writings from the 1920s.* Boston: Harvard Business School Press.

[3]Thompson, L., Valley, K. L., & Kramer, R. M. (1995). The bittersweet feeling of success: An examination of social perception in negotiation. *Journal of Experimental Social Psychology, 31*(6), 467–492.

[4]Fry, W. R., Firestone, I. J., & Williams, D. L. (1983). Negotiation process and outcome of stranger dyads and dating couples: Do lovers lose? *Basic and Applied Social Psychology, 4,* 1–16; Thompson, L., & DeHarport, T. (1998). Relationships, good incompatibility, and communal orientation in negotiations. *Basic and Applied Social Psychology, 20*(1), 33–44; Kurtzberg, T., & Medvec, V. H. (1999). Can we negotiate and still be friends? *Negotiation Journal, 15*(4), 355–362.

have identical preferences across all issues is small, and, as we will see, *it is differences in preferences, beliefs, and capacities that may be profitably traded off to create joint gain.*[5]

Can Other Issues Be Brought In?

Another strategy is to bring additional issues into the negotiation. For example, in a four-day negotiation between the City of San Marino, California, and the local firefighters association, the key issue was salary. Firefighters wanted an increase. The negotiators searched for several options by connecting benefits to wages, allowing cost savings to be distributed to firefighters, and taking on additional duties (thereby increasing incomes). In addition, management spent a great deal of time providing the firefighters with information on cost-benefit analyses, operating costs, and other relevant budgetary information so that all parties could evaluate which options were the most practical and beneficial. This information sharing contributed not only to this negotiation but provided helpful information for future organizational discussions.[6] Similarly, when Mark Lazarus of Turner Broadcasting was negotiating with NBA Commissioner David Stern in 2001, he brought in several issues, including the number of regular season games, rights to Western Conference finals, rights to the NBA All-Star game, a stake in the new cable network, and the integration of AOL into the deal.[7] In short, the more moving parts, the better the potential deal.

Can Side Deals Be Made?

In many situations, people are strictly cautioned not to make side deals or side payments. In contrast, the ability to bring other people into negotiations to make side deals may increase the size of the bargaining pie. For example, consider the side deal that AT&T made with Comcast Corporation in 1999. For a while, AT&T was in a vigorous battle with Comcast for the acquisition of MediaOne Group, Inc. A win-win deal was created when AT&T provided Comcast with a number of its cable systems and about 2 million additional cable subscribers; in return, Comcast paid AT&T $9 billion, or about $4,500 per subscriber, for the additional customers. Most important for AT&T, Comcast withdrew its $48 billion bid for MediaOne. Thus, by offering a valuable side deal, AT&T was able to satisfy its competitor.[8]

Do Parties Have Different Preferences Across Negotiation Issues?

If parties have different strengths of preference across the negotiation issues, then a win-win negotiation is possible.[9] Consider the orange-splitting example. Essentially, the situation involves two issues: the juice and the rind. One sister cares more about the juice; the other cares more about the rind. If only a single issue (the orange) was involved or if both sisters wanted the juice much more than the rind, then an integrative agreement would not be possible.

---

[5]Lax, D. A., & Sebenius, J. K. (1986). *The manager as negotiator.* New York: Free Press.
[6]Quinn, S. R., Bell, D., & Wells, J. (1997). Interest-based negotiation: A case study. *Public Personnel Management, 26*(4), 529–533.
[7]Larson, A. (2003, June 9). Atlanta falcon: With his keen business instinct and sharp negotiating skills, Mark Lazarus has soared through the ranks of Turner. *Adweek,* p. SR14.
[8]Hofmann, T. (1999, December 27). The year in review: Media players set torrid pace. *Dow Jones Business News.*
[9]Froman, L. A., & Cohen, M. D. (1970). Compromise and logroll: Comparing the efficiency of two bargaining processes. *Behavioral Science, 30,* 180–183.

A PYRAMID MODEL

True win-win or integrative negotiations leave no resources underutilized. We distinguish three "levels" of integrative, or win-win, agreements. The pyramid model presented in Exhibit 4-1 depicts the three levels of integrative agreements. Beginning at the base, each successive level subsumes the properties of the levels below it. Ideally, negotiators should always strive to reach level 3 integrative agreements. Higher levels are progressively more difficult for negotiators to achieve, but they are more beneficial to negotiators.

Level 1 integrative agreements exceed parties' no-agreement possibilities, or reservation points. Reaching an agreement that exceeds parties' no-agreement possibilities creates value relative to their best alternative. Negotiators create value by reaching settlements that are better than their reservation points, or disagreement alternatives.

Level 2 integrative agreements are better for both parties than are other feasible negotiated agreements. In other words, negotiators create value with respect to one negotiated outcome by finding another outcome that all prefer.

The existence of such agreements, by definition, implies that the bargaining situation is not purely fixed-sum: Some agreements yield higher joint gain than do others. By definition, in purely fixed-sum situations, all outcomes sum to the same joint amount, and, therefore, no alternative agreement exists that improves one party's outcome while simultaneously improving or not reducing the outcome of the other party. If negotiators fail to reach agreement in a fixed-sum negotiation when the bargaining zone is positive, they have failed to reach a level 1 agreement. Unlike the pure fixed-sum case, integrativeness is much more difficult to assess in the more common mixed-motive case.

Level 3 integrative agreements are settlements that lie along the **Pareto-optimal frontier** of agreement, meaning that no other feasible agreement exists that would improve one party's outcome while simultaneously not hurting the other party's outcome. Therefore, *any* agreement reached by negotiators in a purely fixed-sum situation

EXHIBIT 4-1   A Pyramid Model of Integrative Agreements

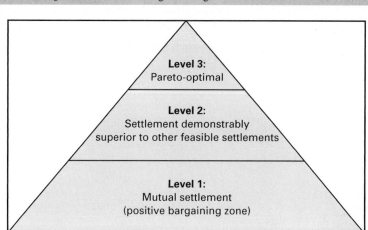

is level 3, leaving no way to improve any negotiator's outcome without making the other party worse off. In reality, it is difficult to determine whether an agreement is level 3, but we will present some helpful techniques.

Reaching level 3 integrative agreements may sound easy enough, but observation of hundreds of executives' performance in business negotiation simulations reveals that fewer than 25% reach level 3 agreements, and of those, approximately 50% do so by chance.[10]

MOST COMMON PIE-EXPANDING ERRORS

If reaching win-win negotiation agreements is the objective of most negotiators, what prevents them from doing so? Negotiators encounter two key problems, which we describe next.

False Conflict

False conflict, also known as **illusory conflict**, occurs when people believe that their interests are incompatible with the other party's interests when, in fact, they are not. For example, in the Cuban Missile Crisis, unbeknownst to the United States, Russia preferred to constrain the Cubans from provocative behavior and to minimize the contributions of the Chinese—an interest held by the United States.[11] Similarly, in a labor strike at the Dow Chemical Company, both union and management preferred the same wage increase; however, neither party realized this fact at the time of the strike.[12]

In 1990, we uncovered a particularly insidious and widespread effect in negotiations: **the lose-lose effect**. A negotiation situation was constructed in which parties had compatible interests on a few of the negotiation issues, meaning both parties wanted the same outcome. At first, it seemed absurd to imagine any outcome occurring other than the parties settling for what was obviously the best solution for themselves and the other party. However, a substantial number of negotiators not only failed to realize that the other party had interests that were completely compatible with their own, but they reached settlements that were less optimal for both parties than some other readily available outcome. When people fail to capitalize on compatible interests, this is known as a lose-lose agreement.[13] In an analysis of 32 different negotiation studies across more than 5,000 people, we found that negotiators failed to realize compatible issues about 50% of the time and fell prey to the lose-lose effect about 20% of the time.[14]

What should negotiators do to avoid lose-lose agreements? First, they should be aware of the fixed-pie perception and not automatically assume that their interests are opposed by the other party. Second, negotiators should avoid making **premature concessions** to the other party (i.e., giving up ground on issues before even being asked). Third, negotiators should develop an accurate understanding of the other party's interests—a skill we will explore shortly.

---

[10]These data are based on executives' performance in negotiation simulations that involve integrative (win-win) potential.
[11]Walton, R. E., & McKersie, R. B. (1965). *A behavioral theory of labor relations.* New York: McGraw-Hill.
[12]Balke, W. M., Hammond, K. R., & Meyer, G. D. (1973). An alternate approach to labor-management relations. *Administrative Science Quarterly, 18*(3), 311–327.
[13]Thompson, L., & Hrebec, D. (1996). Lose-lose agreements in interdependent decision making. *Psychological Bulletin, 120*(3), 396–409.
[14]Ibid.

Fixed-Pie Perception

The **fixed-pie perception** is the belief that the other party's interests are directly and completely opposed to one's own interests.[15] Most untrained negotiators view negotiation as a pie-slicing task: They assume that their interests are incompatible, that impasse is likely, and that issues are settled one by one rather than as packages.[16] For example, in one investigation, negotiators' perceptions of the other party's interests were assessed immediately before, during, and then following a negotiation.[17] Most negotiators (68%) perceived the other's interests to be completely opposed to their own. However, negotiators shared interests that could be profitably traded off and completely compatible.

Unfortunately, banishing the fixed-pie perception is difficult. It is not enough to warn negotiators of its existence.[18] Further, it is not enough for negotiators to have experience.[19] It is not even enough for negotiators to receive feedback about their counterparties' interests to eliminate the fixed-pie perception.[20] We will talk more about how to successfully challenge the fixed-pie perception when we examine biases and creativity (Chapter 8).

Lack of time and effort do not explain lose-lose outcomes and the fixed-pie perception. The biggest detriment to the attainment of integrative agreements is the faulty assumptions we make about the counterparty and the negotiation situation. One of the first realizations negotiators should make is that negotiation is not a purely competitive situation. Rather, most negotiation situations are mixed-motive in nature, meaning that parties' interests are imperfectly correlated with one another. The gains of one party do not represent equal sacrifices by the other. For example, consider a negotiation between two collaborators on a joint project: One is a risk-averse negotiator who values cash up front more than riskier long-term payoffs; the other is more interested in long-term value than in current gains. The two may settle on a contract in which a large lump sum is paid to the risk-averse negotiator, and the other party reaps most of the (riskier) profits in the long term.

Few conflicts are purely win-or-lose.[21] In most mixed-motive negotiations, parties realize at some level that they have two incentives vis-à-vis the other party: cooperation (so that they can reach an agreement and avoid resorting to their BATNAs) and competition (so that they can claim the largest slice of the pie). However, what this analysis misses is the incentive to create value, which is the key to win-win negotiation.

---

[15]Fisher, R., & Ury. W. (1981). *Getting to yes.* Boston: Houghton Mifflin; Bazerman, M. H., & Neale, M. A. (1983). Heuristics in negotiation: Limitations to effective dispute resolution. In M. Bazerman & R. Lewicki (Eds.), *Negotiating in organizations* (pp. 51–67). Beverly Hills, CA: Sage; Thompson, L., & Hastie, R. (1990). Social perception in negotiation. *Organizational Behavior and Human Decision Processes, 47*(1), 98–123.

[16]O'Connor, K. M., & Adams, A. A. (1999). What novices think about negotiation: A content analysis of scripts. *Negotiation Journal, 15,* 135–147.

[17]Thompson & Hastie, "Social perception in negotiation."

[18]Thompson, L. (1991). Information exchange in negotiation. *Journal of Experimental Social Psychology, 27*(2), 161–179.

[19]Thompson, L. (1990). An examination of naïve and experienced negotiators. *Journal of Personality and Social Psychology, 59*(1), 82–90; Thompson, L. (1990). The influence of experience on negotiation performance. *Journal of Experimental Social Psychology, 26*(6), 528–544.

[20]Thompson, L., & DeHarpport, T. (1994). Social judgment, feedback, and interpersonal learning in negotiation. *Organizational Behavior and Human Decision Processes, 58*(3), 327–345.

[21]Deutsch, M. (1973). *The resolution of conflict.* New Haven, CT: Yale University Press.

STRATEGIES THAT DO NOT REALLY WORK

We want to save negotiators time and heartache in their quest to expand the pie by outlining several strategies that might seem to be effective in expanding the pie and reaching win-win agreements but, in fact, do not really work.

Commitment to Reaching a Win-Win Deal

Many negotiators approach the negotiation table committed to reaching a win-win deal. However, commitment to reaching a win-win deal does not guarantee that negotiators will reach a win-win agreement.

Compromise

Negotiators often mistake win-win negotiations for **equal-concession negotiations**. Equal concessions or "splitting the difference" does not really ensure that a win-win negotiation has been reached. Compromise pertains to slicing the pie, not expanding the pie.

Focusing on a Long-Term Relationship

Oftentimes, negotiators believe that focusing on the long-term nature of their relationship with the other party will ensure a win-win deal. Obviously, the long-term relationship is key in negotiation—and we spend an entire chapter (Chapter 6) discussing how to foster the relationship—but establishing a long-term relationship does not translate directly into win-win. Rather, it means that negotiators should have an easier time working to reach win-win.

Adopting a Cooperative Orientation

It is nice when negotiators approach the negotiation table with benevolent attitudes and a cooperative orientation. However, negotiators' intentions to cooperate often keep them from focusing on the right information at the right time. For example, negotiators often attempt to cooperate by revealing their BATNA to the other party; revealing one's BATNA is a pie-slicing, not a pie-expanding, tactic. Negotiators often think cooperation means compromise, and compromises often lead to lose-lose outcomes. For example, in 1996 MasterCard International wanted to determine why it was losing money on some of its promotional deals. Subsequent analysis revealed that MasterCard was attempting to form good relationships with others (i.e., being cooperative), but it was giving away money and promotions and not asking for sufficient compensation in return.[22] This type of situation prompted Pruitt and Carnevale to develop a **dual-concern model** of effective negotiation: high concern for the other party coupled with high concern for one's own interests.[23]

Taking Extra Time to Negotiate

Negotiators often think that, with a little extra time, they can achieve all the joint gains possible in a negotiation. Extra time does not guarantee that negotiators will reach an

---

[22]Kiser, K. (1999, October 1). The new deal. *Training, 36*(10), 116–126.

[23]Pruitt, D. G., & Carnevale, P. J. (1993). *Negotiation in social conflict.* Pacific Grove, CA: Brooks-Cole.

integrative agreement (most negotiators wait until the last few moments of a negotiation to reach an agreement), and the quality of the negotiation does not improve with additional time. Furthermore, people tend to work to fill their time.[24] The same is true for negotiation. For example, we recently gave some people one hour, others two hours, and still others a week (via e-mail) to complete a two-party negotiation exercise. If time really makes a difference in terms of the quality of negotiated agreements, then the one-hour group should be expected to have inferior outcomes in terms of expanding the pie. However, this expectation was not realized: No discernible differences appeared among the three groups, which suggests that more time to negotiate does not improve the quality of negotiated agreements.

STRATEGIES THAT WORK

So much for the strategies that do not work. What does work when it comes to expanding the pie? We identify nine strategies that can help negotiators expand the pie and create win-win negotiations.[25] We order them in terms of the most obvious and intuitive strategies to strategies that are more sophisticated. The first few strategies are especially good to use when negotiating with someone who seems cooperative and trustworthy; the strategies that come later on this list are useful when dealing with extremely tough negotiators.

Perspective-Taking

By taking the perspective of the other party, negotiators attempt to see the world through the counterparty's eyes. Indeed, negotiators who take the perspective of the counterparty are more successful in terms of a number of social enterprises, such as coordinating with others.[26] Perspective taking also enhances problem-solving abilities, including the ability to jointly solve problems at the bargaining table.[27] Consider the following example of losing trees in new building construction. Typically, a building site provides the required replacement trees and counties plant the trees in public parks and along streets. Due to heavy construction, Arlington County lost numerous trees but at the same time ran out of suitable free space on public property to plant new trees. By taking the county's perspective and supporting the importance of an urban canopy, developers negotiated a program to use the tree-loss calculation for owed money instead of owed trees. Developers funded the program in which the county gave away trees to residents to plant on their private property.[28] Perspective-taking ability

---

[24]McGrath, J. E., Kelly, J. R., & Machatka, D. E. (1984). The social psychology of time: Entrainment of behavior in social and organizational settings. *Applied Social Psychology Annual, 5,* 21–44.

[25]Bazerman, M. H., & Neale, M. A. (1982). Improving negotiation effectiveness under final offer arbitration: The role of selection and training. *Journal of Applied Psychology, 67*(5), 543–548.

[26]Galinsky, A., Ku, G., & Wang, C. (2005). Perspective-taking: Fostering social bonds and facilitating coordination. *Group Processes and Intergroup Relations, 8,* 109–125; Galinsky, A. D., Wang. C. S., & Ku, G. (in press). Perspective-takers behave more stereotypically. *Journal of Personality and Social Psychology.*

[27]Richardson, D., Hammock, G., Smith, S., Gardner, W., & Signo, M. (1994). Empathy as a cognitive inhibitor of interpersonal aggression. *Aggressive Behavior, 20,* 275–289.

[28]Schulte, B. (2007, May 31). Sowing a different tomorrow; on a mission to restore urban canopy, Arlington distributes trees to plant on private property. *Washington Post, Virginia Extra,* p. T01.

also enhances negotiators' ability to claim resources[29] and react effectively to the anchoring attempts of the counterparty.[30]

Perspective taking is different from empathy. Whereas perspective taking is a *cognitive* ability to consider the world from another's viewpoint, empathy is the ability to *emotionally* connect with another person.[31] And it is the cognitive capacity that is most important for negotiation success. Negotiators who are either high in perspective-taking ability or are prompted to take the perspective of the counterparty are more successful in identifying and reaching integrative outcomes in negotiation. Perspective takers are more likely than empathizers to discover hidden agreements, achieve maximum joint gains, and secure peace. For these reasons, it is better to get inside the head (but not heart) of your competitive adversaries.[32]

Ask Questions About Interests and Priorities

A negotiator could ask the other party in a negotiation any number of questions (see Exhibit 4-2). However, of the six types of information listed in Exhibit 4-2, only two are truly helpful types of questions to ask in terms of expanding the pie—questions about underlying interests and questions about priorities.[33] Negotiators who ask the counterparty about their preferences are much more likely to reach integrative agreements than negotiators who do not ask the other party about his or her priorities.[34] However, left to their own devices, negotiators fail to ask diagnostic questions. For example, only about 7% of negotiators seek information about the other party's preferences during negotiation, even though it would be dramatically helpful to know such information.[35]

Why are these questions diagnostic with respect to increasing the likelihood of win-win agreements? Two reasons: First, such questions help negotiators discover where the value is. Second, diagnostic questions do not tempt the other party to lie or to misrepresent himself or herself. It is easy to see how asking a person about his or her BATNA or reservation price might induce that person to exaggerate or lie, but it is not immediately clear why or how a negotiator would lie about his or her underlying needs. Thus, diagnostic questions are effective because they do not put negotiators on the defensive.

Provide Information About Your Interests and Priorities

It is a fallacy to believe that negotiators should never provide information to the counterparty.[36] Negotiations would not go anywhere if negotiators did not communicate their interests to the other party. You should negotiate as you would with your fraternal twin: If you do not provide information, neither will the other party. A negotiator should never ask the other party a question that he or she is not willing to

[29]Bazerman & Neale, "Improving negotiation effectiveness."

[30]Galinsky, A., & Mussweiler, T. (2001). First offers as anchors: The role of perspective-taking and negotiator focus. *Journal of Personality and Social Psychology, 81*(4), 657–669.

[31]Galinsky, A. D., Maddux, W. W., Gilin, D., & White, J. B. (2008). Why it pays to get inside the head of your opponent: The differential effects of perspective-taking and empathy in strategic interactions. *Psychological Science, 19*(4), 378-384.

[32]Ibid.

[33]Bazerman, M. H., & Neale, M. A. (1992). *Negotiating rationally.* New York: Free Press.

[34]Thompson, "Information exchange in negotiation."

[35]Ibid.

[36]Bazerman & Neale, *Negotiating rationally.*

EXHIBIT 4-2 Types of Information in Negotiation and How Each Affects Distributive and Integrative Agreements

Type of Information	Definition (example)	Claiming Value	Creating Value
BATNA (and reservation price)	The alternatives a negotiator has outside of the current negotiation (e.g., "If I don't buy your car, I can buy my uncle's car for $2,000.")	Revealing this information severely hurts the ability to maximize negotiator surplus.	Revealing or obtaining this information does not affect ability to reach level 2 or 3 integrative agreements; it might help negotiators reach level 1 integrative agreements.
Position (stated demand)	Usually, a negotiator's opening offer; the behavioral manifestation of his/her target point (e.g., "I will give you $1,500 for your car.")	Opening with an aggressive target point significantly increases the negotiator's surplus (share of the bargaining zone).	This does not affect integrative agreements.
Underlying interests	The underlying needs and reasons a negotiator has for a particular issue (e.g., "I need a car because I need transportation to my job site, which is 15 miles away in a rural zone.")	Revealing this information generally increases the likelihood of obtaining a favorable slice of the pie because negotiators who provide a rationale for their demands are more adept at realizing their targets.	Very important for reaching win-win deals; by (truthfully) revealing underlying interests, negotiators can discover win-win agreements (e.g., one sister tells the other that she wants the orange because she needs to make juice and has no need for rinds).
Priorities	A judgment about the relative importance of the issues to a negotiator (e.g., "I am more concerned about the down payment than I am about the financing for the car.")	Increases a negotiator's surplus indirectly, because if more value is created via sharing priorities, then the probability that a negotiator will get a larger slice of the pie increases.	Vitally important for maximizing the pie (e.g., the sister who said she cared more about the rinds relative to the juice created potential for integrative agreement).
Key facts	Pertains to information that bears on the quality and the value of the to-be-negotiated issues (e.g., "The car has a rebuilt engine and has been involved in a major collision." "The oranges are genetically modified.")	This information can affect the slice of the pie the negotiator obtains in that facts either increase or decrease the value of the to-be-negotiated issues.	Affects the quality of win-win agreements in that failure to reveal key information may lead a negotiator to over- or undervalue a particular resource (e.g., someone who sells "fresh organic orange juice" does not want to have genetically modified oranges as an ingredient).
Substantiation	Argument either made to support one's own position or to attack the other party's position (e.g., "You will get lots of dates if you buy my car because women like it.")	Most dominant type of distributive tactic (24% to 27% of all statements*); can increase a negotiator's slice of the pie because providing a rationale (even an absurd one) can often be effective in obtaining a demand.	A distributive tactic; does not increase win-win negotiation and may, in fact, reduce likelihood of win-win.**

*Carnevale, P. J., & Lawler, E. J. (1986). Time pressure and the development of integrative agreements in bilateral negotiations. *Journal of Conflict Resolution, 30*(4), 636–659.
**Pruitt, D. G. (1981). *Negotiation behavior.* New York: Academic Press; Hyder, E. B, Prietula, M. J., & Weingart, L. R. (2000). Getting to best: Efficiency versus optimality in negotiation. *Cognitive Science, 24*(2), 169–204.

answer truthfully. The important question, then, is not *whether* to reveal information but *what* information to reveal.

By signaling your willingness to share information about your interests (not your BATNA), you capitalize on the powerful principle of reciprocity: If you share information, the other party will often share as well. Negotiators who provide information to the other party about their priorities are more likely to reach integrative agreements than negotiators who do not provide this information.[37] The disclosing negotiator is not placed at a strategic disadvantage. The disclosing negotiator does not earn significantly more or less resources than the counterparty.

Negotiators can exchange six key types of information during negotiation. The skilled negotiator knows how to recognize each. Even more important, the skilled negotiator knows what information is safe (and even necessary) to reveal in order to reach win-win outcomes. The information that negotiators need to share is not information about their BATNAs but, rather, information about their *preferences* and *priorities* across the negotiation issues. (Exhibit 4-2 outlines the six types of information that negotiators can exchange. Exhibit 4-3 supplements Exhibit 4-2 by providing a worksheet to complete prior to negotiation.)

A distinct time course emerges in terms of the unraveling of information during negotiation. Adair and her colleague divided the negotiation into four quarters.[38] During the first quarter, people are more likely to use influence strategies as they battle for power and influence. During the second quarter, priority information peaks as negotiators discuss the issues and share information about their priorities. In the third quarter, negotiators make offers and counteroffers and either support or reject them on the basis of rational argument. In the fourth quarter, negotiators begin to work toward agreement by building on each other's offers.

Even though many negotiators may provide information during a negotiation, the counterparty may not necessarily understand the information. This faulty assumption may be traceable to the **illusion of transparency**.[39] The illusion of transparency occurs when negotiators believe they are revealing more than they actually are (i.e., they believe others have access to information about them when in fact they do not). In one investigation, negotiators judged whether an observer to the negotiation could accurately discern their negotiation goals from their behavior.[40] Negotiators consistently overestimated the transparency of their objectives. Thus, people feel more like an "open book" with respect to their goals and interests in negotiation than they actually are. Negotiators are also not as clear in their messages as they should be. Indeed, when the information exchanged is amenable to multiple interpretations, it can lead to settlement delays and divergent expectations.[41] Conversely, when a single interpretation is obvious, information sharing leads to convergence of expectations and speeds settlement.

---

[37]Thompson, "Information exchange in negotiation."

[38]Adair, W. L., & Brett, J. M. (2005). The negotiation dance: Time, culture and behavioral sequences. *Organization Science, 16*(1), 33–51.

[39]Gilovich, T., Savitsky, K., & Medvec, V. H. (1998). The illusion of transparency: Biased assessments of others' ability to read one's emotional states. *Journal of Personality and Social Psychology, 75*(2), 332–346.

[40]Vorauer, J. D., & Claude, S. (1998). Perceived versus actual transparency of goals in negotiation. *Personality and Social Psychology Bulletin, 24*(4), 371–385.

[41]Loewenstein, G. F., & Moore, D. A. (2004). When ignorance is bliss: Information exchange and inefficiency in bargaining. *Journal of Legal Studies, 33*(1), 37–58.

EXHIBIT 4-3 Preparation Worksheet

Issue	Self	Other
	position / * underlying interest	other party's position on this issue / ☐ other party's underlying interest
	*	☐
	*	☐
	*	☐
	*	☐
Reservation price		
Target		
BATNA		

Instructions:

1. In the left-most column, identify the issues to be negotiated.
2. Then, indicate your "position" in the top part of the triangle and your underlying interest in the lower part of the triangle in the middle column.
3. Next, rank-order the issues from most to least important (using, say, 1 through 5 in the small boxes).
4. Next, make your best assessment of the other party's position, interests, and priorities across the issues.
5. Indicate your reservation price (and attempt to assess the reservation price of the other party).
6. Indicate your target point.
7. Indicate your BATNA (and attempt to assess the other party's BATNA).

Note: *Rating/ranking of importance (e.g., 0–100, 1–5, etc.).

Source: Brett, J. (2007). *Negotiating globally: How to negotiate deals, resolve disputes, and make decisions across cultural boundaries (2nd edition),* San Francisco: Jossey-Bass, p. 17.

Unbundle the Issues

One reason negotiations fail is because negotiators haggle over a single issue, such as price. By definition, if negotiations contain only one issue (e.g., price), they are purely distributive (i.e., fixed-pie). Skilled negotiators are adept at expanding the set of negotiable issues. Adding issues, unbundling issues, and creating new issues can transform a single-issue, fixed-pie negotiation into an integrative, multi-issue negotiation with win-win potential.[42] Integrative agreements require at least two issues. Roger Fisher recounts a situation when he was helping the president of a company sell a building he owned: "He was retiring and wanted $2 million, which he considered a fair price. He had a buyer, but the buyer wouldn't pay that price. I asked the seller, 'What's the worst thing about selling this building?' And he said, 'All of my papers for 25 years are mixed up in my corner office. When I sell the building, I can't throw everything away. I've got to go through that stuff. That's the nightmare I have.'"[43] Then Fisher asked the buyer why he wanted the building. The buyer explained he hoped to use it for hoteling. This knowledge gave Fisher the idea of suggesting that the seller offer the buyer a lease with an option to buy with one contingency: that the president's name be on the corner office for three years. The buyer agreed. In this example, an integrative agreement was reached by unbundling the price and the lease option.

Make Package Deals, Not Single-Issue Offers

Most negotiators make the mistake of negotiating each issue one by one. This approach is a mistake for several reasons: First and foremost, negotiating each issue separately does not allow negotiators to make trade-offs between issues. To capitalize on different strengths of preference, negotiators need to compare and contrast issues and trade them off. Second, it may mean that impasse is more likely, especially if the bargaining zone is narrow and trade-offs are necessary to reach a mutually profitable outcome. Single-issue offers lure negotiators into compromise agreements, which, as we have seen, are usually not the best approach for win-win negotiations.

Make Multiple Offers of Equivalent Value Simultaneously

In some cases, negotiators are disappointed and frustrated to find that their attempts to provide and seek information are not effective. Can negotiators do anything to change the situation? Fortunately, the answer is yes. The strategy of making **multiple offers of equivalent value simultaneously** can be effective even with the most uncooperative of negotiators.[44] The strategy involves presenting the other party with at least two (and preferably more) proposals of *equal value* to oneself. For example, in the Wal-Mart negotiation discussed in Exhibit 4-4, the Sequim county engineer, Don McInnes, responded to the planning director's protests by outlining three different options: (a) widening three roads to a standard 40-foot width; (b) bringing the roadways up to a higher standard (but not to full standard) through a major overhaul; or (c) creating a cul-de-sac at two of the roads.[45]

---

[42]Lax & Sebenius, *The manager as negotiator.*
[43]Fisher, R. (2001, September 1). Doctor YES. *CFO: The Magazine for Senior Financial Executives,* p. 66.
[44]Bazerman & Neale, *Negotiating rationally;* Kelley, H. H., & Schenitzki, D. P. (1972). Bargaining. In C. G. McClintock (Ed.), *Experimental social psychology* (pp. 298–337). New York: Holt, Rinehart, and Winston; Kelley, H. H. (1966). A classroom study of dilemmas in interpersonal negotiations. In K. Archibald (Ed.), *Strategic intervention and conflict* (pp. 49–73). Berkeley: University of California, Institute of International Studies.
[45]Ross, D. (2003, July 30). County proposes mall traffic solution. *Sequim Gazette,* p. A7.

EXHIBIT 4-4 Wal-Mart's Construction Plans

The mayor of Sequim, Washington, and Wal-Mart's attorney fired verbal shots at the county as the appeals hearing for approving Wal-Mart's construction plans concluded. Shortly thereafter, appeals were filed by the Clallam County Department of Community Development, the Jamestown S'Kallam Indian tribe, and the community group, Sequim First, to block the city planning director from allowing a Wal-Mart complex to be built in the small town of Sequim (fewer than 5,000 people). The groups opposed to the new 575,000-square-foot shopping center complex argued that the Wal-Mart would create a traffic nightmare, causing "unsafe driving conditions" on the roads, and the storm-water runoff (from all the concrete and pavement) would put toxins in the city's rivers and streams; they argued that the impact could cause anywhere between a 280% and 500% increase in traffic. And they wanted Wal-Mart to pay—in advance—something to the tune of $100 million to fix the roads. However, Wal-Mart and the mayor of Sequim viewed these protests as a thinly veiled ploy to squeeze a "deep pocket to pay for [the city's] neglect [of its roads]." According to Wal-Mart and the mayor, the county's road maintenance around Sequim had been downright negligent and the county had not kept up the roads. A Wal-Mart analysis of the same roads predicted only a 7% traffic increase. For a while it appeared to be a standoff, and the two sides seemed to be working off completely different data. Then a breakthrough solution was proposed by Mayor Walt Schubert: An independent body would conduct an analysis of possible traffic impacts on the country roads, and Wal-Mart would give the city up to $100,000 if substantial traffic impacts were proven through the independent study. Through this plan, the Wal-Mart could be built and the city could have money to fix the roads.

Source: Ross, D. (2003, July 9). Wal-Mart united against county during hearing. *Sequim Gazette,* pp. A1, A5.

The multiple-offer strategy is threefold:

1. ***Devise multiple-issue offers,*** as opposed to single-issue offers (to get away from sequential bargaining, which can lock people into lose-lose outcomes).
2. ***Devise offers that are all of equal value to yourself*** (leaving yourself many ways to get what you want before making a concession).
3. ***Make all the offers at the same time.*** This last point is the hardest for most people to do because they negotiate like playing tennis: They make one offer and then wait for the other party to "return" a single offer; then they make a concession, and so on. In the multiple-offer strategy, a negotiator presents a "dessert tray" of offers to the other party and invites a response. *Note:* The other party should be cautioned that cherry-picking (e.g., selecting the terms from each option that most suit a negotiator) is not permissible. Rather, the offers are truly package deals.[46]

Negotiators who make multiple equivalent offers enjoy more profitable negotiated outcomes and are evaluated more favorably by the other party.[47] Specifically, they are seen by the other side as being more flexible, and they are more satisfied at the end of the negotiation. Multiple offers increase the discovery of integrative solutions.[48] When issues are packaged together in a single proposal, rather than considered as separate entities, it

[46]Schatzki, M. (1981). *Negotiation: The art of getting what you want.* New York: New American Library.
[47]Leonardelli, G. J., Medvec, V., Galinsky, A. D., & Claussen-Schulz, A. (2008). Building interpersonal and economic capital by negotiating with multiple equivalent simultaneous offers. Under review at *Organizational Behavior and Human Decision Processes.*
[48]Hyder, E. B., Prietula, M. J., & Weingart, L. R. (2000). Getting to best: Efficiency versus optimality in negotiation. *Cognitive Science, 24*(2), 169–204.

is easier to arrange trades or concession. Moreover, when issues are dealt with individually, negotiators tend to compromise on each issue in a sequential fashion.[49] More important, it is **substantiation** (arguments for one's own position or against the other's position) that interferes the most with win-win agreements. According to Hyder and colleagues, "Substantiation, by its very nature, is a seductive strategy that seems not only to be a default behavior, but a persistent one that feeds upon itself and the cognitive resources of the negotiators."[50] Substantiation begets more substantiation.[51]

Negotiators who make multiple, equivalent offers have an edge in five critical aspects: They can (a) be more aggressive in terms of anchoring the negotiation favorably, (b) gain better information about the other party, (c) be more persistent, (d) signal their priorities more effectively, and (e) overcome concession aversion on the part of the other side.[52]

Be Aggressive in Anchoring

Consider how Ken Alex, an attorney at a major international law firm, negotiated a business news database.[53] For the law firm, the database was critical and renewal was necessary. Not doing so would mean a lot more research librarian time, and recent staff cutbacks had reduced the number of librarians. The amount the firm paid for the renewal in the previous year was $52,000. Alex had budgeted $58,000 for this year's renewal. Alex's strategy was to use the simultaneous multiple-offer strategy. Because he knew that one of the key issues for the database service was the contracted value of the database, he reasoned that a 2-year contract with a major firm would be quite valuable for the database company. Moreover, signing up for 2 years was a low-risk strategy for him because he was confident that the firm would want the database again next year. Moreover, it also would represent budget certainty for the firm in highly volatile times. Alex made two proposals that he called A and B. Proposal A was a 1-year renewal at $45,000; proposal B was a 2-year renewal for $43,000 for year 1 and $47,000 for year 2. Ultimately, the database company opted for proposal B, the 2-year renewal.

Gain Better Information About the Other Party

The multiple-offer strategy is based on the strategy of **inductive reasoning**, meaning that a negotiator can deduce what the other party's true interests are and where the joint gains are. (We present more about inductive, as well as deductive, reasoning in Chapter 8 in a discussion of advanced negotiations and creativity.) By listening to the opponent's response, the negotiator learns about the other party's preferences. Thus, the negotiator acts as a "detective" by drawing conclusions based on the counterparties' responses to the multiple offers.

---

[49]Thompson, L., Mannix, E., & Bazerman, M. H. (1988). Group negotiation: Effects of decision rule, agenda, and aspiration. *Journal of Personality and Social Psychology, 54,* 86–95; Weingart, L. R., Bennett, R., & Brett, J. M. (1993). The impact of consideration of issues and motivational orientation on group negotiation process and outcome. *Journal of Applied Psychology, 78,* 504–517.

[50]Hyder, Prietula, & Weingart, "Getting to best," 194.

[51]Weingart, L. R., Hyder, E. B., & Prietula, M. J. (1996). Knowledge matters: The effect of tactical descriptions on negotiation behavior and outcome. *Journal of Personality and Social Psychology, 70,* 1205–1217.

[52]Medvec, V. H., & Galinsky, A. D. (2005). Putting more on the table: How making multiple offers can increase the final value of the deal. *Negotiation, 8,* 4–6.

[53]Personal communication, December 4, 2002. Names have been altered.

Be Persistent and Persuasive Regarding the Value of an Offer

Consider how the multiple-offer strategy helped a team at a major pharmaceutical firm maintain ground in a particularly tense negotiation.[54] "The situation was a divestiture, and we had an issue surface from our side (regarding much more inventory than was originally estimated), a significant surprise that appeared as if we had provided incorrect information at the due diligence stage. The issue was of a very significant magnitude relative to the size of the deal (meaning that they would have to pay a higher amount in some very significant way)." The pharmaceutical firm proposed five options, all of equivalent value, that involved various trade-offs between deferred payment terms, cash on close, and not taking some of the inventory, among other options. The team made the five proposals and then held their collective breath. "We had already had multiday tirades on issues of who owned the pencil sharpeners, so we were braced for the worst attacks." The other team calmly said, "We understand," and the very next day selected one of the options. Says the pharmaceutical team members, "If we had taken the single-option approach, their obvious position would have been to say 'That is your problem, you misled us . . . provide us with the excess inventory for free.'" However, this potential deal killer was avoided and the deal closed much more successfully than ever anticipated.

Overcome Concession Aversion

When people perceive themselves as having more choices (as opposed to only one), they may be more likely to comply. For example, when Ross Johnson, a member of the California Senate was faced with a legislative bill that he hated, he did not kill it outright. Rather, he strategically offered up three amendments he knew would not be accepted but which would make the non–Orange county legislators aware of some issues Johnson felt were important.[55]

Structure Contingency Contracts by Capitalizing on Differences

Negotiators not only have differences in interests and preferences, but they also view the world differently.[56] A book author may believe that the sales will be high; the publisher may believe they will be more modest. Different interpretations of the facts may threaten already tenuous relations. Attempts to persuade the other person may be met with skepticism, hostility, and an escalating spiral of conflict. Differences in beliefs—or expectations about uncertain events—pave the way toward integrative agreements. For example, in the Wal-Mart negotiation presented in Exhibit 4-4, the parties had widely differing beliefs about the impact the shopping complex would have on local traffic, with the city estimating a 500% increase in traffic and Wal-Mart estimating only 7%. Given these differing predictions, it is somewhat ironic to think they might be leveraged to create a workable solution. In fact, it is differences, rather than commonalities, that can be more advantageous in negotiations.[57] The enlightened negotiator realizes that differences in beliefs, expectations, and tastes can create greater value. Most people are uncomfortable when they encounter differences and, instead of leveraging this opportunity, they either downplay their differences or ignore them.

---

[54] Personal Communication, September 14, 2003.
[55] Quach, H. (2002, January 6). "Caveman" and conciliator: Sen. Ross Johnson adroitly plays to both sides of the aisle, and sings, too. *Orange County Register*, p. 1.
[56] Lax & Sebenius, *The manager as negotiator.*
[57] Ibid.

Negotiators can exploit differences to capitalize on integrative agreements in a variety of ways.[58] Consider the following differences and the opportunities they create:

- Differences in the valuation of the negotiation issues
- Differences in expectations of uncertain events
- Differences in risk attitudes
- Differences in time preferences
- Differences in capabilities

Differences in Valuation

Negotiators have different strengths of preference for each issue. For example, in a negotiation for scarce office space, one person is more interested in a large office than a nice view; the other negotiator is more interested in a view than having extra space. They reach an agreement in which one person gets a large, windowless office and the other gets a small office with a great view. The strategy of trading off so as to capitalize on different strengths of preference is known as **logrolling**.[59]

Differences in Expectations

Because negotiation often involves uncertainty, negotiators differ in their forecasts, or beliefs, about what will happen in the future. Consider the case of a woman and her brother who inherited a tool store from their father.[60] The sister expected the profitability of the store to decline steadily; the brother expected the store to succeed. The sister wanted to sell the store; the brother wanted to keep it. A contingent contract was constructed: The brother agreed to buy his sister's share of the store over a period of time at a price based on her bleak assessment of its worth. The sister is guaranteed a certain return; the brother's return is based on the success of the store.

Differences in Risk Attitudes

In other situations, negotiators agree on the probability of future events but feel differently about taking risks.[61] For example, two colleagues may undertake a collaborative project, such as writing a novel, for which they both agree that the probability of success is only moderate. The colleague with an established career can afford to be risk-seeking; the struggling young novelist may be risk-averse. The two may capitalize on their different risk-taking profiles with a contingent contract: The more risk-averse colleague receives the entire advance on the book; the risk-seeking colleague receives the majority of the risky profits after the publication of the novel. Negotiators who have a **gain-frame** (i.e., see the glass as half full) are more likely to logroll or trade off issues in a win-win fashion; conversely, those with a **loss-frame** (i.e., see the glass as half empty) are more likely to accept a contingent contract.[62]

Differences in Time Preferences

People may value the same event quite differently depending on when it occurs.[63] If one party is more impatient than the other, mechanisms for optimally sharing the consequences over time may be devised. Two partners in a joint venture might allocate the ini-

---

[58]Ibid.

[59]Froman & Cohen, "Compromise and logroll."

[60]Personal Communication, April 1993.

[61]Lax & Sebenius, *The manager as negotiator.*

[62]Kray, L. J., Paddock, L., & Galinsky, A. D, (2008). The effect of past performance on expected control and risk attitudes in integrative negotiations. *Negotiations and Conflict Management Research, 1,* 161-178.

[63]Lax & Sebenius, *The manager as negotiator.*

tial profits to the partner who has high costs for time, whereas the partner who can wait will achieve greater profits over a longer, delayed period.

Differences in Capabilities

People differ not only in their tastes, probability assessments, and risk preferences; they also differ in their capabilities, endowments, and skills. Consider two managers who have different resources, capital, and support staff. One manager has strong quantitative skills and access to state-of-the-art computers; the other has strong marketing and design skills. Together, they may combine their differing skills and expertise in a mutually beneficial way, such as in the design of a new product concept. The development of successful research collaborations is fostered by differences in skills and preferences.[64]

Cautionary Note

Capitalizing on differences often entails **contingency contracts**, wherein negotiators make bets based upon different states of the world occurring. For contingency contracts to be effective, they should satisfy the following four criteria: First, they should not create *a conflict of interest.* For example, if a book author, optimistic about sales, negotiates a contingency contract with her publisher such that royalty rates will be contingent upon sales, the contract should not create an incentive for the publisher to attempt to thwart sales. Second, contingency contracts should be *enforceable* and therefore often may require a written contract. Third, contingency contracts should be *clear, measurable, and readily evaluated,* leaving no room for ambiguity. Conditions and measurement techniques should be spelled out in advance.[65] Further, a date or time line should be mutually agreed upon. Finally, contingency contracts require *continued interaction* among parties. We go into more detail about contingency contracts in Chapter 8.

Presettlement Settlements (PreSS)

Presettlement settlements (PreSS) have three characteristics: They are *formal,* in that they encompass specific, binding obligations; *initial,* because they are intended to be replaced by a formal agreement; and *partial,* in that the parties do not address or resolve all outstanding issues.[66] PreSSs involve more than a simple handshake or "gentleman's agreement." Rather, a PreSS occurs in advance of the parties undertaking full-scale negotiations and is designed to be replaced by a long-term agreement. A PreSS resolves only a subset of the issues on which the parties disagree (i.e., partial). In some cases, instead of resolving any of the outstanding issues, a PreSS may simply establish a concrete framework for final negotiations. For example, reaching a workable agreement between United Kingdom broadcasters and independent producers over who owns the rights to exploit TV shows across broadband and mobile platforms could have taken up to a year. Therefore, a quick resolution to generate revenue from new audiences was crucial for both partners. The parties agreed to negotiate an interim code of practice deal before the consensus on a final agreement.[67]

---

[64]Northcraft, G., & Neale, M. A. (1993). Negotiating successful research collaboration. In J. K. Murnighan (Ed.), *Social psychology in organizations: Advances in theory and research.* Upper Saddle River, NJ: Prentice Hall.
[65]Bazerman, M. H., & Gillespie, J. J. (1999). Betting on the future: The virtues of contingent contracts. *Harvard Business Review, 77*(4), 155–160.
[66]Gillespie, J. J., & Bazerman, M. H. (1998). Pre-settlement settlement (PreSS): A simple technique for initiating complex negotiations. *Negotiation Journal, 14*(2), 149–159.
[67]Jones, G. (2006, March 2). Pact warns solution to digital media rights could take a year. *NMA Magazine,* p. 4.

EXHIBIT 4-5 NO-FIST (Normal Operations with a Financial Strike)

Lax and Sebenius proposed a type of presettlement settlement (PreSS) in a letter to the editor of the *Wall Street Journal*. They noted that a planned strike by American Airlines pilots would result in the airline suffering revenue losses of more than $200 million per day. To avoid such a catastrophe, they recommended the following: "Once the [strike] deadline is imminent and negotiations are irretrievably stuck, the parties would agree to continue normal operations but to put some or all of their revenues and salaries into an escrow account controlled by a trusted outside party." No matter how the escrow fund is eventually divided, both parties will be better off relative to a typical strike. NO-FIST produces a Pareto-superior outcome for all concerned parties, including pilots, shareholders, customers, and nonpilot airline employees.

Source: Lax, D. A., & Sebenius, J. K. (1997, February 24). A better way to go on strike. *The Wall Street Journal,* Section A, p. 22. Copyright © 1997 Dow Jones. Reprinted by permission.

Gillespie and Bazerman note that a famous example of PreSS is the 1993 Oslo Accords between Israel and Palestine.[68] The Oslo Accords sought to establish an incremental process of negotiation and reciprocation that would lead to what both parties termed "final-status" talks. The parties agreed to wait to resolve the most difficult issues (e.g., borders, settlements, Jerusalem) until the final-status talks. As an initial step, the Israelis and Palestinians sought to resolve less difficult issues, thereby establishing a political dialogue and working toward formalized relations. For example, the Israelis agreed to release female prisoners, transfer disputed money, and withdraw from Hebron. The Palestinians agreed to revise their national charter, transfer suspected terrorists, and limit the size of the Palestinian police force. Gillespie and Bazerman also noted that the PreSS framework has subsequently floundered due to heated rhetoric and escalating violence. (For another type of PreSS, see Exhibit 4-5.)

Search for Postsettlement Settlements

A final strategy for expanding the pie is one in which negotiators reach an initial settlement that both agree to but spend additional time attempting to improve upon (each from their own perspective). In the **postsettlement settlement strategy**, negotiators agree to explore other options with the goal of finding another that both prefer more than the current one, or that one party prefers more and to which the other is indifferent.[69] The current settlement becomes both parties' new BATNA. For any future agreement to replace the current one, both parties must be in agreement; otherwise, they revert to the initial agreement. It may seem counterintuitive, and perhaps downright counterproductive, to resume negotiations once an acceptable agreement has been reached, but the strategy of postsettlement settlements is remarkably effective in improving the quality of negotiated agreements[70] and in moving an agreement from a level 1 agreement to a level 2 or 3 agreement.

---

[68]Gillespie & Bazerman, "Pre-settlement settlement (PreSS)."
[69]Raiffa, H. (1982). *The art and science of negotiation.* Cambridge, MA: Belknap.
[70]Bazerman, M. H., Russ, L. E., & Yakura, E. (1987). Post-settlement settlements in dyadic negotiations: The need for renegotiation in complex environments. *Negotiation Journal, 3,* 283–297.

Because they can safely revert to their previous agreement, the postsettlement settlement strategy allows both parties to reveal their preferences without fear of exploitation. If better terms are found, parties can be more confident they have reached a level 2 or 3 settlement. If no better agreement is found, the parties may be more confident that the current agreement is level 3.

A STRATEGIC FRAMEWORK FOR REACHING INTEGRATIVE AGREEMENTS

The discovery and creation of integrative agreements is much like problem solving, which requires creativity. Integrative agreements are devilishly obvious after the fact but not before. Because negotiation is an ill-structured task, with few constraints and a myriad of possible "moves," a royal road for reaching integrative agreement does not exist. Look at the decision making model of integrative negotiation in Exhibit 4-6. The model is prescriptive; that is, it focuses on what negotiators *should* do to reach agreement, not what they *actually* do. The model has five major components: resource assessment, assessment of differences, construction of offers and trade-offs, acceptance/rejection of a decision, and renegotiation.

Resource Assessment

Resource assessment involves the identification of the bargaining issues and alternatives. For example, consider an employment negotiation. The bargaining issues may be salary, vacation, and benefits. In this stage, parties identify the issues that are of concern to them in the negotiation. A superset emerges from the combination of both parties' issues.

EXHIBIT 4-6   Decision Making Model of Integrative Negotiation

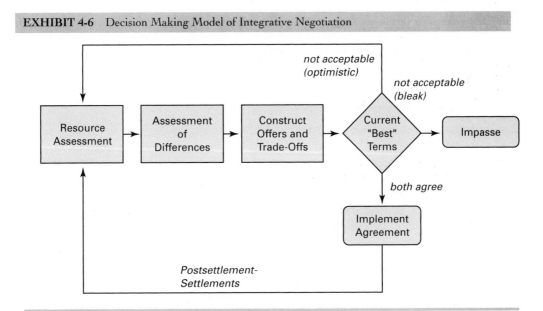

The union of both parties' issue sets forms the **issue mix** of the negotiation. In addition to specifying the issue mix, parties also define and clarify the alternatives for each issue. The ultimate set of options for each issue is a superset of both parties' alternatives.

Later stages of resource assessment move beyond the mere identification of issues and alternatives to more sophisticated processes, namely, the **unbundling** of issues and alternatives and the addition of new issues and alternatives. Unbundling[71] of issues is important in negotiations that center around a single issue. Because mutually beneficial trade-offs require a minimum of two issues, it is important to fractionate conflict into more than one issue. In other instances, it may be necessary to add new issues and alternatives. The process of adding issues and alternatives is facilitated by discussing parties' interests.

Assessment of Differences

Once the issue mix is identified, we should focus on assessing their differences in valuation, probability assessment, risk preferences, time constraints, and capabilities.[72] Eeach party should focus on its most important issues.

Offers and Trade-Offs

In this phase, parties should consider several potential trade-offs among valuations, forecasts, risks, time preferences, and capabilities, and eliminate those dominated by other alternatives. Parties should focus on issues that are of high value to one party and of low cost for the other party to provide. It makes no sense to pursue a trade-off unless what you are offering is more valuable to the other party than what it costs you to provide.

Acceptance/Rejection Decision

At some point, negotiators may identify a set of terms that both find minimally acceptable: It exceeds both parties' reservation points and constitutes a level 1 integrative agreement. However, identification of a minimally acceptable agreement does not necessarily mean that settlement is efficient. Negotiators should continue to explore the possibilities, depending on their costs for time and their subjective assessments of the likelihood of reaching a superior solution. Negotiators' aspirations and goals may influence the search process in negotiation; negotiators who set specific, challenging goals are more likely to continue to search for integrative agreements than do those who do not set goals or who set easy goals.[73]

Prolonging Negotiation and Renegotiation

Two feedback loops emanate from the decision stage: the decision to prolong negotiations and the decision to renegotiate. Negotiators should prolong negotiations when the best agreement on the bargaining table fails to meet both parties' reservation points. Negotiators should reassess the resources by unpacking the initial set of issues and breaking them down into smaller issues that may be traded off. In addition to unpacking issues, negotiators may add issues and alternatives to the bargaining mix. If parties have identified all the issues and alternatives, and they have identified differ-

[71]Lax & Sebenius, *The manager as negotiator.*
[72]Ibid.
[73]Huber, V., & Neale, M. A. (1986). Effects of cognitive heuristics and goals on negotiator performance and subsequent goal setting. *Organizational Behavior and Human Decision Processes, 40,* 342–365.

ences to trade off, but a mutually agreeable solution has not been found, then they should call a halt to the negotiation and pursue their BATNAs. For example, Canadian National Railway representatives met with representatives of the Canadian branch of the United Transportation Union numerous times but could not make any progress toward a national agreement. After 8 months of negotiations, both parties agreed to pursue regional deals as the best alternative to the national agreement.[74]

DO NOT FORGET ABOUT CLAIMING

Sometimes, when negotiators learn about integrative agreements and expanding the pie, they forget about the distributive (pie-slicing) element of negotiation. It is not an effective negotiation strategy to focus exclusively on expanding the pie; the negotiator must simultaneously focus on claiming resources. After all, if a negotiator focused only on expanding the pie, he or she would not benefit because the other party would reap all the added value.

We have witnessed three stages in the evolution of the integrative negotiator. The first stage is what we call the **old-fashioned negotiator**. This type of negotiator comes from the old school of bargaining and believes that one must adopt a tough, hard stance to negotiate successfully. The second stage in the evolution of the negotiator is what we call the **flower child negotiator**: one who gets "turned on" to win-win negotiations and is so busy expanding the pie that he or she forgets to claim resources. Thus, the "flower child" is at a disadvantage in terms of slicing the pie. The third stage is what we call the **enlightened negotiator**, who realizes that negotiation has a pie-expanding aspect but at the same time does not forget to claim resources. Thus, this negotiator protects his or her interests while expanding the pie. If you follow all the strategies outlined in this chapter, you will be an enlightened negotiator.

CONCLUSION

Virtually all negotiators want to reach integrative (or win-win) agreements; however, most negotiators fail to do so, resulting in money and resources being left on the table. In reality, people are usually not aware that their negotiation outcomes are inefficient. The key reasons for lose-lose outcomes are illusory conflict and the fixed-pie perception. The successful creation of win-win negotiation deals involves perspective-taking; asking questions about interests and priorities; providing the counterparty with information about your priorities and preferences (not your BATNA!); unbundling issues; making package deals (not single-issue offers); making multiple offers simultaneously; structuring contingency contracts that capitalize on differences in negotiators' beliefs, expectations, and attitudes; and using pre- and postsettlement settlement strategies. In their attempts to expand the pie, negotiators should not forget about claiming resources.

---

[74]Boyd, J. D. (2007, April 23). CN-UTU rumble on the rails. *Traffic World, 271*(16), 1.

C H A P T E R

Developing a Negotiating Style

Ron Gettelfinger, president of the United Auto Workers (UAW), is a shrewd negotiator. When Delphi's top executives gave themselves bonuses while proposing a slash in workers' wages, he famously called them "hogs slopping at the trough"—later changing that to "swine dining at the trough." However, unlike his predecessor Steve Yokich, Gettelfinger is reserved and straight-laced. He doesn't drink, he takes his wife along on business trips, and his Kentucky drawl makes him sound modest and genuine. Yet he's proved himself to be a tough and determined negotiator at the bargaining table, with a finely honed sense of timing. "He's the hardest-working individual I've ever met," said Robbie Collins, a UAW local president who has participated in contract talks with Gettelfinger. "We went 61 hours straight at one time." His inspiring speeches about the decline of the middle class, growing income inequality in the United States, and the need for a national health plan have provoked even conservative audiences, such as the Detroit Economic Club, to give him standing ovations. But Gettelfinger is also practical. As a trained accountant, he is able to thoroughly study the financial data. "He's aware of how troubled these times are for both the union and the industry," said Harley Shaiken, a labor specialist and professor at the University of California at Berkeley. A devout Catholic, Gettelfinger's positions seem to be based on strong ethical beliefs, and he responds with outrage to anything he recognizes as greed or injustice. Yet despite his sometimes public hostility toward Delphi CEO Steve Miller, Gettelfinger has continued to work with Miller in hopes of instituting a lower wage scale and compensating workers with a lump-sum payment. He is on good terms with most top executives in Detroit, and many recognize him for bringing more integrity to the UAW.[1]

TOUGH VERSUS SOFT NEGOTIATORS

Negotiators often choose between one of two completely different negotiation styles: being tough or being soft.[2] The tough negotiator is unflinching, makes high demands, concedes little, holds out until the very end, and often rejects offers that

---

[1]Tierney, C. (2007, June 22). Facing make-or-break contract talks, fiery UAW boss Ron Gettelfinger has become . . . the pragmatist. *Detroit News*, p. A1.
[2]Bazerman, M. H., & Neale, M. A. (1992). *Negotiating rationally.* New York: Free Press.

are within the bargaining zone. In contrast, the soft negotiator typically offers too many concessions, reveals his or her reservation point, and is so concerned that the other party feels good about the negotiation that he or she gives away too much of the bargaining pie. About 78% of MBA students describe their style as "cooperative"; 22% describe themselves as "aggressive."[3] Neither approach is particularly effective in simultaneously expanding and slicing the pie, and both approaches are likely to lead to outcomes negotiators regret. The tough negotiator often walks away from potentially profitable interactions and gains a reputation for being stubborn. On the other hand, the soft negotiator agrees too readily and never reaps much of the bargaining surplus.

This chapter is designed to help you create a comfortable and effective negotiating style that allows you to (a) expand the pie, (b) maximize your slice, and (c) feel good about the negotiation.

This chapter focuses on motivational orientation; the interests, rights, and power model of disputing; and the influence of emotions and emotional knowledge in negotiations. We provide ways of assessing your style and we profile negotiators who characterize each style. Your job is to do an honest self-assessment of your negotiation style. (See Exhibit 5-1 for a description of Charlene Barshefsky's style.)

Your first response in a negotiation situation is often a good indicator of your instinctive style. Take an honest look at yourself negotiating (audio record or videotape yourself if you have to). Then ask people who are not afraid to give you frank feedback about how they view your style. You will probably be surprised at their responses!

EXHIBIT 5-1   Charlene Barshefsky's Negotiation Style

When Charlene Barshefsky was U.S. trade representative, she would don her signature silk scarves before going to the negotiation table to hammer out deals. She once went without sleep for 51 hours to pound out a trade agreement with Japan; speaking in perfect turns of phrase, she was able to grind down the other side. Her colleagues were so impressed that they nicknamed her "Stonewall" and she was also called "Dragon Lady." In a negotiation with China, she threatened to pack her bags and leave for the airport, cueing her negotiation partner, Gene Sperling, a White House aide, to stalk from the table theatrically after her. Some described Barshefsky as a "sharp instrument," a "woman warrior who is genuinely responsive to people." Armed with the precise speech of a litigator, Barshefsky was enormously skilled in wresting concessions from trading partners. In one negotiation, she did not even need to utter a single word to disconcert her counterpart—when a Japanese finance minister said that the U.S. delegation had to "take or leave" the offer that was on the table, Barshefsky just laughed out loud.

Source: Hua, L. S. (1999, November 21). She's a master of details. *Straits Times,* p. 42. Article by courtesy of SPH–The Straits Times.

---

[3]Lewicki, R. J., & Robinson, R. J. (1998). Ethical and unethical bargaining tactics: An empirical study. *Journal of Business Ethics, 17*(6), 665–682.

MOTIVATIONAL ORIENTATION

People have different orientations toward the process of negotiation. Some are individualists, seeking only their own gain; others are cooperative, seeking to maximize joint interests; and others are competitive, seeking to maximize differences. Exhibit 5-2 depicts eight distinct motivational orientations, ranging from altruism (high concern for others' interests) to aggression (desire to harm the other party) to masochism (desire to harm oneself) and individualism (desire to further one's own interests). Cooperation represents a midpoint between altruism and individualism; martyrdom represents a midpoint between altruism and masochism; sadomasochism represents a midpoint between masochism and aggression; and competition represents a midpoint between aggression and individualism.

Assessing Your Motivational Style

Although Exhibit 5-2 depicts several motivational orientations, the following three are most common: individualism, competition, and cooperation, so we'll focus most on these. (See Exhibit 5-3, specifically.)

EXHIBIT 5-2 A Circumplex of Social Motivations

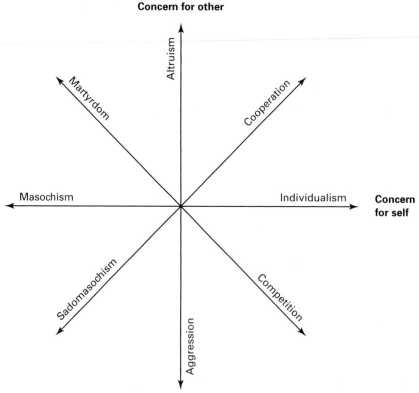

Source: Based on *Cooperation and Helping Behavior*, C. G. McClintock and E. van Avermaet, E. Social values and rules of fairness: A theoretical perspective. In V. J. Derlega and J. Grezlak (Eds.), *Cooperation and helping behavior* (pp. 43–71). New York: Academic Press. Copyright © 1982.

EXHIBIT 5-3   Motivational Styles

	Motivational Style		
	Individualistic	Competitive	Cooperative
Objective	Self-interest	Victory	Joint welfare
View of others	Self-interested	Competitive	Heterogeneous: Some cooperative; some competitive; some individualistic
Situational factors that trigger this motivational orientation	Incentives to maximize own gain	Group competition; when organizations make interpersonal comparisons salient	Social identity; superordinate goals

1. The **individualistic** negotiator prefers to maximize his or her own gain and is indifferent to how much the other person is getting.
2. The **competitive** negotiator prefers to maximize the difference between his or her own profits and those of the other party (i.e., "beat" the other side).
3. The **cooperative** negotiator seeks equality and to minimize the difference between negotiators' outcomes.

For a quick assessment of your own motivational orientation, answer the nine questions in Exhibit 5-4.

Richard Shell has identified helpful strategies and tips designed for cooperative types and competitive types.[4] According to Shell, if you are a cooperative negotiator, you need to become more assertive, confident, and prudent in negotiations to be more effective at pie-expanding and pie-slicing. He outlines seven tools for the overly cooperative negotiator:

1. *Avoid concentrating too much on your bottom line.*   Instead, spend extra time preparing your goals and developing high aspirations.
2. *Develop your BATNA.*   Know your options to negotiating.
3. *Get an agent and delegate the negotiation task.*   It is not an admission of failure to appoint an agent if you think that person can act more assertively for you than you can for yourself.
4. *Bargain on behalf of someone or something else, not yourself.*   Sometimes people feel selfish when they negotiate; to get away from this limiting perception, think about other people, such as your family, your staff, even your "retired self," and negotiate on their behalf.
5. *Create an audience.*   People negotiate more assertively when they have an audience. So, tell someone about your negotiation, make promises, and then report results.
6. *Say "You will have to do better than that because . . . ," not "Yes."*   Cooperative people are programmed to say yes to almost anything. Rehearse not saying yes to everything that is proposed. Indeed, a historical analysis of four crises (including the Bay of Pigs and the Cuban Missile Crisis) reveals that leaders with cooperative-affiliative motivation are more likely to offer concessions.[5]

[4]Shell, G. R. (1999). *Bargaining for advantage: Negotiation strategies for reasonable people.* New York: Viking.
[5]Langner, C., & Winter, D. (2001). The motivational basis of concessions and compromise: Archival and laboratory studies. *Journal of Personality and Social Psychology, 81*(4), 711–727.

EXHIBIT 5-4 Motivational Style Assessment

MOTIVATIONAL STYLE ASSESSMENT

Each question presents three possible distributions of money (A, B, and C) to you and an opponent. Your task is to choose which of these distributions you most prefer. Indicate your true preference, not what you think you should choose. Be honest with yourself and circle only one alternative per question.

	Payoff to You Payoff to Other	A	B	C
1	You	$4,800	$5,400	$4,800
	Other party	$ 800	$2,800	$4,800
2	You	$5,600	$5,000	$5,000
	Other party	$3,000	$5,000	$1,000
3	You	$5,200	$5,200	$5,800
	Other party	$5,200	$1,200	$3,200
4	You	$5,000	$5,600	$4,900
	Other party	$1,000	$3,000	$4,900
5	You	$5,600	$5,000	$4,900
	Other party	$3,000	$5,000	$ 900
6	You	$5,000	$5,000	$5,700
	Other party	$5,000	$1,000	$3,000
7	You	$5,100	$5,600	$5,100
	Other party	$5,100	$3,000	$1,100
8	You	$5,500	$5,000	$5,000
	Other party	$3,000	$1,000	$5,000
9	You	$4,800	$4,900	$5,400
	Other party	$4,800	$1,000	$3,000

Compute your cooperative score by giving yourself one point for:
#1-C, #2-B, #3-A, #4-C, #5-B, #6-A, #7-A, #8-C, #9-A.
Compute your cooperative score by giving yourself one point for:
#1-A, #2-C, #3-B, #4-A, #5-C, #6-B, #7-C, #8-B, #9-B.
Compute your individualist score by giving yourself one point for:
#1-B, #2-A, #3-C, #4-B, #5-A, #6-C, #7-B, #8-A, #9-C.

Source: Kuhlman, D. M., & Marshello, A. (1975). Individual differences in the game motives of own, relative, and joint gain. *Journal of Research in Personality, 9*(3), 240–251. Reprinted by permission of Elsevier via RightsLink.

7. ***Insist on commitments, not just agreements.*** An agreement puts too much trust in the other party; instead, insist upon commitments and specific promises from the other party, with consequences if they are not followed.

Shell also outlines seven tools for competitive people. He cautions that competitive negotiators need to become more aware of others and legitimate their needs.

1. ***Think about pie-expansion, not just pie-slicing.*** Remember that you can increase your slice of the pie by creating a bigger pie.

2. *Ask more questions than you think you should.*   It pays to really understand the other party's objectives and needs.

3. *Rely on standards.*   Other people respond well to arguments based upon standards of fairness and objectivity.

4. *Hire a relationship manager.*   It is not a sign of failure to consult with someone concerning how to manage the "people side" of negotiations.

5. *Be scrupulously reliable.*   Keep your word. Remember the egocentric bias: You see yourself as more honorable than others do, so you have to go overboard. (Recall the data on the "lying" study presented in Chapter 3.)

6. *Do not haggle when you can negotiate.*   Do not view the negotiation as a contest of wills on every little issue. Spend time thinking about all the issues and the big picture. Remember that trade-offs mean you may lose on some issues in return for big gains on other issues.

7. *Always acknowledge the other party and protect that person's self-esteem.*   Do not gloat or brag. Remember that Dale Carnegie said the word other people most like to hear is their own name. So shower them with honest respect.

Strategic Issues Concerning Motivational Style

Once you know your own (and the other party's) motivational style, how can you best use this information? Several strategic issues are relevant when it comes to motivational style.

The Myth of the Hard Bargainer

In Schneider's analysis of more than 700 practicing attorneys, adversarial behavior was regarded by peers to be distinctly ineffective. In fact, more than 50% of the negotiators viewed as adversarial were regarded as ineffective.[6] Simply put, as negotiators become more irritating, stubborn, and unethical, their effectiveness ratings drop.

Similar findings have been obtained by directly observing negotiators (as opposed to self- and other-reports). When both negotiators have a cooperative orientation, they can be more effective in terms of maximizing the pie.[7] For example, in a study of multiparty negotiations, cooperative groups outperformed individualists in terms of pie-expanding.[8] Highly cooperative negotiators use more integrative strategies (such as information exchange), make more proposals for mutual coordination, and use fewer distributive tactics.[9] Moreover, the more cooperatively motivated people present in a negotiation, the more integrative (pie-expanding) information is exchanged.[10] When individualistically motivated negotiators are at the table, distributive strategies increase

---

[6]Schneider, A. K. (2002). Shattering negotiation myths: Empirical evidence on the effectiveness of negotiation style. *Harvard Negotiation Law Review, 7,* 143–233.

[7]Olekalns, M., & Smith, P. L. (1999). Social value orientations and strategy choices in competitive negotiations. *Personality and Social Psychology Bulletin, 25*(6), 657–668; Olekalns, M., & Smith, P. L. (2003). Testing the relationships among negotiators' motivational orientations, strategy choices, and outcomes. *Journal of Experimental Social Psychology, 39,* 101–117; Pruitt, D. G., & Lewis, S. A. (1975). Development of integrative solutions in bilateral negotiation. *Journal of Personality and Social Psychology, 31,* 621–630; Weingart, L. R., Bennett, R., & Brett, J. M. (1993). The impact of consideration of issues and motivational orientation on group negotiation process and outcome. *Journal of Applied Psychology, 78,* 504–517; Weingart, L. R., Brett, J. M., Olekalns, M., & Smith, P.L. (2007). Conflicting social motives in negotiating groups. *Journal of Personality and Social Psychology, 93*(6), 994–1010.

[8]Weingart, Bennett, & Brett, "The impact of consideration."

[9]Olekalns & Smith, "Social value orientations."

[10]Weingart, Brett, & Olekalns, "Conflicting social motives."

(e.g., positional statements and substantiation). Cooperators and individualists take different roads to reach win-win outcomes.[11] Individualists use the multiple-offer strategy and indirect information exchange; in contrast, cooperators share information about interests and priorities directly.

Do Not Lose Sight of Your Own Interests

By arguing that competitive, hard bargaining is not effective, we do not mean that negotiators should turn into "cream puffs."[12] In any negotiation situation, it is important not to lose sight of your own interests. Individualists do not need to worry about this possibility, but cooperators and competitors do. Often, two cooperators end up with a lose-lose agreement because they fail to make their interests known to the other party.[13] Similarly, competitors are often so intent on "beating" the other side they do not pay attention to their own interests. In a sense, they win the battle but lose the war. Thus, it is important that you maintain a high level of concern for your own interests, as well as those of the other party.[14] (Some gender differences have been documented as well when it comes to motivational orientation; see Exhibit 5-5.)

Social Comparison Can Cause Breakdowns in Negotiation

In the negotiations between United Airlines and its pilots in 1999, the union doubled its pay raise demand from 14.5% to 28% immediately upon learning that pilots at Delta had gotten a 20% jump above industry-leading rates.[15] Houston janitors working in

---

EXHIBIT 5-5 Why Do Women Settle for Less?

Lisa Barron began studying how women negotiate while she was in graduate school, after noticing that the men in her master of business administration classes spent a lot of time talking about money—but the women didn't. Barron watched men and women negotiate in mock job interviews. To enhance realism, she had real MBA students negotiate with real hiring managers for marketing positions. She told them to ask for more than the $60,000 starting salary. Men believed they had to advocate for themselves; in contrast, women believed if they did a good job the organization would eventually reward them. Whereas 85% of the men felt comfortable measuring their worth in dollars, 83% of the women were uncomfortable doing so and unsure of their monetary value. At least 70% of men believed they were entitled to more than others, but 71% of the women believed they were entitled to the same as others (cooperative motivation).

Sources: Fisher, M. (2003, July 5). Why do women settle for less: A researcher says female job seekers hate to haggle over pay. *Orange County Register,* p. 1; Barron, L. A. (2003). Ask and you shall receive? Gender differences in negotiators' beliefs about requests for a higher salary. *Human Relations, 56*(6), 635.

---

[11]Olekalns & Smith, "Testing the relationships."

[12]Glick, S., & Croson, R. (2001). Reputations in negotiation. In S. Hoch & H. Kunreuther (Eds.), *Wharton on making decisions* (pp. 177–186). New York: Wiley.

[13]Thompson, L., & DeHarpport, T. (1998). Relationships, good incompatibility, and communal orientation in negotiations. *Basic and Applied Social Psychology, 20*(1), 33–44.

[14]Pruitt, D. G., & Carnevale, P. J. (1993). *Negotiation in social conflict.* Pacific Grove, CA: Brooks-Cole; De Dreu, C. K. W., Weingart, L. R., & Kwon, S. (2000). Influence of social motives on integrative negotiation: A meta-analytic review and test of two theories. *Journal of Personality and Social Psychology, 78*(5), 889–905.

[15]Griffin, G., & Leib, J. (2003, June 9). Flying on fumes: A costly pilots contract, the dot-com meltdown and a failed merger put United in a tailspin and sent executives scrambling to recover. *Denver Post,* p. A01.

buildings owned by Hines Interests asked for a salary increase and family health care benefits after comparing their pay and benefits to janitors in other cities. According to the Service Employees International Union, janitors of Hines-owned buildings in Chicago were making $13.80 an hour plus benefits, while those in Houston earned only $5.30 an hour and received no family health care benefits.[16] As noted in Chapter 3, people are concerned with the payoffs received by others. In one investigation, people were given several choices concerning the division of a pie between themselves and another person (e.g., $300 you/$300 other versus $500 you/$800 other, etc.).[17] They were asked to indicate how satisfactory each division of the pie was. If people were purely individualistic, satisfaction would only be driven by the amount of money for oneself. In fact, people were highly concerned with how much the "other person" received, so much so that people often preferred to earn less money, if it meant that this would equate outcomes between themselves and another person. For example, many people preferred $300 self/$300 other over $500 self/$800 other. When faced with a choice between $300 self/$300 other versus $800 self/$500 other, people still tended to prefer equality but not as strongly as when the self was disadvantaged.

The relationship we have with the other party can affect our own motivational orientation. Consider the following choices:[18]

Choice A: $4,000 for yourself
Choice B: 50% chance at $3,000; 50% chance at $5,000

Which do you choose? We asked 111 MBA students, and most of them (73%) chose the sure thing: choice A. This example confirms the risk-aversion principle we discussed in Chapter 2. We then asked a separate, but comparable, group of MBA students to choose between the following:

Choice C: $4,000 for yourself
         $6,000 for another person
Choice D: Self: 50% chance at $3,000, 50% chance at $5,000
         Other: 50% chance at $7,000, 50% chance at $5,000

A close look at all four choices (A, B, C, and D) reveals that choice C is identical to choice A (except for the payoff to the other person), and choice D is identical to choice B (except for the payoff to the other person). Thus, if people were perfectly rational and consistent, they would choose C over D (given that most choose A over B). However, this outcome dose not occur. People's choices are driven, in large part, by their *relationship* with the other party. Negotiators who have a positive relationship with the other person prefer the sure thing of choice C (56%) over the gamble of choice D; in contrast, those who had a negative relationship with the other person preferred to gamble on D (67%) over C. The type of relationship we have with another person affects our motivational orientation.

Perhaps it is this concern for equality that led to the removal of American Airlines CEO Donald Carty in 2003. When Donald Carty became CEO of American

[16]Sixel, L. M. (2006, September 30). Janitors try to build support: Union asks building owners, managers for help. *Houston Chronicle,* p. 1.
[17]Loewenstein, G. F., Thompson, L., & Bazerman, M. H. (1989). Social utility and decision making in interpersonal contexts. *Journal of Personality and Social Psychology, 57*(3), 426–441.
[18]Ibid.

Airlines in 1998, he was well liked. However, in the aftermath of the September 11, 2001 terrorist attacks, Carty was forced from his position because of tainted relations with American's powerful unions and, in the end, his own board of directors. The reason? The union members, who had recently taken serious wage cuts, discovered Carty and other executives had privately been given bonus plans and lavish pension benefits. It seemed like an inequity of the grandest sort and they would have no part of it.[19]

Distinct differences are evident between the pie-expanding and pie-slicing strategies used by cooperators versus those used by competitors. Cooperators not only increase the size of the pie, they also prefer an equitable division of the pie in comparison to individualists and competitors. Furthermore, cooperation is strongly related to reciprocity: Relative to individualists and competitors, cooperators are more likely to engage in the same level of cooperation as their opponent.[20]

Use the Principle of Reinforcement to Shape Behavior

Negotiators can use basic principles of reinforcement (and punishment) to shape the behavior of their opponents. Reinforcement and punishment can be subtle, and the other party may not even be aware that you are using it. For example, in one study a lecturer stood in front of a class. Half of the class was instructed to look interested, nod their heads, and smile approvingly (positive reinforcement); the other half of the class was told to look bored and disinterested (punishment). After a short time, the instructor moved to the side of the class that was reinforcing his behavior. One of the best ways to encourage the counterparty to engage in a behavior is to reinforce it positively when you see that person using it. It is important to reinforce the behavior immediately after it occurs. Similarly, one of the fastest ways to extinguish behavior you *do not* want the counterparty, to use is simply not to respond.

The Power of Reciprocity

Integrative (pie-expanding) and distributive (pie-slicing) behaviors tend to be reciprocated.[21] Similarly, the tendency is for people to reciprocate the motivational orientation of the other party. If you want to discourage a competitive motivational orientation in the counterparty, then resist the urge to reciprocate it.

Anticipate Motivational Clashes at the Bargaining Table

It is unlikely that the counterparty will have the same motivational orientation as you. What happens when a person with a cooperative orientation negotiates with a competitive person? The cooperator begins the negotiation in a cooperative fashion, but when she realizes that she is facing a competitor, she changes her own style. People with a cooperative orientation behave competitively when paired with a competitive opponent,

---

[19]Kerr, K. (2003, April 25). Carty known as tough CEO who smiled. *Tulsa World*, p. E1.

[20]Van Lange, P. A. M. (1999). The pursuit of joint outcomes and equality in outcomes: An integrative model of social value orientation. *Journal of Personality and Social Psychology, 77*(2), 337–349.

[21]Brett, J. M., Shapiro, D. L., & Lytle, A. (1998). Breaking the bonds of reciprocity in negotiations. *Academy of Management Journal, 41*(4), 410–424; Donohue, W. A. (1981). Analyzing negotiation tactics: Development of a negotiation interact system. *Human Communication Research, 7*(3), 273–287; Putnam, L. L. (1983). Small group work climates: A lag-sequential analysis of group interaction. *Small Group Behavior, 14*(4), 465–494.

whereas competitive players do not change.[22] In another study, when different types of players were faced with a prosocial (cooperative) opponent, prosocial and individualistic players were more likely to cooperate than were competitive players, but they would compete when the other party competed; competitive players competed regardless of the behavior of the other party.[23]

Motivational Convergence

A negotiator's goal orientation (individualistic, cooperative, or competitive) provides an initial strategic approach to negotiations. During negotiation, people's strategies often change in response to how they view the other party and the situation. In particular, when a cooperator meets a competitor, the cooperator is the one to change. Thus, a strong tendency toward convergence of styles is likely to occur at the bargaining table.[24] Convergence of outcomes, as well as bargaining styles, occurs in later stages of negotiation.[25] As deadlines approach, people exchange specific proposals and make concessions.[26]

Epistemic Motivation

Epistemic motivation refers to a person's need to understand his or her world.[27] To reach integrative agreements, negotiators should have not only a cooperative (social) orientation but also a deep understanding of the task (epistemic motivation). Indeed, negotiators who are high in both epistemic and cooperative motivation develop greater trust and reach more integrative agreements than those low in cooperation or low in epistemic motivation.[28]

INTERESTS, RIGHTS, AND POWER MODEL OF DISPUTING

According to Ury, Brett, and Goldberg, negotiators use one of three types of approaches when in the process of conflict or dispute resolution:[29]

1. **Interests:** Negotiators who focus on interests attempt to learn about the other party's underlying needs, desires, and concerns.[30] Interests-based negotiators attempt to reconcile

---

[22]Kelley, H. H., & Stahelski, A. J. (1970). Social interaction basis of cooperators' and competitors' beliefs about others. *Journal of Personality and Social Psychology, 16*(1), 66–91.

[23]McClintock, C. G., & Liebrand, W. B. (1988). Role of interdependence structure, individual value orientation, and another's strategy in social decision making: A transformational analysis. *Journal of Personality and Social Psychology, 55*(3), 396–409.

[24]Weingart, L. R., Brett, J. M., Olekalns, M., & Smith, P. L. (2007). Conflicting social motives in negotiating groups. *Journal of Personality and Social Psychology, 93*(6), 994–1010.

[25]Gulliver, M. P. (1979). The effect of the spatial visualization factor on achievement in operations with fractions. *Dissertation Abstracts International, 39*(9-A), 5381–5382.

[26]Lim, S. G., & Murnighan, J. K. (1994). Phases, deadlines, and the bargaining process. *Organizational Behavior and Human Decision Processes, 58*, 153–171; Stuhlmacher, A. F., Gillespie, T. L., & Champagne, M. V. (1998). The impact of time pressure in negotiation: A meta-analysis. *International Journal of Conflict Management, 9*(2), 97–116.

[27]Kruglanski, A. W. (1989). *Lay epistemics and human knowledge: Cognitive and motivational bases.* New York: Plenum Press.

[28]DeDreu, C., Beersma, B., Stroebe, K., & Euwema, M. (2006). Motivated information processing, strategic choice, and the quality of negotiated agreement. *Journal of Personality and Social Psychology, 90*(6), 927–943.

[29]Ury, W. L., Brett, J. M., & Goldberg, S. B. (1988). *Getting disputes resolved: Designing systems to cut the costs of conflict.* San Francisco: Jossey-Bass.

[30]Fisher, R., & Ury. W. (1991). *Getting to yes* (2nd edition). Boston: Houghton Mifflin.

differing interests among parties in a way that addresses parties' most pressing needs and concerns.

2. ***Rights:*** Negotiators who focus on rights apply standards of fairness to negotiation. Standards may include terms specified by contracts, legal rights, precedent, or expectations based upon norms.

3. ***Power:*** Negotiators who focus on power use status, rank, threats, and intimidation to get their way. Books such as *Guerilla Negotiating: Unconventional Weapons and Tactics to Get What You Want* and *Sue the Bastards!* are power focused.[31]

As an example of the difference between interests-, rights-, and power-based approaches, consider this statement made by an employer: "I am afraid I cannot meet your desired salary requirements, but I do hope you will realize that working in our company is a wonderful opportunity and join us." Before reading further, take a moment to consider how you would respond if an employer made this statement to you. Three different negotiators might respond to the employer's statement in ways unique to their own approach:

1. ***Interests-based response:*** "I am very interested in joining your company if my interests can be met. I would like to share some of my key goals and objectives. I want to learn more about the company's interests, from your standpoint. I should mention right now that salary is a key concern for me. I am the single wage earner in my family, and I have a number of educational loans. You did not mention other aspects of the offer, such as stock options, vacations, and flex time. Can we discuss these issues at this point?"

2. ***Rights-based response:*** "I am very interested in joining your company if we can come up with a fair employment package. I would like to point out that my salary requirements are in line with those of other people joining similar companies. I would think it would be a competitive advantage for your company to offer employment packages that are competitive with those being offered by other companies. I believe that my record and previous experience mean that a higher salary would be fair in this case."

3. ***Power-based response:*** "I am very interested in joining your company, but I must tell you that other companies are offering me more attractive deals at this point. I would like to invite you to reconsider the offer so that I do not have to resort to turning your offer down, given that I think that we make a good match for one another. I hope you will be able to make a competitive offer."

(For a more complete description of interests-, rights-, or power-based approaches, see Exhibit 5-6.)

During the process of negotiating or resolving disputes, the focus may shift from interests to rights to power and back again. For example, in one investigation negotiators' statements were recorded during a negotiation. Each statement was coded in terms of whether it reflected an interests-, rights-, or power-based approach.[32] Parties moved frequently among interests, rights, and power in the same negotiation (23 of 25 dyads), with more emphasis on rights and power in the first and third quarters than in the second and fourth quarters.

---

[31]Levinson, C., Smith, M., & Wilson, O. (1999). *Guerilla negotiating: Unconventional weapons and tactics to get what you want.* New York: Wiley; Fox, G., & Nelson, J. *Sue the bastards! Everything you need to know to go to—or stay out of—court.* Chicago: Contemporary Books.
[32]Lytle, A. L., Brett, J. M., & Shapiro, D. L. (1999). The strategic use of interests, rights and power to resolve disputes. *Negotiation Journal, 15*(1), 31–49.

EXHIBIT 5-6   Approaches to Negotiation

	Approach		
	Interests	Rights	Power
Goal	Self-interest Dispute resolution Understanding others' concerns	Fairness Justice	Winning Respect
Temporal focus	Present (What needs and interests do we have right now?)	Past (What has been dictated by the past?)	Future (What steps can I take in the future to overpower others?)
Distributive strategies (pie-slicing)	Compromise	Often produces a "winner" and a "loser"; thus, unequal distribution	Often produces a "winner" and a "loser"; thus, unequal distribution
Integrative strategies (pie-expansion)	Most likely to expand the pie via addressing parties' underlying needs	Difficult to expand the pie unless focus is on interests	Difficult to expand the pie unless focus is on interests
Implications for future negotiations and relationship	Greater understanding Satisfaction Stability of agreement	Possible court action	Resentment Possible retaliation Revenge

Assessing Your Approach

Consider the United Airlines pilots' negotiation of 2000 to analyze the moves in the negotiation in terms of interests, rights, and power:

- *Union power move:*   United's pilots expected a new contract on April 12, 2000, and many were angry when it did not happen. They began refusing to work overtime and started calling in extra sick days. This reaction caused immediate disruptions to United's flight schedule, which required voluntary overtime by pilots to function normally. Management also noticed that pilots were taxiing more slowly, correcting flight plans at the last minute, and insisting on repairs of minor items.
- *Management rights move:*   Management warned that if such tactics were organized by the union, they would be illegal. The company began compiling evidence it could take to court, including union communiqués encouraging pilots to "work to rule" (in other words, to do everything to the letter of the contract).
- *Union power move:*   Pilots stopped conducting training flights for new hires, leaving a pool of 120 pilots who could not fly. In July, 20 California-based first officers called in sick in one day, forcing the company to cancel virtually its entire schedule of Asia-bound fights. In Colorado Springs, pilots abandoned a plane full of passengers on the ramp because their duty time was up, and United couldn't find replacements to get the plane to Denver. A clandestine pilot newsletter, circulated in August, urged pilots to "slow down" and give United "a Labor Day that they'll never forget."

- *Management rights and power move:*   In November, with the busy Thanksgiving weekend approaching, United took its mechanics to court, seeking $66 million in damages (rights). The company also fired and disciplined some of them (power).

Next, we present each approach in greater detail. Which one characterizes you?

Interests

Interests are a person's needs, desires, concerns, fears—in general, the things a person cares about or wants. Interests underlie people's positions in negotiation (the things they *say* they want). Reconciling interests in negotiation is not easy. It involves understanding interests, devising creative solutions, and looking for trade-offs. We discussed some negotiation strategies in Chapters 3 and 4, such as fashioning trade-offs or logrolls among issues, searching for compatible issues, devising bridging solutions, and structuring contingency contracts. It is difficult to immediately address interests in a negotiation because people adopt positional tendencies and because emotions can often conceal interests. Negotiators who use an interests-based approach frequently ask other parties about their needs and concerns and, in turn, disclose their own needs and concerns.

Rights

Steve Clayborn of Grovetown, Georgia, shocked a nurse and caused a scene at Doctors Hospital when he refused to sign a standard consent form unless he could "pencil in some changes."[33] Consider the moves of Nike CEO Phil Knight and Will Vinton of Vinton Studios that resembled a complicated game of corporate chess.[34] Each time Knight tried to make a move, Vinton blocked it, using his rights under the company's complicated stock ownership structure. Knight would not put more money into the company unless it issued new stock. However, Vinton found a legal loophole that would allow him to buy enough stock to regain control of Vinton Studios. Eventually, Knight fired Vinton and paid him no severance.

The United Steel Workers (USW) Union is known for invoking successorship clauses to get what it wants. In most cases, these clauses simply require that the potential buyer of a plant adhere to a collective-bargaining agreement. But the USW altered its clauses to state that before a plant can be sold a successor company and the union must agree on a new labor contract, giving the union the ability to "approve" the sale of a steel plant. When Wheeling-Pittsburgh, a leading steel company, struck a partnership deal with Brazil's CSN, the union did not like the idea. Union leaders believed CSN would benefit significantly while the American workers would receive very little. Invoking the rights of the successorship clause it had negotiated earlier with Wheeling-Pittsburgh, the union rejected the possibility of a merger between the two companies.[35]

These examples illustrate that a common negotiation style is to rely on some independent standard with perceived legitimacy or fairness to determine who is right in

---

[33]Mogul, M. (2003, July 12). The art of the deal: Professional haggler shares bargaining skills. *Augusta Chronicle,* p. C7.

[34]Manning, J., & Turnquist, K. (2003, May 25.) Squabble in 'Toon Town. *Oregonian,* p. D01.

[35]Wysocki Jr., B., Maher, K., & Glader, P. (2007, May 9). New clout—A labor union's power: Blocking takeover bids; steel-company buyers learn they must get USW on their side. *Wall Street Journal,* p. A1.

a situation. Some rights are formalized by law or contract. Others are socially accepted standards of behavior, such as reciprocity, precedent, equality, and seniority (e.g., "I want a higher salary because it would be consistent with the incentive structure in this organization"). Rights are rarely clear-cut. They often differ from situation to situation, and sometimes, contradictory standards apply. For example, a productive employee may want a salary increase based upon extreme productivity, yet the organization may focus on seniority. Reaching an agreement on rights, where the outcome will determine who gets what, can often be exceedingly difficult, frequently leading negotiators to involve a third party to determine who is right. The prototypical rights procedure involves **adjudication,** in which disputants present evidence and arguments to a neutral third party with the power to hand down a binding decision. Negotiators who use a rights-based approach frequently say things like "I deserve this" or "This is fair." (See the cartoon in Exhibit 5-7 for a humorous example of a rights-based move.)

EXHIBIT 5-7   Humorous Example of a Rights-Based Move in a Divorce

"Your wife's also asking that you rot in hell for eternity, but I think that's negotiable."

Source: © The New Yorker Collection 1999 Michael Masline from cartoonbank.com. All Rights Reserved.

EXHIBIT 5-8   Power Moves

At 12:01 on the morning of May 1, 2000, the TV screen went blue on Time Warner Cable's WABC-TV feed, and a scrolling message in block letters began: "DISNEY HAS TAKEN ABC AWAY FROM YOU." After four months of fruitless negotiations over the rights to retransmit ABC signals over cable, Time Warner yanked ABC stations off its systems in 11 cities, including Houston, Philadelphia, Raleigh, and New York, during a critical period for setting ratings and ad rates. The "alert" aired on WABC-TV Channel 7 in New York, whose cable subscribers in 3.5 million homes went without their local ABC station. Time Warner said it wanted to extend talks until the end of the year, but ABC only offered an extension through May 24—the end of the sweeps. Time Warner laid blame squarely on Disney, ABC's corporate parent. "Disney is trying to inappropriately use its ownership of ABC television stations to extract excessive and unreasonable terms for its cable TV channels—terms that would add hundreds of millions of dollars in cost for Time Warner and its cable customers," said Fred Dressler, senior vice president of programming for Time Warner Cable. Disney wanted higher fees for the cable rights to ABC and broader distribution by Time Warner for Disney's own cable programming, especially ESPN. The Cable Act of 1992 entitles over-the-air networks to compensation from cable systems that carry network signals. The agreement between Disney's ABC and Time Warner Cable expired on December 31, 1999. ABC blamed the impasse on Time Warner: "This is a punitive act, but Time Warner is only punishing their own customers through their cable system," said Tom Kane, president and general manager of WABC.

Source: From *Fading to Black* by M. Larson in ADWEEK, May 8, 2000, 41(19), p. C50. Reprinted by permission of Nielsen Business Media, Inc.

Power

Power is the ability to coerce someone to do something he or she would not otherwise do. Exercising power typically means imposing costs on the other side or threatening to do so. Exercising power may manifest itself in acts of aggression, such as sabotage, physical attack, or withholding benefits derived from a relationship. A prime example of a power move occurred when Time Warner yanked ABC stations off its systems in 11 cities at the beginning of the May sweeps period in 2000, a critical time for setting ratings and ad rates. Television viewers saw the words "DISNEY HAS TAKEN ABC AWAY FROM YOU" scrolling across the screen in block letters.[36] (See Exhibit 5-8 for the complete story.)

Within a relationship of mutual dependence (e.g., labor and management; employee and employer), the question of who is more powerful rests on who is more dependent. In turn, one's degree of dependency on the other party rests on how satisfactory the alternatives are for satisfying one's interests. The better the alternative, the less dependent one is. Power moves include behaviors that range from insults and ridicule to strikes, beatings, and warfare.

The variety of power tactics have in common the intent to coerce the other side to settle on terms more satisfactory to the wielder of power. For example, Kim Jong Il, president of North Korea, was described as "cunning and cruel, with street-fighter instincts."[37] Moreover, he was not above using brinksmanship—threatening to drive himself and others over the edge. However, Wendy Sherman, the former senior

---

[36]Larson, M. (2000, May 8). Fading to black. *Adweek, 41*(19), C50.
[37]Zielenziger, M. (2003, January 12). Crazy like a fox and steel-tough. *Patriot-News Harrisburg,* p. A20.

U.S. State Department official who negotiated with Kim in the Clinton administration, said, "He is not crazy. . . . He is intelligent and he is totally conscious about what he is doing."[38] His strategy is to push just far enough. Just before the U.S. government gets really angry, he stops the provocations and comes to the negotiation table.

Two types of power-based approaches are **threats** (in which one or both parties makes a threat) and **contests** (in which parties take action to determine who will prevail).[39] Determining who is more powerful without a decisive and potentially destructive power contest may be difficult because power is ultimately a matter of perception. Despite objective indicators of power (e.g., financial resources), parties' perceptions of their own and each other's power do not often coincide. Moreover, each side's perception of the other's power may fail to take into account the possibility that the other will invest greater resources in the contest than expected, out of fear that a change in the perceived distribution of power will affect the outcomes of future disputes. Many power contests involve threatening avoidance (e.g., divorce), actually engaging in it temporarily to impose costs on the other side (e.g., striking or breaking off diplomatic relations), or ending the relationship altogether.

Strategic Issues Concerning Approaches

Negotiators should keep in mind the following principles when choosing their approach.

The Principle of Reciprocity

The style you use in negotiation will often be reciprocated by the other party. In one investigation, reciprocity rates were interests (42%), followed by power (27%) and rights (22%).[40] Thus, before negotiation, you should evaluate the pros and cons of interests, rights, and power. In general, interests are less risky than rights and power, as we will see later.

Interests Are Effective for Pie-Expansion

Focusing on interests can usually resolve the problem underlying the dispute more effectively than focusing on rights or power. A focus on interests can help uncover "hidden" problems and help identify which issues are of the greatest concern to each party. Put the focus on interests early in the negotiations. This suggestion raises an obvious question: If interests are effective, why doesn't everyone use them? Ury, Brett, and Goldberg identify several reasons, including lack of skill, the tendency to reciprocate rights and power, and strong cultural or organizational norms.[41]

How to Refocus Your Opponent on Interests (and Move Them from Rights and Power)

Suppose you enter a negotiation with an interests-based approach, but your opponent is focusing steadily on rights or power. This is making you angry, and you find yourself starting to reciprocate power and rights out of sheer self-defense. Yet you also realize this behavior is creating a lose-lose situation. How do you break out of the spiral of reciprocity? Consider two strategies: personal strategies (that you, as a person, can use

[38]Ibid.

[39]Ury, Brett, & Goldberg, *Getting disputes resolved.*

[40]Lytle, Brett, & Shapiro, "The strategic use of interests."

[41]Ury, Brett, & Goldberg, *Getting disputes resolved.*

in a face-to-face situation) and structural strategies (steps that an organization can take to create norms that engender an interests-based culture).[42]

Personal Strategies

Do Not Reciprocate! If you want to extinguish a behavior, resist the urge to reciprocate.[43] By not reciprocating, you can refocus your opponent. In one investigation, when the other negotiator reciprocated, the focal negotiator stayed with rights and power arguments 39% of the time; however, when the other did not reciprocate, the focal negotiator stayed with rights and power arguments only 22% of the time (and, hence, was refocused 78% of the time).[44] For example, Rex Tillerson, CEO of ExxonMobil, led tense negotiations for access to underwater fields off Russia's Sakhalin Island. At one point, a Russian minister let his anger show in a disagreement over a permit and slammed his fist on the bargaining table. Instead of getting angry and reciprocating the minister's behavior, Mr. Tillerson remained calm, realizing the extensive talks required a gentle touch. He feared the Russian officials would be offended by the Exxon leaders, thinking, "Here come the powerful Americans that won the Cold War, and now they're going to come in and tell us all how messed up we are and how we got it all wrong," Mr. Tillerson recalled. "You make yourself very aware of it, and almost go out of your way to make sure there's nothing that conveys such a sentiment."[45]

Provide Opportunities to Meet.   Often, rights- and power-based approaches emerge when parties are out of touch and uncertain about the intentions of the other side. Getting parties together for informal discussions can move them toward interests. When people are face-to-face, they often can't help but feel some compassion for the other party. Moreover, differences don't have an opportunity to fester. When the Boston Red Sox's top executives thought they were going to lose their chance to sign Daisuke Matsuzaka, the Japanese pitching star, they boarded a private jet to southern California. Unable to come to an agreement and fearful that Scott Boras, Matsuzaka's agent, was not negotiating faithfully, they went on an unsolicited visit to Boras's neighborhood, forcing him to negotiate face-to-face. The tactic worked. Just days later, Matsuzaka boarded the plane back to Boston with the Red Sox executives.[46]

Don't Get Personal: Use Self-Discipline.   Make sure that you stay focused on the conflict and the issues. Many negotiators begin to attack the other party's character. In their classic book, *Getting to Yes,* Fisher and Ury advocate separating the people from the problem. Moreover, the same phenomenon characterizes successful marriages![47] Gottman and Levenson tracked couples over a 14-year period.[48] Based upon an initial observation of the couples' fighting style early in their marriage, the researchers were

---

[42]Ibid.

[43]Fisher, R., Ury, W., & Patton, B., *Getting to yes;* Ury, Brett, & Goldberg, *Getting disputes resolved.*

[44]Lytle, Brett, & Shapiro, "The strategic use of interests."

[45]Ball, J. (2006, March 8). The new act at Exxon; CEO Tillerson, prototype of Texas oilman, must focus on delicate global diplomacy. *Wall Street Journal,* p. B1.

[46]Curry, J. (2006, December 14). After forcing issue, Red Sox on verge of Matsuzaka deal. *New York Times,* p. D1.

[47]Fisher & Ury, *Getting to yes.*

[48]Gottman, J. M., & Levenson, R. W. (2000). The timing of divorce: Predicting when a couple will divorce over a 14-year period. *Journal of Marriage & the Family, 62*(3), 737–745.

able to predict which couples got divorced and which stayed together with 93% accuracy. The biggest determinant of divorce was not the amount of arguing, nor the amount of anger, but the use of personal attacks.

Use Behavioral Reinforcement.   Make sure that you are not rewarding the other party's rights- or power-based behavior. In other words, if you have been planning on making a concession, do not offer it to the other party immediately after he or she has misbehaved or acted out. If you do, you reward the very behavior you want to extinguish. One of the most effective ways to extinguish a behavior is simply not to react. If you do react, you may be unconsciously rewarding the behavior (e.g., if the other party benefits from the attention associated with a conflict spiral). Recall that rewards include things such as eye contact, head nods, smiling, and other types of nonverbal approval.

Making unilateral concessions is not effective for refocusing negotiations. In one study, concession making was less effective in refocusing negotiations from rights and power (60% refocused), as were other uncontentious communications (77% refocused).[49] Why? A unilateral concession may be seen as a reward for contentious behavior; therefore, it may encourage the repetition of such behavior.

Send a Mixed Message.   In other words, reciprocate but add an interests-based proposal. Reciprocation is instinctive, especially under stress.[50] Thus, you may find that your opponent is making you angry and you need to "flex your muscles." One effective strategy is to reciprocate rights or power, but *combine* it with interests-based questions or proposals.[51] Sending the counterparty a "mixed message" (rights and interests) gives them a chance to choose what to reciprocate—interests, rights, or power.

Try a Process Intervention.   Process interventions are tactics that are interests-based with the goal of moving the counterparty back to interests-based negotiation. Effective processes can include any of the pie-expanding strategies we discussed in Chapter 4 (e.g., multiple offers, revealing information about priorities, etc.), as well as several other dispute resolution strategies (indicated next). In a direct test of the effectiveness of process interventions, Ury, Brett, and Goldberg examined the percentage of time that a negotiator successfully extinguished a rights or power move by the opponent.[52] Least effective was reciprocation (66%); the most effective method was process intervention (82% success rate). Other methods included the mixed-message approach (74% success rate), and simply resisting the urge to reciprocate (self-discipline; 76% success rate).

Let's Talk and Then Fight.   Another strategy is to agree to talk for 20 minutes or so, and then argue. By agreeing up front on a process, both parties commit implicitly to listening to one another at least temporarily.

Strategic Cooling-Off Periods.   It is easy to muster a rights-based response or power display in the heat of conflict. After all, an interests-based approach requires deeper levels of cognitive processing and the ability to get past the more obvious rights and power issues that are likely to surface. Thus, it often serves parties' interests to build in

[49]Lytle, Brett, & Shapiro, "The strategic use of interests."
[50]Lerner, H. G. (1985). *The dance of anger.* New York: Harper and Row.
[51]Ury, Brett, & Goldberg, *Getting disputes resolved.*
[52]Ibid.

some cooling-off periods that allow them to better assess their own needs and interests, independent of rights and power issues.

Paraphrasing. Many times, negotiators will have difficulty in their attempts to turn a rights- or power-based argument into an interests-based discussion. It is important for negotiators not to abandon their interests-based approach but, rather, to persist in their attempt to understand the other party's underlying needs. Stephen Covey suggests that parties to conflict should be forced to empathize with each other.[53] He has a strict ground rule: "You can't make your point until you restate the other person's point to his or her satisfaction."[54] People are often so emotionally invested that they cannot listen. According to Covey, they pretend to listen. So he asks the other party, "Do you feel understood?" The other party always says, "No, he mimicked me, but he doesn't understand me." The negotiator gets to state a point only after satisfying the other party. (For an example of this intervention, see Exhibit 5-9.)

EXHIBIT 5-9 Resolving Differences

The following is a summary of an intervention led by Steven Covey between two parties who had no trust for one another:

The president of Company A asked Covey to act as a third-party facilitator in a lawsuit with Company B, the key reason being that there was no trust between the parties.

Covey stated that the disputants did not actually need a third party because they possessed the power to handle the conflict themselves. Covey suggested putting all the issues on the table and asking if they would be willing to search for a solution. Covey called the president of Company B and made the invitation. The president of Company B declined the offer and said he wanted the legal process to handle it.

The president of Company A suggested that he send his material and documents to Company B and meet face-to-face. He promised not to bring an attorney and told Company B president that he could bring his attorney if he wished. He further said it was not even necessary that Company B president speak. They could just have lunch. In short, there was nothing to lose and possibly everything to gain.

The presidents met for lunch and Company A president said, "Let me see if I can make your case for you since you are not going to speak." Company A president tried to show genuine empathy and took pains to describe Company B president's position in depth. He then asked if his understanding was correct or not.

At this point, the silence was broken. The president of Company B spoke up and said that the summary was 50 percent accurate but he wanted to correct some inaccuracies. At that point, the attorney advised Company B president to not say another word. At this juncture Company B president told the attorney to shut up because he could feel the power of the dialogue that was happening.

The lunch meeting progressed with both parties standing shoulder-to-shoulder making notes, using flip charts, and brainstorming alternatives. At the close of the lunch, the disagreement was resolved.

Source: Based on Covey, S. R. (1999). Resolving differences. *Executive Excellence*, *16*(4), 5–6.

---

[53]Covey, S. R. (1999). Resolving differences. *Executive Excellence, 16*(4), 5–6.
[54]Ibid.

Label the Process.   If the counterparty uses a rights- or power-based approach after you have tried to focus on interests, it might be useful to point out and label the strategy you see the counterparty using. Recognizing or labeling a tactic as ineffective can neutralize or refocus negotiations.[55]

Structural Strategies   The following structural strategies are ones suggested by Ury, Brett, and Goldberg in their book *Getting Disputes Resolved.*[56] The authors suggest several methods whereby dispute resolution systems can be designed and used within organizations, some of which are described here in detail. Each of these strategies is designed to reduce the costs of handling disputes and to produce satisfying, durable resolutions.

Put the Focus on Interests.   The parties involved should attempt to negotiate, rather than escalate to adjudication, which can be achieved by establishing a known negotiation procedure. For example, Ury, Brett, and Goldberg note that when International Harvester introduced a new procedure for oral (rather than written) handling of grievances at the lowest possible level, the number of written grievances plummeted to almost zero.[57] Some organizations stay focused on interests via use of a **multistep negotiation procedure,** in which a dispute that is not resolved at one level of the organizational hierarchy moves to progressively higher levels. Another strategy is the **wise counselor,** in which senior executives are selected to consider disputes. By creating **multiple points of entry,** negotiators can have several points of access for resolving disputes. In some instances, **mandatory negotiations** can provide a way for reluctant negotiators to come to the table. By providing **skills and training** in negotiation, people will be better prepared to negotiate in an interests-based fashion. Finally, by providing opportunities for **mediation** in which a third party intervenes, negotiators can often focus on interests.

Build in "Loop-Backs" to Negotiation.   According to Ury, Brett, and Goldberg, interests-based procedures will not always resolve disputes, yet a rights or power contest can be costly and risky.[58] Structural solutions provide procedures that encourage negotiators to turn back from contests to negotiation. These methods are what Ury, Brett, and Goldberg call "loop-back" procedures:

- ***Looping back from rights.***   Some loop-back procedures provide information about a negotiator's rights, as well as the likely outcome of a rights contest. Consider **information procedures** in which databases are created that can be accessed by negotiators who want to research the validity and outcome of their claims. **Advisory arbitration** is a method whereby managers are provided with information that would likely result if arbitration were to be carried out or the dispute were to go to court. **Minitrials** are procedures whereby "lawyers" (high-level executives in the organization who have not been involved previously) represent each side and present evidence and arguments that are heard by a neutral judge or advisor. Minitrials put negotiation in the hands of people who are not emotionally involved in the dispute and who have the perspective to view it in the context of the organization's broad interests.

---

[55]Fisher, Ury, & Patton, *Getting to yes.*
[56]Ury, Brett, & Goldberg, *Getting disputes resolved,* p. 42.
[57]Ibid., pp. 42–43.
[58]Ibid., p. 52.

- *Looping back from a power conflict.*   A variety of strategies can be used to move parties away from power contests back to interests. **Crisis procedures,** or guidelines for emergency communication written in advance, can establish communication mechanisms between disputants. For example, in disputes between the United States and the Soviet Union, a hotline served a crisis procedure purpose; in addition, U.S. and Soviet officials established nuclear risk reduction centers, staffed 24 hours in Washington and Moscow, for emergency communications.[59] Finally, **intervention by third parties** can halt power contests. For example, when Detroit public school teachers were unsatisfied with their pay, they went on strike and entered negotiations that went on for over two weeks. Unable to come to an agreement, Mayor Kwame Kilpatrick stepped in. He called everyone into his office, where negotiations continued for the next 11 hours. They dealt with one issue at a time, finally settling on a definitive agreement.[60]

Provide Low-Cost Rights and Power Backups.

Should interests-based negotiation fail, it is useful to have low-cost rights and power backup systems. **Conventional arbitration** is less costly than court or private adjudication. Ury, Brett, and Goldberg note that 95% of all collective bargaining contracts provide for arbitration of disputes.[61] **Med-arb** is a hybrid model in which, if mediation fails, the mediator serves as an arbitrator. With the threat of arbitration in the air, parties are often encouraged to reach a negotiated solution. In **final-offer arbitration,** the arbitrator does not have authority to compromise between parties' positions but, rather, must accept one of the final offers made. Thus, each party has an incentive to make a final offer appear the most reasonable in the eyes of the neutral third party. **Arb-med** is also a hybrid model traced from South Africa in which an arbitrator makes a decision and places it in a sealed envelope. The threat of the arbitrator's decision sits on a table and is destined to be opened unless the parties reach mutual agreement. Arb-med is more effective than conventional arbitration.[62]

Build in Consultation Beforehand and Feedback Afterward.

Notification and consultation between parties prior to taking action can prevent disputes that arise through sheer misunderstanding. They can also reduce the anger and hostility that often result when decisions are made unilaterally and abruptly. **Postdispute analysis and feedback** is a method whereby parties learn from their disputes to prevent similar problems in the future. Similarly, by establishing a **forum,** consultation and postdispute analysis can be institutionalized to create an opportunity for discussion.

Provide Skills and Resources.

Oftentimes, people find themselves embroiled in conflict and negotiation when they never expected it. The extent to which they do not have the resources or skills to resolve disputes can often lead to rights- and power-based actions (i.e., lawsuits or firings). However, when these same people have been given skills in interests-based negotiations, they can often create opportunity from conflict in a way that benefits for everyone concerned.

---

[59]Ibid., p. 55.
[60]MacDonald, C., & Jun, C. (2006, September 3). How mayor brokered end of school strike; No wage givebacks, but benefits cut. *Detroit News*, p. A1.
[61]Ury, Brett, & Goldberg, *Getting disputes resolved*, p. 56.
[62]Conlon, D. E., Moon, H., & Ng, K. Y. (2002). Putting the cart before the horse: The benefits of arbitrating before mediating. *Journal of Applied Psychology, 87*(5), 978–984.

High Costs Associated with Power and Rights

Focusing on who is right or who is more powerful usually leaves at least one person perceiving himself or herself as a loser. Even if you are the winner in these situations, the problem is that losers often do not give up but appeal instead to higher courts or plot revenge. Rights are less costly than power, generally—power costs more in resources consumed and opportunities lost. For example, strikes cost more than arbitration, and violence costs more than litigation. Costs are incurred not only in efforts invested but also from the destruction of each side's resources. Power contests often create new injuries and a desire for revenge. Interests are less costly than rights. In summary, focusing on interests, compared to rights and power, produces higher satisfaction with outcomes, better working relationships, and less recurrence; it may also mean lower transaction costs.

Know When to Use Rights and Power

Despite their general effectiveness, focusing on interests is not enough: Resolving all disputes by reconciling interests is neither possible nor desirable.[63] The problem is that rights and power procedures are often used when they are not necessary; a procedure that should be the last resort too often becomes the first move. Rights and power may be appropriate to use in the following situations:[64]

- ***The other party refuses to come to the table.***   In this case, no negotiation is taking place, and rights and power are necessary for engagement.
- ***Negotiations have broken down and parties are at an impasse.***   A credible threat, especially if combined with an interests-based proposal, may restart negotiations. For example, when union clerical workers at the Ports of Los Angeles and Long Beach were unable to come to an agreement in their labor contract negotiations, they threatened a crippling strike. Accounting for 40% of the nation's cargo container traffic and for 12% of southern California's economic activity, a strike at the two ports would be extremely costly, even if it only lasted few days. A few hours later, all issues were finally resolved, and the strike was averted.[65]
- ***The other party needs to know you have power.***   Sometimes, people need to wield power simply to demonstrate they have it.[66] However, the consequences of imposing willpower can be costly. Your threats must be backed up with actions to be credible. Furthermore, the weaker party may fail to fully comply with a resolution based on power, thus requiring the more powerful party to engage in expensive policing.
- ***Someone violates a rule or breaks the law.***   In this situation, it is appropriate to use rights or power.
- ***Interests are so opposed that agreement is not possible.***   Sometimes, parties' interests are so disparate that agreement is not possible. For example, when fundamental values are at odds (e.g., abortion beliefs), resolution can occur only through a rights contest (a trial) or power contest (a demonstration or legislative battle).
- ***Social change is necessary.***   To create social impact, a rights battle may be necessary. For example, consider the case of *Brown v. Board of Education,* which laid important groundwork for the elimination of racial segregation.
- ***Negotiators are moving toward agreement and parties are "positioning" themselves.***   In other words, parties are committed to reaching a deal, and now they are dancing in the bargaining zone.

---

[63]Ury, Brett, & Goldberg, *Getting disputes resolved,* p. 15.
[64]Ibid., p.16.
[65]White, R. (2007, July 27). All hands on board at ports: A tentative contract deal, reached after negotiators declared an impasse, averts a strike by clerical workers. *Los Angeles Times,* p. C1.
[66]Ury, Brett, & Goldberg, *Getting disputes resolved,* p. 16.

Know How to Use Rights and Power

We made the point that negotiators need to know when to use rights and power. However, simply recognizing when to use these strategies does not guarantee success. Following are some key issues the negotiator needs to take into consideration when using rights and power and, in particular, when making a threat.[67]

Threaten the Other Party's Interests   To effectively make a threat, a negotiator needs to attack the other party's underlying interests. Rights and power should challenge the opponents' long-term and highly valued interests. Otherwise, the other party will feel little incentive to comply with your threat. Consider how American Airlines attempted to jump-start negotiations with its union members in 2003 by threatening their most basic interests.[68] Company negotiators gave each union group a written outline, called a "term sheet," that clearly laid out the financial impact of bankruptcy: $500 million in pay and benefit cuts beyond the $1.62 billion the airline requested. The result was that the union leaders became anchored on this number: The pilot's board quickly huddled at union offices and came up with 10 concessions that would raise the needed amount.

Clarity   Negotiators need to be clear about what actions are needed by the other party. For example, nine days after al-Qaeda's terrorist attacks on the United States in 2001, President George W. Bush issued a clear threat: He demanded that the Taliban turn over Osama bin Laden and the leaders of his terrorist network and shut down the terrorist training camps in Afghanistan; otherwise, the United States would "direct every resource at our command—every means of diplomacy, every tool of intelligence, every instrument of law enforcement, every financial influence and every necessary weapon of war—to the destruction and to the defeat of the global terror network."[69]

Credibility   Power-based approaches typically focus on the future (e.g., "If you do not do such-and-such, I will withdraw your funding"). To be effective, the other party must believe that you have the ability to carry out the threat. If you are not seen as credible, people will call your bluff. Ideally, it is desirable to convince the other party you have power without actually having to exert it.

Do Not Burn Bridges   It is important to leave a pathway back to interests-based discussion. Ury, Brett, and Goldberg call it the "loop-back to interests."[70] Threats are expensive to carry out; thus, it is critical that you are able to turn off a threat, allowing the other party to save face and reopen negotiations. If you do not provide yourself with a loop-back to interests, you force yourself to carry out the threat. Furthermore, after you use your threat, you lose your power and ability to influence. Lytle, Brett, and Shapiro suggest that if you are going to use rights or power, you should use the following sequence: (a) state a specific, detailed demand and deadline; (b) state a specific, detailed, credible threat (which harms the other side's interests); and (c) state a specific, detailed, positive consequence that will follow if the demand is met.[71]

---

[67]Brett, J. M. (2007). *Negotiating globally: How to negotiate deals, resolve disputes, and make decisions across cultural boundaries,* 2nd edition. San Francisco, CA: Jossey-Bass.
[68]Torbenson, E. (2003, April 3). American Airlines pilots agree to plan to avoid bankruptcy. *Dallas Morning News.*
[69]Espo, D. (2001, September 20). Bush says U.S. will use 'every resource' to defeat global terrorism. *Associated Press Newswires.*
[70]Ury, Brett, & Goldberg, *Getting disputes resolved,* p. 52.
[71]Lytle, Brett, & Shapiro, "The strategic use of interests."

EMOTIONS AND EMOTIONAL KNOWLEDGE

Emotions are inevitable in conflict and negotiations. We need to be concerned about our own emotional expression, as well as that of the counterparty. Moreover, negotiators vary in terms of how accurate they are in assessing the emotional expression of others.

Emotions and Moods

For the purposes of this chapter, **emotions** are relatively fleeting states that are usually fairly intense and often a result of a particular experience. In general, emotions are characterized into two broad classes: positive emotions, such as love, joy, and happiness, and negative emotions, such as sadness, fear, anxiety (see Exhibit 5-10). **Moods** are more chronic and more diffuse, meaning that whereas emotions are a result of, and can be directed at, certain events or people, moods are usually not directed at someone. Unlike emotions, which are very specific, such as anger, regret, relief, gratitude, and so on, moods are often classified as simply "being in a good mood" or a "bad mood." Emotions and moods can be either a consequence or a determinant of negotiation behavior and outcomes.

Expressed Versus Felt Emotion

People vary in terms of their ability and willingness to express (as well as control) their emotions. There are implications for people who express too much emotion and, conversely, for those who attempt to suppress emotions.

Negotiators should resist the urge to gloat or show signs of smugness following negotiation.[72] In one investigation, some negotiators gloated following their negotiation ("I really feel good about the negotiation—I got everything I wanted!"). Other negotiators made self-effacing remarks (such as "I really didn't do that well"). Later, negotiators who

EXHIBIT 5-10 Distinct Emotions

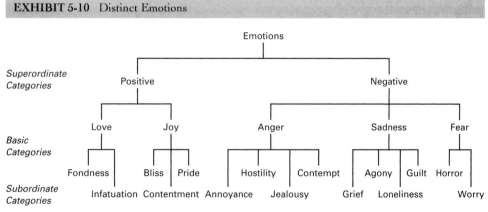

Source: Fischer, K. W., Shaver, P. R., & Carnochan, P. (1990). How emotions develop and how they organize development. *Cognition and Emotion, 4,* 81–127. Reprinted by permission.

---

[72]See also Raiffa, H. (1982). *The art and science of negotiation.* Cambridge, MA: Belknap.

overheard the other party gloat or make self-effacing remarks were given an opportunity to provide valuable stock options to these same parties. Those parties who gloated received significantly fewer stock options than those who made the self-effacing remark.[73]

Genuine Versus Strategic Emotion

Perhaps the key question when it comes to emotion at the bargaining table concerns whether emotions are **genuine** (behavioral manifestations of felt emotions) or **strategic** (carefully designed orchestration to take the counterparty off guard). The effectiveness of three different strategic emotions (positive emotion, negative emotion, and poker face [no emotion]) was tested in a distributive bargaining situation.[74] The positive and poker-face strategies were distinctly more effective than the negative emotional strategy in obtaining a favorable outcome from a counterparty. (See Exhibits 5-11 and 5-12 to assess your own strategic use of emotion.)

In another investigation, Three strategic uses of emotion were examined: expressing truly felt emotions, hiding felt emotions, and feigning unfelt emotions.[75] When it comes to anger, hiding truly felt anger and feigning anger benefit negotiators in terms of monetary outcomes. Feigning rapport with the counterparty is especially useful for garnering concessions, as is feigning resentment. Elation or joy, however, is an emotion that is best kept hidden from the counterparty.

EXHIBIT 5-11 Emotional Styles

	Rational	Positive	Negative
Focus	Conceal or repress emotion	Create positive emotion in other party Create rapport	Use irrational-appearing emotions to intimidate or control other party
Distributive strategies (pie-slicing)	Citing norms of fair distribution	Compromise for the sake of the relationship	Threats Often tough bargaining
Integrative strategies (pie-expansion)	Systematic analysis of interests	Positive emotion stimulates creative thinking	Negative emotion may inhibit integrative bargaining
Implications for future negotiations and relationship	Not likely to say or do anything regrettable, but also may come across as "distant"	Greater feelings of commitment to relationship partner	Pressure to carry out threats or lose credibility

---

[73]Thompson, L., Valley, K. L., & Kramer, R. M. (1995). The bittersweet feeling of success: An examination of social perception in negotiation. *Journal of Experimental Social Psychology, 31*(6), 467–492.
[74]Kopelman, S., Rosette, A., & Thompson, L. (2004). The three faces of Eve: Strategic displays of positive, negative, and neutral emotion in negotiations. *Organizational Behavior and Human Decision Processes, 99*(1), 81–101.
[75]Levine, R., Amanatullah, E., & Morris, M. Untangling the web of emotional deceit: A new methodology for the study of strategic emotional expression in negotiations. Working paper. Columbia University.

EXHIBIT 5-12   Emotional Style Questionnaire

Read each statement, and indicate whether you think it is true or false for you in a negotiation situation. Force yourself to answer each one as generally true or false (i.e., do not respond with "I don't know").

1. In a negotiation situation, it is best to "keep a cool head."
2. I believe that in negotiations you can "catch more flies with honey."
3. It is important to me that I maintain control in a negotiation situation.
4. Establishing a positive sense of rapport with the other party is key to effective negotiation.
5. I am good at displaying emotions in negotiation to get what I want.
6. Emotions are the downfall of effective negotiation.
7. I definitely believe that the "squeaky wheel gets the grease" in many negotiation situations.
8. If you are nice in negotiations, you can get more than if you are cold or neutral.
9. In negotiation, you have to "fight fire with fire."
10. I honestly think better when I am in a good mood.
11. I would never want to let the other party know how I really felt in a negotiation.
12. I believe that in negotiations you can "catch more flies with a flyswatter."
13. I have used emotion to manipulate others in negotiations.
14. I believe that good moods are definitely contagious.
15. It is very important to make a very positive first impression when negotiating.
16. The downfall of many negotiators is that they lose personal control in a negotiation.
17. It is best to keep a "poker face" in negotiation situations.
18. It is very important to get the other person to respect you when negotiating.
19. I definitely want to leave the negotiation with the other party feeling good.
20. If the other party gets emotional, you can use it to your advantage in a negotiation.
21. I believe that it is important to "get on the same wavelength" as the other party.
22. It is important to demonstrate "resolve" in a negotiation.
23. If I sensed that I was not under control, I would call a temporary halt to the negotiation.
24. I would not hesitate to make a threat in a negotiation situation if I felt the other party would believe it.

Scoring Yourself
   Computing your "R" score: Look at items #1, #3, #6, #11, #16, #17, #20, #23. Give yourself 1 point for every "true" answer and subtract 1 point for every "false" answer. Then combine your scores for your R score (rational).
   Computing your "P" score: Look at items #2, #4, #8, #10, #14, #15, #19, #21. Give yourself 1 point for every "true" answer and subtract 1 point for every "false" answer. Then combine your scores for your P score (positive).
   Computing your "N" score: Look at items #5, #7, #9, #12, #13, #18, #22, #24. Give yourself 1 point for every "true" answer and subtract 1 point for every "false" answer. Then combine your scores for your N score (negative).

One type of strategic emotion is feigned liking. Presumably negotiators feign liking as a way of gaining favor and achieving their ultimate interaction goals. However, using "fake" emotions can take its toll on the negotiator: People who fake positive emotion are more likely to feel stress and actually get lower service delivery ratings (e.g., ratings by customers).[76]

---

[76]Grandey, A. (2003). When "the show must go on": Surface acting and deep acting as determinants of emotional exhaustion and peer-rated service delivery. *Academy of Management Journal, 46*(1), 86–96.

Negative Emotion

Another use of strategic or feigned emotion is the use of anger. Negotiators who use negative emotion feign temper tantrums as a way of threatening the counterparty to make a concession. It makes a difference whether the anger is "real" or "strategic." Negotiators who are really angry and feel little compassion for the counterparty are less effective in terms of expanding the pie than are happy negotiators.[77] Moreover, they are not as effective in terms of slicing the pie.[78] In contrast, negotiators who are "strategically angry" are more likely to gain concessions from their opponent because the counterparty will assume the angry person is close to their reservation point.[79] Angry negotiators induce fear in their opponent, and their opponents are more likely to succumb when they are motivated.[80] For example, before the annexation of Austria, Hitler met to negotiate with the Austrian chancellor, von Schuschnigg. At some point, in this dark historical meeting, Hitler's emotional style became very angry:

> [He] became more strident, more shrill. Hitler ranted like a maniac, waved his hands with excitement. At times he must have seemed completely out of control. . . . Hitler may then have made his most extreme coercive threats seem credible. . . . [He threatened to take von Schuschnigg into custody, an act unheard of in the context of diplomacy.] He insisted that von Schuschnigg sign an agreement to accept every one of his demands, or he would immediately order a march into Austria.[81]

The effect of negative emotions on negotiator behavior are also influenced by the alternatives available to negotiators. When a negotiator acts angry, he or she is communicating "toughness"; recipients who have particularly poor alternatives are most affected by such displays and therefore make more concessions.[82] The motivations and goals of the negotiator also influence the degree to which they react to the counterparty's display of negative emotion. For example, whereas negotiators do tend to make more concessions to an angry opponent than to a happy one, this tends to be more true when negotiators are motivated to understand the other party, such as when they are not under time pressure (and, therefore, have resources to engage in thought processing).[83]

The use of strategic negative emotion is not limited to displays of anger and temper tantrums. Displays of helplessness, pouting, and hurt feelings also can be used to manipulate others in negotiations. For example, Effa Manley, a female baseball player,

---

[77]Allred, K. G., Mallozzi, J. S., Matsui, F., & Raia, C. P. (1997). The influence of anger and compassion on negotiation performance. *Organizational Behavior and Human Decision Processes, 70*(3), 175–187.
[78]Allred, K. G. (2000). Anger and retaliation in conflict: The role of attribution. In M. Deutsch & P. T. Coleman (Eds.), *The handbook of conflict resolution: Theory and practice* (pp. 236–255). San Francisco: Jossey-Bass.
[79]van Kleef, G. A., De Dreu, C. K. W., & Manstead, A. S. R. (2004). The interpersonal effects of anger and happiness in negotiations. *Journal of Personality and Social Psychology, 86*(1), 57–76.
[80]Ibid.
[81]Raven, B. H. (1990). Political applications of the psychology of interpersonal influence and social power. *Political Psychology, 11*(3), 515.
[82]Sinaceur, M., & Tiedens, L. (2006). Get mad and get more than even: When and why anger expression is effective in negotiation. *Journal of Experimental Social Psychology, 42,* 314–322.
[83]van Kleef, De Dreu, & Manstead, "The interpersonal effects of anger."

was not above shedding tears to get what she wanted at the negotiation table. Pittsburgh sports writer Wendell Smith recalls, "If she did not get what she wanted, Mrs. Manley would wrinkle up her pretty face and turn on the sprinkling system."[84] Acting somewhat insane can achieve similar effects, such as when AOL's Myer Berlow would announce to his opponents during the middle of negotiations that his favorite movie was *The Godfather* and he would quote his philosopher-hero, Machiavelli, by saying "it is safer to be feared than loved."[85]

The type of negative emotion expressed may elicit very different reactions from counterparties. For example, one investigation examined how negotiators responded to an opponent who was disappointed or worried (supplication) with a guilty or regretful opponent (appeasement) versus an unemotional opponent. Negotiators conceded more when the opponent showed supplication (disappointment and worry) and conceded the least when the opponent showed guilt.[86]

Emotional Intelligence

Emotional intelligence is the ability of people (and negotiators) to understand emotions in themselves and others and to use emotional knowledge to effect positive outcomes. Whereas research and theory on emotional intelligence encourage people to be aware of their emotions, a large body of research indicates emotions, especially negative ones, can often thwart people's ability to make good decisions. For example, decision makers experiencing high levels of emotional stress often undergo incomplete search, appraisal, and contingency-planning thought processes.[87] For this reason, it is important to draw a distinction between *expressing* emotion and *feeling* emotion. Even though a negotiator may feel emotion, he or she may not express that emotion.

Positive Emotion

Expressing positive emotion might have positive consequences in negotiations.[88] People process information differently when in a positive mood, as opposed to a negative or neutral mood.[89] Good moods promote creative thinking,[90] which, in turn, leads to innovative problem solving.[91] For example, in one investigation, negotiators watched a funny movie and were given a gift. These negotiators reached more integrative outcomes and generated more creative ideas than negotiators who did not

---

[84]Moritz, O. (2003, June 20). First lady Effa Manley. *New York Daily News*, p. 33.
[85]Klein, A. (2003, June 15). Lord of the flies, *Washington Post*, p. W06.
[86]van Kleef, G., DeDreu, C., & Manstead, A. (2006). Supplication and appeasement in conflict and negotiation: The interpersonal effects of disappointment, worry, guilt and regret. *Journal of Personality and Social Psychology, 91*(1), 124–142.
[87]Janis, I. L., & Mann, L. (1977). *Decision making: A psychological analysis of conflict, choice, and commitment.* New York: Free Press.
[88]Kumar, R. (1997). The role of affect in negotiations: An integrative overview. *Journal of Applied Behavioral Science, 33*(1), 84–100; Kramer, R., Pommerenke, P., & Newton, E. (1993). The social context of negotiation: Effects of social identity and accountability on negotiator judgment and decision making. *Journal of Conflict Resolution, 37,* 633–654.
[89]Isen, A. M. (1987). Positive affect, cognitive processes, and social behavior. In L. Berkowitz (Ed.), *Advances in experimental social psychology: Vol. 20* (pp. 203–253). San Diego, CA: Academic Press, Inc.
[90]Isen, Daubman, & Nowicki, "Positive affect."
[91]Carnevale, P. J., & Isen, A. (1986). The influence of positive affect and visual access on the discovery of integrative solutions in bilateral negotiations. *Organizational Behavior and Human Decision Processes, 37,* 1–13.

watch the movie and were not given a gift.[92] Negotiators who are in a positive mood use more cooperative strategies, engage in more information exchange, generate more alternatives, and use fewer contentious tactics than do negative or neutral-mood negotiators.[93]

Emotions in negotiation can create a self-fulfilling prophecy, in which negotiators' emotions stimulate those emotions in the counterparty. In one investigation, people in a job-contract negotiation achieved lower joint gains when they experienced high levels of anger and low levels of compassion toward each other than when they experienced positive emotion.[94] Furthermore, angry negotiators were less willing to work with each other and more likely to retaliate.[95]

When people are experiencing a positive mood, they are more creative, generate integrative information, and are more flexible in conveying their thoughts.[96] Why does positive emotion work? It is largely due to a combination of the self-fulfilling prophecy, information processing, and the fact that positive affect is associated with more creative and varied cognitions. For example, people who experience positive emotion see relationships among ideas and link together nontypical category exemplars.[97] This response builds rapport, which, in turn, helps to avoid impasse and facilitates the negotiation process.[98]

Emotional Intelligence and Negotiated Outcomes

The relationship between measured emotional intelligence (EQ) and negotiation outcomes is not totally straightforward.[99] On one hand, framing negotiations in affective (as opposed to purely cognitive-intellectual) terms allows negotiators to be more involved and positive, but they simultaneously have lower levels of trust and use of cooperative

[92]See also Allred, Mallozzi, Matsui, & Raia, "The influence of anger"; Barry, B., & Oliver, R. L. (1996). Affect in dyadic negotiation: A model and propositions. *Organizational Behavior and Human Decision Processes, 67*(2), 127–144; Forgas, J. P. (1996). The role of emotion scripts and transient moods in relationships: Structural and functional perspectives. In G. J. O. Fletcher & J. Fitness (Eds.), *Knowledge structures in close relationships: A social psychological approach* (pp. 275–296). Mahwah, NJ: Erlbaum.
[93]Carnevale & Isen, "The influence of positive affect."
[94]Allred, Mallozzi, Matsui, F., & Raia, "The influence of anger."
[95]Ibid.
[96]Baron, R. A. (1990). Environmentally induced positive affect: Its impact on self-efficacy, task performance, negotiation, and conflict. *Journal of Applied Social Psychology, 20*(5), 368–384; Isen, A. M., Daubman, K. A., & Nowicki, G. P. (1987). Positive affect facilitates creative problem solving. *Journal of Personality and Social Psychology, 52*, 1122–1131; Isen, A. M., Niedenthal, P. M., & Cantor, N. (1992). An influence of positive affect on social categorization. *Motivation and Emotion, 16*(1), 65–78.
[97]Forgas, J. P. (1998). On feeling good and getting your way: Mood effects on negotiator cognition and bargaining strategies. *Journal of Personality and Social Psychology, 74*(3), 565–577; Isen, Niedenthal, & Cantor, "An influence of positive affect on social categorization."
[98]Drolet, A. L., & Morris, M. W. (2000). Rapport in conflict resolution: Accounting for how nonverbal exchange fosters cooperation on mutually beneficial settlements to mixed-motive conflicts. *Journal of Experimental Social Psychology, 36*, 26–50; Moore, D. A., Kurtzberg, T., Thompson, L., & Morris, M. W. (1999). Long and short routes to success in electronically mediated negotiations: Group affiliations and good vibrations. *Organizational Behavior and Human Decision Processes, 77*(1), 22–43; Thompson, L., Nadler, J., & Kim, P. (1999). Some like it hot: The case for the emotional negotiator. In L. Thompson, J. Levine, & D. Messick (Eds.), *Shared cognition in organizations: The management of knowledge* (pp. 139–162). Mahwah, NJ: Erlbaum.
[99]For reviews, see Fulmer, I. S., & Barry, B. (2004). The smart negotiator: Cognitive ability and emotional intelligence in negotiation. *International Journal of Conflict Management, 15*(3), 245–272.

negotiation tactics.[100] People who are high in measured emotional intelligence experience greater subjective outcomes in negotiation than do people lower in emotional intelligence, however, high EQ negotiators achieve lower objective outcomes.[101] Apparently, people high in emotional intelligence feel better emotionally and create objective value for their counterparty but not for themselves.

Accuracy

The ability to accurately read emotions in others, particularly the counterparty, is important for successful outcomes. Indeed, a consistent positive correlation exists between emotion recognition accuracy (ERA) and goal-oriented performance.[102] Greater recognition of facial expressions predicted how well negotiators did in a buyer-seller negotiation, in terms of both distributive and integrative outcomes.[103]

Self-Efficacy

Part of emotional intelligence is a certain degree of self-efficacy and confidence. Whereas no one likes an overly confident, arrogant person, we admire people who have a quiet, steady belief in themselves and a "can do" attitude. Just as there are many types of negotiation skills, it stands to reason that there are many areas of skill about which negotiators may or may not be self-confident. **Distributive self-efficacy** refers to a negotiator's belief in his or her ability to claim resources effectively (e.g., "gain the upper hand"; "persuade others to make the most concessions"); in contrast, **integrative self-efficacy** refers to a negotiator's belief in her or his ability to create resources (e.g., "establish rapport"; "find tradeoffs").[104]

Strategic Advice for Dealing with Emotions at the Table

Negotiators who understand how emotions work can be more strategic at the bargaining table.

Beware of What You Are Reinforcing

People often make concessions to another person just to shut them up. What they may not realize is that this effectively reinforces the very behavior they are trying to extinguish. Negative reinforcement, or escape behavior, explains the increased likelihood of behavior that eliminates or removes an aversive stimulus.[105] For example, if obnoxious music is emanating from a radio, you will turn off the radio, thus eliminating the unpleasant sounds. In a similar vein, because most people find it unpleasant to be around someone who is openly hostile, negative, and unpredictable, they may

---

[100]Hunt, C., & Kernan, M. (2005). Framing negotiations in affective terms: Methodological and preliminary theoretical findings. *International Journal of Conflict Management, 16*(2), 128–156.

[101]Foo, M., Elfenbein, H., Tan, H., & Aik, V. (2004). Emotional intelligence and negotiation: The tension between creating and claiming value. *International Journal of Conflict Management, 15*(4), 411–436.

[102]For a review, see Elfenbein, H., Foo, M., White, J., Tan, H., & Aik, V. (2007). Reading your counterparty: The benefit of emotion recognition accuracy for effectiveness in negotiation. *Journal of Nonverbal Behavior, 31*(4), 205–233.

[103]Elfenbein, Foo, White, Tan, and Aik, "Reading your counterparty."

[104]Sullivan, B., O'Connor, K., & Burris, E. (2006). Negotiator confidence: The impact of self-efficacy on tactics and outcomes. *Journal of Experimental Social Psychology, 42,* 567–581.

[105]Skinner, B. F. (1938). *The behavior of organisms: An experimental analysis.* New York, London: D. Appleton Century.

be willing to capitulate to the other party just to remove themselves from this aversive situation. Unfortunately, this behavior acts as positive reinforcement for the counterparty. If someone acts irrationally and you acquiesce, you increase the likelihood of that person engaging in negative behavior in the future.

Reevaluation Is More Effective Than Suppression

People often try to suppress emotions. However, suppression may backfire. For example, when people tell themselves not to conjure up certain thoughts, they find it virtually impossible to refrain from thinking those exact thoughts. Indeed, people who spend more time trying to repair their negative moods are the most likely to suffer from persistent emotional problems, such as depression and anxiety.[106] Reevaluation involves acknowledging emotion, but thinking about a different way to view it.

Emotions Are Contagious

If one negotiator conveys positive emotion, the other negotiator is likely to "catch" this positive emotional state and convey positive emotion as well.[107] However, the same is true for negative emotion.

Understand Emotional Triggers

Certain words, when used in negotiation, are loaded and evoke emotion. In one investigation, the emotional impact of six different types of words were measured (see Exhibit 5-13).[108] Of all the different types of words, those that labeled the other person negatively or told the other person what he or she ought to do triggered the greatest anger and frustration.

CONCLUSION

We considered motivational orientation (individualistic, cooperative, or competitive), the interests-, rights-, and power-based model of disputing, and the role of emotion at the bargaining table. The following are the key messages of this chapter:

Get in touch with your own style in an honest and straightforward way. Ask someone else to appraise you honestly, using the diagnostic tools presented in this chapter.

Know your limits and your strengths. We have seen that it is not better to adopt one particular style because each has its own weaknesses and strengths. Knowing your own stylistic limits and strengths is important.

Understand the counterparty. Most naïve negotiators just assume that the counterparty has the same orientation they do.

Expand your repertoire. We often find that people do not feel comfortable with their bargaining style or do not find it effective. This chapter gives negotiators options for expanding their repertoire, especially at critical points during negotiation.

[106]Wegner, D. M., & Wenzlaff, R. M. (1996). Mental control. In E. T. Higgins & A. W. Kruglanski (Eds.), *Social psychology: Handbook of basic principles* (pp. 466–492). New York: Guilford Press.
[107]Hatfield, E., Caccioppo, J. T., & Rapson, R. L. (1992). Primitive emotional contagion. In M. S. Clark (Ed.), *Review of personality and social psychology: Vol. 14, Emotion and social behavior* (pp. 151–177). Newbury Park, CA: Sage.
[108]Schroth, H., Bain-Chekal, J., & Caldwell, D. (2005). Sticks and stones may break bones and words can hurt me: Words and phrases that trigger emotions in negotiations and their effects. *International Journal of Conflict Management, 16*(2), 102–127.

EXHIBIT 5-13   Emotional Trigger Words and Phrases

Type of Emotional Trigger	Example Phrases	Words
Labeling the other person negatively	"You are lying." "Don't be stupid." "You are being unfair." "It was your fault."	Unfair, silly, liar, stupid
Telling the other person what to do or what they can't do	"No way." "You need to. . . ." "You need to give me a better deal."	Can't, must, never, should
Appealing to a higher source; blaming, abdicating responsibility	"From a legal standpoint. . . ." "This is how we've always done it." "You should have known that." "I don't think you understand."	Fair, ethical, moral, better
Rude: not listening, explicative, insincere praise, sarcasm, educating the other	"Yes, but. . . ." "I like you, but. . . ." "With all due respect. . . ." "It is easy to see that. . . ."	Whatever, you always, you never
Labeling your own behavior as superior	"I'm being reasonable." "This is a good deal." "I know what I'm doing."	Reasonable, deserve
Implied threats	"You either comply or else." "We are going to ruin your reputation."	

Source: Adapted from Schroth, H., Bain-Chekal, J., and Caldwell, D. (2005). Sticks and stones may break bones and words can hurt me: Words and phrases that trigger emotions in negotiations and their effects. *International Journal of Conflict Management, 16*(2), 102–127. Reprinted by permission.

CHAPTER 6

Establishing Trust and Building a Relationship

Bill Richardson is a negotiator who has successfully built relationships and established trust with some of the world's toughest political diplomats. Before becoming governor of New Mexico, Mr. Richardson spent many years working as the United States ambassador to the United Nations. His confidence in his ability to make deals where others have failed, and his lack of hesitation in bringing even the most unpleasant adversaries to the negotiating table, have made him a successful negotiator. On one trip to Tokyo, in hopes of gaining support for possible military strikes in Iraq, Mr. Richardson discovered that previous talks with his superior, Madeline Albright, had not gone well. When Dr. Albright's Japanese counterpart asked if he could smoke, Dr. Albright made the mistake of giving him a lecture on the risks of smoking. Their relationship never fully recovered. Mr. Richardson, hoping to get off to a better start, decided to begin his meeting with the Japanese diplomat by pulling a cigar from his jacket and asking if he could smoke. His joke broke the ice, and he returned to the United States with the assurances for which he had hoped. On another trip, Mr. Richardson jokingly asked a Pakistani delegation why it seemed that everyone in Pakistan was named Chaudhuri. But statements like this rarely attracted any negative attention for Mr. Richardson. His warm personality and ability to make jokes, even during aggressive negotiations, brought a higher degree of trust to his relationships. To build a relationship with his North Korean contacts, Mr. Richardson gave them ample attention. After his first trip to North Korea, he took the time to learn the names of their children and their favorite foods. He even acted as host during their trips to Santa Fe. Because North Korean diplomats are often ostracized, his contacts were extremely grateful for his kindness. "I consider some of the North Korean people I've negotiated with friends," he said. "Even though we're ideological adversaries, we trust each other. We wish each other well on the holidays."[1]

THE PEOPLE SIDE OF WIN-WIN

Successful negotiation is not just about money or economic value. Despite the fact that rational behavior is often equated with the maximization of **monetary wealth**, economic models focus on the maximization of **utility**—which can be defined as money but can in-

---

[1]Kantor, J. (2007, December 21). Personal touch for Richardson in envoy role. *New York Times*, p. 1.

clude other considerations, such as trust, security, happiness, and peace of mind. Win-win agreements are those that maximize whatever negotiators care about, whether it's money, relationships, trust, or peace of mind. Curhan, Elfenbein, and Xu surveyed a broad spectrum of laypeople, negotiation researchers, and negotiation practitioners about what they value in a negotiation.[2] Negotiators care about four basic domains: feelings about instrumental outcomes, feelings about themselves, feelings about the process, and feelings about their relationships. Their *Subjective Value Inventory (SVI)* helps negotiators conceptualize their own performance in a negotiation along multiple dimensions—dimensions that may constitute precursors to long-term negotiation value. (See Exhibit 6-1 for the Subjective Value Inventory.)

EXHIBIT 6-1   Subjective Value Inventory

Think about your most recent negotiation. Rate your response to each of the following questions on a scale of 1 to 7, with 1 = not at all; 4 = moderately; and 7 = perfectly true or characteristic.

1. How satisfied are you with your own outcome—i.e., the extent to which the terms of your agreement (or lack of agreement) benefit you?
2. How satisfied are you with the balance between your own outcomes and the outcome(s) of your counterpart(s)?
3. Did you feel like you forfeited or "lost" in this negotiation?
4. Do you think the terms of your agreement are consistent with the principles of legitimacy of objective criteria (e.g., common standards of fairness, precedent, industry practice, legality, etc.)?
5. Did you "lose face" (i.e., damage your sense of pride) in the negotiation?
6. Did this negotiation make you feel more or less competent as a negotiator?
7. Did you behave according to your own principles and values?
8. Did this negotiation positively or negatively impact your self-image or your impression of yourself?
9. Did you feel your counterpart(s) listened to your concerns?
10. Would you characterize the negotiation process as fair?
11. How satisfied are you with the ease (or difficulty) of reaching an agreement?
12. Did your counterpart(s) consider your wishes, opinions, or needs?
13. What kind of "overall" impression did your counterpart(s) make on you?
14. How satisfied are you with your relationship with your counterpart(s) as a result of this negotiation?
15. Did the negotiation make you trust your counterpart(s)?
16. Did the negotiation build a good foundation for a future relationship with your counterpart(s)?

Note about scoring:
• Instrumental outcome (average items 1–4; reverse score #3)
• Feelings about oneself (average items 5–8; reverse score #5)
• Feelings about the process (average items 9–12)
• Feelings about the relationship (average items 13–16)

Source: Based on Curhan, J., Elfenbein, H., and Xu, H. (2006). What do people value when they negotiate? Mapping the domain of subjective value in negotiation. *Journal of Personality and Social Psychology, 91*(3), 493–512.

---

[2]Curhan, J., Elfenbein, H., & Xu, H. (2006). What do people value when they negotiate? Mapping the domain of subjective value in negotiation. *Journal of Personality and Social Psychology, 91*(3), 493–512.

EXHIBIT 6-2 Resources That May Be Exchanged in a Relationship

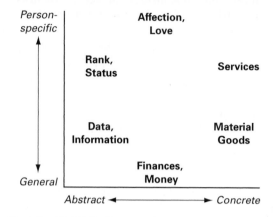

Source: Based on Foa, U., & Foa, E. (1975). *Resource theory of social exchange.* Morristown, NJ: General Learning Press.

Making more money may not always make us feel more successful[3] or more satisfied.[4] Negotiators tend to like proposals that they make or ultimately accept more than other proposals; and they devalue proposals offered by the counterparty, not so much based upon the content of the proposal but upon who is offering it.[5] Even though it is wise to unbundle single-issue negotiations into multi-issue negotiations, those who negotiate a lot of issues actually feel worse about their outcomes.[6] Why? They are more likely to ponder "what might have been" and experience doubts.

Exhibit 6-2 identifies six different types of resources people can exchange: love, money, services, goods, status, and information.[7] Each of these resources varies in terms of **particularism** (how much utility we derive depends on who is providing it—a kiss from one's own child is valued much more than a kiss from a complete stranger) and **concreteness** (how tangible it is). Love and social status are less concrete than services or goods, and love is more particular than money.

---

[3]Thompson, L. (1995). The impact of minimum goals and aspirations on judgments of success in negotiations. *Group Decision Making and Negotiation, 4*, 513–524; Thompson, L., Valley, K. L., & Kramer, R. M. (1995). The bittersweet feeling of success: An examination of social perception in negotiation. *Journal of Experimental Social Psychology, 31*(6), 467–492.

[4]Thompson, Valley, & Kramer, "The bittersweet feeling of success." Galinsky, A., Mussweiler, T., & Medvec, V. H. (2002). Disconnecting outcomes and evaluations: The role of negotiator focus. *Journal of Personality and Social Psychology, 83*(5), 1131–1140.

[5]Curhan, J., Neale, M., & Ross, L. (2004). Dynamic valuation: Preference changes in the context of face-to-face negotiation. *Journal of Experimental Social Psychology, 40*, 142–151.

[6]Naquin, C. (2003). The agony of opportunity in negotiation: Number of negotiable issues, counterfactual thinking, and feelings of satisfaction. *Organizational Behavior and Human Decision Processes, 91*, 97–107.

[7]Foa, U., & Foa, E. (1975). *Resource theory of social exchange.* Morristown, NJ: General Learning Press.

TRUST AS THE BEDROCK OF RELATIONSHIPS

Trust is essential in any human relationship. It is an expression of confidence in another person or group of people that you will not be put at risk, harmed, or injured by their actions.[8] On a practical level, trust means that we could be exploited by someone. Most relationships hold some incentive for people to behave in an untrustworthy fashion.[9]

Three Types of Trust in Relationships

People form three major types of trust relationships with others: deterrence-based trust, knowledge-based trust, and identification-based trust.[10]

Deterrence-Based Trust

Deterrence-based trust is based on consistency of behavior, meaning people will follow through on what they promise to do. Behavioral consistency, or follow-through, is sustained by threats or promises of consequences that will result if consistency and promises are not maintained. The consequences most often used are punishments, sanctions, incentives, rewards, and legal implications. Deterrence-based trust often involves contracts, surveillance, and sometimes punishment. An estimated 66% of the online workforce is monitored by employers.[11] In the Hawthorne plant in the 1940s, the established norm was that workers would not deviate from acceptable levels of production. Whenever a worker was caught over- or underperforming, other plant workers would give him or her a sharp blow to the upper arm (called "binging"). (For another example, see Exhibit 6-3.)

EXHIBIT 6-3   Deterrence-Based Trust

Another striking example of deterrence-based trust is the negotiated agreement between explorer Christopher Columbus and Spain's King Ferdinand and Queen Isabella. Ferdinand and Isabella offered Columbus ships, men, and money to carry the faith and the Spanish flag to the West. However, Columbus refused to agree until his demands were met in writing. He insisted he be knighted and made admiral of the Ocean Sea and viceroy and governor general of all the lands he would discover. He further demanded 10% of whatever would be acquired overseas. A handshake would not suffice. He insisted that the deal be set in writing, and so he drafted a lengthy, detailed agreement between himself and the crown. This move was astonishingly bold, considering the king and queen held the power of life and death over him. The haggling went back and forth, and on April 17, 1492, the Pact of Santa Fe was agreed to by the rulers.

Source: Dworetzky, T. (1998, December 11). Explorer Christopher Columbus: How the West's greatest discoverer negotiated his trips' financing. *Investors' Business Daily,* p. 1BD. Copyright © 1998-2008. Investor's Daily, Inc. Republished with permission.

---

[8]Axelrod, R. (1984). *The evolution of cooperation.* New York: Basic Books.
[9]Kramer, R. M. (1999). Trust and distrust in organizations: Emerging perspectives, enduring questions. *Annual Review of Psychology, 50,* 569–598; Kramer, R. M., Brewer, M. B., & Hanna, B. A. (1996). Collective trust and collective action: The decision to trust as a social decision. In R. M. Kramer & T. R. Tyler (Eds.), *Trust in organizations* (pp. 357–389). Thousand Oaks, CA: Sage.
[10]Shapiro, D. L., Sheppard, B. H., & Cheraskin, L. (1992). Business on a handshake. *Negotiation Journal, 8*(4), 365–377; Lewicki, R. J., & Bunker, B. B. (1996). Developing and maintaining trust in work relationships. In R. M. Kramer & T. R. Tyler (Eds.), *Trust in organizations: Frontiers of theory and research* (pp. 114–139). Thousand Oaks, CA: Sage.
[11]2007 electronic monitoring & surveillance survey: Over half of all employers combined fire workers for e-mail & Internet abuse. (2008, February 28). *Business Wire.*

There are two key problems with deterrence-based trust systems. First, they are expensive to develop and maintain (they require development, oversight, maintenance, and monitoring) and second, they can backfire. The backfiring is based upon the psychological principles of **reactance** (in popular culture, this concept is also known as **reverse psychology**). For example, the presence of signs reading "Do Not Write on These Walls Under Any Circumstances" actually increases the incidence of people's violations of the vandalism norm (as compared to signs that say "Please Do Not Write on These Walls" or the complete absence of signs).[12] Similarly, people take longer to vacate a parking space when they know someone else is waiting for it.[13] People often have a negative reaction when they perceive that someone is controlling their behavior or limiting their freedom. When people think their behavior is controlled by extrinsic motivators, such as sanctions and rewards, intrinsic motivation is reduced.[14] Thus, surveillance may undermine people's motivation to engage in the behaviors that such monitoring is intended to ensure. The fear of monitoring adversely impacted trust among flight attendants at Delta Airlines.[15] Flight attendants came to fear and distrust their passengers because of a policy allowing passengers to write letters of complaint about in-flight service. The climate of distrust was further intensified when flight attendants became suspicious that undercover supervisors were posing as passengers. The system backfired. (We discuss more about deterrence-based trust in Chapter 11.)

Knowledge-Based Trust

Knowledge-based trust is grounded in behavioral predictability, and it occurs when a person has enough information about others to understand them and accurately predict their behavior. Whenever informational uncertainty or asymmetry characterizes a relationship, it provides opportunity for deceit, and one or both parties risk exploitation. Paradoxically, if no risk is present in an exchange situation, exploitation cannot occur, but high levels of trust will not develop.[16] Trust is a consequence or response to uncertainty.[17]

An intriguing example of the development of knowledge-based trust among negotiators concerns the sale of rubber and rice in Thailand.[18] For various reasons, the quality of rubber cannot be determined at the time of sale but, rather, only months later: When rubber is sold, the seller knows the quality of the rubber, but the buyer does not. This is a classic case of one-sided informational asymmetry. In contrast, in

[12]Pennebaker, J. W., & Sanders, D. Y. (1976). American graffiti: Effects of authority and reactance arousal. *Personality and Social Psychology Bulletin, 2,* 264–267.
[13]Ruback, R. B., & Juieng, D. (1997). Territorial defense in parking lots: Retaliation against waiting drivers. *Journal of Abnormal Social Psychology, 27,* 821–834.
[14]Enzle, M. E., & Anderson, S. C. (1993). Surveillant intentions and intrinsic motivation. *Journal of Personality and Social Psychology, 64,* 257–266.
[15]Hochschild, A. R. (1983). *The managed heart: Commercialization of human feeling.* Berkeley: University of California Press.
[16]Thibaut, J., & Kelley, H. H. (1959). *The social psychology of groups.* New York: Wiley.
[17]Kollock, P. (1994). The emergence of exchange structures: An experimental study of uncertainty, commitment and trust. *American Journal of Sociology, 100*(2), 313–345; Granovetter, M. (1973). The strength of weak ties. *American Journal of Sociology, 78,* 1360–1379.
[18]Siamwalla, A. (1978, June). Farmers and middlemen: Aspects of agricultural marketing in Thailand. *Economic Bulletin for Asia and the Pacific,* 38–50; Popkin, S. (1981). Public choice and rural development— free riders, lemons, and institutional design. In C. Russel & N. Nicholson (Eds.), *Public choice and rural development* (pp. 43–80). Washington, DC: Resources for the Future.

the rice market, the quality of rice can be readily determined at the time of sale (no informational uncertainty). It would seem that the rubber market, because of its informational asymmetries, would be characterized by exploitation on the part of sellers who would only sell cheap rubber at high prices, creating a market of lemons.[19] However, buyers and sellers in the rubber market abandoned anonymous exchange for long-term exchange relationships between particular buyers and sellers. Within this exchange framework, growers establish reputations for trustworthiness, and rubber of high quality is sold.

Knowledge-based trust increases dependence and commitment among parties.[20] For example, suppliers who regularly negotiate with certain customers develop highly specialized products for those customers. Such product differentiation can create barriers to switching suppliers. In addition to economic dependence, people become emotionally committed to some relationships. For example, in markets characterized by information asymmetries, once negotiators develop a relationship with someone they find to be trustworthy, they remain committed to the relationship, even when it would be profitable to trade with others.[21] When switching does occur, the party who is "left" feels indignant and violated. For example, the decision of major car manufacturers to switch to lower-cost suppliers left their higher-cost longtime suppliers feeling betrayed. Similarly, people who expect to interact with others in the future are less likely to exploit them, even when given an opportunity.[22] When negotiators anticipate extended relationships, they are more likely to cooperate with customers, colleagues, and suppliers but not with competitors.[23] These relationships and the perception of low mobility among individuals promote development of integrative agreements across interactions, rather than only within given transactions.[24]

Identification-Based Trust

Identification-based trust is grounded in complete empathy with another person's desires and intentions. In identification-based trust systems, trust exists between people because each person understands, agrees with, empathizes with, and takes on the other's values because of the emotional connection between them; thus, they act for each other.[25] Identification-based trust means that other people have adopted your own preferences.

Exhibit 6-4 lists the three types of relationships (personal, business, and embedded) and the three types of trust (deterrence-based, knowledge-based, and identification-based). We indicate the type and nature of interaction that may occur when different types of trust and different types of relationships intersect. Whereas it may seem that

---

[19]Akerlof, G. (1970). The market for lemons: Quality uncertainty and the market mechanism. *Quarterly Journal of Economics, 84*, 488–500.

[20]Dwyer, F. R., Schurr, P. H., & Oh, S. (1987). Developing buyer-seller relationships. *Journal of Marketing, 51*, 11–27; Kollock, "The emergence of exchange structures."

[21]Kollock, "The emergence of exchange structures."

[22]Marlowe, D., Gergen, K., & Doob, A. (1966). Opponents' personality, expectation of social interaction and interpersonal bargaining. *Journal of Personality and Social Psychology, 3*, 206–213.

[23]Sondak, H., & Moore, M. (1994). Relationship frames and cooperation. *Group Decision and Negotiation, 2*, 103–118.

[24]Mannix, E. A., Tinsley, C. H., & Bazerman, M. H. (1995). Negotiating over time: Impediments to integrative solutions. *Organizational Behavior and Human Decision Processes, 62*(3), 241–251.

[25]Lewicki & Bunker, "Developing and maintaining trust."

EXHIBIT 6-4 Trust Relationship Grid

| | *Relationship* | | |
Trust	Personal Relationship	Business Relationship	Embedded Relationship
Deterrence-based	Lack of trust Prenuptial agreements Surveillance	Theory X management Use of threats, punishments, sanctions Surveillance	Use of threats, punishments, sanctions
Knowledge-based	Sympathy for other	Customer-driven focus Assessment of clients' needs	Understanding and appreciation of partners
Identification-based	True empathy for other Investment in other's welfare	Theory Y management Selection of employees who fit corporate culture and its values Restructuring to serve customer	Empathy Development of social identity

personal relationships would be completely grounded in knowledge-based or identification-based trust, it does not always occur. For example, a deterrence-based trust system is put in place when couples get prenuptial agreements or when husbands or wives hire private investigators to monitor the actions of their spouses.

Building Trust: Rational and Deliberate Mechanisms

There are two routes to building trust: the **cognitive route** is based on rational and deliberate thoughts and considerations; the **affective route** is based on intuition and emotion.[26] The cognitive and the affective routes to trust have different triggers and turning points in negotiation.[27]

Let's first consider how to build trust through the cognitive route. (For an examination of how businesspeople attempt to secure trust, see Exhibit 6-5.)

Transform Personal Conflict into Task Conflict

Two basic types of conflict occur in relationships. **Personal conflict**, also known as **emotional conflict**, is personal, defensive, and resentful.[28] Personal conflict is often rooted in anger, personality clashes, ego, and tension. **Task conflict**, also known as

[26]McAlister, D. (1995). Affect- and cognition-based trust as foundations for interpersonal cooperation in organizations. *Academy of Management Journal, 38*(1), 24–59; Lewis, D. & Weigert, A. (1985). Trust as a social reality. *Social Forces, 63*(4), 967–985.

[27]Olekans, M., & Smith, P. (2005). Moments in time: Metacognition, trust, and outcomes in dyadic negotiations. *Personality and Social Psychology Bulletin, 31*(12), 1696–1707.

[28]Guetzkow, H., & Gyr, J. (1954). An analysis of conflict in decision-making groups. *Human Relations, 7,* 367–381; Jehn, K. A. (2000). Benefits and detriments of workplace conflict. *The Public Manager, 29*(2), 24–26.

EXHIBIT 6-5   How Managers Secure Commitment in the Absence of Binding Contracts

52 MBA students were asked to "imagine that you are involved in a negotiation situation where you need to get commitment (i.e., follow-through) from one or more of the people involved. The nature of the negotiation does not involve 'binding contracts.' How do you try to instill a sense of commitment in the absence of any binding contracts?" The responses varied dramatically.

Responses (Left to Right):

- *Persuasion and consciousness-raising* (e.g., "I would reinforce the idea that this is the beginning of a long-term, multiple-contact relationship, and that it is in my counterparty's best interest to think about the repercussions of reneging on future negotiations")
- *Coercion and threat tactics* (e.g., humiliation, punishment, etc.)
- *Nonverbal strategies* (e.g., handshakes, establishing rapport, ". . . look people in the eye, have them look at you, and say to you that they will do what you want them to do . . . ", etc.)
- *Verbal agreements*
- *Behavior modification* (e.g., tit for tat; social modeling)
- *Rewards and benefits*
- *Public commitments* (e.g., ". . . by making the outcome public, the erring party would suffer public embarrassment and suffer loss of reputation. . . .")
- *Alignment of incentives*
- *Collecting information about other's BATNA*
- *Written (nonbinding) agreements*
- *Creation of mutual enemy*
- *Creating escrow or collateral arrangements*

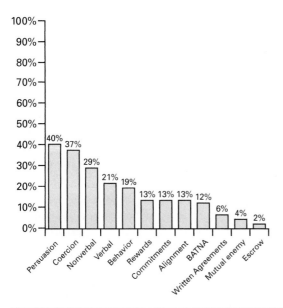

cognitive conflict, is largely depersonalized. It consists of argumentation about the merits of ideas, plans, and projects, independent of the identity of the people involved. Task conflict is often effective in stimulating the creativity necessary for integrative agreement because it forces people to rethink problems and arrive at outcomes that everyone can accept. Personal conflict threatens relationships, whereas task conflict enhances relationships, provided that people are comfortable with it.[29] (For an example of how companies create a forum for conflict, see Exhibit 6-6.)

Agree on a Common Goal or Shared Vision
The importance of a common goal is summed up in a quote by Steve Jobs, associated with three high-profile Silicon Valley companies—Apple, NeXT, and Pixar: "It's okay to

[29]Jehn, K. A. (1997). A qualitative analysis of conflict types and dimensions in organizational groups. *Administrative Science Quarterly, 42,* 530–557.

EXHIBIT 6-6 Creating a Forum for Conflict

Bitter negotiations between the Washington Ballet and its dancers came to an end after months of debate when Joel Schaffer and Gary Eder of the Federal Mediation and Conciliation Service called a meeting among the artistic staff and the dancers, where no notes were taken and concerns were directly addressed, bringing conflict to the forefront. According to dancer Luis Torres, communicating honestly was often difficult in earlier negotiations. "We were involved in legal talk that nobody really understood. Once we got to our own lingo, we were able to understand each other," Torres said. The meeting was meant to "humanize" the conflict, according to Schaffer. He said the meeting allowed those involved "to finally remember how much both sides truly care about the company, and that what both of them were doing in their own way was protecting the future of the company." Dancers and management finally reached agreement, he said, "because both sides wanted it. They just needed a little assistance in finding out a way to get it."

Source: Kaufman, S. (2006, March 7). Dancers, company agree on contract; Washington ballet to extend season after ratification. *Washington Post,* p. C1. Reprinted by permission.

spend a lot of time arguing about which route to take to San Francisco when everyone wants to end up there, but a lot of time gets wasted in such arguments if one person wants to go to San Francisco and another secretly wants to go to San Diego."[30] Shared goals do not imply homogeneous thinking, but they do require everyone to share a vision.

The 2005 departure of Carly Fiorina as chief executive of Hewlett-Packard (HP) illustrates how conflicts can also mask the fact that people never agree fundamentally on the goals of the company. Escalating disagreements between Fiorina and HP's board of directors led to an open discussion of their differences at a company retreat. Several board members expressed concern about the company's performance under Fiorina's leadership. When a *Wall Street Journal* story leaked details of their discussions, Fiorina was furious and shifted her focus to the leak. Board members were also outraged by the leak but felt their concerns regarding the performance of the company were more important. They started to believe it had become impossible to work out their differences with Fiorina. Less than 2 weeks later, during a private meeting, the board members voted to dismiss her.[31]

Capitalize on Network Connections

Negotiators who do not know each other may attempt to build a more trusting relationship by trying to find a common node in their social networks. In other words, they engage in enough discussion to attempt to single out someone whom they both know. However, getting people to talk to someone outside their social network is challenging. An investigation of a weekly business "mixer" revealed that people don't mix as much as would be expected, given the purpose of the mixer.[32] Affect-based trust is high in people who are

[30]Eisenhardt, K. M., Kahwajy, J. L., & Bourgeois, L. J., III. (1997). How management teams can have a good fight. *Harvard Business Review, 75*(4), 77–85 (p. 80).

[31]Murray, A. (2006, September 6). Directors cut: H-P board clash over leaks triggers angry resignation—Perkins slams briefcase, says, "I quit and I'm leaving," as probe fingers a friend—A new era of governance. *Wall Street Journal,* p. A1.

[32]Ingram, P., & Morris, M. (2007). Do people mix at mixers? Structure, homophily, and the "life of the party." *Administrative Science Quarterly, 52,* 558–585.

embedded densely in their networks and among those who provided social support; cognition-based trust is higher in those with whom people engage in instrumental exchanges.[33]

Find a Shared Problem or a Shared Enemy

It is remarkable how the presence of a common enemy can unite people and build trust.[34] This phenomenon happens for several reasons. First, it is often necessary for people to join forces to compete against a common enemy. A shared goal of sorts was established during the Reagan–Gorbachev summit talks. One evening, President Reagan and Soviet leader Mikhail Gorbachev were drinking coffee after dinner on Lake Geneva. Secretary of State George P. Shultz turned to Georgi Kornienko, the Soviet first deputy foreign minister, and accused him of trying to stall summit negotiations on bilateral issues. "You, Mr. Minister, are responsible for this," Shultz declared. Then, turning to Gorbachev, the secretary of state added forcefully, "This man is not doing what you want him to do. He is not getting done what you want done." Reagan took advantage of the situation to create a common bond and looked at Gorbachev: "To hell with what they're doing. You and I will say, 'We will work together to make it come about.'" Reagan and Gorbachev then shook hands. The moment marked a critical turning point in the meeting.[35] A common goal, or common enemy, removes the perception that parties' interests are completely opposed and builds a new value that represents a higher-order principle that all parties find motivating.

Focus on the Future

It is difficult for negotiators to agree on what happened in the past, but if they can forgive and forget and focus on their future together, they can go a long way toward building trust. A new collective bargaining agreement between the San Francisco Opera and the union representing solo singers, chorus members, dancers, and the production staff put an end to a formerly turbulent relationship. In 2003, the union threatened a strike, and during talks in 2004 the union filed a lawsuit to force the company to follow negotiated grievance procedures. However the 2006 negotiations marked the beginning of a more cooperative relationship. According to Shane Gasbarra, the company's director of artistic and music administration, the talks over an electronic media agreement were used as a way to establish trust between the two parties: "There's been a bad history here, and this was a way to move things forward with a more productive partnership."[36]

Building Trust: Psychological Strategies

A variety of psychological tools can be used to enhance and build trust between people. These psychological mechanisms distinguish themselves from the rational, cognitive mechanisms discussed earlier in that people tend not to talk about these factors explicitly; rather, savvy negotiators know how to capitalize on them intuitively.

---

[33]Chua, R., Ingram, P., & Morris, M. (2008). From the head and the heart: Locating cognition- and affect-based trust in managers' professional networks. *Academy of Management Journal, 51,* 436–452.

[34]Sherif, M., Harvey, O. J., White, B. J., Hood, W. R., & Sherif, C. W. (1961). *Intergroup conflict and cooperation: The robber's cave experiment.* Norman: University of Oklahoma Press.

[35]Hoffman, D. (1985, November 23). Tense turning point at summit; key Reagan-Gorbachev handshake calmed atmosphere. *Washington Post,* p. A1.

[36]Kosman, J. (2006, November 9). San Francisco Opera workers ratify 5-year contract including 3 to 4 percent raises. *San Francisco Chronicle,* p. E1.

Similarity

People who are similar to each other like one another.[37] The **similarity-attraction effect** may occur on the basis of little, and sometimes downright trivial, information. Simply put, we like people whom we perceive to be similar to us. Negotiators are more likely to make concessions when negotiating with people they know and like. Savvy negotiators increase their effectiveness by making themselves similar to the other party. Many sales training programs urge trainees to "mirror and match" the customer's body posture, mood, and verbal style because similarities along each of these dimensions actually lead to positive results.[38] Similarity in dress also has dramatic effects. For example, marchers in a political demonstration not only are more likely to sign the petition of a similarly dressed requester but do so without bothering to read it first.[39]

Mere Exposure

The more we are exposed to something—a person, object, or idea—the more we like it. The **mere exposure effect** is extremely powerful and occurs below the level of our awareness.[40] Advertisers know about the mere exposure effect. The more we are exposed to TVs, the more we come to like the product—up to a point.

Instead of having a single-shot negotiation, negotiators could suggest a preliminary meeting over drinks and follow with a few phone calls and unexpected gifts. By the time of the final negotiation, the target negotiator feels as though he or she is interacting with an old friend. Personal connections make a difference, even in the oil industry. Bill Greehey, chairman and former CEO of Valero Energy, says one of his best acquisitions occurred when Valero bought a refinery in Aruba for $365 million. "Of all the bidders, I was the only CEO to visit Aruba," he says. "I met with the prime minister six or seven times." Their talks went well, and when bids finally came in, Valero's package was deemed best, despite the report that a higher price was offered by at least one other bidder. The personal relationship Mr. Greehey had built helped him beat out the higher bidder.[41] (See Exhibit 6-7 for an example of how mere exposure increases liking in classrooms.)

Physical Presence

When students are seated alphabetically in a classroom, friendships are significantly more likely to form between those whose last names begin with the same or a nearby letter.[42] This is what is called the **propinquity effect**. This may not seem important until you

---

[37]Griffin, E., & Sparks, G. G. (1990). Friends forever: A longitudinal exploration of intimacy in same-sex friends and platonic pairs. *Journal of Social and Personal Relations, 7,* 29–46.

[38]LaFrance, M. (1985). Postural mirroring and intergroup relations. *Personality and Social Psychology Bulletin, 11*(2), 207–217; Locke, K. D., & Horowitz, L. M. (1990). Satisfaction in interpersonal interactions as a function of similarity in level of dysphoria. *Journal of Personality and Social Psychology, 58*(5), 823–831; Woodside, A. G., & Davenport, J. W., Jr. (1974). Effects of salesman similarity and expertise on customer purchasing behavior. *Journal of Marketing Research, 11*(2), 198–202.

[39]Suedfeld, P., Bochner, S., & Matas, C. (1971). Petitioners attire and petition signing by peace demonstrators: A field experiment. *Journal of Applied Social Psychology, 1*(3), 278–283.

[40]Zajonc, R. (1968). Attitudinal effects of mere exposure. *Journal of Personality and Social Psychology, 9* (monograph supplement No. 2, Part 2).

[41]Anders, G. (2006, August 21). The best acquisitions start with a CEO who charms sellers. *Wall Street Journal,* p. B1.

[42]Segal, M. W. (1974). Alphabet and attraction: An unobtrusive measure of the effect of propinquity in a field setting. *Journal of Personality and Social Psychology, 30*(5), 654–657.

EXHIBIT 6-7   Mere Exposure Increases Liking

The effects of mere exposure on liking are demonstrated clearly in the classroom. In one investigation, student A attended 15 sessions of a course. For each session, she arrived before the class began, walked down the aisle, and sat at the front where other students could see her. Student B did the same thing but attended only 10 lectures. Student C came to class only 5 times. Student D never showed up. At the end of the term, the students in the class were shown slides of students A, B, C, and D and were asked to indicate how "familiar" they found each one; how attractive they found each one; and how similar they believed each one was to them. The number of classes attended had a dramatic impact on attraction and similarity but not on familiarity.

Source: Moreland, R. L., & Beach, S. R. (1992). Exposure effects in the classroom: The development of affinity among students. *Journal of Experimental Social Psychology, 28*(3), 255–276. Reprinted by permission of Elsevier via RightsLink.

---

consider the fact that you may meet some of your closest colleagues, and perhaps even a future business partner, merely because of an instructor's seating chart! Similarly, people given a corner seat or an office at the end of a corridor make fewer friends in their organization.[43] If an instructor changes seat assignments once or twice during the semester, each student becomes acquainted with additional colleagues.[44] To further see the power of the propinquity effect, consider the entering class of the Maryland State Police Training Academy.[45] Trainees were assigned to their classroom seats and to their dormitory rooms by the alphabetical order of their last names. Sometime later, trainees were asked to name their three best friends in the group; their choices followed the rules of alphabetization almost exactly. Larsons were friends with Lees, not with Abromowitzes or Xiernickes, even though they were separated by only a few yards.[46]

For another example, consider friendship formation among couples in apartment buildings. In this particular case, residents had been assigned to their apartments at random as vacancies opened up, and nearly all of them were strangers when they moved in. When asked to name their three closest friends in the entire housing project, 65% named friends in the same building. Among those living in the same building, the propinquity effect was in play: 41% of next-door neighbors indicated they were close friends, compared to only 22% who lived two doors apart and only 10% who lived on the opposite ends of the hall.

The propinquity effect has an impact on **functional distance**. Certain aspects of architectural design make it more likely that some people will come into contact with each other more often than with others, even though physically the distances between them might be the same. For example, more friendships were made with people on the same floor than on another floor, presumably because climbing stairs requires more effort than walking down the hall.

---

[43]Maisonneuve, J., Palmade, G., & Fourment, C. (1952). Selective choices and propinquity. *Sociometry, 15,* 135–140.

[44]Byrne, D. (1961). Interpersonal attraction and attitude similarity. *Journal of Abnormal and Social Psychology, 62,* 713–715.

[45]Segal, "Alphabet and attraction."

[46]Byrne, "Interpersonal attraction"; Kipnis, D. (1957). Interaction between bomber crews as a determinant of sociometric choice. *Human Relations, 10,* 263–270.

Reciprocity

According to the **reciprocity principle**, we feel obligated to return in kind what others have offered or given to us. This principle is one that all human societies subscribe to—it is a rule permeating exchanges of all kinds.[47] Feelings of indebtedness are so powerful that, if unresolved, they are carried into the future and are passed on to the next generation to repay. People feel upset and distressed if they have received a favor from another person and are prevented from returning it.

Madeleine Albright (U.S. Secretary of State, 1997–2001) knew the power of reciprocity. One of Albright's first public meetings with members of Congress was an appearance to testify before the House Appropriations Subcommittee chaired by Republican Harold Rogers. Albright needed to be on good terms with Rogers because his subcommittee's jurisdiction included the State Department's operating budget. For the occasion, Albright carried with her a big box, gift-wrapped in red, white, and blue ribbon. Inside was a book of photographs. Albright had learned that Rogers had lost all his papers and photographs in a fire at his home, a disaster that had erased many souvenirs of his career and compounded the grief caused by the recent death of his wife. Albright instructed embassies in countries he had visited to provide copies of photos taken on those occasions, and compiled them in an album she bestowed on him right there in the committee hearing room.[48]

Not surprisingly, people are aware of the powerful grip that reciprocity has on them. People often will turn down favors and rewards from others because they do not want to feel obligated. For example, suppose the counterparty provides us with a favor, gift, or service that we never invited and perhaps even attempted to avoid. Our attempts to return it have been denied, and we are left with the unwanted gift. Even under these circumstances, the reciprocity rule may operate. Thus, we should beware of the unsolicited gift from our real estate agent, the courtesy token from our business associate, and the free lunch from the consulting firm. When faced with these situations, we should acknowledge the favor and then, if we still feel indebted, we should return the favor on a similar level.

Reciprocity is made even more difficult when parties place different value on aspects of a relationship. For example, trustors focus primarily on the risk associated with trusting someone, whereas trusted parties (those who are in a position to reciprocate) base their decisions on the level of economic benefits they have received.[49] Unfortunately, neither party is particularly sensitive to the factors that affect their counterpart's decision.

Schmoozing

Small talk often seems to serve no obvious function. The exchange of pleasantries about the weather or our favorite basketball team seems to be purposeless, except for conforming to social etiquette. However, **schmoozing** has a dramatic impact on our liking and trust of others. For example, even a short exchange can lead people to develop

---

[47]Gouldner, A. W. (1960). The norm of reciprocity: A preliminary statement. *American Sociological Review, 25,* 161–179.
[48]Lippmann, T.W. (2000, June 3). Madame Secretary. *National Journal,* p. 1736.
[49]Malhotra, D. (2004). Trust and reciprocity decision: The differing perspectives of trustors and trusted parties. *Organizational Behavior and Human Decision Processes, 94,* 61–73.

trust.[50] According to Susan Pravda, co-managing partner of the Boston law office of Epstein, Becker, and Green, schmoozing is an important part of negotiations. She advises, "Don't walk in and start going through your list. If they have a baby picture on the desk, it doesn't hurt to say, 'Oh, is that a new grandchild?' People like to talk about themselves. It can segue into what you're trying to achieve."[51]

Flattery

People like others who appreciate and admire them. People are more likely to trust others who like them and to respond more favorably when they are flattered. It would seem that the positive pie-slicing effects of flattery would be reversed if the flatterer is suspected of having ulterior motives; however, even if people suspect the flatterer has another reason for flattering them, this behavior can still increase liking and trust under some conditions.[52] The most strategic type of flattery, in terms of advancing one's own interest, is to flatter another person on a personally important dimension about which he or she feels somewhat insecure.[53] John Wakeham, previous chief whip for Margaret Thatcher, says about Westminster politics, "I was absolutely fascinated by how Westminster actually works . . . the smoke-filled rooms, the nods and the winks. As a businessman, I found it more comprehensible than most politicians do. One thing I learnt as chief whip was the infinite capacity of human beings to absorb flattery."[54]

Self-Disclosure

Self-disclosure means sharing information about oneself with another person. It is a way of building a relationship with another person by making oneself vulnerable, in that the self-disclosing negotiator is providing information that could potentially be exploited. Self-disclosure also explicitly invites the other person to reciprocate the disclosure, thereby increasing trust.

What Leads to Mistrust?

One of the biggest threats to trust in a relationship is a **breach**, or **defection**. A breach occurs when one or both people violate the trust that has been built between them. For example, on March 19, 2003, U.S. President George W. Bush issued orders to begin "striking selected targets of military importance to undermine Saddam Hussein's ability to wage war." According to the United States, Saddam Hussein had engaged in a breach of trust by placing "Iraqi troops and equipment in civilian areas, attempting to use innocent men and women as shields for his own military," and demonstrating disregard for "conventions of war [and] rules of morality."[55]

---

[50]Morris, M., Nadler, J., Kurtzberg, T., & Thompson, L. (2002). Schmooze or lose: Social friction and lubrication in e-mail negotiations. *Group Dynamics: Theory, Research, and Practice, 6*(1), 89–100.

[51]Lancaster, H. (1998, January 27). You have to negotiate for everything in life, so get good at it. *Wall Street Journal,* p. B1.

[52]Jones, E. E., Stires, L. K., Shaver, K. G., & Harris, V. A. (1968). Evaluation of an ingratiator by target persons and bystanders. *Journal of Personality, 36*(3), 349–385.

[53]Ibid.

[54]Perkins, A. (2000, January 15). John Wakeham, Lord fixit. *The Guardian,* p. 6.

[55]Bush declares war: U.S. President George W. Bush has announced that war against Iraq has begun (2003, March 19). *CNN.com.* Retrieved on July 1, 2008 from http://www.cnn.com/2003/US/03/19/sprj.irq.int.bush .transcript

Miscommunication

In some cases, a real breach of trust does not occur but a miscommunication occurs that causes one or more parties to interpret it as such. Miscommunication is more likely when parties are not in regular contact, especially when they have little face-to-face contact.

Dispositional Attributions

Negotiators often make dispositional, as opposed to situational, attributions for the questionable behavior of the other party, which can threaten trust levels.[56] A **dispositional attribution** is one that calls into question another person's character and intentions by citing them as the cause of a behavior or incident (e.g., arrogance, greed, etc.). In contrast, a situational attribution cites one or more situational factors as the cause of a behavior or incident (e.g., a traffic jam, the faulty mail-delivery system, etc.). Assigning these dispositional attributions to their opponents' behaviors can threaten the trust between negotiators and the other party because it is much more difficult for people to respond to a dispositional attribution than a situational one. For example, Kramer and Wei examined how people interpret ambiguous and slightly negative social interactions (i.e., when a person you know does not acknowledge you when you walk past).[57] The power or status differential is significant in interpreting these situations. The high-power person who does not acknowledge a colleague usually reported having a busy day or, more often, not even being aware of the other person. In contrast, the low-power person was often extremely paranoid and upset, believing that the high-power person was attempting to ostracize or punish them. Thus, the low-power person pieces together a dispositional attribution for what is really a situational case.

Focusing on the "Bad Apple"

In a team or group, one person may have a reputation for being less trustworthy, tougher, or less easy to work with than other members of the group. We call this person the "bad apple," and bad apples can stand out. The problem is that people's impression of the bad apple can spoil their impression of the entire bunch. For example, in simulated negotiations between labor and management groups, negotiators were significantly less likely to trust the group as a whole than any individual in the group.[58] It seems the "bad apple" in the group called the entire group's trustworthiness into question.

Repairing Broken Trust

Violations of trust are common in negotiation. When trust has been broken, it is often in both parties' interests to attempt to repair the trust because broken relationships are often costly in terms of the emotions involved and the opportunities lost. Trust that is

[56]Morris, M. W., Larrick, R. P., & Su, S. K. (1999). Misperceiving negotiation counterparties: When situationally determined bargaining behaviors are attributed to personality traits. *Journal of Personality and Social Psychology, 77,* 52–67.

[57]Kramer, R. M., & Wei, J. (1999). Social uncertainty and the problem of trust in social groups: The social self in doubt. In T. R. Tyler & R. M. Kramer (Eds.), *The psychology of the social self: Applied social research* (pp. 145–168). Mahwah, NJ: Erlbaum.

[58]Naquin, C. (1999). Trust and distrust in group negotiations. Unpublished dissertation, Kellogg Graduate School of Management, Northwestern University, Evanston, IL.

EXHIBIT 6-8   Steps Toward Repairing Broken Trust

Step 1:	Arrange a personal meeting.	**Step 7:**	Test your understanding.
Step 2:	Put the focus on the relationship.	**Step 8:**	Formulate a plan.
Step 3:	Apologize.	**Step 9:**	Think about ways to prevent a future problem.
Step 4:	Let them vent.		
Step 5:	Do not get defensive.	**Step 10:**	Do a relationship checkup.
Step 6:	Ask for clarifying information.		

---

harmed by untrustworthy behavior can be effectively restored when people observe a consistent series of trustworthy actions; however, trust harmed by the same untrustworthy actions and deception never fully recovers, even when the victim receives a promise and an apology and observes a consistent series of trustworthy actions.[59] We now outline a process for repairing broken trust. (See Exhibit 6-8 for a summary.)

Step 1: Arrange a Personal Meeting

When trust has been violated, one person (party) either directly or indirectly accuses the other (target) of doing something that was unfair. The target's first reaction is often one of surprise combined with denial, and he or she may feel a need to exonerate himself or herself. The target should suggest a face-to-face meeting with the party as quickly as possible. Indeed, verbal explanations are more effective than written explanations.[60]

Step 2: Put the Focus on the Relationship

Instead of launching into discussions of who is right or who is wrong, the focus should be put on what both people care about: the relationship. Often, both people will readily agree the relationship is worth saving. Consider how superagent and attorney Leigh Steinberg negotiated quarterback Drew Bledsoe's multiyear contract with New England Patriots owner Bob Kraft. Their first meeting took place in a loud, crowded hotel lobby during the National Football League (NFL) owners' conference. As they led up to their bargaining positions, other people were interrupting them, thus making it difficult to talk or build a connection. In the midst of the interruptions and chaos, Kraft proposed $29 million over 7 years. Steinberg countered with $51 million. Insulted, angry, and shaking his head, Kraft got up and walked out. In the second meeting, 6 months later, Steinberg asked Kraft to dinner at a quiet Italian restaurant. He let Kraft vent anger and frustration over Bledsoe's proposed salary. It came out that Kraft had interpreted the high counteroffer as a signal that Bledsoe wanted nothing to do with the team and instead wanted to be a free agent. Calmly, Steinberg assured Kraft that Bledsoe wanted to stay. He explained that in the hubbub of the lobby 6 months earlier,

---

[59]Schweitzer, M., Hershey, J., & Bradlow, E. (2006). Promises and lies: Restoring violated trust. *Organizational Behavior and Human Decision Processes, 101*(1), 1–19.
[60]Shapiro, D. L., Buttner, E. H., & Barry, B. (1994). Explanations: What factors enhance their perceived adequacy? *Organizational Behavior and Human Decision Processes, 58*(3), 346–368.

Steinberg had not been able to create the solid rapport they had that evening and had not been able to establish an atmosphere of trust. That night, they settled on $42 million. Says Steinberg, "The key to successful negotiations is to develop relationships, not conquests."[61]

Step 3: Apologize

Sincerity is important. Targets should apologize for their behavior and accept responsibility for their actions. The expression of remorse following a wrongful act can mitigate punishment. But resist the urge to immediately blurt out an apology: Apologies offered later in a conflict are more impactful and effective than those offered immediately.[62] Later apologies are more effective because the "victim" has had an opportunity for self-expression and feels more understood. If the target does not feel at fault, then he or she should apologize in a way that takes ownership for his or her actions or behavior, yet does not necessarily accept the party's version of the violator's intentions. For example, a target might tell a party "I am very sorry that I did not consult you before preparing the report." By saying this, the target does not agree with the party's accusation that the violator attempted to take more credit for the report; rather, the target only identifies the action as being hurtful for the victim. Indeed, when companies acknowledge they have committed acts that threaten their legitimacy (e.g., newspaper claims of illegal conduct), they are more successful in blunting criticism when they point to external, mitigating circumstances (e.g., company norms, budgetary problems, etc.).[63]

Step 4: Let Them Vent

It is important for people to express their anger, rage, disappointment, and feelings of betrayal over an event. Merely talking about negative events can actually be part of the cure.[64] Research on procedural justice indicates that having a chance to express their disappointment often helps people take a significant step in the healing process.[65]

Step 5: Do Not Get Defensive

Instinctively, targets will attempt to defend their own honor. However, it is important not to behave defensively, no matter how misinformed or wrong you believe the other party to be. It is appropriate to tell the other person you view the situation differently and to point out that the situation can be viewed in many ways. Only after the party has had an opportunity to vent and explain his or her perspective should the violator attempt to tell the party, in clear and simple terms, what his or her intentions were. For example, a target might say, "My intention was to submit the report and not bother too many people with unnecessary requests to edit it."

---

[61]Dworetzky, T. (1998, September 22). Sports superagent Leigh Steinberg. *Investors' Business Daily,* p. A6.

[62]Frantz, C. M., & Bennigson, C. (2005). Better late than early: The influence of timing on apology effectiveness. *Journal of Experimental Social Psychology, 41*(2), 201–207.

[63]Elsbach, K. D. (1994). Managing organizational legitimacy in the California cattle industry: The construction and effectiveness of verbal accounts. *Administrative Science Quarterly, 39*(1), 57–88; Bies, R. J., Shapiro, D. L., & Cummings, L. L. (1988). Causal accounts and managing organizational conflict: Is it enough to say it's not my fault? *Communication Research, 15*(4), 381–399.

[64]Pennebaker, J. W., Hughes, C. F., & O'Heeron, R. C. (1987). The psychophysiology of confession: Linking inhibitory and psychosomatic processes. *Journal of Personality and Social Psychology, 52,* 781–793.

[65]Lind, E. A., & Tyler, T. R. (1988). *The social psychology of procedural justice.* New York: Plenum.

Step 6: Ask for Clarifying Information

Targets should invite the party to provide clarifying information in a nondefensive fashion. For example, a target might say "Am I wrong in thinking you did not ask to be listed on the report?" or "Did you receive the draft copy I sent last week?"

Step 7: Test Your Understanding

If a person feels understood, the chances for rebuilding trust are greatly increased. It is helpful if one party can truly empathize with the other's perspective (e.g., "I can understand why you felt out of the loop. I have felt that way before, too"). The ability to understand emotion in others is one aspect of emotional intelligence.[66] Indeed, a negotiator's ability to understand emotion is directly related to how satisfied the other party feels, independent of the monetary value of the outcome.[67]

Step 8: Formulate a Plan

A major stumbling block in the trust rebuilding process is that parties have different ideas about what is fair. The egocentric bias once again rears its ugly head with most harmdoers perceiving themselves as more beneficent than the harmed. However, the mere fact of asking the harmed what he or she needs can go a long way toward rebuilding trust. In an empirical investigation of breaches of trust, harmdoers who asked "What can I do?" were more successful in rebuilding cooperation than those who did not ask or asked "What will it take?"[68] Penance is critical to trust in mixed-motive relationships.[69] Aggravating a counterparty after a breach by making offers of penance that do not seem sincere may further antagonize. In contrast, volunteering to do penance, even in small amounts, is particularly effective.

In a major investigation of how people repair trust, a key finding was that the speed and amount of "trust recovery" are significantly moderated by the *promises* that a person makes.[70] No one should underestimate the power of the spoken word, especially when it contains an apology. For example, verbal explanation can dramatically dampen people's negative reactions to aversive behavior.[71] However, when it comes down to truly rebuilding cooperation, the power of the deed exceeds the power of the spoken word. "Substantive amends have significantly more positive effects than explanations alone [on rebuilding cooperation]."[72]

Step 9: Think About Ways to Prevent a Future Problem

Do not just try to remedy the past; rather, think about a way to make sure this problem, and any others like it, does not occur in the future. This effort may take some time, but it is well worth it.

---

[66]Mayer, J. D., Salovey, P., & Caruso, D. (2000). Models of emotional intelligence. In R. J. Sternberg (Ed.), *The handbook of emotional intelligence* (pp. 396–420). New York: Cambridge University Press.

[67]Mueller, J. S., & Curhan, J. R. (2006). Emotional intelligence and counterpart mood induction in a negotiation. *International Journal of Conflict Management, 17,* 110–128.

[68]Bottom, W., Gibson, K. S., Daniels, S., and Murnighan, J. K. (2002). When talk is not cheap: Substantive penance and expressions of intent in rebuilding cooperation, *Organization Science, 13*(5), 497–513.

[69]Ibid.

[70]Schweitzer, Hershey, & Bradlow, "Promises and lies."

[71]Bottom, Gibson, Daniels, & Murnighan, "When talk is not cheap."

[72]Ibid., p. 497.

Step 10: Do a Relationship Checkup

It is often wise to pull out your planners and decide upon a lunch or coffee meeting in a month or so to discuss how each party is feeling about the situation and occurrences since the breach of trust occurred. It is also helpful to schedule this date during the first meeting because it may seem awkward to bring it up after this time. This step ensures that parties will have a reason to meet and an opportunity to talk things through at a later date.

REPUTATION

One thing a negotiator definitely needs to protect is his or her reputation. According to Glick and Croson, you don't have to be a famous real estate tycoon for others to have an impression of you.[73] Managers' reputations are built fairly quickly in negotiation communities.[74] The reputations people gain affect how others deal with them. As a case in point, they describe the reputation held by Donald Trump:

> Real estate developer Donald Trump has a well-publicized reputation as a hard-line negotiator. In an article describing Trump's negotiations with the Taj Mahal Casino Resort's bondholders, Trump's advisors tell how after a deal is agreed upon, he always comes back requesting something more. Well-informed counterparts, familiar with his reputation, are prepared for this tactic and anticipate it in deciding how many concessions to make during the pre-agreement stage. Similarly, Trump has a reputation for storming out of negotiations in the middle of talks. An anonymous participant in the bondholders negotiation above said, "You know Donald's going to get up and leave, you just don't know when."[75]

Glick and Croson cite the Silicon Valley as an example of a negotiation community, where an active technology trade press helps generate a rich flow of information regarding reputations. Because venture capitalists co-invest with various firms, they share information. Moreover, because time is money, you might not even get on a calendar unless your reputation is good. Our impressions of others are formed quickly and immediately, sometimes within the first few minutes of meeting someone, because the judgments we make about people are often automatic.[76] Not surprisingly, we form impressions of people on the basis of limited information. Reputations are often more extreme and polarized than the person they represent; they can be summed up by four words: **judgmental**, **consistent**, **immediate**, and **inferential**. The reputations assigned to others tend to be highly evaluative, meaning that they are either "good" or "bad."[77] Furthermore, the reputations we assign to others are highly internally consistent. Once

[73]Glick, S., & Croson, R. (2001). Reputations in negotiation. In S. Hoch & H. Kunreuther (Eds.), *Wharton on making decisions* (pp. 177–186). New York: Wiley.
[74]Ibid.
[75]Ibid., p. 178.
[76]Bargh, J. A., Lombardi, W. J., & Higgins, E. T. (1988). Automaticity of chronically accessible constructs in person-situation effects on person perception: It's just a matter of time. *Journal of Personality and Social Psychology, 55*(4), 599–605.
[77]Osgood, C. E., Suci, G. J., & Tannenbaum, P. H. (1957). *The measurement of meaning.* Urbana: University of Illinois Press.

we decide that someone is trustworthy, other qualities about this person are perceived as consistent with this favorable impression. This tendency gives rise to the **halo effect**, which is the propensity to believe that people we trust and like are also intelligent and capable.

Of course, the halo effect can work in the opposite direction. The **forked-tail effect** means that once we form a negative impression of someone, we tend to view everything else about them in a negative fashion. For this reason, it is difficult to recover from making a bad impression.

Reputations are based on a combination of firsthand and secondhand information.[78] Firsthand information is based on our direct experience with someone. Secondhand information is based on what we hear about someone else's experience with someone.

Glick and Croson undertook an investigation of the reputations earned by 105 students enrolled in a class.[79] They rated one another, on the basis of firsthand experience, from the least cooperative to the most cooperative:

- *Liar-manipulator*   (will do anything for advantage)
- *Tough but honest*   (very tough and makes few concessions but will not lie)
- *Nice and reasonable*   (makes concessions)
- *Cream puff*   (makes concessions and is conciliatory regardless of what the other does)

The major finding from their multiweek investigation was that people act much tougher when dealing with someone who has the reputation of being a liar (61% reported using classic distributive, pie-slicing tactics with these people). Against tough negotiators, this behavior dropped to 49%, and integrative tactics (pie-expanding tactics) were used 35% of the time. Against nice negotiators, only 30% used distributive tactics and 64% used integrative tactics. Against cream puffs, 40% used distributive tactics, and only 27% used integrative tactics. People use tough or manipulative tactics in a defensive fashion with liars and tough negotiators, and they use them in an opportunistic fashion with cream puffs.

Repairing a tarnished reputation is a lot like attempting to build trust. People will look at your behavior more than your words, so it is important to act in a trustworthy fashion—not just to talk in a trustworthy fashion.

RELATIONSHIPS IN NEGOTIATION

Relationships affect the process and outcome of negotiation and, in turn, processes and outcomes influence relationships. Thus, relationships influence not only the process of how people negotiate but also their choice of an interaction partner.[80] Negotiators who reach impasse find themselves getting caught in "distributive spirals" in which they interpret their performance as unsuccessful, experience negative emotions, and develop negative perceptions of their negotiation counterparts and the entire negotiation process.[81] Moreover, negotiators who reach an impasse in a prior negotiation are more

---

[78]Glick & Croson, "Reputations in negotiation."
[79]Ibid.
[80]McGinn, K. L. (2006). Relationships and negotiations in context. In L. Thompson (Ed.), *Negotiation theory and research: Frontiers of social psychology* (pp. 129–144). New York: Psychology Press.
[81]O'Connor, K. M., Arnold, J. A. & Burris, E. R. (2005). Negotiators' bargaining histories and their effects on future negotiation performance. *Journal of Applied Psychology, 90*(2), 350–362.

likely to do the same in their next negotiation or to reach low-value (lose-lose) deals compared to negotiators who were successful in reaching agreement (i.e., reaching a level 1 agreement).[82] Moreover, this effect holds true even when the negotiator is dealing with a different person. Thus, if a negotiator has "baggage" from the past, it affects his or her ability to go forward. Incidental emotions from the past (e.g., anger stemming from an argument with a spouse) can influence trust even more dramatically in an unrelated setting (e.g., the likelihood of trusting a coworker).[83] In short, anger about anything—even in our past with another person—makes us less likely to trust anyone else in the future.

People often feel better about pie-slicing and are in a better position to expand the pie when they have a good relationship and trust one another. For example, Pruitt and Carnevale find that a high concern for oneself and the other party is most likely to lead to integrative (win-win) outcomes.[84] Levels of cooperation decrease as social distance increases between people.[85] When reaching agreement is important, negotiators who have a relationship are more likely to reach a win-win agreement than negotiators who do not have a relationship.[86]

Most people negotiate in their personal lives. For example, people negotiate with spouses, friends, and neighbors.[87] People also negotiate on a repeated basis with others in their personal life who do not necessarily fall into the categories of "friends" or "family" (e.g., homeowners negotiating with contractors; parents negotiating with other parents concerning carpool arrangements; parents negotiating with nannies concerning child care; etc.). In addition to negotiating in our personal lives, we also negotiate in our business lives, with colleagues, supervisors, and staff members. In some cases, our personal life is intermingled with our business life in relationships we cannot easily classify as strictly personal or strictly business but, rather, as a little or a lot of both. We refer to this type of relationship as an "embedded" relationship.[88] We will expose the relevant implicit norms and rules that lurk under each of these three types of relationships and their implications for trust in negotiations. The behavior of people in relationships is guided by shared sets of rules.[89] Individuals in relationships seek to abide by the rules of relationships and not to violate the expectations of others.

---

[82]Ibid.

[83]Dunn, J., & Schweitzer, M. (2005). Feeling and believing: The influence of emotion on trust. *Journal of Personality and Social Psychology, 88*, 736–748.

[84]Pruitt, D. G., & Carnevale, P. J. (1993). *Negotiation in social conflict.* Pacific Grove, CA: Brooks-Cole; for an overview, see Rubin, J. Z., Pruitt, D. G., & Kim, S. H. (1994). *Social conflict: Escalation, stalemate and settlement.* New York: McGraw-Hill.

[85]Buchan, N., Croson, R., & Dawes, R. M. (2002). Swift neighbors and persistent strangers: A cross-cultural investigation of trust and reciprocity in social exchange. *American Journal of Sociology, 108*(1), 168–206.

[86]Kray, L., Thompson, L., & Lind, A. (2005). It's a bet! A problem solving approach promotes the construction of contingent agreements. *Personality and Social Psychology Bulletin, 31*(8), 1039–1051.

[87]See Valley, K., Neale, M. A., & Mannix, E. (1995). Friends, lovers, colleagues, strangers: The effects of relationship on the process and outcome of dyadic negotiations. In R. J. Bies, R. J. Lewicki, & B. H. Sheppard (Eds.), *Research on negotiation in organizations: Handbook of negotiation research: Vol. 5* (pp. 65–93). Greenwich, CT: JAI Press.

[88]Uzzi, B. (1997). Social structure and competition in interfirm networks: The paradox of embeddedness. *Administrative Science Quarterly, 42*, 35–67.

[89]Argyle, M., & Henderson, M. (1984). The rules of relationships. In S. Duck & D. Perlman (Eds.), *Understanding personal relationships: An interdisciplinary approach.* Beverly Hills, CA: Sage; Clark, M., & Mills, J. (1979). Interpersonal attraction in exchange and communal relationships. *Journal of Personality and Social Psychology, 37*, 12–24.

Negotiating with Friends

Most people negotiate quite often, even in the most intimate of personal relationships. For example, consider how James and Lloyd Maritz decided to negotiate their differences about how to manage their business. In 1950, they decided to cut the company in half and, following Solomon's rule, one brother did the dividing and the other brother got to choose first.[90]

McGinn and Keros examined negotiations among strangers and friends and found that one of three patterns emerges early on:[91]

- *Opening up*   (complete and mutual honesty)
- *Working together*   (cooperative problem solving)
- *Haggling*   (competitive attempt to get the best possible deal for oneself)

These negotiators use one of three dynamic processes: trust-testing, process clarification, and emotional punctuation—when they have difficulty moving through the interaction. When strangers interact, they often immediately begin in haggling mode. In contrast, friends begin to open up almost immediately.

Why People Are Uncomfortable Negotiating with Friends

A motto followed by many people is "Friends should not do business." People are extremely reluctant to negotiate with friends if it means money, goods, or services change hands. People who do negotiate with friends report feeling uncomfortable.[92] According to Kurtzberg and Medvec, "Friendship dictates that we should be concerned with fairness and the other person's welfare, while negotiations dictate that we should get a good deal for ourselves."[93] These two dictates are in conflict with one another. The reason for the discomfort is traceable to the fact that most friendships are built on **communal norms**, which mandate that we should take care of people we love, respond to their needs, and not "keep track" of who has put in what.[94] Thus, the communal norm prescribes that we should be sensitive to the needs of people we love or like and attempt to meet those needs, rather than trying to maximize our own interests. The opposite of communal norms are **exchange norms**, which basically state that people should keep track of who has put what into a relationship and they should be compensated based on the value and quality of their inputs. Thus, people need to have a mental accounting system of sorts that records who has done what.

The truth is that we negotiate with our friends all the time. For example, we make child-care arrangements with neighbors, plan parties and vacations together, and even purchase jointly shared equipment together (e.g., snowblowers). Friends don't call these activities "negotiations"; rather, they say they are "working things out," "making plans," "figuring things out," and so on. Above all, in these interactions, people are careful not to exchange money, and sometimes go to great and strange lengths in order to avoid it.

---

[90]Bailey, J. (2002, August 12). A CEO's legacy: Sons wage battle over family firm. *Wall Street Journal,* p. A1.
[91]McGinn, K. L., & Keros, A. T. (2002). Improvisation and the logic of exchange in socially embedded transactions. *Administrative Science Quarterly, 47,* 442–473.
[92]Kurtzberg, T., & Medvec, V. H. (1999). Can we negotiate and still be friends? *Negotiation Journal, 15*(4), 355–362.
[93]Ibid., p. 356.
[94]Clark & Mills, "Interpersonal attraction."

Friends Are Less Competitive with Each Other

Not surprisingly, friends are less competitive with each other than they are with strangers.[95] Friends exchange more information, make more concessions, make fewer demands, and are more generous with one another.[96] Consequently, negotiators who are in a relationship are often unable to profitably exploit opportunities to create value. The oft-observed pattern in which people in close relationships reach monetarily inefficient outcomes but increase their relational satisfaction is known as the "O. Henry Effect."[97] In O. Henry's story "The Gift of the Magi," the main characters—husband and wife—are madly in love with each other but engage in an inefficient exchange in a desperate attempt to provide each other with a Christmas gift. When relationship partners sacrifice instrumental value, they actually increase their relational satisfaction.

Friends May Not Reach Level 3 Integrative Agreements

Friends and lovers are too willing to compromise.[98] Friends are reluctant to engage in the firm flexibility maxim that is often required to reach level 3 integrative agreements. In short, friends believe that reaching an impasse may permanently damage their relationship, so they settle quickly. Yet, as we have seen in our discussion of integrative agreements in Chapter 4, it is important to focus on differences of interest and maintain high aspirations to reach level 3 integrative outcomes. When people compromise quickly because they want to avoid conflict and minimize the threat of impasse, they are likely to leave value on the table. In short, they satisfice rather than optimize. Too much focus on the relationship can lead to satisficing, rather than optimizing.[99] As can be seen in Exhibit 6-9, when both negotiators have a high relational focus, there is a tendency to satisfice. When one negotiator has a high relationship focus and the other does not, there is distancing; when both are low in relationship focus, there is trading; it is only when both negotiators are moderately focused on the relationship that integrating occurs.

Friendship and the Mismanagement of Agreement

Organizational psychologist Jerry Harvey's story of the road to Abilene (see Exhibit 6-10) epitomizes the notion that among family and friends, conflict is to be avoided at all costs, even if it means a lose-lose outcome for all involved.[100] The need for friends to maintain the illusion of agreement means that important differences in preferences, interests, and beliefs are often downplayed or buried. Paradoxically, it is precisely these kinds of differences that *should* surface in any negotiation to enable negotiators in per-

---

[95]For a review, see Valley, Neale, & Mannix, "Friends, lovers, colleagues."

[96]Mandel, D. R. (2006). Economic transactions among friends. *Journal of Conflict Resolution, 50*(4), 584–606.

[97]Curhan, J., Neale, M., Ross, L., & Rosencranz-Engelmann, J. (in press). Relational accommodation in negotiation: Effects of egalitarianism and gender on economic efficiency and relational capital. *Organizational Behavior and Human Decision Processes.*

[98]Fry, W. R., Firestone, I. J., & Williams, D. L. (1983). Negotiation process and outcome of stranger dyads and dating couples: Do lovers lose? *Basic and Applied Social Psychology, 4,* 1–16; Thompson, L., & DeHarpport, T. (1998). Relationships, good incompatibility, and communal orientation in negotiations. *Basic and Applied Social Psychology, 20*(1), 33–44.

[99]Gelfand, M., Major, V., Raver, J., Nishi, L., & O'Brien, K. (2006). Negotiating relationally: The dynamics of the relational self in negotiations. *Academy of Management Review, 31*(2), 427–451.

[100]Harvey, J. (1974). The Abilene Paradox: The management of agreement. *Organizational Dynamics, 3*(1), 63–80.

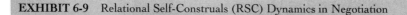

EXHIBIT 6-9   Relational Self-Construals (RSC) Dynamics in Negotiation

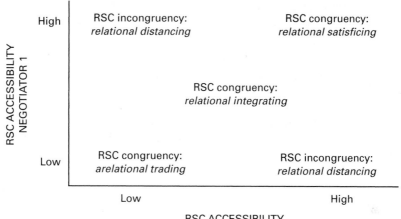

Source: Gelfand, M., Major, V., Raver, J., Nishi, L., & O'Brien, K. (2006). Negotiating relationally: The dynamics of the relational self in negotiations (Figure 2, p. 440). *Academy of Management Review, 31*(2), 427–451. Reprinted by permission.

sonal relationships to fashion value-added trade-offs and develop contingency contracts. Somehow, friends and families need a way to make their differences known so they can capitalize on them in a win-win fashion.

If We Have to Negotiate, We Should Divide It Down the Middle
When it comes to dividing the pie, friends use an **equality rule** (thereby allocating equal shares to everyone involved), whereas strangers and business associates use an **equity rule**—otherwise known as a **merit-based rule**—in which those who have contributed more are expected to receive more.[101] Unfortunately, equality norms may promote compromise agreements, thereby inhibiting the discovery of integrative trade-offs. However, norms of equality are not blindly applied by people in close relationships. For example, friends who differ in their ability and effort in a joint task will favor the less able but more diligent partner in the allocation of resources.[102] Similarly, people in communal relationships will meet others' needs, with no expectation of remuneration.[103] Equity, in which outcomes are allocated proportional to inputs, is a hallmark feature of the business world. For example, most of us do not expect to earn the same exact salary as our colleagues; we earn salaries based upon various contributions and inputs to the specific business situation. However, equity does not seem to have a legitimate role in personal relationships.

---

[101] Austin, W. (1980). Friendship and fairness: Effects of type of relationship and task performance on choice of distribution rules. *Personality and Social Psychology Bulletin, 6,* 402–408.
[102] Lamm, H., & Kayser, E. (1978). An analysis of negotiation concerning the allocation of jointly produced profit or loss: The roles of justice norms, politeness, profit maximization, and tactics. *International Journal of Group Tensions, 8,* 64–80.
[103] Clark & Mills, "Interpersonal attraction."

EXHIBIT 6-10 The Abilene Paradox

The July afternoon in Coleman, Texas (population 5,607), was particularly hot—104 degrees as measured by the Walgreen's Rexall Ex-Lax temperature gauge. In addition, the wind was blowing fine-grained West Texas topsoil through the house. But the afternoon was still tolerable—even potentially enjoyable. There was a fan going on the back porch; there was cold lemonade; and finally, there was entertainment. Dominoes. Perfect for the conditions. The game required little more physical exertion than an occasional mumbled comment, "Shuffle 'em," and an unhurried movement of the arm to place the spots in the appropriate perspective on the table. All in all, it had the markings of an agreeable Sunday afternoon in Coleman—that is, it was until my father-in-law suddenly said, "Let's get in the car and go to Abilene and have dinner at the cafeteria."

I thought, "What, go to Abilene? Fifty-three miles? In this dust storm and heat? And in an un-air-conditioned 1958 Buick?"

But my wife chimed in with "Sounds like a great idea. I'd like to go. How about you, Jerry?" Since my own preferences were obviously out of step with the rest I replied, "Sounds good to me," and added, "I just hope your mother wants to go."

"Of course I want to go," said my mother-in-law. "I haven't been to Abilene in a long time."

So into the car and off to Abilene we went. My predictions were fulfilled. The heat was brutal. We were coated with a fine layer of dust that was cemented with perspiration by the time we arrived. The food at the cafeteria provided first-rate testimonial material for antacid commercials.

Some four hours and 106 miles later we returned to Coleman, hot and exhausted. We sat in front of the fan for a long time in silence. Then, both to be sociable and to break the silence, I said, "It was a great trip, wasn't it?"

No one spoke. Finally my mother-in-law said, with some irritation, "Well, to tell the truth, I really didn't enjoy it much and would rather have stayed here. I just went along because the three of you were so enthusiastic about going. I wouldn't have gone if you all hadn't pressured me into it."

I couldn't believe it. "What do you mean 'you all'?" I said. "Don't put me in the 'you all' group. I was delighted to be doing what we were doing. I didn't want to go. I only went to satisfy the rest of you. You're the culprits."

My wife looked shocked. "Don't call me a culprit. You and Daddy and Mama were the ones who wanted to go. I just went along to be sociable and to keep you happy. I would have had to be crazy to want to go out in heat like that."

Her father entered the conversation abruptly. "Hell!" he said.

He proceeded to expand on what was already absolutely clear. "Listen, I never wanted to go to Abilene. I just thought you might be bored. You visit so seldom I wanted to be sure you enjoyed it. I would have preferred to play another game of dominoes and eat the leftovers in the icebox."

After the outburst of recrimination we all sat back in silence. Here we were, four reasonably sensible people who, of our own volition, had just taken a 106-mile trip across a godforsaken desert in a furnace-like temperature through a cloud-like dust storm to eat unpalatable food at a hole-in-the-wall cafeteria in Abilene, when none of us had really wanted to go. In fact, to be more accurate, we'd done just the opposite of what we wanted to do. The whole situation simply didn't make sense.

Source: Harvey, J. (1974). The Abilene Paradox: The management of agreement. *Organizational Dynamics, 3*(1), 63–80. Reprinted by permission of Elsevier via RightsLink.

Negotiating with Businesspeople

In contrast to friendship negotiation, businesspeople are much more likely to use an exchange norm. Exchange norms are rooted in the concept of market pricing. **Market pricing** is a method by which everything is reduced to a single value or utility metric that allows for the comparison of many qualitatively and quantitatively diverse factors.[104] Market pricing allows people to negotiate by making references to ratios of this metric, such as percentage share in a business venture. Money is the prototypical medium of market pricing relationships. Capitalism is the ultimate expression of market pricing. Market pricing can be viewed from another angle as a social influence device. In a true market pricing relationship, people will do virtually anything if offered enough money because "Everyone has his price." However, just because this approach is the predominant business mode, it does not mean people will follow it.

We Choose Our Friends, but Not Our Coworkers

Basically, we (usually) like our friends, but we do not necessarily like the people with whom we do business. Yet this generalization does not excuse us from having to negotiate and deal with them. In fact, we often must deal with people we do not like and may regard to be offensive. For example, a woman might find herself having to negotiate with a male who is a blatant sexist. It is often difficult for people to separate their feelings about someone as a person from the business at hand. (See Exhibit 6-11 for an example of an uncomfortable business relationship.)

Business Relationships Often Have Status and Rank Issues Associated with Them

Most friendships are not hierarchical, meaning that people in friendships do not have different status and rank. In contrast, businesses are generally organized around rank and status—either explicitly (e.g., an organizational chart) or implicitly (e.g., salaries, number of supervisees, office space, etc.). In one investigation, an employment negotiation was simulated: When people believed themselves to be in an "egalitarian" (equal status) relationship, they were less likely to expand the pie but liked one another more. In contrast, when people believed themselves to be in a hierarchical relationship (in which one person

---

EXHIBIT 6-11   Uncomfortable Business Relationships

Uncomfortable business relationships occur when a negotiation involves engaging in interactions that, in a personal context, would take on a different meaning and, thus, might be regarded as inappropriate. For example, consider two managers, a man and a woman, each married, who have late flights arriving in their destination city and very busy schedules, and nevertheless they need to negotiate. They agree to meet at a bar because it is the only location open late enough. However, when they arrive at the bar, the waitstaff treats them as a couple. The situation is embarrassing for the business associates because their relationship is viewed in a different way by those outside the business context than by those on the "inside." This perception has implications for the negotiation; for example, if the waitstaff presents the check to the man, it can potentially create an uncomfortable power dynamic between them. (We will discuss this further in Chapter 7.) Quite often, business opportunities are conducted in the context of social relationships. For this reason, it is difficult to form close relationships across gender lines if they are built through social activities such as playing golf, going to the theater, or meeting for dinner because these practices often have a different meaning between men and women than they do between persons of the same gender.

Source: Uzzi, B. (1997). Social structure and competition in interfirm networks: The paradox of embeddedness. *Administrative Science Quarterly, 42,* 35–67; Etzkowitz, H., Kemelgor, C., & Uzzi, B. (1999). *Social capital and career dynamics in hard science: Gender, networks, and advancement.* New York: Cambridge University Press.

---

[104]Fiske, A. P. (1992). The four elementary forms of sociality: Framework for a unified theory of social relations. *Psychological Review, 99*(4), 689–723.

had more authority), they were more likely to expand the pie but not feel as good about the relationship.[105] As we will see in Chapter 10, in some cultures, it is perfectly acceptable for members of different status and rank to meet each other at the bargaining table. However, in other cultures people find this uncomfortable and insulting.

Swift Trust

Sometimes we need to build trust with people very rapidly, on the basis of little information, and, in many cases, with no expected meaningful future interaction. For example, a temporary partnership involving the need for immediate trust was formed between auctioneer Sotheby's Holdings, Inc., and Rossi & Rossi, a London art dealer, for an exhibition and sale of Tibetan art.[106] The partnership was well-timed, as long-neglected art and objects from Tibet and the Himalayas are of interest to both collectors and buyers. This exhibition marked the first time a major auction house partnered with an independent dealer to sell artwork publicly and far away from the auction block. Normally, the auction house does not own inventory; the new partnership, though, makes Sotheby's a dealer with its own inventory to protect and push. Sotheby's offered Rossi & Rossi the use of its gallery space and promoted the show with its sizeable marketing power in return for a share of the profits from the sale.

The partnership between Sotheby's and Rossi & Rossi is an example of **swift trust**, which is the mechanism that allows people to build trust quickly.[107] Many new business relationships require that strangers come together and produce a product, service, or carry out some task and then immediately disband, perhaps never to see one another again. In contrast, our personal relationships are longer term; we have a past history with family and friends, and we expect to have future interactions with them. Business situations of the twenty-first century increasingly require swift trust, which is necessary among people who have a finite life span in a temporary system. The question is, how do we build trust with no past and no likely future? We deal with this issue in Chapter 11.

The Myth of the One-Shot Business Situation

In the business world, through its web of networked relationships, it is impossible not to experience the consequences of our interactions with others. If these consequences percolate through our business networks, then the situation is technically not a one-shot interaction. Social networks mean that even though the particular people in a business interaction may never interact or see one another again, their companies will interact again, or others in their social network will become apprised of the interaction, which will, in turn, affect the nature of future business interactions. The one-shot business situation may be a virtual impossibility.

When in Business with Friends and Family

Brothers Prestley and Curtis Blake started the Friendly Ice Cream company in 1935; however, the two brothers no longer speak. After decades of working together, Curtis began to think the company needed to spend more money to compete against rivals,

---

[105]Curhan, Neale, Ross, & Rosencranz-Engelmann, "Relational accommodation in negotiation."

[106]Bensinger, K., & Costello, D. (1999, March 19). Art and money. *Wall Street Journal*, p. W16.

[107]Meyerson, D., Weick, K. E., & Kramer, R. M. (1996). Swift trust and temporary groups. In R. M. Kramer & T. R. Tyler (Eds.), *Trust in organizations: Frontiers of theory and research* (pp. 166–195). Thousand Oaks, CA: Sage.

but Prestley was holding onto Depression-era spending habits. The fighting continued. The brothers eventually sold the company to the Hershey Company in 1979. Curtis removed himself from business dealings, while Prestley continued fighting to keep the company going. The one thing both Blake brothers agree on is the disappointment they feel that the company they started together has severed their relationship. "I'm sorry my brother isn't with me on this," Prestley said, "but I'm going to keep going because I know I'm right. I'm going to keep going until I can't go any further." According to Curtis, "I'm very disappointed. He was my best friend for 85 years. It would have been a nice story if we ended up best friends for our entire life."[108]

When friends and family do business, the relationship is more complex and is known as an **embedded relationship**. This relationship would seem to have several advantages, the most important of which is facilitating the nature of business exchange by initiating self-organizing governance arrangements that operate through expectations of trust and reciprocity, rather than expensive deterrence mechanisms.[109] Firms that embedded their bank exchanges in social attachments were more likely to have access to capital and received more favorable interest rates on loans.[110]

Another example of an embedded relationship was that between Magic Johnson (former Los Angeles Lakers' star basketball player) and Jerry Buss (the Lakers' owner). They socialized away from the basketball court and spent nearly every dinner hour together during home games. Formally, they were employer and employee: The employer would pay, and the employee would play. According to Magic Johnson, the two of them developed a relationship outside of their formal business because "he saw me as one of his kids."[111] Says Johnson, "That's why I've never negotiated with him. . . . We never had a negotiation. He said, 'I want to give you this.' I said, 'OK.' He said, 'I want you to coach this team.' I said, 'OK.' It's been like that. It's no contract, you just say, 'OK.' That's how we have it." Buss calls Johnson his hero; Johnson calls Buss his surrogate father.

However, pitfalls to an embedded relationship can also happen. We describe some of them next.

The Emotional Potential Is Higher

When business and friendship combine, the emotional potential can often be overwhelming, and interpersonal conflict can result. For example, if someone has a poor exchange with a neighbor that leaves the friendship in question, it is quite disturbing, but the person can at least travel to work knowing the situation is "contained." Similarly, a person may have a terrible day at work and still be able to go home that evening to take solace in friends and family. Somehow, the separation of work and friendship creates a "buffer zone" for the parties involved. However, when things go awry in an embedded relationship during the course of negotiation, all systems can potentially fail. Consider the Maritz Company, which suffered through three generations of

---

[108]Abelson, J. (2007, March 18). Feuding over Friendly's New England ice cream institution beset by corporate, sibling rivalries. *Boston Globe*, p. A1.
[109]Uzzi, B. (1999). Embeddedness in the making of financial capital: How social relations and networks benefit firms seeking financing. *American Sociological Review, 64*(4), 481–505.
[110]Ibid.
[111]Howard-Cooper, S. (1996, April 23). The odd couple: From beginning, friendship between Buss, Johnson has transcended usual relationship between owner, player. *Los Angeles Times*, p. 1.

feuding.[112] Before Bill Maritz passed away, he wrote at the end of his memoir, "I still find it virtually impossible to understand and accept the lack of respect and feeling my two sons, Peter and Flip, have shown me." Their mother, Phyllis Maritz said, "It would be my greatest hope to see the company sold and out of the family forever. Then perhaps the family could heal." Similarly at the National Association for Stock Car Racing (NASCAR), a contract negotiation escalated into a family feud filled with both personal and public attacks and a malicious fight over control. The clash between Dale Earnhardt Jr. and his stepmother, Teresa Earnhardt, stemmed in part from the death of Dale Earnhardt, who was killed in a crash on the final lap of the 2001 Daytona 500. "The main factor is the ownership part," Earnhardt Jr. said. "It has nothing to do with money and nothing else, really. My father has been gone almost six years now. I want majority ownership." But in 2006, Teresa Earnhardt criticized her stepson publicly. "Right now the ball's in his court to decide on whether he wants to be a NASCAR driver or whether he wants to be a public personality," she said. Earnhardt responded by making scornful remarks about his stepmother and their relationship during a news conference.[113]

Internal Value Conflict

Personal relationships are driven by people's need for acceptance, love, and identity, whereas business relationships are generally guided by a need for achievement and utilitarian goals. In embedded relationships, people often experience more internal value conflict because competence and liking are at battle with one another. For example, we may find someone to be a delightful friend, a wonderful and empathic listener, and a good person with whom to spend time; however, this person may be incompetent at the business task at hand. Conversely, the person who is more competent may be annoying to us. The question is, which of these factors do we respond to in the situation: competence or liking?

Myopia

We have seen that embedded relationships can often reduce the costs associated with surveillance. However, embedded relationships may create myopia if people are reluctant to move beyond their own networks. At the extreme, imagine a cliquish network in which people engage only in business matters with their friends. This interaction may eventually result in a myopic view of reality, if people within the network are biased in their perceptions and not connected to others who may have more or better information. These are **sticky ties**—relationships that emanate from ingrained habits of past social interaction.[114] Most people are reluctant to turn to new, untried partners for information, resources, and the variety of interactions that are required in organizations.

Bottom Line on Relationships

Virtually all of the relationships a person has fit into one of the three types we have described: friendship, pure business, or business friends. How can a negotiator assess the quality of the relationship he or she has with a given person? As a start, you can consider where your relationship stands on each of the dimensions listed in Exhibit 6-12. If

[112]Bailey, "A CEO's legacy."

[113]Bernstein, V. (2007, February 11). Simmering family feud clouds future of team and its namesake. *New York Times*, p. SP10.

[114]Valley, K. L., & Thompson, T. A. (1998). Sticky ties and bad attitudes: Relational and individual bases of resistance to change in organizational structure. In Kramer, R. M., & Neale, M. A. (Eds.), *Power and influence in organizations* (pp. 39–66). Thousand Oaks, CA: Sage.

EXHIBIT 6-12   Summary of Dyadic Dimensions Along Which Relationships Develop

From	*To*
Openness and Self Disclosure	
Limited to "safe," socially acceptable topics	Disclosure goes beyond safe areas to include personally sensitive, private, and controversial topics and aspects of self
Knowledge of Each Other	
Surface, "biographic" knowledge: Impressionistic in nature	Knowledge is multifaceted and extends to core aspects of personality, needs, and style
Predictability of Other's Reactions and Responses	
Limited to socially expected or role-related responses, and those based on first impressions or repeated surface encounters	Predictability of the other's reactions extends beyond stereotypical exchange and includes a knowledge of the contingencies affecting the other's reactions
Uniqueness of Interaction	
Exchanges are stereotypical, guided by prevailing social norms or role expectations	Exchanges are idiosyncratic to the two people, guided by norms that are unique to the relationship
Multimodality of Communication	
Largely limited to verbal channels of communication and stereotypical or unintended nonverbal channels	Includes multiple modalities of communication, including nonverbal and verbal "shorthands" specific to the relationship or the individuals involved; less restrictiveness of nonverbal
Substitutability of Communication	
Little substitution among alternative modes of communication	Possession of and ability to use alternative modes of communication to convey the same message
Capacity for Conflict and Evaluation	
Limited capacity for conflict; use of conflict-avoidance techniques; reluctance to criticize	Readiness and ability to express conflict and make positive or negative evaluations
Spontaneity of Exchange	
Interactions tend to be formal or "comfortably informal" as prescribed by prevailing social norms	Greater informality and ease of interaction; movement across topical areas occurs readily and without hesitation or formality; communication flows and changes direction easily
Synchronization and Pacing	
Except for stereotyped modes of response, limited dyadic synchrony occurs	Speech and nonverbal responses become synchronized; flow of interaction is smooth; cues are quickly and accurately interpreted
Efficiency of Communication	
Communication of intended meanings sometimes requires extensive discussion; misunderstandings occur unless statements are qualified or elaborated	Intended meanings are transmitted and understood rapidly, accurately, and with sensitivity to nuance
Mutual Investment	
Little investment in the other except in areas of role-related or situation interdependencies	Extensive investment in other's well-being and efficacy

Source: Adapted from Galegher, J., Kraut, R. E., & Egido, C. (1990). *Intellectual teamwork: Social and technological foundations of cooperative work*. Mahwah, NJ: Erlbaum.

the majority of the dimensions of your relationship are listed on the right-hand side, an effective relationship has developed.

CONCLUSION

Personal value, which includes goodwill, trust, and respect, is just as important as economic value. Establishing trust and building relationships are essential for effective negotiation. The three types of "trust" relationships discussed in this chapter include deterrence-based trust (based on sanctions and monitoring), knowledge-based trust (based on predictability and information), and identification-based trust (based on true empathy). Trust-building and trust-repairing strategies include transforming personal conflict into task conflict, agreeing on a common goal, capitalizing on network connections, recognizing a shared problem, and focusing on the future. Psychological strategies that often engender trust include similarity, mere exposure, physical presence, reciprocity, schmoozing, flattery, and self-disclosure. And the three common types of relationships in negotiation are business only, friendship only, and multiplex relationships that involve both.

CHAPTER

Power, Persuasion, and Ethics

7

Lenoir, a quiet town in western North Carolina, seemed an unlikely place for a leading high-tech company on the Web. Lenoir had stumbled out from the loss of more than 2,000 jobs because of the closure of seven furniture factories. Yet, Lenoir had just about everything that Google wanted: lots of inexpensive land, access to cheap electricity, huge and faultless warehouses, and excess water capacity for cooling off computers. By playing an aggressive real estate game, Google elicited a stream of promises from local and state officials, all frantic to lure a mighty tech company. During long months of negotiations, Google never failed to remind those officials that it could go elsewhere. In the end, Lenoir agreed to a package of tax breaks, infrastructure upgrades, and other prospects valued at $212 million over 30 years, or more than $1 million for each of the 210 jobs Google hoped to create in Lenoir. However, many people felt bullied by the tactics used by the out-of-town technology giant. "It's simply unconscionable from an ethics standpoint for this company to go in from this very unfair bargaining position," said Robert F. Orr, a former North Carolina Supreme Court justice. "These are business decisions by the smartest businesspeople in the world, and it's just exploiting a desperate town." "There were 18 or 20 drafts of contracts, a lot of ticky-tacky stuff," said T. J. Rohr, an attorney and member of Lenoir's city council (who voted against the final deal), "And a lot of the time it seemed like they were saying, 'It's our way or the highway.'"[1]

The Google example suggests that negotiators often attempt to get as much of the pie as possible. Negotiators who have power are in position to claim the lion's share of the pie. Negotiators should be aware of the two ways the power and persuasion strategies in this chapter can be read. One way is to read it as the *holder* of power. However, negotiators who read this book must be aware that the *counterparty* is reading this or another book; therefore, every strategy and tactic in this chapter could (and probably will) be used against you by the counterparty. Thus, it is important to remember

---

[1]Byrnes, N., & Cowan, C. (2007, July 23). The high cost of wooing Google; states and cities are dangling ever-bigger inducements to attract companies, and the digital giant knows how to drive a hard bargain. *Business Week, 4043,* 50–57.

the "fraternal twin" model that we introduced in Chapter 1. At relevant points in this chapter, we present "defense strategies" that negotiators can use to deal with a source of power or a persuasion tactic employed by the other party during the course of negotiation.

YOUR BATNA IS YOUR MOST IMPORTANT SOURCE OF POWER IN NEGOTIATION

When negotiators have a great BATNA, they have a lot of power. Because negotiators are not willing to settle for less than the value of their BATNA, they can hold out for a greater share of resources. Consider how basketball coach Brenda Oldfield used her BATNA (an offer from Maryland) to leverage an offer from her Minnesota position.[2] When asked what Maryland could offer that Minnesota couldn't, Oldfield responded, "They're offering me more money in three years than I'd make in Minnesota in seven years."[3] Unfortunately, most of the time, people do not have a great BATNA. For this reason, it is imperative that negotiators cultivate and improve their BATNAs prior to negotiating:

- *Keep your options open.*   Your BATNA may be great now, but as we have noted, BATNAs are always changing. Thus, it is important to keep your options open even after you have come to the negotiation table because negotiations could break down for a variety of reasons at any point prior to mutual settlement. For example, the couple who made an offer on your home may retract the offer following an inspection. Consider how NBC kept its options open in negotiations with Bay Area TV station KRON in 2002.[4] For several years, KRON was the carrier of NBC programming in the Bay Area. However, in 2002 NBC looked at an alternative station, KNTV. Interestingly, it was KNTV owners who had been following the feud between NBC and KRON and saw an opportunity. Moreover, KNTV suggested that it pay NBC to make the switch to its station—an unusual form of reverse compensation.
- *Signal your BATNA, but do not reveal it.*   Negotiators often get seduced into revealing their BATNA, but the minute they do, the cat is out of the bag. On the other hand, if the counterparty does not believe you actually have a BATNA, you should signal that you have options, without revealing their exact value. However, alluding to options you do not actually have is **misrepresentation**, which is unethical. It is not misrepresentation to signal to the other party that you have alternative courses of action (if you actually do). In the NBC–KRON negotiations, KRON mistakenly thought that NBC was bluffing about its alternative (KNTV). Thus, when NBC approached KRON—saying "This is the last chance you have, take it or leave it. Pay us $10 million or no deal."—KRON responded by putting out a press release saying it was no longer an NBC affiliate. However, NBC was surprised and said, "We're not finished [negotiating]." Five days later, NBC struck a deal with KNTV.
- *Assess the other party's BATNA.*   It pays to research the other party's BATNA as best you can. Negotiators who even *think* about the counterparty's BATNA do better in terms

---

[2]Schmid, P. (2002, April 1). Director: Oldfield planning to leave, AAU official says "U" coach to move on. *Star-Tribune,* p. 1C.
[3]Ibid., para 13.
[4]Fost, D. (2002, January 13). How NBC, KRON deal fell apart: Animosity, mistrust colored negotiations. *San Francisco Chronicle,* p. G1.

of slicing the pie than those who don't.[5] Do not leave any stone unturned when attempting to assess the counterparty's BATNA. Start your research well before the negotiation begins. Do not wait until you get to the negotiation table: The cues are harder to detect because most negotiators will not reveal their BATNAs. In the NBC example, KRON did not adequately assess NBC's BATNA. They assumed it was worse than it actually was and, thus, no deal was struck. Spend some time before negotiation assessing current data (if you have them), previous years' data, current market trends—anything you can get. Also, use multiple sources. Your investment into researching the other party's BATNA is time well spent. For example, in the 2003 negotiations between the Pentagon and Boeing to lease 100 767 aircraft, the Pentagon had an excellent assessment of Boeing's poor BATNA. It was well-known that commercial orders for the 767 had dried up, and many believed that without the Pentagon contract, Boeing would shut down the 767 production line in Everett, Washington. Lawmakers conjectured the contract would provide 2,500 jobs at Boeing and 8,000 related jobs. Not surprisingly, Boeing made major concessions to close the deal: The price of each plane was negotiated at $131 million, which was $17 million less than Boeing's opening offer ($148 million). Moreover, Boeing had to guarantee that if it sold a tanker to another country for less than $131 million, it would provide a rebate to the United States.[6]

SOURCES OF POWER

We've discussed power in negotiation as stemming primarily from a negotiator's alternative to a negotiated agreement. In addition to a negotiator's BATNA, other possible sources of power are present in negotiation, such as the contribution a negotiator makes to a negotiation.[7] When you bring resources to a negotiation and the other party puts a high value on those resources, your contribution is great. When the bargaining zone is small, BATNAs exert a stronger effect on resource allocation than do contributions; however when the bargaining zone is large, contributions exert a stronger effect than do BATNAs.[8]

ANALYZING YOUR POWER

Power in a negotiation can be analyzed in terms of four vantage points: potential power, perceived power, power tactics, and realized power.[9] A negotiator's **potential power** is the underlying capacity of the negotiator to obtain benefits from an agreement.[10] It is a function of the counterparty's dependence on you. How much someone depends on you in a negotiation is based upon how much he or she values the resources you provide and the value of the alternatives to negotiating with you. **Perceived power** is a negotiator's assessment of each party's potential power, which may or may not square

---

[5]Galinsky, A., & Mussweiler, T. (2001). First offers as anchors: The role of perspective-taking and negotiator focus. *Journal of Personality and Social Psychology, 81*(4), 657–669.
[6]Pope, C. (2003, May 24). Boeing lands major deal. *Seattle Post-Intelligencer,* p. A1.
[7]Kim, P., & Fragale, A. (2005). Choosing the path to bargaining power: An empirical comparison of BATNAs and contributions in negotiation. *Journal of Applied Psychology, 90*(2), 373–381.
[8]Ibid.
[9]Kim, P., Pinkley, R., & Fragale, A. (2005). Power dynamics in negotiation. *Academy of Management Review, 30*(4), 799–822.
[10]Ibid.

with reality. Whereas a negotiator's alternatives affect the distribution of outcomes, perceived power, as well as actual alternatives, affect the integrativeness of outcomes.[11] **Power tactics** comprise what's commonly studied in negotiation behavior and refer to the behaviors designed to use or change the power relationship. **Realized power** is the extent to which negotiators claim benefits from an interaction.

PERSUASION TACTICS

You do not necessarily have to have power to be persuasive. We identify techniques negotiators can use to induce attitude and behavior change in their opponents. However, we need to caution negotiators that power also can be used against them as well.

Two desires are especially important in negotiation: the need to be liked and approved of, and the need to be rational and accurate. Savvy negotiators prey upon people's need to be approved of and respected by others and their need to believe they are rational and logical. Next, we identify two primary routes to persuasion that tap into these two needs.

Two Routes to Persuasion

The two routes to persuasion roughly correspond to our distinction between the mind and heart of the negotiator.[12] The first route is called the **central route** to persuasion. It is direct, mindful, and information-based. Here, activities such as evaluating the strength or rationality of the counterparty's argument and deciding whether its content agrees or disagrees with a negotiator's beliefs tend to occur. When the counterparty's messages are processed via this central route, persuasion will occur to the extent that the arguments presented by a negotiator are convincing and the facts marshaled on their behalf are strong ones. The central route is ideal when dealing with analytical people who focus on information, facts, and data.

The other route is the **peripheral route** to persuasion. In contrast to the central route, little cognitive or mindful work is performed when attempting to persuade someone via the peripheral route. Rather, persuasion, when it occurs, involves a seemingly automatic response to various cues. Typically, the cues relating to a person's prestige, credibility, or likeability are the ones that will be successful when navigating the peripheral route. Persuasion is more likely to occur through the peripheral route when the negotiator is distracted or highly emotionally involved in the situation.

In the next sections, we deal with tactics that can be used via the central route and via the peripheral route. Again, we caution negotiators that all of these tactics can and probably will be used against them at some time in their negotiation career. Therefore, when describing each of these tactics, we indicate a defense strategy a negotiator can use if he or she suspects a particular tactic is being used against him or her. The best defensive system is awareness of these tactics and excellent preparation prior to entering into a negotiation.

---

[11]Wolfe, R., & McGinn, K. (2005). Perceived relative power and its influence on negotiations. *Group Decision and Negotiation, 14,* 3–20.
[12]Chaiken, S., Wood, W., & Eagly, A. H. (1996). Principles of persuasion. In E. T. Higgins & A. W. Kruglanski (Eds.), *Social psychology: Handbook of basic principles* (pp. 702–742). New York: Guilford Press.

Central Route Persuasion Tactics

Central route persuasion tactics involve rational and deliberate strategies that can be used to organize the content and flow of information during a negotiation.

The Power of Agenda

In a negotiation, players explicitly or implicitly follow an agenda. Most commonly, negotiators discuss the issues in a one-by-one, "laundry list" fashion. Negotiations often involve a discussion of who will control the agenda. Tom Smerling, Washington director of the Israel Policy Forum, a group that supports an active U.S. role in Middle East peace talks, notes that virtually every international negotiation starts with a quarrel over the agenda.[13]

As we indicated when discussing integrative negotiation in Chapter 4, we strongly dissuade negotiators from considering issues one at a time. Rather, it is through the **packaging of issues** that integrative opportunities can be discovered. Nevertheless, the savvy negotiator may use the power of agenda not only to expand the pie but also to slice the pie in a manner favorable to himself or herself. The negotiator who lays out the issues in a way that reflects his or her own priorities may be more likely to achieve gains on his or her high-priority issues.

Defense   It is a good idea to discuss what may seem to be an implicit or unspoken agenda (e.g., "I get the sense that you have an agenda of how you would like to cover the issues. I would like to hear your ideas and then tell you mine. Maybe we can come up with an agenda that makes sense for both of us, after hearing each other out.").

The Power of Alternatives

Negotiators who generate several alternatives for each issue may have a bargaining advantage because they formulate alternatives that benefit themselves. Obviously, an infinite number of alternatives may be possible for any given bargaining situation; the savvy negotiator will specify alternatives that are most favorable to himself or herself. Consider a software development deal between two of the fiercest rivals in the industry: Apple and Microsoft. Both companies stunned the world in 1997 with Microsoft buying a $150 million stake in Apple and making a 5-year software development deal to release new versions of Microsoft Office for the Mac. In return, Apple agreed to replace Netscape with Internet Explorer. However, power plays lurked below the surface. Ben Waldman, head of Microsoft's Macintosh development group, sent an e-mail to Bill Gates explaining that Mac Office was a stick Microsoft could use against Apple. "The threat to cancel Mac Office 97 is certainly the strongest bargaining point we have, as doing so will do a great deal of harm to Apple immediately. I also believe that Apple is taking this threat pretty seriously." Not surprisingly, Mac users called the deal "a marriage made in hell."[14]

Defense   You do not need to be too much on the defensive if the counterparty is laying out the alternatives. This factor is helpful for you in trying to assess the counterparty's needs and interests. Make sure that you have thought about your own alternatives, and get those on the table.

---

[13]Slavin, B. (2000, January 5). Negotiators clear first bump in Middle East talks. *USA Today,* p. 6A.
[14]Keizer, G. (2007, May). Office for Mac was almost no more. *Macworld, 24*(5).

The Power of Options

In our chapter on integrative bargaining (Chapter 4), we strongly advocated that negotiators generate several options, all of equal value to themselves. The negotiator who generates options is at a power advantage in the negotiation.

Defense If you find the counterparty suggesting several options, it is actually good news because it suggests that your opponent is not a positional negotiator. However, make sure that you do not offer unilateral concessions. The best way to avoid making unilateral concessions is to generate several options to present to the other party.

Attitudinal Structuring

If a negotiator suspects that the counterparty has an uncertain or unspecified BATNA, he or she can influence the opponent's perception of his or her BATNA. Thus, a negotiator may manipulate the counterparty into revealing his or her BATNA.

Defense The best strategy to use when the counterparty attempts to manipulate your BATNA is to research your BATNA and develop your reservation price before negotiating. Oftentimes, negotiators can be manipulated into revealing their BATNA when an opponent makes the assumption that the negotiator's BATNA is weak. Consider the following interchange between negotiators:

NEGOTIATOR A: You know, it is really a buyer's market out there. I would strongly suggest that you think about my offer [on your house] before you turn it down. There may not be any more buyers for a while.

NEGOTIATOR B: Actually, I have received a lot of interest on my house.

NEGOTIATOR A: In this market? That does not sound very likely to me. In fact, my sister is selling her house, and she has not had an offer yet.

NEGOTIATOR B: Actually, just last week, a buyer from out of state saw my house and said he would most likely make an offer of $230,000 this week. You can ask my agent about it, if you do not believe me.

NEGOTIATOR A: That is so interesting. Just last night my husband and I decided that we would most likely offer $231,000 for your house. Imagine that!

From this interchange, we see negotiator A was successful in getting negotiator B to reveal her BATNA by challenging it.

The Power of Contrast

Negotiators may often invent irrelevant alternatives for the counterparty to consider. The negotiator who proposes these irrelevant alternatives knows the other party will find them unacceptable, but these alternatives create a **psychological contrast effect**. To understand how the contrast effect works, consider the behavior of some real estate agents.[15] Agents who want a prospective buyer to make an offer on a house may show the buyer several houses. They arrange a house-showing day during which they first show the prospective buyer some "doghouses" that may have been on the market for several months because they are extremely unattractive or overpriced. The buyer may become somewhat depressed at the sight of these houses or at the high price tags they carry.

---

[15]Cialdini, R. B. (1993). *Influence: Science and practice.* New York: HarperCollins.

At this point, the agent will show the buyer the houses he or she wants the buyer to seriously consider. This tactic creates a psychological contrast effect because the potential buyer will view these houses much more favorably than the more dilapidated, overpriced alternatives and will be more motivated to make an offer. In negotiation, contrast is often used when the counterparty makes an extreme initial offer and then follows with an offer that appears more reasonable. Acceptance rates of the second offer are higher when it follows the initial extreme offer.

Defense   The best defense against the contrast effect is to set a well-formed target point prior to negotiation. For example, the prospective home buyer should research the market enough to realize what value is available. Negotiators should avoid making premature concessions (i.e., concessions they make before they have tried to get what they want.)

Commitment and Consistency

The **consistency principle** describes the human need to be consistent in our beliefs, feelings, and behaviors. To contradict ourselves, whether in thought or in deed, is a sign of irrationality. Thus, savvy negotiators will often attempt to get a verbal commitment from the counterparty.

What are the implications of the consistency principle for the negotiator? If a negotiator agrees to something (e.g., a particular set of terms, etc.), he or she is motivated to behave in a fashion consistent with his or her verbal commitment. A common bargaining ploy of salespeople is to ask customers about their intentions to buy (e.g., "Are you ready to buy a car today at the right price?"). Most people would agree to this statement because it does not obligate them to buy a particular car. However, powerful psychological commitment processes begin to operate once we acknowledge ourselves to be a "buyer."

Defense   Be careful what you agree to in a negotiation. If a car seller asks whether you are ready to buy a car, do not immediately say "Yes!" but, rather, "That depends on the terms."

Framing Effects: Capitalizing on the Half-Full or Half-Empty Glass

As we saw in Chapter 2, people are risk-averse for gains and risk-seeking when it comes to losses. Recall that the **reference point** defines what a person considers to be the status quo from which gains and losses are evaluated. Savvy negotiators know if they want to induce the counterparty to maintain the status quo—that is, induce risk aversion or conservatism—they should present options as gains relative to a reference point. Similarly, if they want to induce change, they frame choices as losses.

Defense   Determine your reference point prior to entering into a negotiation to avoid being "framed."

Fairness Heuristics: Capitalizing on Egocentric Bias

Fairness is a hot button in negotiation. To the extent that negotiators characterize their offer as "fair," they increase the likelihood that it will be accepted by the other party. However, multiple indexes and measures of fairness exist.

Defense   Be aware of the many rules of fairness (e.g., equity, equality, and need). When an opponent puts forth a fairness ploy, be ready to present a counterargument that is favorable to and consistent with your own perceptions of fairness (see Chapter 3).

Time Pressure

Common intuition states that the negotiator who is under the most time pressure is at a disadvantage in a negotiation. Whereas it is true that the negotiator who needs to come to an agreement more quickly (because his or her BATNA may deteriorate with time) is at a disadvantage, time limits may be an advantage for the negotiator.[16]

Defense　Remember that the party who has the deadline in effect sets the deadline for the other party. Set a limit on how long you will negotiate. A final deadline limits the potential time-related costs. If you face a final deadline, whether or not you set it yourself, make sure those with whom you are negotiating know about the time constraint it puts on them. If they want any deal at all, they will have to come up with an agreement before the deadline.[17]

Peripheral Route Persuasion Tactics

The strategies we describe next work through a fundamentally different mechanism: people's inherent need to be liked, approved of, and respected by others. The negotiator who uses the following strategies manipulates the counterparty's sense of his or her own identity and, through these strategies, attempts to change the counterparty's behavior. Marshaling defense strategies is more difficult in the case of peripheral route persuasion tactics because they often catch us off guard. A good defense is an awareness of common strategies.

Status

Two types of status are relevant in most negotiation situations: primary status characteristics and secondary status characteristics. **Primary status characteristics** refer to indicators of legitimate authority; for example, a person's rank within an organization, the number of supervisees in that person's unit, and a person's various titles and degrees all denote primary status. The impact of status on the conduct of bargaining can be quite enormous. High-status individuals talk more, even when they do not necessarily know more. A high-status person will also generally control when he or she speaks in a conversation. Furthermore, a low-status person will defer to the high-status person in terms of turn-taking in the conversation. These factors can affect pie-slicing in a negotiation. Norm Brodsky, a veteran entrepreneur, reflecting on the terminated sale of his businesses to Nova Records Management, said, "Make sure you know how the buyer makes decisions and who the ultimate decision maker is. Ironically, I've long prided myself on my ability to identify that individual in any negotiation. I sure blew it this time. I thought Nova's board had the final say, but it actually belonged to one board member who had veto power over the board's decisions. I would have known that if I'd asked enough questions in the beginning."[18]

When primary status cues (such as rank and stature in an organization) are absent, or when people of equal status negotiate, people often pay attention to **secondary status characteristics**, which are cues and characteristics that have no legitimate bearing on the allocation of resources or on the norms of interaction, but nevertheless they

---

[16]Moore, D. A. (2004). The unexpected benefits of final deadlines in negotiation. *Journal of Experimental Social Psychology, 40,* 121–127.

[17]Ibid.

[18]Brodsky, N. (2007, July). The offer, part nine. *Inc.*, *29*(7), 59–61.

exert a powerful influence on behavior. Secondary status characteristics are also known as **pseudostatus characteristics** and include sex, age, ethnicity, status in other groups, and cultural background. The three most common secondary status characteristics are gender, age, and race. Men have more influence than women; older people have more influence than younger people; and white people have more influence than black people when it comes to interpersonal interaction.[19] Typically, pseudostatus characteristics are highly visible. Although they have nothing to do with ability, people act as if they do.

Status cues operate quickly, often within minutes after negotiators are seated at the bargaining table. Pseudostatus characteristics should not, in any normative or rational sense, exert an effect on the negotiation; however, they often do. Furthermore, even when a negotiator does not regard these pseudostatus cues to be significant (or even rejects them outright), if someone else at the bargaining table considers them significant, it creates a **self-fulfilling prophesy**.

Gender

Because gender is a secondary status characteristic, it is worth exploring the question of how men and women fare at the bargaining table. Across the board, men are more successful than women in terms of pie-slicing—they inevitably get a bigger slice.[20] When negotiators believe a negotiation simulation is diagnostic of their true negotiation ability, men do even better. Apparently, highly successful female managers from major companies, get tripped up because of the pervasive cultural stereotype that "women are docile." Even though the successful females in our investigation were anything but docile, the mere knowledge that this stereotype about women exists was enough to form a mental roadblock in the negotiations. However, if the cultural stereotype about women was positioned more prominently, perhaps women would be able to attack it mentally. Consequently, when we created a simulation in which the classic female stereotype was explicitly mentioned, the tide turned. Highly competent female MBA students not only actively dismissed the stereotype, but they also claimed more of the pie than did their fellow male MBA students. The message? Stereotypes that lurk below the surface have a way of creeping into the subconscious recesses of our minds and interfering negatively with our performance. By exposing those negative stereotypes—getting them out in the open and then attacking them mentally—women can do much better. This effect is even stronger when people want to make a good impression on others. In one investigation, men and women in high-status roles responded to impression motivation in a way that contradicted classic gender stereotypes: Men actually became more docile, and women responded by acting more assertively.[21]

These results gave us the idea of completely turning the stereotype of women on its head: We created a negotiation simulation in which we clearly told the male and female MBA students that success in negotiation requires people skills—listening, verbal

[19]Mazur, A. (1985). A biosocial model of status in face-to-face groups. *Social Forces, 64,* 377–402.
[20]Kray, L., Thompson, L., & Galinsky, A. (2001). Battle of the sexes: Gender stereotype confirmation and reactance in negotiations. *Journal of Personality and Social Psychology, 80*(6), 942–958; Kray, L., Galinsky, A., & Thompson, L. (2002). Reversing the gender gap in negotiations: An exploration of stereotype regeneration. *Organizational Behavior and Human Decision Processes, 87*(2), 386–409.
[21]Curhan, J., & Overbeck, J. (2008). Making a positive impression in a negotiation: Gender differences in response to impression motivation. *Negotiation and Conflict Management Research, 1*(2), 179–193.

EXHIBIT 7-1 The Verbal and Nonverbal Skills of Power

Madeleine Korbel Albright served as the first female secretary of state in U.S. history and at that time was also the highest-ranking woman ever to serve in the executive branch of government. The tough-talking, wisecracking, former Georgetown University professor sought the job and accepted it eagerly, making no pretense of reluctance and offering no sham modesty about her stellar credentials. During her reign as secretary of state, "Last Word" Albright compiled an impressive list of powerful accomplishments: She forged an alliance that finally faced down Serb aggression in the Balkans and held it together during the war, and she did it without a total rupture with Moscow. At the same time, she kept the Israeli–Palestinian peace negotiations from falling apart completely while Benjamin Netanyahu was prime minister so that Netanyahu's successor, Ehud Barak, could build on a foundation that was still intact. She nursed the relationship with China and opened the door to better relations with Iran. Her secret to power? "Interrupt!" At least that is the advice she gives to young women: "Don't wait for men to solicit your input" (p. 1736). And she walks the talk: In her course at Georgetown, she instituted a no-hand-raising rule because she believes that if students are told to raise their hands before speaking, women will do so but men will not. Her successes with the variety of people she has dealt with reveal her remarkable persuasive skills and her bargaining power.

Source: Based on Robinson, Lewicki & Donahue (2000), Extending and Testing a Five Factor model of Ethical and Unethical Bargaining Tactics: Introducing the SINS Scale. Journal of Organizational Behavior, 21, 649-664.

---

prowess, nonverbal acumen, and so on—all the elements of the classic female stereotype. Sure enough, women performed better under these conditions.[22] The key conclusion is that if a task (such as negotiation) can be positively linked to your own gender stereotype, you can perform better. (See also Exhibit 7-1 for an example of how a powerful female leader has leveraged her role.)

The greater the amount of situational ambiguity in a given situation, the more a negotiation will be affected by gender.[23] In short, when a situation is uncertain or ambiguous, people are prompted to respond on the basis of their gender.

Social Networks

Whereas information power in a negotiation refers to the power associated with *what* you know, network power refers to the power associated with *who* you know. **Social capital** is the power that results from managers' access to other people within and outside of their organization. Social capital is a value that comes from who, when, and how to coordinate through various contacts within and beyond the organization. Mark Isakowitz acts as a negotiator-mediator for businesspeople who want to influence Capitol Hill. The Federation of American Hospitals sought his negotiation skills to kill a Medicare bill. The legislation was supported by high-ranking Republicans, so

---

[22]Kray, Galinsky, & Thompson, "Reversing the gender gap."
[23]Bowles, H., Babcock, L., & McGinn, K. (2005). Constraints and triggers: Situational mechanics of gender in negotiation. *Journal of Personality and Social Psychology, 89*(6), 951–965; Bowles, H., & McGinn, K. (2005). Claiming authority: Negotiating challenges for women leaders. In D. Messick & R. Kramer (Eds.), *The psychology of leadership: New perspectives and research,* (pp. 191-208). Mahwah, NJ: Erlbaum; Pradel, D., Bowles, H., & McGinn, K. (2005, November). When does gender matter in negotiation? *Negotiation,* 3–5.

Isakowitz used networks of a higher order—the party's leadership—to prevent the bill's passage. One day, he staked out the busy crossroads on the second floor of the Capitol between the Rotunda and the door to the House. Standing there, he was guaranteed to spot then–Majority Leader Tom DeLay (R-Texas) and Whip Roy Blunt (R-Missouri). When they appeared, he issued his threat: The hospital industry had produced TV ads that would label as an enemy of health care any lawmaker supporting the bill. The group was willing to spend $4 million to air commercials, and Isakowitz was willing to give them a demo tape right on the spot. The Republicans declined the tape but accepted his threat. Within weeks, the Ways and Means committee killed the Medicare decrease. Hospital stocks stabilized, and the commercials never aired. Such is the power of networks and social capital.[24]

You don't have to be a Capitol Hill lobbyist to leverage social networks. Managers with more social capital get higher returns on their human capital because they are positioned to identify and develop more rewarding opportunities.[25] Negotiators with high network power are those who act as **boundary spanners** by bridging functional gaps in organizations and units. In other words, they are the critical link between people who otherwise would not be in contact. As boundary spanners, they fill a unique spot within the organizational network by bringing together people, knowledge, and information that would not otherwise be brought together. A negotiator's position as a unique link in a network of relationships means that he or she can broker more opportunities than can other members of the network who do not represent unique links within the organization and beyond. Furthermore, negotiators who are boundary spanners are in a position to make or break opportunities for other people. Negotiators who act as boundary spanners broker the flow of information between people and control information. Negotiators who bridge gaps are the people who know about, have a hand in, and exercise more control over rewarding opportunities. They have broader access to information because of their diverse contacts. This access means they are more often aware of new opportunities and have easier access to these opportunities than do their peers—even their peers of equivalent or greater human capital. For this reason, they are also more likely to be discussed as suitable candidates for inclusion in new opportunities and are more likely to be able to display their capabilities because they have more control over the substance of their work, defined by relationships with subordinates, superiors, and colleagues.

Physical Appearance

Physically attractive people are more effective in getting what they want than are less physically attractive people, independent of their actual skills. And the work produced by allegedly attractive people is more highly valued than that produced by less-attractive people. In one investigation, men evaluated an essay with a photo of the supposed author attached—either an attractive or an unattractive woman (as judged by an independent group of people).[26] Even though the essays were identical, men's judgments of the essays were strongly affected by how attractive the woman in each picture was: The

---

[24]Birnbaum, J. (2003, August 11). The persuaders. *Fortune, 148*(3)121–124.
[25]Burt, R. S. (1992). *The social structure of competition.* Cambridge, MA: Harvard University Press.
[26]For a review, see Feingold, A. (1992). Good-looking people are not what we think. *Psychological Bulletin, 111*(2), 304–341.

more attractive the person in the photo, the better the grade given.[27] People think attractive people are more talented, kind, honest, and intelligent than unattractive people.[28] As a consequence, attractive people are more persuasive in terms of changing attitudes[29] and getting what they want.[30] Physical attractiveness has a favorable impact on sales effectiveness[31] and on income levels across a wide range of occupations.[32] (Attractiveness is usually achieved through dress and grooming in most of these investigations.)

The benefits of attractiveness carry through to the negotiation table. Consistent with the idea of a "beauty premium," attractive people are offered more money, but also more is demanded of them.[33]

The evaluation of an employment applicant can be affected by physical attractiveness as well.[34] Attractive people are evaluated more positively and are treated better than unattractive people. Attractive communicators and salespeople are more effective in changing other people's attitudes than unattractive ones.[35] For this reason, sales campaigns often feature an attractive person selling a product or service. Attractive people are often presumed to have other positive qualities as well; for example, they are regarded to be more poised, interesting, sociable, independent, dominant, exciting, sexy, well-adjusted, socially skilled, and successful than unattractive persons.[36] This attribution of positive qualities to attractive people is part of the **halo effect** described in Chapter 6. The underlying message: Be aware of how your judgment (and others') is affected by physical appearance.

Delayed Liking

Should you show your liking for the other party immediately or wait awhile? In terms of gaining compliance from the other party, it is far more effective to *grow* to like the other party.[37] The most effective type of liking (in terms of getting what you want

---

[27]Landy, D., & Sigall, H. (1974). Beauty is talent: Task evaluation as a function of the performer's physical attractiveness. *Journal of Personality and Social Psychology, 29*(3), 299–304.

[28]Eagly, A. H., Ashmore, R. D., Makhijani, M. G., & Longo, L. C. (1991). What is beautiful is good, but . . . : A meta-analytic review of research on the physical attractiveness stereotype. *Psychological Bulletin, 110*(1), 109–128.

[29]Chaiken, S. (1979). Communicator physical attractiveness and persuasion. *Journal of Personality and Social Psychology, 37*(8), 1387–1397.

[30]Benson, P. L., Karabenick, S. A., & Lerner, R. M. (1976). Pretty pleases: The effects of physical attractiveness, race, and sex on receiving help. *Journal of Experimental Social Psychology, 12*(5), 409–415.

[31]Kivisilta, P., Honkaniemi, L., & Sundvi, L. (1994, July 12). *Female employees' physical appearance: A biasing factor in personnel assessment, or a success-producing factor in sales and marketing?* Poster presented at the 23rd International Congress of Applied Psychology, Madrid, Spain; Reingen, P. H., & Kernan, J. B. (1993). Social perception and interpersonal influence: Some consequences of the physical attractiveness stereotype in a personal selling setting. *Journal of Consumer Psychology, 2*(1), 25–38.

[32]Hamermesh, D. S., & Biddle, J. E. (1994). Beauty and the labor market. *The American Economic Review, 84*(5), 1174.

[33]Solnick, S. J., & Schweitzer, M. (1999). The influence of physical attractiveness and gender on ultimatum game decisions. *Organizational Behavior and Human Decision Processes, 79*(3), 199–215.

[34]Dion, K. L. (1972). Physical attractiveness and evaluations of children's transgressions. *Journal of Personality and Social Psychology, 24*(2), 207–213.

[35]Kiesler, C. A., & Kiesler, S. B. (1969). *Conformity.* Reading, MA: Addison-Wesley.

[36]Dion, K. L., & Dion, K. K. (1987). Belief in a just world and physical attractiveness stereotyping. *Journal of Personality and Social Psychology, 52*(4), 775–780; Moore, J. S., Graziano, W. G., & Millar, M. G. (1987). Physical attractiveness, sex role orientation, and the evaluation of adults and children. *Personality and Social Psychology Bulletin, 13*(1), 95–102.

[37]Aronson, E., & Linder, D. (1965). Gain and loss of esteem as determinants of interpersonal attractiveness. *Journal of Experimental Social Psychology, 1*(2), 156–171.

from someone) is to not like the other person immediately. Rather, people who *grow* to like someone are more effective in getting what they want than if they show their liking for the other person immediately. Consider an investigation in which people were given one of four types of evaluations by a peer: completely positive, initially negative and then positive, relentlessly negative, and initially positive and then negative. The recipient of the evaluation feedback was then asked to indicate how much he or she liked the other party. Liking was highest for the other party who was initially negative and later became positive.[38]

To Err Is Human

Negotiators are naturally suspicious of smooth-talking and attractive negotiators. Therefore, it is important to show the counterparty that you are human and have your own foibles and faults. Showing the other person that you have flaws may endear you to them. For example, in one investigation, people listened to someone who was highly competent (i.e., got 92% of difficult exam questions correct). During a subsequent interview, it was revealed that this person was also very competent in other areas—an honor student, editor of the yearbook, and excellent at sports. In another situation, people heard the same person, but this time he spilled coffee on himself during the interview. Even though the person had identical qualifications in both instances, when he made the human error (spilling coffee), he was liked much more than when he was "perfect." In fact, liking increased by 50%.[39]

Priming the Pump

People's judgments and behaviors are affected by **unconscious priming**, which refers to the impact subtle cues and information in the environment have on our behavior (at a level below our conscious awareness).

Consider the following hypothetical scenario: You and a business associate are formulating strategy for the next round of negotiations with an important client. The two of you are discussing your strategy at a local bar, where a big-screen TV is broadcasting a particularly vicious boxing match. You and your associate are not really watching the fight but hear the referee's calls and description of the action in the background. You notice your associate talks about "packing a punch" and "hitting below the belt," and you wonder whether the social context is affecting your associate's judgment about negotiation. You suggest that the two of you walk down the street to the Honey Bear Cafe; the local music that night is a folk group called Brotherly Love. As the two of you are sipping coffee, your associate once again starts talking about the upcoming negotiations. You listen as he talks about "harmony" and "building a community" and wonder again whether features of your location are influencing your friend's judgment. This scenario illustrates how people are often manipulated by cues in the environment that act as primes. Sometimes these cues are random or naturally occurring products of the environment (such as in the bar); sometimes they may be "planted" (by a savvy negotiator). Obviously, it is important to understand how priming certain aspects of the situation may affect our own behavior.

---

[38]Aronson & Linder, "Gain and loss of esteem."
[39]Aronson, E., Willerman, B., & Floyd, J. (1966). The effect of a pratfall on increasing interpersonal attractiveness. *Psychonomic Science, 4,* 227–228.

Reciprocity versus Complementarity

In the previous chapters, we've mentioned the powerful process of reciprocity in negotiation. However, tactics in negotiation are not always met with similar tactics; they can be met with their complement, such as when dominant strategies are met with submissive behavior. Whereas negotiators believe they would behave more competitively with an opponent who acted competitively, they actually behave less competitively, as evidenced by setting lower, less-aggressive reservation prices, making less-demanding counteroffers, and ultimately settling for worse-negotiated outcomes.[40]

Social Proof

According to the **social proof principle**, we look to the behavior of others to determine what is desirable, appropriate, and correct. This behavior is sensible in many respects; if we want to get along with others, it only makes sense to know what they expect. However, this fundamental psychological process can work against us in negotiations if we look toward others—especially the counterparty—to determine an appropriate offer or settlement. For example, new-car dealers target the neighbors of recent customers. Bartenders often "seed" their tip jars, and church ushers "prime" collection baskets with coins. Social proof is why advertisers use the slogans "largest-selling" and "fastest-growing." One tactic, called the **list technique**, involves making a request after a target person has been shown a list of similar others who have already complied. For example, college students and homeowners donated money or blood to a charitable cause in much greater numbers when shown a list of others who had already done so.[41] The more ambiguous the situation, the more likely we are to rely on situational cues and the behavior of others to tell us what to do.

Reactance Technique

Reactance technique (also known as **reverse psychology** or the **boomerang effect**) refers to people's innate need to assert their individual freedom when others attempt to take it away.[42] Negotiators can use an interesting form of reverse psychology to extract what they want and need from the counterparty. (*Warning:* This technique can be extremely risky to use; we argue that negotiators practice with it before negotiating so as not to make fatal errors.)

One strategy for getting a "reaction" from the counterparty is to paraphrase his or her position in a way that makes it sound more extreme than it actually is. For example, consider the following interchange that occurs after two hours of a negotiation in which each negotiator has stopped making concessions:

NEGOTIATOR A: (*with deep sincerity and respect*): So, what you seem to be saying is that you have put your best offer on the table. That is your final

---

[40]Diekmann, K., Tenbrunsel, A., & Galinsky, A. (2003). From self-prediction to self-defeat: Behavioral forecasting, self-fulfilling prophesies, and the effect of competition expectations. *Journal of Personality and Social Psychology, 85*(4), 672–683.

[41]Reingen, P. H. (1982). Test of a list procedure for inducing compliance with a request to donate money. *Journal of Applied Psychology, 67*(1), 110–118.

[42]Brehm, S. S. (1983). Psychological reactance and social differentiation. *Bulletin de Psychologie, 37*(11–14), 471–474.

best offer; there are no other possibilities of any kind. Your offer is a line drawn in the sand.

NEGOTIATOR B: (*looking slightly perplexed*): Well, no, it is not entirely like that. I have tried to be clear about my company's position and feel committed to achieving our goals. And the final offer I made reflects my company's goals.

NEGOTIATOR A: (*with resignation*): I respect a person who makes a commitment, who draws a line in the sand and who will not move an inch from that position. Who has the resolve to stick to his guns, and the tenacity and firmness of an army and . . .

NEGOTIATOR B: (*interrupting negotiator A*): Look, I am not drawing a line in the sand, or anything like that. I am a reasonable person, and I am willing to consider reasonable offers.

NEGOTIATOR A: (*looking incredulous*): You mean you have the power and the freedom to create more options? I was under the impression that you were tied to your position.

NEGOTIATOR B: (*somewhat defensively*): Well, of course, I can do anything I want here—within reason. I can come up with other alternatives.

NEGOTIATOR A: (*with interest*): I am most interested in hearing about your ideas.

Foot-in-the-Door Technique

In the **foot-in-the-door technique**, a person is asked to agree to a small favor or statement (such as agreeing with a question like "Are you ready to buy a car today at the right price?" or signing a petition). Later, the same person is confronted with a larger request (e.g., buying a car or voting with a particular coalition in a departmental meeting). The probability the person will agree to the larger request increases when the person previously agreed to the smaller request.[43] This strategy plays upon people's need to demonstrate consistent behavior.

Door-in-the-Face Technique

Another strategy for gaining compliance is called the **door-in-the-face technique** (or the **rejection-then-retreat tactic**), in which a negotiator asks for a very large concession or favor from the other party—one that the counterparty is almost certain to refuse.[44] When the refusal occurs, the negotiator makes a much smaller request, which is, of course, the option he or she wanted all along. We described this principle in Chapter 3, which admonishes negotiators to state high aspirations. The high aspiration creates a contrast effect, in that the counterparty views any request that is less extreme than the original to be more reasonable.

That's-Not-All Technique

Many negotiators engage in the **that's-not-all technique** (also known as **sweetening the deal**) by offering to add more to a negotiated package or deal. For example, car dealers often add options to the car in question as a "deal closer." Evidence suggests

---

[43]Beaman, A. L., Cole, N., Preston, M., Glentz, B., & Steblay, N. M. (1983). Fifteen years of the foot-in-the-door research: A meta-analysis. *Personality and Social Psychology Bulletin, 9,* 181–186.
[44]Cialdini, R. B. (1975). Reciprocal concessions procedure for inducing compliance: The door-in-the-face technique. *Journal of Personality and Social Psychology, 31*(2), 206–215.

that the that's-not-all technique actually works: In a study involving a bake sale, when patrons asked about cupcake prices and were told that two cupcakes cost $0.75, 40% bought the cupcakes. However, when they were told that one cupcake cost $0.75 and another cupcake would be "thrown in" for free, 73% bought the cupcakes.[45]

The Effects of Power on Those Who Hold Power

People with power are often oblivious to people who have less power.[46] People who are high in power have little or no reason to pay attention to those who are less powerful. After all, the powerful are in control of the situation, and the actions of those who are not as powerful have little effect on the high-power person's well-being. Consequently, those who have more power tend to be less accurate about the situation. In terms of negotiation, people who are higher in power (whether it is a legitimate form of power or not) may be less vigilant and thorough in collecting information from those of lesser power. Those with more power also engage in less "self-monitoring," meaning they don't change their behavior to fit the situation.[47] In one investigation, highly powerful people were secretly videotaped as they interacted with less powerful people. The interchange took place at a social gathering where refreshments were being served. High-power people ate more and messier foods, which resulted in a disheveled appearance.[48] People with a high-power mindset are more likely to act in a risk-seeking fashion and divulge their interests in a negotiation (a form of risky behavior).[49]

The Effects of Power on Those with Less Power

What are the psychological effects of those who have more power on those who have less power? In terms of perception and accuracy, those with less power are highly accurate in perceiving the behaviors and attitudes of those with higher power.[50] This capability makes a lot of sense, especially because those of lesser power are dependent upon those of higher power for important organizational rewards. If someone is in a position to control a variety of organizational benefits that could dramatically affect your well-being, you would probably closely scrutinize his or her behavior. However, this greater accuracy may come at a price. Those who are low in power may exhibit signs of paranoia, believing they are being constantly scrutinized and evaluated by those who are higher in power.[51]

[45]Burger, J. M. (1986). Increasing compliance by improving the deal: The that's-not-all technique. *Journal of Personality and Social Psychology, 51,* 277–283.

[46]Gruenfeld, D. H., Keltner, D. J., & Anderson, C. (2003). The effects of power on those who possess it: How social structure can affect social cognition. In G. Bodenhausen & A. Lambert (Eds.), *Foundations of social cognition: A festschrift in honor of Robert S. Wyer, Jr.* (pp. 237–261). Mahwah, NJ: Erlbaum.

[47]Snyder, M. (1974). Self-monitoring of expressive behavior. *Journal of Personality and Social Psychology, 30,* 526–537; Gruenfeld, Keltner, & Anderson, "The effects of power."

[48]Gruenfeld, Keltner, & Anderson, "The effects of power."

[49]Anderson, C., & Galinsky, A. (2006). Power, optimism, and risk-taking. *European Journal of Social Psychology, 36,* 511–536.

[50]Fiske, S. T., & Dépret, E. (1996). Control, interdependence, and power: Understanding social cognition in its social context. *European Review of Social Psychology, 7,* 31–61.

[51]Kramer, R. M., & Hanna, B. A. (1988). Under the influence? Organizational paranoia and the misperception of others' influence behavior. In R. M. Kramer & M. A. Neale (Eds.), *Power and influence in organizations* (pp. 145–179). Thousand Oaks, CA: Sage.

ETHICAL NEGOTIATION

Negotiation creates incentives for people to violate ethical standards of behavior. Some hard-and-fast rules dictate what is ethical in negotiation, but more often negotiators must deal with many shades of gray. Ethics are a manifestation of cultural, contextual, and interpersonal norms that render certain strategies and behaviors unacceptable. Negotiators evaluate tactics on a continuum of "ethically appropriate" to "ethically inappropriate" when deciding whether to use tactics.[52] We address the question of what behaviors are regarded as unethical or questionable in negotiations, what factors give rise to them, and how to develop personal ethical standards. Consider the following example. In 2005 the U.S. Air Force lifted the suspension on Boeing to compete for military contracts. The suspension started after Boeing misused 25,000 pages of documents that had landed in Boeing's hands from a rival, Lockheed Martin, while the two companies competed for contracts. It was also discovered that negotiations were tilted toward Boeing by a high-level Air Force procurement official, Darleen Druyun, who oversaw billion-dollar contracts while negotiating for a job with Boeing and later accepting the $250,000 job. Boeing also hired Druyun's daughter and son-in-law. Boeing's former finance director, Mike Sears, pleaded guilty to ethics charges and was sentenced to four months in prison for illegally hiring Ms. Druyun, who was sentenced to nine months in prison. Prosecutors questioned the role of other executives and admitted that "Rather than react with concern to a questionable 'non-meeting' with a senior government official, these Boeing executives appear to have accepted the negotiations as business as usual." The air force withdrew $1 billion of launch contracts from Boeing and temporarily disqualified it from competing for new agreements until it could prove it had addressed its ethical problems.[53]

Lying

More than anything else, lying is regarded to be unethical (as well as illegal in some cases). A given statement may be defined as **fraudulent** when the speaker makes a knowing misrepresentation of a material fact on which the victim reasonably relies and the fact causes damage. Unpacking this definition, we find several key aspects to lying: (a) The speaker is aware he or she is misrepresenting information (b) regarding a material fact. The other party (c) relies on this fact and (d) by doing so is damaged in some way—economically or emotionally. Consider the case in which a New York City landlord told a prospective tenant that if he did not rent the condo, the landlord could rent it immediately to someone else. In this situation, the landlord misrepresented his BATNA. The tenant relied on this fact to make a lease decision and was economically damaged.

Using this standard of lying, let's examine some of the key concepts we have discussed thus far: positions, interests, priorities, BATNAs, reservation prices, and key facts.

1. ***Positions.***   Positions are the stated demands made by one party to another. Negotiators are under no obligation to truthfully state their position. For example, a prospective employee

---

[52]Robinson, R. J., Lewicki, R. J., & Donahue, E. M. (2000). Extending and testing a five factor model of ethical and unethical bargaining tactics: Introducing the SINS scale. *Journal of Organizational Behavior, 21,* 649–664.

[53]Daniel, C., & Sevastopulo, D. (2005, March 5). Boeing hopes for end to Air Force deals ban. *Financial Times,* p. 7.

negotiating a job contract may tell the employer she feels entitled to a salary of $100,000 per year, when in fact she is willing to accept $85,000. Note that this negotiator is not lying about her BATNA, nor is she implying that she has another job offer; she is just stating that she feels entitled to $100,000. Whereas most negotiators may believe they are being perfectly clear about their positions, negotiators often beat around the bush and are not as clear as they think they are.[54]

2. **Interests.** Recall that interests are the underlying "whys" behind negotiators' positions. In negotiation, it is generally assumed that people are self-interested with no "general duty of good faith." Specifically, according to the U.S. Court of Appeals, 7th Circuit:

> In a business transaction, both sides presumably try to get the best deal. That is the essence of bargaining and the free market. . . . No legal rule bounds the run of business interest. So, one cannot characterize self-interest as bad faith. No particular demand in negotiations could be termed dishonest, even if it seemed outrageous to the other party. The proper recourse is to walk away from the bargaining table, not sue for "bad faith" negotiations. [55]

3. **Priorities and preferences.** A negotiator is entitled to his or her preferences, however idiosyncratic they might be. A negotiator who misrepresents his or her interests is not lying about a material fact. "Estimates of price or value placed on the subject of a transaction and a party's intentions as to an acceptable settlement of a claim"[56] are not material facts for purposes of the rule prohibiting lawyers from making false statements to a third person.

You can appreciate the complexities of sharing (or failing to share) information with the following example: Consider two people who have been hired to act as a project team in a company. The two associates (A and B) are given a large office to share, and they begin to arrange their workplace. The office contains two desks, and the only window can be enjoyed from one of the desks. A conversation between A and B reveals that A wants the desk with the window view and is ready to make sacrifices on other joint resources to get it—like giving up the close parking space and the storage areas. Unbeknownst to A, B has a terrible fear of heights; the window overlooks a steep precipice outside, and frankly, B prefers the other desk that is near an attractive saltwater aquarium. B considers not mentioning her true preference, hoping that she can *appear* to make a sacrifice, and thus extract more resources. This strategy is known as **passive misrepresentation** because a negotiator does not mention true preferences and allows the other party to arrive at an erroneous conclusion. Now, imagine that A surprises B by asking her point-blank which desk B prefers—the one by the window or the aquarium. Does B lie about her preferences? If so, she commits an act of **active misrepresentation** (if she deliberately misleads her opponent). This strategic manipulation ploy is used about 28% of the time.[57]

4. **BATNAs.** As stated in Chapter 2, a negotiator's BATNA is an objective state of affairs and therefore *is* material and subject to litigation. The message: Don't make up offers that don't exist! Negotiators who make up offers that don't exist (or even allude to them) are bluffing. According to Lewicki, a bluff can be a false promise or false threat.[58] A false promise (e.g., "If you do x, I will reward you") and a false threat (e.g., "If you do not do x, I will punish you") are false in the sense that the person stating the threat does not intend to or cannot follow through.

[54]Harinck, F. (2004). Persuasive arguments and beating around the bush in negotiations. *Group Processes and Intergroup Relations, 7*(1), 5–18.
[55]*Feldman v. Allegheny International, Inc.,* 850 F.2d 1217 (IL 7th Cir. 1988).
[56]American Bar Association. (2004). Model rules of professional conduct: Transactions with persons other than clients. Retrieved August 24, 2007, at http://www.abanet.org/cpr/mrpc/rule_4_1_comm.html
[57]O'Connor, K. M., & Carnevale, P. J. (1997). A nasty but effective negotiation strategy: Misrepresentation of a common-value issue. *Personality and Social Psychology Bulletin, 23*(5), 504–515.
[58]Lewicki, R. J. (1983). Lying and deception: A behavioral model. In M. H. Bazerman & R. J. Lewicki (Eds.), *Negotiating in organizations.* Beverly Hills, CA: Sage.

5. *Reservation prices.*   As stated in Chapter 2, a negotiator's reservation price is the quantification of a negotiator's BATNA. A negotiator's stated reservation price (the least or most at which he or she will sell or buy) is not a material fact per se, and thus, whereas it may be reprehensible to lie about one's reservation price, it is not unethical, legally speaking.
6. *Key facts.*   The falsification of erroneous, incorrect information is unethical (and subject to punishment). For example, a home seller who does not disclose known foundation problems is guilty of falsification.

Other Questionable Negotiation Strategies

In addition to lying about positions, interests, preferences, priorities, BATNAs, reservation prices, or material facts, let's consider other strategies negotiators might regard as unethical. (See Exhibit 7-2 for testing a five factor model of ethical and unethical bargaining tactics.)

- *Traditional competitive bargaining.*   In an analysis of MBA students' perceptions of unethical behavior, traditional competitive bargaining behavior, such as hiding one's real bottom line, making very high or low opening offers, and gaining information by asking among one's contacts, was considered to be unethical.[59] Indeed, self-rated

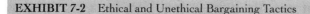

EXHIBIT 7-2   Ethical and Unethical Bargaining Tactics

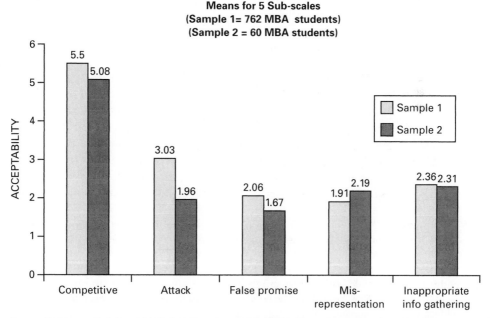

Source: Robinson, R. J., Lewicki, R. J., & Donahue, E. M. (2000). Extending and testing a five factor model of ethical and unethical bargaining tactics: Introducing the SINS scale. *Journal of Organizational Behavior, 21,* 649–664.

Note: Sample 1 is based upon Robinson et al.; sample 2 is based upon an independent sample.

---

[59]Based on Lewicki, R. J., & Robinson, R. J. (1998). Ethical and unethical bargaining tactics: An empirical study. *Journal of Business Ethics, 17*(6), 665–682.

"aggressive" negotiators are more accepting of such tactics than are self-rated "cooperative" negotiators.[60]

- *Manipulation of an opponent's network.*   This tactic involves an attempt to weaken an opponent's position by influencing his or her associate or constituency. For example, consider how state labor unions attempted to use access to social networks to defeat an antitax initiative in the state of Washington.[61] Labor union groups sent e-mails, pretending to be from campaign supporters who were requesting petitions, signs, and stickers. The idea was to get the protax group to waste a lot of money and time sending people pamphlets, stickers, and other items that would ultimately be thrown away. The political director of the Washington State Labor Council, Diane McDaniel, said, "It will cost [the other side] valuable campaign resources to mail hundreds and possibly thousands of packets."

- *Reneging on negotiated agreements.*   In many important negotiations, deals are closed without formal contracts. For example, even in the purchase of houses and cars, an understanding is often reached before official papers have been signed. Even after formal contracts are signed, a period of rescission exists, wherein either party can legally exit from the agreement. However, considerable disagreement and ethical debate concern the issue of whether parties have a right to renege on an agreement once an informal closing (such as a handshake) has occurred.

- *Retracting an offer.*   According to an unwritten rule, once a negotiator puts an offer on the table, he or she should not retract it. This action would be bargaining in bad faith. Even so, negotiators may need to retract offers because a mistake has been made. For example, a newspaper published winning lottery numbers, but a typo was made, and a large number of people believed themselves, mistakenly, to be winners (see Exhibit 7-3). However, what the offering negotiator may see as a mistake is often viewed by the recipient negotiator as bargaining in bad faith.

- *Nickel-and-diming.*   The strategy of continually asking for "just one more thing" after a deal has been closed is annoying to most people. Most people are reluctant to make concessions when they fear the other party will continue to prolong negotiations. Negotiators are more likely to make concessions if they feel they will be successful in closing the deal. Thus, it is often an effective strategy to inform the other party of the terms you need to make the agreement final. Even better, prepare the official paperwork and indicate that you will "sign today" if your terms are met. The prospect of closing a deal is often enough of an enticement for negotiators to agree to the terms proposed by the other party.

EXHIBIT 7-3   Retracting an Offer

On November 5, 1999, the *New York Daily News* printed the wrong numbers in a Scratch 'N' Match lottery game. The *News*, citing game rules, said it would not honor "false winners," but it did announce that it would award the day's regular sum of $192,500 in prizes by holding a drawing the next month between all who sent in winning game cards. Not surprisingly, calls of anger and frustration flooded the hotline and telephone system, and people swarmed the lobby of the *News* building in New York. An elderly security guard in the building was punched and suffered a black eye, and irate game players threatened lawsuits.

Source: McFadden, R. D. (1999, November 6). *Daily News* error: $100,000 dreams turn to nightmare. *New York Times*, p. A1. Reprinted by permission.

---

[60]Ibid.
[61]Postman, D. (2002, April 4). E-mail reveals labor's plot to foil I-776. *Seattle Times*, p. A1.

EXHIBIT 7-4   Sins of Omission

A couple interested in purchasing a house had almost all aspects of a deal worked out on House A. The realtor was aware the couple would have strongly preferred to make an offer on House B, which had sold in the previous month to someone else and, therefore, had not been on the market when the couple was house shopping. The realtor showed the couple House A, and the couple made an offer on it that was accepted. Prior to the closing on House A, House B came on the market again due to a set of completely unforeseeable circumstances. The realtor was aware House B was now on the market but did not inform the couple prior to their closing on House A. It was only following the closing (and after a 7.5% commission was paid to the realtor) that the realtor informed the couple that House B was now on the market and asked the couple if they wanted to put their newly purchased House A on the market and purchase House B.

Did the agent engage in unethical behavior? In the eyes of the real estate agent, because House B was not officially listed and because the couple did not inquire about whether House B was on the market, he did not engage in unethical behavior. In the eyes of the couple, it was unethical for the realtor not to inform them that their preferred house had become available when it did.

Sins of Omission and Commission

Sins of commission (active lying) are regarded as more unethical than sins of omission. (For an example of the complexity of sins of omission, consider the scenario in Exhibit 7-4.) It is possible to withhold information and not be regarded as unethical, but willful shielding from material information does not exculpate the negotiator. In other words, a businessperson should not refuse to see company reports in order to maintain a stance that the company is in financial health.

Costs of Lying

Senator Sam Ervin once remarked that "the problem with lying is you have to remember too damn much."[62] Several costs, or disadvantages, are associated with lying, the first being that the liar can be caught and face criminal charges. Even if the liar is not caught, one's reputation and trustworthiness can be damaged. This event, when it happens repeatedly, can then lead to a culture in which everyone in the organization lies and general suspiciousness increases. Lying also may not be strategic: Because a negotiator who lies about his or her reservation price effectively decreases the size of the bargaining zone, the probability of impasse increases.

Under What Conditions Do People Engage in Deception?

Tenbrunsel and Diekman examined the factors that lead people to engage in deception: the lure of temptation, uncertainty, powerlessness, and anonymity of victims.[63] The more negotiators have to gain economically by lying, the more likely

---

[62]Senate Watergate Hearings. (1974).
[63]Tenbrunsel, A., & Diekmann, K. (2007). When you're tempted to deceive. *Negotiation, 10,* 9–11.

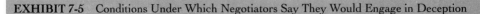

EXHIBIT 7-5 Conditions Under Which Negotiators Say They Would Engage in Deception

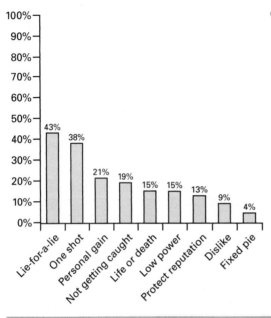

Conditions

- *Lie-for-a-lie:* When I suspect the other party is deceiving me
- *One shot:* In a one-shot situation, with no potential for a long-term relationship
- *Personal gain:* If there was a gain to be had
- *Not getting caught:* If I felt I could get away with it
- *Life or death:* If the situation was "life or death"
- *Low power:* If the other party had more power (i.e., to "level the playing field")
- *Protecting reputation:* When I would not have to worry about my reputation
- *Dislike:* If I did not like the other person
- *Fixed pie:* If the situation was purely distributive

they are to lie.[64] Moreover, the more uncertainty negotiators have about material factors, the more likely they are to lie.

In a survey of MBA students enrolled in a negotiations class, students were asked to describe the conditions under which they personally would engage in deception (defined as lying) in negotiations. Somewhat surprisingly, most people were able to identify situations in which they would lie. Only 2 people out of 47 said they would never deceive. More than 25% said that they would use "white lies" or exaggerations in nearly any negotiation. The most common reason for lying is when we think the other party is lying (see Exhibit 7-5).

Psychological Bias and Unethical Behavior

Ethics are often a problem in negotiations, not so much because people are inherently evil and make trade-offs between profit and ethics or fail to consider other people's interests and welfare but, rather, because of psychological tendencies that foster poor decision making.[65] People may often *believe* they are behaving ethically, but due to self-serving tendencies, problems result and negotiators cry foul.[66]

---

[64]Bazerman, M. H., Tenbrunsel, A. E., & Wade-Benzoni, K. (1998). Negotiating with yourself and losing: Making decisions with competing internal preferences. *Academy of Management Review, 23*(2), 225–241; Grover, S. (2005). The truth, the whole truth and nothing but the truth: The causes and management of workplace lying. *Academy of Management Executive, 19*(2), 148–157.
[65]Messick, D. M., & Bazerman, M. H. (1996). Ethical leadership and the psychology of decision making. *Sloan Management Review, 37*(2), 9–22.
[66]Ibid.

Bounded ethicality. Bounded ethicality refers to the limits of people to make ethical decisions because they are either unaware or fail to fully and deliberately process information.[67]

Illusion of superiority. People view themselves and their actions much more favorably than others view them.[68] People focus on their positive characteristics and downplay their shortcomings. In relative terms, people believe they are more honest, ethical, capable, intelligent, courteous, insightful, and fair than others.

Illusion of control. People believe they have more control over events than they really do. For example, in games of chance, people often feel they can control outcomes.[69] Obviously, this thinking can lead to a type of gambler's fallacy in decision making. However, it can also give rise to ethical problems, such as when people make claims of quality control that cannot be met.

Overconfidence. Most people are overconfident about their knowledge. For example, when people are asked factual questions and then asked to judge the probability that their answers are true, the probability judgments far exceed the accuracy measures of the proportion of correct answers. On average, people claim to be 75% certain, when they are actually correct only 60% of the time.[70] And, people who have unmet goals (presumably because of overconfidence) are more likely to engage in unethical behavior.[71]

Given that our judgments of ethical behavior will be biased, how can negotiators best answer the question of whether a given behavior is ethical? Consider the following:

1. *The front-page test.*   The front-page test, or light-of-day test, poses the following ethical challenge to negotiators: Would you be completely comfortable if your actions and statements were printed in full on the front page of the local newspaper or were reported on the TV news? If not, then your behavior or strategies in question may be regarded as unethical. Another version: "How would I feel if I had to stand before a board of inquiry and describe what I have done?"

2. *Reverse Golden Rule.*   The Golden Rule states, "Do unto others as you would have them do unto you." In this strategy, the negotiator asks himself or herself "If the tables were turned, how would I feel if my opponent did this to me?" If the answer is "I wouldn't like it very much," then it means the behavior in question may be regarded as unethical.

3. *Role modeling.*   "Would I advise others to do this?" or "Would I be proud to see my child act this way?" or "What if everyone bargained this way? Would the resulting society be desirable?"

4. *Third-party advice.*   It is wise to consult a third party (someone who takes an impartial view of the negotiation) to see how that person regards your planned behavior. When consulting the third party, do not reveal your own vote. Describe the event or situation in the third-person voice.

5. *Strengthen your bargaining position.*   Negotiators who have prepared adequately will be less tempted to lie. For example, a negotiator who initiates efforts to improve her BATNA

---

[67]Chugh, D., Banaji, M., & Bazerman, M. (2005). Bounded ethicality as a psychological barrier to recognizing conflicts of interest. In D. Moore, D. Cain, G. Loewenstein, & M. Bazerman, (Eds.), *Conflicts of interest: Problems and solutions from law, medicine and organizational settings.* London: Cambridge University Press.

[68]Taylor, S. E., & Brown, J. (1988). Illusion and well-being: A social-psychological perspective. *Psychological Bulletin, 103,* 193–210.

[69]Langer, E. (1975). The illusion of control. *Journal of Personality and Social Psychology, 32,* 311–328.

[70]Fischhoff, B., Slovic, P., & Lichtenstein, S. (1977). Knowing with certainty: The appropriateness of extreme confidence. *Journal of Experimental Psychology: Human Perception and Performance, 3*(4), 552–564.

[71]Schweitzer, M., Ordonez, L., & Douma, B. (2004). Goal setting as a motivator of unethical behavior. *Academy of Management Journal, 47*(3), 422–432.

does not need to lie about her BATNA. A negotiator who has thought about the factors that affect his reservation price can simply inform the other party, "It's none of your business." And a negotiator who has considered the facts can express an "opinion" based on the facts.

CONCLUSION

A negotiator's BATNA is the most important source of power in a negotiation. Having said that, effective use of power is not simply the threat of exercising one's BATNA. The enlightened negotiator knows a larger slice of the pie can be obtained by creating a larger pie. We outlined two types of influence strategies that appeal to the mind and heart, respectively. The mindful strategies include controlling the agenda, generating alternatives within issues, generating options across issues, attitudinal structuring and contrast, consistency, strategic framing, fairness, and time pressure. The psychological strategies we discussed included: status, gender, social networks, physical appearance, delaying liking, a certain degree of self-effacing behavior, strategic priming, reciprocity and complementarity, social proof, reactance, and foot-in-the-door, door-in-the-face, and the that's-not-all technique.

All negotiators need to be concerned about ethical behavior in negotiation and know that, as with everything else, we don't always see our actions the way others see them. We discussed the moral and strategic disadvantages of lying with respect to the six things negotiators most often lie about (positions, interests, priorities, BATNAs, reservation prices, and key facts). We discussed how bounded ethicality, the illusion of superiority, the illusion of control, and overconfidence might contribute to a negotiator's decision to engage in deception. We suggest that negotiators engage in five "tests" when struggling to decide whether a given behavior is ethical: the front-page test, reverse Golden Rule, role modeling, third-party advice, and strengthening their bargaining position.

CHAPTER 8

Creativity and Problem Solving in Negotiations

Howard County negotiated for months to obtain dental coverage for the Healthy Howard Plan (a plan designed to provide affordable primary and specialty care and medications for 20,000 uninsured residents, including 5,000 children, by drawing on federal programs, local government money, private donations, and user fees). Monthly fees were meant to comprise 60% of the initial plan's budget, but for the county it became clear that providing dental coverage was a challenge. Aetna normally charges $7.50 a month per participant, but this fee was too large to ensure dental coverage for everyone. Aetna did not offer discounts to the general public, but Howard County was an important market for the company, so they negotiated the following deal: For an additional $1.65 monthly fee, the Healthy Howard Plan would offer services from a network of dental providers at significant discounts of 30% to 50%. Aetna recently became one of the insurance providers for county government employees and pledged to award a grant of $57,000 to help with the start-up of the Healthy Howard Plan.[1]

CREATIVITY IN NEGOTIATION

The most creative negotiation agreements, like the Howard-Aetna deal, are often complex agreements that have several moving parts. The creative aspect of negotiation is often ignored by negotiators, who fixate on the competitive aspect of negotiation. This tendency is largely driven by the pervasive **fixed-pie perception**, or the belief that negotiation is a win-or-lose enterprise. Successful negotiation requires creativity and problem solving, and the process of slicing the pie is easier when the pie has been enlarged via creative and insightful problem-solving strategies.

This chapter is the "advanced course" in integrative bargaining. It provides the means by which negotiators can transform their negotiations into win-win enterprises. We invite negotiators to put their problem-solving skills and creativity to the test. Then we take up the topic of creativity in negotiation and what creative negotiation agreements look like. Next, we consider the biggest threats to creative problem solving in negotiations. We conclude by offering an exercise regimen to keep your creative mind sharp.

---

[1]DeFord, S. (2008, March 27). Agreement puts teeth in affordable health care. *Washington Post*, p. T3.

Test Your Own Creativity

Exhibit 8-1 contains 13 problems. Take 30 minutes right now to try to solve these problems. When in doubt, make your best guess, but make an honest attempt at solving each problem. As you go along, make a mental note of your thoughts about each problem as you try to solve it. Read the rest of this chapter before you look up the answers in Exhibit 8-13 (at the end of this chapter). As you read the chapter, see whether any insights come to you, and make note of them as they arise. When it comes to creativity, we can focus on products of negotiation (such as outcomes), the people involved (i.e., the negotiators), and the processes (or the conditions that connect the people to the product).[2]

WHAT IS YOUR MENTAL MODEL OF NEGOTIATION?

Interviews with managers, the research literature, and the most popular published books on negotiation reveal five distinct mental models of negotiation, including haggling, cost-benefit analysis, game playing, partnership, and problem solving.[3] Negotiators' mental models shape their behavior. In other words, if you approach negotiation as a "dog-eat-dog" enterprise, you are going to be much tougher than if you approach negotiation as a "partnership." As you read about these five mental models, think about which one best characterizes your approach to negotiation.

Haggling

Probably the most common mental model of negotiation is what we call the **haggling model**. The image this approach might conjure up is of two dogs fighting over one bone. Resolution in this model comes down to a struggle between two parties, in which each is trying to obtain the biggest share of the pie. The haggling model is based upon a fixed-pie perception of negotiation.

Cost-Benefit Analysis

Some negotiators think of negotiation as a rational, decision making model in which they compute a cost-benefit analysis and attempt to maximize their returns. For example, Robert Rubin, former U.S. Treasury secretary, calculates the odds of almost every decision he faces, using both real and mental yellow pads.[4] He once suggested to the board of the American Ballet Theatre, on which he sat, that it enact a cost reduction by cutting 10% of the swans in *Swan Lake*.

Game Playing

The chess game model of negotiation elevates negotiation from "fighting in the streets" to a battle of wits between two or more highly intelligent people. In game playing, each person has his or her own interests in mind. This game is carried out, however, in an extremely civil and refined fashion. (See Exhibit 8-2 for an example of game playing.)

---

[2]Carnevale, P. (2006). Creativity in the outcomes of conflict. In M. Deutsch, P. T. Coleman & E. C. Marcus (Eds.), *Handbook of conflict resolution* (2nd ed.). San Francisco: Jossey-Bass.
[3]Thompson, L., & Loewenstein, J. (2003). Mental models of negotiation: Descriptive, prescriptive, and paradigmatic implications. In M. A. Hogg & J. Cooper (Eds.), *Sage handbook of social psychology*. London: Sage.
[4]Loomis, C. (2003, December 22). The larger-than-life life of Robert Rubin. *Fortune*, pp. 114–124.

EXHIBIT 8-1   Creativity Test

CARD DECISION*

Look at the following numbers/letters. Each number/letter represents a card. On each of the four cards, a letter appears on one side and a number on the other. Your task is to judge the validity of the following rule: *"If a card has a vowel on one side, then it has an even number on the other side."* Your task is to turn over only those cards that have to be turned over for the correctness of the rule to be judged. What cards will you turn over? [*Circle those cards that you will turn over to test the rule.*]

   E   K   4   7

PERSON IN A ROOM DECISION†

A person has been chosen at random from a set of 100 people, consisting of 30 engineers and 70 lawyers. What is the probability that the individual chosen at random from the group, Jack, is an engineer?

"Jack is a 45-year-old man. He is married and has four children. He is generally conservative, careful, and ambitious. He shows no interest in political and social issues and spends most of his free time on his many hobbies, which include home carpentry, sailing, and mathematical puzzles."

Jack is [*circle one*]:
an engineer   a lawyer

BETTING DECISION‡

Which gamble would you rather play? [*Circle either A or B.*]

   A: 1/3 chance to win $80,000
   B: 5/6 chance to win $30,000
Now, imagine that you have to choose one of the following gambles. Which one will you play? [*Circle either C or D.*]
   C: 50% chance to win $10,000, and 50% chance to lose $10,000
   D: $0

WATER JUGS§

You have been given a set of jugs of various capacities and unlimited water supply. Your task is to measure out a specified quantity of water. You should assume you have a tap and a sink so that you can fill jugs and empty them. The jugs start out empty. You are allowed only to fill the jugs, empty them, and pour water from one jug to another. As an example, consider the following problems 1 and 2:

---

*Wason, P. C., & Johnson-Laird, P. N. (1972). *Psychology of reasoning: Structure and content.* Cambridge, MA: Harvard University Press.

†Kahneman, D., & Tversky, A. (1973). On the psychology of prediction. *Psychological Review, 80,* 237–251.

‡Tversky, A., & Kahneman, D. (1981). The framing of decisions and the psychology of choice. *Science, 211,* 453–458.

§Luchins, A. S. (1942). Mechanization in problem solving. *Psychological Monographs, 5*(46), 1–95.

continued

EXHIBIT 8-1   Creativity Test (*continued*)

Example Problem#	Capacity of Jug A	Capacity of Jug B	Capacity of Jug C	Quantity Desired
1	5 cups	40 cups	18 cups	28 cups
2	21 cups	127 cups	3 cups	100 cups

To solve problem 1, you would fill jug A and pour it into B, fill A again and pour it into B, and fill C and pour it into B. The solution to this problem is denoted by **2A + C**.

   To solve problem 2, you would first fill jug B with 127 cups, fill A from B so that 106 cups are left in B, fill C from B so that 103 cups are left in B, and empty C and fill C again from B so that the goal of 100 cups in jug B is achieved. The solution to this problem can be denoted by **B-A-2C**.

Real Problems

Problem #	Capacity of Jug A	Capacity of Jug B	Capacity of Jug C	Desired Quantity	Solution
1	14 cups	163 cups	25 cups	99 cups	
2	18 cups	43 cups	10 cups	5 cups	
3	9 cups	42 cups	6 cups	21 cups	
4	20 cups	59 cups	4 cups	31 cups	
5	23 cups	49 cups	3 cups	20 cups	
6	15 cups	39 cups	3 cups	18 cups	
7	28 cups	76 cups	3 cups	25 cups	
8	18 cups	48 cups	4 cups	22 cups	
9	14 cups	36 cups	8 cups	6 cups	

STICK PROBLEM[**]

You have six sticks, all of equal length. You need to arrange them to form four triangles that are equilateral and with each side one stick long. (You cannot break any sticks.) Indicate how you would do this.

LETTER SEQUENCE[††]

What is the next letter in the following sequence? OTTFFSS___

CHAIN PROBLEM[‡‡]

The goal of this task is to make a chain (as depicted in the goal state) from the links you are given (in the given state). Please note that it costs $3 to open a link, $5 to close a link. Your total budget is $25.

[**]Scheer, M. (196 3). *Scientific American, 208,* 118–218.
[††]Letter sequence: Source unknown.
[‡‡]De Bono, E. (1967). *The use of lateral thinking.* New York: Penguin.

SUSAN AND MARTHA

Susan and Martha are discussing their children when Susan asks Martha for the ages of her three sons. Martha says, "The sum of their ages is 13 and the product of their ages is the same as your age." Susan replies, "I still do not know their ages." What must Susan's age be?

    a. 24   b. 27   c. 63   d. 36   e. 48

NECKLACE[§§]

A woman has four pieces of chain. Each piece is made of three links. She wants to join the pieces into a single closed ring of chain. To open a link costs 2 cents; to close a link costs 3 cents. All links are now closed. She has only 15 cents. How does she do it?

GOLD CHAIN

Isaac is staying at a motel when he runs short of cash. Checking his finances, he discovers that in 23 days he will have plenty of money, but until then he will be broke. The motel owner refuses to let Isaac stay without paying his bill each day, but because Isaac owns a heavy gold chain with 23 links, the owner allows Isaac to pay for each of the 23 days with one gold link. Then, when Isaac receives his money, the motel owner will return the chain. Isaac is very anxious to keep the chain as intact as possible, so he does not want to cut off any more of the links than absolutely necessary. The motel owner, however, insists on payment each day, and he will not accept advance payment. How many links must Isaac cut while still paying the owner one link for each successive day?
_____links

NINE DOT PROBLEM[***]

Consider the following nine dots. Draw four or fewer straight lines *without lifting your pencil from the paper* so that each of the nine dots has a line through it.

[§§]Wickelgren, W. A. (1974). *How to solve problems.* San Francisco: W. H. Freeman.
[***]Weisberg, R. W., & Alba, J. W. (1981). An examination of the alleged role of "fixation" in the solution of several insight problems. *Journal of Experimental Psychology: General, 110,* 169–192.

continued

EXHIBIT 8-1   Creativity Test (*continued*)

PIGPEN[†††]

Nine pigs are kept in a square pen, as shown in the figure. Build two more square enclosures that would put each pig in a pen by itself.

WATER LILIES[‡‡‡]

Water lilies on a certain lake double in area every 24 hours. On the first day of summer, one water lily is on the lake. On the sixtieth day, water lilies completely cover the lake. On what day is the lake half covered?

BARTENDER PROBLEM[§§§]

A man walks into a bar and asks for a glass of water. The bartender points a shotgun at the man. The man says, "Thank you," and walks out. What is going on in this situation?

[†††]Fixx, J. F. (1972). *More games for the super-intelligent.* New York: Warner Books.
[‡‡‡]Sternberg, R. J., & Davidson, J. E. (1983). Insight in the gifted. *Educational Psychologist, 18,* 51–57.
[§§§]Dayton, T., Durso, F. T., & Shepard, J. D. (1990). A measure of the knowledge reorganization underlying insight. In R. W. Schraneveldt (Ed.), *Pathfinder associative networks: Studies in knowledge organization.* Norwood, NJ: Ablex.

EXHIBIT 8-2   Game Playing

California Tortilla's customers were invited to challenge cashiers to a game of Rock, Paper, Scissors to get a dollar taken off their bill. The World RPS (Rock, Paper, Scissors) Society posted the following advice on *http://www.worldrps.com* to size up one's counterparty: A seemingly intellectually superior counterparty (thus most likely to play paper) can be beat by playing scissors. Rock being the most aggressive throw, the knuckle-dragging cashier type can be beat by playing paper, which symbolizes "the victory of modern culture over barbarism." A contained, clever, user of tools can be beat by playing rock.

Source: Szokan, N. (2007, June 18). If cashier is Cro-Magnon, play paper. *Washington Post,* p. D02.

Partnership

A quite different mental model of negotiation is what we call the **partnership model**, embraced by companies and salespeople who treat their clients as partners. Negotiators who ascribe to the relationship model believe it is important to build rapport between people to nurture a long-term relationship and, in many cases, to make sacrifices in the name of creating long-term goodwill.

Problem Solving

The **problem-solving model** is a mental model of negotiation in which people consider negotiation to be the task of defining and solving a problem. In problem-solving negotiations, two people sit on the same side of the table and attempt to solve a puzzle together. This model focuses on the collaborative or cooperative aspects of the task and involves a great deal of creativity, reframing, and out-of-the-box thinking.

We investigated negotiators' mental models and how they affect performance.[5] Compared to negotiators who fail to reach win-win outcomes, negotiators who reach win-win outcomes are better able to understand the other party's underlying interests. Comparison of the negotiators who reach win-win outcomes revealed they have mental models that are more similar to one another than do negotiators who fail to reach win-win outcomes. Experience-based training was effective in helping negotiators to develop mental models that looked more like expert, win-win models; didactic lecturing was uniquely ineffective—a topic we take up in detail in this chapter.

CREATIVE NEGOTIATION AGREEMENTS

Creativity in negotiation often follows the pattern of the "Monday morning quarterback," meaning that it is easy in hindsight to see creative opportunity in negotiations; however, it often eludes us in the moment. Next, we outline the hallmark characteristics of truly creative negotiations.[6]

Fractionating Problems into Solvable Parts

Most negotiation situations appear to contain a single issue. Fractionating negotiation issues into solvable parts and creating multiple-issue negotiations from what appear to be single-issue negotiations is probably the most important aspect of creative negotiation.[7] For example, consider how the negotiations between members of the United Food and Commercial Workers Local 175 and Wilfrid Laurier University avoided a strike, even when they had a $300,000 deficit with which to deal. They fractionated the bargaining issue from a single issue (wage increases) to several issues, including job security, control over uniforms, parking fees, access to athletic facilities, and overtime costs.[8]

People are good at solving problems when the problems are presented directly to them; however, they are not very good at *defining* problems. Negotiation is mostly about defining a problem rather than solving it (i.e., searching for differences in such a

[5]van Boven, L., & Thompson, L. (2003). A look into the mind of the negotiator: Mental models in negotiation. *Group Processes & Intergroup Relations, 6*(4), 387–404.

[6]Pruitt, D. G., & Carnevale, P. J. (1993). *Negotiation in social conflict.* Pacific Grove, CA: Brooks-Cole.

[7]Lax, D. A., & Sebenius, J. K. (1986). *The manager as negotiator.* New York: Free Press.

[8]Simone, R. (2003, July 29). Food workers help WLU trim deficit. *Kitchener-Waterloo Record,* p. D8.

way that trade-offs can be creative). Psychologists call this task **problem representation**, as opposed to problem solving.

Finding Differences: Issue Alignment and Realignment

Before negotiators can find differences to trade off, they need to align the issues in such a way that permits the issues to be negotiated independently and, ideally, traded off.[9] Linking issues creates a lot of constraints that limit negotiators' abilities to trade off issues. Ideally, negotiators should create issues that are **orthogonal** to one another, such that they can be traded off without having too many implications for other issues. Skilled negotiators know how to realign issues so as to find pockets of opportunity. Consider, for example, the negotiation between architect Daniel Libeskind and developer Larry Silverstein concerning the rebuilding of the World Trade Center site.[10] By identifying additional issues and realigning issues, a negotiated agreement was reached, ending months of heated battles between Silverstein and Libeskind. The impasse centered on how much influence the architect (Libeskind) would have on the design of the first office building to go up at the site—the 1,776-foot tower that defines the rebuilt Trade Center's presence on the Lower Manhattan skyline. The developer (Silverstein) wanted to involve other architects for the largest tower and make changes to the master plan. An agreement was reached between the two by carving out another issue—namely, the development of commercial design guidelines governing future commercial development on the site. Libeskind won this issue, but Silverstein got to hire another firm to serve as design architect and project manager for the Freedom Tower, the first commercial building to be constructed on the site.

Expanding the Pie

Expanding the pie is an important method by which to create integrative agreements. At first glance, it may not seem that expanding the pie is a viable option in many negotiation situations. However, negotiators who labor under the fixed-pie perception may limit their options unnecessarily. Consider, for example, how a negotiation between a fire station and an elementary school was transformed from an impasse to a creative arrangement by expanding the pie.[11] Initially, the school wanted to acquire land to expand, but the fire station blocked that move. So the pie was expanded such that each party paid an unrelated third party for a separate parcel of land. In the final deal, the city gave a 3-acre parcel of land to a private owner, who then gave back to the city 7.5 of his own acres (located nearer to the school and fire station). At this point, the fire station and the school successfully expanded the pie of available land to accomplish both of their goals. Thus, by expanding the pie to include another plot of land that could be "swapped," both parties ultimately achieved what they wanted: The school was able to expand, and the firehouse could make its entrances and exits more convenient and safe.

Bridging

Oftentimes, it is not possible for negotiators to find a compromise solution, and expanding the pie does not work. Furthermore, perhaps neither party can get what it wants in a trade-off that meets their interests. A **bridging** solution creates a new alternative that

---

[9]Lax & Sebenius, *The manager as negotiator.*
[10]Wyatt, E. (2003, July 16). Officials reach an agreement on rebuilding downtown site. *New York Times,* p. 1.
[11]Robertson, G. (1998, February 18). Creative negotiations pay off. *Richmond Times-Dispatch,* p. J3.

meets parties' underlying interests. Bridging alerts us to yet another reason to understand the other party's interests and avoid positional bargaining. If negotiators understand the basic needs of the counterparty, they are more likely to fashion bridging agreements.

Cost Cutting

Sometimes, people are reluctant to negotiate because reaching a resolution seems costly to them. Most people are risk-seeking when it comes to loss, meaning that they are reluctant to make concessions and may behave irrationally when they believe they will have to make concessions. **Cost cutting** is a way of making the other party feel whole by reducing that party's costs. An example of value-added cost cutting occurred in negotiations between The Nature Conservancy and the Great Northern Paper Company.[12] On the surface, we might expect the interests of these two to be a classic fixed-pie—The Nature Conservancy, dedicated to preserving everything from trees to water, should hardly want to work with a company that makes its money by cutting down trees for consumer and industrial use. Kent Wommack of The Nature Conservancy said, "In my 20 years with the Nature Conservancy, I have heard far too often from skeptics that environmentalists and the paper industry can never see eye to eye." But in an unprecedented partnership, The Nature Conservancy assumed $50 million worth of Great Northern's debts. In return, Great Northern Paper agreed to protect a quarter-million acres from development.[13]

Nonspecific Compensation

In a **nonspecific-compensation** negotiated agreement, one negotiator receives what he or she wants, and the other is compensated (or paid) by some method that was initially outside the bounds of the negotiation. For example, Phil Jones, managing director of Real Time, a London-based interactive design studio, recalls an instance where he used nonspecific compensation in his negotiations.[14] The problem was that his client, a Formula 1 motor-racing team, wanted to launch Internet Web sites but did not have the budget to pay him. However, in Phil Jones's eyes, the client was high profile and had creative, challenging projects with which Real Time wanted to get involved. Formula 1 came up with a nonspecific-compensation offer to make the deal go through: tickets to some of the major Formula 1 meetings. It worked. Says Phil Jones, "The tickets are like gold dust . . . and can be used as a pat on the back for staff or as an opportunity to pamper existing clients or woo new ones."

Structuring Contingencies

A major obstacle to reaching negotiated agreements often concerns negotiators' beliefs about some future event or outcome.[15] Impasses often result from conflicting beliefs that are difficult to surmount, especially when each side is confident about the accuracy of his or her prediction and consequently suspicious of the other side's forecasts. Often, compromise is not a viable solution, and each party may be reluctant to change his or her point of view.

---

[12]Analysis: Business deal between Great Northern Paper and The Nature Conservancy to protect a quarter-million acres of Maine woods from development. (2002, August 28). *NPR org.* Retrieved July 12, 2008, at http://www.npr.org/templates/story/story.php?storyId=1149055
[13]Ibid.
[14]Davies, J. (1998, November 1). The art of negotiation. *Management Today,* pp. 126–128.
[15]Lax & Sebenius, *The manager as negotiator.*

Contingent contracts can provide a way out of the mire. With a **contingency** (or contingent) **contract**, differences of opinion among negotiators concerning future events do not have to be bridged; they become the core of the agreement.[16] Negotiators can bet on the future rather than argue about it. In some areas of business, contingency contracts are commonplace. For example, some CEOs agree to tie their salary to a company's stock price.

However, in many business negotiations, contingency contracts are either ignored or rejected out of hand for several reasons.[17] First, people are unaware of how to construct contingency contracts. It often never occurs to people to bet on their differences when they are embroiled in conflict. Second, contingency contracts are often seen as a form of gambling, a high-risk enterprise. Third, no systematic way of thinking about the formulation of such contracts is usually available, meaning that they *appear* to be a good idea, but how to formalize and act upon them remain an enigma. Fourth, many negotiators have a "getting to yes" bias, meaning they focus on reaching common ground with the other party and are reluctant to accept differences of interest, even when this might create viable options for joint gain.[18] Most negotiators think differences of belief are a source of problems in a negotiation. The paradoxical view suggested by the contingency contract strategy states that differences are often constructive. With a contingency contract, negotiators can focus on their real mutual interests, not on their speculative disagreements.[19] When companies fail to find their way out of differences in beliefs, they often go to court, creating expensive delays, litigation costs, loss of control by both parties, and deteriorating BATNAs. (For an example of how negotiators fail to use contingency contracts and suffer costs, see Exhibit 8-3.)

Another advantage of contingency contracts is they provide a nearly perfect lie-detection device. Contingency contracts allow negotiators to test the counterparty's veracity in a nonconfrontational manner, thereby allowing parties to save face. Contingency contracts also allow parties who are concerned about being cheated to safeguard themselves. This fear of being cheated is precisely what Christopher Columbus was worried about when he negotiated an agreement about the New World with Queen Isabella and King Ferdinand. Worried he would risk life and opportunity and gain nothing, Christopher Columbus insisted he be offered an opportunity to contribute one-eighth of the costs of future expeditions and be guaranteed one-eighth of all profits. Unfortunately, the crowns reneged on the deal upon his return, and Columbus had to go to court.[20]

By the same token, contingency contracts can build trust and good faith between negotiators because incentives can be provided for each company to deliver exceptional performance. Therefore, contingency contracts provide a safety net, limiting each company's losses should an agreement go awry unexpectedly. (For a summary of the benefits of contingency contracts, see Exhibit 8-4.)

---

[16]Bazerman, M. H., & Gillespie, J. J. (1999). Betting on the future: The virtues of contingent contracts. *Harvard Business Review, 77*(4), 155–160.
[17]Ibid.
[18]Gibson, K., Thompson, L., & Bazerman, M. H. (1994). Biases and rationality in the mediation process. In L. Heath, F. Bryant, & J. Edwards (Eds.), *Application of heuristics and biases to social issues: Vol. 3*. New York: Plenum.
[19]Bazerman & Gillespie, "Betting on the future."
[20]Dworetzky, T. (1998, December 11). Explorer Christopher Columbus: How the West's greatest discoverer negotiated his trips' financing. *Investors' Business Daily*, p. 1BD.

EXHIBIT 8-3   Failure to Use Contingency Contracts

"Consider how a contingent contract might have changed the course of one of the century's most famous and most fruitless antitrust cases. In 1969, the U.S. Department of Justice [DOJ] filed a suit against IBM, alleging monopolistic behavior. More than a decade later, the case was still bogged down in litigation. Some 65 million pages of documents had been produced, and each side had spent millions of dollars in legal expenses. The DOJ finally dropped the case in 1982, when it had become clear that IBM's once-dominant share of the computer market was eroding rapidly.

During the case's thirteen futile years, IBM and the government had essentially been arguing over differences in their expectations about future events. IBM assumed that its market share would decrease in coming years as competition for the lucrative computer market increased. The government assumed that IBM, as a monopolist, would hold its large market share for the foreseeable future. Neither felt the other's view was valid, and so neither had a basis for compromise.

An efficient and rational way to settle this dispute would have been for IBM and the government to have negotiated a contingent contract—to have placed a wager on the future. They might have agreed, for example, that if by 1975 IBM still held at least 70 percent of the market—its share in 1969—it would pay a set fine and divest itself of certain businesses. If, however, its market share had dropped to 50 percent or lower, the government would not pursue antitrust actions. If its share fell somewhere between 50 percent and 70 percent, another type of contingency would take effect.

Constructing such a contingent contract would not have been easy. There were, after all, an infinite number of feasible permutations, and many details would have to have been hammered out. But it would have been far more rational—and far cheaper—to have the two sides' lawyers devote a few weeks to arguing over how to structure a contingent contract than it was for them to spend years filing motions, taking depositions, and reviewing documents."

Source: Reprinted by permission of Harvard Business Review. From "Betting on the future: The Virtuses of Contingent Contracts" by M. H. Bezerman and J. J. Gillespie, 1999. Copyright© 1999 by the Harvard Business School Publishing Corporation; all rights reserved.

Although we believe contingency contracts can be valuable in many kinds of business negotiations, they are not always the right strategy to use. Bazerman and Gillespie suggest three key criteria for assessing the viability and usefulness of contingency contracts in negotiation:[21]

1. Contingency contracts require *some degree of continued interaction between the parties.* Because the final terms of the contract will not be determined until sometime after the initial agreement is signed, some amount of future interaction between parties is necessary, thereby allowing them to assess the terms of their agreement. Therefore, if the future seems highly uncertain, or if one of the parties is suspected of preparing to leave the situation permanently, contingency contracts may not be wise.

2. Parties need to think about the *enforceability* of the contingency contract. Under a contingency contract, one or more of the parties will probably not be correct about the outcome because the contract often functions as a bet. This outcome creates a problem for the "loser" of the bet, who may be reluctant to reimburse the other party when things do not go his or her way. For this reason, the money in question might well be placed in escrow, thereby removing each party's temptation to defect.

---

[21]Bazerman & Gillespie, "Betting on the future."

EXHIBIT 8-4 The Six Benefits of Contingency Contracts

1. Contingency contracts allow negotiators to *build on their differences*, rather than arguing about them. Do not argue over the future. Bet on it.
2. Contingency contracts allow negotiators to *manage decision making biases*. Although overconfidence and egocentrism can be barriers to effective agreements, contingency contracts use these biases to create a bet.
3. Contingency contracts allow negotiators to *solve problems of trust*, when one side has information that the other side lacks. The less-informed party can create a contingency to protect itself against the unknown information possessed by the other side.
4. Contingency contracts allow negotiators to *diagnose the honesty of the other side*. When one party makes a claim that the other party does not believe, a bet can be created to protect a negotiator against the lie.
5. Contingency contracts allow negotiators to *reduce risk through risk sharing*. The sharing of upside gains and losses not only can reduce risk, but it can also create goodwill by increasing the partnership between the parties.
6. Contingency contracts allow negotiators to *increase the incentive of the parties to perform* at or above contractually specified levels. Contingency contracts should be specifically considered when the motivation of one of the parties is in question.

Source: Reprinted by permission of Harvard Business Review. From "Betting on the future: The Virtues of Contingent Contracts" by M. H. Bezerman and J. J. Gillespie, 1999. Copyright© 1999 by the Harvard Business School Publishing Corporation; all rights reserved.

---

3. Contingency contracts require a high degree of *clarity* and *measurability*. If an event is ambiguous, nonmeasurable, or of a subjective nature, overconfidence, egocentric bias, and a variety of other self-serving biases can make the objective appraisal of a contingency contract a matter of some opinion. Parties should agree up front on clear, specific measures concerning how the contract will be evaluated. For this reason, it is often wise to consult a third party.

THREATS TO EFFECTIVE PROBLEM SOLVING AND CREATIVITY

A variety of human biases and shortcomings threaten people's ability to think creatively. We illuminate the most common threats to effective problem solving and creativity and make suggestions on how to avoid them. A key first step to preventing these biases is *awareness* of their existence.

The Inert Knowledge Problem

People's ability to solve problems in new contexts depends on the accessibility of their relevant knowledge. Simply stated, if a manager is confronted with new business challenges, he or she often consults his or her knowledge base for previous problems that have cropped up in an attempt to see which previous problem solving strategies might be useful in solving the new problem. The **inert knowledge problem** is the inability to access relevant knowledge when we most need it.[22] Simply, the information necessary to solve a new problem is part of a manager's cognitive repertoire but is not accessible

---

[22]Whitehead, A. N. (1929). *The aims of education.* New York: Macmillan.

at the right time. This unavailability is not due to senility or amnesia but, rather, to the peculiar way that our long-term memories are constructed.

A striking dissociation occurs between what is most *accessible* in our memories and what is most *useful* in human problem solving and reasoning. People often fail to recall what is ultimately most valuable for solving new problems.[23] In one investigation, people studied examples containing principles of probability theory and then attempted to solve problems requiring the use of those principles.[24] If the study and test stories were from the same context, people were more likely to be reminded of them than if the stories were from different contexts. In another investigation, participants were given a story to read about a hawk giving feathers to a hunter.[25] Participants were then given one of four stories resulting from combining surface and structural similarities (i.e., a story with similar characters and plot, different characters but same plot, similar characters but different plot, or different characters and different plot). People were more than four times more likely to recall the original story when later shown a story with similar characters than when shown a story with different characters, suggesting that people often fail to recall what is ultimately most valuable for solving new problems.[26] Upon being informed of the correct approach to a negotiation, management students often express regret: "I knew that. I just did not think to use it."

Unfortunately, negotiators in the real world typically do not experience regret because they are not told when they have made learning and application errors. The ability of managers to transfer knowledge from one context to another is highly limited. **Transfer** is the ability to apply a strategy or idea learned in one situation to solve a problem in a different, but relevant, situation. It is important to distinguish **surface-level transfer** from **deep transfer**. Surface-level transfer occurs when a person attempts to transfer a solution from one context to a superficially similar context. However, in most situations it is desirable for people to apply solutions and strategies that have deep, meaningful similarities, rather than superficial ones. Unfortunately, this task proves to be quite difficult for most managers to do. In general, if two problems have similar surface (or superficial) features, managers are more likely to transfer knowledge from one problem situation to the other. Ideally, however, managers want to transfer solutions to problems that have similar deep (or structural) features but may have significantly different superficial features.

As a case in point, consider the "tumor problem" presented in Exhibit 8-5. When presented with this problem, few people successfully solve it; if it is preceded by the fortress problem in Exhibit 8-6, the solution rate rises dramatically.[27] Even though a similar solution can be applied in both problems, because the surface information in each problem is quite different (one deals with a medical situation; the other, a political

---

[23]Forbus, K. D., Gentner, D., & Law, K. (1995). MAC/FAC: A model of similarity-based retrieval. *Cognitive Science, 19*(2), 141–205; Gentner, D., Rattermann, M. J., & Forbus, K. D. (1993). The roles of similarity in transfer: Separating retrievability from inferential soundness. *Cognitive Psychology, 25*(4), 524–575.

[24]Ross, B. H. (1987). This is like that: The use of earlier problems and the separation of similarity effects. *Journal of Experimental Psychology: Learning, Memory and Cognition, 13*(4), 629–639.

[25]Gentner, Rattermann, & Forbus, "The roles of similarity in transfer."

[26]Forbus, Gentner, & Law, "MAC/FAC"; Gentner, Rattermann, & Forbus, "The roles of similarity in transfer."

[27]Gick, M. L., & Holyoak, K. J. (1980). Analogical problem solving. *Cognitive Psychology, 12,* 306–355.

EXHIBIT 8-5   The Tumor Problem

Suppose you are a doctor faced with a patient who has a malignant tumor in his stomach. It is impossible to operate on the patient, but unless the tumor is destroyed, the patient will die. A kind of ray can be used to destroy the tumor. If the rays reach the tumor all at once at a sufficiently high intensity, the tumor will be destroyed. Unfortunately, at this intensity, the healthy tissue the rays pass through on the way to the tumor will also be destroyed. At lower intensities, the rays are harmless to healthy tissue, but they will not affect the tumor either. What type of procedure might be used to destroy the tumor with the rays and, at the same time, avoid destroying the healthy tissue?

Source: Gick, M. L., & Holyoak, K. J. (1980). Analogical problem solving. *Cognitive Psychology, 12,* 306–355. Reprinted by permission of Elsevier via Copyright Clearance Center.

situation), people are often unable to access their knowledge about one of these problems to help them solve the other.

The same problem occurs in negotiation. Studies of MBA students, executives, and consultants acquiring negotiation skills reveal a dramatic inert knowledge problem.[28] Transfer rates are quite low when a key principle needs to be applied to different

EXHIBIT 8-6   The Fortress Story

A small country fell under the iron rule of a dictator. The dictator ruled the country from a strong fortress. The fortress was situated in the middle of the country, surrounded by farms and villages. Many roads radiated outward from the fortress like spokes on a wheel. A great general arose, who raised a large army at the border and vowed to capture the fortress and free the country of the dictator. The general knew that if his entire army could attack the fortress at once, it could be captured. His troops were poised at the head of one of the roads leading to the fortress, ready to attack. However, a spy brought the general a disturbing report. The ruthless dictator had planted mines on each of the roads. The mines were set so that small bodies of men could pass over them safely because the dictator needed to be able to move troops and workers to and from the fortress. However, any large force would detonate the mines. Not only would this blow up the road and render it impassable, but the dictator would destroy many villages in retaliation. A full-scale direct attack on the fortress therefore appeared impossible.

The general, however, was undaunted. He divided his army into small groups and dispatched each group to the head of a different road. When all was ready, he gave the signal, and each group charged down a different road. All of the small groups passed safely over the mines, and the army then attacked the fortress in full strength. In this way, the general was able to capture the fortress and overthrow the dictator.

Source: Gick, M. L., & Holyoak, K. J. (1980). Analogical problem solving. *Cognitive Psychology, 12,* 306–355. Reprinted by permission of Elsevier via Copyright Clearance Center.

---

[28]Loewenstein, J., Thompson, L., & Gentner, D. (1999). Analogical encoding facilitates transfer in negotiation. *Psychonomic Bulletin and Review, 6*(4), 586–597; Loewenstein, J., Thompson, L., & Gentner, D. (2003). Analogical learning in negotiation teams: Comparing cases promotes learning and transfer. *Academy of Management Learning and Education, 2*(2), 119–127; Thompson, L., Loewenstein, J., & Gentner, D. (2000). Avoiding missed opportunities in managerial life: Analogical training more powerful than case-based training. *Organizational Behavior and Human Decision Processes, 82*(1), 60–75; Gentner, D., Loewenstein, J., & Thompson, L. (2003). Learning and transfer: A general role for analogical encoding. *Journal of Educational Psychology, 95*(2), 393–408; for a review, see Loewenstein, J., & Thompson, L. (2000). The challenge of learning. *Negotiation Journal, 16*(4), 399–408.

negotiation situations that involve different surface features. For example, when people are challenged with a negotiation situation involving a theater company that contains the potential for a contingency contract, they are often unable to employ the principle of contingency contracts even when they have received extensive training on this principle in a previous negotiation case involving a different context, such as a family-owned farm. This occurs because we tend to use our previous knowledge only when it seems similar to a new problem. People do not appear able to recognize problems that may benefit from similar problem solving principles and strategies.

The obvious question is this: What can decrease the inert knowledge problem and increase people's ability to transfer knowledge they possess when faced with a situation that could potentially benefit from that knowledge? One answer appears to be quite simple and powerful. It involves making an explicit comparison between two or more relevant cases.[29] To the extent that people mentally compare cases or situations, they are able to create a problem-solving schema that is uncluttered by irrelevant surface information. Thus, problem-solving schemas created through this process of mental comparison are more portable and more likely to be called upon when negotiators are challenged with a novel problem. In the absence of comparison, it is not clear to negotiators which information about a situation is relevant or irrelevant. Furthermore, as helpful as making comparisons can be, recognizing *when* to make them is not always obvious. For example, in our training of MBA students and executives, we frequently present negotiators with several training cases, usually on the same page. Very rarely do negotiators actively compare the cases printed on the same page, even though they contain a similar underlying principle. Thus, the key appears to be making comparisons among experiences, a strategy we elaborate upon later.

The preceding strategy focused on enhancing knowledge transfer by providing negotiators with very similar, specific examples. However, diverse analogical training, wherein negotiators compare several different value-creating strategies, may be more effective.[30] In a related investigation, negotiators were able to engage in successful knowledge transfer by focusing on differences in seemingly unrelated tasks.[31] Specifically, negotiators who were able to think about how others made decisions in versions of the "Monty Hall" game[32] and the multiparty "Ultimatum" game,[33] were more accurate in analyzing a new problem. [34]

Availability Heuristic

Which is more common: words that start with the letter K—for example, *king*—or words with K as the third letter—for example, *awkward?*[35] In the English language,

---

[29] Thompson, Loewenstein, & Gentner, "Avoiding missed opportunities."

[30] Moran, S., Bereby-Meyer, Y., & Bazerman, M. H. (2008). Stretching the effectiveness of analogical training in negotiations: Teaching diverse principles for creating value. *Negotiation and Conflict Management Research, 1*(2), 99–134.

[31] Idson, L., Chugh, D., Bereby-Meyer, Y., Moran, S., Grosskopf, B., & Bazerman, M. (2004). Overcoming focusing failures in competitive environments. *Journal of Behavioral Decision Making, 17,* 159–172.

[32] Nalebuff, B. (1987, Autumn). Puzzles: Choose a curtain, duelity, two point conversions, and more. *Journal of Economic Perspectives, 1,* 157–163.

[33] Messick, D. M., Moore, D. A., & Bazerman, M. H. (1997). Ultimatum bargaining with a group: Underestimating the importance of the decision rule. *Organizational Behavior and Human Decision Processes, 69*(2), 87–101.

[34] Samuelson, W. F., & Bazerman, M. H. (1985). Negotiating under the winner's curse. In V. Smith (Ed.), *Research in experimental economics: Vol. 3* (pp. 105–137). Greenwich, CT: JAI Press.

[35] Kahneman, D., & Tversky, A. (1982). On the study of statistical intuitions. *Cognition, 11*(2), 123–141.

more than twice as many words have K as the third letter than have K as the first letter. Despite this fact, the majority of people guess incorrectly (they assume that more words have K as the first letter), due to the **availability heuristic**. According to the availability heuristic, the more prevalent a group or category is judged to be, the easier it is for people to bring instances of this group or category to mind. This heuristic affects the quality of negotiators' judgments in that they may be biased by the ease with which information can be brought to mind. In another investigation, people were presented with a list of 39 names of well-known people.[36] Nineteen of the people on the list were female; 20 were male. The women happened to be more famous than the men. Afterward, people were asked to judge how many women's names appeared on the list. People dramatically overestimated the number of female names, presumably because they were easier to recall—another illustration of the availability heuristic.

The availability heuristic is associated with the **false consensus effect**.[37] The false consensus effect refers to the fact that most people think others agree with them more than is actually warranted. For example, people who smoke estimate that 51% of others are smokers, but nonsmokers estimate that only 38% of people are smokers.[38] Furthermore, people overestimate the proportion of people who agree with them about their attitudes concerning drugs, abortion, seatbelt use, politics, and even certain brand-name crackers.[39] When a negotiator falls victim to the availability heuristic, the likelihood of employing creative strategies (which are often less available) is severely undermined.

Representativeness

Imagine that you have just met your new boss. She is thin, wears glasses, is soft-spoken, and dresses conservatively. Does your supervisor enjoy poetry or sports? In answering such questions, people make judgments on the basis of a relatively simple rule: The more similar a person is to a group stereotype, the more likely he or she is to also belong to that group. Most people assume the supervisor enjoys poetry. Basically, the more a person *looks* like the stereotype of a group member, the more we are inclined to stereotype them as belonging to that group. The **representativeness heuristic** is based on stereotypes of people, which often have a basis in reality but are frequently outdated and wrong. Furthermore, reliance on stereotypical information leads people to overlook other types of information that could potentially be useful in negotiations. The most important type of information is related to base rates. **Base rates** are the frequency with which some event or pattern occurs in a general population. For example, consider a negotiator interested in purchasing a new car. One source of information concerning the new car is a popular consumer report. This report is based upon thousands of consumer data points and research and therefore is highly reliable. However, in addition to consulting this source, people interested in purchasing a new car

---

[36]Tversky, A., & Kahneman, D. (1973). Availability: A heuristic for judging frequency and probability. *Cognitive Psychology, 5,* 207–232.

[37]Sherman, S. J., Presson, C. C., & Chassin, L. (1984). Mechanisms underlying the false consensus effect: The special role of threats to the self. *Personality and Social Psychology Bulletin, 10,* 127–138.

[38]Ibid.

[39]Nisbett, R. E., Krantz, D. H., Jepson, C., & Kunda, Z. (1995). The use of statistical heuristics in everyday inductive reasoning. In R. E. Nisbett (Ed.), *Rules for reasoning* (pp. 15–54). Hillsdale, NJ: Erlbaum.

often consult their neighbors and friends. Sometimes, a neighbor or friend may have had a personal experience with a car that is quite different from what is reported in the consumer report magazine. Oftentimes, however, people who consult their neighbors and friends will discount perfectly valid information (i.e., the base rate information) and choose to rely upon a single, vivid data point. This error is known as the **base rate fallacy**.

Faulty judgments of probability are associated with what is known as the **gambler's fallacy**, the tendency to treat chance events as though they have a built-in, evening-out mechanism. However, each event is independently determined. As an example, consider the following problem: Suppose you flip a coin and it comes up heads five times in a row. What do you think the next outcome will be? Most people feel that the probability is high that the coin will come up tails. Of course, the probability of a heads or tails outcome is always the same (50%) for each flip, regardless of the previous result. However, most people think that some sequences (such as heads, tails, heads, tails) are far more likely to occur than others (such as a string of heads or a string of tails).[40]

Anchoring and Adjustment

Job candidates are often asked by recruiters to state their salary range. The job candidate, wanting to maximize his or her salary but at the same time not remove himself or herself from consideration because of unrealistic demands, faces a quandary. Similarly, the prospective home buyer struggles with what to make as an opening offer. What factors determine how we make such assessments of value?

People use a reference point as an anchor and then adjust that value up or down as deemed appropriate.[41] For example, a prospective job recruit may have a roommate who just landed a job with a salary of $80,000. The candidate decides to use $80,000 as a starting point. Two fundamental concerns arise with the anchoring-and-adjustment process. First, the anchors we use to make such judgments are often arbitrary.[42] Oftentimes, anchors are selected on the basis of their temporal proximity, not their relevance to the judgment in question. Second, we tend to make insufficient adjustments away from the anchor; we are weighed down by the anchor. (Remember how people's estimates of the number of doctors in Manhattan were affected by their Social Security number!) The message for the negotiator is clear: Carefully select anchors, and be wary if the counterparty attempts to anchor you.

Unwarranted Causation

Consider the following facts:

- Women living in the San Francisco area have a higher rate of breast cancer.
- Women of lower socioeconomic status are less likely to breast-feed their babies.
- People who marry at a later point in life are less likely to divorce.

---

[40]Tversky, A., & Kahneman, D. (1974). Judgment under uncertainty: Heuristics and biases. *Science, 185,* 1124–1131.
[41]Tversky & Kahneman, "Judgment under uncertainty."
[42]Ibid.

Before reading further, attempt to explain each fact. When people are asked to do so, they frequently conclude the following:

- Living in San Francisco causes breast cancer.
- People of lower socioeconomic status are not given postnatal care.
- People become wiser as they grow older.

All of these explanations are reasonable, but they are all unwarranted based upon the information given. The tendency to infer a **causal relationship** between two events is unwarranted because we do not know the direction of causality (for example, it is possible that women with cancer are attracted to the Bay Area). Further, a third variable could be the cause of the event (for example, people who marry later may be richer or more educated). Maybe older, more professional women are attracted to the Bay Area, and this group is statistically more susceptible to cancer. Maybe women of lower socioeconomic status are younger and less comfortable breast-feeding, more likely to be targeted by formula companies, or less likely to get maternity leave. There is a myriad of possible explanations.

Belief Perseverance

The **perseverance effect** is the tendency of people to continue to believe that something is true even when it is revealed to be false or has been disproved.[43] For example, imagine that you have taken an aptitude test and have been told you scored poorly. Later, you learn the exam was misscored. Are you able to erase this experience? Not if you are like most college students, who continue to persevere in their beliefs.[44] Why is this tendency so prevalent? Once a causal explanation is constructed, it is difficult to change it. If you or your counterparty has an erroneous belief about the other, even when it is proven wrong, the belief may still prevail. The important implication is to carefully examine the beliefs you hold about the counterparty and be cognizant of faulty beliefs they may have about you.

Illusory Correlation

Illusory correlation is the tendency to see invalid correlations between events. For example, people often perceive relationships between distinct pieces of information as a mere consequence of their being presented at the same time.[45] For example, in one investigation, people read diagnoses of mental patients.[46] Specifically, people were shown pictures allegedly drawn by these patients and then were given the patients' diagnoses to read. In actuality, there was no correlation at all between the types of pictures the patients allegedly drew and the nature of their diagnoses (paranoia, schizophrenia). Nevertheless, the people reviewing the evidence believed they saw correlations—for example,

---

[43]Ross, L., & Lepper, M. R. (1980). The perseverance of beliefs: Empirical and normative considerations. In R. A. Shweder (Ed.), *New directions for methodology of behavioral science: Fallible judgment in behavioral research.* San Francisco: Jossey-Bass.
[44]Ibid.
[45]Hamilton, D. L., & Gifford, R. K. (1976). Illusory correlation in interpersonal perception: A cognitive basis of stereotypic judgments. *Journal of Experimental Social Psychology, 12,* 392–407.
[46]Chapman, L. J., & Chapman, J. P. (1967). Genesis of popular but erroneous diagnostic observations. *Journal of Abnormal Psychology, 72,* 193–204; Chapman, L. J., & Chapman, J. P. (1969). Illusory correlation as an obstacle to the use of valid psychodiagnostic signs. *Journal of Abnormal Psychology, 74*(3), 271–280.

between a diagnosis of paranoia and a drawing of a very large eye. Even when people are presented with contradictory or ambiguous evidence, they are extremely reluctant to revise their judgments. As another example, suppose you learn during the course of a negotiation with a business representative from country X that 60% of country X's male population is uneducated. Suppose the same day you learn 60% of crimes committed in that country are violent. Although no logical relation connects the two statistics, most people assume a correlation; that is, they assume that uneducated men from country X are responsible for violent crimes. In fact, no relationship exists between the two—it is illusory. Such correlations between separate facts are illusory because they lack an objective basis for the relationships. Rather, our implicit theories are constructed so that we interpret relations between temporally proximate events.

Just World

Most people believe the world is a fair place: People get out of life what they deserve and deserve what happens to them.[47] This mind-set leads to positive evaluations of others who have good things happen to them; for example, most people believe "good" people are likely to win lotteries. Unwarranted negative impressions are produced when others suffer misfortune; for instance, we assume that bad people or ignorant people are victims of crimes.[48] **Blaming-the-victim attributions** are **defensive attributions** because they enable observers to deal with perceived inequities in others' lives and maintain the belief that the world is just.[49] In short, if we believe bad things could easily happen to us (e.g., dying in an airplane crash or losing a limb), the world seems scary and less predictable.

Hindsight Bias

The **hindsight bias** refers to a pervasive human tendency for people to be remarkably adept at inferring a process once the outcome is known but to be unable to predict outcomes when only the processes and precipitating events are known.[50] The hindsight bias, or the "I knew it all along" effect, makes integrative solutions to negotiation situations appear obvious when we see them in retrospect, although before they were discovered, the situation appeared to be fixed-sum.

We are frequently called upon to explain the causes of events, such as the demise of an organization or the success of a particular company. We often perceive events that have already occurred as inevitable. Stated another way, once we know the outcome of an event, we perceive the outcome to be an inevitable consequence of the factors leading to the outcome. This **creeping determinism**[51] accounts for the "Monday morning quarterback" or the "I knew it all along" phenomenon. Therefore, once someone knows the outcome, the events leading up to it seem obvious. The hindsight bias

---

[47]Lerner, M. (1980). *The belief in a just world: The fundamental delusion.* New York: Plenum.
[48]Saunders, D. G., & Size, P. B. (1986). Attitudes about woman abuse among police officers, victims, and victim advocates. *Journal of Interpersonal Violence, 1,* 25–42.
[49]Thornton, B. (1992). Repression and its mediating influence on the defensive attribution of responsibility. *Journal of Research in Personality, 26,* 44–57.
[50]Fischhoff, B. (1975). Hindsight does not equal foresight: The effect of outcome knowledge on judgment under uncertainty. *Journal of Experimental Psychology: Human Perception and Performance, 1,* 288–299.
[51]Ibid.

also accounts for why negotiators often think integrative agreements are obvious after the fact but fail to see them when encountering a novel negotiation.

Functional Fixedness

Functional fixedness occurs when a problem solver bases a strategy on familiar methods.[52] The problem with functional fixedness is that previously learned problem-solving strategies hinder the development of effective strategies in new situations. The person fixates on one strategy and cannot readily switch to another method of solving a problem. In other words, experience in one domain produces in-the-box thinking in another domain. Reliance on compromise as a negotiation strategy may produce functional fixedness.

The notion here is that past experience can limit problem solving. Consider the tumor problem presented in Exhibit 8-5. The solution rate, when people are given the problem by itself, is 37%; however, when people are shown a diagram of an arrow going through a black dot and then given the problem, the solution rate drops to 9%.[53] The diagram of the arrow going through the black dot depicted the function of the X-ray as a single line going through the human body; thus, it blocked people's ability to think of several rays focused on the tumor. Functional fixedness occurs when people have a mental block against using an object in a new way in order to solve a problem. In another example, people are challenged with the problem of how to mount a candle vertically on a nearby screen to function as a lamp. The only materials they are given are a box of matches, a box of candles, and a box of tacks. The creative solution is to mount the candle on top of the matchbox by melting the wax onto the box and sticking the candle to it, then tacking the box to the screen. This elegant solution is much harder to discover when the people are presented with the boxes filled with tacks (i.e., the way the boxes are normally used), rather than emptied of their contents.[54]

Set Effect

Closely related to the problem of functional fixedness is the **set effect**, in which prior experience can also have negative effects in new problem solving situations. Also known as **negative transfer**, prior experience can limit a manager's ability to develop strategies of sufficient breadth and generality. Consider the water jug problem presented in Exhibit 8-1. People who had the experience of working on all the water problems typically used a longer, costlier method to solve the problems. People without the experience of solving the problems almost always discovered the short, direct solution. Mechanized thought and set effects are the arthritis of managerial thinking and the wet blanket on the fires of creativity in negotiation. Consider the following example. Paramount Pictures forged a deal to buy DreamWorks after DreamWorks ended negotiations with rival bidder NBC. The DreamWorks studio, founded by Steven Spielberg, Jeffrey Katzenberg, and David Geffen, had

---

[52]Adamson, R. E., & Taylor, D. W. (1954). Functional fixedness as related to elapsed time and situation. *Journal of Experimental Psychology, 47,* 122–216.
[53]Duncker, K. (1945). On problem solving. *Psychological Monographs, 58,* 270.
[54]Anderson, J. R. (1995). *Cognitive psychology and its implications* (4th ed.). New York: Freeman.

been in on-and-off talks with NBC for several months. For NBC, the inability to close the deal demonstrated the difficulties of a corporate conglomerate running a creative enterprise in the movie business. NBC's analysis of minor deal points caused the DreamWorks situation to drag on for months, giving Paramount and DreamWorks time to get their act together and steal away the deal.[55]

Selective Attention

In negotiations, we are bombarded with information—the counterparty's physical appearance, his or her opening remarks, hearsay knowledge, nonverbal behavior, and so on. However, we perceive about 1% of all information in our stimulus field.[56] Thus, we perceive only a tiny fraction of what happens in the negotiation room. How do we know if we are paying attention to the right cues?

The basic function of our sensory information buffers is to parse and code stimulus information into recognizable symbols. Because external stimuli cannot get directly inside our heads, we cognitively represent stimuli as internal symbols and their interrelations as symbol structures. The sensory buffers—visual, auditory, and tactile—maintain the stimulus as an image or icon while its features are extracted. This activity occurs rapidly and below our threshold of awareness. The features extracted from a given stimulus object comprise a coded description of the object. For example, our interaction with a colleague concerning a joint venture is an event that is real, but our minds are not video cameras that record everything; rather, we use a process known as **selective attention**.

Overconfidence

Consider a situation in which you are assessing the probability that a particular company will be successful. Some people might think the probability is quite good; others might think the probability is low; others might make middle-of-the-road assessments. For the decision maker, what matters most is making an assessment that is accurate. How accurate are people in judgments of probability? How do they make assessments of likelihood, especially when full, objective information is unavailable?

Judgments of likelihood for certain types of events are often more optimistic than is warranted. The **overconfidence effect** refers to unwarranted levels of confidence in people's judgment of their abilities and the occurrence of positive events and underestimates of the likelihood of negative events. For example, in negotiations involving third-party dispute resolution, negotiators on each side believe the neutral third party will adjudicate in their favor.[57] Obviously, this outcome cannot happen; the third party cannot adjudicate in favor of both parties. Similarly, in final-offer arbitration, wherein parties each submit their final bid to a third party who then makes a binding decision between the two proposals, negotiators consistently overestimate the probability that

---

[55]Marr, M., & Kelly, K. (2005, December 10). Paramount to buy DreamWorks. *Wall Street Journal*, p. A3.

[56]Kaplan, S., & Kaplan, R. (1982). *Cognition and environment: Functioning in an uncertain world.* New York: Praeger.

[57]Farber, H. S. (1981). Splitting the difference in interest arbitration. *Industrial and Labor Relations Review, 35,* 70–77; Farber, H. S., & Bazerman, M. H. (1986). The general basis of arbitrator behavior: An empirical analysis of conventional and final offer arbitration. *Econometrica, 54,* 1503–1528; Farber, H. S., & Bazerman, M. H. (1989). Divergent expectations as a cause of disagreement in bargaining: Evidence from a comparison of arbitration schemes. *Quarterly Journal of Economics, 104,* 99–120.

the neutral arbitrator will choose their own offer.[58] Obviously, the probability is only 50% that a final offer will be accepted; nevertheless, typically, both parties' estimates sum to a number greater than 100%. The message is to beware of the overconfidence effect. When we find ourselves to be highly confident of a particular outcome occurring (whether it be the counterparty caving in to us, a senior manager supporting our decision, and so on), it is important to examine why.

Perspective taking has been a common treatment to remedy a number of faulty beliefs in negotiation, such as overconfidence and egocentric behavior. Indeed, leading people to consider other peoples' thoughts and perspective can reduce self-centered judgments such that people claim it is fair for them to take less from a common pool of resources, yet their behavior actually becomes more selfish![59] Moreover, people seem completely unaware of the fact that their personal beliefs about what is fair do not align with their behavior.

The Limits of Short-Term Memory

Short-term memory is the part of our mind that holds the information currently in the focus of our attention and conscious processing. Unfortunately, short-term memory has severely limited capacity; only about five to nine symbols or coded items may be currently active. The "seven plus-or-minus two" rule extends to just about everything we try to remember.[60] Consider, for example, an interaction you might have with the president of a company concerning the details of a consulting engagement. The president tells you many facts about her company; you will recall, on average, five to nine pieces of information. Without deliberate rehearsal, the information in your short-term memory will disappear and be replaced with new information perceived by your sensory registers. Obviously, we perceive much more information than we ultimately store and remember.

CREATIVE NEGOTIATION STRATEGIES

The following strategies are designed to sharpen your creative mind. Thus, they are not specific to negotiation; rather, they are an exercise program for enhancing creativity. Since negotiation, like exercise, is an activity we need to engage in regularly, these strategies can be extraordinarily beneficial for increasing creativity in negotiation.

Multiple Roads Lead to Rome (and an Expert Understanding)

In our research, we have carefully examined the ability of managers to apply what they learn in the classroom to their real-life negotiations. The rates of "positive transfer"

---

[58]Neale, M. A., & Bazerman, M. H. (1983). The role of perspective taking ability in negotiating under different forms of arbitration. *Industrial and Labor Relations Review, 36,* 378–388; Bazerman, M. H., & Neale, M. A. (1982). Improving negotiation effectiveness under final offer arbitration: The role of selection and training. *Journal of Applied Psychology, 67*(5), 543–548.

[59]Epley, N., Caruso, E., & Bazerman, M. (2006). When perspective taking increases taking: Reactive egoism in social interaction. *Journal of Personality and Social Psychology, 91*(5), 872–889.

[60]Miller, G. A. (1956). The magical number seven plus or minus two: Some limits on our capacity for processing information. *Psychological Review, 63,* 81–97.

(applying knowledge learned in one situation to another) are markedly limited.[61] Moreover, even the ability to benefit from our own experience is limited. For example, 100% of the respondents reading a negotiation case that contained win-win potential suggested (suboptimal) compromises.[62] We have found dramatic evidence that when attempting to learn something new (e.g., a key strategy, principle, etc.), it is important to have two (or more) cases or examples, rather than just one. The reason is clear: What is essential about any example or any case taught in a business school is not the details of the case but rather the underlying idea. The ability of a manager to separate the wheat from the chaff, or the core idea from the idiosyncrasies of the example, is limited if embedded in only one case. In fact, one case is no more effective than no cases at all.[63] However, it is not enough simply to be presented with two cases; the manager needs to actively mentally compare the two cases. Moreover, even if the instructor does not provide more than one case, if the manager (or trainee) can think of examples from his or her own experience, it can help significantly.

Feedback

No one can get better without feedback. For example, even star golfers regularly seek feedback on their swings. And when it comes to learning, the more intense and pointed the feedback is, the better. For example, power golf guru Jim McLean charges $500 per hour to give business leaders such as Henry Kravis, Charles Schwab, Ken Chenault, and David Rockefeller direct feedback on just how bad their swing looks.[64] His teaching style is simple and powerful: analyze, be direct, and focus on what needs work. Says McLean, "These [business] people are used to getting results on the job. They want the same from their golf games."[65] If we consider the fact that a near-perfect correlation exists between our ability to negotiate and our ability to successfully run a company, doesn't it make sense to seek feedback on our negotiation ability?

Feedback improves a negotiator's ability.[66] The type and method of feedback matter. For example, in one investigation of business managers' negotiations, negotiators were given one of four types of feedback (allegedly from their counterparty) following a negotiation, ranging from positive to negative, which focused on their abilities or their ethics:[67]

- *Positive-ability feedback*   ("What a skilled negotiator you seem to be.")
- *Negative-ability feedback*   ("What an unskilled negotiator you seem to be.")
- *Positive-ethicality feedback*   ("What an ethical negotiator you seem to be.")
- *Negative-ethicality feedback*   ("What an unethical negotiator you seem to be.")

---

[61]Thompson, Loewenstein, & Gentner, "Avoiding missed opportunities"; Loewenstein, Thompson, & Gentner, "Analogical learning in negotiation teams."

[62]Gentner, Loewenstein, & Thompson, "Learning and transfer."

[63]Loewenstein, Thompson, & Gentner, "Analogical learning in negotiation teams."

[64]Rynecki, D. (2003, August 11). Field guide to power: Power golf guru. *Fortune, 148(3),* p. 126.

[65]Ibid.

[66]Thompson, L., & DeHarpport, T. (1994). Social judgment, feedback, and interpersonal learning in negotiation. *Organizational Behavior and Human Decision Processes, 58*(3), 327–345; Nadler, J., Thompson, L., & van Boven, L. (2003). Learning negotiation skills: Four models of knowledge creation and transfer. *Management Science, 49*(4), 529–540.

[67]Kim, P. H., Diekmann, K. A., & Tenbrunsel, A. E. (2003). Flattery may get you somewhere: The strategic implications of providing positive vs. negative feedback about ability vs. ethicality in negotiation. *Organizational Behavior and Human Decision Processes, 90,* 225–243.

The key question was how the feedback would affect the performance of the nego-tiators in a subsequent negotiation situation. Negotiators who received the negative-ability feedback were the least competitive and achieved the worst individual performance. Ne-gotiators who received the negative-ethicality feedback were the most honest. Negotia-tors who received the positive-ethicality feedback were the most cooperative.[68]

In addition to the type of feedback negotiators give to one another, we examined the type of feedback a coach might give to a negotiator.[69] We first measured managers' baseline performance in an initial negotiation. Then we separated them into one of five different "feedback groups": no feedback (our scientific "control" condition); tradi-tional lecture-style feedback (also known as "didactic feedback"); information-based feedback (wherein negotiators learned about the other party's underlying interests); observational feedback (wherein negotiators watched experts-in-action via videotape for about 15 minutes); and analogical learning (wherein negotiators were given rele-vant cases that all depicted a key negotiation skill). The results? Nearly everything is better than no feedback at all, and nearly anything is better than traditional, class-room-style, didactic learning(see Exhibit 8-7).[70]

EXHIBIT 8-7   Effect of Learning Method on Negotiation Performance

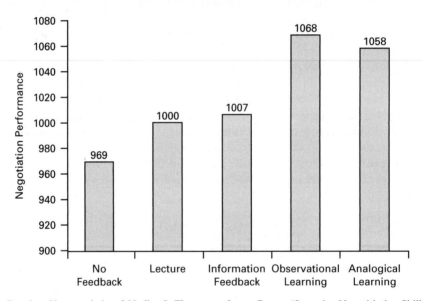

Source: Reprinted by permission. J. Nadler, L. Thompson, L. van Boven, "Learning Negotitiation Skills: Four Models of Knowledge Creation and Transfer." 2003. Management Science *49(4),* 529-540.

---

[68]Ibid.

[69]Nadler, Thompson, & van Boven, "Learning negotiation skills."

[70]For another illustration of how experience-based training is better than instruction-based training, see also van Boven & Thompson, "A look into the mind of the negotiator."

EXHIBIT 8-8   Incubation Effects

Numerous examples of incubation were reported by the famous French mathematician Poincaré including the following: "Then I turned my attention to the study of some arithmetical questions apparently without much success and without a suspicion of any connection with my preceding researches. Disgusted with my failure, I went to spend a few days at the seaside, and thought of something else. One morning, walking on the bluff, the idea came to me, with just the same characteristics of brevity, suddenness, and immediate certainty, that the arithmetic transformations of indeterminate ternary quadratic forms were identical with those of non-Euclidean geometry." (p. 388)

Source: Poincaré, H. (1929). *The foundations of sciences.* New York: Science House.

In an in-depth analysis of feedback in negotiation, two types of information were focused on: how well negotiators understand the counterparty's general priorities among the issues under negotiation, and how much the counterparty gained for a particular offer. Both types of understanding are important for negotiators to improve: Understanding the counterparty's interests is not sufficient to reach integrative outcomes; the additional step of assessment of their gains for each offer is key.[71]

Incubation

Excellent problem solvers frequently report that after trying to solve a problem and getting nowhere, they put the problem aside for hours, days, and even weeks, and upon returning to it, they can see the solution quickly. (For a real-life example of the incubation effect, see Exhibit 8-8.) The incubation phase is usually one step in a process of problem solving detailed in the following list:

1. *Preparation.*   During the preparation phase, the problem solver gathers information and makes preliminary attempts to arrive at a solution. The key here is to understand and define the problem. As we have noted, finding a good problem is the essence of effective negotiation.
2. *Incubation.*   When initial attempts to solve the problem have failed, problem solvers may put the problem aside to work on other activities or even to sleep. Although no one is sure why this tactic helps, people often engage in implicit problem solving at a level below conscious awareness.
3. *Illumination.*   During the illumination phase, the key to a solution often appears. It often happens when people are doing something completely unrelated to solving the problem.
4. *Verification.*   In the verification phase, problem solvers need to check the solution to make sure it works. As an example, think about the necklace problem you were challenged with in Exhibit 8-1, in which you are given four chains to make one necklace on a limited budget. Three groups of people worked on this problem.[72] One group spent 30 minutes trying to solve it, with a solution rate of 55%. A different group spent 30 minutes trying to solve it but was interrupted during the solving period with a 30-minute break. In this group, 64% of participants solved the problem. A third group spent 30 minutes trying to solve the problem but was interrupted in the solving process by a 4-hour break. Of this group, 85% solved the problem. Whereas we do not guarantee that difficult negotiation situations will always be met with illumination after putting the problem aside, it certainly cannot hurt to try.

---

[71]Moran, S., & Ritov, I. (2007). Experience in integrative negotiations: What needs to be learned? *Journal of Experimental Social Psychology, 43,* 77–90.
[72]Silveira, J. M. (1972). Incubation: The effect of interruption timing and length on problem solution and quality of problem processing. *Dissertation Abstracts International, 32*(9-B), 5500.

Rational Problem-Solving Model

The rational problem-solving model, patterned after Pólya, also describes four steps for solving a problem.[73] However, unlike the incubation method, the rational problem-solving model is deliberate and incremental:

1. **Understand the problem.** In this step, the negotiator needs to ask himself or herself: *What is known? What is unknown? What are the data I am using? What are my assumptions?*
2. **Devising a plan.** During this step, the negotiator may ask himself or herself whether past experience is a profitable means of finding a solution method, engaging in a search for similar problems, or perhaps restating the goal of the problem.
3. **Carrying out the plan.** In this step, the negotiator carries out the plan and tests it.
4. **Looking back.** In this step, the negotiator asks himself or herself whether he or she can obtain the result by using another method and looks at how it all fits together. In this step, it is important the negotiator ask what the key takeaway is.

Fluency, Flexibility, and Originality

What is creativity? What constitutes a creative idea? To be considered creative, an idea must be highly original and useful. The last part is the challenge—many people can come up with totally bizarre but useless ideas. One common way of evaluating creativity is via three indexes: fluency, flexibility, and originality.[74]

- **Fluency.** The ability to generate *many solutions* that all fit some requirement; a negotiator who is able to think of several solutions to a conflict (which matches the notion of strength in numbers).
- **Flexibility.** The ability to change approaches to a problem, such as being able to solve a series of tasks requiring a different strategy for each; a negotiator who is able to generate many *different kinds of solutions.*
- **Originality.** The ability to generate *unusual solutions,* such as coming up with unique answers; a negotiator who is able to think of solutions that elude other people.

As a way of thinking about these three indexes of creativity, do the following exercise: See how many possible uses you can think of for a cardboard box. (Give yourself about 10 minutes for this exercise.) Suppose one person who completed this exercise, Geoff, generated two ideas: using the box as a cage for a hamster and as a kennel for a dog. Geoff would receive two points for fluency of ideas because he offered two different ideas, but only one point for flexibility because the ideas are of the same category (i.e., a home for animals). Creative people generate more novel and unusual ways to use a cardboard box. Another person, Avi, generated these unusual ideas for a cardboard box: using it as a god, using it as a telephone (e.g., two boxes and some string), and trading it as currency. Avi would get a score of three points for fluency and three points for flexibility because three separate categories of ideas for use, involving religion, communication, and economics, were used. In addition, Avi's ideas are extremely original.

---

[73]Pólya, G. (1957). *How to solve it: A new aspect of mathematical method* (2nd ed.). New York: Doubleday; Pólya, G. (1968). *Mathematical discovery: Vol. II: On understanding, learning, and teaching problem solving.* New York: Wiley.
[74]Guilford, J. P. (1959). *Personality.* New York: McGraw-Hill; Guilford, J. P. (1967). The nature of human intelligence. *Intelligence, 1,* 274–280.

It is easy to see how flexibility in thought (that is, thinking about different categories of use) can influence originality. Thus, one key for enhancing creativity is to **diversify the use of categories**. By listing possible categories of use for a cardboard box (containers, shelter, building material, therapy, religion, politics, weaponry, communication, etc.), a person's score on these three dimensions could increase dramatically. Thus, a key strategy is to think in terms of *categories* of ideas—not just *number* of ideas. This approach can often help negotiators out of a narrow perspective on a conflict and open up new opportunities for creative solutions.

Brainstorming

Alex Osborn, an advertising executive in the 1950s, wanted to increase the creativity of organizations. He believed one of the main blocks to creativity was the premature evaluation of ideas. He was convinced two heads were better than one when it came to generating ideas—but only if people could be trained to defer judgment of their own and others' ideas during the idea-generation process. Therefore, Osborn developed the most widespread strategy used by organizations to encourage creative thought: brainstorming.

Brainstorming is a technique used by a large number of companies and organizations to unleash the creative group mind and avoid the negative impact of group dynamics on creativity. The goal of brainstorming is to maximize the quantity and quality of ideas. Osborn aptly noted that quantity is a good predictor of quality: A group is more likely to discover a really good idea if it has a lot of ideas from which to choose, but brainstorming involves more than mere quantity. Osborn believed that the ideas generated by one person in a team could stimulate ideas in other people in a synergistic fashion.

Osborn believed the collective product could be greater than the sum of the individual parts if certain conditions were met. Hence, he developed rules for brainstorming. Contrary to popular corporate lore that brainstorming sessions are wild and crazy free-for-alls where anything goes, brainstorming has defined rules,[75] which are still widely used today. In fact, several companies post the brainstorming guidelines and roles prominently in their meeting rooms (see Exhibit 8-9). However, people do not often use these rules for negotiations.

Convergent Versus Divergent Thinking

Two key skills are involved in creative thinking: divergent thinking and convergent thinking.[76] **Convergent thinking** proceeds toward a single answer, such as the expected value of a 70% chance of earning $1,000 is obtained by multiplying $1,000 by 0.7 to reach $700. **Divergent thinking** moves outward from the problem in many possible directions and involves thinking without boundaries. It is related to the notion of flexibility of categories and originality of thought. Divergent thinking *is* out-of-the-box thinking.

Many of the factors that make up creative problem solving seem most closely related to divergent thinking. However, ideas eventually need to be evaluated and acted

[75]Osborn, A. F. (1957). *Applied imagination.* New York: Scribner; Osborn, A. F. (1963). *Applied imagination* (3rd ed.). New York: Scribner.
[76]Guilford, *Personality*; Guilford, "Nature of human intelligence."

EXHIBIT 8-9 Rules for Brainstorming

Expressiveness: Group members should express any idea that comes to mind, no matter how strange, weird, or fanciful. Group members are encouraged not to be constrained nor timid. They should freewheel whenever possible.

Nonevaluation: Do not criticize ideas. Group members should not evaluate any of the ideas in any way during the generation phase; all ideas should be considered valuable.

Quantity: Group members should generate as many ideas as possible. Groups should strive for quantity; the more ideas, the better. Quantity of ideas increases the probability of finding excellent solutions.

Building: Because all of the ideas belong to the group, members should try to modify and extend the ideas suggested by other members whenever possible.

Source: Based on Osborn, A. F. (1957). *Applied imagination:* (Rev. Ed.). New York: Scribner.

---

upon, which is where convergent thinking comes in. In convergent thinking, a negotiator judges and evaluates the various ideas presented in relation to their feasibility, practicality, and overall merit.

People working independently excel at divergent thinking because no cognitive or social pressures constrain their thought. In short, they are not subject to conformity pressures. In contrast, people are much less proficient at divergent thinking. To avoid social censure, people assess the norms of the situation and conform to them. In contrast, groups excel compared to individuals when it comes to convergent thinking. Groups are better at judging the quality of ideas. This ability suggests that an effective design for promoting creativity in negotiation involves separating the generation of ideas—leaving this task to individual team members—and then evaluating and discussing the ideas as a team. (However, divergent thinking is not always looked upon favorably; see Exhibit 8-10.)

Deductive Reasoning

To be effective at negotiation, negotiators must be good at deductive, as well as inductive, reasoning. First we take up the topic of **deductive reasoning**, or the process of

---

EXHIBIT 8-10 Divergent Thinking

Divergent thinking (or creative thinking) is often not rewarded in schools or organizations. For example, Getzels and Jackson observed that teachers prefer students who have high IQs but are not high in creativity. High-IQ students and managers tend to gauge success by conventional standards (i.e., to behave as teachers expect them to and seek careers that conform to what others expect of them). In contrast, highly creative people use unconventional standards for determining success, and their career choices do not usually conform to expectations. Most educational training, including that of MBAs, favors logical or convergent thinking and does not nurture creative or divergent thinking.

Source: Getzels, J. W., & Jackson, P.W. (1962). *Creativity and intelligence: Explorations with gifted students.* New York: Wiley.

drawing logical conclusions. For example, most people have some kind of training in solving logical syllogisms, such as the ones in Exhibit 8-11. The difficulty in solving these syllogisms does not imply that managers are unintelligent; rather, it indicates that formal logic and individual (or psychological) processes are not necessarily the same. However, many people violate rules of logic on a regular basis. Some of the most common violations of the rules of logic are the following:

- *Agreement with a conclusion.*   The desirability of the conclusion often drives people's appraisal of reality. This behavior, of course, is a form of wishful thinking, as well as an egocentric bias. The tendency is strong for people to judge the conclusions they agree with as valid, and the conclusions they disagree with as invalid.
- *Cognitive consistency.*   People have a tendency to interpret information in a fashion that is consistent with information they already know. The tendency for people to judge conclu-

---

EXHIBIT 8-11   Sample Syllogisms

Pick the conclusions about which you can be sure:

1. All S are M. All M are P. Therefore,
   a. All S are P.
   b. All S are not P.
   c. Some S are P.
   d. Some S are not P.
   e. None of these conclusions is valid.
2. As technology advances and natural petroleum resources are depleted, the securing of petroleum from unconventional sources becomes more imperative. One such source is the Athabasca tar sands of northern Alberta, Canada. Because some tar sands are sources of refinable hydrocarbons, these deposits are worthy of commercial investigation. Some kerogen deposits are also sources of refinable hydrocarbons. Therefore:
   a. All kerogen deposits are tar sands.
   b. No kerogen deposits are tar sands.
   c. Some kerogen deposits are tar sands.
   d. Some kerogen deposits are not tar sands.
   e. None of the above.
3. The delicate Glorias of Argentina, which open only in cool weather, are all Sassoids. Some of the equally delicate Fragilas, found only in damp areas, are not Glorias. What can you infer from these statements?
   a. All Fragilas are Sassoids.
   b. No Fragilas are Sassoids.
   c. Some Fragilas are Sassoids.
   d. Some Fragilas are not Sassoids.
   e. None of the above.
   If you think like most people, you think that problem 1 is probably the easiest to solve (the answer is a). However, problems 2 and 3 generate much higher error rates (75% error rate for problem 2, with most errors due to picking answer c instead of e; 90% error rate for problem 3, mainly due to picking d instead of e).

Source: Based on Stratton, R. P. (1983). Atmosphere and conversion errors in syllogistic reasoning with contextual material and the effect of differential training. Unpublished master's thesis, Michigan State University, East Lansing. In R. E. Mayer (Ed.), *Thinking, problem-solving, and cognition.* New York: W. H. Freeman and Company.

EXHIBIT 8-12   The Hospital Problem

A certain town is served by two hospitals. In the larger hospital, about 45 babies are born each day, and in the smaller hospital, about 15 babies are born each day. As you know, about 50% of all babies are boys. However, the exact percentage varies from day to day. Sometimes it may be higher than 50%, sometimes lower. For a period of one year, each hospital recorded the days in which more than 60% of the babies born were boys. Which hospital do you think recorded more such days?

1. The larger hospital
2. The smaller hospital
3. About the same (within 5 percent of each other)

Source: Tversky, A., & Kahneman, D. (1974). Judgment under uncertainty: Heuristics and biases. *Science, 185,* 1124–1131. Used with permission from AAAS.

sions to be true, based upon whether the information agrees with what they already know to be true, illustrates the need for consistency in one's belief structure.

- *Confirmation bias.*   People have a strong tendency to seek information that confirms what they already know. A good example of this bias is the card task presented in Exhibit 8-1.

Inductive Reasoning

Inductive reasoning is a form of hypothesis testing, or trial and error. In general, people are not especially good at testing hypotheses, and they tend to use confirmatory methods. A good example is the card task in Exhibit 8-1. Another example is the availability heuristic we discussed previously, which states that judgments of frequency tend to be biased by the ease with which information can be called to mind.

For example, people make inaccurate judgments when estimating probabilities. Consider the problem in Exhibit 8-12.[77] When people are asked to answer this question, 22% select the first answer (i.e., the larger hospital), 22% select the second answer (i.e., the smaller hospital), and 56% select the third answer (i.e., both hospitals). They seem to make no compensation for large versus small sample sizes. They believe that an extreme event (for example, 60% of births being male) is just as likely in a large hospital as in a small one. In fact, it is actually far more likely for an extreme event to occur within a small sample because fewer cases are included in the average. People often fail to take sample size into account when they make an inference.

In summary, managers do not form generalizations (reason inductively) in ways that statistics and logic suggest. When people make inferences about events based on their experience in the real world, they do not behave like statisticians. Rather, they seem to be heavily influenced by salient features that stand out in their memory, and they are swayed by extreme events even when the sample size is small.

---

[77]Tversky & Kahneman, "Judgment under uncertainty."

Flow

According to Csikszentmihalyi, **autotelic experience**, or **flow**, is a particular kind of experience so engrossing and enjoyable that it becomes worth doing, even though it may have no consequences beyond its own context.[78] Creative activities in life, such as music, sports, games, and so on, are typical sources for this kind of experience. Of course, people never do anything purely for its own sake—their motives are always a combination of intrinsic and extrinsic considerations. For example, filmmakers may make films for the joy of creating something artistic but also because the film may make money or win an Academy Award. Similarly, managers and executives create new products and ideas not only because they enjoy doing so but also because the products will make the company more profitable. However, if people are only motivated by extrinsic rewards, they are missing a key ingredient in terms of experience. In addition to external rewards, they can also enjoy an activity, such as negotiation, for its own sake.

This kind of intense flow experience is not limited to creative endeavors. It is also found in the most mundane activities in the personal and business world, such as going to work every day, interacting with people, and so on. An important condition for the flow experience is that a person feels his or her abilities match the opportunities for action. If the challenges are too great for a person's skill, intense anxiety, or **choking**, can occur. However, if the person's skills outweigh the challenges of the experience, he or she may feel bored. In a negotiation, this effect of flow means the process of working through differences, satisfying underlying needs, and creating value is more important than the content of the particular negotiation. To the extent that negotiation is viewed as unpleasant, uncomfortable, or a struggle, flow (and the creative process that can ensue from flow) is less likely to occur.

CONCLUSION

Effective negotiation requires creative thinking. The ability to think creatively is affected by a negotiator's mental model of negotiation. We identified five common mental models: haggling, cost-benefit analysis, game playing, partnership, and problem solving. Creative negotiations involve fractionating problems into several, simpler parts; finding differences to exploit; expanding the pie; bridging; cost cutting; nonspecific compensation; and structuring contingency contracts. We reviewed several of the biggest threats to creativity in negotiation, including the inert knowledge problem, availability bias, representativeness, anchoring and adjustment, unwarranted causation, illusory correlation, hindsight bias, functional fixedness, selective attention, and overconfidence. We described several strategies for rethinking almost any negotiation problem, including feedback, incubation, brainstorming, divergent (as opposed to convergent) thinking, deductive as well as inductive reasoning, and psychological flow.

---

[78]Csikszentmihalyi, M. (1997). *Finding flow: The psychology of engagement with everyday life.* New York: Basic Books.

EXHIBIT 8-13 Answers to Creativity Test

CARD DECISION[*]

Correct answer: E and 7.

Averaging over a large number of experiments,[†] it has been found that 89% of people select E, which is a logically correct choice because an odd number on the other side would disconfirm the rule. However, 62% also choose to turn over the 4, which is not logically informative because neither a vowel nor a consonant on the other side would have falsified the rule. Only 25% elect to turn over the 7, which is a logically informative choice because a vowel behind the 7 would have falsified the rule. Only 16% elect to turn over K, which would not be an informative choice.

PERSON IN A ROOM DECISION[‡]

Correct answer: Jack is a lawyer.

This problem illustrates a classic base-rate problem. We are given information that the probability of any one person selected is equivalent to the stated base rates; the normatively appropriate solution is 30%, thus making it more likely that Jack is a lawyer. Yet, most people choose to ignore base rate information and assume that Jack is an engineer. An answer that goes against explicitly stated probability theory runs the risk of being one based on stereotypes. Groups may be more likely to defend the stereotype decision.

BETTING DECISION[§]

Correct answer: A (for the first bet).

The normatively appropriate logic here is to use expected value theory, in which the expected value of a risky choice is determined by the value of the payoff multiplied by its probability. Using this technique, the expected value of bet A is $8 \times 0.3333 = 2.66. The expected value of bet B is ($3 \times 0.8333 = 2.5). Thus, bet A maximizes expected value. However, many people overweight high probabilities and end up choosing bet B. Groups tend to be riskier than individuals, so groups often choose riskier decisions, whether they are normatively appropriate or not. For the second bet, either answer is normatively correct because their expected values are the same.

WATER JUGS[**]

Problem solvers can become biased by their experiences to prefer certain problem solving operators in solving a problem. Such biasing of the problem solution is known as a **set effect**. Also known as the **Einstellung effect**, or **mechanization of thought**, this can paradoxically lead to worsened performance. The Einstellung effect involves remembering a particular sequence of operations, and it is memory for this sequence that is blinding managers to other possibilities. In this series of problems, all problems except 8 can be solved by using the B-2C-A method. For problems 1 through 5, this solution is the simplest, but for problems 7 and 9, the simpler

[*]Wason, P. C., & Johnson-Laird, P. N. (1972). *Psychology of reasoning: Structure and content.* Cambridge, MA: Harvard University Press.

[†]Oaksford, M., & Chater, N. (1994). A rational analysis of the selection task as optimal data selection. *Psychological Review, 101*(4), 608–631.

[‡]Kahneman, D., & Tversky, A. (1973). On the psychology of prediction. *Psychological Review, 80,* 237–251.

[§]Tversky, A., & Kahneman, D. (1981). The framing of decisions and the psychology of choice. *Science, 211,* 453–458.

[**]Luchins, A. S. (1942). Mechanization in problem solving. *Psychological Monographs, 5*(46), 1–95.

solution of A + C also applies. Problem 8 cannot be solved by the B-2C-A method but can be solved by the simpler solution of A-C. Problems 6 and 10 are also solved more simply as A-C than B-2C-A.

Of the participants who received the whole setup of 10 problems, 83% used the B-2C-A method on problems 6 and 7, 64% failed to solve problem 8, and 79% used the B-2C-A method for problems 9 and 10. The performance of people who worked on all 10 problems was compared with the performance of people who saw only the last 5 problems. These people did not see the biasing B-2C-A problems. Fewer than 1% of these people used B-2C-A solutions, and only 5% failed to solve problem 8. Thus, the first 5 problems can create a powerful bias for a particular solution. This bias hurt solution of problems 6 through 10.

STICK PROBLEM[††]

Correct answer: Form a tetrahedron (something like a pyramid).
Most people take the six sticks and form a square with an X in it. However, this solution is not acceptable because the triangles are not equilateral—each has a 90-degree angle. Another incorrect answer that is common is to form three of the sticks in a triangle and overlay them on another triangle upside down; this produces four triangles, but the sides of the triangle are not one stick in length. To solve the problem, the solver must think in three dimensions, making a pyramid with a triangle base. This is a general class of problem situations that often involve "insight"—a rearrangement of the parts in a certain way to solve a problem.

LETTER SEQUENCE[‡‡]

Correct answer: E.
The answer to this Eureka problem is E. The letters are the first seven letters of the first eight digits: one, two, three, four, five, six, seven, and eight.

CHAIN PROBLEM[§§]

Open one chain and put links between the other three.

SUSAN AND MARTHA

Correct answer: 36.
This is a disjunctive decision task. It is a Eureka problem, and the answer must be calculated. Only 14 combinations yield a total of 13 (e.g., 1, 1, 11; 1, 2, 10; 1, 3, 9, etc.), and only two of these have the identical product (1, 6, 6 and 2, 2, 9). If we assume Susan knows her own age, she would still be confused only if she were 36.

NECKLACE[***]

Initially, people tend to break a link on each chain, attach it to another chain, and then close it. The more elegant (and cheaper) solution is to break a single three-link piece and use its links to attach others. It costs 6 cents to open three links. The total connection cost is 9 cents, yielding a 15-cent necklace.

[††]Scheer, M. (1963). *Scientific American, 208,* 118–218.

[‡‡]Source unknown.

[§§]De Bono, E. (1967). *The use of lateral thinking.* New York: Penguin

[***]Wickelgren, W. A. (1974). *How to solve problems.* San Francisco, CA: W. H. Freeman.

continued

EXHIBIT 8-13   Answers to Creativity Test (*continued*)

GOLD CHAIN

Correct answer: 2.

The chain puzzle is a Eureka problem. Many groups answer 11 because that would involve cutting only every other link. The correct answer, however, is 2. If the fourth and eleventh links are cut, all the values from 1 to 23 can be obtained by getting "change" back from the motel owner. Separate links (the fourth and the eleventh) are given on days 1 and 2, but on day 3 the three-link unit is given to the owner, who returns the separate links. These links are then used to pay on days 4 and 5, but on day 6 the six-link unit is used, and the owner returns the others as change. The process can be continued for 23 days.

NINE DOT PROBLEM[†††]

Correct answer: See Panels 3 and 4.

Most people implicitly assume that the lines must be drawn within an imaginary boundary, as shown in the second panel of the diagram. One possible solution that is preferred by "experts" is given in the third panel of the diagram. The problem solver must go outside the self-imposed square boundary. Another creative solution uses lines that do not go through the center of the dots, as shown in the fourth panel of the diagram. This solution involves overcoming another self-imposed limit on the problem—namely, realizing it is not necessary to draw the lines through the center of each dot.

Thus, one major kind of conceptual block is the tendency to impose too many constraints on the problem (that is, to represent the problem in a way that limits the potential kinds of solutions). Overcoming the conceptual blocks is similar to overcoming functional fixedness or Einstellung; instead, look for alternative ways of representing the problem.

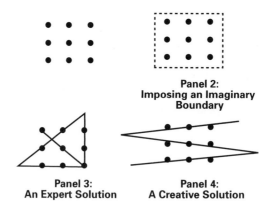

Panel 2:
Imposing an Imaginary
Boundary

Panel 3:
An Expert Solution

Panel 4:
A Creative Solution

[†††]Weisberg, R. W., & Alba, J. W. (1981). An examination of the alleged role of "fixation" in the solution of several insight problems. *Journal of Experimental Psychology: General, 110,* 169–192.

PIGPEN[‡‡‡]

Correct answer: See diagram.
This is an "insight" problem. Most people assume that each pigpen must be square. The solution involves diamond-shaped pens.

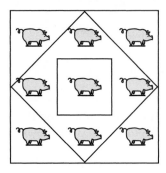

WATERLILIES[§§§]

Correct answer: Day 59.
This is a pure "insight" problem. People initially approach the problem as one involving a linearly increasing quantity and simply divide the total time in half. However, because the lilies increase exponentially in area, this approach is incorrect, and another representation is needed. Such a change in representation can occur when the participant tries to imagine what happens as the pond fills up and he or she works backward from the last day, rather than carrying out a formal analysis of the problem.

BARTENDER PROBLEM[****]

The man who walked into the bar had the hiccups. The bartender realized this and attempted to scare the daylights out of the man by pointing a gun at him. Some people are able to solve this problem immediately; others are not. This is a Eureka problem.

[‡‡‡]Fixx, J. F. (1972). *More games for the super-intelligent.* New York: Warner Books.

[§§§]Sternberg, R. J., & Davidson, J. E. (1983). Insight in the gifted. *Educational Psychologist, 18,* 51–57.

[****]Dayton, T., Durso, F. T., & Shepard, J. D. (1990). A measure of the knowledge reorganization underlying insight. In R. W. Schraneveldt (Ed.), *Pathfinder associative networks: Studies in knowledge organization.* Norwood, NJ: Ablex.

CHAPTER

Multiple Parties, Coalitions, and Teams

In May 2003, CEOs at every company on the *Fortune* 1000 and *Fortune* Global 500 opened a letter to discover they would be sued if anyone anywhere in their company had used Linux—the free, open-source operating system sweeping corporate IT departments. A little known company named SCO Group, headquartered in Lindon, Utah, had sent the letter. Two months earlier, SCO had filed a $1 billion lawsuit against IBM, claiming that Big Blue had taken chunks of SCO-owned Unix code and sprinkled it into Linux. According to Darl McBride, the CEO of SCO, some companies were misusing Unix code by inserting it into other programs they were using, a privilege they needed to pay SCO for in the form of an additional license. The leverage that SCO had in fighting IBM was by involving IBM's customers. The more SCO could scare Big Blue's customers, the more power SCO had. To make things more complicated, Ralph Yarro, the head of Canopy Group, owned 43 percent of SCO. Canopy, owned by Noorda, is made up of 35 start-up companies. When McBride got rebuffed by IBM, he flew to the Florida office of Boies, Schiller, and Flexner for a meeting with the anti-Microsoft litigator David Boies, who agreed to take up the case on a combination contingency and hourly-fee basis. In the meantime, Microsoft called BayStar Capital managing partner Lawrence Goldfarb to ask if he would consider investing in SCO. Finally, in 2007 a federal court in Utah ruled that Novell, not SCO, owned the copyright to Unix. The ruling stated that SCO had only licensed Unix from Novell and declared that Novell had the authority to force SCO to drop its claim against IBM.[1]

The opening example indicates that negotiation situations are not purely one-on-one situations. Often, other people are at the table and behind the scenes. Some are negotiators; some are agents; others are constituents. To negotiate

---

[1]Lashinsky, A. (2003, July 21). Penguin slayer. *Fortune, 148(2),* 85–90; Kersetter, J. (2004, March 22). Microsoft versus Linux. *Business Week, 3875,* 14; Winstein, K. J., & Bulkeley, W. M. (2007, August 11). Court ruling gives Novell copyright in Unix system. *Wall Street Journal,* p. A3.

effectively in groups, negotiators need all of the skills we have described thus far, and then some. We discuss the skills specific to multiparty negotiation in this chapter.

The SCO-IBM dispute illustrates a complex assortment of players. At the primary table are SCO and IBM. When IBM becomes a reluctant negotiator, SCO puts leverage on IBM's hidden or secondary table—its customers. SCO's second table includes the Canopy Group, which is an extension of Noorda, and BayStar Capital, which is connected to SCO. Ultimately, Novell enters the negotiation.

ANALYZING MULTIPARTY NEGOTIATIONS

How might we analyze the negotiation between SCO and IBM? The negotiation involves a myriad of players, relationships, and issues. In the example in Exhibit 9-1, two principals are involved in the multiparty negotiation: SCO and IBM. Noorda, the Canopy Group, BayStar Capital, and Novell are potential principals. A coalition may include SCO and Microsoft, SCO and IBM customers, or IBM and Novell. Further, other companies are in positions similar to IBM (in terms of receiving the letter) and may act as coalition partners. Negotiations within and between organizations are embedded in an intricate web of interdependent relationships and interests. Just as a complete understanding of human anatomy requires analyses at the levels of cell chemistry, tissues, organs, and organ

EXHIBIT 9-1 SCO-IBM Negotiations Structure

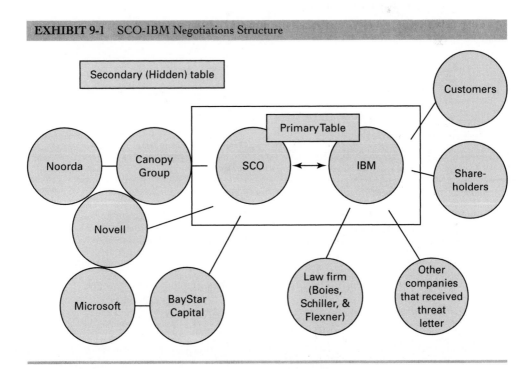

systems, a complete understanding of negotiation within and between organizations requires analysis at several levels.[2]

In this chapter, we review six levels of analysis beyond one-on-one negotiation: (1) multiparty negotiations, (2) coalitions, (3) principal-agent relationships, (4) constituencies, (5) team negotiation, and (6) team-on-team negotiations, or intergroup negotiations (see Exhibit 9-2). For each level, we identify key challenges and suggest practical advice and strategies for maximizing negotiation effectiveness.

EXHIBIT 9-2 Levels of Analysis in Multiparty Negotiation

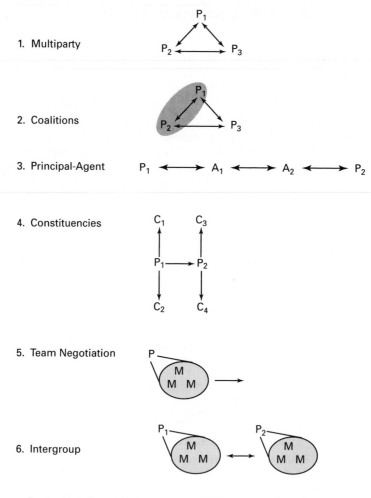

P, principal; C, constituency group; M, group member; A, agent

[2] Thompson, L., & Fox, C. (2000). Negotiation within and between groups in organizations: Levels of analysis. In M. Turner (Ed.), *Groups at work: Advances in theory and research*. Hillsdale, NJ: Erlbaum.

MULTIPARTY NEGOTIATIONS

A **multiparty negotiation** is formed when a group of three or more individuals, each representing his or her own interests, attempts to resolve perceived differences of interest.[3] The involvement of more than two principals at the negotiation table complicates the situation enormously. Social interactions become more complex, information-processing demands increase exponentially, and coalitions form. Yet groups make more accurate judgments and more readily aggregate information than do individuals.[4]

Key Challenges of Multiparty Negotiations

We present four key challenges of multiparty negotiations and follow with some practical advice.

Dealing with Coalitions

A key difference between two-party and group negotiations is the potential for two or more parties within a group to form a coalition to pool their resources and exert greater influence on outcomes.[5] A **coalition** is a (sub)group of two or more individuals who join together in using their resources to affect the outcome of a decision in a mixed-motive situation[6] involving at least three parties.[7] Coalition formation is one way that otherwise weak group members may marshal a greater share of resources. Coalitions involve both cooperation and competition. Members of coalitions cooperate with one another in competition against other coalitions but compete against one another regarding the allocation of rewards the coalition obtains.

Formulating Trade-Offs

Integrative agreements are more difficult to fashion in multiparty negotiations because the trade-offs are more complex. In a multiparty negotiation, integrative trade-offs may be achieved either through circular or reciprocal logrolling.[8] **Circular logrolling** involves trade-offs that require each group member to offer another member a concession on one issue while receiving a concession from yet another group

[3]Bazerman, M. H., Mannix, E., & Thompson, L. (1988). Groups as mixed-motive negotiations. In E. J. Lawler & B. Markovsky (Eds.), *Advances in group processes: Theory and research: Vol. 5.* Greenwich, CT: JAI Press; Kramer, R. M. (1991). The more the merrier? Social psychological aspects of multiparty negotiations in organizations. In M. H. Bazerman, R. J. Lewicki, & B. H. Sheppard (Eds.), *Research on negotiations in organizations: Handbook of negotiation research: Vol. 3* (pp. 307–332). Greenwich, CT: JAI Press.

[4]Bottom, W. P., Ladha, K., & Miller, G. J. (2002). Propagation of individual bias through group judgment: Error in the treatment of asymmetrically informative signals. *Journal of Risk and Uncertainty, 25*(2), 147–163.

[5]For a review, see Komorita, S. S., & Parks, C. D. (1995). Interpersonal relations: Mixed-motive interaction. *Annual Review of Psychology, 46,* 183–207.

[6]Komorita & Parks, "Interpersonal relations"; Murnighan, J. K. (1978). Models of coalition behavior: Game theoretic, social psychological, and political perspectives. *Psychological Bulletin, 85,* 1130–1153.

[7]Gamson, W. (1964). Experimental studies in coalition formation. In L. Berkowitz (Ed.), *Advances in experimental social psychology: Vol. 1.* New York: Academic Press.

[8] Palmer, L. G., & Thompson, L. (1995). Negotiation in triads: Communication constraints and tradeoff structure. *Journal of Experimental Psychology: Applied, 2,* 83–94.

member on a different issue. A circular trade-off is typified by the tradition of drawing names from a hat to give holiday gifts to people. People receive a gift from one person and give a gift to yet another person. Ideally, we give gifts that are more appreciated by the recipient than by the giver. In contrast, **reciprocal trade-offs** are fashioned between two members of a larger group. Reciprocal trade-offs are typified in the more traditional form of exchanging presents. Circular trade-offs are more risky than reciprocal trade-offs because they involve the cooperation of more than two group members.

Voting and Majority Rule

Groups often simplify the negotiation of multiple issues among multiple parties through voting and decision rules. However, if not used wisely, decision rules can thwart effective negotiation, both in terms of pie-expansion and pie-slicing. A number of problems are associated with voting and majority rule.[9]

Problems with Voting and Majority Rule   **Voting** is the procedure of collecting individuals' preferences for alternatives on issues and selecting the most popular alternative as the group choice. The most common procedure used to aggregate preferences of team members is **majority rule**. However, majority rule presents several problems in the attainment of efficient negotiation settlements. Despite its democratic appeal, majority rule fails to recognize the strength of individual preferences. One person in a group may feel very strongly about an issue, but his or her vote counts the same as the vote of someone who does not have a strong opinion about the issue. Consequently, majority rule does not promote integrative trade-offs among issues. Groups negotiating under unanimous rule reach more efficient outcomes than groups operating under majority rule.[10]

Although **unanimity rule** is time-consuming, it encourages group members to consider creative alternatives to expand the size of the pie and satisfy the interests of all group members. Because strength of preference is a key component in the fashioning of integrative agreements, majority rule hinders the development of mutually beneficial trade-offs. Voting in combination with other decision aids, such as agendas, may be especially detrimental to the attainment of efficient outcomes because it prevents logrolling.[11]

---

[9]For an overview, see Bottom, W. P., Eavey, C. L., Miller, G. J., & Victor, J. N. (2000). The institutional effect on majority rule instability: Bicameralism in spatial policy decisions. *American Journal of Political Science, 44*(3), 523–540; Bottom, W. P., Handlin, L., King, R. R., & Miller, G. J. (2002). Institutional modifications of majority rule. In C. Plott & V. Smith (Eds.), *Handbook of experimental economics results.* Amsterdam: North Holland.

[10]Beersma, B., & De Dreu, C. K. W. (2002). Integrative and distributive negotiation in small groups: Effects of task structure, decision rule, and social motive. *Organizational Behavior and Human Decision Processes, 87*(2), 227–252; Mannix, E. A., Thompson, L., & Bazerman, M. H. (1989). Negotiation in small groups. *Journal of Applied Psychology, 74*(3), 508–517; Thompson, L., Mannix, E., & Bazerman, M. H. (1988). Group negotiation: Effects of decision rule, agenda, and aspiration. *Journal of Personality and Social Psychology, 54,* 86–95.

[11]Mannix, Thompson, & Bazerman, "Negotiation in small groups"; Thompson, Mannix, & Bazerman, "Group negotiation."

Other problems arise with voting. Within groups that demonstrate "egoistic" motives (as opposed to prosocial motives), majority rule leads to more distributive and less integrative behavior.[12] Group members may not agree upon a method for voting; for example, some members may insist upon unanimity, others may argue for a simple majority rule, and still others may advocate a weighted majority rule. Even if a voting method is agreed upon, it may not yield a choice. For example, a group may not find a majority if the group is evenly split. Voting does not eliminate conflicts of interest but, instead, provides a way for group members to live with conflicts of interest; for this reason, majority rule decisions may not be stable. In this sense, voting hides disagreement within groups, which threatens long-term group and organizational effectiveness.

Voting Paradoxes   Consider a three-person (Raines, Warner, and Lassiter) product development team. The three are in conflict over which design to use—A, B, or C. The preference ordering is depicted in Exhibit 9-3. Everyone is frustrated, and the group has argued for hours. As a way of resolving the conflict, Warner suggests voting between designs A and B. In that vote, A wins and B is discarded. Warner then proposes that the group vote between A and C. In that vote, C wins. Warner then declares that design C be implemented. Lassiter concludes that the group vote was fair and agrees to develop design C. However, Raines is perplexed and suggests taking another vote. Warner laughs and says, "We just took a vote and you lost—so just accept the outcome!" Raines glares at Warner and says, "Let's do the vote again, and I will agree to accept the outcome. However, this time I want us to vote between B and C first." Warner has no choice but to go along. In this vote, B is the clear winner and C is eliminated. Next, the vote is between A and B, and A beats B. Raines happily declares A the winner. Lassiter then jumps up and declares that the whole voting process was fraudulent but cannot explain why.

Raines, Warner, and Lassiter are victims of the **Condorcet paradox**, which demonstrates that the winners of majority rule elections will change as a function of the *order* in which alternatives are proposed. Alternatives that are proposed later, as opposed to earlier, are more likely to survive sequential voting.[13] Thus, clever

EXHIBIT 9-3   Manager's Preferences for Product Designs

Manager	Design A	Design B	Design C
Raines	1	2	3
Warner	2	3	1
Lassiter	3	1	2

---

[12]Beersma & De Dreu, "Integrative and distributive negotiation."
[13]May, K. (1982). A set of independent, necessary and sufficient conditions for simple majority decisions. In B. Barry & R. Hardin (Eds.), *Rational man and irrational society.* Beverly Hills, CA: Sage.

negotiators arrange to have their preferred alternatives entered at later stages of a sequential voting process.

The unstable voting outcomes of the product development team point to a larger concern known as the **impossibility theorem**.[14] This theorem states that the derivation of group preference from individual preference is indeterminate. Simply put, no method can combine group members' preferences in a way that guarantees group preference is maximized when groups contain three or more members and are facing three or more options. In other words, even though each manager's preferences are transitive, the group-level preference is intransitive.

Strategic Voting The problem of indeterminate group choice is further compounded by the temptation for members to **strategically misrepresent** their true preferences so that a preferred option is more likely to be favored by the group.[15] For example, a group member may vote for his least-preferred option to ensure that the second choice option is killed. Raines could have voted strategically in the first election to ensure that his preferred strategy was not eliminated in the first round.

Consensus Agreements **Consensus agreements** require the consent of all parties to the negotiation before an agreement is binding. However, consensus agreements do not imply unanimity. For an agreement to be unanimous, parties must agree inwardly as well as outwardly. Consensus agreements imply that parties agree *publicly* to a particular settlement, even though their *private* views about the situation may be in conflict.

Although consensus agreements are desirable, they precipitate several problems. They are time-consuming because they require the consent of all members, who are often not in agreement. Second, they often lead to compromise, in which parties identify a lowest common denominator acceptable to all. Compromise agreements are an extremely easy method of reaching agreement and are compelling because they appear to be fair, but they are usually inefficient because they fail to exploit potential Pareto-improving trade-offs.[16]

Communication Breakdowns

In a perfect communication system, a sender transmits a message that is accurately received by a recipient. Errors are possible at three different points: The sender may fail to send a message; the message may be sent but is inaccurate or distorted; or, an accurate message is sent but is distorted or not received by the recipient. In a multiparty

[14]Arrow, K. J. (1963). *Social choice and individual values.* New Haven, CT: Yale University Press.

[15]Chechile, R. (1984). Logical foundations for a fair and rational method of voting. In W. Swapp (Ed.), *Group decision making.* Beverly Hills, CA: Sage; Ordeshook, P. (1986). *Game theory and political theory: An introduction.* Cambridge, England: Cambridge University Press; Plott, C. (1976). Axiomatic social choice theory: An overview and interpretation. *American Journal of Political Science, 20,* 511–596; Plott, C., & Levine, M. (1978). A model of agenda influence on committee decisions. *American Economic Review, 68,* 146–160.

[16]For a discussion of "the sufficient consensus standard" applied to negotiations in South Africa and Northern Ireland, see Mnookin, R. H. (2003). Strategic barriers to dispute resolution: A comparison of bilateral and multilateral negotiation. *Journal of Institutional and Theoretical Economics, 159*(1), 199–220.

environment, the complexity grows when several people are simultaneously sending and receiving messages. The extent to which communication is restricted influences how the pie is divided. For example, parties with weaker BATNAs benefit from a more constrained communication structure, especially if they are the conduit of communication.[17] In contrast, negotiators with stronger BATNAs benefit from a more public communication structure that promotes competitive bidding.[18]

Private Caucusing   When groups grow large, communication among all parties is difficult. One way of simplifying negotiations is for negotiators to communicate in smaller groups, thereby avoiding full-group communication. Group members often form private caucuses for strategic purposes. However, private caucusing may cause problems. Full-group communication is more time-consuming but enhances equality of group members' outcomes, increases joint profitability, and minimizes perceptions of competition.[19] However, a caveat accompanies the benefits of full communication. When the task structure requires group members to logroll in a reciprocal fashion (as opposed to a circular fashion), restricted communication leads to higher joint outcomes than full communication. Private caucusing can take many different forms. For example, in 2003 China proposed a caucusing arrangement for restarting multiparty negotiations between the United States and Korea to end the standoff over North Korea's nuclear weapons program.[20] The proposed arrangement called for a multilateral meeting in which bilateral talks would take place on the sidelines. This arrangement addresses North Korea's demand for individual, face-to-face negotiations with the United States, while also addressing U.S. insistence that any new talks involve Japan, South Korea, and China.

Biased Interpretation   People often hear what they want to hear when receiving messages, especially ambiguous ones. For example, when people are given neutral information about a product, they interpret it in a way that is favorable toward their own position. Furthermore, they pay attention selectively to information in a report that favors their initial point of view and ignore or misinterpret information that contradicts their position.

Perspective-Taking Failures   People are remarkably poor at taking the perspective of others. For example, people who are privy to information and knowledge that they know others are not aware of nevertheless act as if others are aware of it, even though it would be impossible for the receiver to have this knowledge.[21] This problem is

---

[17]Bolton, G. E., Chatterjee, K., & McGinn, K. L. (2003). How communication links influence coalition bargaining: A laboratory investigation. *Management Science, 49*(5), 583–598.
[18]Ibid.
[19]Palmer & Thompson, "Negotiation in triads."
[20]Powell, S. (2003, July 16). U.S. scrambles to investigate North Korea's nuclear claim. *Seattle Post-Intelligencer,* p. A1.
[21]Keysar, B. (1998). Language users as problem solvers: Just what ambiguity problem do they solve? In S. R. Fussell & R. J. Kreuz (Eds.), *Social and cognitive approaches to interpersonal communication* (pp. 175–200). Mahwah, NJ: Erlbaum.

known as the **curse of knowledge**.[22] For example, in a simulation, traders who possessed privileged information that could have been used to their advantage behaved as if their trading partners also had access to the privileged information. Perspective-taking deficiencies also explain why some instructors who understand an idea perfectly are unable to teach students the same idea. They are unable to put themselves in their students' shoes to explain the idea in a way the students can understand.

Indirect Speech Acts   Each statement one person makes to another has an intended meaning that is couched in casual conversation. **Indirect speech acts** are the ways in which people ask others to do things—but in indirect ways. For example, consider the various ways of requesting that a person shut a door (see Exhibit 9-4). Each statement can serve as a request to perform that act even though the sentence forms (except for "Close the door") are not requests but assertions and questions. Thus, statements 2 through 9 are indirect speech acts; a listener's understanding of the intention behind a communicator's intention requires an extra cognitive step or two, which can often fail, especially in cases of stress.

Indirect speech acts are a function of the magnitude of the request being made (i.e., trivial requests, such as asking someone for the time of day, are easy to accommodate; asking someone if you can have a job is much more difficult to accommodate), the power the recipient has over the sender, and the social distance in the culture.[23] Thus, as the magnitude of requests increases, the power distance increases, and as the social distance increases, requests made by negotiators will become more indirect. Of course, indirectness can be disastrous for effective communication.

EXHIBIT 9-4   Different Ways to Make a Request That Require Progressively More Inferences and Assumed Common Knowledge on the Part of the Receiver

1. Close the door.
2. Can you close the door?
3. Would you close the door?
4. It might help to close the door.
5. Would you mind awfully if I asked you to close the door?
6. Did you forget the door?
7. How about a little less breeze?
8. It's getting cold in here.
9. I really don't want the cats to get out of the house.

Source: Adapted from Krauss, R. M., & Fussell, S. R. (1996). Social psychological models of interpersonal communication. In E. T. Higgins and A. W. Kruglanski (Eds.), *Social psychology: Handbook of basic principles* (pp. 766–701). New York: Guilford; Levinson, S. C. (1983). *Pragmatics* (p. 264). Cambridge, England: Cambridge University Press.

---

[22]Camerer, C. F., Loewenstein, G., & Weber, M. (1989). The curse of knowledge in economic settings: An experimental analysis. *Journal of Political Economy, 97,* 1232–1254.
[23]Brown, P., & Levinson, S. (1987). *Politeness: Some universals in language use.* Cambridge, England: Cambridge University Press.

Multiple Audience Problem   In some negotiation situations, negotiators need to communicate with another person in the presence of someone who should not understand the message. For example, consider a couple selling a house having a face-to-face discussion with a potential buyer. Ideally, the couple wants to communicate information to one another in a way that the spouse understands but the buyer does not—better yet, in such a way that the buyer is not even aware that a surreptitious communication is taking place. Fleming and Darley call this issue the **multiple audience problem**.[24]

People are quite skilled at communicating information to the intended recipient without the other party being aware.[25] People are able to "tune" their messages to specific audiences. For example, former U.S. president Ronald Reagan was gifted in his ability to send different messages to different audiences within the same speech. Reagan's "evil empire" speech of March 8, 1983, to the National Association of Evangelicals (and, indirectly, the whole world) is a case in point. In the early sections of this speech, Reagan established identification with the evangelical audience through an ethos that exemplified their ideals, even using their technical vocabulary (e.g., "I believe in intercessionary prayer"). The section of his speech dealing with foreign policy was addressed to a complex array of audiences, foreign as well as domestic. The "evil empire" phrase had strong resonance not only with evangelicals but also with opponents of the Soviet Union everywhere, including those in Poland and Czechoslovakia. For the benefit of his diplomatic audiences, however, Reagan carefully avoided specific references to evil actions of the Soviet Union, personally deleting from early drafts all references to chemical warfare in Afghanistan. And the speech's attack on the nuclear freeze movement of that time was balanced with a call for "an honest freeze," a term that created "presence" for his proposal for "extensive prior negotiations on the systems and numbers to be limited and on the measures to ensure effective verification and compliance."[26] To his audience in the international, diplomatic, and arms control communities, including those within the Soviet Union, such praise alluded to extratextual facts that gave this part of the message a pragmatic connotation.[27]

Key Strategies for Multiparty Negotiations

Given that multiparty negotiations are complex and present special challenges, what strategies and practices should negotiators put into place to enhance their ability to expand and slice the pie in a multiparty context? Consider the following strategies.

Know Who Will Be at the Table

Know who will be at the table and understand the interests of the constituencies they represent (the hidden table). Consider the following example. Yucaipa, led by Los

---

[24]Fleming, J. H., & Darley, J. M. (1991). Mixed messages: The multiple audience problem and strategic communication. *Social Cognition, 9*(1), 25–46.

[25]Ibid.

[26]Myers, F. (1999, February). Political argumentation and the composite audience: A case study (p. 65). *Quarterly Journal of Speech, 85*(1), 55–65.

[27]Ibid.

Angeles billionaire Ron Burkle, stirred up controversy after purchasing a controlling stake in Allied, North America's largest hauler in bankruptcy proceedings. Yucaipa was allowed to assist Allied and its investor's Hawk Opportunity Fund contract concession talks with Teamsters. However, Teamsters representatives claimed, "We were getting conflicting proposals from Yucaipa and the company, we didn't know who we were negotiating with." Several outside investors and Allied directors claimed that during the talks Yucaipa was trying to push through its own reorganization plan. Eventually, Yucaipa was asked to leave the negotiations, and in 2007 Hawk Opportunity Fund sued Yucaipa, charging it with racketeering in Yucaipa's takeover of Allied and stating that Yucaipa and the Teamsters "colluded" to "manipulate and abuse" the bankruptcy/reorganization process "for their own benefit."[28]

Manage the Information and Systematize Proposal Making

People experience "information overload" when dealing with multiple parties and multiple issues. It is nearly impossible to keep track of the issues, alternatives, and preferences of each party without some kind of information management device. Negotiators are well advised to develop a matrix that lists each party (along the rows) and each issue (along the columns), and then record each person's preferences for each issue. To the extent that this information can be publicly displayed, it can greatly enhance the ability of the group to find true win-win agreements.

Observations of multiparty negotiations suggest that negotiating groups severely mismanage their time. For example, negotiating groups begin by engaging in distributive bargaining and then transition into integrative bargaining.[29] Groups tend not to make proposals and explore options and alternatives in a systematic fashion. This behavior can lead to **tunnel vision**, which is the tendency for people in group negotiations to underestimate the number of feasible options available. For example, in one of our investigations, we asked people who had just completed a multiparty negotiation how many feasible agreements they thought were possible (the negotiation contained five issues and four to five alternatives within each issue). The modal response was one. On average, people estimated approximately four feasible outcomes for the group (the highest estimate was 12). In fact, feasible outcomes numbered 55! This example illustrates the tunnel vision (and ensuing desperation) that can overtake a group if members fail to systematize their proposal making. We strongly encourage members to make several multi-issue proposals and to keep a record of which proposals have been considered.

Use Brainstorming Wisely

We also encourage groups to use brainstorming wisely. Most groups suggest fewer and lower-quality ideas than do individuals thinking independently.[30] We suggest instructing parties to group negotiation to engage in **brainwriting** prior to meeting

---

[28]Emshwiller, J. R. (2007, May 2). Politics & economics: Controversy, by the truckload; battle for car hauler puts spotlight on Burkle's dealings. *Wall Street Journal*, p. A4.

[29]Olekalns, M., Brett, J. M., & Weingart, L. R. (2004). Phases, transitions and interruptions and interruptions: The processes that shape agreement in multi-party negotiations. *International Journal of Conflict Management: Special Issue on Processes in Negotiation, 14*, 191–211.

[30]Diehl, M., & Stroebe, W. (1987). Productivity loss in brainstorming groups: Toward the solution of a riddle. *Journal of Personality and Social Psychology, 61*, 392–403.

face-to-face.[31] **Brainwriting**, or **solitary brainstorming**, is a strategy whereby group members independently write down ideas for resolving negotiations and then, later, when the group meets, they share those ideas. Brainwriting capitalizes on the fact that individuals are better at generating ideas but groups are superior in terms of evaluating ideas.

Develop and Assign Process Roles

Multiparty negotiations need, at the very least, a timekeeper, a process manager, and a recorder of information. We encourage groups to assign these roles to group members, then to consider what additional process roles will be helpful prior to negotiating and to assign such roles to other parties in the group. These roles can be rotated, so as not to give any particular member an advantage or disadvantage.

Stay at the Table

It is unwise for group members to break away from the table when all parties need to reach agreement.[32] When groups break away from the table, coalitions are more likely to form, which can be detrimental for the group.[33]

Strive for Equal Participation

The problem of **uneven participation**, wherein one or two people do all the talking, thwarts information exchange in groups. As the group grows larger, the uneven participation problem becomes more of an issue.

Allow for Some Points of Agreement, Even If Only on Process

Group negotiations are much more complex than dyadic negotiations. In any given group negotiation, behavior can be studied in terms of the acts of individuals, sequences between individuals, phrases of multiple actors, and breakpoints that signal transitions.[34] Sometimes group negotiations can get bogged down because it takes longer for parties to reach agreements—even on a single issue. Failure to reach agreement on negotiation issues can make group members feel they are not making progress and that negotiations are stalemated. Further, it can create a combative atmosphere. For example, the more persistent cooperative negotiators are in their use of integrative strategies, the better they do for themselves.[35] A good strategy at this point is not to reach agreement just for the sake of reaching settlement but, instead, to agree on the process of reaching settlement. For example, a group member may suggest something like the following:

> I know we have been working for over 2 hours and have not been able to agree on a single issue. We could take this as a sign of failure or ill will, but I do

---

[31]Paulus, P. B. (1998). Developing consensus about groupthink after all these years. *Organizational Behavior and Human Decision Processes, 73*(2–3), 362–374.

[32]Palmer & Thompson, "Negotiation in triads."

[33]Mannix, E. (1993). Organizations as resource dilemmas: The effects of power balance on coalition formation in small groups. *Organizational Behavior and Human Decision Processes, 55*, 1–22.

[34]Brett, J., Weingart, L., & Olekans, M. (2004). Baubles, bangles and beads: Modeling the evolution of negotiating groups over time. In E. Mannix, M. A. Neale, & S. Blount-Lyon (Eds.), *Research on managing groups and teams: Vol. 6* (pp. 39–64), New York: Elsevier.

[35]Kern, M., Brett, J., & Weingart, L. (2005). Getting the floor: Motive-consistent strategy and individual outcomes in multi-party negotiations. *Group Decision and Negotiations, 14*, 21–41.

not think that would be wise. I suggest that we take 10 minutes as a group to list all of the settlements that we have considered and then independently rank them in terms of their favorability. This ranking may give us some sense of where to look for possible agreements.

Avoid the "Equal Shares" Bias

A tendency often emerges in group negotiations to divide things equally among the parties involved (see also Chapter 3, on pie-slicing). This bias is problematic for several reasons. First and foremost, as we saw in Chapter 3, no fair method of allocation is universally acceptable. Multiple criteria of fairness can be justified as "fair" in some sense, and none are necessarily superior to others. Second, pressure is strong in many groups to behave in an egalitarian fashion, but privately, people are not inclined to be egalitarian.

Avoid the Agreement Bias

We caution negotiators against the **agreement bias**, which we described in a previous chapter. Specifically, this behavior occurs when negotiators focus on reaching common ground with the other party and are reluctant to accept differences of interest, even when such acceptance might create viable options for joint gain.

Another word of warning: Don't assume everyone wants to "get to yes." In some negotiation situations, people are paid to break deals and stall agreement. Some parties at the table may not desire to reach settlement but, rather, have an incentive to forestall reaching settlement.

Avoid Sequential Bargaining

Groups often use **sequential bargaining** (and discuss one issue at a time) rather than simultaneous bargaining (where several issues are under consideration at any given time). By independently discussing and voting on each issue, negotiators cannot fashion win-win trade-offs among issues.[36]

COALITIONS

Coalitions face three sets of challenges: (1) the formation of the coalition, (2) coalition maintenance, and (3) the distribution of resources among coalition members. We take up these challenges and provide strategies for maximizing coalition effectiveness.

Key Challenges of Coalitions

Optimal Coalition Size

Ideally, coalitions should contain the minimum number of people sufficient to achieve a desired goal. Coalitions are difficult to maintain because members are tempted by other members to join other coalitions and because agreements are not enforceable.[37]

[36]Mannix, Thompson, & Bazerman, "Negotiation in small groups."; Thompson, Mannix, & Bazerman, "Group negotiation."

[37]Mannix, E., & Loewenstein, G. (1993). Managerial time horizons and inter-firm mobility: An experimental investigation. *Organizational Behavior and Human Decision Processes, 56,* 266–284.

Trust and Temptation in Coalitions

Coalitional integrity is a function of the costs and rewards of coalitional membership; when coalitions are no longer rewarding, people will leave them. Nevertheless, members of coalitions experience a strong pull to remain intact even when it is not rational to do so.[38] According to the **status quo bias**, even when a new coalition structure that offers greater gain is possible, members are influenced by a norm of **coalitional integrity**, such that they stick with their current coalition.[39] Negotiators should form coalitions early so as not to be left without coalitional partners.

Dividing the Pie

The distribution of resources among members of coalitions is complex because a normative method of fair allocation does not exist.[40] Experience and risk tolerance influence the size of the pie coalition negotiators get.[41] For example, novice negotiators often settle for "equal division," but experienced negotiators never do so.[42] Experienced negotiators are much more willing and able to exploit differences in their relative bargaining power. Veteran U.S. politicians such as Sam Rayburn, Lyndon Johnson, and Dan Rostenkowski were known for their ability to exploit their sources of power and build winning coalitions around policy initiatives.[43] To illustrate this observation, consider the following example. Lindholm, Tepe, and Clauson are three small firms producing specialized products, equipment, and research for the rehabilitation medicine community.[44] This area has become a critical, high-growth industry, and each firm is exploring ways to expand and improve its technologies through innovations in the research and development (R&D) divisions. Each firm recently applied for R&D funding from the National Rehabilitation Medicine Research Council (NRMR).

The NRMR is a government agency dedicated to funding research in rehabilitation medicine and treatment. The NRMR is willing to provide funds for the proposed research, but because the firms' requests are so similar, they will fund only a **consortium** of two or three firms. The NRMR will not grant funding to Lindholm, Tepe, or Clauson alone.

The largest of the three firms is Lindholm, followed by Tepe, and then Clauson. The NRMR took a variety of factors into consideration when it put caps on funding, as shown in Exhibit 9-5.

The NRMR strictly stipulated that for a consortium of firms to receive funding, the parties in the consortium (either two or three firms) must be in complete agreement concerning the allocation of resources among firms.

If you are Lindholm, what consortium would you consider to be the best for you? Obviously, you want to be in on some consortium, with either Tepe or Clauson or

---

[38]Bottom, W. P., Eavey, C. L., & Miller, G. J. (1996). Getting to the core: Coalitional integrity as a constraint on the power of agenda setters. *Journal of Conflict Resolution, 40*(2), 298–319.
[39]Ibid.
[40]Raiffa, H. (1982). *The art and science of negotiation.* Cambridge, MA: Belknap.
[41]Bottom, W. P., Holloway, J., McClurg, S., & Miller, G. J. (2000). Negotiating a coalition: Risk, quota shaving, and learning to bargain. *Journal of Conflict Resolution, 44*(2), 147–169.
[42]Ibid.
[43]Ibid.
[44]This example is based on the case Federated Science Fund, written by Elizabeth Mannix, available through the Dispute Resolution Research Center, Kellogg School of Management, Northwestern University (e-mail: drrc@kellogg.northwestern.edu); and the Social Services case, by Raiffa, *The art and science of negotiation.*

EXHIBIT 9-5 Maximum Funding Caps as a Function of Parties in a Consortium

Organizations in Consortium	Cap for R&D Funding
Lindholm alone	0
Tepe alone	0
Clauson alone	0
Lindholm and Tepe	$220,000
Lindholm and Clauson	$190,000
Tepe and Clauson	$150,000
Lindholm, Tepe, and Clauson	$240,000

both, to avoid being left out in the cold. But what is the best division of resources within each of those consortiums? Suppose you approach Tepe about a two-way venture, and Tepe proposes receiving half of the $220,000 or $110,000. You argue that you should earn more because you are bigger and bring more synergy to the agreement. You demand $200,000 for yourself, leaving $20,000 for Tepe. At this point, Tepe threatens to leave you and approach Clauson. Tepe argues that Tepe and Clauson can command $150,000 as a consortium without you, and each can receive $75,000. At this point, you argue that you can outbid Tepe's offer to Clauson with $80,000 and keep $110,000 for yourself. Just as Tepe is threatening to overbid you for Clauson, Clauson steps in and tells Tepe that Clauson would want at least $100,000 of the $150,000 pie that Clauson and Tepe together could command. Tepe is frustrated but relents.

You get nervous in your role as Lindholm. You certainly do not want to be left out. You could attempt to get Clauson or Tepe in a consortium. Then a new thought occurs to you: Maybe all three of you can be in a consortium. After all, all three firms command the greatest amount of funding ($240,000). But how should the $240,000 be divided between the three of you? You are the biggest firm, so you propose that you keep half of the $240,000 (or $120,000), that Tepe get $80,000, and that Clauson get $40,000. This allocation strikes you as fair. At this point, Clauson gets upset and tells you that Clauson and Tepe can team up and get $150,000. Clauson thinks your share is unfair and should be reduced to something less than $90,000. You then remind Clauson that you and Tepe can get $190,000 together, of which you certainly deserve at least half, which is better than the $90,000 offer. Then the three of you are at it again in a vicious circle of coalition formation and demolition.

The negotiation between Lindholm, Tepe, and Clauson illustrates the unstable nature of coalitions. In this example, the left-out party is always able to approach one of the two parties in the coalition and offer a better deal, which can then be beaten by the remaining party, ad infinitum. Furthermore, splitting the pie three ways seems to offer no obvious solution. So, what should the three parties do? Is there a solution? Or are the parties destined to go around in circles forever?

Getting Out of the Vicious Circle As a way out of the vicious circle, let's conceptualize the problem as a system of simultaneous equations to solve. Namely,

$$L + T = \$220,000$$
$$L + C = \$190,000$$

$$T + C = \$150,000$$
$$L + T + C = \$240,000$$
$$L + T + C = (\$220,000 + \$190,000 + \$150,000)/2$$
$$= \$560,000/2$$
$$= \$280,000 \text{ total funds needed}$$

However, it is impossible to solve all simultaneous equations. We are $40,000 short of satisfying each party's minimum needs. What should we do? Consider the following three solutions: the core solution, the Shapley solution, and a hybrid model.[45]

The Core Solution.   The core solution is a set of alternatives that are undominated.[46] An alternative is in the core if no coalition has both the power and desire to overthrow it.

The first step in computing the core solution is to determine what would be each party's share if shortage of funds were not an issue. Thus, we solve for L, T, and C shares as follows:

$$(L + T) - (L + C) = \$220,000 - \$190,000$$
$$= (T - C) = \$30,000$$
$$(L + T) - (T + C) = \$220,000 - \$150,000$$
$$= (L - C) = \$70,000$$
$$(T + C) + (T - C) = \$150,000 + \$30,000$$
$$2T = \$180,000$$
$$T = \$90,000$$
$$L + T = \$220,000$$
$$L + \$90,000 = \$220,000$$
$$L = \$220,000 - \$90,000$$
$$L = \$130,000$$
$$L + C = \$190,000$$
$$\$130,000 + C = \$190,000$$
$$C = \$190,000 - \$130,000$$
$$C = \$60,000$$

check:

$$L = \$130,000$$
$$T = \$90,000$$
$$C = \$60,000$$
$$\text{Total} = \$280,000$$

Thus, if we had a total of $280,000, we could solve each equation. But, the harsh reality is that we do not. So, the second step is to get the total down to $240,000 by deducting $40,000 from somewhere. In the absence of any particular argument as to why one party's share should be cut, we deduct an equal amount, $13,333, from each party's share. In the final step, we compute the "core" shares as follows:

Lindholm:	$116,670
Tepe:	$76,670
Clauson:	$46,670

---

[45] Raiffa, *The art and science of negotiation.*
[46] McKelvey, R. D., & Ordeshook, P. C. (1980). Vote trading: An experimental study. *Public Choice, 35,* 151–184.

EXHIBIT 9-6   Analysis of Pivotal Power in the Shapley Model

Order of Joining	Lindholm Added Value	Tepe Added Value	Clauson Added Value
LTC	0	$220,000	$ 20,000
LCT	0	50,000	190,000
TLC	$220,000	0	20,000
TCL	90,000	0	150,000
CLT	190,000	50,000	0
CTL	90,000	150,000	0
Shapley (average)*	98,333	78,333	63,333

*These figures are rounded slightly.

As Lindholm, you are delighted. Tepe agrees, but Clauson is not happy. Clauson thinks that $46,670 is too little and hires a consultant to evaluate the situation. The consultant proposes a different method, called the Shapley model.

The Shapley Model.   Consider a coalition formation in which one player starts out alone and then is joined by a second and third player. The Shapley model determines the overall payoff a player can expect on the basis of his or her **pivotal power**, or the ability to change a losing coalition into a winning coalition. The consultant considers all possible permutations of players joining coalitions one at a time. The marginal value added to each coalition's outcome is attributed to the pivotal player. The Shapley value is the mean of a player's added value (see Exhibit 9-6). When all players bring equal resources, the Shapley value is the total amount of resources divided by the total number of people. This outcome, of course, is the **equal division principle**, as well as the **equity principle**.

When Clauson's consultant presents this report, Clauson is delighted with a share that increased by almost $20,000. Lindholm is nonplussed with a share that decreased. Tepe is tired of all the bickering and proposes they settle for something in between the two proposed solutions.

Raiffa's Hybrid Model.   We have presented two models to solve for shares in coalition situations. The medium-power player's share in both models is identical, but the high- and low-power player's shares fluctuate quite dramatically. It is possible that an egocentric argument could ensue between Lindholm and Clauson as to which model to employ. One solution is a hybrid model in which the mean of the Shapley and core values is computed.[47] This model yields the following shares:

    Lindholm: $107,500
    Tepe: $77,500
    Clauson: $55,000

Tips for Low-Power Players   Each of the three preceding models of fair solutions is compelling and defensible because each makes explicit the logic underlying the division

---

[47] Raiffa, *The art and science of negotiation.*

of resources. It is easy to be a high-power player in coalition situations. However, the real trick is to know how to be an effective low-power player. Weakness can be power if you can recognize and disrupt unstable coalitions. Power is intimately involved in the formation of coalitions and the allocation of resources among coalition members. Power imbalance among coalition members can be detrimental for the group. Compared to egalitarian power relationships, unbalanced power relationships produce more coalitions defecting from the larger group,[48] fewer integrative agreements,[49] greater likelihood of bargaining impasse,[50] and more competitive behavior.[51] Power imbalance makes power issues salient to group members, whose primary concern is to protect their own interests. What is best for the coalition is often not what is best for the organization.

Can an optimal way be found for multiple parties to allocate resources so that group members are not tempted to form coalitions that may hinder group welfare? Usually not. Although several defensible methods can be used to allocate resources among coalition members, no single best way exists.[52]

Strategies for Maximizing Coalitional Effectiveness

What follows are some interpersonal strategies for effectively navigating coalitions.[53]

Make Your Contacts Early

Because of the commitment process, people tend to feel obligated to others with whom they have made explicit or implicit agreements. For this reason, it is important to make contact with key parties early in the process of multiparty negotiation before they become committed to others.

Seek Verbal Commitments

One of the most effective strategies for enhancing coalitional effectiveness is to obtain verbal commitments from people with whom you want to develop trust. Most people feel obligated to follow through with promises they make to others, even when verbal commitments are not legally binding.[54]

Use Unbiased-Appearing Rationale to Divide the Pie

Remember that "fairness" is a psychological construct and is the strongest determinant of negotiators' satisfaction with the outcome and, consequently, their willingness to follow through on their verbal commitments. If one or more members of the coalition regard the proposed allocation of resources to be unfair, the coalition will be less stable, and they will be likely to renege. To the extent to which coalitional members feel that

---

[48]Mannix, "Organizations as resource dilemmas."

[49]Ibid.; McAlister, L., Bazerman, M. H., & Fader, P. (1986). Power and goal setting in channel negotiations. *Journal of Marketing Research, 23,* 238–263.

[50]Mannix, "Organizations as resource dilemmas."

[51]McClintock, C. G., & Liebrand, W. B. (1988). Role of interdependence structure, individual value orientation, and another's strategy in social decision making: A transformational analysis. *Journal of Personality and Social Psychology, 55*(3), 396–409.

[52]For an extensive treatment, see Raiffa, *The art and science of negotiation.*

[53]For structural strategies, see Bottom, Eavey, Miller, & Victor, "The institutional effect on majority rule."

[54]Cialdini, R. B. (1993). *Influence: Science and practice.* New York: HarperCollins.

the distribution of the pie is fair, they are more likely to resist persuasion from others to break away from the coalition.

PRINCIPAL-AGENT NEGOTIATIONS

The reason why principal-agent negotiations are problematic is that "a risk-neutral principal must negotiate an incentive contract to motivate a risk-averse agent to undertake costly actions that cannot be observed."[55] An agent has a stake in the outcome (e.g., a real estate agent earns a commission on the sale of a house). In the SCO negotiation, CEO Darl McBride was an intermediary between SCO and IBM and also between SCO and the Canopy Group, and potentially Noorda.

Many advantages can be realized by using agents to represent one's interests:[56]

- **Expertise.**   Agents usually have more expertise in the negotiation process (e.g., a real estate agent).
- **Substantive knowledge.**   Agents may have more information than the principal about certain areas. For example, a tax attorney has a wealth of information about tax law and exemptions.
- **Networks and special influence.**   Often, people work through agents because they do not know what potential principals might be interested in their product or service.
- **Emotional detachment.**   Agents can provide emotional detachment and tactical flexibility. For example, half of all couples in the United States will eventually divorce; and divorce ranks among life's most stressful events. A "divorce planner" is not an attorney, but rather a person who can act as an agent and bring rationality and perspective to an otherwise too-hot emotional process.[57]
- **Ratification.**   Precisely because an agent does not have authority to make or accept offers (unless directed to do so by the principal), the agent has power in the same way that a car salesperson has limited authority to offer price reductions (without the approval of the owner-manager).
- **Face-saving.**   Agents can provide a face-saving buffer for principals.

However, agency also comes with costs. Because they are usually compensated for their services, agents diminish the resources to be divided among the principals. In addition, ineffective agents complicate the negotiation dynamic and thereby inhibit settlement. Most problematic, the agent's interests may be at odds with those of the principals.[58]

For example, consider a typical home sale involving two principals and two agents. Is it wise for a home buyer to tell her agent her BATNA (how much she is willing to spend for a particular house)? Similarly, should a seller tell his agent the least amount of money he would accept for his home? Agents for home buyers desire higher selling

[55]Bottom, W. P., Holloway, J., Miller, G. J., Mislin, A., & Whitford, A.B. (2006). Pathways to cooperation: Negotiation and social exchange between principal and agent. *Administrative Science Quarterly, 51,* 29–58.
[56]Rubin, J. Z., & Sander, F. E. A. (1988). When should we use agents? Direct vs. representative negotiation. *Negotiation Journal, 4*(4), 395–401.
[57]Grondhal, P. (2003, March 9). Offering a lifeline at marriage's end. *Times Union-Albany,* p. C17.
[58]For an overview of principal-agent issues in economics, see Jensen, M. C., & Meckling, W. H. (1976). Theory of the firm: Managerial behavior, agency costs, and ownership structure. *Journal of Financial Economics, 3,* 305–360.

prices because their fees are based on selling price. For this reason, it may not be in a buyer's interest to reveal to the agent his or her reservation price (i.e., the maximum he or she is willing to pay). In fact, actual home sale prices point to a distinct disadvantage for parties with agents: Selling prices are lowest when the agent knows only the seller's reservation price and highest when the agent knows only the buyer's reservation price.[59] Not surprisingly, when buyers don't reveal their reservation price, their agent spends more time asking them about it.[60]

Agents increase the likelihood of impasse.[61] Agents may be maximally effective only when their interests are aligned with those of the principal. The social relationship the agent has with the principal affects how much effort the principal exerts.[62] The extent to which the agent believes the principal is a "benevolent individual" is directly related to the wage a principal offers an agent. However, money matters as well: The size of the bonus principals offer agents predicts how much effort agents exert.

Disadvantages of Agents

Shrinking ZOPA

Agents shrink the bargaining zone. Thus, using an agent means more parties are claiming a fixed bargaining surplus. A small bargaining zone increases the likelihood of an impasse. (For an example, see Exhibit 9-7.)

Incompatible Incentive Structure

Most agent-principal relationships have an incompatible incentive structure; the agent's interests are not perfectly aligned with those of the principal. Incentive compatibility is the only way to ensure that the agent serves your interests. For this reason, principals should not reveal their BATNAs to their agents under any condition. Agents will routinely ask principals about their BATNAs. Your agent does not need to know your BATNA to effectively negotiate for you. It is unwise to trust someone to effectively represent your interests when their incentives are not aligned with yours. Ultimately, an agent's job is to broker a deal, and thus, agents are motivated to apply pressure to whomever is motivated to reach a deal. Agents have an incentive to make transactions happen; for example, in home buying a buyer's agent is really an employee of the selling company. The agent's preference is the higher price because he or she gets a commission. Furthermore, an agent may give biased information to get an agreement from his or her constituency.

A key question for agents is whether to align with their principal or to align with the other agent.[63] Obviously, certain laws and regulations govern disclosure, but the

---

[59]Valley, K. L., White, S. B., Neale, M. A., & Bazerman, M. H. (1992). Agents as information brokers: The effects of information disclosure on negotiated outcomes. [Special issue: Decision processes in negotiation.] *Organizational Behavior and Human Decision Processes, 51*(2), 220–236.

[60]Valley, K. L., White, S. B., & Iacobucci, D. (1992). The process of assisted negotiations: A network analysis. *Group Decision and Negotiation, 2,* 117–135.

[61]Bazerman, M. H., Neale, M. A., Valley, K., Zajac, E., & Kim, P. (1992). The effect of agents and mediators on negotiation outcomes. *Organizational Behavior and Human Decision Processes, 53,* 55–73.

[62]Bottom, Holloway, Miller, Mislin, & Whitford, "Pathways to cooperation."

[63]Dunn-Jensen, L., Kurtzberg, T., & Matsibekker, C. (2005). Multiparty e-negotiations: Agents, alliances, and negotiation success. *International Journal of Conflict Management, 16*(3), 245–264.

EXHIBIT 9-7 The Bargaining Zone, Maximum Surplus, and Agent Commission Rates for a House Sale

Commission	Seller RP* [adjusted from $410,000/ (1 − c)]	Bargaining Zone [Buyer RP ($440,000) − Seller RP*]	Buyer Maximum Surplus	Seller Maximum Surplus	Agents' Surplus Range
0% (for sale by owner)	$410,000	$30,000	$30,000	$30,000	$0
2%	$418,367	$21,633	$21,633	$21,200	$8,367–$8,800
4%	$427,083	$12,917	$12,917	$12,400	$17,083–$17,600
5%	$431,578	$8,422	$8,422	$8,000	$21,579–$22,000
6%	$436,170	$3,830	$3,830	$3,600	$26,170–$26,400

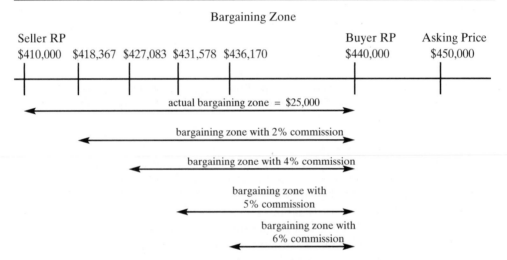

Note: RP = reservation price. In this example, assume that the house is originally listed for sale at $450,000; assume that the buyer's reservation price is $440,000 and the seller's reservation price is $410,000. If no agency fees were involved, the bargaining range is $30,000 (i.e., any price between $410,000 and $440,000). The agent commission fees mean that the seller must adjust his or her reservation price upward. For example, if the agent commission rate is 6%, the seller cannot sell below $436,170.

question is which social bond is most important for the final agreement. Agents initially show greater loyalty to their principals, but over time their loyalty to the other agent is greater. Moreover, to the extent that the across-the-table relationship among agents is strong, the likelihood of agreement is greater and settlements occur in the middle of the bargaining zone. Most notably, to the extent that the agents are socially similar (i.e., graduated from the same school, etc.) and familiar with each other, they are more likely to forge a bond.

Communication Distortion
Because agents often do the negotiating (rather than the principal), more communication distortion may occur. Any one message can be sent in an infinite number of ways.

Message tuning refers to how senders tailor messages for specific recipients. People who send messages (e.g., "I have no fuel"; "I did not receive the attached file") edit their messages in a way they think best suits the recipient. For example, people give longer and more elaborate street directions and instructions to people whom they presume to be nonnatives or unfamiliar with a city.[64] Also, senders capitalize on the knowledge that they believe the recipient to already hold. For this reason, negotiators may send shorter, less complete messages to one another because they believe that they can capitalize on an existing shared knowledge base. However, negotiators often overestimate the commonality of information they share with others. Consequently, the messages they send become less clear.

Message senders present information that they believe will be favorably received by the recipient, and therefore they distort messages.[65] For example, when people present a message to an audience they believe is either for or against a particular topic, they err in the direction of adopting the audience's point of view. It is as if they know that the messenger who brings unwelcome news is endangered—so one way of dealing with this factor is to modify the news.

Loss of Control

Because an agent is negotiating in your stead, you are giving up control over the process of negotiation and, ultimately, the outcome. Indeed, agents are more active in a negotiation than principals.[66]

Agreement at Any Cost

Because agents have an incentive to reach agreement, they may fall prey to the **getting to yes bias** in which agreement becomes more important than the contents of the deal.[67] Simply stated, the desire to reach agreement quickly and efficiently may lead agents to withhold information from principals that might impede a deal.

Strategies for Working Effectively with Agents

Shop Around

Do not assume the first agent you meet is uniquely qualified to represent you. Ask the agent how he or she will successfully represent your interests. Ask the agent about what is expected of you. Ask the agent about the nature of your relationship and what obligations, if any, you have to one another. Many real estate agents have easy-exit clauses that allow principals to remove agents without difficulty; in the absence of this clause, a principal might be committed to an agent for a lengthy period of time. For example, Darcy Bouzeous negotiates talent contracts for sports stars and media

[64]Krauss, R. M., & Fussell, S. R. (1991). Perspective-taking in communication: Representations of others' knowledge in reference. *Social Cognition, 9,* 2–24.

[65]Higgins, E. T. (1999). "Saying is believing" effects: When sharing reality about something biases knowledge and evaluations. In L. Thompson, J. M. Levine, & D. M. Messick (Eds.), *Shared cognition in organizations: The management of knowledge.* Mahwah, NJ: Erlbaum.

[66]Valley, White, & Iacobucci, "Process of assisted negotiations."

[67]Gibson, K., Thompson, L., & Bazerman, M. H. (1994). Biases and rationality in the mediation process. In L. Heath, F. Bryant, & J. Edwards (Eds.), *Application of heuristics and biases to social issues: Vol. 3.* New York: Plenum.

EXHIBIT 9-8   Questions That Potential Home Buyers Should Ask Real-Estate Agents

1. Can you represent me as a buyer's agent?
2. How will you find me homes?
3. How can you leverage my down payment, interest rate, and monthly payment?
4. What different points will you be able to negotiate on my behalf?
5. How long have you been selling real estate full time?
6. What can I expect in terms of communication?
7. Does your contract have an "easy exit" clause in it?
8. Under what conditions will you cut your commission?

Source: Based on Ron Holdridge, Re/Max Metro Realty, Seattle, Washington.

---

personalities. Bouzeous says, "I do not believe in having a retention agreement. If they do not like what I've done, I do not think they have to be stuck with me."[68] Ask agents about their negotiation training and strategies. (See Exhibit 9-8 for some suggested questions to ask an agent.)

Know Your BATNA Before Meeting with Your Agent

Do your homework before meeting with your agent. Know your own BATNA. Prepare questions to ask your agent that will allow you to test the soundness of your BATNA, but do not reveal your BATNA. For example, a home seller might say, "I would like to find out what average sale prices are for this type of home."

Communicate Your Interests to Your Agent Without Giving Away Your BATNA

One of the most challenging tasks for a negotiator is to communicate his or her interests, priorities, and preferences but not reveal his or her BATNA. You can help your agent to help you most effectively by listing, in order of priority, your key interests and what you perceive to be the alternatives for meeting those interests. Anticipate that your agent will ask you about your BATNA. When this question comes up (and it will!), focus the conversation onto your priorities (e.g., "I am not sure how helpful it is to tell you the most money I am willing to pay for the house you showed me today. However, I am really interested in a home within this school district area and a double garage. In fact, I would be willing to pay more for those features than a master suite and an updated kitchen").

Capitalize on the Agent's Expertise

Good agents have a wealth of expertise. Ask them about what they perceive to be their key strategies for targeting opportunities for you and closing deals.

Tap into Your Agent's Sources of Information

Agents, by virtue of their professional affiliations and networks, have access to a lot of information. However, you should not expect that passivity on your part will lead your agent to provide you with information. Rather, you need to ask your agent to provide

---

[68] Bednarski, P. (1990, October 22). When stars need pacts, she's hired. *Chicago Sun-Times,* p. 35.

key information for you. If your agent is unwilling or unable to do so, interview another agent and see whether he or she can provide the information.

Discuss Ratification

By nature of the principal-agent relationship, an agent's authority is limited with respect to making certain concessions or types of agreements (i.e., your agent cannot reduce or increase your offer without explicit direction from you). Thus, agents may effectively resist making too many and too deep concessions that you might impulsively make in the heat of negotiation. In this sense, your agent provides a buffer zone between yourself and the other party.

Use Your Agent to Help Save Face

Sometimes, negotiators make what they regard to be perfectly reasonable proposals that are insulting to the other party. When this situation happens (and if the counterparty is insulted), negotiations may start on a losing course. In an agent-mediated negotiation, you can attempt to salvage damaged egos and relationships by blaming your agent.

Use Your Agent to Buffer Emotions

In keeping with this point about saving face, agents can be an effective emotional buffer between parties who may either dislike one another or are irrational (see Chapter 5 on bargaining styles). Effective agents will put a positive "spin" on the communications by each party and effectively "tune into" their principal's needs.

CONSTITUENT RELATIONSHIPS

When a negotiating party is embedded within an organization, several peripheral players may have an indirect stake in the outcome and may influence the negotiation process. A **constituent** is on the "same side" as a principal but exerts an independent influence on the outcome through the principal. Constituents can be used to exert pressure on the other side of the table.

By the same token, constituencies can also exert pressure on negotiators. For example, in the United States–North Korea dispute over nuclear weapon proliferation, China was an involved constituent. China sent an envoy to the North Korean capital and proposed a formula for restarting negotiations. Moreover, China exerted pressure on both sides to find a diplomatic solution.[69]

We distinguish three types of constituencies: superiors, who have authority over principals; subordinates, who are under the authority of principals; and constituencies, the party whom the principal represents—that is, for whom the principal is responsible and to whom the principal is accountable (constituencies are represented by C in Exhibit 9-2). In the chapter opening example, IBM is accountable to its major shareholders and customers, who are ostensibly on their side but may have interests of their own. Further, the SCO group has dual accountability to the Canopy Group (as 43% owners), as well as its investor BayStar Capital, and ultimately to Noorda as the parent company of Canopy.

---

[69] Kahn, J. (2003, July 16). As U.S. and North Korea glower, China pushes for talks. *New York Times,* p. 3.

Challenges for Constituent Relationships

Identification

Constituent representatives must think about how they want to identify themselves/their side in a negotiation. One choice involves using personal language (e.g, "I believe") or collective language (e.g., "we believe"). Ironically, collective language is not always preferred by constituency members. When constituency members are not highly identified with their group, they rate advocates as more likeable and more effective when they use personal rather than collective language.[70]

Accountability

Negotiators at the bargaining table comprise the primary relationship in negotiation. The relationship parties share with their constituents is the **second table**.[71] Constituents do not have to be physically present at the negotiation table for their presence to be strongly felt.[72] Negotiators who are accountable to their constituents make higher demands and are less willing to compromise in negotiation than those not accountable to constituents.[73] Gender affects accountability. Women, as compared to men, believe they are more generous when representing a group; conversely, men don't believe this. When it comes to actual behavior, men are significantly more self-interested when they are responsible for a group as compared to when they are acting only on behalf of themselves; female representatives don't behave differently whether they are representing a group or just themselves.[74]

The second table has a paradoxical effect on the primary table. Representatives of constituents often are not given power to enact agreements; that is, the representative is not monolithic.[75] In some cases, this restriction would seem to reduce his or her power at the bargaining table, but the opposite can be true. The negotiator whose "hands are tied" is often more effective than the negotiator who has the power to ratify agreements. Anyone who has ever negotiated a deal on a new car has probably experienced the "My hands are tied" or "Let me take it to the boss" ploy, in which the salesperson induces the customer to commit to a price that requires approval before a deal is finalized.

---

[70]Hornsey, M., Blackwood, L., & O'Brien, A. (2005). Speaking for others: The pros and cons of group advocates using collective language. *Group Processes and Intergroup Relations, 8*(3), 245–257.
[71]Ancona, D. G., Friedman, R. A., & Kolb, D. M. (1991). The group and what happens on the way to "yes." *Negotiation Journal, 7*(2), 155–173.
[72]Kramer, R., Pommerenke, P., & Newton, E. (1993). The social context of negotiation: Effects of social identity and accountability on negotiator judgment and decision making. *Journal of Conflict Resolution, 37,* 633–654; Pruitt, D. G., & Carnevale, P. J. (1993). *Negotiation in social conflict.* Pacific Grove, CA: Brooks-Cole; Tetlock, P. E. (1985). Accountability: A social check on the fundamental attribution error. *Social Psychology Quarterly, 48,* 227–236.
[73]Ben-Yoav, O., & Pruitt, D. G. (1984). Accountability to constituents: A two-edged sword. *Organizational Behavior and Human Processes, 34,* 282–295; Carnevale, P. J., Pruitt, D. G., & Britton, S. (1979). Looking tough: The negotiator under constituent surveillance. *Personality and Social Psychology Bulletin, 5,* 118–121; O'Connor, K. M. (1997). Groups and solos in context: The effects of accountability on team negotiation. *Organizational Behavior and Human Decision Processes, 72,* 384–407.
[74]Song, F., Cadsby, C., & Morris, T. (2004). Other-regarding behavior and behavioral forecasts: Females versus males as individuals and as group representatives. *International Journal of Conflict Management, 15*(4), 340–363.
[75]Raiffa, *The art and science of negotiation.*

Accountability to collateral actors is an inevitable aspect of organizational life.[76] At least two motivational processes are triggered by accountability: decision making vigilance and evaluation apprehension.

Decision Making Vigilance   Decision makers who are accountable for their actions consider relevant information and alternatives more carefully.[77] Accountability increases thoughtful, deliberate processing of information and decreases automatic, heuristic processing.[78] Accountability would seem to uniformly improve the quality of decisions made by negotiators and increase the likelihood of integrative agreements.

However, decision accountability may not always promote more thorough and unbiased processing of information if organizational actors are partisan to a particular view.[79] Imagine a situation in which an observer watches a videotape of people negotiating. Some observers are told to take an objective and impartial view of the situation; other observers are instructed to take the perspective of one of the parties. Further, some observers are told they will be accountable for their actions and behaviors (e.g., they must justify their decisions to others who will question them), whereas others are not accountable. After watching the tape, observers indicate what they think each negotiator wanted. Accountable partisans fall prey to the fixed-pie assumption because they are motivated to reach a particular conclusion. However, nonpartisan observers are willing to reach whatever conclusion the data will allow, and their judgments are therefore driven by the evidence, not their desires.

Evaluation Apprehension and Face-Saving   Negotiators who are accountable for their behaviors are concerned with how they are viewed by others. When people are concerned what others will think, they use face-saving strategies and make their actions appear more favorable to relevant others. Negotiators who want to save face will be more aggressive and uncompromising so they will not be viewed as weak. Negotiators who are accountable to constituents are more likely to maintain a tough bargaining stance, make fewer concessions, and hold out for more favorable agreements compared to those who are not accountable.[80] A **diffusion of responsibility** occurs across members of the team.[81]

Conflicts of Interest

Negotiators often face a conflict between their goals and those of their constituency. For the manager interested in effective dispute resolution, it is important to understand the relationships negotiators share across the bargaining table and the hidden

---

[76] Tetlock, "Accountability"; Tetlock, P. E. (1992). The impact of accountability on judgment and choice: Toward a social contingency model. *Advances in Experimental Social Psychology, 25,* 331–376.

[77] Tetlock, "Accountability"; Tetlock, "Impact of accountability."

[78] See also Chaiken, S. (1980). Heuristic versus systematic information processing and the use of source versus message cues in persuasion. *Journal of Personality and Social Psychology, 39*(5), 752–766; Fiske, S. T., & Neuberg, S. L. (1990). A continuum of impression formation, from category-based to individuating processes: Influences of information and motivation on attention and interpretation. In M. P. Zanna (Ed.), *Advances in experimental social psychology: Vol. 23* (pp. 1–74). New York: Academic Press.

[79] Thompson, L. (1995). "They saw a negotiation": Partisanship and involvement. *Journal of Personality and Social Psychology, 68*(5), 839–853.

[80] Carnevale, P. J., & Pruitt, D. G. (1992). Negotiation and mediation. *Annual Review of Psychology, 43,* 531–582.

[81] O'Connor, "Groups and solos in context."

table of constituent relationships.[82] Consider a negotiation involving teams of two people who are either personally acquainted or strangers to one another. Each team reports to a manager. Some teams report to a "profit-oriented" manager who instructs the team to "serve the interests of the group at all costs." Some teams report to a "people-oriented" manager who instructs the team to maximize interests while maintaining harmonious intergroup relations. Teams who report to the "profit" supervisor claim a greater share of the resources than do teams who report to the "people" supervisor and teams not accountable to a manager.[83] When team members are acquainted, no differences occur in relative profitability. Why? Negotiators are more likely to maximize profit when the goal is clear and they do not share a previous relationship.

Strategies for Improving Constituent Relationships

Communicate with Your Constituents
Representatives need to understand their constituents' interests, not just their positions. Moreover, when constituents feel heard, they are less likely to take extreme action. In many cases, representatives act too early (before they understand their constituency's real needs)so as to demonstrate their competence.

Do Not Expect Homogeneity of Constituent Views
Constituencies are often composed of individuals and subgroups with different needs and interests. On some level, they realize they can achieve more through collective action and representation, but be aware of heterogeneity of views within the constituency.

Educate Your Constituents on Your Role and Your Limitations
Constituents, like other people, suffer from egocentric bias, meaning they view the world from their own perspective in a self-serving fashion. They often see your role as one of educating the other side about the reality of the situation. They may often believe your task is easier than it really is. It is important to clearly define your role to your constituents early on in the process. Set realistic expectations. Do not characterize yourself as an "evangelist" for their "crusade." Share with your constituents all possible outcomes, not just the favorable ones they think will occur.

Help Your Constituents Do Horizon Thinking
Horizon thinking involves making projections about future outcomes. People have a difficult time thinking about future events,[84] tend to under- or overestimate the duration of future emotional states,[85] and fail to account for positive or negative circum-

---

[82] Kolb, D. (1983). *The mediators.* Cambridge, MA: MIT Press.

[83] Peterson, E., & Thompson, L. (1997). Negotiation teamwork: The impact of information distribution and accountability on performance depends on the relationship among team members. *Organizational Behavior and Human Decision Processes, 72*(3), 364–383.

[84] Gilbert, D. T., & Wilson, T. D. (2000). Miswanting: Some problems in the forecasting of future affective states. In J. P. Forgas (Ed.), *Feeling and thinking: The role of affect in social cognition. Studies in emotion and social interaction, Second series* (pp. 178–197). New York: Cambridge University Press.

[85] Gilbert, D. T., Pinel, E. C., Wilson, T. D., Blumberg, S. J., & Wheatley, T. P. (1998). Immune neglect: A source of durability bias in affective forecasting. *Journal of Personality and Social Psychology, 75*(3), 617–638.

stances that could arise.[86] You can help your constituents develop a sound BATNA and realistic aspirations by helping them to engage in horizon thinking.

TEAM NEGOTIATION

Consider the following situations:

- A husband and wife negotiate with a salesperson on the price of a new car
- A group of disgruntled employees approach management about wages and working conditions
- A large software company approaches a small software company about an acquisition

In all of these examples, people join together on one side of the bargaining table as a team. Presumably, in each of these cases, one member could do all of the negotiating for the team, but teams believe they will be more effective as a united group. Unlike solo negotiators, members of negotiating teams may play different roles for strategic reasons, such as "good cop–bad cop."[87] Are teams effective at exploiting integrative potential at the bargaining table? A comparison of three types of negotiation configurations (team vs. team, team vs. solo, and solo vs. solo negotiations) revealed that the presence of at least one team at the bargaining table increased the size of the pie.[88]

Why are teams so effective? Negotiators exchange much more information about their interests and priorities when at least one team is at the bargaining table than when two individuals negotiate.[89] Information exchange leads to greater judgment accuracy about parties' interests,[90] which promotes integrative agreement.[91] The **team effect** is quite robust: It is not even necessary that team members privately caucus with one another to be effective.[92] In negotiations with integrative potential, teams outperform solos; however, in extremely competitive tasks, teams are more likely to behave in a competitive fashion.[93]

---

[86]Loewenstein, G. F., & Schkade, D. (1999). Wouldn't it be nice? Predicting future feelings. In D. Kahneman & E. Diener (Eds.), *Well-being: The foundations of hedonic psychology* (pp. 85–105). New York: Russell Sage Foundation; Schkade, D. A., & Kahneman, D. (1998). Does living in California make people happy? A focusing illusion in judgments of life satisfaction. *Psychological Science, 9*(5), 340–346; Wilson, T. D., Wheatley, T. P., Meyers, J., Gilbert, D. T., & Axsom, D. (2000). Focalism: A source of durability bias in affective forecasting. *Journal of Personality and Social Psychology, 78,* 821–836.

[87]Brodt, S., & Tuchinsky, M. (2000). Working together but in opposition: An examination of the "good cop/bad cop" negotiating team tactic. *Organizational Behavior and Human Decision Processes, 81*(2), 155–177.

[88]Thompson, L., Peterson, E., & Brodt, S. (1996). Team negotiation: An examination of integrative and distributive bargaining. *Journal of Personality and Social Psychology, 70*(1), 66–78; see also Morgan, P., & Tindale, R. S. (2002). Group vs. individual performance in mixed-motive situations: Exploring the inconsistency. *Organizational Behavior and Human Decision Processes, 87*(1), 44–65.

[89]O'Connor, "Groups and solos in context."; Carnevale, P. J. (2007). Team effects in bilateral negotiation. Unpublished manuscript, Marshall School of Business, University of Southern California, Los Angeles, CA; Thompson, Peterson, & Brodt, "Team negotiation."

[90]Ibid.

[91]Thompson, L. (1991). Information exchange in negotiation. *Journal of Experimental Social Psychology, 27*(2), 161–179.

[92]Thompson, Peterson, & Brodt, "Team negotiation."

[93]Morgan & Tindale, "Group vs. individual performance."

The presence of a team at the bargaining table increases the integrativeness of joint agreements,[94] but what about the distributive component? Do teams outperform their solo counterparts? Not necessarily. Nevertheless, both teams and solo players believe teams have an advantage—a **team efficacy effect**.[95] Even in situations in which teams reap greater shares of profit than their solo counterparts, solos are still better off negotiating with a team than with another solo player. The solo negotiator earns less than the team, but the amount of jointly available resources is greater in the team-solo negotiation than in the solo-solo negotiation. The **team halo effect** refers to the fact that teams tend not to be blamed for their failures, as much as do individuals, holding constant the nature of the failure.[96] Rather, teams simply are given a lot of credit for their successes but are not blamed for their failures. The reason is that people have an easier time imagining how an *individual* might have done something better than imagining how a *team* might have done something better.

Challenges That Face Negotiating Teams

For a comprehensive review, see Brodt and Thompson.[97]

Picking Your Teammates

Consider the following criteria for choosing and evaluating teammates:

1. **Negotiation expertise.**   People with good negotiation skills may be worth their weight in gold if, for example, they are able to devise an integrative solution to a complex conflict situation. A negotiation expert can streamline preparation, make sure the team avoids the four major sandtraps of negotiation (see Chapter 1), avoids destructive conflict strategies, and instigates a creative problem-solving process.
2. **Technical expertise.**   It helps to have someone with technical expertise in the domain of interest. For example, when house buying, it is valuable to have someone who is skilled in architecture, plumbing, electricity, and so on. Furthermore, by tapping into the technical expertise of our teammates, we can prioritize our own interests.
3. **Interpersonal skills.**   It often helps to have people with good interpersonal skills on a negotiating team, even if they are not specifically trained in negotiation. Negotiation involves many interpersonal skills, such as the ability to establish rapport, communicate effectively, and redirect a power- or rights-based argument to one focusing on interests.[98]

How Many on the Team?

Two or three heads can be better than one, but at some point conformity pressures increase with group size, peaking at about five and then leveling off.[99] As teams grow in size, coordination problems increase.

---

[94]Ibid; O'Connor, "Groups and solos in context."; Carnevale, *Team effects in bilateral negotiation.*

[95]O'Connor, "Groups and solos in context."; Carnevale, *Team effects in bilateral negotiation;* Thompson, Peterson, & Brodt, "Team negotiation."

[96]Naquin, C., & Tynan, R. (2003). The team halo effect: Why teams are not blamed for their failures. *Journal of Applied Psychology, 88*(2), 332–340.

[97]Brodt, S., & Thompson, L. (2001). Negotiating teams: A levels of analysis approach. *Group Dynamics: Theory, Research, and Practice, 5*(3), 208–219.

[98]Ury, W. L., Brett, J. M., & Goldberg, S. B. (1988). *Getting disputes resolved: Designing systems to cut the costs of conflict.* San Francisco: Jossey-Bass.

[99]Latané, B. (1981). The psychology of social impact. *American Psychologist, 36,* 343–356.

Communication on the Team

Communication, or **information pooling**, is facilitated if members are acquaintances or share a relationship. For example, when the clues for solving a murder mystery game are distributed among group members, groups of friends are more likely to pool their diverse information than are groups of strangers.[100]

Team Cohesion

Cohesion is the strength of positive relations within a team,[101] the sum of pressures acting to keep individuals in a group,[102] and the result of all forces acting on members to remain in a group.[103] Cohesive groups perform better than less cohesive groups.[104] The three sources of cohesion are (a) attraction to the group or resistance to leaving the group, (b) morale and motivation, and (c) coordination of efforts.

Different kinds of bonds keep teams together. **Common-identity groups** are composed of members who are attracted to the group; the individual members may come and go. **Common-bond groups** are composed of members who are attracted to particular members in the group.[105]

Information Processing

Organizational members often negotiate as a team or a group because no single person has the requisite knowledge and expertise required to negotiate effectively. Thus, knowledge is distributed among team members. How effective are teams at utilizing knowledge that is distributed among members?

The issue of how teams decide who is responsible for storing and retaining information is crucial to the effectiveness of the team. Trade-offs are involved in the storage of information. It is more efficient for each team member to be responsible for a particular piece of information so that each member is not overwhelmed by too much data. However, as storage space is minimized, so are the chances of successfully retrieving the desired information. Furthermore, groups are less likely to consider and discuss information that is shared only by a subset of its members. They suffer from the **common information bias**.[106]

Members of groups are not privy to the same facts and information. People rely on others for information. In fact, members of product development teams rely on informal social exchanges more than technical reports for information. Teams can be more efficient by dividing the labor among members. However, distributed cognition is risky because

[100]Gruenfeld, D. H., Mannix, E. A., Williams, K., & Neale, M. A. (1996). Group composition and decision making: How member familiarity and information distribution affect process and performance. *Organizational Behavior and Human Decision Processes, 67*(1), 1–15.

[101]Evans, C. R., & Dion, K. L. (1991). Group cohesion and performance: A meta-analysis. *Small Group Research, 22,* 175–186.

[102]Back, K. W. (1951). Influence through social communication. *Journal of Abnormal Social Psychology, 46,* 9–23.

[103]Festinger, L. (1950). Informal social communication. *Psychological Review, 57,* 271–282.

[104]Evans & Dion, "Group cohesion and performance."

[105]Prentice, D. A., Miller, D. T., & Lightdale, J. R. (1994). Asymmetries in attachments to groups and to their members: Distinguishing between common-identity and common-bond groups. *Personality and Social Psychology Bulletin, 20,* 484–493.

[106]Gigone, D., & Hastie, R. (1993). The common knowledge effect: Information sharing and group judgment. *Journal of Personality and Social Psychology, 65,* 959–974; Stasser, G. (1992). Pooling of unshared information during group discussion. In S. Worchel, W. Wood & J. A. Simpson (Eds.), *Group processes and productivity* (pp. 48–67). Newbury Park, CA: Sage.

information may be lost to the entire group if a team loses one of its members. Thus, groups face a dilemma: divide responsibility, which increases members' dependence upon each individual member, or share information, which is clumsy and redundant.

Strategies for Improving Team Negotiations

Prepare Together

Preparing for a negotiation as a team is much more effective than if all members prepare separately. Team preparation is so important that we developed a worksheet for effective team preparation (see Exhibit 9-9). Preparing together creates a transactive memory system in which group members understand the information others have and how and when to access it. For example, groups in one investigation were given instructions on how to assemble a transistor radio. Some groups trained together; in other groups, individuals trained individually (or with a different group). When it came to actual performance, groups who had trained together outperformed those who had trained individually or with different groups.[107]

Plan Scheduled Breaks

Make sure that you schedule breaks into your negotiation to allow team members to meet privately. For example, Ralph Szygenda of General Motors (GM) summoned six suppliers for several rounds of intense weeklong negotiations during which GM representatives met with teams from each bidder every day for 5 days. For the tech companies, these "sessions were like barefoot marathons." IBM assigned a team of 500 people worldwide, and in later negotiation rounds, they set up a war room, where team members would gather any time to resolve issues that had been raised in negotiations.[108]

A word of caution: Many teams spend too much time in private caucus and not enough time at the table. This behavior is ultimately not effective for negotiation.

Assess Accountability

It is important to assess the extent to which team members are accountable to others outside of the team. For example, when teams are accountable to a supervisor, they are more effective than when they negotiate strictly on their own behalf.[109]

INTERGROUP NEGOTIATION

People who represent different social groups often negotiate with members of other groups.[110] For example, members of a student council and university administrators, union and management negotiators, and groups of students from rival universities are all examples of intergroup negotiators. On a larger scale, nations negotiate with other nations.

[107]Moreland, R. L., Argote, L., & Krishnan, R. (1996). Socially shared cognition at work. In J. L. Nye & A. M. Brower (Eds.), *What's social about social cognition?* Thousand Oaks, CA: Sage.

[108]Hamm, S. (2005, December 19). GM's way or the highway; With $15 billion in deals to disburse, it's changing the tech outsourcing biz. *Business Week, 3964,* 48.

[109]Peterson & Thompson, "Negotiation teamwork."

[110]Deutsch, M. (1973). *The resolution of conflict.* New Haven, CT: Yale University Press; Klar, Y., Bar-Tal, D., & Kruglanski, A. W. (1988). Conflict as a cognitive schema: Toward a social cognitive analysis of conflict and conflict termination. In W. Stroebe, A. Kruglanski, D. Bar-Tal, & M. Hewstone (Eds.), *The social psychology of intergroup conflict.* Berlin: Springer-Verlag; Sherif, M. (1936). *The psychology of social norms.* New York: Harper and Row.

EXHIBIT 9-9   Preparing for Your Team-on-Team Negotiation

Team-on-team negotiation can be an advantage over solo negotiation if the team prepares properly. Here are some guidelines:

Step 1:   Individual Preparation
- Identify the issues.
- Identify your BATNA.
- Determine what *you* believe to be your team's "worst-case" scenario.
- Determine what *you* believe to be your team's "best-case" scenario.
- Write down these scenarios and be prepared to share them with the members of your team.

Step 2:   As a Team, Decide on Your Procedures for Running the Preparation Meeting
- Who is going to run the meeting (i.e., who is going to summarize, synthesize, etc.)?
- What materials do you need to be effective (calculator, flipcharts, computer, etc.), and who is bringing them?
- What is your timeline, and who will enforce it so that the team arrives at the negotiation table prepared and refreshed?

Step 3:   As a Team, Clarify Facts and Information (*Note:* You are not discussing strategy yet!)
- Develop a "Positions and Interests" chart.
- Prioritize your issues. Understand the reasons for your priorities.
- Identify what you think the other party's priorities are.
- Identify what information you need from the other party.
- Determine your BATNA.
- What do you know about the other party's BATNA?
- Identify your worst-case scenario (reservation price).
- Identify your best-case scenario (target).
- As you complete the preceding tasks, make a list of questions to research.
- Identify information that is too sensitive to reveal at any point under any condition (get clarification and closure within the team on this point).
- Identify information that you are willing to share with the other team if they inquire (get clarification and closure within the team on this point).

Step 4:   Strategy
- As a team, plan your OPENING OFFER. (*Note:* It is not advisable to simply want the "other party" to open; you need to be able to put something on the table at some point.)
- Choose a *lead negotiator* (speaker).
- Choose a *lead strategist* (listener and strategic watchdog).
- Choose an *accountant* to run the numbers.
- Choose a *scribe* to keep track of offers. Decide on a signal to adjourn for a private caucus.

The toll in death, suffering, and displacement caused by intergroup conflict has reached staggering proportions. The number of American casualties in the United States-Iraq war has reached over 4,000.[111]

[111]Griffis, M. (2008, July 17). Casualties in Iraq: The human cost of occupation. Retrieved July 30, 2008 from http://antiwar.com/casualties/

Challenges of Intergroup Negotiations

Stereotyping

In intergroup negotiations, parties identify with their organization and often hold negative impressions about members of the other organizations.[112]

Changing Identities

People identify with many different social groups.[113] For example, a student might consider a relevant group to be the other students in his or her study group, the class as a whole, marketing majors in general, or the entire student body. At any given time, one group might be more or less salient to the student: At a football game, students might identify most strongly with the entire student body; in a dining hall, students might identify most strongly with a particular dorm or floor.

Imagine you are in an organization in which marketing and finance are distinct subgroups located on different floors of a building. Contrast that arrangement to a situation in which marketing and finance are not separate functional units but, instead, are part of the same product team. What happens in the case in which a marketing manager negotiates with a financial manager? Negotiations among individuals representing different social groups are less mutually beneficial than negotiations among individuals who perceive themselves as belonging to a larger social organization—one that encompasses all those present at the bargaining table.[114] When people define their social identity at the level of the organization, they are more likely to make more organizationally beneficial choices than when social identity is defined at an individual or subgroup level. For example, when group members are instructed to consider features they have in common with another group, behavior toward out-groups is much more generous than when they consider features that are distinct.[115]

In-Group Bias

Five beliefs propel groups toward conflict: superiority, injustice, vulnerability, distrust, and helplessness.[116] These deeply entrenched beliefs can trigger destructive action. Moreover, to the extent that groups receive social support from their fellow in-group members, such beliefs can lead to even greater intergroup conflict.[117] Group distinctions and social boundaries may be created on the basis of completely arbitrary distinctions.[118] In one investigation, participants were divided into two groups on the basis of an

---

[112]Kramer, R. M. (1991). The more the merrier? Social psychological aspects of multiparty negotiations in organizations. In M. H. Bazerman, R. J. Lewicki, & B. H. Sheppard (Eds.), *Research on negotiations in organizations: Handbook of negotiation research: Vol. 3* (pp. 307–332). Greenwich, CT: JAI Press; for reviews, see Stroebe, W., Kruglanski, A. W., Bar-Tal, D., & Hewstone, M. (Eds). (1988). *The social psychology of intergroup conflict.* Berlin: Springer-Verlag; Worchel, S., & Austin, W. G. (Eds.). (1986). *Psychology of intergroup relations.* Chicago: Nelson-Hall.

[113]Kramer, "The more the merrier?"

[114]Ibid.

[115]Kramer, R. M., & Brewer, M. (1984). Effects of group identity on resource use in a simulated commons dilemma. *Journal of Personality and Social Psychology, 46,* 1044–1057.

[116]Eidelson, R. J., & Eidelson, J. I. (2003). Dangerous ideas: Five beliefs that propel groups toward conflict. *American Psychologist, 58*(3), 182–192.

[117]Wildschut, T., Insko, C. A., & Gaertner, L. (2002). Intragroup social influence and intergroup competition. *Journal of Personality and Social Psychology, 82*(6), 975–992.

[118]Tajfel, H. (1970). Experiments in intergroup discrimination. *Scientific American, 223,* 96–102.

arbitrary procedure (random draws from a box).[119] Then, individuals negotiated with either a member of their "own group" or the "other group." Even though the information concerning the negotiation situation was identical in both respects, negotiations with members of out-groups were anticipated to be more contentious than negotiations with members of in-groups; further, the mere anticipation of negotiation with an out-group member led to increased **in-group bias**, positive evaluations of one's own group relative to the out-group. In another investigation, people allocating money between their group and a competing group took a significantly greater share of the monetary funds than people allocating between themselves and a competing individual.[120]

When we anticipate negotiations with out-group members, we are more likely to engage in **downward social comparison**.[121] We evaluate the competitor to be less attractive on a number of organizationally relevant dimensions (such as intelligence, competence, and trustworthiness) than members of our group. However, after successful negotiation with out-groups, intergroup relations improve, and downward social comparison virtually disappears.[122] Negotiation with out-group members is threatening to organizational actors, but to the extent that integrative agreements are feasible, negotiation has remarkable potential for improving intergroup relations. Although our initial expectations may be quite pessimistic, interactions with members of opposing groups often have a beneficial impact on intergroup relations if several key conditions are met, such as mutual dependence for goal attainment.[123]

People of high status, those of low status who have few alternatives, and members of groups who have an opportunity to improve their group are most likely to identify with their own group. Members of groups with lower perceived status display more in-group bias than members of groups with higher perceived status.[124] However, high-status group members show more in-group bias on group status-related dimensions, whereas low-status group members consider the in-group superior on alternative dimensions.[125]

Extremism

Groups in conflict often misperceive each other's beliefs. Parties in conflict do not have an accurate understanding of the views of the other party and exaggerate the position of the other side in a way that promotes the perception of conflict.[126] Each side views the

---

[119]Thompson, L. (1993). The impact of negotiation on intergroup relations. *Journal of Experimental Social Psychology, 29*(4), 304–325.

[120]Diekmann, K. (1997). Implicit justifications and self-serving group allocations. *Journal of Organizational Behavior, 18*, 3–16.

[121]Wills, T. A. (1981). Downward comparison principles in social psychology. *Psychological Bulletin, 90*, 245–271.

[122]Thompson, L. (1993). The impact of negotiation on intergroup relations. *Journal of Experimental Social Psychology, 29*(4), 304–325.

[123]Aronson, E., & Bridgeman, D. (1979). Jigsaw groups and the desegregated classroom: In pursuit of common goals. *Personality and Social Psychology Bulletin, 5*, 438–446.

[124]Ellemers, N., Van Rijswijk, W., Roefs, M., & Simons, C. (1997). Bias in intergroup perceptions: Balancing group identity with social reality. *Personality and Social Psychology Bulletin, 23*(2), 186–198.

[125]Ellemers, N., & Van Rijswijk, W. (1997). Identity needs versus social opportunities: The use of group level and individual level identity management strategies as a function of relative group size, status, and in-group identification. *Social Psychology Quarterly, 60*(1), 52–65.

[126]Robinson, R. J., Keltner, D., Ward, A., & Ross, L. (1994). Actual versus assumed differences in construal: "Naïve realism" in intergroup perception and conflict. *Journal of Personality and Social Psychology, 68*, 404–417; Ross, L., & Ward, A. (1996). Naïve realism in everyday life: Implications for social conflict and misunderstanding. In T. Brown, E. S. Reed, & E. Turiel (Eds), *Values and knowledge. The Jean Piaget symposium series* (pp. 103–135). Mahwah, NJ: Erlbaum.

other as holding more extreme and opposing views than is really the case. And people perceive more disagreement with rivals about values that are central to their own party's ideological position than those that are central to their rival's position.[127] Moreover, people believe their adversaries are actually motivated by their opposition to their own core values rather than by the promotion of the adversaries' core values.

Consider the 1986 Howard Beach incident involving the death of a young African-American man who was struck by a passing car as he attempted to escape from a group of white pursuers in the Howard Beach neighborhood of New York City. A trial ultimately led to the conviction of some (but not all) of the young man's pursuers. Many details of the case were ambiguous and controversial, leading each party to have exaggerated perceptions of the other parties' views, thereby exacerbating the perception of differences in opinion. Partisans on either side of the affirmative action debate greatly overestimate the liberalism of proponents and the conservatism of opponents.[128] The same polarization effect is found for other policy issues, such as abortion and immigration.

Why does this extremism occur? According to the **naïve realism** principle, people expect others to hold views of the world similar to their own.[129] When conflict erupts, people are initially inclined to sway the other party with evidence. When this tactic fails to bridge interests, people regard dissenters as extremists who are out of touch with reality.

Strategies for Optimizing Intergroup Negotiations

Consider the following strategies in intergroup negotiations.

Separate Conflict of Interest from Symbolic Conflict

Conflict between groups does not always arise from competition over scarce resources. Many conflicts between groups do not have their roots in resource scarcity but, rather, in fundamental differences in values.[130] For example, conflicts are judged as more difficult to resolve when they occur between members of different groups than members of the same group, holding constant the nature of the conflict.[131] Consider for example, the strong protests made against busing by people whose lives are not affected by it.[132] Presumably, people who do not have children or grandchildren are not affected by busing. However, they tend to have strong feelings about it. Busing does not represent an economic issue to them but, rather, a symbolic issue. It is important to understand which issues are symbolic and which are economic. Moreover, adversaries are more optimistic about intergroup negotiation when they are exposed to the actual, rather than assumed, views of their counterparts.[133]

---

[127]Chambers, J., & Melnyk, D. (2007). Why do I hate thee? Conflict misperceptions and intergroup mistrust. *Personality and Social Psychology Bulletin, 32*(10), 1295–1311.

[128]Sherman, D. K., Nelson, L. D., & Ross, L. D. (2003). Naïve realism and affirmative action: Adversaries are more similar than they think. *Basic and Applied Social Psychology, 25*(4), 275–289.

[129]Ross & Ward, "Naïve realism in everyday life."

[130]Bobo, L. (1983). Whites' opposition to busing: Symbolic racism or realistic group conflict? *Journal of Personality and Social Psychology, 45*(6), 1196–1210.

[131]Ybarra, O., & Ramon, A. (2004). Diagnosing the difficulty of conflict resolution between individuals from the same and different social groups. *Journal of Experimental Social Psychology, 40*, 815–822.

[132]Sears, D. O., & Allen, H. M., Jr. (1984). The trajectory of local desegregation controversies and Whites' opposition to busing. In N. Miller & M. Brewer (Eds.), *Groups in contact: The psychology of desegregation* (pp. 123–151). New York: Academic Press.

[133]Sherman, Nelson, & Ross, "Naïve realism and affirmative action."

Search for Common Identity

To the extent groups in conflict can share a common identity, conflict and competition decreases dramatically.[134] People in organizations can identify at different levels within their organization (e.g., person, group, department, unit, organization as a whole, etc.). In one investigation, groups were told to focus on their group identities. Other groups who were involved in an objectively identical conflict were told to focus on the collective organization. Cooperation was greatly increased when groups focused on the collective, rather than their group, identities. Moreover, the stronger the group identification, the more likely it is that groups develop a shared understanding that leads to more integrative outcomes.[135] Finding common identity may be more efficacious when dealing with outgroup members than actually understanding their underlying interests. Negotiations with in-group members are more cooperative when they share information about their underlying self-interests. Conversely, negotiations with out-group members are more cooperative when they don't share information about their underlying interests.[136]

Avoid the Out-Group Homogeneity Bias

Suppose three white managers watch a videotape of a discussion among members of a mixed-race group, composed of three African-American men and three Caucasian men. After watching the videotape, the managers are presented with the actual text of the conversation and asked to indicate who said what. They are very good at remembering whether an African-American or Caucasian person made a particular comment, but their accuracy in terms of differentiating which African-American male said what is abysmal.[137] Within-race (or within-group) errors are more prevalent than between-race errors because people categorize members of out-groups not as individuals but, simply, as "black Americans." It is important for people to treat members of out-groups as individuals.

Contact

The **mere contact** strategy is based on the principle that greater contact among members of diverse groups increases cooperation among group members. Unfortunately, contact does not always lead to better intergroup relations, and in some cases it may even exacerbate negative relations among groups. For example, contact between African-Americans and Caucasians in desegregated schools does not reduce racial prejudice;[138] little relationship is noted between interdepartmental contact

[134]Kramer, R. M., & Brewer, M. (1986). Social group identity and the emergence of cooperation in resource conservation dilemmas. In H. Wilke, C. Rutte, & D. Messick (Eds.), *Experimental studies of social dilemmas*. Frankfurt, Germany: Peter Lang.

[135]Swaab, R., Postmes, T., van Beest, I., & Spears, R. (2007). Shared cognition as a product of, and precursor to, shared identity in negotiations. *Personality and Social Psychology Bulletin, 33*(2), 187–199.

[136]Harinck, F., & Ellemers, N. (2006). Hide and seek: The effects of revealing one's personal interests in intra- and intergroup negotiations. *European Journal of Social Psychology, 36,* 791–813.

[137]Linville, P. W., Fischer, G. W., & Salovey, P. (1989). Perceived distributions of the characteristics of in-group and out-group members: Empirical evidence and a computer simulation. *Journal of Personality and Social Psychology, 57,* 165–188.

[138]Gerard, H. (1983). School desegregation: The social science role. *American Psychologist, 38,* 869–878; Schofield, J. W. (1986). Black and white contact in desegregated schools. In M. Hewstone & R. J. Brown (Eds.), *Contact and conflict in intergroup encounters* (pp. 79–92). Oxford, England: Blackwell.

and conflict in organizations;[139] and college students studying in foreign countries become increasingly negative toward their host countries the longer they remain in them.[140]

Several conditions need to be in place before contact can have its desired effect of reducing prejudice.

- *Social and institutional support.*   For contact to work, a framework of social and institutional support is needed. That is, people in positions of authority should be unambiguous in their endorsement of the goals of the integration policies. This support fosters the development of a new social climate in which more tolerant norms can emerge.
- *Acquaintance potential.*   A second condition for successful contact is that it be of sufficient frequency, duration, and closeness to permit the development of meaningful relationships between members of the groups concerned. Infrequent, short, and casual interaction will do little to foster more favorable attitudes and may even make them worse.[141] This type of close interaction will lead to the discovery of similarities and disconfirm negative stereotypes.
- *Equal status.*   The third condition necessary for contact to be successful is that participants have equal status. Many stereotypes of out-groups comprise beliefs about the inferior ability of out-group members to perform various tasks. If the contact situation involves an unequal-status relationship between men and women—for example, with women in the subordinate role (e.g., taking notes, acting as secretaries)—stereotypes are likely to be reinforced rather than weakened.[142] If, however, the group members work on equal footing, prejudiced beliefs become hard to sustain in the face of repeated experience of task competence by the out-group member.
- *Shared goal.*   When members of different groups depend on each other for the achievement of a jointly desired objective, they have instrumental reasons to develop better relationships. The importance of a shared group goal is a key determinant of intergroup relations. Sometimes a common enemy is a catalyst for bonding among diverse people and groups. For example, by "waging a war against cancer," members of different medical groups and laboratories can work together.
- *Cross-group friendships.*   Sometimes it is not necessary for groups to have real contact with one another to improve intergroup relations. If group members know that another member of their own group has a friendship or relationship with a member of the out-group, or a cross-group friendship, in-group members have less negative attitudes toward the out-group.[143] It is not necessary that all members of a group have cross-group friendships; merely knowing that one member of the group does can go a long way toward reducing negative out-group attitudes.

Many of these strategies are preventative and can help ward off unhealthy, destructive competition between groups. What steps can a manager take to deal with conflict after it has erupted?

---

[139]Brown, R. J., Condor, F., Mathew, A., Wade, G., & Williams, J. A. (1986). Explaining intergroup differentiation in an industrial organization. *Journal of Occupational Psychology, 59,* 273–286.

[140]Stroebe, W., Lenkert, A., & Jonas, K. (1988). Familiarity may breed contempt: The impact of student exchange on national stereotypes and attitudes. In W. Stroebe, A. W. Kruglanski, D. Bar-Tal, & M. Hewstone (Eds.), *The social psychology of intergroup conflict* (pp. 167–187). New York: Springer-Verlag.

[141]Brewer, M. B., & Brown, R. J. (1998). Intergroup relations. In D. T. Gilbert, S. T. Fiske, & G. Lindzey (Eds.), *The handbook of social psychology: Vol. 2* (4th ed.) (pp. 554–594). New York: McGraw-Hill.

[142]Bradford, D. L., & Cohen, A. R. (1984). *Managing for excellence.* New York: Wiley.

[143]Wright, S. C., Aron, A., McLaughlin-Volpe, T., & Ropp, S. A. (1997). The extended contact effect: Knowledge of cross-group friendships and prejudice. *Journal of Personality and Social Psychology, 73*(1), 73–90.

The GRIT Strategy

The Graduated and Reciprocal Initiative in Tension Reduction, or **GRIT model**, is a model of conflict reduction for warring groups. Originally developed as a program for international disarmament negotiations, it also can be used to deescalate intergroup problems on a smaller, domestic scale.[144] The goals of this strategy are to increase communication and reciprocity between groups while reducing mistrust, thereby allowing for deescalation of hostility and creation of a greater array of possible outcomes. The model prescribes a series of steps that call for specific communication between groups in the hope of establishing the "rules of the game." Other stages are designed to increase trust between the two groups as the consistency in each group's responses demonstrates credibility and honesty. Some steps are necessary only in extremely intense conflict situations in which the breakdown of intergroup relations implies a danger for the group members.

Mikhail Gorbachev's decisions in the period from 1986 to 1989 closely resemble the GRIT model.[145] Gorbachev made a number of unilateral concessions that resulted in serious deescalation of world tensions in this period. On two occasions, the Soviets stalled resumption of atmospheric nuclear testing despite their inability to extend the prior treaty with the Reagan administration. They then agreed twice to summit meetings, despite the Reagan administration's refusal to discuss the Star Wars defense system. They then agreed to the Intermediate-Range Nuclear Forces (INF) Treaty (exceeding the United States' requests for verification) with continued refusal by the United States to bargain about Star Wars. Next came agreements on the Berlin Wall and the unification of Germany. Eventually, even the staunchly anti-Communist/anti-Soviet Reagan-Bush regime had to take notice. These events led to a period of mellowing tensions between these two superpowers (see Exhibit 9-10).

Although the GRIT model may seem overly elaborate and therefore inapplicable to most organizational conflicts, the model clarifies the difficulties inherent in establishing

---

EXHIBIT 9-10   GRIT Strategy: Gradual Reduction in Tension

1. Announce your general intentions to deescalate conflict and your specific intention to make an initial concession.
2. Execute your initial concession unilaterally, completely, and publicly. Provide as much verification and documentation as possible.
3. Invite reciprocity from the other party. Expect the other party to react to these steps with mistrust and skepticism. To overcome this, consider making another concession.
4. Match any reciprocal concessions made by the other party. Invite more.
5. Diversify the nature of your concessions.
6. Maintain your ability to retaliate if the other party escalates conflict. Any such retaliation should be carefully calibrated to match the intensity of the other party's actions.

Source: Based on Barron, R. S., Kerr, N. L., & Miller, N. (1992). *Group process, group decision, group action* (p. 151). Pacific Grove, CA: Brooks/Cole.

---

[144]Osgood, C. E. (1979). GRIT 1 (Vol. 8, No. 1, 0553–4283). Dundas, Ontario: Peace Research Reviews.
[145]Barron, R. S., Kerr, N. L., & Miller, N. (1992). *Group process, group decision, group action.* Pacific Grove, CA: Brooks/Cole.

mutual trust between parties that have been involved in prolonged conflict. Although some of the stages are not applicable to all conflicts, the importance of clearly announcing intentions, making promised concessions, and matching reciprocation are relevant to all but the most transitory conflicts.

CONCLUSION

Multiparty negotiations require all of the pie-slicing and pie-expanding skills of two-party negotiations, and then some. The key challenges of multiparty negotiations are the development and management of coalitions, the complexity of information management, voting rules, and communication breakdowns. We discussed several different levels of analysis involved in multiparty negotiations and key strategies to finesse each situation, including coalition management, principal-agent relationships, team negotiation, intergroup negotiation, and dealing with constituencies. Exhibit 9-11 summarizes the six levels of analysis, the key challenges facing the negotiator at each level, and the best strategies to surmount these challenges.

EXHIBIT 9-11 Summary of Challenges and Strategies for Each Level of Multiparty Analysis

Level of Analysis	Challenges	Strategies
Multiparty negotiation	Coalition formation Difficulty formulating trade-offs Voting paradoxes • Strategic voting • Majority rule suppresses strength of preference Communication breakdowns • Private caucusing • Biased interpretation • Perspective-taking failures • Indirect speech acts • Multiple audience problem	Know who will be at the table Systematize proposal making Use brainstorming wisely Develop and assign process roles Stay at the table Strive for equal participation Allow for some points of agreement Avoid the "equal shares" bias Avoid the "agreement bias" Avoid sequential bargaining
Coalitions	Optimal coalition size Trust and temptation Dividing the pie	Core solution Shapley model Raiffa's hybrid model Make contacts early Seek verbal commitments Use unbiased-appearing rationale to divide the pie
Principal-agent relationships	Conflicting incentives Shrinking bargaining zone Communication distortion Loss of control Agreement at any cost	Shop around Know your BATNA before meeting your agent Communicate interests, but do not reveal your BATNA Capitalize on agent's expertise Tap into agent's sources of information Discuss ratification Use agent for saving face Use agent to buffer emotions

Principal-constituency relationships	Identification
	Accountability
	• Evaluation apprehension
	• Face-saving
	Conflicts of interest
		Understand constituents' interest
		Do not expect homogeneity
		    within constituencies
		Educate constituents on your role
		    and limitations
		Help constituents do horizon thinking

Team negotiation	Choosing teammates How many on the team? Communication within the team Team cohesion Information processing	Prepare as a team (not separately) Plan scheduled breaks (to regroup) Determine accountability
Intergroup negotiation	Stereotyping Changing identities In-group bias Extremism	Separate conflict of interest from symbolic conflict Search for common identity Avoid outgroup homogeneity bias Contact GRIT strategy

CHAPTER

Cross-Cultural Negotiation

₁₀

When President George W. Bush met with Crown Prince Abdullah of Saudi Arabia to discuss rising oil prices and the Israeli-Palestinian conflict, something surprising occurred: The two held hands while walking at the president's Texas ranch. While it may have seemed odd to many Americans, the gesture is considered an expression of affection between men in Saudi Arabia, and it can be interpreted as an insult if a man chooses not to touch another in greeting. President Bush followed Arab custom by kissing Abdullah on each cheek and then walking with him, hand in hand.[1] After September 11, 2001, when it was determined that 15 of the 19 hijackers came from Saudi Arabia, tension grew between the United States and Saudi Arabia. Criticisms of the Saudis and their ties to the Bushes abounded, spurred on by filmmaker Michael Moore and CIA veteran Robert Baer.[2] Yet President Bush allowed the meeting with Abdullah to begin on friendly terms by participating in Saudi customs. The image of the two men holding hands represented a repaired trust and a mutual respect, and the talks were dubbed a success by both sides.

Negotiations between people of different cultures often stir up deeply held values and beliefs; behaviors that seem normative in one culture might meet with severe censure and even legal action in other cultures. Cultural intelligence is essential for effective negotiation. Cross-cultural negotiations do not always go smoothly (see Exhibit 10-1 for an example of a failed cross-cultural negotiation). Most managers cannot expect to negotiate only with people of their own country or culture throughout their career. In fact, North Americans are a minority—about 7% of the world's population. To get a better sense of the world's composition, imagine that the world's population is only 100 people. In this case, the population would include 55 Asians, 21 Europeans, 9 Africans, 8 South Americans, and 7 North Americans.[3]

---

[1]Fattah, H. M. (2005, May 1). Why Arab men hold hands. *New York Times,* p. 4.
[2]Dickey, C. (2005, May 3). Shadowland: "Sharon had better listen". *Newsweek.com.* Retrieved July 17, 2008, from http://www.newsweek.com/id/51652
[3]Triandis, H. C. (1994). *Culture and social behavior* (pp. 29–54). New York: McGraw-Hill.

EXHIBIT 10-1   Failed Cross-Cultural Negotiation

Just when the executives of Millicom International Cellular were getting ready to board a plane for Beijing to celebrate the sale of their company to China Mobile Communications, China called off the $5.3 billion deal. After months of negotiations between the Chinese company and Millicom, a mobile phone company with 9 million customers in developing countries, the failed deal demonstrated the differences between negotiating styles in China and those in Europe and the United States. In China, the last-minute departure was considered a smart corporate strategy because the company managed to avoid overpaying for a group of assets that would have been difficult to manage. But the sudden exit frustrated and angered European and U.S. negotiators. With no warning from China Mobile about its intentions, the failed deal upset the stock market and didn't allow Millicom time to secure a new bidder.

Source: Timmons, H. & Greenlees, D. (2006, July 14). Art of the deal meets the China syndrome. *New York Times,* p. C6. Reprinted by permission.

When people from different cultures get together to negotiate, they may fail to reach integrative agreements.[4] Failure to expand the pie has a number of undesirable effects, including (but not limited to) feelings of exploitation, souring of a potentially rewarding relationship, and the destruction of potential global relationships.

Often, value is left on the table because people are not prepared for the challenges of cross-cultural negotiation. This chapter provides a business plan for effective cross-cultural negotiation. We begin by defining culture; then we identify the key dimensions by which culture affects judgment, motivation, and behavior at the bargaining table. Next, we identify the biggest barriers to effective intercultural negotiation and provide strategies for effective cross-cultural negotiation.

LEARNING ABOUT CULTURES

This chapter does not provide a crash course on how to negotiate with people of different cultures. Thus, we do not offer advice on a country-by-country basis for two reasons.

First, doing so would be contrary to the book's focus, which is to provide negotiation skills that work across people and situations. We do not want to promote cultural stereotypes. By making a generic list of characteristics for cultures, we magnify stereotypes, which is neither practical nor informative. Most people prefer to be considered unique individuals, yet we are often too quick to lump together people from the same country.

A more useful approach is to develop a framework for thinking about culture. Jeanne Brett distinguishes **stereotypes** from **prototypes**. Prototypes recognize that substantial variation is likely even within a culture.[5] Using a prototype approach provides several advantages. A great deal of diversity can be found among people in any culture. Within cultures, key personality traits vary, and different traits are associated

---

[4]Brett, J. M. (2007). *Negotiating globally: How to negotiate deals, resolve disputes, and make decisions across cultural boundaries*(2nd ed). San Francisco: Jossey-Bass.
[5]Ibid.

with better performance within certain cultures but not others.[6] A cultural framework is sensitive to heterogeneity within cultural groups.

Second, most cultures are different today than they were 10 years ago. We need a dynamic framework that allows us to learn how cultures change and grow. This chapter provides a means by which to expose our own cultural beliefs and those of others, how to avoid mistakes, and how to profit from intercultural negotiations.[7]

Defining Culture

Many people conceive of culture strictly in terms of geography; however, culture does not pertain just to nations and countries. Rather, culture is the unique character of a social group, the values and norms shared by its members that set it apart from other social groups.[8] Culture encompasses economic, social, political, and religious institutions. It also reflects the unique products produced by these groups—art, architecture, music, theatre, and literature.[9] Cultural institutions preserve and promote a culture's ideologies. Culture influences our mental models of how things work, behavior, and cause-and-effect relationships. To broaden our thinking about culture, consider the possible cultural differences contained in all of the following:

- Families
- Social groups and departments in an organization
- Organizations
- Industries
- States
- Regions
- Countries
- Societies (e.g., foraging, horticultural, pastoral, agrarian, industrial, service, information)
- Continents
- Hemispheres

Nations, occupational groups, social classes, genders, races, tribes, corporations, clubs, and social movements may become the bases of specific subcultures. When thinking about culture and diversity, avoid the temptation to think of it as a single dimension (e.g., country of origin); culture is a complex whole, and it is best to use many criteria to discern one culture from another.

Culture as an Iceberg

We use Schneider's model of culture as an iceberg.[10] Typically, about one-ninth of an iceberg is visible; the rest is submerged. As Exhibit 10-2 indicates, the top (visible) part of the cultural iceberg is the behaviors, artifacts, and institutions that characterize a culture. This portion includes things such as traditions, customs, habits, and other immediately visible

---

[6]Liu, L., Friedman, R., & Chi, S. (2005). "Ren Qing" versus the "Big Five": The role of culturally sensitive measures of individual difference in distributive negotiations. *Management and Organization Review, 1*(2), 225–247.

[7]For an extensive treatment, see Brett, *Negotiating globally.*

[8]Lytle, A. L., Brett, J. M., & Shapiro, D. L. (1999). The strategic use of interests, rights and power to resolve disputes. *Negotiation Journal, 15*(1), 31–49.

[9]Brett, *Negotiating globally.*

[10]Schneider, S. C. (1997). *Managing across cultures.* Upper Saddle River, NJ: Prentice Hall; see also Brett, *Negotiating globally,* for an extensive review.

EXHIBIT 10-2   Culture as an Iceberg

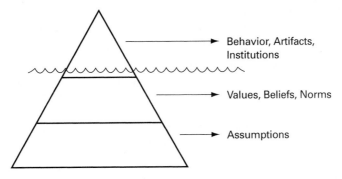

Source: Adapted by Susan Schneider (HEC University of Geneva) from Schein, E. H. (1985). *Organizational culture and leadership,* p. 14. San Francisco: Jossey-Bass. Reprinted by permission.

stimuli. These behaviors and artifacts are an expression of deeper-held values, beliefs, and norms. Driving these values and norms are fundamental assumptions about the world and humanity. The artifacts and customs that characterize a culture are not arbitrary; rather, they are manifestations about fundamental values and beliefs about the world.

CULTURAL VALUES AND NEGOTIATION NORMS

We identify three dimensions of culture, based on Brett (see Exhibit 10-3):[11]

- Individualism versus collectivism
- Egalitarianism versus hierarchy
- Direct versus indirect communication

These three dimensions refer to motivation, influence, and information, respectively.[12] **Individualism-collectivism** refers to the basic human motive concerning preservation of the self versus the collective. **Egalitarianism-hierarchy** refers to the means by which people influence others, either laterally or hierarchically. Finally, **direct-indirect communication** refers to the manner in which people exchange information and messages.

Individualism Versus Collectivism

A key way in which cultures differ is with respect to individualism and collectivism.[13]

---

[11]Brett, *Negotiating globally;* Gelfand, M. J., & Brett, J. M. (Eds.) (2004). *The handbook of negotiation and culture: Theoretical advances and cultural perspectives* Palo Alto, CA: Stanford University Press.
[12]Brett, *Negotiating globally.*
[13]Triandis, *Culture and social behavior;* Hofstede, G. (1980). *Culture's consequences: International differences in work-related values.* Beverly Hills, CA: Sage; Schwartz, S. (1994). Beyond individualism/collectivism: New cultural dimensions of values. In H. C. Triandis, U. Kim, & G. Yoon (Eds.), *Individualism and collectivism* (pp. 85–117). London: Sage; for a review, see Gelfand, M. J., Bhawuk, D. P. S., Nishii, L. H., & Bechtold, D. (2004). Individualism and collectivism: Multilevel perspectives and implications for leadership. In R. J. House, P. J. Hanges, M. Javidan, P. W. Dorfman, & Vipin Gupta (Eds.), *Culture, leadership, and organizations: The GLOBE study of 62 cultures.* Thousand Oaks, CA: Sage.

EXHIBIT 10-3   Dimensions of Culture

Cultural Dimension		
Goal: **Individual versus collective orientation**	*Individualists/Competitors:* Key goal is to maximize own gain (and perhaps the difference between oneself and others); source of identity is the self; people regard themselves as free agents and independent actors.	*Collectivists/Cooperators:* Key goal is to maximize the welfare of the group or collective; source of identity is the group; individuals regard themselves as group members; focus is on social relations.
Influence: **Egalitarianism versus hierarchy**	*Egalitarians:* Do not perceive many social obligations; often regard BATNA to be major source of bargaining power.	*Hierarchists:* Regard social order to be important in determining conflict management strategies; subordinates are expected to defer to superiors; superiors are expected to look out for subordinates.
Communication: **Direct versus indirect**	*Direct Communicators:* Engage in explicit, direct information exchange; ask direct questions; not affected by situational constraints; face-saving issues likely to arise.	*Indirect Communicators:* Engage in tacit information exchange such as storytelling, inference-making; situational norms.

Source: Brett, J. M. (2007). *Negotiating globally: How to negotiate deals, resolve disputes, and make decisions across cultural boundaries.* (2nd ed) San Francisco: Jossey-Bass. Reprinted by permission.

Individualism

In the discussion in Chapter 5 on bargaining style, we outlined three motivational orientations: individualistic, competitive, and cooperative. Individualism, as a cultural style, epitomizes the individualistic motivational orientation.[14] In individualistic cultures, the pursuit of happiness and regard for personal welfare are paramount. People in individualistic cultures give priority to their personal goals, even when these goals conflict with those of their family, work group, or country. Individual happiness and expression are valued more than collective and group needs. People from individualistic cultures enjoy having influence and control over their world and others. Consequently, individual accomplishments are rewarded by economic and social institutions. Furthermore, legal institutions in individualist cultures are designed to protect individual rights. One implication of individualism concerns the use of distributive tactics. People

---

[14]For simplicity, we include competitive style with individual style.

who are more self-interested are motivated to use more tactics that increase their bargaining power. Indeed, U.S. MBA students are more tolerant of certain kinds of ethically questionable tactics than are non-U.S. MBA students studying in the United States.[15] Specifically, U.S. MBA students are more accepting of competitive bargaining tactics and bluffing, which raises the possibility that U.S. negotiators may be perceived as less ethical by their international counterparts.[16] On the other hand, U.S. negotiators are significantly less accepting of misrepresentation to the counterparty's network. The norm in the United States of not spreading stories, particularly to the network of friends, is well entrenched.

Collectivism

Collectivist cultures are rooted in social groups, and individuals are viewed as members of groups. People in collectivist cultures give priority to in-group goals. The dominant motive is concern for, and belonging to, the group. People of collectivist cultures view their work groups and organizations as fundamental parts of themselves. Collectivists are concerned about how the results of their actions affect members of their in-group; they share resources with in-group members, feel interdependent with in-group members, and feel involved in the lives of in-group members.[17] In contrast to individualistic cultures that focus on influence and control, people from collectivist cultures emphasize the importance of adjustment. Collectivist cultures are more concerned with maintaining harmony in interpersonal relationships with the in-group than are individualistic cultures. Social norms and institutions promote the interdependence of individuals through emphasis on social obligations and the sacrifice of personal needs for the greater good. Legal institutions place the greater good of the collective above the rights of the individual, and political and economic institutions reward classes of people as opposed to individuals.[18]

Whereas individualists want to save face and are concerned with their personal outcomes, collectivists are concerned with others' outcomes as well. An analysis of U.S. and Hong Kong negotiations reveal that U.S. negotiators are more likely to subscribe to self-interest and joint problem-solving norms, whereas Hong Kong Chinese negotiators are more likely to subscribe to an equality norm.[19] Further, U.S. negotiators are more satisfied when they maximize joint gain, and Hong Kong Chinese negotiators are happier when they achieve outcome parity. The tendency of North Americans to engage in self-enhancement, an individualistic trait, is more than skin deep. In one investigation of Canadians (individualists) and Japanese (collectivists), behaviors were covertly measured.[20] Canadians were reluctant to conclude they had performed worse

---

[15]Lewicki, R. J., & Robinson, R. J. (1998). Ethical and unethical bargaining tactics: An empirical study. *Journal of Business Ethics, 17*(6), 665–682.

[16]Ibid.

[17]Billings, D. K. (1989). Individualism and group orientation. In D. M. Keats, D. Munroe, & L. Mann (Eds.), *Heterogeneity in cross-cultural psychology* (pp. 22–103). Lisse, The Netherlands: Swets and Zeitlinger; Hui, C. H., & Triandis, H. C. (1986). Individualism-collectivism: A study of cross-cultural researchers. *Journal of Cultural Psychology, 17,* 225–248.

[18]Brett, *Negotiating globally.*

[19]Tinsley, C. H., & Pillutla, M. M. (1998). Negotiating in the United States and Hong Kong. *Journal of International Business Studies, 29*(4), 711–728.

[20]Heine, S. J., Takata, T., & Lehman, D. R. (2000). Beyond self-presentation: Evidence for self-criticism among Japanese. *Personality and Social Psychology Bulletin, 26*(1), 71–78.

than their average classmate (self-enhancement); in contrast, Japanese were hesitant to conclude that they had performed better. In short, they self-criticized. Individualism and collectivism represent a continuum with substantial within-culture variation. One factor that can push people toward behaving more in line with their native cultural values is **accountability pressure**—simply the extent to which they are answerable for conducting themselves in a certain manner.[21]

Implications for Negotiation
Individualism-collectivism involves a variety of implications for the conduct of negotiation. We will outline seven of them:

1. Social networks
2. Cooperation
3. In-group favoritism
4. Social loafing versus social striving
5. Emotion and inner experience
6. Dispositionalism versus situationalism
7. Preferences for dispute resolution

Social Networks   Members of different cultures differ in terms of the density of their work friendships (i.e., how many friendships they share at work), the overlap of instrumental and socioemotional ties (i.e., whether the people they seek for information are also the ones whom they seek for comfort and emotional support), the closeness of the tie, the longevity of the tie, and whether the network relationships are directed upward, laterally, or downward. For example, interpersonal trust is an important element of Chinese **guanxi** networks (see Exhibit 10-4). Affect-and cognition-based trust are more interconnected among Chinese managers than U.S. managers. [22] In one study, U.S. and Hong Kong students negotiated with someone whom they believed to be a friend or a

---

EXHIBIT 10-4   Guanxi Networks

Anyone interested in doing business in a Chinese environment will quickly learn the term guanxi. Literally speaking guanxi means "connections" or "relations." More figuratively, guanxi are the personal bonds that are established between people who may do business together. Having the right personal connection is a stronger predictor of success in the Chinese business environment than in Western cultures. Western businesspeople who have worked in China often experience difficulty establishing trust and breaking into the local social networks. If one desires cognition-based trust from a Chinese counterpart, one cannot ignore the affect-based trust with which it is closely intertwined.

Source: Based on Chua, R., & Morris, M. (2006). Dynamics of trust in Guanxi networks. In Y. Chen (Ed.), *Research on managing groups and teams: National culture and groups.* Oxford, England: JAI Press.

---

[21]Gelfand, M. J., & Realo, A. (1999). Individualism-collectivism and accountability in intergroup negotiations. *Journal of Applied Psychology, 84*(5), 721–736.
[22]Chua, Roy Y. J., M. W. Morris, and P. Ingram. (in press). Guanxi versus networking: Distinctive configurations of affect- and cognition-based trust in the networks of Chinese and American managers. *Journal of International Business Studies.*

stranger from their own culture. The Hong Kong students changed their behavior more when interacting with a friend than did the U.S. students.[23] Whereas U.S. managers are equally likely to trust and reciprocate with a partner, as well as with someone in the network (whom they don't know directly), collectivist managers only trust and reciprocate when interacting with the relationship.[24] Perhaps this is why many realty agents report that Hispanics are often perplexed by the U.S. culture's habit of not meeting the seller of a home they are buying.[25] Similarly, agents with whom the Hispanic principal works are often treated as part of the extended family, with invitations to life cycle events.

Morris, Podolny, and Ariel examined four cultures—North American, Chinese, German, and Spanish—and proposed that each culture developed social networks within the organization according to a different set of norms (see Exhibit 10-5).[26] North American business relationships are characterized by a market orientation in which people form relationships according to the market standard of whether it is profitable. Practically, this tendency means North Americans form ties without the prior basis of friendship, paying attention only to instrumentality. Chinese business relationships are characterized by a familial orientation, in which employees make sacrifices for the welfare of the organization. Sharing resources within the in-group, loyalty, and deference to superiors characterize network relationships. German business relationships are characterized by legal-bureaucratic orientation, formal categories, and rules. In addition, Spanish business relationships are characterized by affiliative orientations,

EXHIBIT 10-5   Dominant Norms of Business Relations

Culture	Dominant Attitude	Business Relationships
North American: *Market norms*	Economic individualism	Short-lived Low-multiplexity
Chinese: *Familial norms*	Filial loyalty Economic collectivism	Directed upward to powerful
German: *Legal-bureaucratic norms*	Economic collectivism	Bounded by formal rules Low affectivity
Spanish: *Affiliative norms*	Self-expressive collectivism	Long-lived High affectivity

Source: In P. C. Earley & H. Singh (Eds.), "Innovation in International and Cross-Cultural Management," pp. 52-90. Thousand Oaks, CA: Sage Publications. Rprinted by permission of Sage Publications via Copyright Clearance Center.

[23]Chan, D. K. S., Triandis, H. C., Carnevale, P. J., Tam, A., & Bond, M. H. (1994). Comparing negotiation across cultures: Effects of collectivism, relationship between negotiators, and concession pattern on negotiation behavior. Unpublished manuscript, Department of Psychology, University of Illinois at Urbana–Champaign.

[24]Buchan, N., Croson, R., & Dawes, R. M. (2002). Swift neighbors and persistent strangers: A cross-cultural investigation of trust and reciprocity in social exchange. *American Journal of Sociology, 108*(1), 168–206.

[25]Gendler, N. (2003, June 14). Hispanic home buyers. *Star-Tribune,* p. 4H.

[26]Morris, M. W., Podolny, J. M., & Ariel S. (2000). Missing relations: Incorporating relational constructs into models of culture. In P.C. Earley & H. Singh (Eds.), *Innovations in international and cross-cultural management* (pp. 52–90). Thousand Oaks, CA: Sage Publications.

such as sociability and friendliness. A controlled cross-national comparison of network relationships in Citibank supported these network norms.[27]

Cooperation   People from collectivist cultural traditions engage in more cooperative behavior in mixed-motive interactions than do people from individualistic cultures.[28] For example, Japanese negotiators are more cooperative (and, in turn, expect others to be more cooperative) than are U.S. negotiators.[29] Greater cooperation in the face of uncertainty and the potential for exploitation imply that people from collectivist cultures place greater emphasis on the needs and goals of their group and are more likely to be willing to sacrifice personal interests for the attainment of group goals. Americans are more likely to remember situations in which they *influenced* others; in contrast, Japanese people are more likely to remember situations in which they *adjusted* to others (a form of cooperation).[30] An examination of Japanese and U.S. newspaper stories on conflict revealed that Japanese newspapers more frequently make reference to mutual blame than do U.S. newspapers, presumably because ascribing blame to both parties affords the maintenance of the social unit and is less threatening to the collective.[31] Moreover, Americans who successfully influenced others reported feeling very *efficacious* (a typical individualistic emotion), whereas Japanese people who adjusted reported feeling *related* (a collectivist emotion).

Awareness of different cultural norms can be a powerful bargaining strategy. For example, consider the negotiations that took place in Kyoto in 1997 to reach a pact on global warming. For more than a week, the negotiators at the Kyoto climate-change conference haggled over the terms of a treaty that would focus on reducing global warming. In the last hours of the negotiation, all of the world's industrialized nations had agreed to firm targets for reducing six different greenhouse gases—all but Japan, that is. The Japanese had been assigned the most modest goal: cut emissions 6% below 1990 levels by the year 2012, compared with 7% for the United States and 8% for the 15 nations of the European Union. The Japanese would not budge. Their limit was 5%. So the U.S. delegation called Washington to report the impasse, and at 2:00 a.m. an exhausted Vice President Al Gore got on the phone with Japanese Prime Minister Ryutaro Hashimoto. Gore's cross-cultural skills were sharp: He first praised Hashimoto for Japan's leadership in playing host to the conference (focusing on hierarchical cultural norms), and then he pointed out how bad it would look for the host country to derail the agreement over a measly percentage point (focusing on collective well-being). It worked.[32]

[27]Morris, Podolny, & Ariel, "Missing relations."

[28]Cox, T. H., Lobel, S. A., & McLeod, P. L. (1991). Effects of ethnic group cultural differences in cooperative and competitive behavior on a group task. *Academy of Management Journal, 34*(4), 827–847.

[29]Wade-Benzoni, K. A., Okumura, T., Brett, J. M., Moore, D. Tenbrunsel, A. E., & Bazerman, M. H. (2002). Cognitions and behavior in asymmetric social dilemmas: A comparison of two cultures. *Journal of Applied Psychology, 87*, 87–95.

[30]Morling, B., Kitayama, S., & Miyamoto, Y. (2002). Cultural practices emphasize influence in the United States and adjustment in Japan. *Personality and Social Psychology Bulletin, 28*(3), 311–323.

[31]Gelfand, M. J., Nishii, L. H., Holcombe, K. M., Dyer, N., Ohbuchi, K–I., & Fukuno, M. (2001). Cultural influences on cognitive representations of conflict: Interpretations of conflict episodes in the United States and Japan. *Journal of Applied Psychology, 86*(6), 1059–1074.

[32]Lemonick, M. (1997, December 22). Turning down the heat. *Time,* p. 23.

In-Group Favoritism   In-group favoritism is the strong tendency to favor the members of one's own group more than those in other groups, even when one has no logical basis for doing so. The in-group bias is so powerful that even when groups are formed on the basis of an arbitrary procedure, such as by drawing lots or random assignment, people evaluate their group members more positively and reward them with more resources than members of the out-group.[33] Members of collectivist cultures display more in-group favoritism than members of individualistic cultures. For example, making group boundaries salient creates more competitive behavior among members of collectivist cultures than among members of individualistic cultures.[34] Moreover, members of collectivistic cultures become more competitive when they perceive their group to be in the minority.[35] In-group favoritism often has positive effects for members of in-groups, but it can be deleterious for members of out-groups and for intergroup relations (see Chapter 9 for more on intergroup negotiation). However, according to Gabriel and Gardner, you don't have to be from a collectivist culture to show collectivist behavior, such as in-group favoritism; rather, everyone has an "interdependent" and an "independent" self, which can be "triggered."[36] And bicultural individuals are often able to spontaneously trigger either self, depending upon which cultural cue is present.[37] (See Exhibit 10-6 for an example of how priming works.)

Social Loafing versus Social Striving   **Social loafing** is the tendency for people to work less hard and contribute less effort and resources in a group context than when working alone. For example, people clap less loudly, work less hard, and contribute less when working in a group, as opposed to working alone.[38] Social loafing should occur less in collectivist cultures than in individualist cultures, presumably because individualist cultures do not reward group effort but collectivist cultures do. In a study of social loafing among management trainees in the United States and the People's Republic of China, American students loafed (individual performance declined in a group setting), but Chinese students did not.[39] In fact, among Japanese participants, the opposite pattern occurred in the group: **Social striving**—collectivist concerns for the welfare of the group—increased people's motivation and performance.[40] Self-serving biases, such as egocentrism (as discussed in Chapter 3) are more prevalent in individualistic cultures, such as the United States, in which the self is served by focusing on positive attributes and desire to stand out and be better than others. In contrast, members of collectivist

---

[33]Tajfel, H. (1982). Social psychology of intergroup relations. *Annual Review of Psychology, 33,* 1–39.

[34]Espinoza, J. A., & Garza, R. T. (1985). Social group salience and interethnic cooperation. *Journal of Experimental Social Psychology, 21,* 380–392.

[35]Ibid.

[36]Gabriel, S., & Gardner, W. L. (1999). Are there "his" and "her" types of interdependence? The implications of gender differences in collective and relational interdependence for affect, behavior, and cognition. *Journal of Personality and Social Psychology, 75,* 642–655.

[37]Fu, J., Chiu, C., Morris, M., & Young, M. (2007). Spontaneous inferences from cultural cues: Varying responses of cultural insiders and outsiders. *Journal of Cross-Cultural Psychology, 38*(1), 58–75.

[38]Kerr, N. L. (1983). Motivation losses in small groups: A social dilemma analysis. *Journal of Personality and Social Psychology, 45,* 819–828.

[39]Earley, P. C. (1989). Social loafing and collectivism: A comparison of the United States and the People's Republic of China. *Administrative Science Quarterly, 34,* 565–581.

[40]Shirakashi, S. (1985). Social loafing of Japanese students. *Hiroshima Forum for Psychology, 10,* 35–40; Yamaguchi, S., Okamoto, K., & Oka, T. (1985). Effects of coactors' presence: Social loafing and social facilitation. *Japanese Psychological Research, 27,* 215–222.

EXHIBIT 10-6   Priming Individualism and Collectivism

Everyone needs to be individualistic at times and more collectivistic, or group-focused, at times. In a series of investigations, we "primed" U.S. managers to be either individualistic (focused on the self) or relational (focused on others). To create this focus, we had the U.S. managers read a story about a leader who had an important decision to make—choosing a successor. In one version of the story, the leader chooses someone on the basis of personal talent and merit (individualistic value); in the other version of the story, the leader chooses someone on the basis of his relationship to him (collectivistic value). Then, we watched how the U.S. managers resolved a dispute. The U.S. managers who were in a position of power in a dispute were significantly more generous and cooperative if they had previously read the collectivistic story. In contrast, the U.S. managers who had read the individualistic story were significantly more self-interested.

In another twist, we then had teams of managers negotiate against other teams. We hypothesized that if we used the same collectivistic prime, it would increase the negotiator's loyalty to his or her team but would lead to significantly more in-group favoritism and less generosity across the table. That's exactly what happened. Negotiators were more generous when they were "primed" with interdependence (rather than independence) in a one-on-one (dyadic) negotiation (see panel A). However, the tables turned when the priming occurred in a group setting: Negotiators primed with interdependence were less generous. In panel B, we see the likelihood of impasse follows the same pattern: With interdependent negotiators, they are *least* likely to impasse when they are one-on-one and *most* likely to impasse when they are team-on-team.

The message? Self-interested or other-focused behavior can be triggered in negotiations with subtle primes. Triggering collectivism in a two-party situation will lead the powerful person to be more generous across the table; however, in a team situation, collectivism leads to greater in-group favoritism (to the tune of more than $80,000). Groups primed for collectivism were more successful in avoiding costly court action than were those who were primed to be independent—even though the facts in the situation, their bargaining reservation prices, and other details were objectively identical. In fact, no one who was primed with interdependence escalated to court action, but 20% of those with an independent focus did.

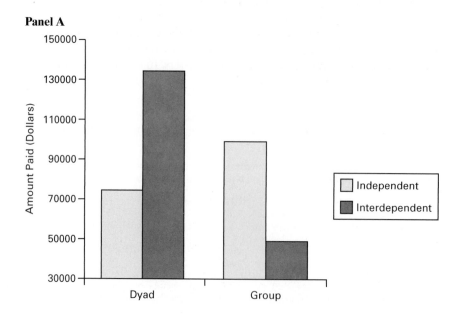

Panel A

Panel B

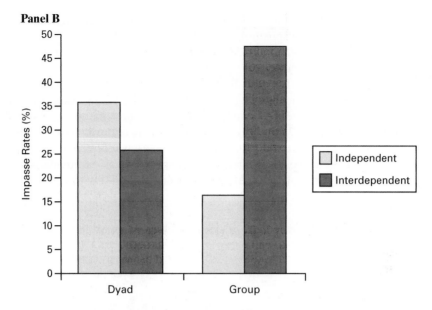

Source: Howard, E., Thompson, L., & Gardner, W. (2007). The role of the self-concept and the social context in determining the behavior of power holders: Self-construal in intergroup versus dyadic dispute resolution negotiations. *Journal of Personality and Social Psychology, 93*(4), 614–631.

cultures are less likely to hold a biased, self-serving view of themselves; rather, the self is served by focusing on negative characteristics in order to "blend in."[41]

Emotion and Inner Experience   Collectivists and individualists differ in the ways they describe emotional experience, with Chinese using more somatic and social words than Americans. For example, when Chinese and Americans are both speaking English during emotional events, less acculturated Chinese Americans used more somatic (e.g., dizzy) and more social (e.g., friend) words than European Americans.[42]

Dispositionalism Versus Situationalism   **Dispositionalism** is the tendency to ascribe the cause of a person's behavior to his or her character or underlying personality. **Situationalism** is the tendency to ascribe the cause of a person's behavior to factors and forces outside of a person's control. For example, suppose you are in the midst of a high-stakes negotiation, and you place an urgent call to your negotiation partner. Your partner does not return your call; yet you know your partner is in town because you contacted the office assistant. What is causing your partner's behavior? It is possible our partner is irresponsible (dispositionalism); similarly, it is possible your partner never got your message (situationalism). Depending upon what you think is the true cause, your behavior toward your partner will be different—anger versus forgiveness, perhaps.[43]

[41]Gelfand, M. J., Higgins, M., Nishii, L. H., Raver, J. L., Dominguez, A., Murakami, F., Yamaguchi, S., & Toyama, M. (2002). Culture and egocentric perceptions of fairness in conflict and negotiation. *Journal of Applied Psychology, 87*(5), 833–845.

[42]Tsai, J., Simeonova, D., & Watanabe, J. (2007). Somatic and social: Chinese Americans talk about emotion. *Personality and Social Psychology Bulletin, 30*(9), 1226–1238.

[43]Rosette, A. S., Brett, J. M., Barsness, Z., & Lytle, A. L. (2008). When cultures clash electronically: The impact of email and culture on negotiation behavior. Under review at *Journal of International Business Studies*.

People from individualistic cultures view causality differently than do members of collectivist cultures. Dispositionalism is more widespread in individualistic than in collectivist cultures. To see how deep-seated these cultural differences are, look at Exhibit 10-7, panels A and B.

In Exhibit 10-7, panels A and B, the dark fish swims on a trajectory that deviates from that of others (indicated by the darkest arrows). When asked to describe what was going on in videotapes of swimming fish whose movements were similar to those illustrated in Exhibit 10-7, members of individualistic cultures (Americans) perceived more influence of internal factors (dispositionalism), whereas members of collectivist cultures (Chinese) perceived more external influence (situationalism) on the blue fish's motions.[44] Specifically, Chinese people were more likely to view the fish as want-

EXHIBIT 10-7 Dispositionalism Versus Situationalism

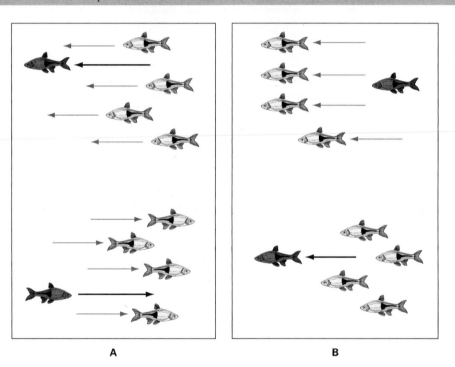

A   B

Diagrams showing trajectories of fish. In A, the group joins the individual (top), and the individual joins the group (bottom). In B, the group leaves the individual (top), and the individual leaves the group (bottom.)

Source: Adapted from Morris, M. W., & Peng, K. (1994). Culture and cause: American and Chinese attributions for social and physical events. *Journal of Personality and Social Psychology, 67*(6), 949–971

---

[44]Morris, M. W., & Peng, K. (1994). Culture and cause: American and Chinese attributions for social and physical events. *Journal of Personality and Social Psychology, 67*(6), 949–971.

ing to achieve harmony, whereas Americans were more likely to view the dark fish as striking out on its own. Similarly, an investigation of stories in American and Chinese newspapers reveals that English-language newspapers are more dispositional and Chinese-language newspapers are more situational when explaining the same crime stories.[45] Specifically, when newspaper articles about "rogue trader" scandals were analyzed, U.S. papers made more mention of the individual trader involved, whereas Japanese papers referred more to the organization.[46] Similarly, when a team member behaves in a maladjusted way, U.S. participants are more likely to focus on the member's traits, whereas the Hong Kong participants focus on situational factors. East Asians, for example, are more sensitive to both external constraints and group influences (as compared to Westerners), but only when there is information about the situation to discount personality traits.[47] Moreover, East Asian people first assign responsibility for events to the collectivity or organizational unit and then extend responsibility to the manager representing that group, thus leaders are held responsible through proxy logic.[48] Dispositionalism also affects biases. People from individualistic cultures, such as the United States, are more likely to fall prey to the fixed-pie bias than are people from collectivistic cultures, such as Greece.[49]

Preferences for Dispute Resolution   Four types of dispute resolution procedures characterize how different cultures resolve disputes: bargaining, mediation, adversarial adjudication, and inquisitorial adjudication. In **bargaining**, or negotiation, two disputants retain full control over the discussion process and settlement outcome. In **mediation**, disputants retain control over the final decision, but a third party guides the process. In **adversarial adjudication**, a judge makes a binding settlement decision, but disputants retain control of the process. In **inquisitorial adjudication**, disputants yield to a third party control over both the process and the final decision. Collectivist cultures such as China differ from individualistic cultures such as the United States in terms of preferences for dispute resolution.[50] For example, when it comes to resolving conflict, Japanese managers prefer to defer to a higher-status person, Germans prefer to regulate behavior via rules, and Americans prefer an interests model that relies on resolving underlying interests.[51] One investigation examined differences between

[45]Ibid.

[46]Menon, T., Morris, M. W., Chiu, C., & Hong, Y. (1999). Culture and construal of agency: Attribution to individual versus group dispositions. *Journal of Personality and Social Psychology, 76*(5), 701–717.

[47]Valenzuela, A., Srivastava, J., & Lee, S. (2005). The role of cultural orientation in bargaining under incomplete information: Differences in causal attributions. *Organizational Behavior and Human Decision Processes, 96,* 72–88.

[48]Zemba, Y., Young, M., & Morris, M. (2006). Blaming leaders for organizational accidents: Proxy logic in collective- versus individual-agency cultures. *Organizational Behavior and Human Decision Processes, 101*(1), 36–51.

[49]Gelfand, M. J., & Christakopoulou, S. (1999). Culture and negotiator cognition: Judgment accuracy and negotiation processes in individualistic and collectivistic cultures. *Organizational Behavior and Human Decision Processes, 79*(3), 248–269.

[50]Leung, K. (1987). Some determinants of reactions to procedural models for conflict resolution: A cross-national study. *Journal of Personality and Social Psychology, 53*(5), 898–908; Morris, M. W., Leung, K., & Iyengar, S. S. (2004). Person perception in the heat of conflict: Negative trait attributions affect procedural preferences and account for situational and cultural differences. *Asian Journal of Social Psychology, 7*(2), 127–147.

[51]Tinsley, C. H. (1998). Models of conflict resolution in Japanese, German, and American cultures. *Journal of Applied Psychology, 83*(2), 316–323; Tinsley, C. H. (2001). How we get to yes: Predicting the constellation of strategies used across cultures to negotiate conflict. *Journal of Applied Psychology, 86*(4), 583–593.

Chinese and American commercial arbitrators. Chinese arbitrators make higher awards for interfirm contract violations than do Americans, presumably because the Chinese arbitrators actually make greater internal attributions, even when observing the actions of a group.[52] Furthermore, cultural differences in attributional tendencies (i.e., collectivists view behavior as a function of situation; individualists view behavior as a function of disposition) create even more of a gap between preferences. Specifically, when negotiators encounter a disagreeable person across the bargaining table, individualists attribute that person's behavior to underlying disposition and desire more formal dispute resolution procedures; in contrast, collectivists are more likely to ascribe behavior to situational factors and prefer informal procedures.[53]

Egalitarianism Versus Hierarchy

A key factor that influences behavior across cultures is the means by which people influence others and the basis of power in relationships. Some cultures have relatively permeable status boundaries and are egalitarian. Other cultures have relatively fixed status boundaries in which influence is determined by existing hierarchical relationships. We describe these relationships in greater detail in the following subsections.

Egalitarian Power Relationships

In egalitarian power relationships, everyone expects to be treated equally. Egalitarian power relationships do not mean that everyone is of equal status, but rather that status differences are easily permeated. Social boundaries that exist within organizations are permeable, and superior social status may be short-lived. Egalitarian cultures empower members to resolve conflict themselves. Furthermore, the base of power in negotiations may differ; in egalitarian cultures, one's BATNA and information are key sources of power (and status and rank are irrelevant). This same power base is not necessarily true in hierarchical cultures.

Hierarchical Power Relationships

In some cultures, great deference is paid to status; status implies social power and is not easily permeated or changed. Social inferiors are expected to defer to social superiors who, in return for privilege, are obligated to look out for the needs of social inferiors.[54] Conflict threatens the stability of a hierarchical society because it implies either that social inferiors have not met expectation or that social superiors have not met the needs of social inferiors.[55] The norm in hierarchical cultures is not to challenge high-status members; thus, conflict is less frequent between members of different social ranks than in egalitarian cultures.[56] Furthermore, conflict between members of the same social rank in hierarchical cultures is more likely to be handled by deference to a superior than by direct confrontation between social equals.[57] In cultures, as in organizations, hierarchy reduces conflict by providing norms for interaction. For this reason, when managers who are superior to

---

[52]Friedman, R., Liu, W., Chen, C., & Chi, S-C. (2007). Casual attribution for interfirm contract violation: A comparative study of Chinese and American commercial arbitrators. *Journal of Applied Psychology, 92*(3), 856–864.
[53]Morris, Leung, & Iyengar, "Person perception."
[54]Leung, "Some determinants of reactions."
[55]Brett, *Negotiating globally.*
[56]Ibid.
[57]Leung, "Some determinants of reactions."

disputants intervene in conflicts (in China and Japan), they behave more autocratically and decide on more conservative outcomes; conversely, when managers who are superiors to disputants intervene (in Western cultures) they generally involve the disputants themselves and obtain integrative outcomes that go beyond contract-related mandates.[58]

To examine which countries were collectivist and which were hierarchical, Hofstede analyzed the responses that IBM employees gave to a values questionnaire.[59] The respondents were diverse in nationality, occupation within IBM, age, and sex. Exhibit 10-8

EXHIBIT 10-8   Position of Countries on Power Distance and Individualism

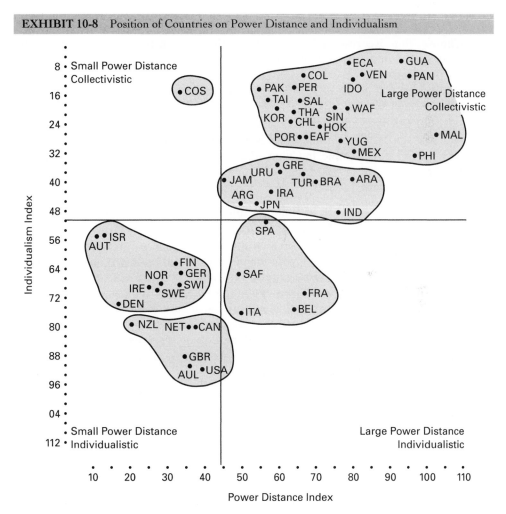

Source: Geert Hofstede, Culture's Consequences: Comparing Values, Behaviors, Institutions and Organizations Across Nations, (2nd ed.). Thousand Oaks, California: SAGE Publications, 2001.

[58]Brett, J., Tinsley, C., Shapiro, D., & Okumura, T. (2007). Intervening in employee disputes: How and when will managers from China, Japan, and the US act differently. *Management and Organization Review, 3*(2), 183–204.

[59]Hofstede, *Culture's consequences.*

presents a grid of where different countries fall in terms of individualism and power distance. Power distance reflects the tendency to see a large distance between those in the upper part of a social structure and those in the lower part of that structure.

It is clear from Exhibit 10-8 that individualism and power distance are highly correlated: Countries high in collectivism are also high in power distance. The most collectivist high-power countries are Venezuela, several other Latin American countries, the Philippines, and Yugoslavia. The most individualistic, low-power-distance countries are Austria and Israel.

Implications for Negotiation

Choose Your Representative   Cultural differences in power sources and power displays can be dramatic and unsettling because power is the basis for pie-slicing. One of the first issues that negotiators must consider prior to intercultural negotiations is determining who will do the negotiating. In egalitarian cultures, power is usually determined by one's BATNA and, thus, it is not unusual for persons of different status to find themselves at the bargaining table. In contrast, in hierarchical cultures power is associated with one's position and rank, and it is insulting to send a lower-rank employee to meet with a CEO. For example, in China, relationships follow people, not organizations. The ideal negotiator is an "old friend of China" with whom the Chinese have had positive experiences or owe favors.[60]

Understand the Network of Relationships   In cultures that have hierarchical power relationships, negotiations often require several levels of approval, all the way to the top. For example, in one failed negotiation, the central government of China voided the long-standing agreement of McDonald's with the Beijing city government because leases of longer than 10 years require central government approval.[61] In the centralized Chinese authority structure, negotiators seldom have the authority to approve the final deal. One by-product of this authority structure is that Chinese negotiators will attempt to secure a deal that is clearly weighted in their favor, so it will be easier to persuade the higher authorities that the Chinese "won" the negotiation.

Face Concerns   Saving and giving face are important in hierarchical cultures.[62] Face-maintaining behavior raises the esteem of the negotiator in the eyes of his or her superiors and will in turn help them give face to their stakeholders. In Western culture, people whose face is threatened act more assertively; in contrast, members of Eastern cultures act more passively.[63] Flattery is a common form of Chinese face-saving.[64] Pachtman cautions:

> Be aware of the effect flattery has on you; the proper response is not "thank you," but a denial and an even bigger compliment in return. Apologies are an-

---

[60]Pachtman, A. (1998, July 1). Getting to "hao!" *International Business,* pp. 24–26.

[61]Ibid.

[62]Ting-Toomey, S. (1988). Intercultural conflict styles: A face negotiation theory. In Y. Kim & W. Gudykunst (Eds.), *Theories in intercultural communication* (pp. 213–235). Newbury Park, CA: Sage.

[63]Brew, F. P., & Cairns, D. R. (2004). Styles of managing interpersonal workplace conflict in relation to status and face concerns: A study with Anglos and Chinese. *International Journal of Conflict Management, 15*(1), 27–56.

[64]Pachtman, "Getting to 'hao!'"

other powerful way to give face, but can obligate the apologizer; be prepared with a token concession in case the Chinese decide to "cash in" on your apology. (p. 25)[65]

The Conduct of Negotiation   A Western view of negotiation holds that each party is expected to voice its own interests, and a back-and-forth exchange will occur. An Eastern view of negotiation is quite different. For example, negotiation among Japanese persons is similar to that of father and son, according to Adler.[66] The status relationship is explicit and important. The son (seller) carefully explains his situation and asks for as much as possible because he will have no chance to bicker once the father (buyer) decides. The son (seller) accepts the decision because it would hurt the relationship to argue and because he trusts the father (buyer) to care for his needs.

Direct versus Indirect Communications

Direct versus indirect information sharing is a cultural dimension that refers to the amount of information contained in an explicit message versus implicit contextual cues.[67] For example, different cultures have different norms about information-sharing strategies in negotiation.[68] Broadly speaking, some cultures' norms favor direct communication, whereas in other cultures, people communicate in an indirect, discreet fashion. The indirect-direct communication dimension has a direct implication for how much people should rely on contextual cues.[69]

Direct Communication

In a direct communication culture, such as the United States, messages are transmitted explicitly and directly, and communications are action-oriented and solution-minded.[70] The meaning is contained in the message; information is provided explicitly, without nuance.[71] Furthermore, information is **context-free**, meaning the message has the same meaning regardless of the context. In negotiations, these factors mean parties will often ask direct questions about interests and alternatives.

Indirect Communication

In some cultures, people avoid direct confrontation when conflict occurs. The meaning of communication is inferred rather than directly interpreted; the context of the message stimulates preexisting knowledge that is then used to gain understanding.[72] In negotiations, asking direct questions is not normative; rather, making a lot of proposals is a matter of indirect communication.[73] The pattern of proposals allows inferences to be

[65] Ibid, p. 25.

[66] Adler, N. J. (1991). *International dimensions of organizational behavior.* Boston: PWS-Kent.

[67] Hall, E. T. (1976). *Beyond culture.* Garden City, NJ: Anchor Press.

[68] Ibid.

[69] Hall, E. T., & Hall, M. R. (1990). *Understanding cultural differences.* Yarmouth, ME: Intercultural Press; Cohen, R. (1991). *Negotiating across cultures: Communication obstacles in international diplomacy.* Washington, DC: United States Institute of Peace Press.

[70] Ting-Toomey, "Intercultural conflict styles."

[71] Brett, *Negotiating globally.*

[72] Ibid.

[73] Brett, J. M., Shapiro, D. L., & Lytle, A. (1998). Breaking the bonds of reciprocity in negotiations. *Academy of Management Journal, 41*(4), 410–424.

EXHIBIT 10-9   Direct and Indirect Communication Cultures

Direct Communication Cultures	Indirect Communication Cultures
Germany	Japan
United States	Russia
Switzerland	France
Scandinavian cultures	Arabs
	Mediterranean peoples
	In general, cultures in which people have extensive information networks among family, friends, colleagues, and clients and in which people are involved in close, personal relationships

Source: Brett, J. M. (2007). *Negotiating globally: How to negotiate deals, resolve disputes, and make decisions across cultural boundaries* (2nd ed.). San Francisco: Jossey-Bass. Reprinted by permission.

made about what is important to each party and where points of concession might be. Indirect cultures (such as Japan) transmit messages indirectly and implicitly, and communication is elusive.[74] For example, Japanese negotiators are less likely to say "No" and more likely to remain silent than U.S. negotiators when confronted with an option that is not favorable.[75] (For a classification of direct and indirect communication cultures, see Exhibit 10-9.)

Culture affects how negotiators share information. Negotiators from direct cultures prefer sharing information directly, asking questions, and getting (in return for giving) answers. In contrast, negotiators from indirect cultures prefer sharing information indirectly, telling stories in an attempt to influence their opponents, and gleaning information from proposals.[76] Cultural norms and values have implications for the reciprocity principle in negotiation. In an investigation of intracultural and intercultural negotiation between the United States and Japan, negotiators reciprocated culturally normative behaviors.[77] U.S. negotiators were more likely to reciprocate direct information exchange; in contrast, Japanese negotiators were more likely to reciprocate indirect information exchange.

Implications for Negotiation

Information Necessary to Reach Integrative Agreements   Getting information out on the table is critical for expanding the pie; relying on context alone to convey information necessary to craft integrative agreements is not enough.[78] Adair examined inte-

---

[74]Ting-Toomey, "Intercultural conflict styles."

[75]Graham, J. L., & Sano, Y. (1984). *Smart bargaining: Doing business with the Japanese.* Cambridge, MA: Ballinger; March, R. M. (1990). *The Japanese negotiator: Subtlety and strategy beyond Western logic* (1st paperback ed.). New York: Kodansha International.

[76]Brett, J. M., Adair, W. A., Lempereur, A., Okumura, T., Shikhirev, P., Tinsley, C., & Lytle, A. (1998). Culture and joint gains in negotiation. *Negotiation Journal, 14*(1), 61–86.

[77]Adair, W. L., & Brett, J. M. (2005). The Negotiation dance: Time, culture, and behavioral sequences in negotiations. Organization Science, 16, 33-51.

[78]Brett, Adair, Lempereur, Okumura, Shikhirev, Tinsley, & Lytle, "Culture and joint gains in negotiation."

grative sequences in same and mixed-culture negotiations. Managers from Hong Kong, Japan, Russia, and Thailand used more indirect integrative strategies (e.g., making multiple offers at same time); in contrast, managers from Israel, Germany, Sweden, and the United States used direct integrative strategies (e.g., asking for priority information).[79] People from indirect cultures seamlessly enter into a "dance" of complementary, indirect information exchange.[80] For example, by complementing priority information and offers, negotiators from indirect cultures supplement the information that may not have been sufficiently conveyed through reciprocal offers.

Because indirect communication requires more complex and subtle communication skills, direct communicators often find it difficult or impossible; in contrast, indirect communicators can be direct, when necessary.[81]

Brett and colleagues investigated negotiation strategies in six cultures: France, Russia, Japan, Hong Kong, Brazil, and the United States. Cultures that used direct (as opposed to indirect) information-sharing strategies or a combination of direct and indirect strategies reached the most integrative, pie-expanding agreements.[82] Furthermore, exchanging information about preferences and priorities was insufficient. For example, in the same study of intracultural negotiations involving the United States, Japan, Brazil, France, Russia, and Hong Kong, negotiators from Russia and Hong Kong generated the lowest joint gains, or integrative agreements.[83] Russia and Hong Kong are indirect communication countries. However, Japanese negotiators had high joint gains, even though they also are an indirect communication culture. The difference is that Japanese negotiators engaged in more direct information exchange (i.e., asking questions) than the negotiators from Russia or Hong Kong. Thus, making comparisons and contrasts to identify trade-offs and direct reactions appears to be essential.[84] Moreover, offers have different effects across cultures. Early offers generate higher joint gains for Japanese negotiators but lower joint gains for U.S. negotiators.[85] Conversely, direct exchange of information about interests and issues generates higher joint gains for U.S. negotiators but lower joint gains for Japanese negotiators.[86]

In direct cultures, the process of deal making comes first; in other cultures, the relationship comes first and provides a context for making deals. Frank Lee, a native of Taiwan, who launched Global Intelligence Consultation in San Diego, says, "In negotiations with Chinese, the first 30 minutes are just warming up." If Americans force Chinese negotiators to get down to business too quickly, conflicts can arise.[87]

---

[79]Adair, W. (2003). Integrative sequences and negotiation outcome in same- and mixed-culture negotiation. *International Journal Conflict Management, 14,* 273–296.

[80]Adair, W., & Brett, J. M. (2005). The negotiation dance: Time, culture, and behavioral sequences in negotiation. *Organization Science, 16*(1), p33–51.

[81]Hall, *Beyond culture.*

[82]Brett, Adair, Lempereur, Okumura, Shikhirev, Tinsley, & Lytle, "Culture and joint gains in negotiation."

[83]Ibid.

[84]Ibid.

[85]Adair, W., Weingart, L., & Brett, J. (2007). The timing and function of offers in U.S. and Japanese negotiations. *Journal of Applied Psychology, 92*(4), 1056–1068.

[86]Ibid.

[87]Simons, C. (2005, September 6). Companies try to learn China's ways. *Atlanta Journal-Constitution,* p. C1.

Dispute Resolution Preferences   U.S. managers often feel satisfied with their outcomes following interests-based negotiations.[88] However, other cultures use different dispute resolution strategies, often with equally satisfying results.[89] For example, U.S. managers prefer to use interests-based methods, such as discussing parties' interests and synthesizing multiple issues.[90] In one investigation, U.S. managers were more likely than Hong Kong Chinese managers to resolve a greater number of issues and reach more integrative outcomes; in contrast, Hong Kong Chinese managers were more likely to involve higher management in conflict resolution[91] and choose a relationally connected third party.[92] One way people from indirect cultures communicate their disapproval is by shaming others. For example, Chinese managers show a stronger desire to shame and teach moral lessons compared to U.S. managers.[93] In collectivist cultures, shaming is a common form of social control.[94] In contrast, U.S. managers are more likely to choose a direct approach in response to conflict.

KEY CHALLENGES OF INTERCULTURAL NEGOTIATION

We identify eight common intercultural challenges.

Expanding the Pie

Negotiators have more difficulty expanding the pie when negotiating across cultures than within a culture. A landmark study of five countries (Japan, Hong Kong, Germany, Israel, and the United States), examined intracultural (within the same culture) negotiations versus intercultural (across cultures) negotiations. Negotiations between Japan and the United States resulted in a smaller expansion of the pie than did intracultural negotiations (Japan–Japan and U.S.–U.S. negotiations).[95] Another study examined joint gains in intra- and inter-cultural negotiations between Japanese and U.S. negotiators and found that joint gains were significantly lower in intercultural negotiations, as opposed to intracultural negotiations.[96] The key reason appeared to be the degree to which parties understood the priorities of the counterparties and the opportunity for exploiting compatible issues. In cross-cultural negotiations, negotiators' bargaining styles did not match, meaning they had less understanding of the counterparty's priorities and consequently did not create as much value. Each culture expected the other

[88]Tinsley, "How we get to yes."
[89]Ibid.
[90]Tinsley, C. H., & Brett, J. M. (2001). Managing workplace conflict in the United States and Hong Kong. *Organizational Behavior and Human Decision Processes, 85*(2), 360–381.
[91]Ibid.
[92]Fu, J., Morris, M., Lee, S-I., Chao, M., Chiu, C., & Hong, Y. (2007). Epistemic motives and cultural conformity: Need for closure, culture, and context and determinants of conflict judgments. *Journal of Personality and Social Psychology, 92*(2), 191–207.
[93]Tinsley, C. H., & Weldon, E. (2003). Responses to a normative conflict among American and Chinese managers. *International Journal of Cross-Cultural Management, 3*(2), 183–234.
[94]Creighton, M. R. (1990). Revisiting shame and guilt cultures: A forty-year pilgrimage. *Ethos, 18,* 279–307; Demos, J. (1996). Shame and guilt in early New England. In R. Harre & W. G. Parrott (Eds.), *The emotions* (pp. 74–88). London: Sage.
[95]Brett, *Negotiating globally.*
[96]Brett, J. M., & Okumura, T. (1998). Inter- and intracultural negotiation: U.S. and Japanese negotiators. *Academy of Management Journal, 41*(5), 495–510.

culture to adopt its own style of negotiating. For example, North Americans expected others to talk directly, whereas people from indirect cultures expected to use other, implicit forms of communication, such as heuristic trial and error. U.S. negotiators exchange information directly and avoid using influence strategies when negotiating intra- and interculturally. In contrast, Japanese negotiators exchange information indirectly and use influence when negotiating intraculturally but adapt their behaviors when negotiating interculturally.[97]

Dividing the Pie

We pointed to a number of biases when it comes to thinking about fairness, and these biases are magnified when people of different cultures sit down to negotiate.

As compared to other cultures, people from the United States are more unabashedly self-interested and, consequently, often have higher aspirations. We pointed out that aspirations manifest themselves in first offers negotiators make and spirations are strongly predictive of the ultimate slice of the pie negotiators receive. Indeed, U.S. negotiators who have higher aspirations than their opponents achieve greater profit than managers from China and Japan, primarily because these collectivist cultures are not as self-interested.[98]

Sacred Values and Taboo Trade-Offs

Sacred values, or protected values, are the beliefs, customs, and assumptions that form the basis of a group or culture's belief system.[99] Sacred values are, by definition, those values and beliefs people regard to be so fundamental that they are not discussible nor debatable. Sacred values resist trade-offs with other values, particularly economic values. When people contemplate buying or selling "sacred objects," they are more likely to distort the price, refuse to answer questions, and express moral outrage and cognitive confusion.[100] However, when it is in their economic interest, people may turn a blind eye to taboo trade-offs.[101] Consider the reaction that John Poindexter, a retired rear admiral, received in 2003 when he put forth a plan for the Pentagon to run a "terrorist futures-trading market"—an online trading parlor that would reward investors who could accurately forecast terrorist attacks, assassinations, and coups.[102] The day after the plan was announced, Poindexter was forced to resign from his position

[97]Adair, W., Okumura, T., & Brett, J. M. (2001). Negotiation behavior when cultures collide: The U.S. and Japan. *Journal of Applied Psychology, 86*(3), 371–385.
[98]Chen, Y., Mannix, E., & Okumura, T. (2003). The importance of who you meet: Effects of self- versus other-concerns among negotiators in the United States, the People's Republic of China, and Japan. *Journal of Experimental Social Psychology, 39,* 1–15.
[99]Baron, J., & Spranca, M. (1997). Protected values. *Organizational Behavior and Human Decision Processes, 70*(1), 1–16; Tetlock, P. E., Peterson, R., & Lerner, J. (1996). Revising the value pluralism model: Incorporating social content and context postulates. In C. Seligman, J. Olson, & M. Zanna (Eds.), *The psychology of values: The Ontario Symposium* (Vol. 8). Mahwah, NJ: Erlbaum.
[100]McGraw, A. & Tetlock, P. (2005). Taboo trade-offs, relational framing, and the acceptability of exchanges. *Journal of Consumer Psychology, 15*(1), 2–15.
[101]Ibid.
[102]Schmitt, E. (2003, August 1). Poindexter will be quitting over terrorism betting plan. *New York Times,* p. A11.

EXHIBIT 10-10 Sacred Values

Instructions: The following list contains actions some people oppose. Some of these activities are happening right now, and others are not. Suppose those in favor of each were willing to pay a great deal of money to see the action carried out. Please answer these questions with a "Yes," "No," or "Not Sure," according to whether you would accept money to perform these actions.

Actions:
1. Destruction of natural forests by human activity, resulting in the extinction of plant and animal species forever
2. Raising the IQ of normal children by giving them (completely safe) drugs
3. Using genetic engineering to make people more intelligent
4. Performing abortions of normal fetuses in the early stages of pregnancy
5. Performing abortions of normal fetuses in the second trimester of pregnancy
6. Fishing in a way that leads to the painful death of dolphins
7. Forcing women to be sterilized because they are retarded
8. Forcing women to have abortions for the purposes of population control
9. Putting people in jail for expressing nonviolent political views
10. Letting people sell their organs (for example, a kidney or an eye) for whatever price they could command
11. Refusing to treat someone who needs a kidney transplant because he or she cannot afford it
12. Letting a doctor assist in the suicide of a consenting terminally ill patient
13. Letting parents sell their daughter in a bride auction (i.e., the daughter becomes the bride of the highest bidder)
14. Punishing people for expressing nonviolent political opinions

Source: Adapted from Baron, J., & Spranca, M. (1997). Protected values. *Organizational Behavior and Human Decision Processes, 70*(1), 1–16. Reprinted by permission of Elsevier via Rights Link.

because several people, including Democratic senators Byron Dorgan (North Dakota) and Ron Wyden (Oregon), called it "morally repugnant." (For an example of how to assess sacred or protected values, see Exhibit 10-10. "Yes" or "Not Sure" answers imply the value is secular, or tradeable; "No" answers imply the value is sacred.)

Sacred values are the opposite of secular values, which are issues and resources that can be traded and exchanged. Within a culture, a near-universal ascription to sacred values generally exists, with some notable exceptions. However, between cultures, extreme conflict may occur when one culture regards an issue to be sacred and another treats it as secular. Taboo trade-offs take place when sacred values are proposed for exchange or trade.[103]

Most people are horrified and shocked when parents offer to sell their children, citizens sell their right to a jury trial, and immigrants buy voting privileges. A thin line separates acceptable from taboo trade-offs. On a purely rational level, these exchanges simply reflect the powerful trade-off principle we discussed in Chapter 4 on integrative bargaining.

---

[103]Tetlock, Peterson, & Lerner, "Revising the value pluralism model."

The trade-off principle is ideal for handling scarce resource conflicts containing issues that are fungible. Principles of rationality (see Appendix 1) assume people can compare and trade resources in a way that maximizes their outcomes. Rational bargaining theory assumes everything is comparable and has a price (see Appendix 1). However, the notion of trading becomes unconscionable in some conflict situations.[104] People sometimes refuse to place a monetary value on a good or even think of trading it. To even suggest a trade is cause for moral outrage and can sour negotiations. Attaching a monetary value to a bottle of wine, a house, or the services of a gardener can be a cognitively demanding task, but it raises no questions about the morality of the individual who proposes the sale or trade. In contrast, attaching monetary value to human life, familial obligations, national honor, and the ecosystem seriously undermines one's social identity or standing in the eyes of others.[105] In a dispute concerning the construction of a dam that would remove native Indians from their ancestral land, a Yavapai teenager said, "The land is our mother. You don't sell your mother."[106]

Proposals to exchange sacred values (e.g., body organs) for secular ones (e.g., money, time, or convenience) constitute taboo trade-offs. Given the inherently sacred values that operate in many countries, the familiar notions of trading and logrolling, so important to interests-based negotiation, are likely to be considered unacceptable and reprehensible to members of different cultures.

Sacred and secular issues are culturally defined, with no absolutes.[107] Sociocultural norms affect the sacredness of certain positions, such as smoking, which is now generally considered baneful but in the recent past was completely acceptable. The sanctity of issues is also influenced by the labels and names used to define conflicts. For example, in 1994 all three members of Alaska's congressional delegation began referring to the part of the Arctic National Wildlife Refuge (ANWR) that would be subject to oil exploration as the "Arctic Oil Reserve." The group believed this term was more accurate because that part of the refuge was not officially classified as either wilderness or refuge. Environmentalists, on the other hand, objected to this term and did not even like the use of the acronym ANWR because they worried that unless the words "wildlife refuge" were clearly stated, the public would not understand the value of the land.

Truly sacred values cannot exist because we make value trade-offs every day, meaning that everyone "has their price." The implication is that with sufficient compensation, people are willing to trade off a "sacred" value. The critical issue is not how much it takes to compensate someone for a sacred issue but, instead, what factors allow trade-offs to occur on sacred issues.

The term **sacred** describes people's preferences on issues on which they view themselves as uncompromising. It immediately becomes obvious, however, that labeling an issue as sacred may be a negotiation ploy, rather than a reflection of heartfelt value. By anointing certain issues as sacred and removing them from bargaining consideration, a negotiator increases the likelihood of a favorable settlement. The strategy is similar to

---

[104]Ibid.

[105]Schlenker, B. R. (1980). *Impression management: The self-concept, social identity, and interpersonal relations.* Belmont, CA: Brooks-Cole.

[106]Espeland, W. (1994). Legally mediated identity: The national environmental policy act and the bureaucratic construction of interests. *Law and Society Review, 28*(5), 1149–1179.

[107]Tetlock, Peterson, & Lerner, "Revising the value pluralism model."

the irrevocable commitment strategy.[108] We refer to issues that are not really sacred, but are positioned as such, as **pseudosacred**.[109] Thus, for example, if the Yavapai Indians would trade 1 acre of land for a hospital, new school, or money, then the land is not truly sacred but pseudosacred.

Biased Punctuation of Conflict

The **biased punctuation of conflict** occurs when people interpret interactions with their adversaries in self-serving and other-derogating terms.[110] An actor, A, perceives the history of conflict with another actor, B, as a sequence of B-A, B-A, B-A, in which the initial hostile or aggressive move was made by B, causing A to engage in defensive and legitimate retaliatory actions. Actor B punctuates the same history of interaction as A-B, A-B, A-B, however, reversing the roles of aggressor and defender. The biased punctuation of conflict is a frequent cause of warfare. Consider the long, sad history of international conflict between the Arabs and Israelis. Each country chooses different historical moments of origin in order to justify its own claims to land and thus casts the other country in the role of the invader.

Negotiation behaviors are a continuous stream of cause-and-effect relationships in which each person's actions influence the actions of others.[111] To an outside observer, their interaction is an uninterrupted sequence of interchanges. However, people who are actively engaged in conflict do not always see things this way. Instead, they organize their interactions into a series of discrete causal chunks,[112] a process known as **causal chunking** or **punctuation**.[113] Causal chunks influence the extent to which people are aware of their influence on others, as well as their impressions of others. Two kinds of chunking patterns are self-causal and other-causal. People form self-causal chunks (e.g., "My action causes my partner's action") when they possess an offensive set, other-causal chunks when they possess a defensive set.

Disagreement about how to punctuate a sequence of events and a conflict relationship is at the root of many cross-cultural disputes.

Ethnocentrism

If egocentrism refers to unwarranted positive beliefs about oneself relative to others, then **ethnocentrism** refers to unwarranted positive beliefs about one's own group relative to other groups.[114] We noted in Chapter 9 that most people display an in-group bias by evaluating members of their own group more favorably than members of out-groups and re-

---

[108]Schelling, T. (1960). *The strategy of conflict*. Cambridge, MA: Harvard University Press.

[109]We are indebted to Max Bazerman for this term; Thompson, L., & Gonzalez, R. (1997). Environmental disputes: Competition for scarce resources and clashing of values. In M. Bazerman, D. Messick, A. Tenbrunsel, & K. Wade-Benzoni (Eds.), *Environment, ethics, and behavior* (pp. 75–104). San Francisco: New Lexington Press; Wade-Benzoni, Okumura, Brett, Moore, Tenbrunsel, & Bazerman, "Cognitions and behavior."

[110]Kahn, R. L., & Kramer, R. M. (1990). *Untying the knot: De-escalatory processes in international conflict.* San Francisco: Jossey-Bass.

[111]Jones, E. E., & Gerard, H. B. (1967). *Foundations of social psychology.* New York: Wiley.

[112]Swann, W. B., Pelham, B. W., & Roberts, D. C. (1987). Causal chunking: Memory and inference in ongoing interaction. *Journal of Personality and Social Psychology, 53*(5), 858–865.

[113]Whorf, B. L. (1956). Science and linguistics. In J. B. Carroll (Ed.), *Language, thought, and reality: Selected writings of Benjamin Whorf.* New York: Wiley.

[114]LeVine, R. A., & Campbell, D. T. (1972). *Ethnocentrism: Theories of conflict, ethnic attitudes, and group behavior.* New York: Wiley.

ward members of their own group more resources than members of out-groups, even when allocations of resources do not affect their own welfare.[115] Ethnocentrism, or the universal strong liking of one's own group and the simultaneous negative evaluation of out-groups, generates a set of universal reciprocal stereotypes in which each culture sees itself as good and the other culture as bad, even when both groups engage in the same behaviors. The behavior may be similar, but the interpretation is not: "We are loyal, they are clannish; we are brave and willing to defend our rights, they are hostile and arrogant."

Even when members of groups do not know one another and never interact, people show in-group favoritism.[116] However, conflict between groups and intergroup bias do not always arise from competition over scarce resources. Much intergroup bias stems from fundamental differences in cultural values. Symbolic conflict can occur between cultural groups due to clashes of values and fundamental beliefs.

One unfortunate by-product of in-group favoritism is the tendency to view people from different cultures as more alike than they really are. Thus, the phrase "They all look alike" means that within-race and within-culture errors are more prevalent than between-race or between-cultural errors because people categorize members of other cultures not as individuals but as part of a group. As an example, consider the long-standing conflict between pro-choice and pro-life activists on the abortion issue (see Exhibit 10-11).

Stereotypes are another manifestation of ethnocentrism. Stereotypes of cultural groups are common; however, they often do not have a basis in reality. The problem is

---

EXHIBIT 10-11   Stereotyping the Other Party

As an example of how members of groups tend to stereotype the other party, consider the conversation that occurred between Naomi Wolf, author of the best-seller *The Beauty Myth,* and Frederica Mathewes-Green, a syndicated religion columnist and author of a book entitled *Right Choices.* Try to figure out which woman made which of the following comments during a discussion in 1996:

> Where the pro-life movement has made its mistake is to focus only on the baby, and not the woman.... You can boil 25 years of the pro-life rhetoric down to three words: "It's a baby." There's a whole industry to promote bonding with the wanted fetus, yet unwanted fetuses are treated as though they are unwanted lumps of batter.

The criticism of the pro-life movement's "It's a baby" focus came from Mathewes-Green, one of the movement's own. The criticism of the pro-choice movement's "unwanted lumps of batter" rhetoric came from Wolf, a staunch abortion-rights supporter.

When Wolf and Mathewes-Green met to talk, Wolf said it was the first time she had ever "knowingly been in the presence of a pro-lifer." To her surprise, the other side was willing to have a conversation. And Mathewes-Green acknowledged that the pro-life movement had invited being stereotyped by "focusing only on the baby and not the woman."

Source: Shirk, M. (1996, June 10.) Women go beyond rhetoric. *St. Louis Post-Dispatch*, p. 11B. Reprinted by permission of St. Louis Post-Dispatch.

---

[115]Doise, W. (1978). *Groups and individuals: Explanations in social psychology*. Cambridge, England: Cambridge University Press.
[116]Brewer, M. (1979). In-group bias in the minimal intergroup situation: A cognitive-motivational analysis. *Psychological Bulletin, 86,* 307–324; Tajfel, "Social psychology"; Tajfel, H., & Turner, J. (1986). The social identity theory of intergroup behavior. In S. Worchel & W. Austin (Eds.), *Psychology of intergroup relations* (pp. 7–24). Chicago: Nelson-Hall.

that if people act as if stereotypes are true, they are likely to create a self-fulfilling prophecy, whereby the stereotypes affect behavior. For example, Americans described their Japanese counterparts as being "poker-faced" or displaying no facial expressions in a negotiation simulation. However, in the laboratory, a camera focused on each person's face during an intercultural negotiation recorded all facial expressions and revealed no differences in the number of facial expressions (smiles and frowns) between the Americans and Japanese. Americans are simply not able to "read" Japanese expressions, and they wrongly describe them as "expressionless."[117]

Affiliation Bias

Affiliation bias occurs when people evaluate a person's actions on the basis of his or her affiliations rather than on the merits of the behavior itself. For example, when football fans watch a game, they believe the other side commits more infractions than does their own team.[118] Consider the following actions a country could take: establishing a rocket base close to the borders of a country with whom it has strained relations; testing a new assault weapon; or establishing trade relations with a powerful country. People's perceptions of the acceptability of these actions differ dramatically as a function of the perceived agent. For example, during the time of the Cold War, U.S. citizens regarded the preceding actions to be much more beneficial when the United States was the one responsible than when what was then the U.S.S.R. engaged in the same actions.[119] People perceive the same objective behavior as either sinister or benign, merely as a consequence of the agent's affiliation.

Faulty Perceptions of Conciliation and Coercion

During World War II, the American journalist Edward R. Murrow broadcasted nightly from London, reporting on the psychological and physical consequences of the Nazi bombing of British cities.[120] Contrary to Nazi intent, the bombing did not move the British toward surrender. It had quite the opposite effect, strengthening rather than diminishing British resolve to resist German domination. Shortly after the United States entered World War II, the Americans joined the British in launching costly bombing raids over Germany. In part, the intent was to decrease the German people's will to resist. Later research reported by the Office of Strategic Services that compared lightly and heavily bombed areas found only minimal differences in civilians' will to resist.

Several other conflicts follow the same psychological pattern, such as Pearl Harbor, South Africa, and North Vietnam. All of these instances point to important differences in countries' perceptions of what will be effective in motivating an enemy and what will be effective in motivating themselves or their allies. Coercion is viewed as more effective with our enemies than with ourselves, whereas conciliation is viewed as

[117]Graham, J. L. (1993). The Japanese negotiation style: Characteristics of a distinct approach. *Negotiation Journal, 9*(2), 123–140.

[118]Hastorf, A., & Cantril, H. (1954). They saw a game: A case study. *Journal of Abnormal and Social Psychology, 49,* 129–134.

[119]Oskamp, S. (1965). Attitudes toward U.S. and Russian actions: A double standard. *Psychological Reports, 16,* 43–46.

[120]Rothbart, M., & Hallmark, W. (1988). In-group and out-group differences in the perceived efficacy of coercion and conciliation in resolving social conflict. *Journal of Personality and Social Psychology, 55,* 248–257.

more effective with ourselves than with our enemies. The unfortunate consequence, of course, is that this perception encourages aggressive rather than constructive action.

Three key reasons explain why this behavior occurs.[121] A preference for punitive strategies with one's enemies may reflect a desire to inflict injury or pain, as well as a desire to influence behavior in a desired direction. The relative preference for punishment is based on an incompatible desire to both injure and modify the behavior of the enemy. Alternatively, people may be inclined to use more coercive strategies with an counterparty because the appearance of toughness conveys information about their motives and intentions, which, in the long run, may bring about the desired result. Finally, the mere creation of mutually exclusive, exhaustive social categories (e.g., "them" and "us") leads to different assumptions about members of such groups: More favorable attributes are assigned to in-group than to out-group members.[122] Social categorization processes may be particularly powerful in cross-cultural disputes because of stereotypes.

Naïve Realism

A heated debate among English teachers concerns which books should be on the required reading list for U.S. high school students. The Western Canon Debate features traditionalists, who prefer to have classics on the reading list, and revisionists, who believe the reading list should be more racially, ethnically, and sexually diversified. In one study, traditionalists and revisionists were interviewed about their own and the other party's preferred books.[123] Most strikingly, each party exaggerated the views of the other side in a way that made their differences bigger rather than smaller. Traditionalists viewed revisionists to be much more extreme than they really were; revisionists viewed traditionalists to be much more conservative. In fact, the groups agreed on 7 out of the 15 books on the reading list! Nevertheless, each group greatly exaggerated the difference between their own and the other's belief systems in a way that exacerbated the conflict. Further, people perceived the other side to be more uniform in their views, whereas they perceived their own views to be more varied and heterogeneous.[124] This faulty perception, of course, leads to beliefs such as "They're all alike." Ideological conflict is often exacerbated unnecessarily as partisans construe the other person's values to be more extremist and unbending than they really are.

The **fundamental attribution error** occurs when people explain the causes of the behavior of others in terms of their underlying dispositions and discount the role of situational factors.[125] Many environmental disputes involve a group that is believed to be interested in the economic development of the environment and an opposing group that represents the interests of the ecosystem. According to the fundamental attribution

---

[121]Rothbart & Hallmark, "In-group and out-group differences."

[122]Brewer, "In-group bias"; Tajfel, H. (1970). Experiments in intergroup discrimination. *Scientific American, 223*, 96–102.

[123]Robinson, R. J., & Keltner, D. (1996). Much ado about nothing? Revisionists and traditionalists choose an introductory English syllabus. *Psychological Science, 7*(1), 18–24.

[124]Linville, P. W., Fischer, G. W., & Salovey, P. (1989). Perceived distributions of the characteristics of in-group and out-group members: Empirical evidence and a computer simulation. *Journal of Personality and Social Psychology, 57*, 165–188.

[125]Ross, L. (1977). The intuitive psychologist and his shortcomings: Distortions in the attribution process. In L. Berkowitz (Ed.), *Advances in experimental social psychology* (Vol. 10) (pp. 173–220). Orlando, FL: Academic Press.

error, when each group is asked to name the cause of the dispute, each attributes the negative aspects of conflict to the dispositions of the other party. Specifically, developers regard environmentalists to be fanatic lunatics; environmentalists regard developers to be sinister and greedy.

PREDICTORS OF SUCCESS IN INTERCULTURAL INTERACTIONS

Your pharmaceutical company wants to expand its international base. You are charged with the task of selecting a few managers to participate in a special global initiatives assignment in various countries. You know that failure rates as high as 70% can be avoided.[126] These costs include not only the lost salary of an executive, the cost of transporting the family, and the cost of setting up an office abroad but also damage to your organization, lost sales, on-the-job mistakes, and loss of goodwill. Unfortunately, ready-made personality measures are not good predictors of success abroad. The following characteristics have some value in predicting success:[127]

- Conceptual complexity: People who are conceptually complex (think in terms of shades of gray, rather than black and white) show less social distance to different others[128]
- Broad categorization: People who use broad categories adjust to new environments better than do narrow categorizers[129]
- Empathy
- Sociability
- Critical acceptance of stereotypes
- Openness to different points of view
- Interest in the host culture
- Task orientation
- Cultural flexibility (the ability to substitute activities in the host culture for own culture-valued activities)
- Social orientation (the ability to establish new intercultural relationships)
- Willingness to communicate (e.g., use the host language without fear of making mistakes)
- Patience (suspend judgment)
- Intercultural sensitivity
- Tolerance for differences among people
- Sense of humor
- Skills in collaborative conflict resolution

ADVICE FOR CROSS-CULTURAL NEGOTIATIONS

Global negotiations are characterized by differences that emerge at interpersonal behavioral levels and are manifestations of more deep-seated societal and institutional differences.[130] Negotiators should avoid arguing about the inherent legitimacy of a social system and instead focus on understanding at the interpersonal level. Brett re-

[126]Copeland, L., & Griggs, L. (1985). *Going international.* New York: Random House.
[127]Martin, J. N. (1989). Intercultural communication competence. *International Journal of Intercultural Relations, 13,* 227–428; Triandis, *Culture and social behavior.*
[128]Gardiner, G. S. (1972). *Aggression.* Morristown, NJ: General Learning Corp.
[129]Detweiler, R. (1980). The categorization of the actions of people from another culture: A conceptual analysis and behavioral outcome. *International Journal of Intercultural Relations, 4,* 275–293.
[130]Tinsley, C. H., Curhan, J. R., & Kwak, R. S. (1999). Adopting a dual lens approach for examining the dilemma of differences in international business negotiations. *International Negotiation, 4,* 5–22.

EXHIBIT 10-12   Advice for International Negotiators

1. Acknowledge differences at the individual and societal levels.
2. Trade off differences in preferences and abilities.
3. Ask questions to ensure understanding of the other party's perspective.
4. Understand the norms and the meaning underlying them.
5. Avoid arguing the inherent legitimacy of a social system.
6. Be prepared to manage bureaucratic interactions with governments.

Source: Tinsley, C. H., Curhan, J. R., & Kwak, R. S. (1999). Adopting a dual lens approach for examining the dilemma of differences in international business negotiations. *International Negotiation.*

searched and proposed several strategies to improve cross-cultural effectiveness.[131] (See Exhibit 10-12 for Tinsley's similar suggestions.) A discussion of Brett's prescriptive advice appears in the following sections.[132]

Anticipate Differences in Strategy and Tactics That May Cause Misunderstandings

Negotiators from different cultures differ in terms of three major dimensions that affect their negotiation behavior and style: individualism-collectivism, hierarchy-egalitarianism, and direct-indirect communications. The negotiator who is able to anticipate differences in terms of these three dimensions is going to be at a pie-expanding and pie-slicing advantage in intercultural negotiations. Further, when encountering differences, the negotiator who is aware of cultural differences will not make negative attributions about the counterparty but will, instead, view discomfort as a natural consequence of different cultural styles.

Analyze Cultural Differences to Identify Differences in Values That Expand the Pie

We noted in Chapter 4 (integrative negotiation) and Chapter 8 (creativity in negotiation) that differences, rather than similarities, between negotiators can open windows for expanding the pie and creating joint gain. Presumably, more degrees of difference are present between members of different cultures than members of the same culture. The level of differences means that the amount of integrative, or win-win, potential is higher in intercultural negotiations, as opposed to intracultural negotiations. The culturally enlightened negotiator will search for differences in beliefs, values, risk profiles, expectations, and abilities that can be used to leverage opportunities for joint gain, such as through the creation of value-added trade-offs (logrolling) and the construction of contingency contracts.

Recognize That the Other Party May Not Share Your View of What Constitutes Power

The other party's estimate of his or her power may be based on factors you think are irrelevant to the negotiation. Negotiators from egalitarian cultures should be prepared to

---

[131]Brett, *Negotiating globally, 4,* 5-22. Courtesy of Brill.
[132]Ibid.

present information about their company and products, even when they think such information should have no bearing on the outcome. In failing to make a presentation comparable to the one made by the negotiator from the hierarchical culture, negotiators from egalitarian cultures risk appearing weak. By the same token, negotiators from hierarchical cultures should be aware that power-based persuasion, although normative in deal-making negotiations in their own cultures, is not normative in egalitarian cultures. Furthermore, in egalitarian cultures, power-based persuasion is likely to be reciprocated and may lead to impasse.[133] One American businessperson suffered due to a lack of understanding about cultural behavioral styles. After long, hard bargaining, a U.S. firm landed a large contract with a Japanese firm. At the signing ceremony, however, the Japanese executive began reading the contract intently. His scrutiny seemed endless. The American panicked and offered to take $100 off each item. What the U.S. executive did not know was that the Japanese president was merely demonstrating authority, not backing out.[134]

Avoid Attribution Errors

An **attribution error** is the tendency to ascribe someone's behavior or the occurrence of an event to the wrong cause. For example, people often attribute behaviors of others to their underlying personality (e.g., a smile from another person is often attributed to a "good" disposition; similarly, a frown is presumed to be a manifestation of a grouchy personality).[135] However, the behavior of others is more often a reflection of particular features of the situation, rather than enduring personality traits. Negotiators who are interculturally naïve are more likely to fall prey to the fundamental attribution error than are people who are interculturally sensitive, who are more likely to view behavior as a manifestation of cultural and situational norms.

Find Out How to Show Respect in the Other Culture

One of the most important preparatory steps a negotiator can take when commencing intercultural negotiation is to find out how to show respect in the other culture. It is a fallacy to assume that the other culture will have the same customs as one's own culture and that ignorance of customs will be forgiven. In one simulation, parties on opposite sides of the table attempted to show respect by studying the cultural style of the other and adapting to it (see Exhibit 10-13). (For an example of a failure to show respect in another culture, see Exhibit 10-14.)

Find Out How Time Is Perceived in the Other Culture

Perceptions of time differ dramatically across cultures.[136] Consider, for example, the lengthy negotiations between the Chinese government and Philip Morris International. After more than three years of negotiations, the Chinese government selected three domestic cigarette brands, of the hundreds sold, to market abroad in partnership

---

[133]Brett & Okumura, "Inter- and intracultural negotiation."

[134]Cultural differences can make or break a deal. (1986, February 10). *Chicago Sun-Times,* p. 60.

[135]Ross, B. H. (1987). This is like that: The use of earlier problems and the separation of similarity effects. *Journal of Experimental Psychology: Learning, Memory and Cognition, 13*(4), 629–639.

[136]Alon, I., & Brett, J. (2007, January). Perceptions of time and their impact on negotiations in the Arabic-speaking Islamic world. *Negotiation Journal, 23,* 55–73.

EXHIBIT 10-13   An Experiment in Cultural Perspective-Taking

Two professors—Shyam Kamath and Martin Desmaras—arranged for a realistic mock negotiation between U.S. managers and Brazilians. Most of the time, executives from different cultures are not prepared for one another, but the managers in this situation went overboard: Each party carefully researched the other party's cultural style and decided to adapt its own bargaining style to it. The strange result was a situation in which the Brazilians wanted to get down to business immediately and the Americans avoided negotiations while attempting to establish relationships before talking about any contract details. Said one American, "What really surprised us was that they wanted to get down to business right away. We knew better than to push them into a decision at the start, but they came in with their price offer right away." Said the Brazilians, "They [the Americans] seemed to want to take more time at the start. Our side acted more like Americans." Kim Smith, business development manager for Hertz Corp., said, "I began to worry that if their side acted like Americans and we acted like Brazilians, we wouldn't get anything done."

Source: Transnational executive education exercise shows Brazilians, Americans must negotiate past cultural difference. (2003, June 5). *Ascribe News.* Reprinted by permission.

---

with PMI. According to PMI Chief Executive Andre Calantzopoulos, the negotiations were delayed partly because of cultural differences. "By Chinese standards, urgency is in terms of decades, versus U.S. companies, where urgency is next quarter."[137]

Cooperative and competitive behaviors in global negotiations wax and wane across four stages: relational positioning, identifying the problem, generating solutions, and reaching agreement.[138] Cultural differences occur at these stages, perhaps the most notable being that direct cultures use more rational arguments in stages 3 and 4. Differences in how time unfolds may lead Westerners to want to talk (i.e., discuss their feelings with the goal of repairing frayed relationships); however, the meaning of such talk may not be shared by people from culturally different backgrounds.[139] Instead of talking directly about feelings, Westerners may be advised to consider visual and aesthetic outlets.

EXHIBIT 10-14   Failing to Show Respect in Another Culture Can Lead to Conflict

In 1992, the Walt Disney Company undertook a $5 billion EuroDisney theme park project in Paris. It began with great visions of a united workforce wearing Disney dress and adopting American grooming. Behavioral codes banned alcohol in the park, and meetings were conducted in English. The French perceived these requirements and restrictions as an unnecessary cultural imposition. They retaliated with insults, storming out of training meetings, and initiating lawsuits. The French press joined in by launching an anti-Disney campaign, and French railroad workers regularly initiated strikes from the Paris-EuroDisney train for months. The annual employee turnover hit a crippling 25 percent, pushing up labor costs by 40 percent. Disney paid a heavy price before making amends.

Source: Based on Mishra, B. & Sinha, N. (1999, November 8). Cross-cultural booby traps. *Economic Times.*

---

[137]Zamiska, N., Ye, J., & O'Connell V. (2008, January 30). Chinese cigarettes to go global. *Wall Street Journal,* p. B4.
[138]Adair & Brett, "The negotiation dance."
[139]Glinow, M. A., Shapiro, D. L., & Brett, J. M. (2004). Can we talk, and should we? Managing emotional conflict in multicultural teams. *Academy of Management Review, 29*(4), 578–592.

Know Your Options for Change

Succeeding in international business requires that people gain international, as well as business, competence.[140] You have done your homework, researched the counterparty's culture, and have a good idea of what to expect during the meeting and which customs are important. You have also uncovered an unsettling fact: In your client's culture, women are regarded as property and second-class citizens. They are not supposed to be opinionated or hold jobs with decision making importance. Imagine you are a man and your key business associate is a woman, trained at an Ivy League university and well-versed in cultural issues and your client's strategic situation. For you both to sit at the bargaining table would be an insult to your client. Your supervisor is pressing you to open the door to this client's company. What do you do?

It is difficult to imagine leaving one's colleague behind; you need her skills and, moreover, you do not want to break up your partnership. Yet, bringing her involves an inevitable culture clash. Further, shutting the door on this client shuts the door on the entire country. You have thoughts about enlightening your client but wonder whether a five-minute lesson from you can overcome centuries of discrimination sewn into the fabric of a country.

The manager who identifies this situation early on is in a better situation to positively address it than is the manager who naïvely steps off the plane with the issue unresolved.

Sometimes, options for change are driven by skill sets—or lack thereof. Most Americans are monolingual, compared to other cultures. Furthermore, members of other cultures know that Americans are monolingual, and so they adapt accordingly. For example, in interactions between North Americans and Mexicans, Mexican bilingual managers immediately switched to English when interacting with North Americans; however, North American linguistic accommodation was a rare occurrence.[141]

Before reading further, think about what courses of action you might take. Berry described four ways for two cultures to relate to each other (see Exhibit 10-15).[142] The first issue is whether the individual (or group) finds it valuable to maintain distinct cultural identity and characteristics. The second issue is whether the individual (or group) desires to maintain relationships with other (cultural) groups.

- ***Integration*** is a type of acculturation whereby each group maintains its own culture and also maintains contact with the other culture. Thus, you bring your associate to the meetings and clearly uphold your firm's egalitarian attitudes, yet you also make it clear that you have a strong desire to build relationships with the other group.
- ***Assimilation*** occurs when a group or person does not maintain its culture but does maintain contact with the other culture. You leave your associate at home and try to follow the mores of the other party's culture.
- ***Separation*** occurs when a group or individual maintains its culture but does not maintain contact with the other culture. You bring your associate to the meetings and remain oblivious to the other group's culture, or you tell your supervisor you do not want this assignment.

---

[140]Matsumoto, D. (1996). *Culture and psychology.* Pacific Grove, CA: Brooks-Cole.
[141]Lindsley, S. L. (1999, June). A layered model of problematic intercultural communication in U.S.-owned maquiladoras in Mexico. *Communication Monographs, 66*(2), 145–167.
[142]Berry, J. W. (1980). Acculturation as varieties of adaptation. In A. Padilla (Ed.), *Acculturation: Theory, models, and some new findings.* Boulder, CO: Westview.

EXHIBIT 10-15   Acculturation Framework

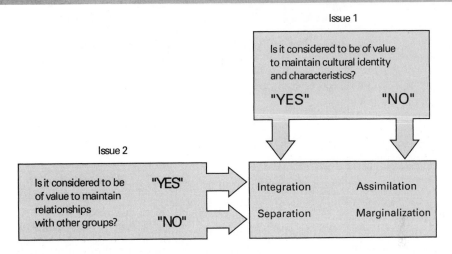

Issue 1

Is it considered to be of value to maintain cultural identity and characteristics?

"YES"   "NO"

Issue 2

Is it considered to be of value to maintain relationships with other groups?

"YES"

"NO"

Integration   Assimilation

Separation   Marginalization

Source: Reprinted by permission of John W. Berry.

- *Marginalization*   occurs when neither maintenance of the group's own culture nor contact with the other culture is attempted. You leave your associate at home and do not attempt to understand the cultural values of the other firm. Marginalization is the most unfavorable condition.[143]

CONCLUSION

Negotiating across cultures is a necessity for success in the business world because globalization is a major objective of most companies. Unfortunately, cross-cultural negotiations frequently result in less effective pie expansion than do intracultural negotiations. Part of the problem is a lack of understanding cultural differences. We used Brett's tripartite model of culture and identified individualism-collectivism, egalitarianism-hierarchy, and direct-indirect communication as key dimensions of cultural differences.[144] Key challenges of intercultural negotiation are expanding the pie, dividing the pie, dealing with sacred values and taboo trade-offs, biased punctuation of conflict, ethnocentrism, the affiliation bias, faulty perceptions of conciliation and coercion, and naïve realism. Negotiators should analyze cultural differences to identify differences in values that could expand the pie, recognize different conceptions of power, avoid attribution errors, find out how to show respect in other cultures, find out how time is perceived, and assess options for change, including integration, assimilation, separation, and marginalization.

---

[143]Berry, J. W., Poortinga, Y. H., Segall, M. H., & Dasen, P. R. (1992). *Cross-cultural psychology: Research and applications*. New York: Cambridge University Press.
[144]Brett, *Negotiating globally.*

CHAPTER

Tacit Negotiations and Social Dilemmas

The Kyoto Protocol, first negotiated in 1997, asked developed countries to cut emissions by an average of 5 percent (compared with 1990 levels) by 2012. However, in the years following the original negotiations, numerous meetings on climate change failed to produce the results needed to curb the environmental effects of global warming. When government ministers from around the world met in Nairobi for the United Nations talks on climate change in 2006, the negotiations were dominated by this dilemma: Each country could promise to cut greenhouse gas emissions, and take steps to do so, or it could refuse. If one, or many, of the countries refused, any country agreeing to cut its emissions would risk damaging the competitiveness of its economy. However, the refusal of every country to meet the necessary commitments would lead to an increased rate of global warming. Japan, fearing it would give competitive advantage to China in manufacturing industries, refused to speed up commitments to reduce emissions. The United States and Australia had both previously rejected the protocol, causing other countries to hesitate. Canada resisted pressure at the Nairobi meeting, concerned it would no longer be able to compete against the United States in many of its industries. The 2006 talks ended with few countries agreeing to take action, while their greenhouse gas emissions climbed.[1]

So far in this book, we have focused on negotiation situations in which people seek to reach mutual agreement in terms of a binding contract, called **explicit negotiations**. In contrast, many negotiations that occur within and between parties are conducted by actions and pledges, such as the Kyoto Protocol. We call these situations **tacit negotiations**.[2] In tacit negotiations, negotiators are interdependent with respect to outcomes, but they make independent decisions. Negotiators' outcomes are determined by the actions they take and the actions taken by others. People can either behave in a cooperative fashion (e.g., agreeing to reduce emissions) or in a competitive fashion (e.g., refusing to reduce emissions).

---

[1]Harvey, F. (2006, December 6). Lose-lose: The penalties of acting alone stall collective effort on climate change. *The Financial Times*, p. 17.
[2]Schelling, T. (1960). *The strategy of conflict.* Cambridge, MA: Harvard University Press.

EXHIBIT 11-1   Two Major Types of Negotiation Situations

Cooperative Negotiations	Noncooperative Negotiations
• Contract is explicit. • Mutual understanding (people know what they are getting before they agree). • People negotiate via proposals and counterproposals and can use words to explain and justify their offers. • People usually come to the table voluntarily.	• Contract is tacit. • People often do not know what others will do. • People negotiate through their behaviors and actions (rather than their promises of what they will do). • People are often pulled into negotiations without wanting to be involved.

Source: Adapted from Nash, J. (1951). Non-cooperative games. *Annals of Mathematics, 54*(2), 286–295; Nash, J. (1953). Two-person cooperative games. *Econometrica, 21,* 129–140.

The distinction between these two different types of negotiation situations was first articulated by the famous mathematician John Nash, who referred to one branch of negotiations as "cooperative games" and the other as "noncooperative games."[3] In using the terms "cooperative" and "noncooperative", Nash was not referring to the motivations or behaviors of the parties involved but, rather, to how the underlying situation was structured. (See Exhibit 11-1 for the difference between the two main types of negotiations.)

In negotiations, our outcomes depend on the actions of others. The situation that results when people engage in behaviors that maximize self-interest but lead to collective disaster, such as a bidding war, greenhouse gases, or negative campaigning, is a **social dilemma**. In this chapter, we discuss two kinds of social dilemmas: two-person dilemmas and multiperson dilemmas. The two-person dilemma is the **prisoner's dilemma**; the multiperson dilemma is a social dilemma. They are dilemmas because the choices available to negotiators are risky. Some choices risk exploitation; others risk antagonizing others. We discuss how dilemmas may be effectively handled by individuals, teams, and even countries.

BUSINESS AS A SOCIAL DILEMMA

Business competitors routinely face social dilemmas. Some industries seem particularly vicious, such as telecommunications companies. For example, in 2007 Comcast was taken by surprise when Verizon marketed and launched a new TV service. After once mocking the possibility that Verizon would ever pose a threat, Comcast later admitted it was losing customers to the phone company. Chief Operating Officer Steve Burke threatened that Comcast would "come out swinging" by adopting more competitive pricing plans in an attempt to draw customers away from Verizon.[4]

---

[3]Nash, J. (1951). Non-cooperative games. *Annals of Mathematics, 54*(2), 286–295; Nash, J. (1953). Two-person cooperative games. *Econometrica, 21,* 129–140.
[4]Searcy, D., & Kumar, V. (2008, February 15). Comcast plans $7 billion buyback—dividend payment also is part of move to satisfy holders. *Wall Street Journal,* p. B4.

In contrast, other industries have attempted to find points of cooperation that can align their competitive goals. For example, in 2006 German software company SAP formed an alliance with Microsoft, its biggest competitor. The companies decided to join forces to create Duet, a product that allows a Microsoft spreadsheet to pull in data from an SAP accounting program. SAP CEO Henning Kagermann said the goal was not to compete with Microsoft but, rather, to combine each company's skills to "focus on what you can do for the customer."[5] In 1998, two national dairy companies using separate advertising campaigns agreed to create a single marketing plan to increase milk sales in the United States. Dairy Management, Inc., which used the "Got Milk?" campaign, and the National Fluid Milk Processor Promotion Board, which used a popular collection of advertisements in which celebrities wear milk mustaches, coordinated campaigns to increase total fluid milk sales by 4% by the year 2000.[6] Willingness to engage in generic advertising (e.g., advertising the local mall instead of one's own store) is a common form of interfirm cooperation. A simulation of generic advertising revealed companies confronting a declining trend contributed significantly more dollars to generic advertising; moreover, it positively influenced their expectations that others would contribute as well.[7]

THE PRISONER'S DILEMMA

Thelma and Louise are common criminals who have just been arrested on suspicion of burglary. Law enforcement has enough evidence to convict each suspect of a minor breaking-and-entering crime but insufficient evidence to convict the suspects on a more serious felony charge of burglary and assault. The district attorney immediately separates Thelma and Louise after their arrest. Each suspect is approached separately and presented with two options: confess to the serious burglary charge or remain silent (do not confess). The consequences of each course of action depend on what the other decides to do. The catch is that Thelma and Louise must make their choices independently. They cannot communicate with each other in any way prior to making an independent, irrevocable decision. The decision situation each suspect faces is illustrated in Exhibit 11-2, which indicates Thelma and Louise will go to prison for as many as 15 years, depending upon what the other partner chooses. Obviously, it is an important decision. Imagine you are advising Thelma. Your concern is not morality or ethics; you are simply trying to get her a shorter sentence. What do you advise her to do?

Ideally, it is desirable for both suspects to not confess, thereby minimizing the prison sentence to 1 year for each (cell A). This option is risky, however. If one confesses, then the suspect who does not confess goes to prison for the maximum sentence of 15 years—an extremely undesirable outcome (cell B or C). In fact, the most desirable situation from the standpoint of each suspect would be to confess and have the other person not confess. Then, the confessing suspect would be released, and his or her

---

[5]Coy, P. (2006, August 21). Sleeping with the enemy. *Business Week, 3998,* 96.

[6]Elliott, S. (1998, February 6). Milk promoters agree to cooperate. *New York Times,* p. D17.

[7]Krishnamurthy, S., Bottom, W. P., & Rao, A. G. (2003). Adaptive aspirations and contributions to a public good: Generic advertising as a response to decline. *Organizational Behavior and Human Decision Processes, 92,* 22–33.

EXHIBIT 11-2   Consequences of Thelma and Louise's Behaviors

		Thelma	
		Do not confess (remain silent)	**Confess**
Louise	**Do not confess (remain silent)**	**A** Thelma: 1 yr Louise: 1 yr	**B** Thelma: 0 yrs Louise: 15 yrs
	Confess	**C** Thelma: 15 yrs Louise: 0 yrs	**D** Thelma: 10 yrs Louise: 10 yrs

Note: Entries represent prison-term length.

partner would go to prison for the maximum sentence of 15 years. Given these contingencies, what should Thelma do? Before reading further, stop and think about what you think is her best course of action.

The answer is not easy, which is why the situation is a dilemma. It will soon be demonstrated that when each person pursues the course of action that is most rational from her point of view, the result is mutual disaster. That is, both Thelma and Louise go to prison for 10 years (cell D). The paradox of the prisoner's dilemma is that the pursuit of individual self-interest leads to collective disaster. The conflict between individual and collective well-being derives from rational analysis. It is easy for Thelma and Louise to see that each could do better by cooperating, but it is not easy to know *how* to implement this behavior. The parties can get there only with coordinated effort.

Cooperation and Defection as Unilateral Choices

We will use the prisoner's dilemma situation depicted in Exhibit 11-2 to analyze decision making. We will refer to the choices that players make in this game as **cooperation** and **defection**, depending upon whether they remain silent or confess. The language of cooperation and defection allows the prisoner's dilemma game structure to be meaningfully extended to other situations that do not involve criminals but nevertheless have the same underlying structure, such as whether an airline company should bid for a smaller company, or whether a cola company or politician should engage in negative advertising. However, prisoner's dilemmas don't just describe criminals and business strategy; in fact, the prisoner's dilemma was initially developed to provide a compelling analysis of the negotiations between the United States and the Soviet Union. Each country sought to develop and deploy arsenals of nuclear arms they thought necessary for military defense. In the 1960s, public concern increased over the nuclear arms race.

Rational Analysis

We use the logic of game theory to provide a rational analysis of this situation. In our analysis, we consider three different cases: (a) one-shot, nonrepeated play situations (as in the case of Thelma and Louise); (b) the case in which the decision is repeated for a finite number of terms; and (c) the case in which the decision is repeated for a potentially infinite number of trials or the end is unknown.

Case 1: One-Shot Decision

Game theoretic analysis relies on the principle of **dominance detection**: A dominant strategy results in a better outcome for player 1 no matter what player 2 does.

To illustrate the dominance principle, suppose you are Thelma and your partner in crime is Louise. First, consider what happens if Louise remains silent (does not confess). Thus, we are focusing on the first row in Exhibit 11-2. Remaining silent puts you in cell A: You both get 1 year. This outcome is not too bad, but maybe you could do better. Suppose you decide to confess. In cell B, you get 0 years and Louise gets 15 years. Certainly no prison sentence is much better than a 1-year sentence, so confession seems like the optimal choice for you to make, given that Louise does not confess.

Now, what happens if Louise confesses? In this situation, we focus on row 2. Remaining silent puts you in cell C: You get 15 years, and Louise gets 0 years, which is not very good for you. Now, suppose you confess. In cell D, you both get 10 years. Neither outcome is splendid, but 10 years is certainly better than 15 years. Given that Louise confesses, what do you want to do? The choice amounts to whether you want to go to prison for 15 years or 10 years. Again, confession is the optimal choice for you.

No matter what Louise does (remains silent or confesses), it is better for Thelma to confess. Confession is a dominant strategy; under all possible states of the world, players in this game should choose to confess. We know that Louise is smart and has looked at the situation the same way as Thelma and has reached the same conclusion. In this sense, mutual defection is an **equilibrium outcome**, meaning no player can unilaterally (single-handedly) improve her outcome by making a different choice.

Thus, both Thelma and Louise are led through rational analysis to confess, and they collectively end up in cell D, where they both go to prison for a long time. This outcome seems both unfortunate and avoidable. Certainly, both suspects would prefer to be in cell A than in cell D. Is escape possible from the tragic outcomes produced by the prisoner's dilemma? Are we doomed to collective disaster in such situations?

It would seem that players might extricate themselves from the dilemma if they could communicate, but we already noted that communication is outside the bounds of the noncooperative game. Further, because the game structure is noncooperative, any deals that players might make with one another are nonbinding. For example, antitrust legislation prohibits companies from price fixing, which means any communication that occurs between companies regarding price fixing is unenforceable, not to mention punishable by law.

What other mechanism might allow parties in such situations to avoid the disastrous outcome produced by mutual defection? One possibility is to have both parties make those decisions over time, thereby allowing them to influence one another. Suppose the parties did not make a single choice but instead made a series of choices and received feedback about the other player's choice after each of their decisions. Perhaps repeated interaction with the other person would provide a mechanism for parties to coordinate their actions. If the game is to be played more than once, players might reason that cooperation may be elicited in subsequent periods by cooperating on the first round. We consider that situation next.

Case 2: Repeated Interaction Over a Fixed Number of Trials

Instead of making a single choice and living with the consequence, suppose Thelma and Louise were to play the game in Exhibit 11-2 a total of 5 times. It might seem strange to think about criminals repeating a particular interaction, so it may be useful to think about two political candidates deciding whether to engage in negative campaigning (hereafter referred to as "campaigning"). Term limits in their state dictate that they can run and hold office for a maximum of 5 years. An election is held every year. During any election period, each candidate makes an independent choice (to campaign or not), then learns of the other's choice (to campaign or not). After the election, the candidates consider the same alternatives once again and make an independent choice; this interaction continues for five separate elections.

We use the concept of dominance as applied previously to analyze this situation, but we need another tool that tells us how to analyze the repeated nature of the game. **Backward induction** is the mechanism by which a person decides what to do in a repeated game situation by looking backward from the last stage of the game.

We begin by examining what players should do in election 5 (the last election). If the candidates are making their choices in the last election, the game is identical to that analyzed in case 1, the one-shot case. Thus, the logic of dominant strategies applies, and we are left with the conclusion that each candidate will choose to campaign. Now, given that we know each candidate will campaign in the last election, what will they do in the fourth election?

From a candidate's standpoint, the only reason to cooperate (or to not campaign) is to influence the behavior of the other party in the subsequent election. In other words, a player might signal willingness to cooperate by making a cooperative choice in the preceding period. We have already determined that it is a foregone conclusion that both candidates will defect (choose to campaign) in the last election, so it is futile to choose the cooperative (no campaigning) strategy in the fourth election. So, what about the third election? Given that candidates will not cooperate in the last election, nor in the second-to-last election, they would find little point to cooperating in the third-to-last election for the same reason that cooperation was deemed to be ineffective in the second-to-last election. As it turns out, this logic can be applied to every election in such a backward fashion. Moreover, this reasoning is true in any situation with a finite number of elections. This realization leaves us with the conclusion that defection remains the dominant strategy even in the repeated trial case.[8]

This result is disappointing. It suggests that cooperation is not possible even in long-term relationships. It runs counter to intuition, observation, and logic, however. We must consider another case, arguably more realistic of the situations we want to study in most circumstances, in which repeated interaction continues for an infinite or indefinite amount of time.

---

[8]Formally, if the prisoner's dilemma is repeated finitely, all Nash equilibria of the resulting sequential games have the property that the noncooperative outcome, which is Pareto-inferior, occurs in each period, no matter how large the number of periods.

Case 3: Repeated Interaction for an Infinite or Indefinite Amount of Time

In the case in which parties interact with one another for an infinite or indefinite amount of time, the logic of backward induction breaks down. No identifiable endpoint from which to reason backward exists. We are left with forward-thinking logic.

If we anticipate playing a prisoner's dilemma game with another person for an infinitely long or uncertain length of time, we reason that we might influence their behavior with our own behavior. We may signal a desire to cooperate on a mutual basis by making a cooperative choice in an early trial. Similarly, we can reward and punish their behavior through our actions.

Under such conditions, the game theoretic analysis indicates that cooperation in the first period is the optimal choice.[9] Should our strategy be to cooperate no matter what? No! If a person adopted cooperation as a general strategy, it would surely lead to exploitation. So, what strategy would be optimal to adopt? Before reading further, stop and indicate what strategy you think is best.

The Tournament of Champions

In 1981, Robert Axelrod, a leading game theorist, spelled out the contingencies of the prisoner's dilemma game and invited members of the scientific community to submit a strategy to play in a prisoner's dilemma tournament. To play in the tournament, a person had to submit a strategy (a plan that would tell a decision maker what to do in every trial under all possible conditions) in the form of a computer program written in FORTRAN code. Axelrod explained that each strategy would play all other strategies across 200 trials of a prisoner's dilemma game. He further explained that the strategies would be evaluated in terms of the maximization of gains across all opponents they faced. Hundreds of strategies were submitted by eminent scholars from around the world.

The Winner Is a Loser

The winning strategy of the tournament was the simplest strategy submitted. The FORTRAN code was only four lines long. The strategy was called **tit-for-tat** and was submitted by Anatol Rapoport. Tit-for-tat accumulated the greatest number of points across all trials with all of its opponents. The basic principle for tit-for-tat is simple: Tit-for-tat always cooperates on the first trial, and on subsequent trials it does whatever its opponent did on the previous trial. For example, suppose tit-for-tat played against someone who cooperated on the first trial, defected on the second trial, and then cooperated on the third trial. Tit-for-tat would cooperate on the first trial and the second trial, defect on the third trial, and cooperate on the fourth trial.

Tit-for-tat never beat any of the strategies it played against. Because it cooperates on the first trial, it can never do better than its opponent. The most tit-for-tat can do is earn as much as its opponent. If it never wins (i.e., beats its opponent), how can tit-for-tat be so successful in maximizing its overall gains? The answer is that it induces cooperation from its opponents.

---

[9]Kreps, D. M., Milgrom, P., Roberts, J., & Wilson, R. (1982). Rational cooperation in the finitely repeated prisoner's dilemma. *Journal of Economic Theory, 27,* 245–252.

Psychological Analysis of Why Tit-for-Tat Is Effective

Not Envious.   One reason why tit-for-tat is effective is that it is not an envious strategy. Tit-for-tat never aims to beat its opponent. Tit-for-tat can never earn more than any strategy it plays against. Rather, the tit-for-tat strategy seeks to maximize its own gain in the long run.

Nice.   Tit-for-tat always begins the interaction by cooperating. Furthermore, it is never the first to defect; thus, tit-for-tat is a nice strategy. This feature is important because it is difficult for people to recover from initial defections. Competitive, aggressive behavior often sours a relationship. Moreover, aggression often begets aggression. The tit-for-tat strategy neatly avoids the costly mutual escalation trap that can lead to the demise of both parties.

Tough.   A strategy of solid cooperation would be easily exploitable by an opponent. Tit-for-tat can be provoked: It will defect if the opponent invites competition. Tit-for-tat reciprocates defection, an important feature of its strategy. By reciprocating defection, tit-for-tat conveys the message that it cannot be taken advantage of. Indeed, tit-for-tat players effectively move competitive players away from them, thus minimizing noncooperative interaction.[10]

Forgiving.   We noted that tit-for-tat is tough in that it reciprocates defection. It is also a forgiving strategy in the sense that it reciprocates cooperation, another important feature. It is often difficult for people in conflict to recover from defection and end an escalating spiral of aggression. Tit-for-tat's eye-for-an-eye strategy ensures its response to aggression will never be greater than what it received.

Simple.   Another reason why tit-for-tat is so effective is that it is simple. People can quickly figure out what to expect from a player who follows it. When people are uncertain or unclear about what to expect, they are more likely to engage in defensive behavior. When uncertainty is high, people often assume the worst about another person. Predictability increases interpersonal attraction.

In summary, tit-for-tat is an extremely stable strategy. Negotiators who follow it often induce their opponents to cooperate. However, few who play prisoner's dilemma games actually follow tit-for-tat. For example, in our analysis of more than 600 executives playing the prisoner's dilemma game, the defection rate is nearly 40%, and average profits are only one-tenth of the possible maximum! But tit-for-tat is not uniquely stable; other strategies are stable as well. For example, solid defection is a stable strategy. Two players who defect on every trial have little reason to do anything else. Once someone has defected, it is difficult to renew cooperation.

Recovering from Defection

Suppose you are the manager of a large health maintenance organization (HMO). The health care industry is highly competitive, with different companies vying to capture market share by touting low deductibles and so on. You have analyzed the situation with your competitors to be a noncooperative game. You have thought about how your

---

[10]Van Lange, P. A. M., & Visser, K. (1999). Locomotion in social dilemmas: How people adapt to cooperative, tit-for-tat and non-cooperative partners. *Journal of Personality and Social Psychology, 77*(4), 762–773.

competitor must view the situation, and you have decided to take a cooperative approach and *not* engage in negative advertising. Later that week, you learn that your opponent has taken out a full-page ad in the *Wall Street Journal* that denigrates your HMO by publicizing questionable statistics about your mortality rates, quotes from angry patients, and charges about negligent physicians. You counter with some negative TV spots. You are spending a lot of money and are angry. Can you stop this escalating spiral of defection? Probably so, if you consider the following strategies.

Make Situational Attributions   We often blame the incidence of escalating mutually destructive conflict on others' ill will and evil intentions. We fail to realize that we might have done the same thing as our competitor had we been in his or her shoes. Why? We punctuate events differently than do our opponents. We see our behavior as a defensive *response* to the other. In contrast, we view the other as engaging in unprovoked acts of aggression. The solution is to see the other side's behavior as a response to our own actions. In the preceding situation, your competitor's negative ad campaign may be a payback for your campaign a year ago.

One Step at a Time   Trust is not rebuilt in a day. We rebuild trust incrementally by taking a series of small steps that effectively "reward" the other party if they behave cooperatively. For example, the GRIT (graduated reduction in tension relations) strategy (reviewed in Chapter 9) calls for parties in conflict to offer small concessions.[11] This approach reduces the risk for the party making the concession.

Getting Even and Catching Up   As we saw in Chapter 3, people are especially concerned with fairness. One way of rebuilding trust is to let the other party "get even" and catch up. The resurrection of a damaged relationship may depend on repentance on the part of the injurer and forgiveness on the part of the injured.[12] Even more surprising is that small amends are as effective as large amends in generating future cooperation.

Make Your Decisions at the Same Time   Imagine you are playing a prisoner's dilemma game like that described in the Thelma and Louise case. You are told about the contingencies and payoffs in the game and then asked to make a choice. The twist in the situation is that you are either told that your opponent (a) has already made her choice earlier that day, (b) will make her choice later that day, or (c) will make her choice at the same time as you. In all cases, you will *not* know the other person's choice before making your own. When faced with this situation, people are more likely to cooperate when their opponent's decision is temporally contiguous with their own decision (i.e., when the opponent makes her decision at the same time.)[13] Temporal contiguity fosters a causal illusion: the idea that our behavior at a given time can influence the behavior of others. This logical impossibility is not permissible in the time-delayed decisions.

---

[11]Osgood, C. E. (1979). GRIT 1 (vol. 8, no. 1, 0553–4283). Dundas, Ontario: Peace Research Reviews.
[12]Bottom, W., Daniels, S., Gibson, K. S., and Murnighan, J. K. (2002). When talk is not cheap: Substantive penance and expressions of intent in rebuilding cooperation. *Organization Science, 13*(5), 497–513.
[13]Morris, M. W., Sim, D. L. H., & Girrotto, V. (1995). Time of decision, ethical obligation, and causal illusion: Temporal cues and social heuristics in the prisoner's dilemma. In R. Kramer & D. Messick (Eds.), *Negotiation as a social process* (pp. 209–239). Thousand Oaks, CA: Sage.

In the prisoner's dilemma game, people make choices simultaneously; therefore, one's choice cannot influence the choice the other person makes on a given trial, only in subsequent trials. That is, when Thelma makes her decision to confess or not, it does not influence Louise, unless she is telepathic. However, people *act as if* their behavior influences the behavior of others, even though it logically cannot.

In an intriguing analysis of this perception, Douglas Hofstadter wrote a letter, published in *Scientific American,* to 20 friends (see Exhibit 11-3). Hofstadter raised the question of whether one person's action in this situation can be taken as an indication of what all people will do. He concluded that if players are indeed rational, they will

---

EXHIBIT 11-3   Letter from Douglas Hofstadter to 20 Friends in *Scientific American*

Dear____ :

I am sending this letter by special delivery to 20 of you (namely, various friends of mine around the country). I am proposing to all of you a one-round Prisoner's Dilemma game, the payoffs to be monetary (provided by *Scientific American*). It is very simple. Here is how it goes.

Each of you is to give me a single letter: *C* or *D*, standing for "cooperate" or "defect." This will be used as your move in a Prisoner's Dilemma with *each* of the 19 other players.

Thus, if everyone sends in *C,* everyone will get $57, whereas if everyone sends in *D*, everyone will get $19. You can't lose! And, of course, anyone who sends in *D* will get at least as much as everyone else. If, for example, 11 people send in *C* and nine send in *D*, then the 11 *C*-ers will get $3 a piece from each of the other *C*-ers (making $30) and will get nothing from the *D*-ers. Therefore, *C*-ers will get $30 each. The *D*-ers in contrast, will pick up $5 a piece from each of the *C*-ers (making $55) and will get $1 from each of the other *D*-ers (making $8), for a grand total of $63. No matter what the distribution is, *D*-ers always do better than *C*-ers. Of course, the more *C*-ers there are, the better *everyone* will do!

By the way, I should make it clear that in making your choice you should not aim to be the *winner* but simply to get as much *money* for yourself as possible. Thus, you should be happier to get $30 (say, as a result of saying *C* along with 10 others, even though the nine *D*-sayers get more than you) than to get $19 (by saying *D* along with everyone else, so that nobody "beats" you.) Furthermore, you are not supposed to think that at some later time you will meet with and be able to share the goods with your coparticipants. You are not aiming at maximizing the total number of dollars *Scientific American* shells out, only at maximizing the number of dollars that come to *you*!

Of course, your hope is to be the *unique* defector, thereby really cleaning up: with 19 *C*-ers, you will get $95 and they will each get 18 times $3, namely $54. But why am I doing the multiplication or any of this figuring for you? You are very bright. So are the others. All about equally bright, I would say. Therefore, all you need to do is tell me your choice. I want all answers by telephone (call collect, please) *the day you receive this letter.*

It is to be understood (it *almost* goes without saying, but not quite) that you are not to try to consult with others who you guess have been asked to participate. In fact, please consult with no one at all. The purpose is to see what people will do on their own, in isolation. Finally, I would appreciate a short statement to go along with your choice, telling me *why* you made this particular one.

Yours,
Doug H.

---

either all choose to defect or all choose to cooperate. Given that all players are going to submit the same answer, which choice would be more logical? It would seem that co-operation is best (each player gets $57 when they all cooperate and only $19 when they all defect). At this point, the logic seems like magical thinking: A person's choice at a given time influences the behavior of others at the same time. Another example: People explain that they have decided to vote in an election so that others will, too. Of course, it is impossible that one person's voting behavior could affect others in a given election, but people act as if it does. Hofstadter argues that decision makers wrestling with such choices must give others credit for seeing the logic they themselves have seen. Thus, we need to believe that others are rational (like ourselves) and that they believe that everyone is rational. Hofstadter calls this rationality **superrationality**. For this reason, choosing to defect undermines the very reasons for choosing it. In Hofstadter's game, 14 people defected, and 6 cooperated. The defectors received $43; the cooperators received $15. Robert Axelrod was one of the participants who defected, and he remarked that a one-shot game offers no reason to cooperate.

SOCIAL DILEMMAS

Sometimes, managers find themselves involved in a prisoner's dilemma that contains several people. In these types of situations, negotiators find themselves choosing between cooperative strategies and self-interested strategies. The multiperson prisoner's dilemma is known as a social dilemma. (See Exhibits 11-4 and 11-5 for volunteer dilemmas and ultimatum dilemmas.) In general, people behave more competitively (in a self-interested fashion) in social dilemmas as compared to prisoner's dilemmas. Why do they act this way?

First, the prisoner's dilemma involves two parties; the social dilemma *involves several people*. People behave more competitively in groups than in two-person situations.[14]

Second, the *costs of defection are spread out,* rather than concentrated upon one person. Simply stated, when one person makes a self-interested choice and others choose to cooperate, everyone but the defector absorbs some (but not all) of the cost. Thus, the defecting person can say to himself or herself that everyone is suffering a lit-

---

EXHIBIT 11-4   Volunteer Dilemma

The volunteer dilemma is a situation in which at least one person in a group must sacrifice his or her own interests to better the group. An example is a group of friends who want to go out for an evening of drinking and celebration. The problem is that not all can drink if one person must safely drive everyone home. A "designated" driver is a volunteer for the group. Most organized entities would not function if no one volunteered. The act of volunteering strengthens group ties.

Source: Murnighan, J. K., Kim, J. W., & Metzger, A. R. (1993). The volunteer dilemma. *Administrative Science Quarterly, 38*(4), 515–538. Reprinted by permission of Administrative Science Quarterly.

---

[14]Insko, C. A., Schopler, J., Graetz, K. A., Drigotas, S. M., Currey, D.P., Smith, S.L., Brazil, D., & Bornstein, G. (1994). Interindividual-intergroup discontinuity in the prisoner's dilemma game. *Journal of Conflict Resolution, 38*(1), 87–116.

EXHIBIT 11-5   Ultimatum Dilemma

In an ultimatum bargaining situation, one person makes a final offer—an ultimatum—to another person. If the other person accepts the offer, then the first player receives the demand that he or she made, and the other player agrees to accept what was offered to him or her. If the offer is refused, then no settlement is reached (i.e., an impasse occurs) and negotiators receive their respective reservation points.

How should we negotiate in ultimatum situations? What kind of a final offer should we make to another person? When the tables are turned, on what basis should we accept or refuse a final offer someone makes to us?

Suppose someone with a $100 bill in hand comes to you and the person sitting on the bus beside you. This person explains that the $100 is yours to share with the other person if you can propose a split to which the other person will agree. The only hitch is that the division you propose is a once-and-for-all decision: You cannot discuss it with the other person, and you have to propose a take-it-or-leave-it split. If the other person accepts your proposal, the $100 will be allocated accordingly. If the other person rejects your proposal, no one gets any money, and you do not have the opportunity to propose another offer. Faced with this situation, what should you do? (Before reading further, indicate what you would do and why.)

It is useful for us to solve this problem using the principles of decision theory and then see whether the solution squares with our intuition. Once again, we use the concept of backward induction, working backward from the last period of the game. The last decision in this game is an ultimatum. In this game, player 2 (the person beside you on the bus) must decide whether to accept the proposal offered by you or reject the offer and receive nothing. From a rational standpoint, player 2 should accept any positive offer you make to him or her because, after all, something (even 1 cent) is better than nothing.

Now we can examine the next-to-last decision in the game and ask what proposal player 1 (you) should make. Because you know that player 2 should accept any positive offer greater than $0, the game theoretic solution is for you to offer $0.01 to player 2 and demand $99.99 for yourself. This proposal is a **subgame perfect equilibrium** because it is rational within each period of the game.[*] In other words, even if the game had additional periods to be played in the future, your offer of $99.99 (to you) and $0.01 to the other person would still be rational at this point.

Contrary to game theoretic predictions, most people do not behave in this way. That is, most player 1s propose amounts substantially greater than $0.01 for player 2, often around the midpoint, or $50. Further, player 2s often reject offers that are not 50–50 splits.[†] Thus, some player 2s choose to have $0 rather than $1 or $2—or even $49. Player 1s act nonrationally, and so do player 2s. This response seems completely counter to one's interests, but as we saw in Chapter 2, people are often more concerned with how their outcomes compare to others than with the absolute value of their outcomes.[‡]

Croson also found that acceptance rates are driven by how much information the responder has about the size of the total pie.[§] When the responder does not know the size of the pie and receives a dollar offer, she is much more likely to reject it.

---

[*]Selten, R. (1975). Re-examination of the perfectness concept for equilibrium points in extensive games. *International Journal of Game Theory, 4*, 25–55.
[†]Pillutla, M. M., & Murnighan, J. K. (1995). Being fair or appearing fair: Strategic behavior in ultimatum bargaining. *Academy of Management Journal, 38*(5), 1408-1426.
[‡]See Loewenstein, G. F., Thompson, L., & Bazerman, M. H. (1989). Social utility and decision making in interpersonal contexts. *Journal of Personality and Social Psychology, 57*(3), 426–441; Messick, D. M., & Sentis, K. P. (1979). Fairness and preference. *Journal of Experimental Social Psychology, 15*(4), 418–434.
[§]Croson, R. (1996). Information in ultimatum games: An experimental study. *Journal of Economic Behavior & Organization, 30*, 197–212.

tle bit, rather than a lot. This mindset may lead people to be more inclined to serve their own interests.

Third, social dilemmas are *riskier* than prisoner's dilemmas. In the two-person dilemma, a certain minimal payoff to parties can be anticipated in advance. However, this outcome is not true in a social dilemma. The worst-case scenario is when the negotiator chooses to cooperate and everyone else defects. The costs of this situation are great. Greater risk and more uncertainty lead people to behave in a more self-interested, competitive fashion.

Fourth, social dilemmas *provide anonymity* that prisoner's dilemmas do not. Whereas anonymity is impossible in two-party situations, in social dilemmas people can "hide among the group." When people feel less accountable, they are more inclined to behave in a self-interested, competitive fashion.

Finally, people in social dilemmas *have less control* over the situation. In a classic, two-party prisoner's dilemma, people can directly shape and modify the behavior of the other person. Specifically, by choosing defection, one person may punish the other; by choosing cooperation, he or she can reward the other. This logic is the beauty of the tit-for-tat strategy. However, in a social dilemma, if someone defects, one person cannot necessarily punish the other on the next round because others will also be affected and, as we have seen, the costs of defection are spread out. For example, consider a classic social dilemma as illustrated by the Organization of the Petroleum Exporting Countries (OPEC). OPEC is a group of mostly Middle Eastern nations that have all agreed to reduce their production of oil. Lowering the volume of available oil creates greater demand, and oil prices go up. Obviously, each member of OPEC has an incentive to increase its production of oil, thus creating greater profit for itself. However, if all members violate the OPEC agreement and increase the production of oil, demand decreases, and so does the price of oil, thus driving down profits for the entire group.

The Tragedy of the Commons

Imagine you are a farmer. You own several cows and share a grazing pasture known as a "commons" with other farmers. One hundred farmers share the pasture. Each farmer is allowed to have one cow graze. Because the commons is not policed, it is tempting for you to add one more cow. By adding another cow, you can double your utility, and no one will really suffer. If everyone does the same thing, however, the commons will be overrun and the grazing area depleted. The cumulative result will be disastrous. What should you do in this situation if you want to keep your family alive?

The analysis of the **tragedy of the commons**[15] may be applied to many real-world problems, such as pollution, use of natural resources, and overpopulation. In these situations, people are tempted to maximize their own gain, reasoning that their pollution, failure to vote, and polystyrene cups in the landfill will not have a measurable impact on others. However, if everyone engages in this behavior, the collective outcome is disastrous: Air will be unbreathable, not enough votes will support a particular candidate in an election, and landfills will be overrun. Thus, in the social dilemma the rational pursuit of self-interest produces collective disaster.

---

[15]Hardin, G. (1968). The tragedy of the commons. *Science, 162,* 1243–1248.

In the social dilemma situation, each person makes behavioral choices similar to those in the prisoner's dilemma: to benefit oneself or the group. As in the prisoner's dilemma, the choices are referred to as "cooperation" and "defection". The defecting choice always results in better personal outcomes, at least in the immediate future, but universal defection results in poorer outcomes for everyone than with universal cooperation.

A hallmark characteristic of social dilemmas is that the rational pursuit of self-interest is detrimental to collective welfare. This factor has serious and potentially disastrous implications. (In this sense, social dilemmas contradict the principle of hedonism and laissez-faire economics.) Unless some limits are placed on the pursuit of personal goals, the entire society may suffer.

Types of Social Dilemmas

The two major forms of the social dilemma are **resource conservation dilemmas** (also known as **collective traps**) and **public goods dilemmas** (also known as **collective fences**).[16] In the resource conservation dilemma, people take or harvest resources from a common pool (like the farmers in the commons). Examples of the detrimental effects of individual interest include pollution, harvesting (of fossil fuels), burning of fossil fuels, water shortages, and negative advertising (see Exhibit 11-6 a, b for actual ads). The defecting choice occurs when people consume too much. The result of overconsumption is collective disaster. For groups to sustain themselves, the rate of consumption cannot exceed the rate of replenishment of resources.

In public goods dilemmas, people contribute or give resources to a common pool or community. Examples include donating to public radio and television, paying taxes, voting, doing committee work, and joining unions. The defecting choice is to not contribute. Those who fail to contribute are known as **defectors** or **free riders**. Those who pay while others free ride are affectionately known as **suckers**.

Think of resource conservation dilemmas as situations in which people *take* things; and think of public goods dilemmas as situations in which people must *contribute*. Moreover, both kinds of dilemmas—taking too much and failing to contribute—can occur within an organization or between different organizations (see Exhibit 11-7 for examples).

How to Build Cooperation in Social Dilemmas

Most groups in organizations could be characterized as social dilemma situations.[17] Members are left to their own devices to decide how much to take or contribute for common benefit. Consider an organization in which access to supplies and equipment, such as computers, photocopy paper, stamps, and envelopes, is not regulated. Each member may be tempted to overuse or hoard resources, thereby contributing to a rapid depletion of supply.

---

[16]Messick, D. M., & Brewer, M. (1983). Solving social dilemmas: A review. In L. Wheeler & P. Shaver (Eds.), *Review of personality and social psychology: Vol. 4* (pp. 11–44). Beverly Hills, CA: Sage.
[17]Kopelman, S., Weber, J. M., & Messick, D. M. (2002). Factors influencing cooperation in commons dilemmas: A review of experimental psychological research. In E. Ostrom et al. (Eds.), *The drama of the commons* (pp. 113–156). Washington, DC: National Academy Press; Mannix, E. (1993). Organizations as resource dilemmas: The effects of power balance on coalition formation in small groups. *Organizational Behavior and Human Decision Processes, 55,* 1–22.

EXHIBIT 11-6 (a)   Example of Negative (Competitive) Advertising

Since the 1970s, in a trend toward "comparative advertising," companies have compared their product with competitors' products and pointed out the advantages of their own product and the disadvantages of the competitors' products. Hardly any industry has managed to avoid comparative advertising. Advertisers have battled over milk quality, fish oil, beer taste, electric shavers, cola, coffee, magazines, cars, telephone service, banking, credit cards, and peanut butter. The ads attack the products and services of other companies. What is the effect of the attack ad? For the consumer, attack ads keep prices down and quality high. However, it can also lead to consumer resentment toward the industry. The effect is much more serious for the advertisers, who can effectively run each other out of business.

YOU WON'T FIND THE FASTEST GROWING DOCUMENT OUTPUT COMPANY UNDER X.

(You won't find it under C or M for that matter, either.)

Here's an interesting fact. The name of the fastest growing major document output company isn't Xerox, Canon, or Mita. It's Savin. That's right, Savin.

After all, Savin not only has the award-winning, multi-functional digital imaging systems today's networked offices require, we're also committed to becoming the fastest, most responsive name in the business. With smart, energetic, highly-trained Savin professionals willing to do whatever it takes to give you the satisfaction and service you deserve.

To find out more about Savin's full line of black & white and full-color digital imaging solutions, as well as our unshakable commitment to service, contact us at **1-800-234-1900** or www.savin.com. Or look in your card file under S.

savin
WE'VE GOT WHAT IT TAKES TO WIN YOU OVER™
SAVIN CORPORATION, 333 LUDLOW ST., STAMFORD, CT 06904

©1999 Savin Corporation

Source: Courtesy of The Savin Corporation, Stamford, Connecticut.

EXHIBIT 11-6 (b)   Example of Explicit Comparative Advertising

Business Class Legroom

Delta BusinessElite	36.5"
Continental	31"
British Airways	24"
Lufthansa	23"
American Airlines	22"

Business Class Recline

Delta BusinessElite	160°
Continental	152°
British Airways	140°
Lufthansa	135°
American Airlines	132°

Nonstop European Destinations

Delta BusinessElite	23
Continental	17
American Airlines	12
British Airways	3
Lufthansa	3

Nonstop destinations from the U.S.

Concierge Service At Every Gateway

Delta BusinessElite	Yes
Continental	No
British Airways	No
Lufthansa	No
American Airlines	No

Looks great on paper.
Feels even better in person.

Presenting Delta BusinessElite.™

There are a lot of reasons to fly Delta's new BusinessElite,

but don't take our word for it. Experience it for yourself.

With more personal space than other leading airlines' business

classes, and our convenient BusinessElite Concierge service at all

32 intercontinental destinations, we think you'll agree. BusinessElite

to Europe, Japan, India and Brazil simply outclasses business class.

BUSINESS *elite*
▲ Delta Air Lines

For reservations, visit us at www.bizelite.com or call Delta Air Lines at 1-800-241-4141. Or see your Travel Agent today.

Personal space is defined as the sum of legroom and recline. Legroom based on measurements taken from the foremost point of the bottom seat cushion to the back of the seat in front of it using non-bulkhead seats on a widebody aircraft of Continental (DC10-30), British Airways (747-200), Lufthansa (A340-300) and American Airlines (767-300). ©1999 Delta Air Lines, Inc.

Source: Courtesy of Delta Air Lines, Atlanta, Georgia.

EXHIBIT 11-7   Different Kinds of Social Dilemmas

	Taking	Contributing
Internal (intraorganizational)	Resources (e.g., money, real estate, staffing) Budget fudging	Committee work Recognition
External (interorganizational)	Price competition Brand competition Overharvesting Pollution	Paying taxes Public television

Many individual characteristics of people have been studied, such as gender, race, Machiavellianism, status, age, and so on.[18] Few, if any, individual differences reliably predict behavior in a prisoner's dilemma game. In fact, people cooperate more than rational analysis would predict. Many investigations use a single trial or fixed number of trials in which the rational strategy is solid defection. When the game is infinite or the number of trials is indefinite, however, people cooperate less than they should. What steps can the negotiator take to build greater cooperation and trust among organization members? Two major types of approaches for maximizing cooperation are **structural strategies** (which are often institutional changes) and **psychological strategies** (which are usually engaged in by the organizational actor; see Exhibit 11-8).

Structural Strategies

Structural strategies involve fundamental changes in the way that social dilemmas are constructed. They are usually the result of thoughtful problem solving and often produce a change in incentives.

Align Incentives   Monetary incentives for cooperation, privatization of resources, and a monitoring system increase the incidence of cooperation. For example, by putting in

EXHIBIT 11-8   Summary of Strategies for Maximizing Cooperation in Social Dilemmas

Structural Strategies	Psychological Strategies
Align incentives	Psychological contracts
Monitor behavior	Superordinate goals
Regulation	Communication
Privatization	Personalize others
Tradable permits	Social sanctions
	Focus on benefits of cooperation

Source: Brett, J., & Thompson, L. (2003). *Negotiation strategies for managers.* Executive course, Kellogg School of Management, Northwestern University, Evanston, IL. Reprinted by permission of Jeanne Brett.

---

[18]For a review, see Kopelman, Weber, & Messick, "Factors influencing cooperation."

"high-occupancy vehicle" lanes on major highways, single drivers are motivated to car-pool. However, realignment of incentives can be time-consuming and expensive.

Often, defectors are reluctant to cooperate because the costs of cooperation seem exorbitantly high. For example, people often defect by not paying their parking tickets because the price is high and they have several tickets. In some cases, city officials have allowed for amnesty delays for delinquent parking tickets, whereby people can cooper-ate at a cost less than they expected. Some U.S. cities have adopted similar policies to induce people to return borrowed library books.

Cooperation can also be induced through reward and recognition in organizations. Recognition awards, such as gold stars, employee-of-the-month awards, and the like are designed to induce cooperation rather than defection in a variety of organizational social dilemmas.

In some instances, cooperation can be induced by increasing the risk associated with defection. For example, some people do not pay their state or federal income tax in the United States. This behavior is illegal, and if a defector is caught he or she can be convicted of a crime. The threat of spending years in jail often lessens the temptation of defection. However, most tacit negotiations in organizations are not policed in this fashion, and, therefore, defection is more tempting for would-be defectors.

Monitor Behavior   When we monitor people's behavior, they often conform to group norms. The same beneficial effects also occur when people monitor their own behavior. For example, when people meter their water consumption during a water shortage, they use less water.[19] Moreover, people who meter their water usage express greater concern with the collective costs of overconsumption during a drought.

One method of monitoring behavior is to elect a leader. For example, people often will be in favor of electing a leader when they receive feedback that their group has failed at restricting harvests from a collective resource.[20] When a leader is introduced into a social dilemma situation, especially an autocratic leader, individual group mem-bers might fear restriction of their freedom.[21] People are more reluctant to install lead-ers in public goods situations (contributing) than in common resource situations (taking) because it is more threatening to give up decision freedom over private prop-erty than over collective property.[22]

Regulation   Regulation involves government intervention to correct market imper-fections with the idea of improving social welfare. Examples include rationing, in which limits are placed on access to a common-pool resource (i.e., water use). Regulation also occurs in other markets, such as agriculture. The telephone industry in the United States is a heavily regulated industry; in 1934 Congress created the Federal Communications

[19]Van Vugt, M., & Samuelson, C. D. (1999). The impact of personal metering in the management of a nat-ural resource crisis: A social dilemma analysis. *Personality and Social Psychology Bulletin, 25*(6), 731–745.

[20]Messick, D. M., Wilke, H., Brewer, M. B., Kramer, R. M., Zemke, P. E., & Lui, L. (1983). Individual adapta-tions and structural change as solutions to social dilemmas. *Journal of Personality and Social Psychology, 44*(2), 294–309; Rutte, C. G., & Wilke, H. A. M. (1984). Social dilemmas and leadership. *European Journal of Social Psychology, 14,* 105–121.

[21]Van Vugt, M., & De Cremer, D. (1999). Leadership in social dilemmas: The effects of group identification on collective actions to provide public goods. *Journal of Personality and Social Psychology, 76*(4), 587–599.

[22]van Dijk, E., Wilke, H., & Wit, A. (2003). Preferences for leadership in social dilemmas: Public good dilemmas versus common resource dilemmas. *Journal of Experimental Social Psychology, 39,* 170–176.

Commission (FCC) to oversee all wire and radio communication (e.g., radio, broadcast, telephone). Even though regulation does not always result in a system that encourages responsible behavior (cf. the moral hazard problem created by the Federal Deposit Insurance Corporation system), the intent of regulation is to protect public (social) interests.

Privatization The basic idea of privatization is to put public resources under the control of specific individuals or groups: public lands in private hands. The rationale is that public resources will be better protected if they are under the control of private groups or individuals. For example, protracted battles over public lands in New Mexico prompted the U.S. Congress to develop a national preserve that is not administered by federal land managers but by a board of nine private trustees appointed by the president.[23] Valles Caldera, New Mexico, is a 90,000-acre volcanic bowl with scenic overlooks. The federal government bought the land 2 years ago for $100 million. The trustees, who include experts in ranching, forestry, government, and conservation, decide what activities to allow based upon their sense of what best serves the common good. For example, 700 cows graze in Caldera's grassy valleys—a temporary arrangement to help 40 local ranchers stricken by drought. Hikers are only allowed to enter by bus, at a cost of more than $40 each. Moreover, the region contains rich oil and gas reserves, timbering potential, and great hunting with thousands of elk.

Another example: Hawaii's Sea Grant, partnering with the Oceanic Institute, works with government and private organizations to examine biological, environmental, and economic feasibility of offshore aquaculture in the Pacific region. The moi, a fish farmed by Hawaiian researchers, is highly valued by Hawaiians but is depleted in local waters. Moi grow well in captivity and reach market size in only 6 to 8 months. At the end of the first season, for example, the Hawaii Offshore Aquaculture Research Project (HOARP) harvested more than 19 tons of moi. In the second year, the stocking density of the fish doubled, with an overall harvest over 34 tons.[24]

Tradable Permits Tradable environmental allowance (TEA) governance structures are another way of navigating social dilemmas. In TEA arrangements, instead of competing for scarce resources (like the right to pollute), companies purchase the rights to pollute or to use scarce resources.[25] The idea is that users will treat these rights as they would conventional property and, thus, conserve resources carefully.[26] Tradable permits

[23]In New Mexico, a land management "experiment." (2002, September 23). *NPR.org*. Retrieved July 12, 2008, at http://www.npr.org/programs/morning/features/2002/sept/vallescaldera

[24]Reid, T. (2002, Spring). Raising food fish in sea cages: A Hawai'i first! *Makai, University of Hawai'i Sea Grant College Program Newsletter*, p. 9. Retrieved July 3, 2008, at http://www.soest.hawaii.edu/SEA-GRANT/communication/makai/pdf/Makai-Spring2002.pdf

[25]Brett, J. M., & Kopelman, S. (2004). Cross-cultural perspectives on cooperation in social dilemmas. In M. Gelfand & J. Brett (Eds.), *The handbook of negotiation and culture: Theoretical advances and cultural perspectives* (pp. 395–411). Palo Alto, CA: Stanford University Press.

[26]Ackerman, B. A., & Stewart, R. B. (1988). Reforming environmental law: The democratic case for market incentives. *Columbia Journal of Environmental Law, 13*, 171–199; Kriz, M. (1998). After Argentina. *National Journal, 30*(49), 2848–2853; Tipton, C. A. (1995). Protecting tomorrow's harvest: Developing a national system of individual transferable quotas to conserve ocean resources. *Virginia Environmental Law Journal, 14*, 381–421.

have been successfully used for managing fisheries, water supply, and air and water pollution in many different countries.[27] For example, in the fishing industry, the total allowable catch (or TAC) is set by government agencies and subsequently allocated to associations or individual users. As in the case of pollution, these allocations can be traded by individuals or companies.

Psychological Strategies

In contrast to structural strategies, which often require an act of government or layers of bureaucracy to enact, psychological strategies are inexpensive and only require the wits of the influence agent.

Psychological Contracts   Legal contracts involve paperwork and are similar to the deterrence-based trust mechanisms we discussed in Chapter 6. In contrast, **psychological contracts** are commonly known as "handshake deals." They are not binding in a court of law, but they create a psychological pressure to commit. People are more likely to cooperate when they promise to cooperate. Although such promises are nonbinding and are therefore "cheap talk," people nevertheless act as if they are binding. The reason for this behavior, according to the **norm of commitment**, is that people feel psychologically committed to follow through with their word.[28] The norm of commitment is so powerful that people often do things that are completely at odds with their preferences or that are highly inconvenient. For example, once people agree to let a salesperson demonstrate a product in their home, they are more likely to buy it. Homeowners are more likely to consent to have a large (over 10 feet tall), obtrusive sign in their front yard that says "Drive Carefully" when they agree to a small request made the week before.[29]

Superordinate Goals   Our behavior in social dilemmas is influenced by our perceptions about what kinds of behavior are appropriate and expected in a given context. In an intriguing examination of this idea, people engaged in a prisoner's dilemma task. In one condition, the game was called the "Wall Street game," and in another condition, the game was called the "community game."[30] Otherwise, the game, the choices, and the outcomes were identical. Although rational analysis predicts that defection is the optimal strategy no matter what the name, in fact, the incidence of cooperation was three times as high in the community game as in the Wall Street game, indicating that people are sensitive to situational cues as trivial as the name of the game. Indeed, people behave more competitively in social dilemmas involving economic decisions compared to those involving noneconomic decisions.[31]

---

[27]Tietenberg, T. (2002). The tradable permits approach to protecting the commons: What have we learned. In E. Ostrom, T. Dietz, N. Dolsak, P. C. Stern, S. Sonich, & E. U. Weber (Eds.), *The drama of the commons* (pp. 197–232). Washington, DC: National Academy Press.

[28]Cialdini, R. B. (1993). *Influence: Science and practice.* New York: HarperCollins.

[29]Freedman, J. L., & Fraser, S. C. (1966). Compliance without pressure: The foot-in-the-door technique. *Journal of Personality and Social Psychology, 4,* 195–203.

[30]Liberman, V., Samuels, S. M., & Ross, L.(2004). The name of the game: Predictive power of reputations versus situational labels in determining prisoner's dilemma game moves. *Personality and Social Psychology Bulletin, 30,* 1175-1185.

[31]Pillutla, M. M., & Chen, X. (1999). Social norms and cooperation in social dilemmas: The effects of context and feedback. *Organizational Behavior and Human Decision Processes, 78*(2), 81–103.

Communication A key determinant of cooperation is communication.[32] If people are allowed to communicate with the members of the group prior to making their choices, cooperation increases dramatically.[33]

Two reasons explain this increase in cooperation.[34] First, communication enhances group identity or solidarity. Second, communication allows group members to make public commitments to cooperate. Verbal commitments in such situations indicate the willingness of others to cooperate. In this sense, they reduce the uncertainty people have about others in such situations and provide a measure of reassurance to decision makers. Of the two explanations, it is the commitment factor that is most important.[35]

In our investigations on the relative effectiveness of verbal face-to-face communication as compared to written-only or no communication, people who communicate face-to-face are much more likely to reach a mutually profitable deal because they are able to coordinate on a price above each party's BATNA.[36] Commitments also shape subsequent behavior. People are extremely reluctant to break their word, even when their words are nonbinding. If people are prevented from making verbal commitments, they attempt to make nonverbal ones.

The other reason why communication is effective in engendering cooperation is that it allows group members to develop a shared group identity. Communication allows people to get to know one another and feel more attached to their group. People derive a sense of identity from their relationships to social groups.[37] When our identity is traced to the relationships we have with others in groups, we seek to further the interests of these groups. This identification leads to more cooperative, or group-welfare, choices in social dilemmas.

Social identity is often built through relationships. For example, as a consequence of population growth, the politics of water distribution, and five years of drought, California had widespread shortages of water in 1991. Residents of many areas were encouraged to voluntarily conserve water and were subjected to regulations imposed by the Public Utilities Commission. A telephone survey of hundreds of residents of the San Francisco area revealed that people were more willing to support authorities when they had strong relational bonds to the authorities.[38] The effectiveness of authorities in eliciting cooperation in water-shortage dilemmas is linked to the social bonds they share with community members.

---

[32]Komorita, S. S., & Parks, C. D. (1994). *Social dilemmas*. Madison, WI: Brown and Benchmark; Liebrand, W. B. G., Messick, D. M., & Wilke, H., Eds. (1992). *Social dilemmas: Theoretical issues and research findings*. Oxford, England: Pergamon Press; Messick & Brewer, "Solving social dilemmas"; Sally, D. F. (1995). Conversation and cooperation in social dilemmas: Experimental evidence from 1958 to 1992. *Rationality and Society, 7*(1), 58–92.

[33]Sally, "Conversation and cooperation in social dilemmas."

[34]Dawes, R. M., van de Kragt, A. J. C., & Orbell, J. M. (1990). Cooperation for the benefit of us—Not me, or my conscience. In J. Mansbridge (Ed.), *Beyond self-interest* (pp. 97–110). Chicago: University of Chicago Press.

[35]Kerr, N. L., & Kaufman-Gilliland, C. M. (1994). Communication, commitment, and cooperation in social dilemma. *Journal of Personality and Social Psychology, 66*(3), 513–529.

[36]Valley, K., Thompson, L., Gibbons, R., & Bazerman, M. H. (2002). How communication improves efficiency in bargaining games. *Games and Economic Behavior, 38,* 127–155.

[37]Tajfel, H. (1979). The exit of social mobility and the voice of social change: Notes on the social psychology of intergroup relations. *Przeglad Psychologiczny, 22*(1), 17–38.

[38]Tyler, T. R., & Degoey, P. (1995). Collective restraint in social dilemmas: Procedural justice and social identification effects on support for authorities. *Journal of Personality and Social Psychology, 69*(3), 482–497.

Personalize Others   People often behave as if they were interacting with an entity or organization rather than a person. For example, an embittered customer claims that the airline refused her a refund when in fact it was a representative of the airline who did not issue a refund. To the extent that others can be personalized, people are more motivated to cooperate than if they believe they are dealing with a dehumanized bureaucracy. Even more important is that people see you as a cooperator. People cooperate more when others have cooperated in a previous situation.[39]

For example, Knez and Camerer created a simulation that resembled the transfer of cooperative norms in small firms (which are largely cooperative) as firms grow larger and become more like prisoner's dilemmas (which pit self-interest against cooperation).[40] Some managers shared a history of coordinating their behavior; others did not. Those who had a history of coordinating their actions together were more likely to cooperate in a subsequent prisoner's dilemma situation. Further, the difference was dramatic: Those who had a previous history cooperated in the prisoner's dilemma game about 71% of the time, whereas others without a history only cooperated 15% to 30% of the time.

Still another reason why people cooperate is that they want to believe they are nice. For example, one person attributed his decision to make a cooperative choice in the 20-person prisoner's dilemma game to the fact that he did not want the readers of *Scientific American* to think he was a defector.[41] This behavior is a type of impression management.[42] **Impression management** raises the question of whether people's behavior is different when it is anonymous than when it is public. The answer appears to be yes. However, it is not always the case that public behavior is more cooperative than private behavior. For example, negotiators who are accountable to a constituency often bargain harder and are more competitive than when they are accountable for their behavior.[43]

Social Sanctions   Social sanctions are punishments that are administered in a community or a group when defection occurs. Unlike legal sanctions, social sanctions are not economic penalties and fines but, rather, might be a form of reprimand. Consider for example what Bertreice Dixon did when she learned that her son had bullied another student over an iPod. Dixon made her son wear a large sandwich board and parade on the corner of a busy intersection. The sign on the sandwich board explained his behavior, and his mother even made him ring a bell and wear a hat with the letter "d" on it for dumb. Clearly, the son was shamed and embarrassed by the mother's social sanctioning of his behavior.[44]

Focus on Benefits of Cooperation   The probability that a person will make a particular choice in a social dilemma is a function of the attraction of that choice in terms of

[39]Pillutla & Chen, "Social norms and cooperation."

[40]Knez, M., & Camerer, C. (2000). Increasing cooperation in prisoner's dilemmas by establishing a precedent of efficiency in coordination games. *Organizational Behavior and Human Decision Processes, 82*(2), 194–216.

[41]Hofstadter, D. (1983). Metamagical thinking. *Scientific American, 248,* 14–28.

[42]Goffman, E. (1959). *The presentation of self in everyday life.* Garden City, NY: Doubleday.

[43]See Carnevale, P. J., Pruitt, D. G., & Seilheimmer, S. (1981). Looking and competing: Accountability and visual access in integrative bargaining. *Journal of Personality and Social Psychology, 40,* 111–120.

[44]Dudzik, K. (2007, June 1). Public punishment for boy accused of bullying. *Fox16.com.* Retrieved on July 11, 2008 from http://www.fox16.com/news/local/story.aspx?content_id=add62b3f-a938-4f6c-95cd-3045c3b651af

its ability to return a desirable outcome immediately.[45] Our attraction to a choice is usually a reflection of our ability to imagine or mentally simulate good outcomes.[46] In a direct examination of people's ability to think positively in a prisoner's dilemma game, participants were instructed to think about some alternatives that were "worse" or "better" than what actually happened; then they played some more. The results were startling: Negotiators' subsequent cooperation with their partner was directly related to the number of best-case scenarios they generated, and negotiators who generated worst-case scenarios defected a lot.[47] The message? Thinking about how good we can be greatly increases cooperation.

How to Encourage Cooperation in Social Dilemmas When Parties Should Not Collude

In the examples thus far, we've suggested ways negotiators can entice others to cooperate. However, in many situations, it is illegal for parties to cooperate. Consider, for example, the problem of price-fixing among companies within an industry. One example concerns how a pharmaceutical company might respond to the entry of a new competitor in a particular class of a drug. Brett suggests the following principles to encourage cooperation in social dilemmas when companies should not privately collude:[48]

- *Keep your strategy simple.*   The simpler your strategy, the easier it is for your competitors to predict your behavior. The correspondence is nearly one-to-one between uncertainty and competitive behavior: Greater uncertainty leads to more competitive behavior;[49] thus it helps to minimize uncertainty for your competitors.
- *Signal via actions.*   The adage that behaviors speak louder than words is important.
- *Do not be the first to defect.*   As we have seen, it is difficult to recover from escalating spirals of defection. Thus, do not be the first to defect.
- *Focus on your own payoffs, not your payoffs relative to others.*   Social dilemmas trigger competitive motives (as discussed in Chapter 5). The competitive motive is a desire to "beat" the other party. Instead, focus on your profits.
- *Be sensitive to egocentric bias.*   As we discussed, most people view their own behavior as more cooperative than that of others. We see ourselves as more virtuous, more ethical, and less competitive than others see us. When planning your strategy, consider the fact that your competitors will see you less favorably than you perceive yourself.

[45]Anderson, C. M., & Camerer, C. (2000). Experience-weighted attraction learning in sender-receiver signaling games. *Economic Theory, 16,* 689–718; Camerer, C., & Ho, T. H. (1998). Experience-weighted attraction learning in coordination games: Probability rules, heterogeneity, and time-variation. *Journal of Mathematical Psychology, 42,* 305–326; Camerer, C., & Ho, T. H. (1999). Experience-weighted attraction learning in games: Estimates from weak-link games. In D. V. Budescu, I. Erev, & R. Zwick (Eds.), *Games and human behavior* (pp. 31–51). Mahwah, NJ: Erlbaum; Camerer, C., & Ho, T. H. (1999). Experience-weighted attraction learning in normal form games. *Econometrica, 67,* 827–874.
[46]Parks, C. D., Sanna, L. J., & Posey, D. C. (2003). Retrospection in social dilemmas: How thinking about the past affects future cooperation. *Journal of Personality and Social Psychology, 84*(5), 988–996.
[47]Ibid.
[48]Brett, J. M. (2007). *Negotiating globally: How to negotiate deals, resolve disputes, and make decisions across cultural boundaries* (2nd ed). San Francisco: Jossey-Bass.
[49]Kopelman, Weber, & Messick, "Factors influencing cooperation."

ESCALATION OF COMMITMENT

Suppose you make a small investment in a start-up Internet company that seems to have great potential. After the first quarter, you learn that the company suffered an operating loss. You cannot recover your investment; your goal is to maximize your long-term wealth. Should you continue to invest in the company? Consider two possible choices in this situation:

1. Losing the small amount of money you have already invested
2. Taking additional risk by investing more money in the company, which could turn around and make a large profit or plummet even further

The reference point effect described in Chapter 2 would predict that most negotiators would continue to invest in the company because they have already adopted a "loss frame" based upon their initial investment. Suppose you recognize that the Internet company did not perform well in the first period and you consider your initial investment to be a sunk cost—that is, water under the bridge. In short, you adapt your reference point. Now, ask yourself which of the following would be the wiser choice:

1. Not invest in the company at this point (a sure outcome of $0)
2. Take a gamble and invest more money in a company that has not shown good performance in the recent past

Under these circumstances, most people choose not to invest in the company because they would rather have a sure thing than a loss. A negotiator's psychological reference point also influences the tendency to fall into the escalation trap. Recall that negotiators are risk-seeking when it comes to losses and risk-averse for gains. When negotiators see themselves as trying to recover from a losing position, chances are they engage in greater risk than if they see themselves as starting with a clean slate. Like the gambler in Las Vegas, negotiators who are hoping to hold out longer than their opponent (as in a strike) have fallen into the escalation trap. Most decision makers and negotiators do not readjust their reference point. Rather, they fail to adapt their reference point and continue to make risky decisions, which often prove unprofitable.

The **escalation of commitment** refers to the unfortunate tendency of negotiators to persist with a losing course of action, even in the face of clear evidence that their behaviors are not working and the negotiation situation is quickly deteriorating. The two types of escalation dilemmas are personal and interpersonal. In both cases, the dilemma is revealed when a person would do something different if he or she had not already been involved in the situation.

Personal escalation dilemmas involve only one person, and the dilemma concerns whether to continue with what appears to be a losing course of action or to cut one's losses. Continuing to gamble after losing a lot of money, investing money in a car or house that continues to malfunction or deteriorate, and waiting in long lines that are not moving are examples of personal escalation dilemmas. To stop, in some sense, is to admit failure and accept a sure loss. Continuing to invest holds the possibility of recouping losses.

Interpersonal escalation dilemmas involve two or more people, often in a competitive relationship, such as negotiation. Union strikes are often escalation dilemmas, and so is war. Consider the situation faced by Lyndon Johnson during the early years of the

Vietnam War. Johnson received the following memo from George Ball, then undersecretary of state:

> The decision you face now is crucial. Once large numbers of U.S. troops are committed to direct combat, they will begin to take heavy casualties in a war they are ill-equipped to fight in a noncooperative if not downright hostile countryside. Once we suffer large casualties, we will have started a well-nigh irreversible process. Our involvement will be so great that we cannot—without national humiliation—stop short of achieving our complete objectives. Of the two possibilities I think humiliation will be more likely than the achievement of our objectives—even after we have paid terrible costs. [50]

In escalation dilemmas, negotiators commit further resources to what appears to unbiased observers to be a failing course of action. In most cases, people fall into escalation traps because initially the situation does not appear to be a losing enterprise. The situation becomes an escalation dilemma when the persons involved in the decision would make a different decision if they had not been involved up until that point, or when other objective persons would not choose that course of action. Often, in escalation situations, a decision is made to commit further resources to "turn the situation around," such as in the case of gambling (personal dilemma) or making a final offer (interpersonal dilemma). The bigger the investment and the more severe the possible loss, the more prone people are to try to turn things around.

The escalation of commitment process is illustrated in Exhibit 11-9. [51] In the first stage of the escalation of commitment, a person is confronted with questionable or

---

EXHIBIT 11-9   Escalation of Commitment

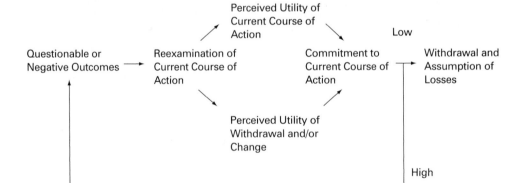

Source: Adapted from Ross, J., & Staw, B. M. (1993, August). Organizational escalation and exit: Lessons from the Shoreham Nuclear Power Plant. *Academy of Management Journal, 36*(4), 701–732. Reprinted by permission.

---

[50]*The Pentagon papers.* (1971). As published by *The New York Times,* based on the investigative reporting by Neil Sheehan, written by Neil Sheehan [and others]. Articles and documents edited by G. Gold, A. M. Siegal, and S. Abt. New York, Toronto: Bantam.
[51]Ross, J., & Staw, B. M. (1993, August). Organizational escalation and exit: Lessons from the Shoreham Nuclear Power Plant. *Academy of Management Journal, 36*(4), 701–732.

negative outcomes (e.g., a rejection of one's offer by the counterparty, decrease in market share, poor performance evaluation, a malfunction, or hostile behavior from a competitor). This external event prompts a reexamination of the negotiator's current course of action, in which the utility of continuing is weighted against the utility of withdrawing or changing course. This decision determines the negotiator's commitment to his or her current course of action. If this commitment is low, the negotiator may make a concession, engage in integrative negotiations (rather than distributive negotiations), or possibly revert to his or her BATNA. If this commitment is high, however, the negotiator will continue commitment and continue to cycle through the decision stages.

When negotiators receive indication that the outcomes of a negotiation may be negative, they should ask themselves, "What are the personal rewards for me in this situation?" In many cases, the *process* of the negotiation itself, rather than the *outcome* of the negotiation, becomes the reason for commencing or continuing negotiations. This reasoning leads to a self-perpetuating reinforcement trap, wherein the rewards for continuing are not aligned with the actual objectives of the negotiator. Ironically, people who have high, rather than low, self-esteem are more likely to become victimized by psychological forces; people with high self-esteem have much more invested in their ego and its maintenance than do those with low self-esteem.[52] Sometimes face-saving concerns lead negotiators to escalate commitment; some negotiators worry they will look silly or stupid if they back down from an initial position. Ego protection often becomes a higher priority than the success of the negotiation.

Avoiding the Escalation of Commitment in Negotiations

Most negotiators do not realize they are in an escalation dilemma until it is too late. Complicating matters is the fact that, in most escalation dilemmas, a negotiator (like a gambler) might have some early "wins" or good signs that reinforce their initial position. How can a negotiator best get out of an escalation dilemma?

The best advice is to adopt a policy of risk management: Be aware of the risks involved in the situation; learn how to best manage these risks; and set limits, effectively capping losses at a tolerable level. It is also important to find ways to get information and feedback about the negotiation from a different perspective.

Set Limits
Ideally, a negotiator should have a clearly defined BATNA. At no point should a negotiator make or accept an offer that is worse than his or her BATNA.

Avoid Decision Myopia
A negotiator should get several perspectives on the situation. Ask people who are not personally involved in the negotiation for their appraisal. Be careful not to bias their evaluation with your own views, hopes, expectations, or other details, such as the cost of extricating yourself from the situation, because that will only predispose them toward your point of view, which is not what you want—you want an honest, critical assessment.

---

[52]Taylor, S. E., & Brown, J. (1988). Illusion and well-being: A social-psychological perspective. *Psychological Bulletin, 103,* 193–210.

Recognize Sunk Costs

Probably the most powerful way to escape escalation of commitment is to simply recognize and accept **sunk costs**, which are basically water under the bridge: money (or other commitments) previously spent that cannot be recovered. It is often helpful for negotiators to consider removal of the project, product, or program. In this way, the situation is redefined as one in which a decision will be made immediately about whether to invest; that is, if you were making the initial decision today, would you make the investment currently under consideration (as a continuing investment), or would you choose another course of action? If the decision is not one you would choose anew, you might want to start thinking about how to terminate the project and move on to the next one.

Diversify Responsibility and Authority

In some cases, it is necessary to remove or replace the original negotiators from deliberations precisely because they are biased. One way to carry out such a removal is with an external review: appointing someone who does not have a personal stake in the situation.

Redefine the Situation

Often, it helps to view the situation not as the "same old problem" but as a new one. Furthermore, it often helps to change the decision criteria. For example, Indonesia's state-owned oil and gas company, PT Pertamina, and Exxon Mobil eventually resolved a dispute over a plan to develop the country's Cepu oil field, years after negotiations began, by redefining the situation. Negotiations with Exxon were exhausted over who would manage the oil field. Pertamina demanded that control should alternate between Exxon and Pertamina every 5 years during the 30-year contract Exxon signed with the Indonesian government in September 2006. When a new president director of Pertamina, Ari Sumarno, was elected, he quickly dropped the demand, opening the way for an agreement. The original issue over control was redefined: Instead of alternating control, it was agreed that Exxon would appoint the organization's general manager, while a Pertamina executive would be deputy general manager.[53]

CONCLUSION

Prisoner's dilemmas and social dilemmas are characterized by the absence of contracts and enforcement mechanisms. In these dilemmas, people choose between acting in a self-interested fashion or in a cooperative fashion, which makes the negotiator vulnerable to exploitation. Strategic pie-expanding and pie-slicing strategies in the two-person prisoner's dilemma can be achieved via the tit-for-tat strategy, but tit-for-tat works only with two players in a repeated game. However, many tacit negotiations within and between organizations involve more than two players and are called social dilemmas. The best way to ensure cooperation in social dilemmas is to align incentives, monitor behavior, practice regulation and privatization, use tradable permits, communicate with involved parties, personalize others, and focus on the benefits of cooperation. Escalation dilemmas occur when people invest in what is (by any objective standards) a losing course of action. People can deescalate via setting limits, getting several perspectives, recognizing sunk costs, diversifying responsibility, and redefining the situation.

---

[53]Pura, R. and Sudrajat, D. (2006, March 14). Energy: Exxon, Pertamina end dispute over $2 billion Indonesia oil field. *Wall Street Journal*, p. A13.

CHAPTER

Negotiating Via Information Technology

12

During the 2007–2008 Writers Guild of America (WGA) strike, both the guild leadership and the Hollywood studios kept an eye on the blog *www.artfulwriter.com*, demonstrating how powerful the Internet can be when used as a public sounding board during union negotiations. Traffic on the Web site increased as the debate between the two sides heated up. The negotiations intensified when the union set a deadline for a strike authorization vote and some of the bargaining sessions buckled. The main issue in the negotiations was concern about compensation for the use of content on the Internet and other digital platforms.[1] As the talks continued, writers began to use the blog as a place to publicly discuss what needed to be done next. When screenwriter Craig Mazin, co-writer of *Scary Movie 3,* decided to post on the blog about his reasons for voting "yes" to authorize a strike, 180 comments were posted from his readers, some identifying themselves, others remaining anonymous. Hollywood began looking to the blog for indicators of how guild members felt about a strike, and Mazin claimed that he got "nervous calls from the guild" about some of his posts. "The blog has been a bit of a touchstone and a bellwether as a place where I can go either as a board member or as a writer to take the temperature reading," said Aaron Mendelsohn, a WGA board member who was also a member of the union's negotiating committee. "There's no water cooler, so often writers have to turn to these message boards and blogs to get a sense of what everyone else is thinking," he added.

This chapter examines the impact of information technology on negotiation, with a particular focus on electronic negotiations (e-negotiations). We describe a model of social interaction, the place-time model, and use it to evaluate the impact of information technology on negotiation. The model focuses on negotiators who either negotiate in the same or different physical location and at the same or different time. For each of these cases, we describe what to expect and ways to deal with the limitations of that communication mode. We follow this discussion with a section on

---

[1]Sanders, P. (2007, October 10). Blog is Hollywood's must-see; Screenwriters check in as the plot thickens in talks for contract. *Wall Street Journal,* p. B4.

how information technology affects negotiation behavior. We then describe strategies to help negotiators expand and divide the pie effectively.

PLACE-TIME MODEL OF SOCIAL INTERACTION

The **place-time model** describes four models of interaction: same place + same time; different place + different time; same place + different time; different place + same time (Exhibit 12-1).[2] As might be suspected, negotiation behavior unfolds differently in face-to-face situations than in electronic forums.

One consideration is **richness**, or the potential information-carrying capacity of the communication medium.[3] Face-to-face communication is relatively "rich," whereas formal, written messages, such as memos and business correspondence, are relatively "lean" (see Exhibit 12-2).[4] Face-to-face communication conveys the richest information because it allows for the simultaneous observation of multiple clues, including body language, facial expression, and tone of voice, thereby providing people with a greater awareness of context. In contrast, formal numerical documentation conveys the least-rich information, providing few clues about the context. In addition, geographical propinquity and time constraints affect negotiations.

Let's consider each of the four types of communications in the place-time model in greater detail.

Face-to-Face Communication

Face-to-face negotiation is the clear preference of most negotiators and rightly so. Face-to-face contact is crucial in the initiation of relationships and collaborations, and people are more cooperative when interacting face-to-face than via other forms of communication.

EXHIBIT 12-1 Place-Time Model of Interaction

	Same Place	Different Place
Same Time	Face-to-face	Telephone Videoconference
Different Time	Single text editing Shift work	E-mail Voice mail

---

[2]See also Englebart, D. (1989, November). Bootstrapping organizations into the 21st century. Paper presented at a seminar at the Software Engineering Institute, Pittsburgh, PA; Johansen, R. (1988). *Groupware: Computer support for business teams*. New York: Free Press.
[3]Drolet, A. L., & Morris, M. W. (2000). Rapport in conflict resolution: Accounting for how nonverbal exchange fosters cooperation on mutually beneficial settlements to mixed-motive conflicts. *Journal of Experimental Social Psychology, 36,* 26–50.
[4]Daft, R. L., & Lengel, R. H. (1984). Information richness: A new approach to managerial behavior and organization design. *Research in Organization Behavior, 6,* 191–223; Daft, R. L., Lengel, R. H., & Trevino, L. K. (1987). Message equivocality, media selection, and manager performance: Implications for information systems. *MIS Quarterly, 11*(3), 355–366.

EXHIBIT 12-2   Psychological Distancing Model

FACE-TO-FACE (Kinetic, Visual, Paralinguistic, Linguistic)	TWO-WAY TV (Visual, Paralinguistic, Linguistic)	TELEPHONE (Paralinguistic, Linguistic)	COMPUTER MESSAGING (Linguistic)

CLOSE ———————————— PSYCHOLOGICAL ———————————— REMOTE
DISTANCE

Source: Adapted from Wellens, A. R. (1989, September). Effects of telecommunication media upon information sharing and team performance: Some theoretical and empirical findings. *IEEE AES Magazine*, p. 14.

Face-to-face negotiations are particularly important when negotiators meet for the first time. This meeting is when norms of interaction are established and when misunderstandings should be resolved. Negotiators are more cooperative when interacting face-to-face than over the telephone.[5] Face-to-face communication (as opposed to using the telephone) fosters the development of interpersonal synchrony and rapport and thus leads to more trusting, cooperative behavior.[6] Face-to-face meetings are ideal for wrestling with complex negotiations. "Nearly any mode of communication during bargaining increases the efficiency of outcomes."[7] According to Valley and colleagues, who investigated face-to-face versus writing-only and telephone negotiations, face-to-face negotiators reach more integrative (win-win) outcomes and more balanced distributions of surplus (even pie-slicing) than writing-only or telephone negotiations.[8] Further, writing-only negotiations had a higher incidence of impasse, and telephone negotiations increased the likelihood of losing buyers and highly profitable sellers.

In most companies, the incidence and frequency of face-to-face communication are nearly perfectly predicted by how closely people are located to one another: Employees who work in the same office or on the same floor communicate much more frequently than those located on different floors or in different buildings. And, a few paces can have a huge impact. For example, communication frequency between R&D researchers drops off logarithmically after only 5 to 10 meters of distance between offices.[9] Workers

[5]Drolet & Morris, "Rapport in conflict resolution."
[6]Ibid.
[7]Valley, K. L., Moag, J., & Bazerman, M. H. (1998). A matter of trust: Effects of communication on the efficiency and distribution of outcomes (p. 212). *Journal of Economic Behavior and Organizations, 34,* 211–238.
[8]Ibid.
[9]Allen, T. J. (1977). *Managing the flow of technology: Technology transfer and the dissemination of technological information within the R&D organization.* Cambridge, MA: MIT Press.

in adjacent offices communicate twice as often as those in offices on the same floor, including via e-mail and telephone transmissions.[10]

Just what do people get out of face-to-face contact that makes it so important for smooth negotiations? First, face-to-face communication is easier and therefore more likely to occur than are other forms of communication. We underestimate how many negotiations occur from chance encounters, which virtually never happen in any mode but face-to-face because of perceived effort. Negotiations of opportunity are very important for long-term business success.

Second, although it is seldom consciously realized, people rely primarily on nonverbal signals to help them conduct social interactions. One estimate is that 93% of the meaning of messages is contained in the nonverbal part of communication, such as voice intonation.[11] (See also Appendix 2 on nonverbal communication.) For example, journalist Paul Andrews spent several weeks researching car shopping in hopes of using the indexing and search capabilities of the Web and making further offers and negotiating via e-mail. However, once all forms were filled in, the journalist got numerous e-mails from local dealerships. None would give him the price and all wanted to talk it over.[12] Perhaps this nonverbal factor is why business executives endure the inconvenience of travel across thousands of miles and several time zones so they can negotiate face-to-face.

The emphasis on the human factor is not just old-fashioned business superstition. Important behavioral, cognitive, and emotional processes are set into motion when people meet face-to-face. Face-to-face negotiation allows people to develop rapport—the feeling of being "in sync" or "on the same wavelength" with another person—and rapport is a powerful determinant of whether they develop trust. Nonverbal (body orientation, gesture, eye contact, head nodding) and paraverbal (speech fluency, use of "uh-huhs," etc.) behaviors are key to building rapport. When the person we are negotiating with sits at a greater distance; has an indirect body orientation, backward lean, and crossed arms; and avoids eye contact, we feel less rapport than when the same person sits with a forward lean and an open body posture and maintains steady eye contact.

However, we do not always have the luxury of meeting face-to-face. People often turn to the telephone, but even then, people do not always reach their party. Some estimates suggest up to 70% of initial telephone attempts fail to reach the intended party.[13]

Same Time, Different Place

The same-time, different-place mode, in which people negotiate in real time but are not physically in the same place, is often the alternative to face-to-face negotiations. The most common means is via telephone (telephone tag is different time, different place); videoconferencing is another example. Hewlett-Packard (HP) and other tech-

---

[10]Galegher, J., Kraut, R. E., & Egido, C. (Eds.). (1990). *Intellectual teamwork: Social and technological foundations of cooperative work.* Hillsdale, NJ: Erlbaum.

[11]Meherabian, A. (1971). *Silent messages.* Belmont, CA: Wadsworth.

[12]Andrews, P. (2005, February 28). Web hasn't transformed car shopping. *Seattle Times,* p. C1.

[13]Philip, G., & Young, E. S. (1987). Man-machine interaction by voice: Developments in speech technology. Part I: The state-of-the-art. *Journal of Information Science, 13,* 3–14.

nology firms began to sell something called "telepresence"—an improved version of videoconferencing with better speed and quality of transmission. HP charges $350,000, Cisco up to $299,000, for every such room. Videoconferencing leaders Polycom and Tandberg are also switching to telepresence.[14]

In telephone conversations, people lack facial cues; in videoconferencing, they lack real-time social cues, such as pauses, mutual gaze, and another person's nonverbal response to what is being said (looking away, rolling their eyes, or shaking or nodding their head).

Next, we identify four key challenges to same-time, different-place negotiations.

Loss of Informal Communication

Probably the most limiting aspect of same-time, different-place negotiations is the inability to chat informally in the hall or inside offices. The impromptu and casual conversations that negotiators have in a restroom, by a water cooler, or walking back from lunch are often where the most difficult problems are solved and the most important interpersonal issues are addressed. Often, stalemated negotiations get resolved outside of the official bargaining forum. Beyond a short distance, people do not benefit from the spontaneous exchanges that occur outside of formal meetings. Many companies clearly realize the informal communication that occurs in their organizations is what is most important and most critical, and they are doing something about it. For example, instant messaging is used on an increasing basis among employees in companies. Written as short, rapid responses, instant messages are used to schedule one-on-one meetings and for "back channel" communications during sales calls.[15] However, they can be more prone to spontaneous emotion than e-mail.

Lost Opportunity

Negotiations do not occur just when people are in disagreement and haggling over scarce resources. In fact, many negotiations are negotiations of opportunity—something like entrepreneurial joint ventures. Negotiations of opportunity, because they are not planned, usually occur during informal, chance encounters.

Separation of Feedback

Another negative impact of physical separation is the absence of feedback. Greater distance tends to block the corrective feedback loops provided in face-to-face negotiations. One manager contrasted how employees who worked in his home office negotiated with him, compared to employees 15 kilometers away.[16] Engineers in the home office would drop by and catch him in the hall or at lunch: "I heard you were planning to change project X," they would say. "Let me tell you why that would be stupid." The manager would listen to their points, clarify some details, and all would part better informed. In contrast, employees at the remote site would greet his weekly visit with formally

---

[14]Business: Far away yet strangely personal; Behold, telepresence. (2007, August). *The Economist, 384*(8543), 63.

[15]Shaw, R.(2003, November 12). Workplace messaging offers rewards, risks. *Investors' Business Daily.*

[16]Armstrong, D. J., & Cole, P. (1995). Managing distances and differences in geographically distributed work groups. In S. E. Jackson & M. N. Ruderman (Eds.), *Diversity in work teams: Research paradigms for a changing workplace* (pp. 187–215). Washington, DC: American Psychological Association.

prepared objections, which took much longer to discuss and were rarely resolved as completely as the more informal hallway discussions. In short, negotiators interacting remotely do not get the coincidental chances to detect and correct problems on a casual basis.

Friedman and Currall's model of the four key problems with e-mail cite diminished feedback as a key, causal determinant of conflict escalation, along with minimized social cues, excessively long e-mails, and anger.[17]

Negotiation Timing

Conflicts are expressed, recognized, and addressed more quickly if negotiators work in close proximity. A manager can spot a problem and "nip it in the bud" if he or she works near his or her employees. When people are physically separated, the issues are more likely to go unresolved; this tendency contributes to an escalating cycle of destructive negotiation behavior.

Although many disadvantages of distance can be listed when it comes to negotiation, it is not always a liability for negotiators. The formality of a scheduled phone meeting can compel each party to better prepare for the negotiation and to address the issues more efficiently. Also, it can create a "buffer zone" between parties, meaning it might be a good thing if one party does not see the other rolling his or her eyes.

Different Time, Same Place

In the different-time, same-place mode, negotiators interact asynchronously but have access to the same physical document or space. An example might be shift workers who pick up the task left for them by the previous shift; another example would be two collaborators working on the same electronic document. One colleague finishes and then gives the text to a partner, who further edits and develops it. Although people seldom realize it, they negotiate quite frequently in an asynchronous fashion.

Different Place, Different Time

In the different-place, different-time model, negotiators communicate asynchronously in different places. Just as the telephone became an important medium for working out deals, the Internet is rapidly becoming the medium of choice for many "technobargainers."[18] The most common example is electronic mail (e-mail): Jerry, who is in Seattle, sends a message to Sally, who is in Japan. With e-mail, parties do not have to be available simultaneously for negotiation to occur.[19] For example, nearly half of all mortgage shoppers use the Internet to do research on mortgages. When borrowers are

---

[17]Friedman, R., & Currall, S. (2003). Conflict escalation: Dispute exacerbating elements of e-mail communication. *Human Relations, 56*(11), 1325–1347.

[18]Kiser, K. (Oct. 1, 1999). The new deal. *Training. 36*(10), 116-126.

[19]For an overview of the dynamics of e-mail negotiation, see Nadler, J., & Shestowsky, D. (2006). Negotiation, information technology, and the problem of the faceless other. In L. Thompson (Ed.), *Negotiation theory and research* (pp. 145–172), New York: Psychology Press, Taylor & Francis Group; Thompson, L., & Nadler, J. (2002). Negotiating via information technology: Theory and application. *Journal of Social Issues, 58*(1), 109–124; McGinn, K. L., and Wilson, E. J. (2004, March). How to negotiate successfully online. *Negotiation, 2*(3), 3–5; McGinn, K. L., & Croson, R. (2004). What do communication media mean for negotiations? A question of social awareness. In M. Gelfand & J. Brett (Eds.), *The handbook of negotiation and culture: Theoretical advances and cultural perspectives and negotiation* (pp. 334–349). Palo Alto, CA: Stanford University Press.

ready to buy a home, they may submit financial information on Web sites such as *LowerMyBills.com* and *LendingTree.com* and then receive loan offers, via e-mail, from lenders and brokers.[20]

We identify four key biases that affect the ability of people to negotiate via e-mail.

Temporal Synchrony Bias

The **temporal synchrony bias** is the tendency for negotiators to behave as if they are communicating synchronously when in fact they are not. certainly E-negotiators are aware that e-mail is, in fact, asynchronous communication, but they often discount this or ignore some of its implications. One of the aspects of negotiation that negotiators like is the ability to make proposals and counteroffers, almost in a tennis-game-like fashion. Raiffa refers to this interaction as the "negotiation dance."[21] However, e-negotiations disrupt the natural dance of face-to-face negotiation. There is less turn-taking in negotiations conducted via e-mail than in face-to-face negotiations.[22] Moreover, the volume of turn-taking or "dancing" within negotiations predicts schmoozing behavior (e.g., small talk) and facilitates trust and rapport.[23]

Conversational turn-taking makes the process of negotiation seem smoother and more natural, but it also serves an important informational function: It allows people to correct misunderstandings immediately, which is somewhat similar to the double-loop learning idea (Chapter 1). In face-to-face interactions, receivers and senders typically engage in a process of rapid correction of information.[24] However, in e-negotiations, negotiators are faced with the mysterious task of interpreting impoverished communication without the opportunity for clarification. Thus, e-negotiators are forced to make more assumptions than face-to-face negotiators. Indeed, e-negotiators ask fewer clarifying questions than do face-to-face negotiators.[25]

Burned Bridge Bias

The **burned bridge bias** is the tendency for e-negotiators to engage in more risky interpersonal behaviors (e.g., making threats and demands and ultimatums) in an impoverished medium than they do when face-to-face. When people communicate face-to-face, they conform to what psychologists call a "politeness ritual," in which they nod, smile, make direct eye contact, and make verbalizations ("uh-huh," etc.) that affirm the other person and strengthen the relationship between negotiators. Thus, the politeness ritual sets the stage for trust and rapport between negotiators who are navigating a mixed-motive relationship. Indeed, negotiators who are successful in building positive rapport are more

---

[20]Tedeschi, B. (2008, January 13). Getting started, via the Web. *New York Times* (Real Estate Desk), p. 6.
[21]Raiffa, H. (1982). *The art and science of negotiation.* Cambridge, MA: Belknap.
[22]Morris, M. W., Nadler, J., Kurtzberg, T., & Thompson, L. (2002). Schmooze or lose: Social friction and lubrication in e-mail negotiations. *Group Dynamics: Theory, Research, and Practice, 6*(1), 89–100.
[23]Ibid.
[24]Higgins, E. T. (1999). "Saying is believing" effects: When sharing reality about something biases knowledge and evaluations. In L. Thompson, J. M. Levine, & D. M. Messick (Eds.), *Shared cognition in organizations: The management of knowledge.* Mahwah, NJ: Erlbaum; Krauss, R. M., & Chiu, C. (1998). Language and social behavior. In D. T. Gilbert, S. T. Fiske, & G. Lindzey (Eds.), *The handbook of social psychology* (4th ed.) (pp. 41–88). New York: McGraw-Hill.
[25]Morris et al., "Schmooze or lose."

likely to build trust.[26] For this reason, evaluators in performance appraisals offer more negative feedback to their peers when using e-mail than when using traditional paper-form methods.[27] E-mail appraisers report lower feelings of social obligation.

Several reasons explain why e-negotiators may burn relationship bridges. First, they experience less personal accountability for the relationship. E-negotiations occur in a social vacuum. In contrast, face-to-face negotiations often take place in a richly grounded social network; in this sense, individuals feel greater accountability for their behaviors.[28] Indeed, observers of face-to-face interactions are able to immediately assess the "felt rapport" between interactants. Further, observers appear to pay attention to the right cues: The greater the synchrony of the nonverbal displays, the more likely an outsider will judge that a high level of rapport is present in the interaction.[29]

Second, negotiators often use more aggressive strategies because they don't think about the future of their relationship. Again, the accountability factor plays a role with many e-communicators failing to recognize their e-communications are permanent. Even though e-mails can be "deleted," they are actually retrievable from most computer systems. Yet people act as if the messages are ephemeral.[30] For example, in his congressional hearing, Oliver North was extremely careful in his spoken interviews (presumably aware that the camera was on him, indelibly recording every utterance); however, he was obviously much more lax in his computer mail.[31]

Squeaky Wheel Bias

The **squeaky wheel bias** is the tendency for negotiators to adopt an adversarial negotiation style (similar to the demanding, negative emotional style described in Chapter 5) when communicating via e-mail—whereas the same negotiator might use a positive emotional style in a face-to-face interaction. Indeed, people are more likely to engage in counternormative social behavior when interacting via e-mail.[32] They focus more on the content of the task and less on the etiquette of the situation. For example, bad news is conveyed to superiors with less delay through e-mail than in face-to-face encounters.[33] In a direct comparison of face-to-face negotiations versus e-negotiations, people negotiating via e-mail were more likely to negatively confront one other.[34] Rude, impulsive behavior, such as "flaming," increases when people interact through e-mail, in part because people pay more attention to the content of the message and less attention to the style of the message. One investigation of flaming suggests that people are eight times more likely to flame in e-communication than in face-to-face

[26]Ibid.

[27]Kurtzberg, T., Naquin, C., & Belkin, L. (2005). Electronic performance appraisals: The effects of e-mail communication on peer ratings in actual and simulated environments. *Organizational Behavior and Human Decision Processes, 98*, 216–226.

[28]Wicklund, R. A., & Gollwitzer, P. M. (1982). *Symbolic self-completion.* Hillsdale, NJ: Erlbaum.

[29]Bernieri, F. J. (1991). Interpersonal sensitivity in teaching interactions. *Personality and Social Psychology Bulletin, 17*(1), 98–103; Bernieri, F. J., Davis, J., Rosenthal, R., & Knee, C. (1994). Interactional synchrony and rapport: Measuring synchrony in displays devoid of sound and facial affect. *Personality and Social Psychology Bulletin, 20*, 303–311.

[30]Sproull, L., & Keisler, S. (1991). *Connections: New ways of working in the networked organization.* Cambridge, MA: MIT Press.

[31]Ibid.

[32]Keisler, S., & Sproull, L. (1992). Group decision making and communication technology. *Organizational Behavior and Human Decision Processes, 52*, 96–123.

[33]Sproull & Keisler, *Connections.*

[34]Morris et al., "Schmooze or lose."

communication.[35] Conflict escalates more quickly and frequently in e-negotiations, which creates a roadblock to effective integrative negotiation.

In a study of disputes on SquareTrade, an online mediation service that deals with disputes that arise on eBay, the expression of anger by disputants decreases the likelihood that disputants will resolve their dispute. The reason is that the anger expressed by one party generates an angry response from the other party.[36] Examinations of the text data from these eBay disputes among buyers and sellers revealed a higher likelihood of settlement when people provided a causal account of the dispute and a lower likelihood of settlement when they expressed negative emotions or made commands.[37]

When social context cues are missing or weak, people feel distant from others and somewhat anonymous. They are less concerned about making a good impression, and humor tends to fall apart or to be misinterpreted. The expression of negative emotion is no longer minimized because factors that keep people from expressing negative emotion are not in place when they communicate via information technology. Simply, in the absence of social norms that prescribe the expression of positive emotion, people are more likely to express negative emotion. One MBA student lost a job when he sent his supervisor an e-mail message that was perceived as insensitive. The student was using e-mail to renegotiate his job responsibilities and proceeded to outline what he saw as problems within the organization and the people who were running it. Shortly thereafter, he was called into a meeting with the senior staff, and everyone was holding a copy of his e-mail.[38] Not surprisingly, the tendency for people to "flame" one another via e-mail has led some to attempt to humanize e-communication.

Sinister Attribution Bias

People often misattribute the behavior of others to their underlying character traits while ignoring the influence of temporary, situational factors.[39] The **sinister attribution bias** refers to the tendency for e-communicators to ascribe diabolical intentions to the other party.[40] Kramer coined the term "sinister attribution error" to refer to the tendency of people to attribute malevolent motives to people we don't know or who represent the out-group.[41] Attributing sinister motives to out-group members is especially prevalent in e-communication in which the absence of social cues leads to feelings of social isolation and distance. Indeed, e-negotiators are more likely to mistrust and suspect the other party of lying or deceiving them, relative to negotiators interacting face-to-

---

[35]Dubrovsky, V. J., Keisler, S., & Sethna, B. N. (1991). The equalization phenomenon: Status effects in computer-mediated and face-to-face decision-making groups. *Human-Computer Interaction, 6*(2), 119–146.
[36]Friedman, R., Anderson, C., Brett, J., Olekalns, M., Goates, N., & Lisco, C. (2004). The positive and negative effects of anger on dispute resolution: Evidence from electronically mediated disputes. *Journal of Applied Psychology, 89*(2), 369–376.
[37]Brett, J., Olekalns, M., Friedman, R., Goates, N., Anderson, C., & Lisco, C. (2007). Sticks and stones: Language, face, and online dispute resolution. *Academy of Management Journal, 50*(1), 85–99.
[38]Kaiser, "The new deal."
[39]Ross, L. (1977). The intuitive psychologist and his shortcomings: Distortions in the attribution process. In L. Berkowitz (Ed.), *Advances in experimental social psychology: Vol. 10* (pp. 173–220). Orlando, FL: Academic Press.
[40]Thompson & Nadler, "Negotiating via information technology".
[41]Kramer, R. M. (1995). Dubious battle: Heightened accountability, dysphoric cognition, and self-defeating bargaining behavior. In R. Kramer & D. Messick (Eds.), *Negotiation as a social process* (pp. 95–120). Thousand Oaks, CA: Sage.
[42]Fortune, A., & Brodt, S. (2000). Face to face or virtually, for the second time around: The influence of task, past experience, and media on trust and deception in negotiation. Working paper, Duke University, Fuqua School of Business, Durham, NC.

face.[42] Yet e-negotiators were, in fact, no more likely than face-to-face negotiators to deceive the other party. In short, the situation provided no factual basis to fuel the increased suspicion of the other party.

A key question concerns how information technology affects negotiation performance. Exhibit 12-3 summarizes the main findings concerning how information technology—and in particular, e-negotiations—affects economic measures of performance (level 1 integrative agreements, distributive outcomes) and social measures of

EXHIBIT 12-3 Information Technology's Effect on Negotiator Performance

	E-negotiations vs. Face-to-Face	Enhanced E-negotiations (via schmoozing, in-group status, etc.) vs. Nonenhanced E-negotiations
Impasse rates (finding the ZOPA)		Brief personal disclosure over e-mail reduces likelihood of impasse. Out-group negotiations result in more impasses than in-group negotiations.
Integrative behavior (e.g., multi-issue offers)	E-negotiators make more multi-issue offers.	Brief telephone call prior to e-negotiations improves joint outcomes.
Pie size (expanding the pie)	Mixed results, with some investigations finding that face-to-face results in better joint profits; other studies indicating no difference.	
Distributive behaviors (e.g., threats, etc.)		Negotiators concerned about group's reputation use more aggressive strategies, leading to lower outcomes than negotiators focused on own reputation.
Pie-slicing (distributive outcomes)	Computer-mediated negotiations result in more equal pie-slices than do face-to-face.	
Trust and rapport	Less rapport in e-negotiations.	Brief telephone call prior to e-negotiation increases cooperation and relationship quality. Negotiators who attempt to build rapport build more trust than those who try to dominate.

Source: Table partially based on Thompson, L., & Nadler, J. (2002). Negotiating via information technology: Theory and application. *Journal of Social Issues, 58*(1), 109–124.

performance (e.g., trust, respect, etc.)[43] Negotiators who communicate face-to-face are more likely to reach deals and avoid impasses than are e-negotiators. Further, the likelihood of reaching a mutually profitable negotiation (and avoiding impasse) is a function of the richness of the communication. For example, when negotiators are allowed to communicate in writing or face-to-face, they are more likely to settle in the ZOPA as compared to negotiators who do not interact and just make offers.[44] Considerable debate continues to surround the question of whether information technology hurts or hinders the ability of negotiators to expand the pie. When face-to-face negotiations were compared with computer-mediated negotiations, computer-mediated outcomes were equally or more integrative than were face-to-face outcomes.[45] Computer-mediated negotiations resulted in outcomes that were more fair, as judged in terms of being more equal in value.[46]

INFORMATION TECHNOLOGY AND ITS EFFECTS ON SOCIAL BEHAVIOR

In addition to affecting negotiated outcomes, information technology has an extremely powerful effect on social behavior in general.[47] Many people are surprised at their behavior when communicating via e-mail. To be successful, negotiators must understand how their own behavior is affected by technology.

Trust

Relative to face-to-face negotiations, people who negotiate online trust each other less even before beginning the negotiation, and trust each other less after the online interaction.[48] The low levels of trust negotiators have for one another even before the negotiation suggest that negotiators bring different expectations to electronic bargaining than to face-to-face negotiations. Not surprisingly, online negotiators report less desire for future relationships with the other party, less confidence in their performance, and less overall satisfaction.

Status and Power: The "Weak Get Strong" Effect

In face-to-face interactions, people do not contribute to conversation equally. Walk into any classroom, lunch discussion, or business meeting, and it will be immediately obvious that one person in a two-party group does most of the talking, and a handful of

---

[43]See also McGinn, K. L., & Croson, R. (2004). What do communication media mean for negotiations? A question of social awareness. In M. Gelfand & J. Brett (Eds.), *The handbook of negotiation and culture: Theoretical advances and cultural perspectives and negotiation*
(pp. 334–349). Palo Alto, CA: Stanford University Press.
[44]McGinn, K. L., Thompson, L., & Bazerman, M. H. (2003). Dyadic processes of disclosure and reciprocity in bargaining with communication. *Journal of Behavioral Decision Making, 16,* 17–34.
[45]Croson, R. (1999). Look at me when you say that: An electronic negotiation simulation. *Simulation and Gaming, 30*(1), 23–37.
[46]Ibid.
[47]Keisler & Sproull, "Group decision making."
[48]Naquin, C., & Paulson, G. (2003). Online bargaining and interpersonal trust. *Journal of Applied Psychology, 88*(1), 113–120.

people do more than 75% of the talking in a larger group. For example, in a typical four-person group, two people do more than 62% of the talking; in a six-person group, three people do over 70% of the talking; and in a group of eight, three people do 70% of the talking.[49] Even when performance depends on contributions, participation is not equal.

So who dominates most face-to-face discussions and negotiations? Almost without exception, status predicts domination. Higher-status people talk more, even if they are not experts on the subject. Not surprisingly, managers speak more than subordinates, and men speak more than women. If no inherent organizational status system is obvious, negotiators look for symbols of status such as gender, age, and race. However, such symbols are superficial. Situational factors also affect perceived status. The person who sits at the head of the table talks more than those on the sides, even if the seating arrangement is arbitrary.[50] Appearance can affect status: Those in business suits talk more than others. Dynamic cues can define status, such as nodding in approval, touching (high-status people touch those of lower status but not vice versa), hesitating, and frowning. For example, Channel 5 news in the United Kingdom had to announce a ban on "noddies"—staged occurrences of reporters reacting to interviewees—in a rather heavy-handed attempt to win back the trust of viewers. Astonishingly, the BBC's Alan Yentob was using shots of himself nodding along in interviews he did not conduct. The body-language specialist Robert Phipps describing the nod as a powerful aid to social interaction claims, "If you want others to agree with you just nod."[51]

What happens when negotiators interact via technology, such as electronic mail? The traditional status cues are missing, and the dynamic cues are distinctly less impactive, which has a dramatic effect on negotiation behavior. Power and status differences are minimized. People in traditionally weak positions in face-to-face negotiations become more powerful when communicating via information technology because status cues are harder to read.[52] In a direct test of this idea, some managers negotiate via e-mail and some negotiate via instant messaging.[53] Instant messaging is more like face-to-face interaction because negotiators need to respond quickly and in real time. For example, when someone is asked in instant message mode about the quality of a product, the seller needs to provide an answer quickly and assuredly. We hypothesized that instant messaging would be an advantage when negotiators had a strong bargaining position but would backfire when negotiators had a weak bargaining position because they would be "exposed" and could not easily run for cover. This was exactly the result we found: Sellers who had strong arguments for their product fared particularly well in instant messaging because they could, verbally bamboozle the buyers; however, sellers who had weaker arguments were not able to hold their own in instant messaging and

---

[49]Shaw, M. E. (1981). *Group dynamics: The psychology of small group behavior* (3rd ed.). New York: McGraw-Hill.

[50]Strodtbeck, F. L., & Hook, L. H. (1961). The social dimensions of a 12-man jury table. *Sociometry, 24*(4), 397–415.

[51]Guardian Leader pages. (2007, September 8). Leading article: In praise of. . . nodding. *The Guardian,* p. 38.

[52]Sproull & Keisler, *Connections.*

[53]Loewenstein, J., Morris, M. W., Chakravarti, A., Thompson, L., & Kopelman, S. (2005). At a loss for words: Dominating the conversation and the outcome in negotiation as a function of intricate arguments and communication media. *Organizational Behavior and Human Decision Process, 98,* 28–38.

did much better negotiating via traditional e-mail. The message: If you have a strong bargaining position, face-to-face interaction is ideal; if you have a weak bargaining position, impoverished media can add an important buffer.

The very nature of e-mail hides traditional status cues. When people receive e-mail from others, they often do not know the sender's status or, for that matter, where the person works or if they are at a company. People who would normally not approach others in person are much more likely to initiate e-mail exchange. Traditional, static cues such as position and title are not as obvious in e-mail. It is often impossible to tell whether you are communicating with a president or a clerk on e-mail because traditional e-mail simply lists only the person's name, not his or her title. Addresses are often shortened and may be difficult to comprehend. Even when they can be deciphered, e-mail addresses identify the organization, but not the subunit, job title, social importance, or level in the organization of the sender. Dynamic status cues, such as dress, mannerisms, age, and gender, are also missing in e-mail. In this sense, e-mail acts as an equalizer because it is difficult for high-status people to dominate the discussion. The absence of these cues leads people to respond more openly and less hesitatingly than in face-to-face interaction. People are less likely to conform to social norms and other people when interacting via electronic communication.

Overall, the amount of participation will be less in electronic versus face-to-face communication, but the contributions of members will be more equal.[54] For example, when groups of executives meet face-to-face, men are five times more likely than women to make the first decision proposal. When those same groups meet via computer, women make the first proposal as often as men do.[55] Furthermore, the time to complete a task is longer on e-mail than in face-to-face interaction, probably because people talk much faster than they write.

Social Networks

In traditional organizations, social networks are determined by who talks to whom; in the new organization, social networks are determined by who communicates with whom via technology. People on the periphery who communicate electronically become better integrated into their organization.[56] Computerized interaction increases the resources of low-network people.

The nature of social networks that shape negotiation behavior changes dramatically when information technology enters the picture as a form of communication. E-mail networks, or connection between people who communicate via e-mail, increase the information resources of low-network people. When people need assistance (e.g., information or resources), they often turn to their immediate social network. When such help is not available, they use weak ties, such as relationships with acquaintances or strangers, to seek help that is unavailable from friends or colleagues. However, a

[54]For a review, see McGrath, J. E., & Hollingshead, A. B. (1994). *Groups interacting with technology.* Thousand Oaks, CA: Sage.

[55]McGuire, T., Keisler, S., & Siegel, J. (1987). Group and computer-mediated discussion effects in risk decision-making. *Journal of Personality and Social Psychology, 52*(5), 917–930.

[56]Eveland, J. D., & Bikson, T. K. (1988). Work group structures and computer support: A field experiment. *Transactions on Office Information Systems, 6*(4), 354–379.

problem arises: In the absence of personal relationships or the expectation of direct reciprocity, help from weak ties might not be forthcoming or could be of low quality.

Some companies, particularly global companies and those in the fields of information technology and communications, rely on e-mail and employees within the company forming connections with each other on the basis of no physical contact. The incentives for taking the time to assist someone who is dealing with a problem and is located in a different part of the world are quite minuscule.

Another possibility is to catalog or store information in some easily accessible database. In a technical company, this database would include published reports and scientific manuals. However, engineers and managers do not like to consult technical reports to obtain needed information; most of the information they use to solve their problems is obtained through face-to-face discussions. People in organizations usually prefer to exchange help through strong collegial ties, which develop through physical proximity, similarity, and familiarity. In the late 1990s, several industries predicted buyers and sellers would use Web sites to find one another and would, thereby, disrupt traditional distribution channels and drive down prices. Yet, of the 1,500 business-to-business (B2B) exchanges started, only 43% remain.[57] Buyers place a premium on long-term relationships with vendors.

Is it sending or receiving messages that expands one's social network and ultimate organizational commitment? The amount of e-mail a person sends (but not receives) predicts commitment.[58] Thus, e-mail can provide an alternate route to letting people have a voice if they are low contributors in face-to-face meetings.

Risk Taking

Consider the following choices:

> Option 1: $20,000 return over 2 years
> Option 2: 50% chance of $40,000 return; 50% chance of nothing

Obviously, option 1 is the "safe" (riskless) choice; option 2 is the risky choice. However, these two options are mathematically identical, meaning people should not favor one option over the other (see also Appendix 1). When posed with these choices, most people are risk-averse, meaning they select the option that has the sure payoff as opposed to holding out for the chance to win big (or, equally as likely, not win at all). Consider what happens when the following choice is proposed:

> Option 1: Sure loss of $20,000 over 2 years
> Option 2: 50% chance of losing $40,000; 50% of losing nothing

Most managers are risk-seeking and choose option 2. Why? According to the **framing effect** (see chapter 2),[59] people are risk-averse for gains and risk seeking for losses. This tendency can lead to self-contradictory, quirky behavior. By manipulating the reference point, a person's choices change.

---

[57] Cannella, C. (2003, August 1). Why online exchanges died. *Inc., 25*(8), 28.
[58] Sproull & Keisler, *Connections.*
[59] Kahneman, D., & Tversky, A. (1979). Prospect theory: An analysis of decision under risk. *Econometrica, 47,* 263–291.

Groups tend to make riskier decisions than do individuals given the same choice. Thus, risk-seeking is greatly exaggerated in groups who meet face-to-face. Paradoxically, groups who make decisions via electronic communication are risk-seeking for both gains and losses.[60] Furthermore, executives are just as confident of their decisions whether they are made through electronic communication or face-to-face communication. For example, in comparisons of people negotiating face-to-face, by e-mail, or through a combination of both, people who use only e-mail reach more impasses.[61] According to Shell, "People tend to escalate disagreement when they focus on the issues and position without the benefit of the contextual, personal information that comes across when we speak or go face-to-face with our counterpart."[62]

Rapport and Social Norms

Building trust and rapport is critical for negotiation success. The greater the face-to-face contact between negotiators and the greater the rapport, the more integrative the outcomes are likely to be. Rapport is more difficult to establish with impoverished mediums of communication.[63] For example, Drolet and Morris tested the hypothesis that visual access between negotiators fosters rapport and facilitates cooperation and pie expansion.[64] They instructed some negotiators to stand face-to-face or side-by-side (unable to see each other) in a simulated strike negotiation. Face-to-face negotiators were more likely to coordinate on a settlement early in the strike, resulting in higher joint gains. Further, rapport was higher between face-to-face negotiators than between side-by-side negotiators. In a different investigation, comparisons were made between face-to-face, videoconference, and audio-only negotiation interactions.[65] Face-to-face negotiators felt a greater amount of rapport than did negotiators in the videoconference and audio-only conditions. Further, independent observers judged face-to-face negotiators to be more "in sync" with each other. Face-to-face negotiators trusted each other more and were more successful at coordinating their decisions.

Paranoia

On the TV show *Saturday Night Live,* Pat (Julia Sweeney) was a character whose sex was unknown. Pat had an androgynous name, wore baggy clothes, and did not display any stereotypical male or female characteristics or preferences. Most people found it maddening to interact with Pat without knowing his or her gender. Gender ambiguity also happens when interacting via technology. It is generally impolite to ask someone whether he or she is a man or woman. Therefore, we are left feeling uncertain. Uncertainty, consequently, increases paranoia. Paranoid people are more likely to assume the worst about another person or situation.[66]

---

[60]McGuire, Keisler, & Siegel, "Group and computer-mediated discussion."
[61]Shell, G. R. (1999). *Bargaining for advantage: Negotiation strategies for reasonable people.* New York: Viking.
[62]Ibid, p. 106.
[63]Drolet & Morris, "Rapport in conflict resolution."
[64]Ibid.
[65]Ibid.
[66]Kramer, "Dubious battle."

When technological change creates new social situations, traditional expectations and norms lose their power. People invent new ways of behaving. Today's electronic technology is impoverished in social cues and shared experience. People "talk" to other people, but they do so alone.[67] As a result, their messages are likely to display less social awareness. The advantage is that social posturing and sycophancy decline. The disadvantage is that politeness and concern for others also decline. Two characteristics of computer-based communication—the plain text and perceived ephemerality of messages—make it relatively easy for a person to forget or ignore his or her audience and consequently send messages that ignore social boundaries, disclose the self, and are too blunt.[68]

Did the following exchange occur in a meeting room or via the Internet?

NEGOTIATOR A: If I do not get your answer by tomorrow, then I assume that you agree with my proposal.

NEGOTIATOR B: From my perspective, I do not see any rationale or any incentive to transfer this revolutionary technology to your division.

NEGOTIATOR A: I do not have to remind you that pushing the issue up the corporate ladder can prejudice both our careers.

NEGOTIATOR B: Your offer is ridiculous.

NEGOTIATOR A: It is my final offer.

Most people correctly note that this exchange occurred on the Internet. The phenomenon of flaming suggests that through electronic mail, actions and decisions (not just messages) might become more extreme and impulsive.[69]

STRATEGIES FOR ENHANCING TECHNOLOGY-MEDIATED NEGOTIATIONS

Often, negotiators do not have the luxury of face-to-face meetings for the duration of their negotiations. Under such circumstances, what strategies can be employed to enhance successful pie-expansion and pie-slicing? Consider the following tactics.

Initial Face-to-Face Experience

The effectiveness of virtual and face-to-face teams was compared as they worked on a brainstorming exercise and a negotiation exercise.[70] Virtual teams worked better on the brainstorming exercise, but face-to-face teams did better on the negotiation exercise. Moreover, even though the face-to-face teams communicated better initially (during the early stages of a project), as virtual teams gained experience, they communicated as openly and shared information as effectively as face-to-face teams.[71] According to Alge, "A manager who wants to put a working group together for a long,

---

[67]Sproull & Keisler, *Connections.*
[68]Ibid.
[69]Ibid.
[70]Alge, B. J., Wiethoff, C., & Klein, H. J. (2003). When does the medium matter? Knowledge-building experiences and opportunities in decision-making teams. *Organizational Behavior and Human Decision Processes, 91,* 26–37.
[71]Ibid.

complex project should choose a team whose members are in the same location or initially invest the resources to give the team members an opportunity to get to know each other. Then, as teams become more experienced and familiar with each other and the technology, they can exchange ideas more effectively using 'lean' Internet media that lack the nonverbal communication, social cues, and nuances that exist in face-to-face interactions."[72]

Oftentimes, people develop rapport on the basis of a short face-to-face meeting, which can reduce uncertainty and build trust. Face-to-face contact humanizes people and creates expectation for negotiators to use in their subsequent long-distance work together. For example, Christopher H. Browne, managing director of Tweedy Browne Company, a New York–based investment-management firm, is a self-professed "e-mail junkie." When he presented the University of Pennsylvania with a gift of $10 million, it was his suggestion that they hammer out the details about payment and purpose of the gift online. However, he was careful to make this suggestion after an initial face-to-face meeting about the gift with university officials. Four days and several e-messages later, the deal was completed. Both Browne and university officials said the process could have taken weeks had they relied on telephone calls and faxes. University officials said they were going to make a personal trip to New York to thank Browne: "Even though this [the deal] was done in cyberspace, we don't want to lose sight of the fact that there are real people involved."[73]

One-Day Videoconference/Teleconference

If an initial, face-to-face meeting is out of the question, an alternative may be to get everyone online so that at least people can attach a name to a face. Depending upon the size of the team and locations of different members, this alternative may be more feasible than a face-to-face meeting. For example, in one investigation, negotiators who had never met one another were instructed to have a short phone call prior to commencing e-mail-only negotiations.[74] The sole purpose of the phone call was to get to know the other person. The simple act of chatting and exchanging personal information built rapport and overcame some of the communication difficulties associated with the impoverished medium of e-mail. Another group did not have an initial phone call with its opponent. Negotiators who engaged in the initial phone conversation found that their attitudes toward their opponents changed; negotiators who had chatted with their opponent felt less competitive and more cooperative before the negotiation began, compared with negotiators who had not chatted with their opponent. In the end, negotiators who had made personal contact with their opponent felt more confident that future interaction with the same person would go smoothly. A relationship of trust was thus developed through the rapport-building phone call prior to the negotiation. Not surprisingly, negotiators who had had an initial phone call were less likely to reach impasse and achieved higher joint gains compared to those who did not have the initial phone call. The simple act of making an effort to establish a personal relationship

---

[72]Lillich, M. (2003, April 23). Researcher details management challenge: Getting real results from virtual teams. *Ascribe Higher Education News Service.*
[73]Carlson, S. (2000, February 9). Penn officials use e-mail to negotiate a $10-million gift. *Chronicle of Higher Education,* 1–2.
[74]Morris et al., "Schmooze or lose."

through telephone contact before engaging in e-mail negotiations can have dramatic positive consequences.

Schmoozing

Schmoozing (as described in Chapter 6) is our name for non–task-related contact between people, which has the psychological effect of having established a relationship with someone.[75] The effectiveness of electronic schmoozing has been put to the test, and the results are dramatic: Schmoozing increases liking and rapport and results in more profitable business deals than when people simply "get down to business."[76] Negotiators who schmoozed (on the phone) developed more realistic goals, resulting in a larger range of possible outcomes, and were less likely to reach an impasse compared to nonschmoozers. The key mediating factor was rapport. Moreover, the negotiators who schmoozed on the phone prior to getting down to the business of e-negotiation expressed greater optimism about a future working relationship with the other party, compared to negotiators who did not schmooze.[77]

Another route to building trust and rapport is to build a shared social identity. For example, e-negotiations between managers at the same university (company) versus negotiations between competitor universities (companies) reveals that membership in the same university (company) reduces the likelihood of impasse in e-negotiations.[78] In contrast, negotiators who do not share social ties with their counterpart consistently underperform on the key measures of negotiator performance.

Perhaps the most attractive aspects of schmoozing are that it is relatively low cost and it is efficient. Merely exchanging a few short e-mails describing yourself can lead to better business relations. However, you should not expect people to naturally schmooze—at least at the outset of a business relationship. Team members working remotely have a tendency to get down to business. As a start toward schmoozing, tell the other person something about yourself that does not necessarily relate to the business at hand (e.g., "I really enjoy sea kayaking"); also, provide a context for your own work space (e.g., "It is very late in the day, and there are 20 people at my door, so I do not have time to write a long message"). Furthermore, ask questions that show you are interested in the other party as a person; this approach is an excellent way to search for points of similarity. Finally, provide the link for the next e-mail or exchange (e.g., "I will look forward to hearing your reactions on the preliminary report, and I will also send you the tapes you requested").

CONCLUSION

We used the place-time model of social interaction to examine how the medium of communication affects negotiation. We examined how the use of information technology affects social behavior. In particular, we focused on how non–face-to-face interaction

---

[75]Moore, D. A., Kurtzberg, T., Thompson, L., & Morris, M. W. (1999). Long and short routes to success in electronically mediated negotiations: Group affiliations and good vibrations. *Organizational Behavior and Human Decision Processes, 77*(1), 22–43; Morris et al., "Schmooze or lose."
[76]Moore, Kurtzberg, Thompson, & Morris, "Long and short routes."
[77]Morris et al., "Schmooze or lose."
[78]Moore, Kurtzberg, Thompson, & Morris, "Long and short routes."

results in more actual airtime than does the same group meeting face-to-face. Part of the reason is that cues about someone's status and authority are not as evident when not face-to-face. We discussed social networks and how information technology effectively expands the potential reach and influence of managers. We noted that people are more likely to display risk-seeking behavior (i.e., choosing gambles over sure things) when interacting via information technology, as opposed to face-to-face. Probably the biggest threat to effective negotiation in non–face-to-face settings is the loss of rapport and the tendency for people to be less conscious of social norms, such as politeness rituals. We discussed several methods for enhancing technology-mediated negotiations, including an initial face-to-face experience (so that negotiators can establish social norms) a one-day videoconference, and schmoozing.

Appendix 1

Are You a Rational Person? Check Yourself

The purpose of this appendix is to help you assess your own rationality. First, we present the key principles of **individual rationality**, which focuses on how people make independent decisions. Then we present and discuss **game theoretic rationality**, which focuses on how people make interdependent decisions.

Why Is It Important to Be Rational?

Let's first consider why it is important for a negotiator to be rational. Rational models of negotiation behavior offer a number of important advantages for the negotiator:

- *Pie-expansion and pie-slicing.* Models of rational behavior are based upon the principle of maximization such that the course of action followed guarantees the negotiator will maximize his or her interests (whether that interest is monetary gain, career advancement, prestige, etc.). In short, the best way to maximize one's interests is to follow the prescriptions of a rational model.
- *Learning and personal growth.* The rational models we present in this appendix make clear and definitive statements regarding the superiority of some decisions over others. Thus, they do not allow you to justify or rationalize your behavior. The truth may hurt sometimes, but it is a great learning experience.
- *Measure of perfection.* Rational models provide a measure of perfection or optimality. If rational models did not exist, we would have no way of evaluating how well people perform in negotiations nor what they should strive to do. We would not be able to offer advice to negotiators because we would not have consensus about what is a "good" outcome. Rational models provide an ideal.

- *Diagnosis.* Rational models serve a useful diagnostic purpose because they often reveal where negotiators make mistakes. Because rational models are built on a well-constructed theory of decision making, they offer insight into the mind of the negotiator.
- *Dealing with irrational people.* Negotiators often follow the norm of reciprocity. A negotiator who is well-versed in rational behavior can often deal more effectively with irrational people.
- *Consistency.* Rational models can help us be consistent. Inconsistency in our behavior can inhibit learning. Furthermore, it can send the counterparty ambiguous messages. When people are confused or uncertain, they are more defensive and trust diminishes.
- *Decision Making.* Rational models provide a straightforward method for thinking about decisions and a way of choosing among options, which, if followed correctly, will produce the "best" outcome for the chooser, maximizing his or her own preferences (as we will see in this appendix).

As the cartoon in Exhibit A1-1 suggests, people's behavior is not always rational. Even so, principles and assumptions derived from rational models are still a fundamental part of our "mix" for understanding human behavior.

Individual Decision Making

Negotiation is ultimately about making decisions. If we cannot make good decisions on our own, joint decision making will be even more difficult. Sometimes our decisions are trivial, such as whether to have chocolate cake or cherry pie for dessert. Other times, our decisions are of great consequence, such as choosing a career or a spouse. Our decisions about how to spend the weekend may seem fundamentally different from deciding

EXHIBIT A1-1

Source: Copyright © 1994, *The Economist* Newspaper Ltd. All rights reserved. Reprinted with permission. Further reproduction prohibited. www.economist.com.

what to do with our entire life, but some generalities cut across domains. Rational decision making models provide the tools necessary for analyzing any decision. The three main types of decisions are riskless choice, decision making under uncertainty, and risky choice.

Riskless Choice

Riskless choice, or decision making under certainty, involves choosing between two or more readily available options. For example, a choice between two apartments is a riskless choice, as is choosing among 31 flavors of ice cream or selecting a book to read. Often, we do not consider these events to be decisions because they are so simple and easy. However, at other times, we struggle when choosing among jobs or careers, and we find ourselves in a state of indecision.

Imagine you have been accepted into the MBA program at your top two choices: university X and university Y. This enviable situation is an **approach-approach conflict**, meaning that in some sense, you cannot lose—both options are attractive; you need only to decide which alternative is best for you. You have to make your final choice by next week. In front of you is a large stack of brochures, descriptions, and information about the schools. How should you begin to analyze the situation?

To analyze this decision situation, we will employ a method known as **multiattribute utility technique** (or **MAUT**).[1] According to MAUT, a decision maker should follow 5 steps: (a) identify the alternatives, (b) identify dimensions or attributes of the alternatives, (c) evaluate the utility associated with each dimension, (d) weight or prioritize each

[1]For an overview, see Baron, J. (1988). *Decision analysis and utility measurement. Thinking and deciding* (pp. 330–351). Boston: Cambridge University Press.

dimension in terms of importance, and (e) make a final choice.

Identification of Alternatives The first step is usually quite straightforward. The decision maker simply identifies the relevant alternatives. For example, you would identify the schools to which you had been accepted. In other situations, the alternatives may not be as obvious. In the case that you did not get any acceptance letters, you must brainstorm new options.

Identification of Attributes The second step is more complex and involves identifying the key attributes associated with the alternatives. The attributes are the features of an alternative that make it appealing or unappealing. For example, when choosing among schools, relevant attributes might include the cost of tuition, reputation of the program, course requirements, placement options, weather, cultural aspects, family, and faculty.

Utility The next step is to evaluate the relative utility or value of each alternative for each attribute. For example, you might use a 1-to-5 scale to evaluate how each school rates on each of your identified attributes. You might evaluate the reputation of university X very highly (5) but the weather as very unattractive (1); you might evaluate university Y's reputation to be moderately high (3) but the weather to be fabulous (5). MAUT

assumes preferential independence of attributes (i.e., the value of one attribute is independent of the value of others).

Weight In addition to determining the evaluation of each attribute, the decision maker also evaluates how important that attribute is to him or her. The importance of each attribute is referred to as **weight** in the decision process. Again, we can use a simple numbering system, with 1 representing relatively unimportant attributes and 5 representing very important attributes. For example, you might consider the reputation of the school to be very important (5) but the cultural attributes of the city to be insignificant (1).

Making a Decision The final step in the MAUT procedure is to compute a single, overall evaluation of each alternative. For this task, first multiply the utility evaluation of each attribute by its corresponding weight, and then sum the weighted scores across each attribute. Finally, select the option that has the highest overall score.

We can see from the hypothetical example in Exhibit A1-2 that university X is a better choice for the student compared to university Y. However, it is a close decision. If the importance of any of the attributes were to change (e.g., tuition cost, reputation, climate, or culture), then the overall decision could change. Similarly, if the evaluation of

---

EXHIBIT A1-2 Multiattribute Decision Making

Attribute (weight)	University Y (evaluation)	University X (evaluation)
Tuition cost (4)	Inexpensive (5)	Expensive (1)
Reputation (5)	Medium (3)	High (5)
Climate (3)	Lousy (1)	Great (5)
Culture (1)	Good (4)	Poor (1)

Utility of University (Y) = (4*5) + (5*3) + (3*1) + (1*4) = 42
Utility of University (X) = (4*1) + (5*5) + (3*5) + (1*1) = 45

any attributes changes, then the final choice may change. Decision theory can tell us how to choose, but it cannot tell us how to weight the attributes that go into making choices.

According to the **dominance principle**, one alternative dominates another if it is strictly better on at least one dimension and at least as good on all others. For example, imagine university Y had been evaluated as a 5 in terms of tuition cost, a 5 in reputation, a 4 in climate, and a 4 in culture; and university X had been evaluated as a 1, 5, 4, and 3, respectively. In this case, we can quickly see that university Y is just as good as university X on two dimensions (reputation and climate) and better on the two remaining dimensions (tuition cost and culture). Thus, university Y dominates university X. Identifying a dominant alternative greatly simplifies decision making: If one alternative dominates the other, we should select the dominant option.

The example seems simple enough. In many situations, however, we are faced with considering many more alternatives, each having different dimensions. It may not be easy to spot a dominant alternative. What should we do in this case? The first step is to eliminate from consideration all options dominated by others and to choose among the nondominated alternatives that remain.

The dominance principle as a method of choice seems quite compelling, but it applies only to situations in which one alternative is clearly superior to others. It does not help us with the agonizing task of choosing among options that involve trade-offs among highly valued aspects. We now turn to situations that defy MAUT and dominance detection.

Decision Making Under Uncertainty

Sometimes we must make decisions when the alternatives are uncertain or unknown. These situations are known as **decision making under uncertainty** or **decision making in ignorance**.[2] In such situations, the decision maker has no idea about the likelihood of events. Consider, for example, a decision to plan a social event outdoors or indoors. If the weather is sunny and warm, it would be better to hold the event outdoors; if it is rainy and cold, it is better to plan the event indoors. The plans must be made a month in advance, but the weather cannot be predicted a month in advance. The distinction between risk and uncertainty hinges upon whether probabilities are known exactly (e.g., as in games of chance) or whether they must be judged by the decision maker with some degree of imprecision (e.g., almost everything else). Hence, "ignorance" might be viewed merely as an extreme degree of uncertainty when the decision maker has no clue (e.g., probability that the closing price of Dai Ichi stock tomorrow on the Tokyo stock exchange is above 1,600 yen).

Risky Choice

In decision making under uncertainty, the likelihood of events is unknown; in **risky choice** situations, the probabilities are known. Most theories of decision making are based on an assessment of the probability that some event will take place. Because the outcomes of risky choice situations are not fully known, outcomes are often referred to as "prospects." Many people cannot compute risk accurately, even when the odds are perfectly known, as in the case of gambling. (See Exhibit A1-3 for some odds associated with winning the lottery.)

Negotiation is a risky choice situation because parties cannot be completely certain about the occurrence of a particular event. For instance, a negotiator cannot be certain that mutual settlement will be reached because negotiations could break off as each party opts for his or her BATNA.

---

[2]Yates, J. F. (1990). *Judgment and decision making.* Upper Saddle River, NJ: Prentice Hall.

EXHIBIT A1-3 Understanding Risk and Probability

Millions of people purchase lottery tickets and gamble—every week and every day. But do they really understand the stakes? Consider these statistics:

- If you toss a coin 26 times, your odds of getting 26 heads in a row are greater than the chance that your Powerball ticket will win you the jackpot.
- To have a reasonable chance of winning the Massachusetts lottery by purchasing a lottery ticket each week, you would need to persist for 1.6 million years.
- If you drive 10 miles to buy a Powerball ticket, you are 16 times more likely to die en route in a car crash than to win.
- If you are an average British citizen who buys a ticket in Britain's National Lottery on Monday, you are 2,500 times more likely to die before the Saturday draw than to win the jackpot. Viewers of the lottery draw are 3 times more likely to die during the 20-minute program than to win.

Source: Adapted from Myers, Intuition: Its Powers and Perils (2002), p 224. Reprinted by permission of Yale University Press.

To understand risky choice decision making in negotiations, we need to understand expected utility theory.

Expected Utility Theory   Utility theory has a long history, dating back to the sixteenth century when French noblemen commissioned their court mathematicians to help them gamble. Modern utility theory is expressed in the form of gambles, probabilities, and payoffs. Why do we need to know about gambling to be effective negotiators? Virtually all negotiations involve choices, and many choices involve uncertainty, which makes them gambles. Before we can negotiate effectively, we need to be clear about our own preferences. Utility theory helps us do that.

EU is a theory of choices made by an individual actor.[3] It prescribes a theory of "rational behavior." Behavior is rational if a person acts in a way that maximizes his or her decision utility or the anticipated satisfaction from a particular outcome. The maximization of utility is often equated with the maximization of monetary gain. But satisfaction can come in many nonmonetary forms as well. Obviously, people care about things other than money. For example, weather, culture, quality of life, and personal esteem are all factors that bear on a job decision, in addition to salary.

EU is based on revealed preferences. People's preferences or utilities are not directly observable but must be inferred from their choices and willful behavior. To understand what a person really wants and values, we have to see what choices he or she makes. Actions speak louder than words. In this sense, utility maximization is a tautological statement: A person's choices reflect personal utilities; therefore, all behaviors may be represented by the maximization of this hypothetical utility scale.

EU is based on a set of axioms about preferences among gambles. The basic result of the theory is summarized by a theorem stating that if a person's preferences satisfy the specified axioms, then the person's behavior maximizes the expected utility. Before we can talk about what rational behavior is, we need to understand what a utility function is.

---

[3]von Neumann, J., & Morgenstern, O. (1947). *Theory of games and economic behavior.* Princeton, NJ: Princeton University Press.

Utility Function A **utility function** is the quantification of a person's preferences with respect to certain objects such as jobs, potential mates, and ice cream flavors. Utility functions assign numbers to objects and gambles that have objects as their prizes (e.g., flip a coin and win a trip to Hawaii or free groceries). For example, a manager's choice to stay at her current company could be assigned an overall value, say a 7 on a 10-point scale. Her option to take a new job might be assigned a value of either 10 or 2, depending on how things work out for her at the new job. One's current job is the sure thing; the alternative job, because of its uncertainty, is a gamble. How should we rationally make a decision between the two?

We first need to examine our utility function. The following seven axioms guarantee the existence of a utility function. The axioms are formulated in terms of preference-or-indifference relations defined over a set of outcomes.[4] As will become clear, the following axioms provide the foundation for individual decision making, as well as negotiation or joint decision making.

Comparability A key assumption of EU is that everything is comparable. That is, given any two objects, a person must prefer one to the other or be indifferent to both; no two objects are incomparable. For example, a person may compare a dime and a nickel or a cheeseburger and a dime. We might compare a job offer in the Midwest to a job offer on the West Coast. Utility theory implies a single, underlying dimension of "satisfaction" associated with everything. We can recall instances in which we refused to make comparisons, however, which often happens in the case of social or emotional issues such as marriage and children. However, according to utility theory, we need to be able to compare everything to be truly

rational. Many people are uncomfortable with this idea, just as people can be in conflict about what is negotiable.

Closure The **closure property** states that if x and y are available alternatives, then so are all of the gambles of the form (x, p, y) that can be formed with x and y as outcomes. In this formulation, x and y refer to available alternatives; p refers to the probability that x will occur. Therefore, (x, p, y) states that x will occur with probability p, otherwise y will occur. The converse must also be true: $(x, p, y) = (y, 1 - p, x)$, or y will occur with probability $(1 - p)$, otherwise x will occur.

For example, imagine you assess the probability of receiving a raise from your current employer to be about 30%. The closure property states that the situation expressed as a 30% chance of receiving a raise (otherwise, no raise) is identical to the statement that you have a 70% chance of not receiving a raise (otherwise, receiving a raise).

So far, utility theory may seem to be so obvious and simple that it is absurd to spell it out in any detail. However, we will soon see how people violate basic "common sense" all the time and, hence, behave irrationally.

Transitivity Transitivity means that if we prefer x to y and y to z, then we should prefer x to z. Similarly, if we are indifferent between x and y and y and z, then we will be indifferent between x and z.

Suppose your employer offers you one of three options: a transfer to Seattle, a transfer to Pittsburgh, or a raise of $5,000. You prefer a raise of $5,000 over a move to Pittsburgh, and you prefer a move to Seattle more than a $5,000 raise. The **transitivity property** states that you should therefore prefer a move to Seattle over a move to Pittsburgh. If your preferences were not

---

[4]See also Coombs, C. H., Dawes, R. M., & Tversky, A. (1970). *Mathematical psychology: An elementary introduction.* Upper Saddle River, NJ: Prentice Hall.

transitive, you would always want to move somewhere else. Further, a third party could become rich by continuously "selling" your preferred options to you.

Reducibility The **reducibility axiom** refers to a person's attitude toward a compound lottery, in which the prizes may be tickets to other lotteries. According to the reducibility axiom, a person's attitude toward a compound lottery depends only on the ultimate prizes and the chance of getting them as determined by the laws of probability; the actual gambling mechanism is irrelevant:

$$(x, pq, y) = [(x, p, y), q, y]$$

Suppose that the dean of admissions at your first-choice university tells you that you have a 25% chance of getting accepted to the MBA program. How do you feel about the situation? Now, suppose the dean tells you that you have a 50% chance of not being accepted and a 50% chance you will have to face a lottery-type admission procedure, wherein half the applicants will get accepted and half will not. In which situation do you prefer to be? According to the reducibility axiom, both situations are identical. Your chances of getting admitted into graduate school are the same in each case: exactly 25%. The difference between the two situations is that one involves a **compound gamble** and the other does not.

Compound gambles differ from simple ones in that their outcomes are themselves gambles rather than pure outcomes. Furthermore, probabilities are the same in both gambles. If people have an aversion or attraction to gambling, however, these outcomes may not seem the same. This axiom has important implications for negotiation; the format by which alternatives are presented to negotiators—in other words, in terms of gambles or compound gambles—strongly affects our behavior.

Substitutability The **substitutability axiom** states that gambles that have prizes about which people are indifferent are interchangeable. For example, suppose one prize is substituted for another in a lottery but the lottery is left otherwise unchanged. If you are indifferent to both the old and the new prizes, you should be indifferent about the lotteries. If you prefer one prize to the other, you will prefer the lottery that offers the preferred prize.

For example, imagine you work in the finance division of a company and your supervisor asks you how you feel about transferring to either the marketing or sales division in your company. You respond that you are indifferent. Then your supervisor presents you with a choice: You can be transferred to the sales division, or you can move to a finance position in an out-of-state parent branch of the company. After wrestling with the decision, you decide you prefer to move out of state rather than transfer to the sales division. A few days later, your supervisor surprises you by asking whether you prefer to be transferred to marketing or to be transferred out of state. According to the substitutability axiom, you should prefer to transfer because, as you previously indicated, you are indifferent to marketing and sales; they are substitutable choices.

Betweenness The **betweenness axiom** asserts that if x is preferred to y, then x must be preferred to any probability mixture of x and y, which in turn must be preferred to y. This principle is certainly not objectionable for monetary outcomes. For example, most of us would rather have a dime than a nickel and would rather have a probability of either a dime or a nickel than the nickel itself. But consider nonmonetary outcomes, such as skydiving, Russian roulette, and bungee jumping. To an outside observer, people who skydive apparently prefer a probability mixture of living and dying over either one of them alone; otherwise, one can easily either stay alive or kill oneself without ever skydiving. People who like to risk their lives appear to contradict the betweenness axiom. A more careful analysis reveals, however, that this situation, strange as it may be, is not incompatible with the betweenness axiom. The actual outcomes involved in skydiving are (a) staying alive after skydiving, (b) staying alive without skydiving, or (c) dying while skydiving. In choosing to skydive, therefore, a person prefers a probability mix of (a) and (c) over (b). This analysis reveals that "experience" has a utility.

Continuity or Solvability   Suppose that of three objects—A, B, and C—you prefer A to B and B to C. Now, consider a lottery in which there is a probability, p, of getting A and a probability of $1-p$ of getting C. If $p = 0$, the lottery is equivalent to C; if $p = 1$, the lottery is equivalent to A. In the first case, you prefer B to the lottery; in the second case, you prefer the lottery to B. According to the **continuity axiom**, a value, p, that falls between 0 and 1 indicates your indifference between B and the lottery. This sounds reasonable enough.

Now consider the following example involving three outcomes: receiving a dime, receiving a nickel, and being shot at dawn.[5] Certainly, most of us prefer a dime to a nickel and a nickel to being shot. The continuity axiom, however, states that at some point of inversion, some probability mixture involving receiving a dime and being shot at dawn is equivalent to receiving a nickel. This derivation seems particularly disdainful for most people because no price is equal to risking one's life. However, the counterintuitive nature of this example stems from an inability to understand very small probabilities. In the abstract, people believe they would never choose to risk their life but, in reality, people do so all the time. For example, we cross the street to buy some product for a nickel less, although

by doing so we risk getting hit by a car and being killed.

In summary, whenever these axioms hold, a utility function exists that (a) preserves a person's preferences among options and gambles and (b) satisfies the **expectation principle**: The utility of a gamble equals the expected utility of its outcomes. This utility scale is uniquely determined except for an origin and a unit of measurement.

Expected Value Principle   Imagine you have a rare opportunity to invest in a highly innovative start-up company. The company has developed a new technology that allows cars to run without gasoline. The cars are fuel efficient, environmentally clean, and less expensive to maintain than regular gasoline-fueled cars. On the other hand, the technology is new and unproven. Further, the company does not have the resources to compete with the major automakers. Nevertheless, if this technology is successful, an investment in the company at this point will have a 30-fold return. Suppose you just inherited $5,000 from your aunt. You could invest the money in the company and possibly earn $150,000—a risky choice. Or you could keep the money and pass up the investment opportunity. You assess the probability of success to be about 20%. (A minimum investment of $5,000 is required.) What do you do?

The dominance principle does not offer a solution to this decision situation because it provides no clearly dominant alternatives. But the situation contains the necessary elements to use the **expected value principle**, which applies when a decision maker must choose among two or more prospects, as in the previous example. The "expectation" or "expected value" of a prospect is the sum of the objective values

---

[5]von Neumann & Morgenstern, *Theory of games and economic behavior.*

of the outcomes multiplied by the probability of their occurrence.

For a variety of reasons, you believe there is a 20% chance the investment could result in a return of $150,000, which mathematically is $0.2 \times \$150,000 = \$30,000$. There is an 80% chance the investment will not yield a return, or $0.8 \times \$0 = \$0$. Thus, the expected value of this gamble is $30,000 minus the cost, or $-\$5,000$, $= \$25,000$.

The expected value principle dictates that the decision maker should select the prospect with the greatest expected value. In this case, the risky option (with an expected value of $30,000) has a greater expected value than the sure option (expected value of $0).

A related principle applies to evaluation decisions, or situations in which decision makers must state, and be willing to act upon, the subjective worth of a given alternative. Suppose you could choose to "sell" to another person your opportunity to invest. What would you consider to be a fair price to do so? According to the expected-value evaluation principle, the evaluation of a prospect should be equal to its expected value. That is, the "fair price" for such a gamble would be $25,000. Similarly, the opposite holds: Suppose your next-door neighbor held the opportunity but was willing to sell the option to you. According to the expected value principle, people would pay up to $25,000 for the opportunity to gamble.

The expected value principle is intuitively appealing, but should we use it to make decisions? To answer this question, it is helpful to examine the rationale for using expected value as a prescription. Let's consider the short-term and long-term consequences.[6] Imagine that you will inherit $5,000 every year for the next 50 years. Each year, you must decide whether to invest the inheritance in a start-up company (risky choice) or keep the money (the sure choice). The expected value of a prospect is its long-run average value. This principle is derived from a fundamental principle: the **law of large numbers**.[7] The law of large numbers states that the mean return will get closer and closer to its expected value the more times a gamble is repeated. Thus, we can be fairly sure that after 50 years of investing your money, the average return would be about $25,000. Some years you would lose, others you would make money, but on average your return would be $25,000. When you look at the gamble this way, it seems reasonable to invest.

Now imagine the investment decision is a once-in-a-lifetime opportunity. In this case, the law of large numbers does not apply to the expected-value decision principle. You will either make $150,000, make nothing, or keep $5,000. No in-between options are possible. Under such circumstances, you can often find good reasons to reject the guidance of the expected value principle.[8] For example, suppose you need a new car. If the gamble is successful, buying a car is no problem. But if the gamble is unsuccessful, you will have no money at all. Therefore, you may decide that buying a used car at or under $5,000 is a more sensible choice.

The expected value concept is the basis for a standard way of labeling risk-taking behavior. For example, in the previous situation you could either take the investment gamble or receive $25,000 from selling the opportunity to someone else. In this case, the "value" of the sure thing (i.e., receiving

---

[6]Yates, *Judgment and decision making.*

[7]Feller, W. (1968). *An introduction to probability theory and its applications: Vol. 1* (3rd ed.). New York: Wiley; Woodroofe, M. (1975). *Probability with applications.* New York, McGraw-Hill.

[8]Yates, *Judgment and decision making.*

$25,000) is identical to the expected value of the gamble. Therefore, the "objective worth" of both alternatives is identical. What would you rather do? Your choice reveals your **risk attitude**. If you are indifferent to the two choices and are content to decide on the basis of a coin flip, you are **risk-neutral** or **risk-indifferent**. If you prefer the sure thing, then your behavior may be described as **risk-averse**. If you choose to gamble, your behavior is classified as **risk-seeking**.

Although some individual differences occur in people's risk attitudes, people do not tend to exhibit consistent risk-seeking or risk-averse behavior.[9] Rather, risk attitudes are highly context dependent. The fourfold pattern of risk attitudes predicts people will be risk-averse for moderate- to high-probability gains and low-probability losses, and risk-seeking for low-probability gains and moderate- to high-probability losses.[10]

Expected Utility Principle How much money would you be willing to pay to play a game with the following two rules: (a) An unbiased coin is tossed until it lands on heads; (b) the player of the game is paid $2 if heads appears on the opening toss, $4 if heads first appears on the second toss, $8 on the third toss, $16 on the fourth toss, and so on. Before reading further, indicate how much you would be willing to pay to play the game.

To make a decision based upon rational analysis, let's calculate the expected value of the game by multiplying the payoff for each possible outcome by the probability that it will occur. Although the probability of the first head appearing on toss n becomes progressively smaller as n increases, the probability never becomes zero. In this case, note that the probability of heads for the first time on any given toss is $(1/2)^n$, and the payoff in each case is (2^n); hence, each term of the infinite series has an expected value of $1. The implication is that the value of the game is infinite.[11] Even though the value of this game is infinite, most people are seldom willing to pay more than a few dollars to play it. Most people believe the expected value principle produces an absurd conclusion in this case. The observed reluctance to pay to play the game, despite its objective attractiveness, is known as the **St. Petersburg paradox**.[12]

How can we explain such an enigma? We might argue that expected value is an undefined quantity when the variance of outcomes is infinite. Because, in practice, the person or organization offering the game could not guarantee a payoff greater than its total assets, the game was unimaginable, except in truncated and therefore finite form.[13] So what do we do when offered such a choice? We have decided that to regard it as "priceless" or even to pay hundreds of thousands of dollars would be absurd. So, how should managers reason about such situations?

Diminishing Marginal Utility The reactions people have to the St. Petersburg game are consistent with the proposition that people decide among prospects not according to their expected objective values but, rather, according to their expected subjective values. In other words, the psychological value of money does not increase proportionally as the objective amount increases. To be

[9]Slovic, P. (1962). Convergent validation of risk taking measures. *Journal of Abnormal and Social Psychology, 65*(1), 68–71; Slovic, P. (1964). Assessment of risk taking behavior. *Psychological Bulletin, 61*(3), 220–233.

[10]Tversky, A., & Kahneman, D. (1992). Advances in prospect theory: Cumulative representation of uncertainty. *Journal of Risk and Uncertainty, 5,* 297–323; Tversky, A., & Fox, C. (1995). Weighing risk and uncertainty. *Psychological Review, 102*(2), 269–283.

[11]Lee, W. (1971). *Decision theory and human behavior.* New York: Wiley.

[12]Bernoulli, D. (L. Sommer, Trans.). (1954). Exposition of a new theory on the measurement of risk. (Original work published in 1738.) *Econometrica, 22,* 23–36.

[13]Shapley, L. S. (1977). The St. Petersburg paradox: A con game? *Journal of Economic Theory, 14,* 353–409.

sure, virtually all of us like more money rather than less money, but we do not necessarily like $20 twice as much as $10. And the difference in our happiness when our $20,000 salary is raised to $50,000 is not the same as when our $600,000 salary is raised to $630,000. Bernoulli proposed a logarithmic function relating the utility of money, *u*, to the amount of money, *x*. This function is **concave**, meaning that the utility of money decreases marginally. Constant additions to monetary amounts result in less and less increased utility. The principle of **diminishing marginal utility** is related to a fundamental principle of psychophysics, wherein good things satiate and bad things escalate. The first bite of a pizza is the best; as we get full, each bite brings less and less utility.

The principle of diminishing marginal utility is simple, yet profound. It is known as the **everyman's utility function**.[14] According to Bernoulli, a fair price for a gamble should not be determined by its expected (monetary) value but, rather, by its expected utility. Thus, the logarithmic utility function in Exhibit A1-4 yields a finite price for the gamble.

According to EU, each of the possible outcomes of a prospect has a utility (subjective value) that is represented numerically. The more appealing an outcome is, the higher its utility. The expected utility of a prospect is the sum of the utilities of the potential outcomes, each weighted by its probability. According to EU, when choosing among two or more prospects, people should select the option with the highest expected utility. Further, in evaluation situations, risky prospects should have an expected utility equal to the corresponding "sure choice" alternative.

EU principles have essentially the same form as expected value (EV) principles. The difference is that expectations are computed using objective (dollar) values in EV models as opposed to subjective values (utility) in EU models.

Risk-Taking A person's utility function for various prospects reveals something about his or her risk-taking tendencies. If a utility function is concave, a decision maker will always choose a sure thing over a prospect whose expected value is identical to that sure thing. The decision maker's be-

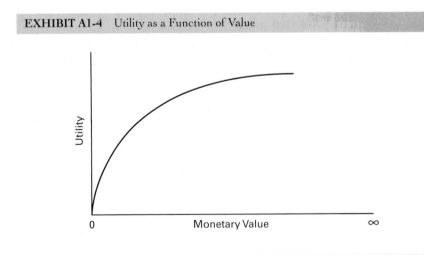

EXHIBIT A1-4 Utility as a Function of Value

---

[14]Bernoulli, "Exposition of a new theory."

EXHIBIT A1-5   Risk Attitudes

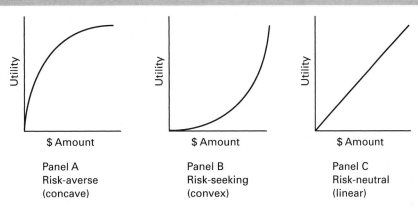

Panel A	Panel B	Panel C
Risk-averse	Risk-seeking	Risk-neutral
(concave)	(convex)	(linear)

havior is risk-averse (Exhibit A1-5, Panel A). The risk-averse decision maker would prefer a sure $5 over a 50–50 chance of winning $10 or nothing—even though the expected value of the gamble [0.5($10) + 0.5($0) = $5] is equal to that of the sure thing. If a person's utility function is convex, he or she will choose the risky option (Exhibit A1-5, Panel B). If the utility function is linear, his or her decisions will be risk-neutral and, of course, identical to those predicted by expected value maximization (Exhibit A1-5, Panel C).

If most peoples' utility for gains are concave (i.e., risk-averse), then why would people ever choose to gamble? Bets that offer small probabilities of winning large sums of money (e.g., lotteries, roulette wheels) ought to be especially unattractive, given that the concave utility function that drives the worth of the large prize is considerably lower than the value warranting a very small probability of obtaining the prize.

Consider the following two options. Which would you choose?

Option A: 80% probability of earning $40,000, otherwise $0

Option B: Earn $30,000 for sure

If you are like most people, you chose B. Only a small number of people (20%) choose A.

Now, consider two different options:

Option C: 20% probability of earning $40,000, otherwise $0

Option D: 25% probability of earning $30,000, otherwise $0

Faced with this choice, a clear majority (65%) choose option C over option D (the smaller, more likely payoff).[15]

However, in this example, the decision maker violates EU, which requires consistency between the A versus B choice and the C versus D choice. In Exhibit A1-6, Branch 1 depicts the C versus D choice [i.e., 25% chance of making $3,000 (otherwise $0) or 20% chance of making $4,000 (otherwise $0)]. In Branch 2 of Exhibit A1-6, another stage has been added to the gamble between A and B, which effectively makes the two-stage gamble in Branch 2 identical to the one-stage gamble in Branch 1. Because Branch 1 is objectively identical to Branch 2, the decision maker should not make different choices. Stated another way, in the A versus B and C versus D choices, the ratio is the same: (0.8/1) = (0.20/0.25). However, people's preferences usually reverse. According

[15]Adapted from Kahneman, D., & Tversky, A. (1979). Prospect theory: An analysis of decision under risk. *Econometrica, 47,* 263–291.

EXHIBIT A1-6 Allais Paradox Decision Tree

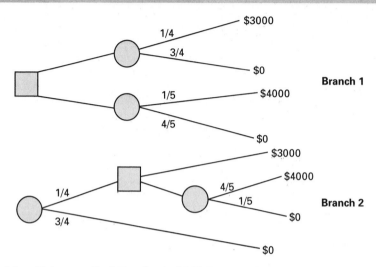

Source: Adapted from Kahneman, D., & Tversky, A. (1979). Prospect theory: An analysis of decision under risk. *Econometrica, 47,* 263–291.

to the **certainty effect**, people have a tendency to overweight certain outcomes relative to outcomes that are merely probable. The reduction in probability from certainty (1) to a degree of uncertainty (0.8) produces a more pronounced loss in attractiveness than a corresponding reduction from one level of uncertainty (0.2) to another (0.25). People do not think rationally about probabilities. Those close to 1 are often (mistakenly) considered sure things. On the flip side is the **possibility effect**: the tendency to overweight outcomes that are possible relative to outcomes that are impossible.

Decision Weights Decision makers transform probabilities into psychological decision weights. The decision weights are then applied to the subjective values. Prospect theory proposes a relationship between the probabilities' potential outcomes and the weights those probabilities have in the decision process.

Exhibit A1-7 illustrates the **probability weighting function** proposed by cumulative prospect theory. It is an inverted-S function that is concave near 0 and convex near 1. The probability-weighting function offers several noteworthy features.

Extremity Effect People tend to overweight low probabilities and underweight high probabilities.

Crossover Point The **crossover probability** is the point at which objective probabilities and subjective weights coincide. Prospect theory does not pinpoint where the crossover occurs, but it is definitely lower than 50%.[16]

Subadditivity Adding two probabilities, p_1 and p_2, should yield a probability $p_3 = p_1 + p_2$. For example, suppose you are an investor considering three stocks: A, B, and C. You assess the probability that stock A will close 2 points higher today than yesterday to be 20%, and you assess the probability that

---

[16]Kahneman & Tversky, "Prospect theory."

EXHIBIT A1-7   A Weighting Function for Decision Under Risk

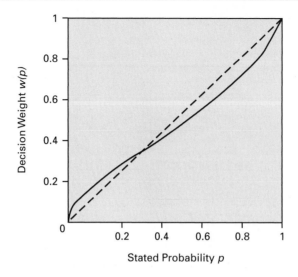

Source: Based on Fox, C. R. & Tversky, A. (1998). A belief-based model of decision under uncertainty. *Management Science, 44,* 879–896. Copyright © by The Econometric Society.

stock B will close 2 points higher today than yesterday to be 15%. The stocks are two different companies in two different industries and are completely independent. Now consider the price of stock C, which you believe has a 35% probability of closing 2 points higher today. The likelihood of a 2-point increase in either stock A or B should be identical to the likelihood of a 2-point increase in stock C. The probability-weighting relationship, however, does not exhibit additivity. That is, for small probabilities, weights are subadditive, as we see from the extreme flatness at the lower end of the curve. It means that most decision makers consider the likely increase of either stocks A or B to be less likely than an increase in stock C.

Subcertainty   Except for guaranteed or impossible events, weights for complementary events do not sum to 1. One implication of the **subcertainty** feature of the probability-

weight relationship is that for all probabilities, p, with $0 < p < 1$, p(p) + p($1 - p$) < 1.

Regressiveness   According to the **regressiveness principle**, extreme values of some quantity do not deviate very much from the average value of that quantity. The relative flatness of the probability-weighting curve is a special type of regressiveness, suggesting that people's decisions are not as responsive to changes in uncertainty as are the associated probabilities. Another aspect is that nonextreme high probabilities are underweighted and low ones are overweighted.

The subjective value associated with a prospect depends on the decision weights and the subjective values of potential outcomes. Prospect theory makes specific claims about the form of the relationship between various amounts of an outcome and their subjective values.[17] Exhibit A1-8 illustrates the generic prospect theory value function.

---

[17]Kahneman & Tversky, "Prospect theory."

EXHIBIT A1-8   A Hypothetical Value Function

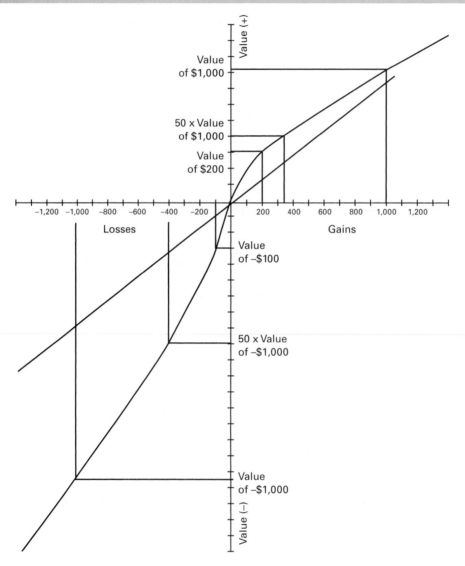

Source: Based on the Econometric Society.

Three characteristics of the value function are noteworthy. The first pertains to the decision maker's reference point. At some focal amount of the pertinent outcome, smaller amounts are considered losses and larger amounts gains. That focal amount is the negotiator's reference point. People are sensitive to changes in wealth.

A second feature is that the shape of the function changes markedly at the reference point. For gains, the value function is concave, exhibiting diminishing marginal value. As the starting point for increases in gains becomes larger, the significance of a constant increase lessens. A complementary phenomenon occurs in the domain of losses: Constant changes in the negative direction away from the reference point also assume diminishing significance the farther from the reference point the starting point happens to be.

Finally, the value function is noticeably steeper for losses than for gains. Stated another way, gains and losses of identical magnitude have different significance for people; losses are considered more important. We are much more disappointed about losing $75 than we are happy about making $75.

Combination Rules How do decision weights and outcome values combine to determine the subjective value of a prospect? The amounts that are effective for the decision maker are not the *actual* sums that would be awarded or taken away but are instead the *differences* between those sums and the decision maker's reference point.

Summing Up: Individual Decision Making

Decisions may sometimes be faulty or irrational if probabilities are not carefully considered. A negotiator's assessment of probabilities affects how he or she negotiates. Clever negotiators are aware of how their *own* decisions may be biased, as well as how the decisions of others may be manipulated to their own advantage. Now that we know about how individuals make decisions, we are ready to explore multiparty, or interdependent, decision making.

Game Theoretic Rationality

Each outcome in a negotiation situation may be identified in terms of its utility for each party. In Exhibit A1-9, for example, party 1's utility function is represented as u_1; party 2's utility function is represented as u_2. Remember that utility payoffs represent the satisfaction parties derive from particular commodities or outcomes, not the actual monetary outcomes or payoffs themselves. A bargaining situation like the one in Exhibit A1-9 has a feasible set of utility outcomes, or *F*, defined as the set of all its possible utility outcomes for party 1 and party 2 and by its

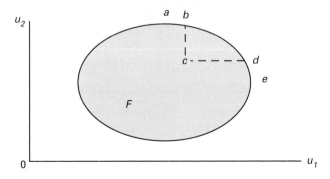

EXHIBIT A1-9   Set of Feasible Bargaining Outcomes for Two Negotiators

Source: Adapted from The New Palgrave Dictionary of Economics by John Eatwell, Murray Milgate, and Peter Newman. Copyright © 1987, 1989 by the MacMillan Press, Lotd. Used by permission of W. W. Norton & Company, Inc.

conflict point, c, where $c = (c_1, c_2)$; c represents the point at which both parties would prefer not to reach agreement (the reservation points of both parties).

Two key issues concern rationality at the negotiation table: one pertains to pie-slicing and one pertains to pie expansion. First, people should not agree to a utility payoff smaller than their reservation point; second, negotiators should not agree on an outcome if another outcome exists that is Pareto-superior, that is, an outcome that is more preferable to one party and does not decrease utility for the other party (e.g., level 3 integrative agreements discussed in Chapter 4).

For example, in Exhibit A1-9, the area F is the feasible set of alternative outcomes expressed in terms of each negotiator's utility function. The triangular area bcd is the set of all points satisfying the individual rationality requirement. The upper-right boundary $abde$ of F is the set of all points that satisfy the joint rationality requirement. The intersection of the area bcd and of the boundary line $abde$ is the arc bd: It is the set of all points satisfying both rationality requirements. As we can see, b is the least favorable outcome party 1 will accept; d is the least favorable outcome party 2 will accept.

The individual rationality and joint rationality assumptions do not tell us how negotiators should divide the pie. Rather, they tell us only that negotiators should make the pie as big as possible before dividing it. How much of the pie should you have?

Nash Bargaining Theory
Nash's bargaining theory specifies how negotiators should divide the pie,[18] which involves "a determination of the amount of satisfaction each individual should expect to get from the situation or, rather, a determination of how much it should be worth to

each of these individuals to have this opportunity to bargain."[19] Nash's theory makes a *specific* point prediction of the outcome of negotiation, the **Nash solution**, which specifies the outcome of a negotiation if negotiators behave rationally.

Nash's theory makes several important assumptions: Negotiators are rational; that is, they act to maximize their utility. The only significant differences between negotiators are those included in the mathematical description of the game. Further, negotiators have full knowledge of the tastes and preferences of each other.

Nash's theory builds on the axioms named in EU by specifying additional axioms. By specifying enough properties, we exclude all possible settlements in a negotiation, except one. Nash postulates that the agreement point, u, of a negotiation, known as the Nash solution, will satisfy the following five axioms: uniqueness, Pareto-optimality, symmetry, independence of equivalent utility representations, and independence of irrelevant alternatives.

Uniqueness The **uniqueness axiom** states that a unique solution exists for each bargaining situation. Simply stated, one and only one best solution exists for a given bargaining situation or game. In Exhibit A1-10, the unique solution is denoted as u.

Pareto-Optimality The bargaining process should not yield any outcome that both people find less desirable than some other feasible outcome. The Pareto-optimality (or efficiency) axiom is simply the joint rationality assumption made by von Neumann and Morgenstern and the level 3 integrative agreement discussed in Chapter 4.[20] The **Pareto-efficient frontier** is the set of outcomes corresponding to the entire set of agreements that leaves no portion of the

[18]Nash, J. (1950). The bargaining problem. *Econometrica, 18,* 155–162; Nash, J. (1953). Two-person cooperative games. *Econometrica, 21,* 129–140.
[19] Nash, "The bargaining problem", p. 155.
[20]von Neumann & Morgenstern, *Theory of games and economic behavior.*

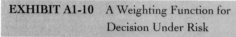

EXHIBIT A1-10 A Weighting Function for Decision Under Risk

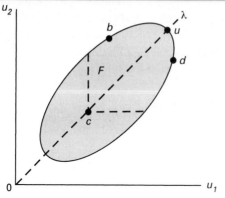

Source: Adapted from Harsanyi, J. C. (1990). *Bargaining.* In J. Eatwell, M. Milgate & P. Newman (Eds), *The New Palgrave: A Dictionary of Economics,* New York: Norton, 54–67.

sands, and in some cases, millions of dollars on it. The money is yours to keep, provided you and the other party (e.g., a car dealer, employer, seller, business associate, etc.) agree how to divide it. Obviously, you want to get as much money as you can, which is the distributive aspect of negotiation. Imagine for a moment you and the other negotiator settle upon a division of the money that both of you find acceptable. However, imagine you leave half or one-third or some other amount of money on the table. A fire starts in the building, and the money burns. This scenario is equivalent to failing to reach a Pareto-optimal agreement. Most of us would never imagine allowing such an unfortunate event to happen. However, in many negotiation situations, people do just that—they leave money to burn.

total amount of resources unallocated. A given option, *x,* is a member of the Pareto frontier if, and only if, no option *y* exists such that *y* is preferred to *x* by at least one party and is at least as good as *x* for the other party.

Consider Exhibit A1-10: Both people prefer settlement point *u* (u_1, u_2), which eliminates *c* (c_1, c_2) from the frontier. Therefore, settlement points that lie on the interior of the arc *bd* are Pareto-inefficient. Options that are not on the Pareto frontier are dominated; settlements that are dominated clearly violate the utility principle of maximization. The resolution of any negotiation should be an option from the Pareto-efficient set because any other option unnecessarily requires more concession on the part of one or both negotiators.

Another way of thinking about the importance of Pareto-optimality is to imagine that in *every* negotiation, whether it be for a car, a job, a house, a merger, or some other situation, a table sits with hundreds, thou-

Symmetry In a **symmetric bargaining** situation, the two players have exactly the same strategic possibilities and bargaining power. Therefore, neither player has any reason to accept an agreement that yields a lower payoff than that of the opponent.

Another way of thinking about symmetry is to imagine interchanging the two players. This alteration should not change the outcome. In Exhibit A1-10, symmetry means that u_1 will be equal to u_2. The feasible set of outcomes must be symmetrical with respect to a hypothetical 45-degree line, λ, which begins at the origin 0 and passes through the point *c*, thereby implying that $c_1 = c_2$. Extending this line out to the farthest feasible point, *u*, gives us the Nash point, wherein parties' utilities are symmetric.

The symmetry principle is often considered to be the fundamental postulate of bargaining theory.[21] When parties' utilities are known, the solution to the game is straightforward.[22] As we already noted, however,

[21]Harsanyi, J. (1962). Bargaining in ignorance of the opponent's utility function. *Journal of Conflict Resolution, 6,* 29–38.
[22]Nash, "The bargaining problem."

players' utilities are usually not known. This uncertainty reduces the usefulness of the symmetry principle. That is, symmetry cannot be achieved if a negotiator has only half of the information.[23]

The Pareto-optimality and symmetry axioms uniquely define the agreement points of a symmetrical game. The remaining two axioms extend the theory to asymmetrical games in which the bargaining power is asymmetric.

Independence of Equivalent Utility Representations Many utility functions can represent the same preference. Utility functions are behaviorally equivalent if one can be obtained from the other by an order-preserving linear transformation (for example, by shifting the zero point of the utility scale or by changing the utility unit). A distinguishing feature of the Nash solution outcome is that it is independent of the exchange rate between two players' utility scales; it is invariant with respect to any fixed weights we might attach to their respective utilities.

The solution to the bargaining game is not sensitive to positive linear transformations of parties' payoffs because utility is defined on an interval scale. Interval scales, such as temperature, preserve units of measurement but have an arbitrary origin (i.e., zero point) and unit of measurement. The utility scales for player 1 and player 2 in Exhibit A1-10 have an arbitrary origin and unit of measurement.

For example, suppose you and a friend are negotiating to divide 100 poker chips. The poker chips are worth $1 each if redeemed by you and worth $1 each if redeemed by your friend. The question is this: How should the two of you divide the poker chips? The Nash solution predicts that the two of you should divide all the chips and not leave any on the table (Pareto-optimality principle). Further, the Nash solution predicts that you should receive 50 chips and your friend should receive 50 chips (symme-

try principle). So far, the Nash solution sounds fine. Now, suppose the situation is slightly changed. Imagine the chips are worth $1 each if redeemed by you, but they are worth $5 each if redeemed by your friend. (The rules of the game do not permit any kind of side payments or renegotiation of redemption values.) Now, how should the chips be divided? All we have done is transform your friend's utilities using an order-preserving linear transformation (multiply all her values by 5) while keeping your utilities the same. The Nash solution states that you should still divide the chips 50–50 because your friend's utilities have not changed; rather, they are represented by a different, but nevertheless equivalent, linear transformation.

Some people have a hard time with this axiom. After all, if you and your friend are really "symmetric," one of you should not come out richer in the deal. But consider the arguments that could be made for one of you receiving a greater share of the chips. One of you could have a seriously ill parent and need the money for an operation; one of you might be independently wealthy and not need the money; or one of you could be a foolish spendthrift and not deserve the money. Moreover, there could be a disagreement: One of you regards yourself to be thoughtful and prudent but is regarded as silly and imprudent by the other person. All of these arguments are outside the realm of Nash's theory because they are **indeterminate**. Dividing resources to achieve monetary equality is as arbitrary as flipping a coin.

But in negotiation, doesn't everything really boil down to dollars? No. In Nash's theory, each person's utility function may be normalized on a scale of 0 to 1 so that his or her "best outcome" = 1 and "worst outcome" = 0. Therefore, because the choices of origin and scale for each person's utility function are unrelated to one another, actual numerical levels have no standing in

[23]Schelling, T. (1960). *The strategy of conflict.* Cambridge, MA: Harvard University Press.

theory, and no comparisons of numerical levels can affect the outcome.

This axiom has serious implications. Permitting the transformation of one player's utilities without any transformation of the other player's utilities destroys the possibility that the outcome should depend on interpersonal utility comparisons. Stated simply, it is meaningless for people to compare their utility with another. The same logic applies for comparing salaries, the size of offices, or anything else.

However, people do engage in interpersonal comparisons of utility (Chapter 3). The important point is that interpersonal comparisons and arguments based on "fairness" are inherently subjective, which leaves no rational method for fair division.

Independence of Irrelevant Alternatives
The **independence of irrelevant alternatives** axiom states that the best outcome in a feasible set of outcomes will also be the best outcome in any smaller subset of feasible outcomes that still contains that outcome. For example, a subset of a bargaining game may be obtained by excluding some of the irrelevant alternatives from the original game, without excluding the original agreement point itself. The exclusion of irrelevant alternatives does not change the settlement.

Consider Exhibit A1-10: The Nash solution is point *u*. Imagine the settlement options in the half-ellipse below the 45-degree line are eliminated. According to the independence of irrelevant alternatives axiom, this change should not affect the settlement outcome, which should still be *u*.

This axiom allows a point prediction to be made in asymmetric games by allowing them to be enlarged to be symmetric. For example, imagine that the game parties play is an asymmetric one like that just described (that is, the half-ellipse below the 45-degree line is eliminated). Such a bargaining problem would be asymmetric, perhaps with player 2 having an advantage. According to Nash, it is useful to expand the asymmetric game to be one that is symmetric—for example, by including the points in the lower half of the ellipse that mirrors the half-ellipse above the 45-degree line. Once these points are included, the game is symmetric, and the Nash solution may be identified. Of course, the settlement outcome yielded by the new, expanded game must also be present in the original game.

The independence of irrelevant alternatives axiom is motivated by the way negotiation unfolds.[24] Through a process of voluntary mutual concessions, the set of possible outcomes under consideration gradually decreases to just those around the eventual agreement point. This axiom asserts that the winnowing process does not change the agreement point.

In summary, Nash's theorem states that the unique solution possesses these properties. Nash's solution selects the unique point that maximizes the geometric average (i.e., the product) of the gains available to people as measured against their reservation points. For this reason, the Nash solution is also known as the **Nash product**. If all possible outcomes are plotted on a graph whose rectangular coordinates measure the utilities that the two players derive from them, as in Exhibit A1-9 and Exhibit A1-10, the solution is a unique point on the upper-right boundary of the region. The point is unique because two solution points could be joined by a straight line representing available alternative outcomes achievable by mixing, with various odds, the probabilities of the original two outcomes, and the points on the line connecting them would yield higher products of the two players' utilities. In other words, the region is presumed convex by reason of the possibility of probability mixtures, and the convex region has a single maximum-utility-product point, or Nash point.

[24]Harsanyi, J. C. (1990). Bargaining. In J. Eatwell, M. Milgate, & P. Newman (Eds.), *The new Palgrave: A dictionary of economics* (pp. 54–67). New York: Norton.

A p p e n d i x 2

Nonverbal Communication and Lie Detection

The purpose of this appendix is to help you (a) be a better reader of nonverbal communication and (b) be a better sender of nonverbal communication.

What Are We Looking for in Nonverbal Communication?

What exactly do we mean by nonverbal communication? **Nonverbal communication** is anything that is "not words." Specifically, it includes the following:

- *Vocal cues or paralinguistic cues.* Paralinguistic cues include pauses, intonation, and fluency. Vocal cues, such as tone and inflection, are nonverbal; they include speech volume, pace, and pitch.
- *Facial expressions.* Smiling, frowning, or expressing surprise. "Facial expressions are books without covers."[1]
- *Eye contact.* A high level of held gazing can be interpreted as a sign of liking or friendliness. However, in other cultures, prolonged eye contact is a sign of dominance or aggression.[2]
- *Interpersonal spacing.* The distance between people when they talk or communicate.
- *Posture.* How people hold and orient their body, including opening their arms and chest, etc.
- *Body movements.* When people are experiencing greater arousal, or nervousness, they tend to make more movements.
- *Gesture.* The three basic kinds of gestures are (a) **emblems**, which symbolize certain messages, such as the North American thumbs-up for "okay," and the finger on the lips for "quiet;" (b) **illustrators**, which em-

bellish a verbal message, such as the widening of hands and arms when talking about something that is large; and (c) **adaptors**, which include things like touching one's nose or twitching in such a way that does not embellish or illustrate a particular point.
- *Touching.* Touching another person (in an appropriate way) often leads to positive reactions.

Nonverbal communication is informative because it is relatively irrepressible in that people cannot control it. What nonverbal signals do negotiators look for, and what do they reveal? To address this question, we conducted a survey of 50 MBA students who had recently completed a multiparty negotiation. The majority of students relied on three nonverbal cues as a window into other party's true feelings and intentions: (a) eye contact (people who are lying avoid looking the other party straight in the eyes); (b) closed body posture ("When he leans toward me while he talks, I tend to trust him more"); and (c) nervousness, twitching, and fidgeting (if people play with their shoestrings, tap their pen, bite their lip, or indicate any other nervous tension, it usually signals anxiety and nervousness). Other indicators mentioned, although much less frequently included, are lack of gestures (too much stillness), emotional outbursts, and autonomic responses, such as sweating and blushing.

What particular nonverbal behaviors do negotiators notice that lead them to distrust

---

[1]DePaulo, B. M., & Friedman, H. S. (1998). Nonverbal communication. In D. T. Gilbert, S. T. Fiske, & G. Lindzey (Eds.), *The handbook of social psychology* (4th ed.). New York: McGraw-Hill.
[2]Ellsworth, P. C., & Carlsmith, J. M. (1973). Eye contact and gaze aversion in aggressive encounters. *Journal of Personality and Social Psychology, 33,* 117–122.

EXHIBIT A2-1   Nonverbal Behaviors

What nonverbal behaviors mean you should not trust someone?	What nonverbal behaviors mean you should trust someone?
• Fidgeting • Excessive smiling; sheepish smiles • Overly serious tone; lack of emotion • Averting eyes; lack of eye contact • Being too quiet	• Direct speech • Open gestures and behavior • Smiling • Pointing

Note: These behaviors are perceived to be linked to trust; they are not actually indicative of trust.

someone? (See Exhibit A2-1 for a list of such behaviors.)

Next, we consider three aspects of nonverbal communication that can affect the nature and outcome of negotiation: (a) gender differences, in terms of ability and accuracy, (b) nonverbal abilities of powerful and dominant people, and (c) nonverbal abilities of charismatic people.[3] Obviously, power and charisma have implications for success at the bargaining table.

Are Women More "Nonverbally Gifted" Than Men?

Popular culture has it that women are more nonverbally sensitive than men. And scientific evidence backs up this claim: Women *are* more skilled in terms of **nonverbal expression**.[4] In general, women are more open, expressive, approachable, and actively involved in social interaction than men. Their faces are more readable than men's, and they smile and gaze at other people and approach them more closely than do men. Women are

also gazed at more, and approached more closely than men.[5] During interactions, women seem more focused on the other person, and they also elicit more warmth and less anxiety from others.[6] However, the sexes are held to different standards of appropriate expressivity; women are typically considered more expressive, and men are viewed as more composed.[7] Women anticipate greater costs and fewer rewards than men if they fail to express positive emotion in response to someone else's good news.[8]

Nonverbal expressiveness is linked with social power. Greater expressivity is required by those of lower social status and power.[9] In many organizations, women traditionally have lower social status than men. Indeed, in studies of visual dominance (measured as the ratio of time a person spends looking at his or her partner while speaking relative to the time spent looking while listening), women are often less dominant. High-power people are more visually dominant than low-power people.[10] When women

---

[3]DePaulo & Friedman, "Nonverbal communication."

[4]Ibid.; Hall, J. A. (1984). *Nonverbal sex differences: Communication accuracy and expressive style.* Baltimore: Johns Hopkins University Press.

[5]Hall, *Nonverbal sex differences.*

[6]Abramowitz, C. V., Abramowitz, S. I., & Weitz, L. J. (1976). Are men therapists soft on empathy? Two studies in feminine understanding. *Journal of Clinical Psychology, 32*(2), 434–437.

[7]Hall, *Nonverbal sex differences.*

[8]Stoppard, J. M., & Gun-Gruchy, C. (1993). Gender, context, and expression of positive emotion. *Personality and Social Psychology Bulletin, 19*(2), 143–150.

[9]Henley, N. M. (1977). *Body politics: Power, sex, and non-verbal communication.* Upper Saddle River, NJ: Prentice Hall.

[10]Dovidio, J. F., & Ellyson, S. L. (1982). Decoding visual dominance: Attributions of power based on relative percentages of looking while speaking and looking while listening. *Social Psychology Quarterly, 45*(2), 106–113.

have uncertain support in a leadership position, men express more visual dominance than women.[11] When people show more visual dominance, they are perceived as more powerful. Furthermore, when women and men are assigned to different power roles, low-power people (regardless of gender) are better able to read their partner's cues.[12]

In terms of **nonverbal reception**, women are no better than men at recognizing covert messages, such as discrepant or deceptive communication (which we discuss later). However, when people are being truthful, women are more accurate than men; however, when people are being deceptive (i.e., when the negotiator is pretending to like someone), women are less accurate than men.[13]

In short, women are better at detecting feelings but are not necessarily better at detecting deception, because anyone who is inferior in status is more sensitive to states of mind of superiors. For example, when women and men are assigned to be supervisors or subordinates in organizational simulations, no differences are evident in emotional sensitivity between genders: Subordinates, regardless of gender, are more sensitive than their superiors.

Dominance

People often assert dominance and power through nonverbal cues. Dominant people sit higher, stand taller, talk louder, and have more space and more resources than non-dominant people. Dominant people are more likely to invade others' space (e.g., putting their feet up on their own or someone else's desk), make more expansive gestures, walk in front of others, sit in front of others or sit at the head of a table, interrupt more often, control time, and stare the other party down more, but they tend to look away more often when the other party is speaking.[14]

High social power is reliably indicated by patterns of looking while speaking and listening. People with less power look more when listening than when speaking. In contrast, more powerful people look about the same amount when listening as when speaking.[15] When people interact with a dominant person, they often respond by decreasing their postural stance (i.e., they often behave more submissively); in contrast, people who interact with a submissive person often increase their stance (i.e., they behave more assertively).[16] Interestingly, liking between people is greater when the interaction is complementary as opposed to reciprocal, meaning that dominance in response to submission and submission in response to dominance result in greater liking between people than dominance in response to dominance and submission in response to submissiveness. In short, people (whether they are dominant or submissive) are more comfortable and like each other more when interacting with people who are not like themselves.[17]

[11]Brown, C. E., Dovidio, J. F., & Ellyson, S. L. (1990). Reducing sex differences in visual displays of dominance: Knowledge is power. *Personality and Social Psychology Bulletin, 16*(2), 358–368.

[12]Snodgrass, S. E. (1985). Women's intuition: The effect of subordinate role on interpersonal sensitivity. *Journal of Personality and Social Psychology, 49*(1), 146–155; Snodgrass, S. E. (1992). Further effects of role versus gender on interpersonal sensitivity. *Journal of Personality and Social Psychology, 62*(1), 154–158.

[13]DePaulo, B. M., Epstein, J. A., & Wyer, M. M. (1993). Sex differences in lying: How women and men deal with the dilemma of deceit. In M. Lewis & C. Saarni (Eds.), *Lying and deception in everyday life* (pp. 126–147). New York: Guilford Press; Rosenthal, R., & DePaulo, B. M. (1979). Sex differences in accommodation in nonverbal communication. In R. Rosenthal (Ed.), *Skill in nonverbal communication: Individual differences* (pp. 68–103). Cambridge, MA: Oelgeschlager, Gunn, and Hain; Rosenthal, R., & DePaulo, B. M. (1979). Sex differences in eavesdropping on nonverbal cues. *Journal of Personality and Social Psychology, 37*(2), 273–285.

[14]DePaulo & Friedman, "Nonverbal communication."

[15]Exline, R. V., Ellyson, S. L., & Long, B. (1975). Visual behavior as an aspect of power role relationships. In P. Pliner, L. Krames, & T. Alloway (Eds.), *Advances in the study of communication and affect: Vol. 2. Nonverbal communication of aggression* (pp. 21–52). New York: Plenum.

[16]Tiedens, L. Z., & Fragale, A. R. (2003). Power moves: Complementary in dominant and submissive nonverbal behavior. *Journal of Personality and Social Psychology, 84*(3), 558–568.

[17]Ibid.

When men and women have equal knowledge, power, and expertise (or when men have more), men behave *visually* as though they really are more powerful. However, when women have the advantage, they "look" like powerful people more often than men.[18]

Personal Charisma

Charisma is a social skill having to do with verbal and nonverbal expressiveness. People vary strikingly in the intensity, expansiveness, animation, and dynamism of their nonverbal (and verbal) behaviors.[19] Differences in expressiveness are linked directly to affection, empathy, influence, and professional success, as well as to interpersonal experiences, such as the regulation of one's own emotional experiences and physical and mental health.

Expressiveness, or **spontaneous sending**, is the ease with which people's feelings can be read from their nonverbal expressive behaviors when they are not trying to deliberately communicate their feelings to others.[20] Expressiveness instantly makes a difference in setting the tone of social interactions. Even commonplace interpersonal behaviors, such as walking into a room and initiating a conversation[21] or greeting someone who is approaching[22] suggest this social skill is immediately influential. Why? Expressive people make better first impressions and, even over time, they are better liked than unexpressive people.[23] Expressive people are considered to be more attractive than unexpressive people.[24] Furthermore, expressive people capture people's attention[25] and then "turn on" the expressive behavior of other people.[26] Expressive people are good actors, feigning convincing expressions of feelings they are not actually experiencing.[27] It follows that they are also good liars.[28]

The most interpersonally successful communicators are nonverbally sensitive, nonverbally expressive, nonverbally self-controlled, and motivated to perform for their "audiences."[29] In social interactions, expressive people can "set the tone and frame the field."[30]

[18]Dovidio, J. F., Brown, C. E., Heltman, K., Ellyson, S. L., et al. (1988). Power displays between women and men in discussions of gender-linked tasks: A multichannel study. *Journal of Personality and Social Psychology, 55*(4), 580–587; Dovidio, J. F., Ellyson, S. L., Keating, C. F., Heltman, K., et al. (1988). The relationship of social power to visual displays of dominance between men and women. *Journal of Personality and Social Psychology, 54*(2), 233–242.
[19]Friedman, H. S., Prince, L. M., Riggio, R. E., & DiMatteo, M. R. (1980). Understanding and assessing nonverbal expressiveness: The Affective Communication Test. *Journal of Personality and Social Psychology, 39*(2), 333–351; Halberstadt, A. G. (1991). Toward an ecology of expressiveness: Family socialization in particular and a model in general. In R. S. Feldman & B. Rime (Eds.), *Fundamentals of nonverbal behavior: Studies in emotion and social interaction* (pp. 106–160). New York: Cambridge University Press; Manstead, A. S. R. (1991). Expressiveness as an individual difference. In R. S. Feldman & B. Rime (Eds.), *Fundamentals of nonverbal behavior: Studies in emotion and social interaction* (pp. 285–328). New York: Cambridge University Press.
[20]Buck, R. (1984). On the definition of emotion: Functional and structural considerations. *Cahiers de Psychologie Cognitive, 4*(1), 44–47; Notarius, C. I., & Levenson, R. W. (1979). Expressive tendencies and physiological response to stress. *Journal of Personality and Social Psychology, 37*(7), 1204–1210.
[21]Friedman, H. S., Riggio, R. E., & Casella, D. F. (1988). Nonverbal skill, personal charisma, and initial attraction. *Personality and Social Psychology Bulletin, 14*(1), 203–211.
[22]DiMatteo, M. R., Friedman, H. S., & Taranta, A. (1979). Sensitivity to bodily nonverbal communication as a factor in practitioner-patient rapport. *Journal of Nonverbal Behavior, 4*(1), 18–26.
[23]Cunningham, M. R. (1986). Measuring the physical in physical attractiveness: Quasi-experiments on the sociobiology of female facial beauty. *Journal of Personality and Social Psychology, 50*, 925–935.
[24]DePaulo, B. M., Blank, A. L., Swaim, G. W., & Hairfield, J. G. (1992). Expressiveness and expressive control. *Personality and Social Psychology Bulletin, 18*(3), 276–285.
[25]Sullins, E. S. (1989). Perceptual salience as a function of nonverbal expressiveness. *Personality and Social Psychology Bulletin, 15*(4), 584–595.
[26]Buck, "On the definition of emotion."
[27]Buck, R. (1975). Nonverbal communication of affect in children. *Journal of Personality and Social Psychology, 31*(4), 644–653.
[28]DePaulo, Blank, Swaim, & Hairfield, "Expressiveness and expressive control."
[29]DePaulo & Friedman, "Nonverbal communication."
[30]Ibid. p. 14.

EXHIBIT A2-2	Cues for Detecting Lies	

Cue	Perceived	Actual
Facial movements	yes	no
Speech hesitation	yes	yes
Changes in pitch	yes	yes
Speech errors	yes	yes
Speech rate	yes	no
Response length	no	yes (short for liars)
Blinking	(no data)	yes (more for liars)
Pupil dilation	(no data)	yes
Touching self	no	yes
Postural shifts	yes	no
Gaze	yes	no

Perceived: what people think are cues that indicate deception.

Actual: what clues can truly indicate deception.

Source: Adapted from Telling lies: Clues to Deceit in the Marketplace, Politics, and Marriage by Paul Ekman. Copyright © 2001, 1992, 1985 by Paul Ekman. Used by permission of W. W. Norton & Company, Inc.

Detecting Deception

Nonverbal sensitivity (in terms of accuracy) is a plus in negotiation, as it is in most social interaction. For instance, doctors who are good at reading body language have more satisfied patients.[31] Students who are nonverbally sensitive learn more than less sensitive students.[32] However, nonverbal sensitivity is difficult to achieve. As a skill, it is not correlated with intelligence, and it is very "channel-specific": Skill at understanding facial expression and body movements is measurably different from skill at understanding tone of voice.[33] Nonverbal sensitivity improves with age.[34] (See Exhibit A2-2 for a list of the cues that are relevant when detecting lies.)

Reading and sending nonverbal messages in negotiation is one thing; detecting deception (and pulling off deception) is another.[35] Obviously, it is to a negotiator's advantage to accurately detect deception at the negotiation table. In fact, relying on nonverbal cues may be our only hope of detecting deception. People believe that either liars cannot control their nonverbal behaviors and therefore these behaviors will "leak out" and betray the liar's true feelings, or

[31]DiMatteo, M. R., Hays, R. D., & Prince, L. M. (1986). Relationship of physicians' nonverbal communication skill to patient satisfaction, appointment noncompliance, and physician workload. *Health Psychology, 5*(6), 581–594.

[32]Bernieri, F. J. (1991). Interpersonal sensitivity in teaching interactions. *Personality and Social Psychology Bulletin, 17*(1), 98–103.

[33]DePaulo, B. M., & Rosenthal, R. (1979). Telling lies. *Journal of Personality and Social Psychology, 37*(10), 1713–1722.

[34]Buck, "On the definition of emotion"; Zuckerman, M., Blanck, P. D., DePaulo, B. M., & Rosenthal, R. (1980). Developmental changes in decoding discrepant and nondiscrepant nonverbal cues. *Developmental Psychology, 16*(3), 220–228.

[35]For reviews, see Croson, R. (2005). Deception of economics experiments. In C. Gerschlager (Ed.), *Deception in markets: An economic analysis* (pp. 113–130). Basingstoke, England: Palgrave-Macmillan; Schweitzer, M. (2001). Deception in negotiations. In S. Hoch & H. Kunreuther (Eds.), *Wharton on making decisions* (pp. 187–200). New York: Wiley.

liars simply will not control all of their nonverbal cues.[36]

Unfortunately, no foolproof nonverbal indicators of deception have been discovered. In fact, most people cannot tell from demeanor when others are lying.[37] Accuracy rates are close to chance levels.[38] People who have been professionally trained (e.g., law enforcement groups) are more accurate.[39] For example, law enforcement officers and clinical psychologists are very accurate in judging videotapes of people who are lying or telling the truth.[40]

There are many things to lie about in negotiation. Some lies may be complete falsifications (such as falsifying an inspection report or pretending another buyer will be calling at any moment with an offer); other lies may be exaggerations (exaggerating the appraised value of a property, exaggerating the attractiveness of one's BATNA). It is more difficult for liars to successfully carry off hard lies (i.e., complete falsifications of information) than to carry off easy lies (exaggerations). Consequently, it is easier for negotiators to detect complete falsifications.

What should you do to maximize the chances of catching a lie in negotiation? It is generally not an effective lie-detection strategy to ask people whether they are lying. Usually, they will say no. So what can you do? Several direct methods, as well as some indirect methods, may be helpful.[41]

Direct Methods

Triangulation   One of the best methods of lie detection is questioning. The process of asking several questions, all designed as cross-checks on one another, is known as **triangulation**. For example, if a person wants to accurately assess the time of day, relying on only one clock can be risky. A better method is to use two or three clocks or different timepieces. Similarly, if a person wants to "catch" a liar, a good strategy is to examine nonverbal cues, verbal cues, and perhaps outside evidence as well.

Direct questions are particularly effective in curtailing lies of omission; however, they may actually increase lies of commission.[42] Detectives and lawyers ask several questions of people they think might be lying. Their questions are designed so that inconsistencies emerge if a person is lying. It is very difficult for even the best of liars to be perfectly consistent in all aspects of a lie.

Objective Evidence   Another direct fashion is to focus on inconsistencies and vagueness. And, in the case of inconsistency, ask for evidence; if appropriate, suggest contingencies. When people buy a used car, they often don't simply rely on the owner's claims of its reliability; rather, they seek an objective, expert opinion. For example, they often have an experienced mechanic inspect the car. This additional assessment is what we mean by **objective evidence**.

---

[36]Ekman, P., & Friesen, W. V. (1969). Nonverbal leakage and clues to deception. *Psychiatry, 32*(1), 88–106.
[37]Ekman, P., O'Sullivan, M. O., & Frank, M. G. (1999). A few can catch a liar. *Psychological Science, 10*(3), 263–266.
[38]See DePaulo, B. M. (1994). Spotting lies: Can humans learn to do better? *Current Directions in Psychological Science, 3*(3), 83–86; DePaulo, B. M., Lassiter, G. D., & Stone, J. I. (1982). Attentional determinants of success at detecting deception and truth. *Personality and Social Psychology Bulletin, 8*(2), 273–279; Zuckerman, M., Koestner, R., & Driver, R. (1981). Beliefs about cues associated with deception. *Journal of Nonverbal Behavior, 6*(2), 105–114.
[39]Ekman, O'Sullivan, & Frank, "A few can catch a liar."
[40]Ibid.
[41]See also Schweitzer, "Deception in negotiations."
[42]Schweitzer, M., & Croson, R. (1999). Curtailing deception: The impact of direct questions on lies and omissions. *International Journal of Conflict Management, 10,* 225–248.

Linguistic Style   Telling lies often requires creating a story about an experience or attitude that does not exist. Consequently, false stories are qualitatively different from true stories. Compared to truth-tellers, liars have less cognitive complexity (shades of gray) in their stories, use fewer self-references and fewer other-references, and use more negative-emotion words.[43] Liars hesitate more and have more speech errors. Further, their response length to questions is shorter.

Indirect Methods

Enrich the Mode of Communication   It is usually easier to catch a liar when communicating face-to-face than when communicating via telephone or e-mail. If negotiations have been proceeding by phone, written correspondence, or e-mail, the negotiator who wants to catch a lie should insist on a face-to-face interaction. First, people are less likely to lie face-to-face than they are when on the telephone or e-mail. Second, it is easier to detect a lie in a face-to-face interaction partly because it is much more difficult for liars to monitor themselves when the communication modality is multichanneled (as it is in face-to-face negotiations). Telltale signs of lying are often found in nonverbal "leakage," such as in the hands or body, rather than the face or words, which liars usually carefully monitor.[44] For example, liars tend to touch themselves more and blink more than truth-tellers.

Do Not Rely on a Person's Face   Most people look at a person's face when they want to detect deception, but this focus is not always effective. Perceivers are able to detect deception at greater-than-chance levels from every individual channel or combination of channels with the exception of one: the face.[45] In fact, people are better off when they cannot see another's face. Facial expressions are misleading at worst and, at best, are of qualified use as cues to deceit. Gaze is not diagnostic in detecting a liar.

Tone of Voice   Paying attention to tone of voice is a better indicator of deception than is facial expression.[46] Useful information can come through the voice, which people do not often consider or detect. People's pitch is higher when they are lying than when they are telling the truth; they speak more slowly and with less fluency and engage in more sentence repairs.[47]

Microexpressions   Deception can be detected in the face if you are specially trained to look for microexpressions (or if you have a videotape you can play back to look for microexpressions). **Microexpressions** are expressions people show on their face for about one tenth of a second. These expressions reveal how a person is truly feeling, but because of social pressure and self-presentation they are quickly wiped away. As an example, consider an investigation in which the facial expressions of men and women participants were secretly observed while they were interacting with male and female assistants specially trained to act as leaders during a group discussion.[48] The results were clear: Female leaders received more negative nonverbal cues (microexpressions) from other members of the group than did male leaders. Moreover, male leaders also received more positive nonverbal

---

[43]Newman, M. L., Pennebaker, J. W., Berry, D. S., & Richards, J. M. (2003). Lying words: Predicting deception from linguistic styles. *Personality and Social Psychology Bulletin, 29*(5), 665–675.

[44]Ekman, P. (1984). The nature and function of the expression of emotion. In K. Scherer & P. Ekman (Eds.), *Approaches to emotion.* Hillsdale, NJ: Erlbaum.

[45]Zuckerman, M., DePaulo, B. M., & Rosenthal, R. (1981). Verbal and nonverbal communication of deception. In L. Berkowitz (Ed.), *Advances in experimental social psychology: Vol. 14* (pp. 1–59). New York: Academic Press.

[46]DePaulo, Lassiter, & Stone, "Attentional determinants of success."

[47]Ekman, P. (2001). *Telling lies: Clues to deceit in the marketplace, politics, and marriage* (3rd ed.). New York: Norton.

[48]Butler, D., & Geis, F. L. (1990). Nonverbal affect responses to male and female leaders: Implications for leadership evaluations. *Journal of Personality and Social Psychology, 58*(1), 48–59.

cues per minute than did female leaders. These findings emerged even though participants strongly denied any bias against females.

Interchannel Discrepancies   To detect deception, look for inconsistencies among these channels, such as tone of voice, body movements, gestures, and so on. As a general rule, watch the body, not the face, and look for clusters of clues. **Illustrators** are another type of body movement that can provide clues about deception.[49] Illustrators depict speech as it is spoken. It is the hands that usually illustrate speech—giving emphasis to a word or phrase, tracing the flow of thought in the air, drawing a picture in space, or showing an action can repeat or amplify what is being said. Eyebrow and upper eyelid movements can also provide emphasis illustrators, as can the entire body or upper torso. Illustrators are used to help explain ideas that are difficult to put into words. For example, people are more likely to illustrate when asked to define the word "zigzag" than the word "chair." Illustrators increase when people are more involved with what is being said; people illustrate less than usual when they are uninvolved, bored, disinterested, or deeply saddened. Illustrators are often confused with emblems, but it is important to distinguish them because these two kinds of body movements may change in opposite ways when people lie: emblematic slips may increase, whereas illustrators will usually decrease. People who feign concern or enthusiasm can be betrayed by the failure to accompany their speech with increased illustrators, and illustrators decrease when a person does not know exactly what to say. For example, if a liar has not adequately worked out a lie in ad-

vance, the liar will have to be cautious and carefully consider each word before it is spoken.

Eye Contact   People who are lying blink more often, have dilated pupils, and have lower eye contact than truth-tellers. However, blinking rates and dilation of pupils are almost impossible to detect with the naked eye (which is why "gaze" is listed as *not* diagnostic in Exhibit A2-2). Although eye contact is the primary cue used by MBA students to detect deceit, it is not reliable; often, it is irrelevant, primarily because it is something that people can control too readily.

Be Aware of Egocentric Biases   Most negotiators regard themselves as truthful and honest and their opponents as dishonest, indicating an egocentric bias. For example, in our investigation, MBA students thought they deceived others in a 10-week negotiation course 22% of the time, whereas they thought they had been deceived by others 40% of the time.

How Motivation and Temptation Affect Lying and Deception

People are more likely to be deceptive when they are likely to get away with it and especially when their potential gain from deception is highest. In one investigation, people were given enticing prospects for large monetary gain in an ultimatum game if they deceived.[50] Although "proposers" and "responders" chose deceptive strategies almost equally, proposers told more outright lies.[51] Moreover, proposers were more deceptive when their potential profits were highest. Proposers deceived about 13.6% of the time, and responders deceived about 13.9% of the time.[52] **Motivated communication** is not purely opportunistic: If liars feel

---

[49]Ekman, *Telling lies.*

[50]Boles, T., Croson, R., & Murnighan, J. K. (2000). Deception and retribution in repeated ultimatum bargaining. *Organizational Behavior and Human Decision Processes, 83*(2), 235–259.

[51]Ibid.

[52]Croson, "Deception of economics experiments."

that they can "justify" a lie (such as when some uncertainty is involved), they are more likely to lie, even when the costs and benefits for misrepresentation are held constant.[53]

Consider two types of lies: monitoring-dependent and monitoring-independent.[54] **Monitoring-dependent lies** require that the liar monitor the reaction of the target for the lie to be effective; conversely, **monitoring-independent lies** do not require the liar to monitor. If someone wants to lie about a closing date, it would be important to determine what kind of closing date is preferred by the target (one cannot assume early or late). Conversely, if one is attempting to lie about interest rates, it is safe to assume that mortgage holders would uniformly want lower rates; and thus, it is not as important to monitor their reaction to this type of statement. Liars are more likely to tell monitoring-dependent lies when they have visual access (than when they don't). The use of monitoring-independent lies is the same, with or without visual access. In this sense, visual access can actually harm potential targets of deception by increasing their risk of being deceived.

When potential deceivers have high incentives to deceive, they are more emotional.[55] It is hard to conceal these feelings. An exception might be people who have great practice at lying and few qualms about the appropriateness of stretching the truth in a selling context, such as experienced salespersons.[56]

Deception and Secrecy Can Create a Life of Their Own

People who are told to keep a secret can become preoccupied with the secret.[57] The secret becomes more accessible in their memory and absorbs their consciousness (as judged by word association and reaction times). Why? Keeping a secret takes mental control. Often, secrecy is linked to obsession and attraction.[58] For example, in a card-playing game, some pairs were told to engage in "nonverbal communication" with their feet to try to influence the game. They were told to either keep it a secret from the other couple or let it be known. After the game, those players who engaged in more nonverbal, secret communication reported more attraction to the other party than those who did not engage in the secretive behavior.[59]

---

[53]Schweitzer, M., & Hsee, C. (2002). Stretching the truth: Elastic justification and motivated communication of uncertain information. *Journal of Risk and Uncertainty, 25*(2), 185–201.

[54]Schweitzer, M., Brodt, S., & Croson, R. (2002). Seeing and believing: Visual access and the strategic use of deception. *International Journal of Conflict Management, 13*(3), 258–275.

[55]DePaulo, B. M., & Kirkendol, S. E. (1989). The motivational impairment effect in the communication of deception. In J. C. Yuille (Ed.), *Credibility assessment* (pp. 51–70). Dordrecht, The Netherlands: Kluwer.

[56]DePaulo, P. J., & DePaulo, B. M. (1989). Can deception by salespersons and customers be detected through nonverbal behavioral cues? *Journal of Applied Social Psychology, 19*(18, pt. 2), 1552–1577.

[57]Wegner, D. M. (1994). Ironic processes of mental control. *Psychological Review, 101,* 34–52.

[58]Wegner, D. M., Lane, J. D., & Dimitri, S. (1994). The allure of secret relationships. *Journal of Personality and Social Psychology, 66*(2), 287–300.

[59]Wegner, D. M., Shortt, J. W., Blake, A. W., & Page, M. S. (1990). The suppression of exciting thoughts. *Journal of Personality and Social Psychology, 58,* 409–418.

Appendix 3

Third-Party Intervention

Sometimes, despite the best of intentions, the bargaining process breaks down, and negotiators are unable to reach an agreement on their own. When this happens at the international level, war results. Indeed, 434 international crises occurred between December 1918 and December 2005.[1] When impasse occurs at the individual level, negotiators may pursue legal action. Sometimes parties try third-party intervention in an effort to avoid court action. Third-party intervention can be an excellent means of reaching settlement when the costs of disagreement are high.

Some negotiators make mediation-arbitration contingencies in the event of disagreement, thereby promising in advance to avoid legal action. For example, as the first wave of Y2K-inspired lawsuits began to emerge, a group of the largest companies vowed not to let the litigation grow into a torrent. A dozen multinational corporations, including General Mills, McDonald's Corp., Philip Morris, and Bank of America,

signed a commitment to use mediation, not litigation, for Y2K disputes with supply-chain partners and vendors.[2]

We review the roles of third parties, key challenges facing third parties, and strategies for enhancing the effectiveness of third-party intervention.

Common Third-Party Roles

A third party may intervene in a dispute in a number of ways.[3]

Mediation

Mediation is a procedure whereby a third party assists disputants in achieving a voluntary settlement (i.e., the mediator cannot impose a settlement on the disputants). Mediation offers the possibility of discovering underlying issues and promoting integrative agreements.[4] Mediation produces a high settlement rate (typically 60–80%), though settlement is not guaranteed.[5] Mediation serves an important face-saving function: Each party can make concessions

[1]Brecher, Michael, and Jonathan Wilkenfeld. International Crisis Behavior Project, 1918-2004 [Computer file]. ICPSR09286-v7. College Park, MD: Michael Brecher and Jonathan Wilkenfeld, University of Maryland [producers], 2007. Ann Arbor, MI: Inter-university Consortium for Political and Social Research [distributor], 2007–12–14.

[2]McKendrick, J. (1999). The third way: Mitigate, not litigate Y2K beefs. *Midrange Systems, 12*(2), 52.

[3]For a more complete discussion, see Rubin, J. Z., Pruitt, D. G., & Kim, S. H. (1994). *Social conflict: Escalation, stalemate and settlement.* New York: McGraw-Hill; McGrath, J. E. (1966). A social psychological approach to the study of negotiations. In R. V. Bowers (Ed.), *Studies on behavior in organizations* (pp. 101–134). Athens: University of Georgia Press.

[4]McEwen, C. A., & Maiman, R. J. (1984). Mediation in small claims court: Achieving compliance through consent. *Law and Society Review, 18,* 11–49.

[5]Hoh, R. (1984). The effectiveness of mediation in public-sector arbitration systems: The Iowa experience. *Arbitration Journal, 39*(2), 30–40; Kochan, T. A. (1979). Dynamics of dispute resolution in the public sector. In B. Aaron, J. R. Grodin, & J. L. Stern (Eds.), *Public-sector bargaining* (pp. 150–190). Washington, DC: BNA Books; Kressel, K., & Pruitt, D. G. (1989). Conclusion: A research perspective on the mediation of social conflict. In K. Kressel & D. G. Pruitt (Eds.), *Mediation research* (pp. 394–435). San Francisco: Jossey-Bass.

without appearing weak.[6] Disputants often see mediation procedures as fair.[7]

Arbitration

Arbitration is a procedure whereby a third party holds a hearing, at which time disputants state their position on the issues, call witnesses, and offer supporting evidence for their respective positions.[8] After the hearing, the arbitrator issues a binding settlement. The greatest advantage of arbitration is that it always produces a settlement. Moreover, the mere threat of arbitration often motivates parties to settle voluntarily.[9] Like mediation, arbitration allows disputants to "save face" with their constituents because they can always blame the arbitrator if the imposed settlement is unsatisfactory.[10] The two major types of arbitration are traditional arbitration and final-offer arbitration.

Traditional Arbitration In **traditional arbitration**, each side submits a proposed settlement to the arbitrator, who is at liberty to come up with settlement terms to which both sides must agree. Oftentimes, the final settlement may be a midpoint between the settlement terms submitted by either party. For example, on *Cybersettle.com,* an online out-of-court settlement service, the algorithm immediately imposes a final settlement outcome that is midway between the last two offers submitted by either party. Thus, each side has an incentive to shape the

arbitrator's final judgment by submitting an offer that is self-serving.

An obvious disadvantage of traditional arbitration is that parties may reason that the third party will impose a settlement midway between the two final proposals submitted. This expectation leads the parties to submit extreme final proposals. The tendency for disputants to exaggerate their demands and reduce their level of concession making is known as the **chilling effect**.[11]

Final-Offer Arbitration Final-offer arbitration was developed in response to the chilling-effect problem of traditional arbitration.[12] In **final-offer arbitration**, the disputants submit final proposals to the arbitrator, who then chooses one of the two final settlements to impose. Thus, the incentive of the parties involved is to submit a settlement that will be viewed as most fair in the eyes of the arbitrator.

Mediation-Arbitration

Recognizing the strengths (and weaknesses) of mediation and arbitration, some scholars and practitioners have advocated the adoption of hybrid procedures: mediation-arbitration and arbitration-mediation.[13] **Mediation-arbitration** (hereafter **med-arb**) consists of two phases: (a) mediation followed by (b) arbitration if mediation fails to secure an agreement by a predetermined deadline. The same third party serves as both mediator

---

[6]Ross, W. H., & Conlon, D. E. (2000). Hybrid forms of third-party dispute resolution: Theoretical implications of combining mediation and arbitration. *Academy of Management Review, 25*(2), 416–427.

[7]Karambayya, R., & Brett, J. M. (1989). Managers handling disputes: Third-party roles and perceptions of fairness. *Academy of Management Journal, 32,* 687–704; Pierce, R. S., Pruitt, D. G., & Czaja, S. J. (1993). Complainant-respondent differences in procedural choice. *International Journal of Conflict Management, 4,* 199–122; Ross, W. H., Conlon, D. E., & Lind, E. A. (1990). The mediator as leader: Effects of behavioral style and deadline certainty on negotiator behavior. *Group and Organization Studies, 15,* 105–124.

[8]Ross & Conlon, "Hybrid forms."

[9]Farber, H. S., & Katz, H. (1979). Why is there disagreement in bargaining? *American Economic Review, 77,* 347–352.

[10]Marmo, M. (1995). The role of fact finding and interest arbitration in "selling" a settlement. *Journal of Collective Negotiations in the Public Sector, 14,* 77–97; Rose, J. B., & Manuel, C. (1996). Attitudes toward collective bargaining and compulsory arbitration. *Journal of Collective Negotiations in the Public Sector, 25,* 287–310.

[11]Notz, W. W., & Starke, F. A. (1987). Arbitration and distributive justice: Equity or equality? *Journal of Applied Psychology, 72,* 359–365.

[12]Farber, H. S. (1981). Splitting the difference in interest arbitration. *Industrial and Labor Relations Review, 35,* 70–77.

[13]For a review, see Ross & Conlon, "Hybrid forms."

and arbitrator.[14] Thus, arbitration is only engaged if mediation fails.

Arbitration-Mediation

Arbitration-mediation (hereafter **arb-med**) consists of three phases.[15] In phase one, the third party holds an **arbitration hearing**. At the end of this phase, the third party makes a decision, which is placed in a sealed envelope and is not revealed to the parties. The second phase consists of **mediation**. The sealed envelope containing the third party's decision is displayed prominently during the mediation phase. Only if mediation fails to produce a voluntary agreement by a specified deadline do the parties enter the third phase, called the **ruling phase**. Here, the third party removes the ruling from the envelope and reveals the binding ruling to the disputants.[16] To ensure that the envelope contains the original ruling and not a later decision (e.g., a ruling created after the mediation phase), the third party can ask a disputant from each side to sign the envelope across the seal at the beginning of mediation. The greatest benefit of arb-med is that it encourages disputants to settle their differences themselves.[17]

In a direct test of the effectiveness of med-arb and arb-med, disputants in the arb-med procedures settled in the mediation phase of their procedure more frequently and achieved settlements of higher joint benefit than did disputants in the med-arb procedure.[18]

Key Choice Points in Third-Party Intervention

Each of the four key types of third-party intervention are formal but more informal types of intervention are also possible. We now consider some key choice points of third-party intervention.

Outcome Versus Process Control

The key aspect in any type of third-party intervention involves the control held by the third party. The ability to control the outcome is the key distinction between mediation and arbitration. **Outcome control** refers to the ability of the third party to impose a final, binding settlement on the parties. In contrast, **process control** refers to the ability of the third party to control the discussions, questions, and process of communication.

The mediator has process control but not outcome control (i.e., the power to impose a settlement). In arbitration, third parties have process and outcome control. Arbitration may be passive or inquisitive, and the arbitrator can have full discretion to impose any kind of settlement or can have constraints, such as the requirement to choose one side's final offer.

Formal Versus Informal

The roles of many, perhaps most, third parties are defined on the basis of some formal understanding among the disputants or on the basis of legal precedents or licensing and certification procedures. Third-party roles are effective to the extent that they are acknowledged by the disputants as implying a legitimate right to be in the business of resolving conflicts. Formal roles include professional mediator, arbitrator, or ombudsperson. However, a variety of informal third-party roles exist, such as a friend who intervenes in a marriage dispute.

Invited Versus Uninvited

Most commonly, a third party intervenes at the request of one or both of the principals.

---

[14]Kagel, J. (1976). Comment. In H. Anderson (Ed.), *New techniques in labor dispute resolution* (pp. 185–190). Washington, DC: BNA Books.

[15]For a review see Ross & Conlon, "Hybrid forms."

[16]Cobbledick, G. (1992). Arb-med: An alternative approach to expediting settlement. Unpublished manuscript, Harvard Program on Negotiation, Harvard University, Boston; Sander, F. E. A. (1993). The courthouse and alternative dispute resolution. In L. Hall (Ed.), *Negotiation: Strategies for mutual gain* (pp. 43–60). Newbury Park, CA: Sage.

[17]Ross & Conlon, "Hybrid forms."

[18]Conlon, D. E., Moon, H., & Ng, K. Y. (2002). Putting the cart before the horse: The benefits of arbitrating before mediating. *Journal of Applied Psychology, 87*(5), 978–984.

For example, a divorcing couple may seek the services of a divorce mediator. Such invited roles are effective for two reasons: First, the invitation to intervene suggests that at least one of the parties is motivated to address the dispute in question. Second, the invitation makes the third party appropriate, acceptable, and desirable, thereby increasing clout and legitimacy. An example of an uninvited role is a customer in an airport witnessing a conflict between a flight agent and a passenger.

Interpersonal Versus Intergroup

Third parties typically intervene in disputes between individuals. In more complex situations, third-party intervention can occur in disputes between groups or nations.

Content Versus Process Orientation

Some third-party roles focus primarily on the content of a dispute, such as the issues or resources under consideration. Others focus more on the process of decision making and on the way in which decisions are taking place. Arbitrators (and to a lesser extent, mediators) are typically content oriented. In contrast, marriage counselors are more process focused (i.e., they try to get each party to listen to one another, etc.).

Facilitation, Formulation, or Manipulation

Mediators use any of three styles: facilitation, formulation and manipulation.[19] **Facilitation,** also known as communication, is characterized by mediators who serve as a channel of communication among disputing parties. Mediators who are facilitators occasionally reveal information they have gathered independently and thereby clarify misconceptions. For example, in a 1990 crisis between India and Pakistan, the U.S. delegation to Pakistan communicated that Pakistan's military was inferior and that the United States did not intend to help Pakistan in a war.[20] In contrast, **formulation** involves a substantive contribution to negotiations by conceiving and proposing new solutions. For example, during the 1992 crisis between Liberia and Sierra Leone, the Economic Community of West African States (ECOWAS) successfully structured the bargaining process and proposed the outcome to which the parties ultimately agreed. Finally, **manipulation** occurs when the mediator uses his or her position and leverage to influence the bargaining process, such as by offering incentives or even threats. For example, during the 1972 crisis between North Yemen and South Yemen, the mediator, Colonel Qaddhafi of Libya, threatened to hold captive the delegation leaders of both sides if they did not reach agreement. Moreover, he offered both sides nearly $50 million in annual aid if they did reach agreement. In a test of the effectiveness of each style in international crisis mediations, manipulation had the strongest effect on the likelihood of reaching a formal agreement and contributing to crisis abatement. Facilitation had the greatest influence on increasing the prospects for lasting tension reduction.[21]

Disputant Preferences

What types of mediation are most preferred by disputants? Participants in mediation generally preferred (a) control over outcome, such that a neutral third party would help disputants reach a mutually satisfactory resolution; (b) control over process such that disputants would relay information on their own behalf without the help of a representative and (c) either substantive rules that disputants would have agreed to before the resolution process or the rules typically used in court.[22]

[19]Beardsley, Quinn, Biswas, & Wilkenfeld, "Mediation style."
[20]Ibid.
[21]Ibid.
[22]Shestowsky, D. (2004). Procedural differences in alternative dispute resolution. *Psychology, Public Policy and the Law, 10*(3), 211–249.

Challenges Facing Third Parties

A number of challenges face the third party.[23]

Increasing the Likelihood That Parties Reach an Agreement if a Positive Bargaining Zone Exists

Effective third-party intervention not only assesses whether a positive bargaining zone exists, but it also helps parties reach agreement if it does. If settlement is not likely, it is to both parties' advantage to realize this issue quickly and exercise their BATNAs. For example, an increasing number of divorcing couples settle their financial disputes through face-to-face cooperation rather than courtroom confrontations.[24] The benefit of mediation, as opposed to the courtroom, is that the parties can talk and, as a result, often reach settlement quicker. One man estimated that he saved more than $10,000 in attorney fees by settling financial issues with his wife during a pair of 2-hour mediation sessions. Moreover, rather than focusing on their "legal rights," they focused on their "future needs" (i.e., an interests rather than a rights focus; see Chapter 5). However, if the divorcing couple is emotional, it may not work.

Promoting a Pareto-Efficient Outcome

It is not enough for third parties to help negotiators reach agreement. Ideally, they should strive for Pareto-optimal win-win agreements. Obviously, this type of agreement will not happen if the third party is not properly trained in integrative bargaining strategies or places a higher premium on reaching agreement over reaching a win-win agreement. Third parties should not let the desperation of the negotiators narrow their own view of the possibilities for integrative agreement.

Promoting Outcomes That Are Perceived as Fair in the Eyes of Disputants

When people feel that a deal is fair, they are more likely to agree to it, less likely to renege on it, and more likely to come to the table in the future. Third parties can be (negatively) affected by an acrimonious relationship among disputants. Mediators' interventions are most likely to be win-win when the relationship among the negotiators is positive and genuine; conversely, mediators are more likely to propose fixed-pie solutions when the negotiators' relationship is negative and not genuine.[25]

Improving the Relationship Between Parties

Ideally, effective third-party intervention should increase the level of trust between parties.

Empowering Parties in the Negotiation Process

A skilled mediator not only helps parties reach integrative settlements but also improves the ability of parties to reach settlements on their own. Ideally, the ability of negotiators to effectively resolve conflict and reach effective outcomes should be enhanced via the influence of a third party.

Debiasing Negotiators

Biased perceptions run rampant among negotiators, even in the best of circumstances. When conflict has escalated and parties are emotional, biased perceptions escalate further. Third parties should attempt, whenever possible, to debias negotiations. Unfortunately, a number of biases lurk in the jungle of conflict, including the following:

---

[23]Bazerman, M. H., & Neale, M. A. (1992). *Negotiating rationally* New York: Free Press.
[24]Silverman, S. (2003, June 22). Divorce mediation gains popularity. *The Pantagraph*, p. A1.
[25]Thompson, L., & Kim, P. H. (2000). How the quality of third parties' settlement solutions are affected by the relationship between negotiators. *Journal of Experimental Psychology: Applied, 6*(1), 1–16.

Exaggeration of Conflict Bias One pervasive bias exaggerates differences between oneself and the opposite party (in negotiation) and even in third parties (in mediation).[26] For example, when students from rival universities watch the same videotape of a football game, they perceive their own team as committing fewer infractions than those attributed to their team by the opposing side.[27] People underestimate the extent to which their beliefs are shaped by subjective construal rather than by direct perception of objective reality.[28]

Examination of partisans of both sides of contemporary social conflict (e.g., liberal versus conservative groups, pro-life versus pro-choice groups) reveal that partisans overestimate the extremity and consistency of the view of the other side.[29] Consider a deep-rooted conflict between the Nez Perce Tribe and local nontribal governments that operate within the boundaries of the Nez Perce Reservation.[30] Overall, disputants were more defensive than offensive. **Offensive behavior** is any attempted actions that benefit one's own side relative to the other side, and **defensive behavior** is antipathy toward actions that harm one's own side to the other side's benefit.[31] Disputants consistently exaggerated the offensiveness of the other side

and underestimated the defensiveness of the other side.

Hostile Media Bias Sometimes, parties on both sides of a conflict will view an even-handed media report to be partial to the other side. For example, news accounts of the 1982 Beirut Massacre were judged by partisans on both sides of the Arab-Israeli conflict to be partial to the other side.[32] Similarly, in another investigation, negotiators role-played an organizational mediation. Both sides to the conflict perceived the mediator to be partial to the opponent. Even when a mediator is partial to a particular side, that party often fails to realize this partiality and assumes the mediator is biased against it.

Overconfidence Bias In general, disputants overestimate the extent to which their beliefs are shared by a third party. For example, when negotiators are asked to estimate the likelihood of prevailing in final-offer arbitration, they are overconfident that the third party will favor their proposal.[33] Parties on both sides of the dispute estimate a greater than 50% chance of prevailing. Obviously, they cannot both be right.

The hostile media bias and the overconfidence bias seem to be contradictory. That is, how can people feel the mediator is simultaneously taking the view of the other side

---

[26]Morris, M. W. (1995). Through a glass darkly: Cognitive and motivational processes that obscure social perception in conflicts. Paper presented at the Academy of Management Meetings, Vancouver, BC.

[27]Hastorf, A., & Cantril, H. (1954). They saw a game: A case study. *Journal of Abnormal and Social Psychology, 49,* 129–134.

[28]Griffin, D. W., & Ross, L. (1991). Subjective construal, social inference, and human misunderstanding. In M. P. Zanna (Ed.), *Advances in experimental social psychology: Vol. 24* (pp. 319–359). San Diego, CA: Academic Press.

[29]Robinson, R. J., Keltner, D., Ward, A., & Ross, L. (1994). Actual versus assumed differences in construal: "Naïve realism" in intergroup perception and conflict. *Journal of Personality and Social Psychology, 68,* 404–417.

[30]Allred, K. G., Hong, K., & Kalt, J. P. (2002). Partisan misperceptions and conflict escalation: Survey evidence from a tribal/local government conflict. Paper presented at the International Association of Conflict Management, Park City, UT.

[31]Ibid.

[32]Vallone, R. P., Ross, L., & Lepper, M. (1985). The hostile media phenomenon: Biased perception and perceptions of media bias in coverage of the "Beirut Massacre." *Journal of Personality and Social Psychology, 49,* 577–585.

[33]Bazerman & Neale, *Negotiating rationally;* Neale, M. A., & Bazerman, M. H. (1983). The role of perspective taking ability in negotiating under different forms of arbitration. *Industrial and Labor Relations Review, 36,* 378–388.

and also agreeing with their own position? The apparent inconsistency stems from the nature of the judgment made by negotiators.[34] In a direct test of this question, negotiators' perceptions of mediator behavior were examined in a realistic simulation of an organization. Each negotiator simultaneously displayed an egocentric (overconfidence) bias, evaluating his or her behavior as more successful than that of the counterparts. However, when asked about the amount and content of the mediator's attention to disputants, they saw themselves as coming up short. Each party perceived the mediator spent more time talking and listening to the counterparty, allowing more faulty arguments from the counterparty, and showing less resistance to the counterparty's persuasion attempts. Also, both sides perceived the mediator as less receptive to their concerns and less active in exploring their interests than those of the counterparty.

Maintaining Neutrality

Nothing guarantees that third parties are neutral.[35] In fact, third parties evince many of the biases that plague principals, such as framing effects.[36] Even a neutral mediator may be mistakenly viewed as partial to one's adversary.[37] Also, third parties may have a bias to broker an agreement at any cost, which may be disadvantageous to the principals—if no positive bargaining zone exists. Finally, the threat of third-party intervention

may inhibit settlement if principals believe an arbitrator is inclined to impose a compromise settlement. For this reason, final-offer arbitration may be more effective than traditional arbitration.[38]

Managers are often called on to resolve disputes in organizations.[39] In contrast to traditional arbitrators and mediators, managers may have a direct stake in the outcome and an ongoing relationship with the disputants. In addition, managers are more likely to have technical expertise and background knowledge about the dispute. Although several intervention techniques are available to managers, they often choose techniques that maximize their own control over the outcome.[40]

Strategies for Enhancing Effectiveness of Third-Party Intervention

What steps can negotiators take to maximize the effectiveness of third-party intervention?

Test Your Own Position

A good scientist will set up an experiment that includes "blinds." For example, in testing the effectiveness of a particular drug, one group of patients might be given the drug and the other group a placebo or sugar pill. The experimenters further blind themselves to which group was given what and assesses the

[34]Morris, M. W., & Su, S. K. (1995). The hostile mediator phenomenon: When each side perceives the mediator to be partial to the other. Unpublished manuscript, Stanford University Graduate School of Business, Palo Alto, CA.

[35]Gibson, K., Thompson, L., & Bazerman, M. H. (1994). Biases and rationality in the mediation process. In L. Heath, F. Bryant, & J. Edwards (Eds.), *Application of heuristics and biases to social issues: Vol. 3.* New York: Plenum.

[36]Carnevale, P. J. (1995). Property, culture, and negotiation. In R. M. Kramer & D. M. Messick (Eds.), *Negotiation as a social process: New trends in theory and research* (pp. 309–323). Thousand Oaks, CA: Sage.

[37]Morris & Su, "The hostile mediator phenomenon."

[38]Farber, "Splitting the difference"; see also Chelius, J. R., & Dworkin, J. B. (1980). The economic analysis of final-offer arbitration as a conflict resolution device. *Journal of Conflict Resolution, 24,* 293–310; Raiffa, H. (1982). *The art and science of negotiation.* Cambridge, MA: Belknap.

[39]Tornow, W. W., & Pinto, P. R. (1976). The development of a managerial job taxonomy: A system for describing, classifying, and evaluating executive positions. *Journal of Applied Psychology, 61,* 410–418.

[40]Karambayya & Brett, "Managers handling disputes"; Sheppard, B. H. (1984). Third-party intervention: A procedural framework. In B. M. Staw & L. L. Cummings (Eds.), *Research in organizational behavior: Vol. 6.* Greenwich, CT: JAI Press.

outcome. The same should be true for your own negotiation position. For example, if you find yourself in a dispute with a merchant or neighbor, describe the situation to the third party in such a way so as not to indicate what role you are playing in the dispute. Then ask the third party for an honest opinion.

Role-Play a Third Party in Your Own Dispute

Describe your negotiation situation to some colleagues who might be willing to play the roles involved. Then take on the role of a third party in the situation. Try to come up with a solution which both parties find agreeable.

Training in Win-Win Negotiation

Perhaps no other skill is as important as the ability to focus on expanding the size of the bargaining zone by discovering interests and then fashioning value-added trade-offs.

Appendix 4

Negotiating a Job Offer

When negotiating a job, you need all the essential skills covered in Part I (Chapters 1, 2, 3, and 4). In addition, you should be comfortable with your own bargaining style (and know its limits; see Chapter 5). You should be well versed in building trust and rapport (Chapter 6) and know the dynamics of power (Chapter 7) and how to increase creativity (Chapter 8). This appendix is designed to provide you with even more skills for this all-important negotiation that will recur throughout your life. We organized this appendix into three phases: preparation, in vivo process, and postoffer.

Preparation

Salary negotiations are extremely important because they affect your livelihood and welfare for years to come. A misassumption can have dramatic effects on your quality of life.

Step 1: Figure Out What You Really Want

This step sounds easy enough, but for a 28-year-old, it means an ability to project forward in time and to be concerned with things such as retirement and benefits. Karen Cates of the Kellogg School recommends working through a checklist of needs and wants (see Exhibit A4-1).[1] Cates further suggests a practical, step-by-step approach to compensation and benefits (see Exhibit A4-2).

Step 2: Do Your Homework

Research the company and the industry. The Internet allows people to get information quickly and easily, especially when it comes to salaries. Several Web sites offer salary surveys, job listings with specified pay levels, and even customized compensation analyses. However, for many jobs, Web-based pay information represents only a starting point. In other words, Web sites can only tell you if you are in the ballpark and can stop you from underbidding yourself.

It is important to do your homework so you don't ask for something that has already been institutionalized. For example, many companies have on-site chefs because they realized it just does not make sense to break at noon, have everyone get in cars, and go elsewhere for lunch.

Step 3: Determine Your BATNA and Your Aspiration

A negotiator always has a BATNA. Some students will claim agitatedly that they do not have a BATNA because they do not have any job offers in hand. They may not have an *attractive* BATNA, but they inevitably have courses of action if they do not get a job offer. Perhaps they will simply "extend" their job search indefinitely; perhaps they will travel abroad; perhaps they will do freelance or volunteer work, take a research assistantship at a university, or search for a nonprofessional job while they continue their career search. All of these options are possible BATNAs; they should be assessed and the best one focused upon and evaluated carefully.

Our BATNAs are never as attractive as we would like them to be. The rare times when we have two or more fabulous job

---

[1]Cates, K. (1997). Tips for negotiating a job offer. Unpublished manuscript, Kellogg School of Management, Northwestern University, Evanston, IL.

EXHIBIT A4-1   Checklist of Needs and Wants

Necessary Living Expenses	Additional Living Expenses
Housing (including utilities)	Recreation and entertainment (vacations, events, activities, books, etc.)
Auto	
Computer	Services (professional and household)
Child care	Continuing education
Insurance (auto, home, life, professional)	Children's expenses (lessons, schooling)
Personal (food, medical, clothing, household)	Gifts, charity
Student loan debt service	
Taxes (income, property, etc.)	

Source: Cates, K. (1997). Tips for negotiating a job offer. Unpublished manuscript, Kellogg School of Management, Northwestern University, Evanston, IL. Used by permission of Karen Cates.

offers in hand, two bids on our house, and lucrative investment opportunities, we can afford to push for a lot more in negotiations. Obviously, you are in a much better position to successfully negotiate an attractive compensation package if your BATNA is attractive. As we stated in Chapter 2, your BATNA is dynamic, and it is important not to be passive about it.

It is important to think about how we might improve upon our BATNA. Most negotiators do not spend adequate time attempting to improve their current situation. As a result, they approach negotiations feeling more desperate than they should.

Step 4: Research the Employer's BATNA
Developing your BATNA is only half the work that needs to be done before the negotiation. The next step is to determine the other party's BATNA, which requires tapping into multiple sources of information.

Step 5: Determine the Issue Mix
You have made your best assessment of the employer's BATNA. The negotiation is fast approaching. Now what? The next step is to determine the issues that are important to you in this negotiation. Do not make the mistake of letting the employer define the issues for you. Be ready to talk about your interests and needs.

EXHIBIT A4-2   Compensation and Benefits

Compensation	Retirement	Paid Leave	Protection
Salary	Pension/401K	Vacation, sick, and personal days	Insurance (life, disability, health, other)
Bonus	Guaranteed pay plans (supplemental unemployment)	Training time	
Other variable pay		Holidays and special travel considerations	Care plans (child, elder)
Stock/equity interest	Savings plans		Wellness programs

Source: Cates, K. (1997). Tips for negotiating a job offer. Unpublished manuscript, Kellogg School of Management, Northwestern University, Evanston, IL.

After you determine which issues are important from your perspective, go back through your list and attempt to create an even more detailed list, breaking down each of the issues into smaller and smaller subsets. Breaking up the issues into smaller subsets does two things. First, it allows the negotiator (you) to be much more specific about what is important (e.g., the paid aspect of a vacation or the number of days allowed off). Second, it provides much greater opportunity for creative agreements.

In addition to focusing on the issues and concerns of importance to you, anticipate the other party's perspective. Again, information and research can help here.

Step 6: Prepare Several Scenarios

Most likely, the negotiations will not go as planned. Rather than being caught off guard, prepare your response to several different scenarios, including the following:

- The employer agrees immediately to your counteroffer.
- The employer makes a low-ball offer (in your eyes) and flatly states, "This is our final offer."
- The employer makes one small concession.
- The employer asks you to make a reasonable offer.

Step 7: Consider Getting a "Coach"

Job coaches can help people advance their careers and achieve their compensation goals. They are people who help managers plan their future. The way that Peter Goodman, CEO of MyJobCoach, puts it, "If you have a legal issue, you go to a lawyer for advice. When doing financial planning, you go to an accountant. So why would you not go to a career coach when planning your career, the area where you spend over 70% of your waking life?" Every month, about 400 to 500 new members join the International Coach Federation (the career coach trade group) and in 2007 about 30,000 career coaches were working worldwide.[2] CEOs have always taken coaching seriously, at least when it comes to negotiating their compensation packages. For example, Joseph Bachelder has negotiated job contracts for top corporate executives for 23 years.[3] His hourly rate of $975 did not deter George Fisher (Eastman Kodak), Patricia Russo (Lucent), Lou Gerstner, Jamie Dimon (Bank One), and executives at Allied Signal and IBM. He also negotiates severance for departures, including that of Jack Grubman, former Salomon Smith Barney telecom analyst. In his typical role, he invites CEOs to talk about their financial goals. Bachelder employs a Ph.D. mathematician, B. Roslyn Abramov, to help leverage the number-crunching showdowns. He is not reluctant to remind companies that terminated executives can be important witnesses in continuing litigation. Moreover, savvy companies often suggest that their employees use Bachelder. For example, Lucent suggested that Richard McGinn, dismissed as CEO in October 2000, use Bachelder. Company management reasoned that his expertise in wrapping up matters ultimately would serve Lucent well. In other cases, ousted executives want to restart their careers quickly and be freed from a thicket of noncompete clauses. One such client, Jamie Dimon (previously Citigroup), hired Bachelder to ensure that he could take the helm of Bank One and take six of his former colleagues with him.

In Vivo: During the Negotiation Itself

You have done your preparation. Now it is time for the actual negotiation.

---

[2]Weiss, T. (2007, November 9). Who needs a career coach? *Forbes.com.* Retrieved March 19, 2008, from http://www.forbes.com/business/2007/11/09/jobs-professional-work-lead-careers-cx_tw_1109coach.html

[3]Anders, G. (2003, June 25). Upping the ante: As some decry lavish CEO pay, Joe Bachelder makes it happen. *Wall Street Journal*, p. A1.

*Think About the Best Way to Position
and Present Your Opening Offer*

Remember to back up your offer with a compelling rationale. Use objective standards. Focus and select those standards that are favorable to you, and be prepared to indicate why standards unfavorable to you are inappropriate.

Assume the Offer Is Negotiable

Do not ask "Can I negotiate the offer you have made?" Always assume the offer is negotiable and articulate your needs and interests. Cates advises saying the following: "I have some questions about the insurance coverage that I would like to talk about if we can" or "I have some concerns about the moving allowance, and I need to talk to you about it."[4] A survey conducted by the Society for Human Resource Management found that 8 out of 10 recruiters were willing to negotiate pay and benefits with job applicants, but only one-third of the job applicants surveyed said they felt comfortable negotiating.[5] Most job applicants do not push employers at the negotiating table. The failure to negotiate a first offer from an employer can cost workers a lot of money. "A 22-year-old who secures a $2,000 increase in annual salary at his or her first job will, because of the compounding effects of years of raises to follow, most likely generate roughly $150,000 in extra income over the course of a 40-year career."[6] The effect is even more dramatic for an MBA student negotiating a $90,000 job offer. What's more, if you do not negotiate what you want in that brief window between your receipt of a job offer and your acceptance of it, you may never get it. Your power is greatest when you are responding to "their offer" because it is the one time the employer may want you more than you want them.[7] (For a list of things to ask for in your negotiation, see Exhibit A4-3.)

EXHIBIT A4-3 Things to Ask for When Negotiating an Offer

Some things to ask for when negotiating an offer (other than a higher salary, which is always worth asking for):

- Extra vacation days
- Flexible scheduling
- Telecommuting
- Delaying your start date to have time off between jobs
- Personal days and parental leaves
- Gas reimbursement
- Public transportation reimbursement
- Increased family benefits

- Supplemental insurance coverage
- Increased job training
- Gym memberships
- Food delivery
- Concierge services
- Dry cleaning services
- Education grants
- Tuition reimbursement
- Adoption assistance

Source: Brandon, E. (2006, June 14). Negotiating for job perks; ask and you might receive. *US News and World Report.* Retrieved on March 19, 2008 from http://www.usnews.com/usnews/biztech/articles/060614/14benefits.htm; Liveten, S. (2006, October 6). The power of the perk. *Forbes.com.* Retrieved March 19, 2008 from http://www.forbes .com/managing/2006/10/05/leadership-managing-perks-lead-manage-cx_ag_1006perks.html

---

[4]Cates, "Tips for negotiating a job offer."
[5]Clark, K. (1999, November 1). Gimme, gimme, gimme: Job seekers don't realize they can ask for more—lots more. *U.S. News & World Report,* pp. 88–92.
[6]Ibid.
[7]Ibid.

Immediately Reanchor the Interviewer by Reviewing Your Needs and Your Rationale

Indicate your interest in working for the company, and tell the interviewer how your needs (and wants) can be met in a variety of ways. Many candidates reach impasse because employers falsely assumed that the candidates did not want the job when they did. Thus, keep reiterating your heartfelt interest in the company. Cates advises to "get your requests on the table and keep them there."[8] According to Cates, salary negotiations are really about candidates helping recruiters to solve their problems. In other words, let the employer know what would make their offer more appealing. This offer of information may even come to sharing your own prioritization and MAUT analysis of the issues.

Reveal Neither Your BATNA Nor Your Reservation Point

Negotiators have a million ways of asking people about their BATNAs. Asking a potential job recruit about his or her current salary and wage package is one of them. Remember that this information is your business, not the recruiter's. If you are currently employed, redirect the discussion by indicating what it is going to take to move you (e.g., a more exciting job and a wage package commensurate with the job). If you are not employed, explain what it will take to hire you. Ward off direct attacks about your previous salary by explaining that your acceptance of a position depends on the nature of the job offer and wage package.

You should be prepared to take the initiative in the conversation. Practice by role-playing. If the employer attempts to get you to talk about why you are leaving a former job, avoid falling into the trap of trashing a former employer, even if you did have a miserable experience. It is a small world, and a relationship you do not immediately see may be involved. Even more important, the employer will probably get the wrong impression about you (e.g., regard you as a troublemaker or overly critical).

If you have not yet been offered the job but sense that the employer wants to find out what you desire in a job offer, avoid talking about salary or specific terms until you have an offer. You are in a much weaker position to negotiate before you have a job offer than after you are offered a position. If you have been told "Things will work out" or "A job offer is coming," express appreciation and inquire when you will receive formal notice. After that, schedule a meeting to talk about the terms. While you are negotiating, you should assume that everything is negotiable. If you are told that some aspect of the job is "not negotiable," ask questions, such as whether everyone (new hires and veterans) receives the same treatment.

Rehearse and Practice

It is important to plan for negotiation. According to Michael Chaffers, a senior consultant with CMI, a negotiation group in Cambridge, Massachusetts, "A pitch for a raise is no different than making a presentation on any subject: It helps to practice beforehand and even do some role playing. Tell an empty chair what you plan to say to your boss (though you might want to make sure no one's around to see you). If you can find a willing participant, have them play the boss, while acting cantankerous and giving you flack."[9]

Imagine You Are Negotiating on Behalf of Someone Else (Not Just Yourself)

Many people are reluctant to negotiate their job offer because they feel greedy or have a hard time being assertive. However,

---

[8]Cates, "Tips for negotiating a job offer."
[9]Tips from a negotiation coach. (1999, February 11). *Machine Design, 71*(3), 96.

these same people are quite effective when negotiating for a company or for someone else. One solution is to approach a job negotiation as if you were negotiating on behalf of an important company: your own family. If we think about the direct effect our salary will have on our ability to provide for our children, our spouse, and our parents, we can be much more effective. Even the unmarried student without children is well advised to think about the family he or she will have or might have in the not-so-distant future and to negotiate on behalf of those people.

Comparables and Benchmarks

Probably no other information is perceived to be more valuable in the job negotiation process than what similar employers are offering or what current employees are receiving. It is important to keep in mind that such comparables or benchmarks can affect the perceived attractiveness of the job offer in question, but the negotiator may be unaware of this. For example, people are more likely to accept a lower-paying job that pays other employees the same amount than a higher-paying job that pays other employees even more. People do not want to be "underpaid" and would even give up more absolute money if this meant they were treated like others.[10] Concerns for social comparisons (comps) are more important when people evaluate a single option than when they evaluate two options. Moreover, discrepancies in pay (i.e., social comparison concerns) may take priority over absolute salary amounts in situations in which choosing a job that is favorable on social comparison but unfavorable on actual salary can be "justified," as in the case when an inferior (i.e., dominated) alternative is present.[11] An analysis of how MBA students react to job offers revealed that signing bonuses did not affect acceptance rates; rather, job candidates strongly consider how responsive companies are to their questions and whether recruiters are cordial (rather than derogatory).[12]

Postoffer: You Have the Offer, Now What?

Do Not Immediately Agree to the Offer

Do not start negotiating until you have a firm job offer and a salary figure from the employer. Do not prolong things, however; this approach only frustrates the employer. Instead, give the employer positive reinforcement. Cates suggests something like "This looks great. I need to go over everything one last time before we make this official. I will call you at [a specific time]."[13]

Get the Offer in Writing

If the employer says it is not standard to make written offers, be sure to consult with others who would know this (e.g., the company's human resources division). At the very least, inform them you will write down your understanding of the terms and put it in a letter or memo to them. Keep notes for

[10]Bazerman, M. H., Loewenstein, G., & White, S. (1992). Reversals of preference in allocating decisions: Judging an alternative versus choosing among alternatives. *Administrative Science Quarterly, 37,* 220–240; Bazerman, M. H., Schroth, H. A., Shah, P. P., Diekmann, K. A., & Tenbrunsel, A. E. (1994). The inconsistent role of comparison others and procedural justice to hypothetical job descriptions: Implications for job acceptance decisions. *Organizational Behavior and Human Decision Processes, 60,* 326–352; Blount, S., & Bazerman, M. H. (1996). The inconsistent evaluation of comparative payoffs in labor supply and bargaining. *Journal of Economic Behavior and Organizations, 891,* 1–14.

[11]Tenbrunsel, A., & Diekmann, K. (2002). Job-decision inconsistencies involving social comparison information: The role of dominating alternatives. *Journal of Applied Psychology, 87*(6), 1149–1158.

[12]Porter, C., Conlon, D., & Barber, A. (2004). The dynamics of salary negotiations; Effects on applicants' justice perceptions and recruitment decisions. *International Journal of Conflict Management, 15*(3), 273–303.

[13]Cates, "Tips for negotiating a job offer."

yourself regarding the points agreed to during each meeting.

Be Enthusiastic and Gracious

Someone has just made you an offer. Thank them and show your appreciation but do not accept immediately. Say, instead, "Let me go home and think about it." Make an appointment to return the following day and state your negotiating position in person.

Assess the Interviewer's Power to Negotiate with You

Before you begin negotiating or contemplating a counteroffer, determine who in the company has the ability to negotiate. Generally, those persons higher up in the organization are the ones who negotiate and the ones who care most about hiring good people. You should be well-versed about the advantages and disadvantages of negotiating with an intermediary, such as a human resources manager (see Chapter 9 on multiple parties). If you sense that things are not going well in the negotiation, try to bring someone else into the loop. However, make this move in a gracious way, so as not to antagonize the person with whom you are dealing.

State Exactly What Needs to Be Done for You to Agree

A powerful negotiating strategy is to let the employer know exactly what it will take for you to agree. This technique is effective because the employer can put aside any fears about the negotiation dragging on forever and being nickel-and-dimed to death. When you make your demands, though, ground them in logic and clear rationale. Requesting something too far out of whack may lose you the job. Ross Gibson, vice president for human resources at American Superconductor in Boston, says he judges applicants by the way they negotiate—and withdraws

offers from those who come across as immature or greedy.[14]

Do Not Negotiate If You Are Not or Could Not Be Interested

Suppose that you are the lucky person sitting on four job offers, all from consulting firms (A, B, C, and D). You have done enough research, cost-benefit analysis, and soul searching to determine that, in your mind, firms A and B are superior in all ways to firms C and D. The question is: should you let firms C and D off the hook or string them along so as to potentially improve your power position when negotiating with firms A and B? Our advice is to politely inform firms C and D that you will not be accepting their offers at this time. You still have a wonderful BATNA, and it saves everyone a lot of time.

Exploding Offers

Exploding offers are offers that have a "time bomb" element to them (e.g., "The offer is only good for 24 hours"). The question is how to deal with them. In our experience, firms usually do not rescind exploding offers once they have made them (unless, as a matter of courtesy, it is for family, medical, or emergency reasons). Generally, we advise that job candidates who receive an exploding offer above their BATNA seriously consider the offer. It certainly cannot hurt to inform other companies that you have an exploding offer and move up the time of the interview, if at all possible.

Do Not Try to Create a Bidding War

Bidding wars occur regularly on Wall Street, in professional athletics, and in the business world. We do not advise, however, that job candidates attempt to create bidding wars between companies. Rather, we advise job candidates to signal to potential employers that

---

[14]Clark, "Gimme, gimme, gimme."

they have attractive BATNAs, that they do not want to start a bidding war, and that they tell their top-rated company what it would take to get them to work at the company.

Know When to Stop Pushing

According to Cates, it is important to know when to stop negotiating.[15] Cates suggests that negotiators stop when they see one or more of the following signals:

- The other side is not responsive.
- Reciprocal concessions are becoming miniscule.
- After some back and forth the employer says, "Enough!"

Use a Rational Strategy for Choosing Among Job Offers

If you find yourself in the lucky position of having multiple offers, you are then faced with a choice. First, you should recognize this enviable position as an approach-approach conflict. How should you weigh the choices? The simplest way is to use MAUT by constructing a grid listing the choices along a row (e.g., firm A, firm B) and the relevant attributes along a column underneath (e.g., salary, fringe benefits, travel, vacation, bonus, etc.). Then, fill in the grid with the details of the offer and how they "stack up" compared to the others (on a scale of 1 to 5 or 1 to 10 in your mind). Next, you can simply add the columns to find a "winner." A more sophisticated version of this strategy is to multiply each grid value by how important it is before adding columns (with importance defined on a scale of 1 to 5). For example, for most people, salary is highly important (maybe a 5), whereas moving expenses are less important (maybe a 1 or 2). This distinction gives a more fine-grained assessment. (See Appendix 1 for a step-by-step approach to MAUT.)

---

[15]Cates, "Tips for negotiating a job offer."

Name Index

A

Aaron, B., 367
Abelson, J., 155
Abramowitz, C. V., 359
Abramowitz, S. I., 359
Abt, S., 316
Ackerman, B. A., 310
Adair, W. L., 84, 276, 277, 279, 289
Adams, A. A., 79
Adams, S., 59, 63, 64
Adler, N. J., 275
Aik, V., 125
Akerlof, G., 13, 133
Alba, J. W., 187, 216
Alge, B. J., 334
Allen, H. M., Jr., 252
Allen, T. J., 321
Allison, S. T., 69
Alloway, T., 360
Allred, K. G., 122, 124, 372
Alon, I., 288
Amanatullah, E., 120
Ancona, D. G., 242
Anders, G., 4, 14, 138, 377
Anderson, C., 174
Anderson, C. M., 314, 327
Anderson, S. C., 132
Andrews, P., 322
Archibald, K., 86
Argote, L., 248
Argyle, M., 148
Ariel, S., 265, 266
Armstrong, D. J., 323
Arnold, J. A., 147
Aron, A., 254
Aronson, E., 30, 170, 171, 251
Arrow, K. J., 224
Ashmore, R. D., 170
Aubert, V., 30
Austin, W., 58, 151, 250, 283
Axelrod, R., 131
Axsom, D., 245

B

Babcock, L., 70, 168
Back, K. W., 247
Baguioro, L., 32
Bailey, J., 149, 156
Balke, W. M., 78
Ball, J., 112
Banaji, M., 181
Banner, M., 7
Barber, A., 380
Bargh, J. A., 146
Baron, J., 67, 69, 71, 279, 280, 339
Baron, R. A., 124
Barron, L. A., 102
Barron, R. S., 255
Barry, B., 124, 143, 223
Barsness, Z., 269
Bar-Tal, D., 248, 250, 254
Bartunek, J., 27
Bazerman, M. H., 4, 5, 8, 11, 13, 14, 15, 16, 19, 22,
    23, 27, 30, 44, 52, 59, 60, 66, 67, 68, 70, 71, 79,
    81, 82, 86, 88, 91, 92, 96, 103, 133, 176, 180,
    181, 192, 193, 194, 197, 203, 204, 221, 222,
    230, 235, 237, 239, 250, 266, 282, 303, 312,
    321, 329, 370, 372, 373, 380
Beach, S. R., 139
Beaman, A. L., 173
Beardsley, K., 367, 370
Bechtold, D., 261
Bednarski, P., 240
Beersma, B., 105, 222, 223
Belkin, L., 326
Bell, D., 76
Bennett, R., 88
Bennigson, C., 144
Bensinger, K., 154
Benson, P. L., 170
Ben-Yoav, O., 242
Bereby-Meyer, Y., 14, 197
Berkowitz, L., 57, 59, 123, 221, 285, 327, 364
Bernieri, F. J., 326, 362
Bernoulli, D., 347, 348

Subject Index

A

Abilene paradox, 152
Acceptance/rejection decision, 94
Accountability
    constituent relationships and, 242–243
    team, 248
Acculturation, 290–291
Accuracy, emotion recognition, 125
Active misrepresentation, 176
Adjudication, 109
    dispute resolution and cultural differences in
        adversarial and inquisitorial, 271–272
Adjustments, creativity problems and, 199
Adversarial adjudication, dispute resolution and
        cultural differences, 271–272
Adversarial style, ineffectiveness
        of, 101–102
Advertising, comparative, 306–307
Advisory arbitration, 115
Affiliation bias, 284
Agenda, power of, 163
Agents. *See* Principal-agent negotiations
Agreement(s)
    bias, 5, 230
    consensus, 224–225
    creativity and, 189–194
    necessity of, 32
    reaching integrative, 93–95
    reneging on, 178
Alignment of issues, 190
Alternatives
    brainstorming, 17
    evaluating, 17
    identifying, 20, 340
    power of, 163
Anchoring
    adjustment and, 199
    aggressive, 88
    point, 47
Apologizing, 144
Approach-approach conflict, 339
Approaches, dispute resolution
        and, 105–118

Arbitration
    advisory, 115
    conventional, 116
    final offer, 368
    hearing, 368
    mediation and, 368–369
    third-party intervention and, 116, 368–369
    traditional, 368
Aspiration point, 13–14, 47–48
Assessment
    of differences, 94
    of motivational styles, 98–105
    party, 27–29, 39
    resource, 93–94
    risk, 21–24
    self-, 13–27, 39
    situation, 29–39
Assimilation, 290
Attention, selective, 203
Attitudinal structuring, 164
Attractiveness, power and, 169–170
Attributes, identifying, 340
Attribution bias, sinister, 327–328
Attribution error, 285–286, 288
    sinister, 327
Audiences, multiple audience problem, 227
Autotelic experience, 213
Availability heuristic, 197–198

B

Backward induction, 297
Bad apple, 142
Bargaining
    dispute resolution and cultural differences,
        271–272
    ethical and unethical tactics, 175–179
    hard, 12
    sequential, 230
    soft, 12
    surplus, 43
    theory, Nash's, 354–357
    traditional competitive, 177–178
    zone and negotiation dance, 41–44

397

PRAISE FOR *ENGAGE EVERY FAMILY*

The public education system is fully invested in the five family engagement principles Dr. Constantino describes in this book. Without fully engaged family support, many students fall, without grace, in the face of failure. Entire communities are made better because of a genuine concern for students and their families.

—**Jenny McGown**, Superintendent
Klein Independent School District
Klein, Texas

Now more than ever, we need the wisdom, experience, and passion that Steve Constantino brings to the field of family and community engagement. He understands profoundly what it takes to develop and sustain partnerships grounded in mutual trust, respect, and learning between families and schools. From conceptual frameworks to practical, hands-on tools for reflection and activity, this book provides indispensable guidance for laying an unshakable foundation on which schools can thrive.

—**Gina Martinez-Keddy**, Executive Director
Parent Teacher Home Visits

The second edition of this book couldn't be timelier. What so many of us have uncovered during the COVID-19 crisis this year has been the central importance of family in the education of every learner. Often taken for granted, the family role must be fostered, developed, given its place and its due in the educational process to help every student, and in particular, the most disenfranchised, to succeed. In this edition each of the five principles has been embellished and augmented. This is a book that should be open and in use on desks and laptops, as we proceed into this new school year.

—**Paul K. Leather**, Director
Interstate Learning Community
National Center for Innovation in Education

This second edition of *Engage Every Family: Five Simple Principles* is a true treasure! From reflecting on your own experiences to detailed research, Dr. Constantino guides you through best practices to boost and improve family engagement in your organization. Most of all, this book reaffirms that intentionally investing time and resources into building partnerships with families is necessary and a determining factor to student success!

—**Maria Ovalle-Lopez**, Family Engagement Program Coordinator
Klein Independent School District
Klein, Texas

Dr. Constantino's commitment to family engagement through effective and meaningful practice has influenced my work for many years. I am thrilled that this second edition includes critical research and invaluable new practices around equity and trust. We will "Engage Every Family" when we confront our biases, collaborate with our families, and work to build trusting relationships. With this book, Dr. Constantino provides a much-needed roadmap to do just that.

—**Nancy Angevine-Sands**, Founder
With Equal Step

Steve Constantino is the unquestioned guru of effective family engagement, and I welcome his updated take on this crucial topic. If you liked the first edition, you will love the second edition!

—**Anne Holton**, Visiting Professor, Schar School of Policy and Government and at the College of Education and Human Development, George Mason University
Former Secretary of Education, Commonwealth of Virginia

Now, perhaps more than ever, our families and schools must be united and be true partners in education. *Engage Every Family, Second Edition,* is the vehicle to help our school communities come together. Dr. Constantino simplifies this process for all of us. Our elementary school in Colombia has subscribed to the Five Simple Principles and the familial response has been wonderful!

—**David J. Gesualdi**, Principal
Colego Jorge Washington Colombia
Cartagena, Colombia

The principles of *Engage Every Family, Second Edition,* have empowered our principals, division leaders, and teacher leaders to move away from the familiar and routine "check the box" traditional communication and toward powerful, proven strategies of engaging families that directly confront the status quo in order to engage every family. This intentional shift has served as a catalyst for better addressing equitable student access and outcomes. Dr. Steve Constantino outlines strategies and qualitative support tools to practitioners through the use of vivid, contextual stories. His work is authentic because he has practiced, for decades, what he is preaching.

—**S. Scott Baker**, Superintendent
Spotsylvania County Public Schools

Engage Every Family is an essential guide that challenges the misperceptions about disengagement and charts a path for developing relationships of trust with families that have measurable impact on student outcomes. The format provides multiple opportunities to reflect and examine practice as well as guidance to scaffold and deepen the impact of family engagement strategies. I highly recommend this book; it is more than a great read—it is a must-have guide for effective family engagement practice.

—**Michele P. Brooks**, Principal Consultant
Transformative Solutions in Education

Dr. Steve Constantino's approach to family engagement is strength-based and his belief in all families as valued and valuable is unwavering. He invites us to make a difference by exploring our responses to families by examining our beliefs, assumptions, and biases about families rather than by judging families' circumstances. In his discussion about understanding implicit bias, he affirms that the greatest change we can make in regard to engaging every family is in ourselves. How do we move from seeking ways for families to realize the school's agenda, to spending time getting to know families, the knowledge they hold, and the efficacy they possess? Dr. Constantino makes a significant contribution to the field through his deep exploration of the principle Build Family Efficacy. Steve demonstrates that when families believe they can make a positive difference in their children's educational lives they bring to bear their skills, abilities, and resources to do just that. Throughout this entire work, Dr. Constantino develops a conceptualization of family engagement as a process, one that requires a significant cultural shift.

—**Debbie Pushor**, Professor, Curriculum Studies
University of Saskatchewan

I have been a classroom teacher for 29 years, 27 in the middle levels. For the past 10 years, I have been a strong advocate at the State and National levels for middle-school students. I was lucky enough to bring Steve to my school district recently. Using the Five Simple Principles model, he had the entire staff evaluating how it is they engage with our families. The seed was planted, and the process has continued to grow. We all are looking forward to the positive results we see in our students. We are thankful for the guidance of Steve and the ideas presented in this book.

—**David Vroman**, Middle School Teacher
Potsdam Central Schools
Potsdam, NY

Partnerships between schools and families have always been important but are often overlooked. When COVID-19 first shut down our school buildings in early 2020, our households became home schools. Continuous learning and development were much easier for students whose caretakers and teachers already had strong levels of engagement and relationship. For years, Dr. Constantino has been calling out the importance of these partnerships. He is a trusted and authoritative voice on parent and family engagement, sought after by practitioners and leaders across the country and around the world. He has a rare combination of personal wit, sophisticated scholarship, and a practitioner's heart. *Engage Every Family* is a call to action for every educator, everywhere. The work of family and school engagement is more important than ever before, and Dr. Constantino helps us get started and get better at it.

—**Stephanie Malia Krauss**, Senior Director, Special Projects
Jobs for the Future
Staff Consultant to the Youth Transition Funders Group
Author, *Making It: What Today's Kids Need for Tomorrow's World*

Engage Every Family

Second Edition

Engage Every Family

Five Simple Principles

Second Edition

Steven M. Constantino

Foreword by Kirsten Baesler

A Joint Publication

FOR INFORMATION:

Corwin

A SAGE Companyy

2455 Teller Road

Thousand Oaks, California 91320

(800) 233-9936

www.corwin.com

SAGE Publications Ltd.

1 Oliver's Yard

55 City Road

London EC1Y 1SP

United Kingdom

SAGE Publications India Pvt. Ltd.

B 1/I 1 Mohan Cooperative Industrial Area

Mathura Road, New Delhi 110 044

India

SAGE Publications Asia-Pacific Pte. Ltd.

18 Cross Street #10-10/11/12

China Square Central

Singapore 048423

Acquisitions Editor: Ariel Curry

Development Editor: Desirée A. Bartlett

Editorial Assistant: Caroline Timmings

Production Editor: Amy Schroller

Copy Editor: Erin Livingston

Typesetter: Hurix Digital

Proofreader: Talia Greenberg

Indexer: Integra

Cover and Graphic Design: Gail Buschman

Marketing Manager: Sharon Pendergast

Printed in the United States of America

Library of Congress Cataloging-in-Publication Data

Names: Constantino, Steven M., 1958- author.

Title: Engage every family : five simple principles / Steven M. Constantino.

Description: Second edition (revised edition). | Thousand Oaks: Corwin, [2021] | Includes bibliographical references.

Identifiers: LCCN 2020016488 | ISBN 9781071803714 (paperback) | ISBN 9781071803707 (epub) | ISBN 9781071803691 (epub) | ISBN 9781071803684 (ebook)

Subjects: LCSH: Home and school–United States. | Teachers and community–United States. | Parent-teacher relationships–United States. | Communication in education–United States. | School children–Family relationships–United States. | Education–Parent participation–United States.

Classification: LCC LC225.3 .C654 2021 | DDC 371.19/2–dc23

LC record available at https://lccn.loc.gov/2020016488

This book is printed on acid-free paper.

22 23 24 10 9 8 7

Contents

CHAPTER 8   PRINCIPLE #3: BUILD FAMILY EFFICACY   145

CHAPTER 9   PRINCIPLE #4: ENGAGE EVERY FAMILY IN
DECISION MAKING   181

Foreword

After listening to Dr. Steve M. Constantino talk about family engagement, I wished I could begin my education career over again. As a classroom teacher, librarian, vice principal, and even as a school board member, I had not fully realized the importance and power of family engagement and its critical role in promoting student success until I encountered Dr. Constantino. He opened my eyes.

Family engagement has become a priority emphasis in North Dakota education. We have facilitated training sessions in some of our school districts, which have imbued family engagement into the fabric of their educational mission.

Teachers have embraced the idea of getting closer to their students and families (although not without some initial trepidation!). They understand that true, authentic family engagement isn't about doing more, it is about doing things differently. Our teachers are learning to be approachable, and they want to know how they can be more helpful.

Because of what I learned through Dr. Constantino's work, I have formed the Superintendent's Family Engagement Cabinet. It includes family members from across North Dakota, with children in all school grades. They are passionate about working to make sure their students are getting a good education, and I am inspired by their dedication and enthusiasm.

We have a rapidly growing Facebook group, North Dakota Family Engagement, and a PK–12 Alliance to promote family educational involvement. These receive joyful support from my teammates at the Department of Public Instruction, who know a good thing when they see it and are eager to be part of it.

As Dr. Constantino proves in his books and numerous workshops and keynotes, when families are involved in, and supportive of, the education of their children, the student is more successful. You almost don't need research to establish that fact. It makes sense to every family member and educator.

Families want to be involved in the education of their children, but often they're not sure how to go about it. School culture can be hard to understand and even harder to navigate. Dr. Constantino helps to break down those barriers, and empower educators to create a better partnership with families. We must go beyond parent–teacher conferences and family fun nights and encourage broader and deeper relationships.

Dr. Constantino deserves credit for inspiring and facilitating our commitment to improving family engagement in North Dakota. Because of his work, families are becoming more involved in North Dakota education, and our students are the winners in it all!

Read this book and be inspired. I was.

Kirsten Baesler, Superintendent of Public Instruction
State of North Dakota

Preface

If we as educators could successfully teach all children by ourselves, then it seems to me that we would have already done so. The fact that we haven't should be all the motivation or evidence we need that engaging every family in the educational life of their child is essential to desired school outcomes. Why haven't we been more successful in engaging every family in the educational lives of their children? Why do so many of us still struggle with the notion of engaging every family as a viable conduit to improved student learning outcomes?

These are daunting questions.

I have been at this family engagement business for a long time, traveling the country and to different parts of the world to share the message of family engagement and its powerful effects upon student achievement. Over these many years, I have had countless conversations about families and their role in education and, more importantly, how educators can better engage every family.

This book is a continuation of those conversations.

Engage Every Family: Five Simple Principles, Second Edition, outlines a pathway and process for any educator or group of educators to engage every family in the academic lives of children and acts as a framework for implementing best practices to increase the likelihood of engaging every family, including those families that have been traditionally disengaged or disenfranchised from schools.

WHAT'S NEW IN THE SECOND EDITION?

With the advent of the Every Student Succeeds Act and numerous state-level reforms in educational practice and accountability, there is a growing interest in engaging families in the academic lives of children. As more and more schools and districts look to implement effective strategies to engage every family, we learn more about what works and what doesn't, what resonates with educators and what does not. I appreciate the large amount of constructive feedback on the first edition and I am thrilled that we can now bring you a new edition.

Chapter 3, *Understanding Disengagement*, has been retitled to *Equity, Bias, and Family Disengagement*. This title change reflects the important conversations that are taking place about equitable learning outcomes for children and the chapter discusses the role of family engagement in that process. An expanded discussion of implicit bias helps educators to better understand why families are seemingly disengaged and disenfranchised from their children's learning lives.

Changes to the Five Simple Principles Model, Descriptions, and Clarifying Statements

Chapter 5, *An Introduction to the Five Simple Principles,* shares new thinking and updates to the logic model. Additional action research, feedback, and program evaluations from hundreds of workshops have helped refine and update the model and the principle descriptions to more clearly reflect the process and outcomes of the Five Simple Principles.

In Chapter 6, *A Culture That Engages Every Family*, new information about the notion of family academic socialization has been added as well as a new survey to help establish baseline information about school culture and family engagement.

Chapter 7, *Principle #2,* has been changed slightly from *Communicate Effectively and Build Relationships* to *Communicate Effectively and Develop Relationships.* This slight nuance is important because the basis of relationships—trust—has been emphasized more in the descriptors and definitions. There is an expanded section on the procedures, practices, and policies that shape family engagement in every school. Also added is a short but important discussion of the difference between *communication* and *engagement*.

I want to take this opportunity to thank my friend Gina Martinez-Keddy, executive director of the Parent Teacher Home Visit Project, for helping me to update, revise, and expand the section on home visits. Also expanded in Chapter 7 is the discussion of families with limited English proficiency and the important changes and updates to technology as a vehicle for engagement.

Chapter 8 represents one of the biggest changes to the Five Principles Model. *Empower Every Family* has been revised to *Build Family Efficacy.* In workshops across the country and in feedback about the book, what became clear is the confusion the word *empower* caused the reader. Many believed that the word *empower* meant to embolden families to somehow work against the school. Nothing could be further from the original intent. The model, description, and clarifying statements have been augmented to better promote the idea of *family efficacy*, empowering families to work alongside teachers, as a direct conduit to improved learning. An expanded discussion of conferences has been added, as well as a new clarifying statement to support the important research notion of family academic socialization.

In Chapters 6 through 10, which encompass the detailed explanation of each of the five principles, more detailed descriptions and updated research have been added to ensure a firmer foundation for each principle. At the conclusion of each chapter, the qualitative activities designed to help readers understand present conditions in their school with regard to each principle have been changed to a series of questions based on the principle descriptions. These questions help you get to the desired outcome faster.

One of the most often-asked questions in workshops around the country centers on family engagement at the secondary school level. A new chapter—Chapter 4,

Engaging Every Family in Middle and High School—discusses the barriers to secondary school engagement and the steps that can be taken to address these barriers and help family engagement at the secondary level to be as robust as it is at the elementary level.

WHAT ARE THE FIVE SIMPLE PRINCIPLES?

Principle #1: A Culture That Engages Every Family

Principle #2: Communicate Effectively and Develop Relationships

Principle #3: Build Family Efficacy

Principle #4: Engage Every Family in Decision Making

Principle #5: Engage the Greater Community

The book will share in great detail the logic model of the Five Simple Principles and devotes entire chapters to each of them. Below is a brief overview of the principles and why they are important in the overall scheme of connecting family engagement to learning.

1. Principle #1: A Culture That Engages Every Family

    More often than not, desired change in an organization is temporary, sporadic, or fleeting. This happens because the change never permeates to alter the culture of the organization. Therefore, the notion of culture as the leading standard is essential for long-term success and growth.

2. Principle #2: Communicate Effectively and Develop Relationships

    Relationships with every family are absolutely essential in the consistent engagement of families from grade level to grade level and school to school. Relationships and trust are born out of distinct, meaningful, and thoughtful systems of communication that relate a value in reaching out and connecting with every family. Communication, for the purposes of this principle, also includes the important concept of welcoming environments in schools.

3. Principle #3: Build Family Efficacy

    In simple terms, one definition of efficacy is the power of one (or some) to produce an effect. Establishing instructional and curricular processes that are inclusive of families begins to allow families to become immersed in school learning and to enhance and support learning at home.

4. Principle #4: Engage Every Family in Decision Making

Every family needs a voice in certain school decisions, and school leaders must put into place mechanisms that ensure that every voice will be heard. Family engagement in decision making ensures that policies, procedures, and practices have at their core a support for engaging every family.

5. Principle #5: Engage the Greater Community

The key to effective community engagement is to first conceptualize what that engagement should look like, with a clear delineation of desired outcomes. There are rich and deep resources in most communities; however, many schools and districts struggle in leveraging those resources.

EVERY FAMILY AND ALL CHILDREN

"How do you work with parents who don't support the school?" a principal asked me. Later in the book, we'll dive a bit deeper into the potential responses and solutions to the challenge the question presents, but in short, it starts with an examination of what we do right now and how that might need to change.

Most schools are very adept at engaging those who are already engaged. The key to creating family engagement that supports better learning outcomes is to ensure that there is a plan in place that engages every family: families for whom English is not a first language, ethnic and minority families, families that are socioeconomically disadvantaged, and families of students with special needs. Every family, in this case, does truly mean *every* family. And the engagement has better achievement for children—*all* children—as an outcome.

But there is a brutal fact that we must confront. Since we clearly understand that use of the phrase *those students* sets differing expectation levels for student learning and drives expectations that ultimately impact achievement gaps, why then would we label families as *those families* and use that as a determination of our ability to engage them or, perhaps worse, allow it to provide us with a perception that they do not wish to be engaged? Do we value a relationship with a family in poverty? Do we believe it's worth our time?

Because a family is a minority family or a poor family, a nontraditional family, a family with special needs, or a family with a different ethnic or cultural origin has nothing to do with their desire to be engaged and see their children succeed; but these factors seem to drive excuses as to why we don't engage them. It is not family circumstances that determine engagement but our response to those circumstances that will make the difference. This book has a clear premise: to engage every family—period.

CONFRONTING THE NEMESIS OF SKEPTICISM

Too often in education, exposure to new ideas and initiatives has been a ritual of annual staff back-to-school meetings. Educators, especially teachers, have become suspect of most new ideas and even more skeptical of the annual unveiling of "this year's initiatives" by school leadership. They have seen these ideas come and go, with significant monies being spent and little change in student outcomes.

Family engagement practices are not immune from this skepticism, which is often a significant reason for their lack of success. More so than skepticism are educators' perceptions that strategies and efforts to engage every family are futile, largely because of apathy on the part of disengaged families. While there are many challenges to successful family engagement practices, family apathy toward their child's education is rarely one of them.

Engage Every Family: Five Simple Principles confronts the belief of educators who might not think there is value in engaging every family. Too many books start with the assumption that educators value family engagement and are merely looking for ways to improve it. Other books provide research as a way to prove to educators that the concept is viable. Both of these options are important contributions to the body of work but dangerous in their assumptions.

This work is a conversation about family engagement, not an intravenous drip of facts and strategies. It may very well challenge the conventional wisdom of other books, but at the same time, it offers suggestions on how educators can move forward. This book encourages educators to explore, reflect on, and discuss their present ideas, attitudes, assumptions, and beliefs about family engagement before any ideas or strategies are presented.

WHY A FIELD BOOK?

Educators have commented about the need for a working and teaching resource. Providing questions, topics for discussion, activities, case studies, and opportunities for professional reflection will link *Engage Every Family: Five Simple Principles* directly to the experiences of all educators.

Given the constraints on your time, it would be attractive to read through this book and skip over the various activities that are included. You are encouraged not only to read the text but also to delve into the activities and reflections that are provided. To ensure that your school is successful with family engagement, try some or all of the following activities:

- Record your thoughts, ideas, and experiences as you use the book to enhance the degree to which every family is engaged with their children's learning. Fold the corners of pages over and write in the margins.

- If you are working with a group, start a Google Hangout and keep a conversation going. Communicate, converse, collaborate, and reflect on the ideas presented. Have conversations with your colleagues about what you are reading and thinking. It's the best way to apply the presented ideas to your own experiences and set of circumstances. If the work is meaningful and relevant to you as an educator, then the likelihood of it having lasting positive effects is greater.
- Work with groups of colleagues to get a better understanding of the presented concepts and a better understanding of why the effort to engage every family is worth it. Discuss your ideas, your fears, and your dreams with your colleagues.
- Work together to try out new strategies and support each other's efforts. Listen to the thoughts and opinions of others and juxtapose them against your own. This type of collaboration will ensure that great things will occur.

SPECIAL FEATURES THAT WILL HELP YOU ALONG YOUR JOURNEY

Case Studies

Throughout the book, there are case studies of situations that are similar to those that occur every day in our schools. The case studies include questions for discussion and reflection.

Forms, Checklists, and Needs Assessments

Where appropriate, checklists, forms, needs assessments, and other items have been included to assist you as you work through the Five Simple Principles and consider the implementation of the ideas presented.

Scenarios, Questions, and Points to Ponder

The key to this book is to reflect on present practices and, using the framework and ideas presented, to create a new culture inclusive of engaging every family. To that end, there are numerous opportunities for you to respond to short scenarios, answer questions, and ponder in more depth some of the lofty issues we face in education and how family engagement can enhance our practice.

Process Ideas

Family engagement is more a process and less a string of events to which families can attend. When appropriate, there are sections, questions, and activities devoted to the important processes for rich and lasting family engagement.

Where We Are

Throughout the book, you will find opportunities to reflect on where you are. Your reflections should lead you to a better understanding of your current situation and clarify a path toward your desired outcomes.

Graphics and Activities

The book includes activities that you and your colleagues can engage in to support your efforts in engaging every family. Graphics are used to illustrate ideas and allow you to collect information and data about your efforts.

No one book can provide all of the answers and strategies regarding effective family engagement. With that said, this book makes an important point: Strategies without process and culture change are ineffective or short-lived. Let's face it: If family engagement were as simple as implementing lists of strategies, every family would already be engaged.

A cookie-cutter, one-size-fits-all approach to family engagement will ensure that success remains elusive. The ideas and thoughts that *you* create, coupled with the suggestions and information provided, act as a foundation through which the Five Simple Principles can be implemented and measured.

WHAT YOU WILL GET FROM THIS BOOK

There is a return on the investment of the time and energy you will spend reading this book and working through the various activities:

- You will determine the existing culture of your school with regard to family engagement and how you can help change it to be inclusive of every family.
- You will have a deep understanding of the processes and components to truly engage every family in the academic lives of their children, which will result in improved learning outcomes for all.
- You will have the chance to learn, think, reflect, and practice before you implement ideas in your classroom, school, or district. There are numerous activities, questions, and case studies to engage your thinking and actions.
- You will have all of the tools and resources to engage every family!
- You will see results.

AS THE JOURNEY BEGINS

Family engagement is not a cure-all or a panacea for everything that ails our system of education, nor is it the sole solution to our student achievement woes. However, it will move us closer—much closer—to our goal of excellence for every student. Family engagement is a means to an end, a process that results in improved outcomes for all students.

Families who build strong efficacy with the educational lives of their children can make a huge difference in the degree to which their children are successful in school. The concept of family engagement is simple: Involve families in the learning lives of their children and they will become partners and advocates of success.

While the concept may be simple, actually making it happen can be a bit more complicated. This complication could be why we haven't seen more universal or consistent success with engaging every family. Some families, sure. Most families, sometimes. Every family . . . hardly ever. What, then, does it take to engage every family? It is this question that motivates this book.

Engage Every Family: Five Simple Principles was born out of necessity. Educators are strapped for time and money. We are under pressure to perform and have been conditioned to try just about anything to help our students pass the test upon which they (and we) will be graded. We must show developmental growth and mastery of learning, and we must do so with conditions that are rather dire. And we must do so now!

Family engagement is not a quick fix. It is not a strategy that we can slap onto the school and expect to see immediate success. It is not a computer program in front of which we can plop students (or their families) for a period of time and then pronounce them engaged and successful. Strategies without process *always* fail. Always.

There is no one-size-fits-all portion to this book, nor is there any money-back guarantee that implementing a simple set of strategies will suddenly engage every family. *Engage Every Family: Five Simple Principles* is designed to help you change the culture of your school or district and promote the conditions necessary so that families play an important role in the educational lives of their children. The principles are by no means magic. Most importantly, this process will take time and commitment.

It is my sincere hope that this book is just the beginning. The catalyst to these dreams is you. At the end of the day, if this book captures the attention of educators and that attention results in a more universal commitment and ability to engage every family in the educational life of their children, then the stage will be set for greatness.

So, let's get started!

Publisher's Acknowledgments

Corwin gratefully acknowledges the contributions of the following individuals:

Melissa Frans, Assistant Principal
Crete Middle School
Crete, NE

Tanna Nicely, Principal
South Knoxville Elementary
Knoxville, TN

Melissa Nixon, Federal Programs Administrator
NC Department of Public Instruction
Raleigh, NC

Heath Peine, Executive Director of Student Support Services
Wichita Public Schools
Wichita, KS

Cathern Wildey, Adjunct Professor
Nova Southeastern University
Miami Beach, FL

About the Author

For over twenty-five years, **Steven M. Constantino** has captivated thousands of teachers, administrators, school board members, and businesspeople from the United States and around the world. His keynote presentations and workshops have been featured in local, state, regional, national, and international conferences. Working as a high school principal in 1995, he stumbled across research about the effects of family engagement on student learning and was immediately convinced that this was the missing ingredient in helping all children learn.

Dr. Constantino's work quickly gained national prominence, and soon he began traveling the United States, speaking and working with all types of educators, school board members, and businesses to promote sound practices in family engagement that result in increased academic achievement for all students. His natural gifts as a motivating orator, coupled with his knowledge and practical experiences, make him one of the most sought-after speakers in the field of family engagement.

Dr. Constantino began his career as a music teacher and moved through the ranks. In addition to teacher, assistant principal, principal, deputy superintendent, and district superintendent, Dr. Constantino is also the former chief academic officer and acting superintendent of public instruction for the Commonwealth of Virginia. Today, Dr. Constantino is an executive professor at the William & Mary School of Education, where he teaches in the education policy, planning, and leadership department and continues to travel the globe helping schools, districts, and organizations to engage every family.

ACTIVITY

Think Before You Read!

Do not read this book . . . yet.

You have acquired a book about engaging families and the first thing you read from the author is "Do not read this book . . . yet." Odd? Yes. Stay with it!

Before you read a word of this book, please reflect and answer the following questions. Discuss your thoughts with colleagues. Take the time now, before you delve into the ideas for engaging every family, to determine what your personal starting point is.

1. When you think about your career in education, what is your impression of the desire for families to be engaged in the academic lives of their children?

2. Over the course of your career, what percentage of families were truly engaged in the learning lives of their children?

3. Keeping the answer to Question 2 in mind, can you determine any patterns in the type of involvement or noninvolvement you have experienced?

4. What do you think are the key ingredients needed to successfully engage every family in the academic lives of their children?

5. Given your answer to Question 4, how do you think you, your colleagues, your school, or your district should go about acquiring the key ingredients for success?

Answer, reflect, and discuss these questions. Then, start reading.

Record your thoughts and ideas from the questions here. As you read through this book, come back and reflect on what you wrote. Taking the time to record your thoughts and referring back to them will help you see how your thinking may change as you work through this book.

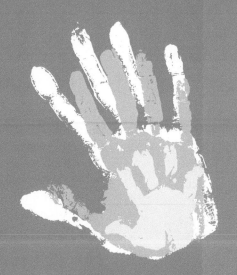

CHAPTER 1

Would Every Family Choose You?

CUSTOMERS MAKE PAYDAYS POSSIBLE

I began my career as a band director and enjoyed every minute of my time teaching and making music with students. As a teacher of music, I taught elective classes. Students were not required to take my class and, if it didn't meet their needs or if their interests took them in different directions, they would drop my class. I learned very quickly that recruitment and retention were my keys to success. As a former superintendent once said to me, "Remember, Mr. Constantino, customers make paydays possible."

A free, public education, for the most part, has always been the only plausible option for most families for a long, long time and is a cornerstone of our democratic society. Every child has a right to an education, and the vast majority of us have taken advantage of this right. Alternatives have always existed, but the percentage of families who would or could take advantage of these options was a small minority.

That is all changing.

There is some debate as to whether or not public education is a right of citizens, good for society, or has simply become a broken idea. Of late, others promote that education is now a commodity. While there is no direct payment for public school services, there is still payment, both in dollars and in societal good, by everyone. With a slight stretch of the definition of *commodity*, it could fit quite well, given the direct competition between public education and the growing number of options open to families with regard to educating their children.

Public education is but one of a number of options open to families who no longer make assumptions or automatically enroll their students in public schools merely because they live in a particular neighborhood. The concept of educational options to families is not a new one, but the availability of these options to a wider range of families is. With the advent of online learning options, the landscape of educational choices is changing, and it is changing quite rapidly.

In my second book, *Engaging All Families: Creating a Positive School Culture by Putting Research into Practice* (2003), I borrowed an idea from a wonderful book titled *Raising Self-Reliant Children in a Self-Indulgent World,* by authors Glenn and Nelsen (1988). In their book, they argue that every parent wants their children to exceed them in their quality of life. Given the complex world in which we live and the financial realities of a postrecession economic society, most families instinctively fear that this will not occur. As a result, they are driven to help their children prosper in any way they can, and for many, the path is the best education available to them.

ACTIVITY

Reflecting on Why

There is a difficult albeit important question that every educator must ask themselves: If families truly have a choice as to where their children will receive an education, will they choose our school district? Our school? My classroom? If your answer to this question is unequivocally yes, then you must ask yourself the logical follow-up question: Why? Why would families choose your school? Why would families choose your classroom or you as a teacher? What is it that is so compelling about your product that a customer will choose it over the growing list of options?

It might be difficult to think of providing an education as a product or service, and it might be more difficult to consider it as an option in an ever-crowded marketplace. Some educators scoff at the idea that education is a business and that we serve customers. There is not enough space here to continue the debate as to whether students are customers or products; both or neither. I've heard it argued just about every way.

When I suggest that we need to learn better customer service in education, I sometimes am plastered with sentiments that suggest that my audience does not agree. More often than not, thank goodness, we inherently understand that customer service is a cornerstone of our continued successful existence. Family engagement and customer service go hand in hand.

I often challenge schools and districts to consider the questions about choice. Then I challenge them to consider taking an action that could very well send a powerful message to families: Not only do we care about their children but we also understand that there are choices and we are grateful that they choose our product.

> If families truly have a choice as to where their children will receive an education, will they choose our school district?

An Idea: We Appreciate You—A Way to Set the Stage to Engage Every Family

If you are looking for a quick way to build trusting relationships, consider this one.

Anybody who flies a great deal listens to endless announcements on the aircraft before they take off, as they fly, and as they land and taxi to the gate. In the myriad of announcements, there is always one that goes something like this: "We know you have a choice in airlines, and we appreciate your choosing us. We hope you will continue to choose our airline in the future."

I have listened to an iteration of this statement more times than I can count. Interestingly, even though I have had more than my fair share of delayed and canceled flights, postponements, and cancellations due to mechanical maladies and other types of issues that cause mayhem in my travel, I stay loyal to one particular airline. Why? Why, when I have so many choices, do I continue to support the airline with which I have been affiliated? Is it convenience? Do I want the air miles that much? Am I on a quest to finally get upgraded to first class? Or do I believe at some level that this particular airline truly *values* me as a customer?

(Continued)

(Continued)

My preferred airline stays in constant communication with me before, during, and after a trip. They want to know my experiences and every time—*every time*—I have responded with a concern, I have received a response. That's impressive. Even more impressive is their communication when they know a problem has occurred and they want feedback as to how they have handled the situation. They even monitor social media for customer dissatisfaction and respond accordingly.

What if we apply this idea to *our* business? At some point, ask every employee of a school district, from the superintendent through the teachers to the support staff, to choose one family at random and call them on the phone. When they answer, simply say:

> *Hi, my name is* [. . .] *and I am calling from* [school/district]. *I just wanted to take a minute to thank you for choosing our* [district/school] *to educate your children. We know you have a choice in how to educate your children, and we appreciate your choosing us. We consider working with your children and your family a privilege.*

Don't say another word. Just listen. Think about the responses you get.

That's it. That's the whole purpose of the message. You simply want your customer to know that you value their decision to use your product/service. Consider for a moment what would occur if every family in your school or district received this call. There would be an exponential increase in relationships and trust.

Every person who makes a phone call like this from your school district should report his or her experience. Was the message received positively? Negatively? As a result of the phone call, did we learn anything about the student or their family that will help us? How can we modify our service to meet the needs of our families in a better manner?

These are all important questions that lead to the ideal of engaging every family. What do you think would happen? What kind of responses do you think you would get? What message will families take away from this simple effort? You won't know unless you try it.

EVERY OPPORTUNITY IS A MARKETING OPPORTUNITY

Consider for a moment a world-famous soda pop company. If I shared the name with you, it would be instantly recognizable. The name of this company and their brand are listed as one of the most recognizable products on the *planet*. That is saying something!

My dear friend and family engagement researcher and expert, Dr. Karen Mapp, often shares a story about this company and how they would pay handsomely to have audiences similar to the ones we get at school events. It would be their marketing dream to work with a captive audience to sell their product or elicit feedback about their product. Yet, we do little to market or elicit feedback for our product when we have these gatherings of families.

When we have families together and listening to us, we should take that opportunity to sell our product to them and explain the meaning and relevance of their child's education to them. We also need to create a culture that helps families share their feedback in a manner they perceive to be both safe and constructive. Maybe we should begin to think of these gatherings as sales opportunities.

If public education is indeed a commodity, then the concept of attracting and retaining customers is not that far-fetched. If you do not believe in the commodity idea, then there is still no harm in helping every family understand why you are the best.

SOME IDEAS TO GET STARTED

The most difficult part of any experience is actually making the decision to begin. All of us have made commitments to making changes that often fall short. On New Year's Eve, many of us resolve to bring a renewed energy and focus to goals in the coming year that have previously eluded us. Sometimes we follow through, sometimes we don't.

The fact that you have this book and you are still reading is an indication that you are ready to start or enhance your efforts to engage every family. It seems appropriate to give you a few things to keep in mind as you get into *Engage Every Family: Five Simple Principles*. Over the years and with mountains of feedback from educators everywhere, a few common themes have emerged. They appear below as a way to draw a starting line and can act as guidelines for you as you begin your venture toward engaging every family.

Keep It Simple

We as educators tend to overthink issues, sometimes to the point of paralysis—we think that change is not worth the time or will not produce the desired result. We take challenges that we face and make the avenues toward potential solutions so complex that resolving the issue seems impossible. We overwhelm ourselves with problems and ultimately become frustrated.

Simply put, we lose hope. We lose hope that we have the energy or power to change anything. We lose hope that things will change regardless of what we do. Let's commit to breaking that cycle. While I would agree with the idea that hope is not a concrete strategy, I would also argue that it is essential to improving organizations. Be sure, however, that hope is not your only strategy.

So, let's keep it simple. Simple translates into more effective action. Breaking down complex ideas into simple ones allows educators with finite amounts of time and resources to actually think and implement the ideas that are presented. Family engagement is not a race. Implementing strategies without the necessary processes and learning will result in little change to your school—or at best, temporary or sporadic change.

You do not have to read this book in a week. As a matter of fact, the longer it takes you to get through the book (assuming you are fully participating in the questions and ideas presented), the more likely your perceptions and actions are changing. As they change, so changes the culture of your school.

Engage Every Family: Five Simple Principles is designed to be simple—simple to discuss, simple to plan, and simple to execute. There are no herculean efforts or large budget expenditures needed to engage every family. As a matter of fact, engaging families is nearly budget neutral. Imagine that—a way to increase student achievement that is almost free. Worth considering, don't you think?

Simple ideas presented by groups of educators supporting each other almost always result in success sooner or later. If it takes a week, a month, or five years, so what? Measurable progress toward a goal is key. Breaking down the progress into simple, logical steps will keep the notion of family engagement very doable in the minds of just about everybody.

Remember the classic question: How do you eat an elephant?

The answer is one piece at a time. Do not expect that by implementing the ideas learned in this book, suddenly or magically every family will be engaged. Consider that we want to engage families, especially those that are disengaged from us, one family at a time.

Time and Patience

We are conditioned to fix everything now, today, this minute. There is no time to think, to explore, to investigate, to research, to pilot, and to assess. Because of the performance pressures placed on schools and educators, we have become a group of people wandering around, educational zombies looking for a quick fix to what ails us. Professional athletes spend 90 percent of their time training and 10 percent of their time performing. For educators, it is exactly the opposite. That's a problem.

There are no quick fixes to the significant challenges we face in education. If there were, we wouldn't have the challenges. The necessary investment to engage every family is one of time and patience. There is no magic wand to wave that will suddenly engage the disengaged or miraculously engage every family by the beginning of the next school year. The process is often a slow one.

The best way to engage every family might very well be one family at a time. In one case, a preschool teacher worked with a family for over a year before the comfort level rose to the point where a relationship could be established.

> The best way to engage every family might very well be one family at a time.

Having patience with families, especially those that have been traditionally disengaged or disenfranchised from our schools, will unquestionably support any effort to reaffirm a commitment to their engagement. Families that are disadvantaged, families for whom English is not a first language, and families whose own school experiences were less than positive all play a role in engagement decisions. These challenges can be overcome. It just takes time and patience.

It is equally important to have patience with educational colleagues who may not see the value in engaging every family. Educators have been made a lot of promises over the years, and many of those promises never materialized. Teachers have become skeptical of educational initiatives, maybe rightfully so. Think of it this way: Family engagement is not an initiative nor is it a new task set in front of you. Consider it the same as doing what we already do but doing it differently, through the lens of engaged families—no new time commitment, no new resources, no new energies, simply doing what we already do . . . differently. Don't think outside the box—blow the box up! Rebuild and reassemble the pieces in a different way.

Not More, Just Different

As a teacher, I remember attending the new school year opening meetings and listening to the leadership share the initiatives for the upcoming year. Over time, the word *initiative* struck fear in my heart. It usually meant that I was going to have to do something else, something new, something for which I may not appreciate the value. I learned to shudder at the word *initiative*.

Family engagement is not an initiative nor is it a race. Family engagement is a commitment to change school culture and, as such,

POINTS TO PONDER

1. Discuss with your colleagues the time you devoted to implementing a new idea and the amount of time you engaged with the idea before you decided to abandon it.

2. Discuss with your colleagues those ideas and strategies that have proven effective. How long did it take to implement and perfect the ideas/strategies before you saw the success you wanted?

3. What role did the amount of time devoted to the new concept play in its ultimate success or failure?

is ongoing and never ending. It is important to keep in mind that not everyone on a school staff or in a school district will suddenly think that engaging families is a great idea. In some cases, there will likely be strong opposition to the idea—even flat-out refusal.

Consider that the implementation of family engagement philosophies, strategies, and practices is not adding new responsibilities to your already full plate. Family engagement takes into consideration what we already do. It merely requires us to act *differently*—no new time, no new energy, no new resources—simply a remolding of what we already have. To engage families means to look at our practices and procedures through a different lens— the lens of families.

During my years as a teacher and building administrator, I marveled at the sharing of ideas and resources among teachers. When one would get a good idea, others would watch to see the results. If the results were good, they would ask the originator of the idea for the information so they could replicate the success. Great methodology is passed among teachers every day. (We'll delve into this idea a bit deeper in the next chapter.)

Educators, similar to the students we teach, are discoverers of knowledge. When presented with good, solid ideas that they see have positive effects on their jobs, the likelihood of their involvement and support of new ideas grows. Engaging every family and promoting the appropriate culture in a school to engage every family takes time and patience. Be encouraging, nurturing, patient, and steadfast. The results will come.

We Already Tried That

It is the rare workshop where I offer more than a handful of new ideas to help engage every family. Quite honestly, schools across the country have captured a plethora of ideas and tailored them to their schools and specific situations. I remember one workshop participant a few years ago who said to me, "Yeah, we did the letter and the phone call and the visit and the food and the childcare and the transportation and three people showed up."

I readily acknowledge that while we continue to find new ways to engage families, especially with technology and social media, most of the great ideas are already out there and have had varying levels of success. So, what is the answer?

It might be time to consider why your efforts, if they were marginally successful, paid so little dividend. Maybe it was the structure or timing of what you did. Perhaps the content didn't resonate with families. Maybe it was the school location that kept families away. Most likely though, the answer lies in the culture that permeates your school. Does everyone value the engagement of every family? How is that value communicated? How do we respond to situations where families do not act as we had hoped with regard to school engagement? What is our response to disengagement? Was the message of your meeting or event meaningful or relevant to families?

Make sure you understand this important fact: No one event or first attempt at engaging every family will bring a thundering herd of families to your doorway. More often than not in communities where family engagement is traditionally low, the successes are small—one family, followed by a few more families, and so forth. If you repeat an event and you increase attendance from three to five people, celebrate that! Don't be discouraged that there were not twenty or thirty people at the event. For many years, I have used this adage: We engage families one family at a time. With time, we hit a tipping point; sometimes it takes a while. Hang in there.

There is another idea about engagement that needs to be discussed. Most of the engagement that impacts student learning happens in homes away from school. I often refer to this as "invisible engagement," engagement you may not see but with which you will see results. This is not to say that workshops and efforts to engage families are fruitless and should be discontinued—quite the contrary. The work we do outside of the home will help promote the efficacy of families when they are with their children and we are not.

In workshops, I usually give the following example of practices that I have witnessed in many schools (including my own!): School staff work tirelessly to create an opportunity for family engagement. They follow all of the appropriate procedures to be an open, welcoming environment and have practiced significant outreach to families. A central idea in the preparation of these events is the notion of its importance. We tend to drive the point home to families about how important it is that they do whatever it is we want them to do (come to a meeting, participate in a workshop, etc.).

When the event occurs and the family attendance is disappointing, it's not what we do next but rather more about what we don't do. We usually are exhausted from our efforts and frustrated with the results. We sulk away and vow never to expend that amount of energy again. We convince ourselves that families are simply apathetic and that our efforts are a waste of time and energy. What we almost never do is follow up with our customer and find out why they didn't attend.

Consider this: If we repeatedly hammer into a family's head that taking a particular action is important and, upon their not taking the desired action, we never say another word, what message have we sent? Exactly! Reinforced in the mind of the parent or family member is the idea that whatever it was, it simply was not that important. That very notion erodes trust in relationships between schools and families.

REALITY, PERCEPTIONS, AND BELIEFS

Our personal belief systems play a powerful role with regard to our desired family engagement outcomes. Families apply the very same thinking. Their personal belief systems and customs also play a large role in determining their level of engagement with their child's education. Understanding that perception is reality for most people underscores the need to carefully examine the belief systems of people and organizations.

> Understanding that perception is reality for most people underscores the need to carefully examine the belief systems of people and organizations.

When a decision is made to undertake a course to engage every family or to increase family engagement, a critical first step is to gauge where everyone is on the subject. Later in the book, ideas and activities will be presented to create a culture for engaging every family. (Hopefully, you took the first step before you ever started reading this chapter.)

Can every family truly be engaged? This question has been debated over the years, and as one can imagine, the answers fall along a continuum between absolutely and absolutely not. It might be interesting to know that many urban and Title I schools have proven that 100 percent engagement is possible. It seems that the answer begins within one's own personal belief system.

Facts, reality, and evidence are clear: There is a strong correlation between family engagement and student learning. Not every family is engaged with their child's education. Every educator does not place the same value on building relationships with every family. Families' experiences with their children's schools shape their engagement practices over time.

Not every school welcomes families. Not every family feels welcome in their child's school. Not every family believes that their voice is heard or that their opinions or ideas matter. It will be imperative that whatever your goals in family engagement, you start with a thorough discussion and reflection on your reality, your perceptions, and your present beliefs on the topic. Not spending this time now will most likely result in very little change, if any.

The ideas below are items that should be completed before you venture into the Five Simple Principles.

WHERE WE ARE

Directions: Have each individual member of your team or school answer the following questions independently and anonymously. Compile the answers to see where your starting point is with regard to engaging every family.

1. What do you believe about family engagement?

2. Do you believe that every family in your (classroom, team, school, etc.) is engaged with their child's learning?

3. If the answer to Question 2 is no, then why do you think there are families who are not engaged?

4. If every family in your (classroom, team, school, etc.) is not engaged, would you welcome their engagement?

5. What would engaging every family look like to you?

FINALLY, THE SECRET TO SUCCESS!

Here is a story that underscores the secret to successfully engaging every family. Read through the story. The point of the story and the secret to success should be clear by the time you finish reading it.

Having numerous issues and stressors in his life, a gentleman made the difficult decision to seek professional counseling. This was a decision that did not come lightly and one that the man debated and rejected many, many times. In the final analysis, though, the man realized that without some assistance, the issues in his life would continue to affect his health and his relationships with the ones he loved. Because of this, he took the large, difficult, and scary step to seek help.

Upon arrival to the counselor's office, the gentleman was immediately put at ease. He was under no obligation to say anything he didn't want to say or take any action he didn't want to take. He was in complete control of the conversation. Almost without knowing it, an hour went by, and the gentleman was asked if he would return the following week. He agreed.

The following week (and several weeks after that) seemed to be a repeat of the first. He talked about all kinds of things, and the individual hours of conversation flew by. After several weeks, he realized he felt a bit better but really couldn't put his finger on why. At his next appointment with the counselor, he decided to ask.

He walked into the meeting, sat down, and asked the counselor the question he had been pondering.

"You feel better because you have discovered the secret," the counselor said.

"The secret? The secret to what?" The gentleman was a bit irritated at the answer given to him.

"The secret to success," answered the counselor. He walked over to his desk and picked up a picture frame and handed it to the gentlemen.

"Please read this out loud, if you will," said the counselor. The gentleman looked at the frame. Inside the frame there was no picture and really no sentence or recognizable word to read. He simply saw the following:

YAGOTTAWANNA

When the gentlemen read it out loud, at that instant, he realized what the word was and what it meant.

"One's personal desire to make a difficult change starts with the very simple idea that we *want* to make the change. Without the intrinsic desire, whatever our goal, it most likely will remain elusive. You have decided to make the change. Therefore, you are." The counselor sat back waiting for a response.

"Yagottawanna, eh?" said the gentleman. "That simple?"

"That simple." The counselor smiled and said not another word. Neither did the gentleman.

The secret to successful family engagement starts with the simple notion that we desire to engage families because we believe that doing so will have a positive impact on the children we serve.

Yagottawanna. It really is that simple.

THE IMPORTANCE OF CARING

There is no question that we have many mountains to climb with regard to reforming and improving our public schools. It seems to be a reasonable conclusion, though, that the mountain that is the easiest to climb is the one that convinces families that we care about their children. Why? Because we do care! I do not recall ever meeting educators who said they simply didn't care about the children they were teaching. Further, convincing families that we care about their children is budget neutral.

The importance of caring is best summarized by another short story. This time, two neighbors, one of whom is a teacher at the local school, are discussing a decision by one of them to move his child from the local public school to a newly organized charter school.

Tom was a staunch supporter of public schools and would be the last one to abandon them. But Tom did just that. Tom removed his children from the local public school and enrolled them in a newly opened charter school. Bill, his friend who was a teacher in the local public school, knew the risks of engaging in a conversation with Tom about his decision but ultimately could not ignore the situation.

"I must admit, you caught me by surprise with your decision about the charter school," Bill said.

"There was a big part of me that was afraid to tell you, given your career and commitment to public schools," Tom responded rather sheepishly. "I want you to know that this was not a decision that we came to lightly."

Bill asked a series of questions to determine the rationale for the decision. "What is it about the education that your kids are getting at their present school that concerns you?" Bill asked. "Or is it a safety issue? I know how much the safety of children weighs on the minds of all parents." Bill thought that if he continued to share potential reasons for the switch, the conversation would go a bit better and he would be closer to understanding the basis for Tom's decision.

"I can't say that I am unhappy with the education my kids are getting. Then again, I really can't judge whether or not what they are getting is appropriate. As far as safety goes, I am more than convinced that the principal and the staff have a good plan for security. I really don't worry about my kids when they are in school."

Bill decided to prod a bit further. "I hear all the time from parents that the lack of challenging curriculum is a real issue. Is that a problem for you?"

"Absolutely not," Tom said. "Sometimes I feel like they are overly challenged and don't have time just to be kids."

"I realize that your kids are tested to death. You do know that the charter schools may require the same kind of testing, don't you?" Bill thought for sure he would hit upon the rationale his friend used to make this decision.

"I am not happy about the testing, but I am smart enough to know that the teachers didn't create this situation. We have our government to thank for that."

Bill paused a moment, a bit confused and wondering how he got this far down the rabbit hole of questions without hitting upon the reasons for the move. "So, let me see if I understand this," Bill started. "You are not unhappy with the education your children are getting and you feel the school is a safe place. You are not trying to escape testing or the laws that govern education. I have to tell you, I am at a loss for why you are moving your children. It sounds like we are doing a pretty good job." As soon as Bill heard his answer, it made perfect sense.

"No, it's none of that. It's just that I feel that the charter school will care more about my children than their present school." Bill asked Tom to elaborate. "I need to know that somebody cares about my kids. I never really hear anything about what goes on in school and outside of typed notes about field trips, money owed, and the need for more tissues and hand sanitizer in the classroom, I don't ever hear anything. I go to the conference every year and it's pretty much the same thing—impersonal, scripted, and irrelevant.

POINTS TO PONDER

1. Reflect on the conversation between Tom and Bill. How did it make you feel?

2. Do you think that this story, which is fictional, could actually occur?

3. Where do you think your school/district is with regard to the issue of caring?

4. What systems could have altered Tom's decision to remove his children from the public school?

5. How do you show families that you care? What more can you do?

6. What ideas can you take away from this story and implement in your school?

"I get a report card with *E*s and *S*s and really can't tell you what the heck they mean. I guess my kids are doing okay, but I don't know that they are. I don't really trust the teachers or staff to care enough about my kids to tell me the truth or, worse yet, to know if there is a problem. I always feel like teachers are put out when I do call and ask a question. I never get the feeling they really want to talk with me. I always feel like when they hang up the phone, they label me a problem parent."

"Considering that your children have not yet attended the charter school, what is it about the experiences you have already had that makes you think the charter school will be different?" Bill asked, not sure if he wanted to hear the answer.

"When we called the school, the lady who answered the phone was pleasant and helpful. She asked me my name and used my name throughout our short conversation. Over and over she said how happy she was that we were considering their school. Within minutes, we had an appointment to visit the school."

Playing the devil's advocate, Bill said, "What if you just ran into one friendly person who has been trained in customer service?"

"That would be one more than exists at our present school," Tom shot back. "But it wasn't just the phone call or the information or the visit. From the first phone call, I felt that we were special, that the school staff really wanted us there. What was really amazing is that within twenty-four hours, all five of the people we met, including two teachers, called us to thank us for visiting their school and once again shared their enthusiasm that we might be coming to their school. I have never had this experience in any school my kids attended."

Bill was stunned. Tom's decision to send his children to a charter school had nothing to do with the quality of education or the perception of a safe school environment but had everything to do with whether or not he perceived that the staff cared about his children. It occurred to Bill at that precise moment that this was the real crisis in our educational system.

The importance of caring about the families we serve cannot be overstated. For the Five Simple Principles to truly assist you in your quest, the whole issue of caring must be discussed at the start.

THE IMPORTANCE OF PROCESS

Strategies without a process produce sporadic and temporary results.

Schools and districts wishing to improve their quality of experiences for staff, students, families, and communities understand that redesigning internal processes of the organization will ultimately lead to improved performance. Schools and districts will need to create processes that are self-sustaining and capable of delivering the required performance objective.

IDEAS TO PROMOTE CARING TO FAMILIES

1. There is nothing more precious to us than someone using our name correctly. Understand the names of your students and their families, especially if they are different because of blended families. Make every contact a personal contact by using that person's name.

2. When families visit the school, give them two name tags. Allow them to put their name on one and their child's name on the other. You will never have to ask a parent who their child is again. Allowing people to make their own name tags will help you understand how to address them in the future. It also makes life easier for teachers and staff members trying to remember names in blended families.

3. Make your first interaction with a family about them, not about you, your classroom, or the course you teach. Demonstrate your desire to learn about them; their family; their customs, rituals, and challenges; and so forth.

4. Whenever possible, have face-to-face conversations or telephone conversations. In this world of mass communication, much is lost in texts, emails, and 140-character messages.

5. Consider home visits (breathe . . . we'll discuss this in more detail later) to those families who are reluctant to participate.

(Continued)

(Continued)

6. When families are invited to an event, take attendance and pay close attention to those who are not there. Call them and tell them you missed them. Offer to share the information with them in another setting. Do not judge their absence or ask them why they were absent; simply reinforce that the information is important and that you want to share it with them.

7. Smile. Don't allow the few negative experiences you may have had with some families to color your attitude toward others.

I bet you can think of other ideas! Write them below:

Available for download at **http://www**.drsteveconstantino.com

We tend to make the time to create the necessary processes for goals and ideas we wish to implement. We often forget the natural dips that occur in organizational effectiveness when we introduce change. Consider Figures 1.1 and 1.2, which help us to understand the implementation of a change.

When we implement a change in an organization, we generally believe that while there may be a few bumps in the road and a few problems to resolve, the change will occur as depicted in Figure 1.1: a slow but steady elevation to our desired state. Unfortunately, this is not usually the case. Change is a messy business. More often than not, it looks more like Figure 1.2.

Change, in any organization, usually plunges some or all of the organization into a chaotic state. More often than not, things get confusing and frustrating before they get better. Then as the change takes hold and the despair turns to acceptance and finally advocacy for the change, the desired state is reached. None of this, however, can be done without explicit processes in place. Strategies without processes do not work.

Figure 1.1

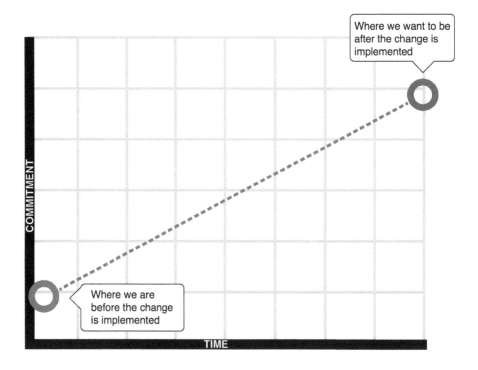

Figure 1.2

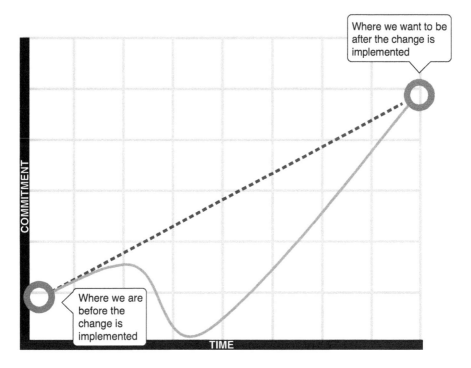

ACTIVITY

Process Exercise

Spend some time reviewing how you process change in your organization.

1. Is your organization used to developing processes that are measured and evaluated over time? If not, what do you think will have to occur in order to become process oriented?

2. Is the leadership of your organization truly committed to the work of family engagement? If so, how will that commitment be translated to your entire organization?

3. Are you willing to examine the culture of your organization, both the positive and negative attributes, in order to bring about improvement?

THE NEED FOR LEADERSHIP

The ingredients to successfully engage every family are as specific as any favorite recipe. Regardless of how well you implement and evaluate your success, if the support of leadership is missing, the recipe will not turn out as expected. Strong, committed, courageous leadership is essential to long-term success.

Several years ago, a question was asked about successful family engagement programs that had been launched in schools around the country. The question was simple: Was there a commonality between those programs that were successful and those that were not? After pondering this question for a while, the answer was clear: Yes. The commonality was supportive and purposeful leadership. Superintendents and central office staff who stood up and set a vision and direction for a school district that was inclusive of families had better results. Principals and building leaders who championed the cause saw more consistent and better measurable results as well.

Of all of the leadership qualities one can possess, it seems that courage is an absolute necessity if leaders wish to engage every family. Changing the direction of organizations and having the will to make changes that can begin as uncomfortable are essential ingredients in engaging every family. Courage comes from facing and overcoming fear. Many people in organizations fear change. Creating the conditions to engage every family will likely be a significant departure from standard practice at your school or in your district.

In many workshops over the years, some teachers and school staff members have approached me to share two specific ideas: First, they want me to know that the concepts and information I am presenting are ones that they believe in and value. The second statement they make is the alarming one. Often, they tell me that they do not perceive that their leadership (district or building) places value on the topic. I have been repeatedly asked what teachers can do to convince leadership that the practice of family engagement is worthwhile and brings about better achievement. My usual response is to persuade them to try the ideas and share the positive results with their leaders as an effort to begin to change the culture.

With these ideas and the notion that families will choose you, the sky is the limit as to your success in engaging every family.

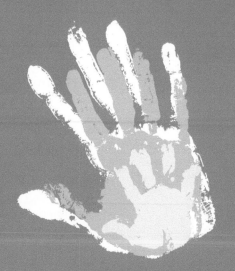

CHAPTER 2

A Quick Note About Motivating Teachers

There is a common theme in the conversations I have with teachers and administrators across the country. Teachers do not feel valued. Morale is at an all-time low. Teachers are losing momentum and are somewhat beleaguered by the constant assault on public education by the media and politicians, the demands on their time, the ever-growing set of standards that must be mastered by all students and new levels of accountability, and the ever-dwindling resources available to public education. Teacher recruitment and retention has become one of the top priorities of school districts, colleges, and state governments as the problem grows with each passing school year.

While I don't deny the reality and severity of these issues, I continue to see progress in student learning. More students are successful in school. In my own district, we have made progress with our students year after year. How can unmotivated, demoralized teachers produce such results? Maybe the answer lies in the degree to which teachers are or can be motivated to be their very best.

In a recent Phi Delta Kappa poll (2014) of 170,000 Americans, 10,000 of which were teachers, teaching was found to be the second most satisfying profession after medicine. The same poll found that in contrast to their overall happiness with their jobs, teachers often rate last or close to the bottom for workplace engagement and happiness.

In the 2019 poll, half the teachers reported they had seriously considered leaving the profession. With that said, however, the poll also has encouraging news—significant numbers of parents and community members will stand up to support teachers (Phi Delta Kappa International, 2019).

Bolman and Deal (2002) articulate the challenge as the failure of "teacher proofing" reform initiatives. Pink (2009) describes the three important factors for motivation in the workplace: autonomy, mastery, and purpose. It is this last notion, purpose, in which family engagement can play a huge role.

Upon entering their chosen profession, a majority of teachers have a strong sense of purpose. Administrators and families that support teachers will allow a teacher to sustain their purpose in advancing the learning of an increasingly diverse country of learners. Students connect to the person who is teaching, not simply the content being taught. Families react in much the same way. Teachers are motivated by a desire to give. Family engagement can considerably enhance this desire.

> To ignore teacher motivation is almost to cast a death knell on the culture of schools and education.

To ignore teacher motivation is almost to cast a death knell on the culture of schools and education. Later, we will learn that culture is made up of the collective beliefs, values, and assumptions of people within the organization. The degree to which people are motivated toward peak performance will go a long way to ensuring a positive and thriving organizational culture.

Research has articulated a great number of positive outcomes when efforts are made to successfully engage families in the academic lives of their children. In a study conducted by Epstein and Becker (1982), a large population of teachers was asked to share what they believed was the largest barrier to their success as a teacher. Interestingly, an overwhelming number of those teachers indicated they wished they had more support from the home for what they were trying to achieve in their classroom.

Family engagement produces a number of positive outcomes for education. One of them is clearly the improved attitudes and morale of teachers. When students do better in school, homework completion rates improve, attendance improves, and student behaviors improve, so does teacher desire and morale (Epstein et al., 2009). When families and teachers are working together on the same page, everybody wins. This collaboration does not happen by itself. It takes a commitment to the idea, reflection on practice, and work toward building trusting relationships with every family.

It's important that we support teachers' efforts to engage families by spending time, energy, and resources to provide effective professional development in the area of family engagement. Teacher satisfaction and student learning both improve for teachers when family engagement is a priority and when teachers feel supported in creating meaningful relationships with all families (Mapp, Carver, & Lander, 2017).

It has been my honor to conduct workshops for educators for many years. More often than not, some workshop participants will confirm with me that they share the same opinions and values about engaging families but wish their superiors or others in charge felt the same way. In some cases, as unbelievable as this may sound, teachers are discouraged by their own leaders from engaging families. In a workshop, one teacher told me, "My principal said that the last thing we needed were parents running around the school all day long."

A very simple step toward engaging every family is to support those educators who are already convinced that the outcomes of family engagement are worth the effort. As this grows, a tsunami of engagement will occur, and good things will start to happen. It's hard to ignore or cast dispersion over progress.

Many schools have instituted parent liaison and specialist positions. These positions, found commonly in schools receiving Title I funding, are dedicated to creating inroads with every family and bridging the gap between home and school. Used effectively, these liaison positions can create an atmosphere of trust in schools and can also serve as a vehicle to connect families with classroom teachers.

While these positions can be critical to the goal of engaging every family, it is important that they not be used as substitutes for the necessary relationships between teachers and families. In some cases, these positions are used to make discipline phone calls or are asked to serve in utility capacities, such as extra help in the cafeteria, hall duty, and duties at arrival and dismissal. If these positions are relegated to these operational tasks, the desired outcome of engaging every family will be lost. Further, if they are used as substitutes for relationships between classroom teachers and families, teacher motivation can suffer.

THREE KINDS OF TEACHERS: A SLIGHTLY HUMOROUS LOOK

In almost every workshop, conference session, or question-and-answer period, I invariably get this question: How do you get teacher buy-in for family engagement?

It's a great question.

I usually start the answer by sharing my opinion of the types of teachers we have in our schools. Mind you, my comments are not based on one shred of research but rather are born from my experiences and observations of teachers over time. These descriptions are meant to be humorous, and while people are laughing, they usually nod their head in agreement. That affirmation provides me with the motivation to share with you "the three types of teachers." Every school usually has these three groups, with minor variations.

Group one is a small group of teachers I call the "happy peppy teachers." They have boundless energy, are creative, and are typically happy morning people. They are the first to offer new ideas and the first to volunteer for just about anything in the school. If there is a sunshine committee, these teachers are on it. If the principal asked them to run naked down the street, they would be shedding clothing as they bolt out the front doors of the school! They are happy, peppy, and full of spirit, energy, and optimism. They never sleep and seem to be at school all the time. Some students believe these teachers are obviously robots and must plug themselves in somewhere to recharge.

Group two is the largest group of teachers; I call them "the wait-and-see-ers." This is a group that does not usually fully commit to doing anything, nor do they refuse to do anything. They simply wait and see. They wait and see if the idea presented will be around in a week or a month. They have seen ideas, practices, procedures, initiatives, and surefire solutions to problems come and go.

They also wait and see if the leadership desiring the action will be around in a week or a month. They have seen them come and go as well.

As a former principal of a school offering the International Baccalaureate (IB) Programme, I once had a teacher say, "I bet you didn't know I was an IB teacher?"

"No," I said, "I didn't know that."

"Yup, *I be* here when you got here and *I be* here when you gone!"

The wait-and-see-ers do just that—they wait and see.

Group three is usually the smallest group of them all, but they pack a powerful punch. I call them the "not-gonna-do-its." No matter what you want, they are simply not going to do it. At meetings, their arms are folded across their chest—that is, at the meetings they actually attend. They can be highly skeptical or, worse yet, negative. No matter what the idea, they will find some way to be critical. The "not-gonna-do-its" are a tough group with which to foster change in an organization.

It is often impossible for leaders to change the mindset of this last small but powerful group of people. The answer lies in changing the culture of the organization. As the genesis of a new culture of relationships and open communication is created, it forces the "not-gonna-do-its" either to conform to the new norm or, in some more drastic cases, leave the organization altogether.

This humorous look at teachers highlights the fact that in every organization there exists a wide continuum of attitudes and assumptions about change, ideas, or initiatives. However, it is important to remember one salient issue: No teacher *wants* to fail.

We have to take some responsibility with regard to the level of skepticism that exists among the teaching force. We have paraded an awful lot of things that were "guaranteed" either to make their lives easier or improve student learning seemingly by magic. Teachers look upon these ideas as passing fads—here today, gone tomorrow. No wonder most of them "wait and see" if something will stick around for a while.

CAN I GET A COPY OF THAT?

Teachers are always willing to share good, practical ideas for improving instruction and learning. Teachers also gravitate quickly to things that work. They watch each other intently, and when a colleague has success, they are quick to replicate those ideas in their own classroom. Proof-of-concept almost guarantees that most teachers will implement the desired practice or idea in their own classroom. However it occurs, one thing is clear: Good ideas spread among teachers.

The implementation of new ideas and change in an organization is not easy. My best advice is to find that small group of happy, peppy teachers and launch the concept. Their colleagues will watch, hidden behind walls and doors, but they will watch. Slowly but surely, the ideas will take root and over time, almost magically, concepts will permeate the culture of a school.

Forcing change that is not prescribed in law or regulation doesn't usually work very well. Teachers are very compliant people. If you force them to do something, whether they like it or not, they will usually do it. If the change demonstrates the results and desired outcomes, teachers incorporate it into their culture. However, if the change doesn't achieve the desired outcomes, the change doesn't last very long, and before you know it, there is no change at all. While some forced change could be argued as necessary, most of this type of organizational change ends up doing nothing more than further driving motivation and morale to a deeper negative level and has the potential to damage leadership credibility. Leading change means leading *cultural* change.

Planting the seeds of ideas, nurturing those ideas, celebrating and replicating successes, and devoting organizational resources to the change are all important ingredients. This is not a book about change theory; however, when thinking about family engagement as a conduit to organizational improvement, the process of change matters.

MY DUMB IDEA

During my years as a building administrator, I launched a lot of new ideas—some good, some not so good. I remember sharing with the faculty a new piece of technology that would revolutionize communication with families; the skepticism ran high—so high, in fact, that one teacher wrote to me anonymously and said in part, "This is the dumbest idea I have ever heard and I have been here for over 25 years and heard a lot of dumb ideas!"

I knew that if we could implement and prove the concept, sooner or later, most teachers would engage. Years later, I got another note, presumably from the same teacher. Unsigned, the note said,

> Three years ago, I told you your telephone idea was dumb. I want to say for the record that I was wrong. In fact, the ideas that you presented have helped all of us be better teachers and most importantly have helped more students be successful.

It is a mistake to ignore the role of motivation in launching a process to engage every family. Understanding the beliefs and values of people within the organization will help leaders better articulate a successful pathway.

In my opinion, the secrets to motivating teachers are simple. First, believe that teachers want to be successful. Second, understand that until a concept is proven, skepticism will run high. Lastly, understand that when the first two conditions are met, teachers will gravitate toward the desired change. Their timeline may not be your timeline, but with nurturing, nudging, and a little patience, the results will be spectacular.

CHAPTER 3

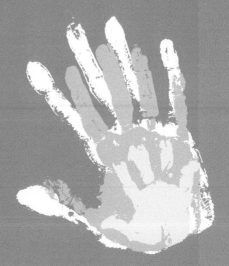

Equity, Bias, and Family Disengagement

To know the true reality of yourself, you must be aware not only of your conscious thoughts, but also of your unconscious prejudices, biases, and habits.

—Anonymous

ISN'T FOREVER LONG ENOUGH?

For all of my career in education, educators have wrestled with achievement gaps between various groups of students. The National Assessment of Educational Progress (NAEP) 2019 report indicates that while some scores are higher overall when compared to scores from a decade ago, they are lower or not significantly different for lower-performing students. We are making little or no progress in closing achievement gaps. It seems as though we have faced this problem forever, which inspires a question: Isn't forever long enough?

At the onset of this book, I challenged you to think about an idea: If we as educators could successfully teach all children by ourselves, then we would have successfully done so already. If we add to that idea the desire to provide equitable outcomes for every student, then the argument for effective family engagement is all the more powerful.

WHAT IS EQUITY?

Traveling the country and working with educators in all different settings provides me with a perspective as to the varying challenges in engaging every family. In the last few years, however, there seems to be one topic that is at the top of every school district's list of goals and improvements. Regardless of the district, location, or community attributes, equity is at the forefront in conversations of educators everywhere. Achieving equitable outcomes for all children, especially the underserved, is a goal of just about every district in our country.

All of us have seen varying depictions of equity in graphic form. Most of the time, equality and equity are juxtaposed to each other to underscore the fundamental difference between the two words. To understand equality, we may have seen students standing at a fence on top of boxes that are of the same dimensions. Even though the boxes are of equal height and dimension, student ability to see over the fence is still not equal. In a second graphic, the boxes are of varying dimensions, which allow all students to see over the fence. The second depiction helps us understand the basic tenets of equity.

> Equity is ensuring that every student has access to the tools, materials, and support they need—exactly when they need it—to meet their learning goals and achieve success.

I suspect there are countless definitions of equity when it comes to educational outcomes. In the spirit of keeping things relatively simple, I believe that equity is ensuring that every student has access to the tools, materials, and support they need—exactly when they need it—to meet their learning goals and achieve success. I don't know that we have to complicate the idea more than that; however, it does raise an interesting question: How then do we ensure that students have what they need, when they need it, when we consider that they spend the vast majority of their time away from school?

Formal out-of-school time (OST) programs recognize the importance of including family engagement processes, such as family literacy, in the design of OST experiences for children. The benefits of family engagement extend to all youth participating in OST programs (Bouffard, Westmoreland, O'Carroll, & Little, 2011). While OST programs are growing around the country, not every school or community can rely on this more-structured approach to providing equitable outcomes for all children. Engaging families by promoting their own efficacy will help move us toward equitable learning outcomes and provide resources and support to students when they are away from school. In order to do so, though, we must first reach past those who are already engaged to those families who are disengaged, disenfranchised, or feel otherwise marginalized by their child's school.

The National Equity Project (2019) lists among its core beliefs the following attributes for the achievement of educational equity:

People lead change. The problems in education today are complex, daunting, and systemic. There is no one program or approach that will solve them. But in every case, people will solve these problems—people working together more effectively, purposefully, openly, and strategically than before.

Solutions must be people focused. Education reform is often conceived and delivered as a technical enterprise: data and accountability, performance management, resource re-allocations, and so on. Program solutions are important in complex education systems, but if we neglect the social and emotional sides of people (culture, race, history, relationships), we will continue to see slow or no progress.

Equity requires dialogue. Urban education systems are oppressive and the people in them are hurting. Students and families are angry, scared, lost, alienated, acting out. Educators are stressed, frustrated, professionally anxious, and turning over at high rates. Progress requires strong alliances across identity and role. Sustainable change requires time and space for talking, listening, thinking, learning, and healing together.

Good data used well makes for good decisions. "Good data" is information about each student that teachers can actually use to make critical decisions now that will improve their teaching and student learning. It also means similar actionable information about families, teachers, schools, districts, and systems. Change should be informed by best practices and research, local data, and qualitative understanding of the people involved.

CULTURALLY RESPONSIVE FAMILY ENGAGEMENT

Children spend the vast majority of their time out of school. It stands to reason that if we want to impact their learning lives, we must commit to understanding the community and culture from which they come. When communication is tailored to family culture and needs, the outcomes for children are likely to improve (Grant & Ray, 2019). Understanding culture is necessary in order to understand the nuances and preferences of how families can and wish to be engaged (Chavkin, 2017).

The growing number of non-English-speaking families challenges teachers with both communication and engagement. Grant and Ray (2019) champion culturally responsive teaching and argue that "it will not be enough only to focus on teaching strategies that are responsive to the families" (p. 27). Similar to culturally responsive teaching, culturally responsive family engagement must include a general understanding and appreciation for culture, family experiences, race, ethnicity, and a conscious understanding of one's own attitude "about children and families that are different from theirs" (Grant & Ray, 2019, p. 27). It is this last idea that can be a daunting proposition for all educators, as it forces us to examine our own beliefs and attitudes—our implicit biases.

Clark-Loque, Lindsey, Quezada, and Jew (2020) answer this call for cultural responsiveness by sharing a cultural proficiency framework, which supports an intersection of "diversity, inclusivity, and equity" (p. 6). Important to this framework is the recognition and confrontation of inequities that exist both in student learning and in responses to families and what happens outside of school.

In their framework, Clark-Loque and colleagues (2020) share the barriers to cultural proficiency:

1. systemic oppression

2. sense of entitlement

3. unawareness of the need to adapt

4. resistance to change

These barriers can have an adverse effect on parents' and families' desires to engage with the school or their perceptions of the school's desire to engage with them. For example, indigenous families that have suffered from colonialism, which attempts to detach them from their language and culture, may struggle with schools to validate their heritage and may wonder if modern schools will continue the quest to introduce their children to inaccurate stereotypes (Garcia, 2019). Cherng (2016) found that student race and ethnicity plays a critical role in how teachers communicate with parents from different racial, ethnic, and immigrant backgrounds, reflecting many existing stereotypes. Gaitan (2012) reminds us that there is little difference between a Latino student's home culture and its connection to their learning. Latino families can feel limited in their own skills and abilities to support their children due to language barriers. Balancing the relationship requires an appreciation of culture, language, and literacy.

IMPLICIT BIAS

Consider these phrases:

Those kids.

That neighborhood.

Those parents.

I know all about that family; I had the older brother In class.

Each of the phrases above can be completely innocent statements or they can harbor significant implicit bias. Every one of us harbors implicit biases. Normally, we are not conscious of these biases; they are usually centered on or about a social group from which inferences are drawn that can lead to stereotyping large groups of people. Implicit bias begins when we are children; through conditioning and learning, those biases can be reinforced.

The Kirwan Institute for the Study of Race and Ethnicity (2019) at the Ohio State University shares characteristics of implicit biases:

- Implicit biases are pervasive. Everyone possesses them, even people with avowed commitments to impartiality, such as judges.
- Implicit and explicit biases are related but distinct mental constructs. They are not mutually exclusive and may even reinforce each other.
- The implicit associations we hold do not necessarily align with our declared beliefs or even reflect stances we would explicitly endorse.
- We generally tend to hold implicit biases that favor our own in-group, though research has shown that we can still hold implicit biases against our in-group.
- Implicit biases are malleable. Our brains are incredibly complex, and the implicit associations that we have formed can be gradually unlearned through a variety of debiasing techniques.

Implicit bias can affect hiring practices in organizations, the type of medical care prescribed or available to patients, and even foul calls in college basketball or the National Basketball Association (NBA). They impact where we live, where we choose to shop or dine, and what we watch on television. It is important to underscore that implicit bias is also pervasive in attitudes and perceptions of families and their engagement with their children's school.

With colleagues, take some time to discuss and reflect what evidence may exist that suggests that implicit bias is hindering relationships with families and students.

WHY DO FAMILIES DISENGAGE?

It is logical for any educator faced with the scenario below to assume that the parent(s) or family of the student is simply apathetic toward

ACTIVITY

A student is struggling in school. The teacher makes repeated attempts to contact the child's family in order to inform them of the issues. Regardless of what effort the teacher makes, there is no response. In a last-ditch effort, a letter is sent home requesting a conference. The letter goes unanswered.

Can you relate to the situation above? What is your first thought when reading it? Before you read any further, in the space below, write down what you believe about the student, the parent/family, and the teacher.

The student:

The parent/family:

The teacher:

their child's success in school. No one would blame a teacher for giving up on trying to engage a seemingly apathetic parent. "There is only so much I can do," said one teacher in complete frustration.

But what if this alleged apathy wasn't apathy at all? What if there were reasons for the behaviors demonstrated by the parent? What if there was a system that could be implemented and strategies that could be employed that would not only prove that the parent was not apathetic but would actually improve the engagement of the parent? Understanding the roots of disengagement helps to reverse the trend.

Hornby (2011) suggests that parents' beliefs about involvement; parents' current life situations; parents' perceptions of the school's desire to engage them; and class, ethnicity, and gender are all factors in parent disengagement. Parents and teachers can often work from different agendas, have differing opinions and attitudes, and use different language.

Challenges to effective and meaningful family engagement exist for both schools and families. Limited resources to engage families with schools create some of the challenges. Most others, however, originate from the beliefs and perceptions of both families and school personnel (Liontos, 1992).

While there may be challenges to family engagement that are specific to particular schools, the most common challenges include teachers' perceptions that engaging families will take more time than they can devote, given the expectations they already have (Caplan, 2000). Even though many poorly educated families support learning, many teachers perceive this not to be the case and believe that these families cannot help their children.

Communication is a huge factor in disengagement. Many times, school efforts to increase family engagement fail because of differing styles and types of communication between schools and families. Languages play a huge role in this problem as well. Other challenges to family engagement include lack of transportation, time, and comfort in engaging with the school. Because many parents had negative school experiences, it is often the norm that they transfer this negativity to their own engagement (Caplan, 2000; Liontos, 1992).

School can be a very unwelcoming place for many families. Whether their personal experiences were negative or, in the case of families with limited English proficiency, the perceived intimidation of schools and families' lack of knowledge of American culture, these feelings all combine to keep them from outwardly engaging with the school. There can also be points of tension and conflict between families and teachers (Baker, 2000; Caplan, 2000; Liontos, 1992).

Some families hold onto the perception that they do not have easy or thorough access to information about school. They believe that teachers blame them when their children have issues in school and feel unwelcome. These same families believe that teachers only share negative information and that teachers wait until things are at a boiling point before communicating with the family.

Teachers, on the other hand, believe that families do not respect them or the job that they do. Teachers are concerned about decisions that are questioned and, in some cases, believe that families encourage their children to be disrespectful to the teacher. Teachers desire more support from homes for what they do in their classrooms (Drake, 2000).

> Fundamentally, your success in engaging every family will come down to what you think about families—every family—and their value as partners to support student learning.

Fundamentally, your success in engaging every family will come down to what you think about families—every family—and their value as partners to support student learning.

ACTIVITY

Consider the following statement from a teacher:

> In my over 30 years of working with students as a teacher and administrator, I have run across all kinds of families—those that are completely uninvolved, those that are too involved, and everything in between. I have worked with students who come from rich families, poor families, immigrant families, families who are homeless, broken families, foster families, incarcerated parents, various races and ethnicities of families, and families that face crises, the likes of which I could never have imagined. In all those years, with all those families, I never ever met one that didn't care about their children.

What do you think when you read this teacher's words? Do you agree or disagree? Why? How does the statement make you feel? Write down what you believe about the statement or any thoughts you have about it:

Now, let's take a look at what the late Ron Edmonds, researcher and founder of the Effective Schools movement, said about our beliefs toward families and their children:

> How many do you need to see? How many effective schools would you have to see to be persuaded of the educability of poor children? If your answer is more than one, then I submit that you have reasons of your own for preferring to believe that pupil performance derives from family background instead of school response to family background. Whether or not we will ever effectively teach the children of the poor is probably far more a matter of politics than of social science and this is as it should be.
>
> We can, whenever and wherever we choose, successfully teach all children whose schooling is of interest to us. We already know more than we need to do that. Whether or not we do it must finally depend on how we feel about the fact that we haven't so far. (as cited in Lake Forest College, 2010)

This statement is built upon research by both academic and field researchers who came to the same conclusions: Given certain organizing and cultural characteristics found in the researched schools and their districts, all children can be taught the intended curriculum and held to high academic standards that enable students to achieve success at the next grade level.

So, then, the important question becomes a very tough question to ask: Do we care? That becomes the salient question when embarking on a process to engage every family. Do we truly care about every child we teach? Do we believe that there is value in all children? Do we believe that there is a benefit in exerting effort to engage every family to children and to ourselves?

It is absolutely imperative that we examine our beliefs and the system of beliefs that drive our schools. Not taking the time to do so will bring about little change not only in family engagement but to any effort we undertake that has at its core a goal for fundamental improvement. It is possible that after close examination, the root of family disengagement could rest with us.

Disengaged people, regardless of who they are, are disengaged for a reason. The reason can be as varied as the disengaged themselves. However, we do know that people are not born disengaged but rather become disengaged. Circumstances present themselves in such a manner that disengagement from an organization or a process is determined to be the best coping option. That is the cycle we need to break.

THE CYCLE OF DISENGAGEMENT

The cycle of family disengagement from schools and education is depicted by Figure 3.1.

The model starts with the premise that people are not born disengaged but become disengaged because of circumstances in their lives.

For example, in the workplace, if a new employee is demonstrating exceptional skills and has garnered the attention of his superiors, his colleagues may resent the fact that his performance is raising standards and expectations. The employee is confronted by his colleagues and, as a result of this exchange, lowers his standards and productivity. This negative catalyst begins a cycle of disengagement.

In education, families can experience negative catalysts in a number of scenarios. Perhaps the assigned teacher is not the teacher a family hoped their child would work with, or perhaps they hold the perception that a child was admonished unfairly by a teacher, leader, or other staff member. Whatever the issue, a negative catalyst is the match that lights the fuse of disengagement.

When confronted with negativity and danger, most people immediately look for ways to protect themselves from the perceived threat. This process of self-preservation is a very normal response to threatening circumstances. While there are many ways one can protect oneself (you have heard the phrase *fight or flight*), the simplest

Figure 3.1   **Disengagement Cycle**

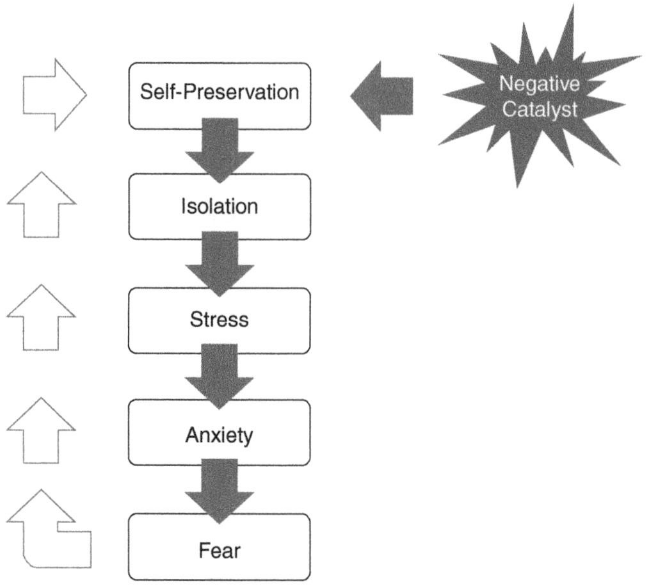

way is for one to isolate oneself from the threat, negative catalyst, or perceived danger. It is at this juncture that educators should reach out and do all that is possible to avoid the self-preservation and isolation that occurs. If we don't, matters tend to get worse.

What causes stress? While there are entire books written on this subject, I think it is safe to say that the nucleus of stress comes from problems or challenges that are not resolved, not easily resolved, or for which there is no perceived resolution. Families in distress over issues, however large or small (negative catalysts), harbor that stress; left unresolved, it often morphs into a form of anxiety. Believing there is an issue with your child at school but feeling helpless or powerless to do anything about it causes stress.

As our world becomes more complicated, it seems that more and more people are anxious, with good cause. Economic recession, terrorism, political polarization, and so forth lead to levels of anxiety in all of us. However, some people have challenges with anxiety that are beyond what the majority of us face. They are in a perpetual state of worry. That worry, left unresolved, allows them to begin to ruminate on problems, causing them to believe things that may or may not be true.

I have explained this phenomenon in workshops by using this example: Several years ago, a fictitious man—I'll call him Bill— suffered from generalized anxiety disorder (GAD). This disorder is characterized by extreme worry and tension, even when there is nothing to worry or be tense about. For example, if he hears a siren or sees an emergency vehicle speed by, his first thought is that one of his family members is hurt or in danger. He often has to contact his family by phone to provide himself reassurance that they have not fallen into harm's way. The extreme worry forces the phone call and hearing the voices of his family resolves the anxiety. Most of us barely pay attention to these things, but people like Bill who suffer from GAD become very concerned about something as simple as a passing siren.

How then does this relate to family disengagement? I am certainly not suggesting in any way that families who are disengaged suffer from disorders such as GAD! I only use that example to illustrate how powerful anxiety can be. Families who are anxious about their children's school experiences often become fearful of the school and fearful of speaking up. They believe that by doing so, they could inadvertently bring harm to their child in the form of retaliation from school personnel. I get a lot of hands raised when I ask audience members if they have ever been the recipient of anonymous communication about their classroom, school, or district. I usually share this dialogue with workshop participants and allow them to finish the conversation. I will do the same with you.

Anonymous caller: You have a problem [describes problem].

Educator: If you will give me your name and number, I will look into the matter and call you back.

Anonymous caller: Oh, I can't do that, because if I do, you will . . . [finish this statement].

> Audiences for years have responded in unison, "Take it out on my child." That's the anxiety that leads to fear.

Fear then triggers a further desire to preserve oneself (or their child, in this case) from danger or retaliation. As families move through this cycle, they become less likely to engage with school personnel and more likely to become disenfranchised from schools. It is this cycle of disengagement that the Five Simple Principles help to eliminate.

This is but one of a number of examples of disengagement. Some families do not feel confident in working with the school because of their own level of education or their own experiences with school. Adult literacy remains a significant barrier for some families. Still other families feel inferior because of the barrier of language. Whatever the reason for disengagement, the important message is that with effort and knowledge, disengagement can be reduced and eliminated.

WHY SOME FAMILIES STAY AWAY FROM SCHOOLS

Consider the plight of the following family.

In the last thirty days, the Jones family had been warned by two utility companies that failure to pay toward their bill would result in termination of service. Mr. Jones, who had been employed in two jobs, was now informed that because of sluggish sales, he was being laid off from his second job. Mrs. Jones found work, but the pay was less than what Mr. Jones made at his former job. In addition to the utilities, the Joneses were also contemplating what to do at the end of the month. It appeared that they would not have enough money to pay their rent as well.

The Jones children arrived home from school and shared with their parents the need for money for a variety of school activities that they wanted to engage in. The Joneses, not wanting to disappoint their children, simply smiled and indicated they would work something out. Unfortunately, they had no idea what they were going to do.

Is it any wonder that a family like the Joneses does not attend school functions or meetings? On any given evening, the family priorities are dominated by ensuring that their living conditions are suitable for their children. They struggle to keep the lights and heat on and food in their home. Often, the Jones children return to school with missing or incomplete homework, and they rarely participate in school events outside of the school day. The Jones family cares deeply about their children; however, they cannot engage with their children's education in a manner that we as educators would like to see.

School perspectives often make a dangerous assumption: Children do not succeed in school because their families do not support the efforts of the school to educate their child (Finders & Lewis, 1994). The assumption of apathy is one of the largest barriers to creating effective relationships with all families.

The idea that disengaged parents are apathetic toward their child's education seems to permeate the attitude of some educators and the culture of schools. We as educators tend to make a huge assumption that if a family is not involved, then the reason can only be apathy. This is a dangerous assumption. There are numerous reasons why families stay away or are disengaged from the educational experiences of their children. In the case of Latino and other immigrant families, school experiences, economic and time constraints, language differences, and cultural practices are all barriers (Finders & Lewis, 1994). Often, factors such as time, distance, and issues of childcare are used as reasons for the lack of engagement, when in actuality, the controlled nature of family–school interactions and the institutionalized nature of relationships are much more common barriers (Smrekar & Cohen-Vogel, 2001).

GATHERING INFORMATION ON DISENGAGEMENT

Conduct a mini-research project. When families seem disengaged from their children's education, reach out and begin a dialogue. Determine why families seem disengaged. Is it time? Fear? Adolescence? Perceived relevance of information? Language barriers? The parents' educational levels? As you reach out and have these crucial conversations, note the reasons for the disengagement from whatever it was you had hoped the family would engage in.

Determine the percentage of parents who said, "I don't care about my child."

The Five Simple Principles are designed first to illustrate why disengagement exists and then to create a system that begins to reverse the trends of disengagement.

These principles are not simply strategies. If we as educators do not believe that engaging every family will bring about improvements in student learning, then there is *not one* strategy that exists that will bring about the desired change. However, if we are willing to examine our own beliefs, confront the brutal facts of our present conditions, and possess both the willingness and patience to change our own destiny, then a world of ideas will be at our disposal and real change will occur.

The principles are designed so that we may reflect on our beliefs and practices as educators and then take the necessary actions to engage every family. Then and only then will change in the learning outcomes for all students become a permanent reality.

THE VERY FEW

My father was a barber for over fifty years, almost until the day he passed away. He quit school at the conclusion of the sixth grade to assist his family financially. My mother, considered by far the most educated in her family, finished high school and began a career as a secretary. Over the years of working for only one company until her retirement, she rose through the ranks to become a department supervisor. Throughout my entire upbringing and well into my adult life, my parents hammered into my head one clear, unwavering message: *You must get an education to succeed in this world . . . and . . . you will!* There were no alternatives presented. My grandmother scoffed at every degree I attained, stating repeatedly at each commencement, "You have to get that doctor's degree and then you'll have something!"

Like many in their generation, my parents were the children of immigrants. Ingrained in them was the simple notion that hard work and sacrifice would provide great rewards, mainly in a better quality of life in a country where opportunity was virtually everywhere. They also believed that their efforts would allow their children access to education and that education would allow their children to succeed as well. My parents' education, though minimal, allowed them to exceed their parents' quality of life, and my education allowed me to exceed my parents' quality of life. Today, however, many families struggle to allow this generational pattern to continue. In greater numbers, our children are struggling to exceed our quality of life, and it scares us.

Engaging families in the school lives of their children is essential to ensuring that all children learn to their fullest potential. I haven't met too many people who disagree with this statement, but I have met countless people who are frustrated by the challenges and obstacles of getting it done. Family structures have changed, communication styles have changed, the structure of jobs and careers has changed, transiency and mobility of families have changed, and education itself has changed.

Some educators hold the belief that families simply don't care to do more (or anything) to support their children and often cite culture or economic status as a reason. Given the statistics of some student performance and the attendance rates of families to school events, it's easy to think this way. But there is an important point that can be made with regard to disengagement and our perception of it.

While there are significant percentages of families who may be disengaged with their children's learning, a very small portion of those families are driven by apathy toward their children's education. It is a poor assumption to think that because someone is disengaged, the reason is always apathy. If we consider the idea that at a minimum, 99 percent of families care about their children's education and want to see their children succeed and surpass them in quality of life, the opportunities to create conditions for this to happen are simply endless.

> It is a poor assumption to think that because someone is disengaged, the reason is always apathy.

It is very common for us to believe that family interest in engaging with schools has something to do with either culture or economics. While we must acknowledge differences in people and families and understand that processes to engage them may be different in different places, the principles recommended in this book are universal and apply to every situation. Those families that disengage with organizations, more often than not, do so because they do not see the value in their participation, the meaningful nature of what that engagement might look like, or how the engagement is relevant to them. Different cultures and economic variances in families might require different strategies to engage them but are clearly not a rationale to explain families' disengagement.

In my travels, I have seen situations in schools and communities where the odds of success seemed hopeless. In a small town in Appalachia, for example, students aspired to follow in the footsteps of their parents and obtain welfare. In many urban settings that I have visited, families were all but invisible at school conferences or meetings designed to assist families in helping their children understand what was being taught in school. In the rural parts of the United States, the distance from family to family and from families to schools convinced educators that trying anything concerning engagement was simply fruitless. None of these situations are hopeless. There is a common thread between every family—their heartfelt desire is that their children exceed them in their quality of life.

If we perceive that we have poor family support, we can change it. The most difficult step is the first one. We must be the catalyst in the process to build relationships and engage families. We must believe there is value in working together, in building a partnership that supports every individual student and family regardless of who they are, what language they speak, or where they come from. School personnel that understand the value and dividends of reaching out to parents and families are poised to ensure that their students will succeed.

Today, even though the world is a very different and complicated place, the dreams and ideals that parents hold for their children are similar to the ideals my parents held for me. Researchers keep asking parents what is important to them, and the answers don't change much: Every one of them wants their own child to exceed them in their quality of life. It's this very notion that drives the importance of engaging families in the academic lives of their children.

The complicated nature of schooling dictates that educators consider the notion of family engagement as a conduit to improved academic outcomes in the same manner they consider other academic, curricular, and instructional reforms. Promoting the efficacy of families to assist in the learning lives of their children taps into the most influential teacher(s) in a child's life: their parent(s) and families.

Every family wants a better life for their children. Engaging families with schools is our best bet to make that happen. Not doing so because there is a chance that a very small percentage of families might not welcome our efforts to engage them doesn't seem prudent.

CASE STUDY: ERNEST B.

Read the case study below. At the conclusion, answer, reflect on, or discuss the questions posed.

Ernest B. was the third of three African American brothers who attended the local high school. His two older brothers dropped out of high school and the oldest brother was serving time in jail for a drug-related crime. Ernest did not know his father and lived with his mother and one brother in a one-room, low-income apartment. Ernest's mother held a job, but income was woefully inadequate for the family.

Desperate, Ernest made the poor decision to steal a purse from a woman he saw walking down the street. Ernest was unsuccessful in his larceny attempt and was caught, arrested, and placed in juvenile detention to await a hearing. The following day in school, the principal was alerted to Ernest's situation. Because of the experiences of Ernest's two older brothers, the relationship between Ernest's mother and the principal was very negative. Any attempt to reach out to Ernest's mother usually ended up in a shouting match or worse. Yet, the thought of Ernest sitting in a jail cell ate away at the principal for most of the day.

Later that day, the principal made a decision to visit Ernest in jail. Upon arrival, the guard opened a gate to allow the principal to enter a group of cells, one of which housed Ernest. Ernest told the guard not to open the cell door because he did not want the principal anywhere near him. Ernest sat on his cot with his elbows on his knees and his head in his hands looking downward toward the floor.

"Ernest, I came here for two reasons today," said the principal. Ernest didn't move or respond. "I'm here because I care about you and I want you to know that regardless of what happens, the sun will rise tomorrow and it will be a new day and a new chance." With those comments, Ernest stood, approached the bars, and stared directly into the principal's eyes. His face was filled with rage.

"You care about me? Really? You come all this way to hand me that line of crap? Well, let me show you how much I care about you." With that, Ernest spat on the principal's shirt. Ernest yelled, swore, and became uncontrollably violent in his cell—so much so that the guard came to the cell and was about to open the door and subdue Ernest. At that moment, Ernest fell onto his bed and sobbed. Ernest cried like never before. The principal was quite shocked at his behavior. Ernest begged the principal to help him and the principal vowed that he would.

"What can I do for you right now?" asked the principal.

"Please fetch my momma," said Ernest, still sobbing.

At that moment, the principal was confronted with a dilemma. How was he supposed to get Ernest's mother when he knew she hated him and blamed him for the problems her older sons faced and undoubtedly would blame him for Ernest's troubles as well? She was never engaged positively with the school, never attended a conference or event, and never answered any teacher when they attempted to communicate. Teachers had long ago given up on communicating with Ernest's mother.

She defended the actions of her sons and continually blamed the school—specifically the principal—for the problems that her sons faced. She had called for the principal's firing and accused him of everything from incompetence to racism. Instinctively, though, regardless of how difficult a visit it might be, he knew he had to go to the home and talk with Ernest's mother.

The principal called his office to inform his secretary that he was headed over to Ernest B.'s house. His secretary asked him if he needed the police. He assured her he did not. He arrived at the apartment complex and walked up three flights of stairs and stared at the apartment door. After collecting himself, he knocked. The door was fastened with a chain that allowed it to open just a few inches, enough for Ernest's mother to see who was standing there.

"What do you want?" she snapped.

"I came here to talk with you about Ernest," said the principal. After an exchange of unpleasant comments, the door closed, the chain was removed, and the door opened. Ernest's mother had already walked away and sat in a chair at the far side of the room. "So, you want to talk about Ernest? Why? Why do you care about my baby boy? He's in jail, right where you want him. Now he ain't gonna be no problem for you no more." Her steely glare made the principal very uncomfortable.

"I understand that you are angry with me, but I have come here because neither one of us alone can help Ernest. We can only do it together. For the sake of your son, can we talk about how to help him?"

"Let me tell you something," started Ernest's mother. "I wouldn't trust you as far as I could throw you. Do you know that when I go to sleep at night, I have a dream? I dream of Ernest graduating from school. And just as he reaches for the diploma, I wake up. I know it's God's way of telling me it ain't ever going to happen. And that is your fault. Now get out of my house before I call the cops and have you arrested for trespassing."

As he walked toward the door, the principal turned and said, "If you change your mind, please come and see me."

"Get out!" the woman yelled as she slammed and chained the door behind the principal.

Two weeks later, sitting in his office mired in paperwork, the principal didn't notice a figure standing in his doorway. "I'm here." The principal looked up and saw Ernest's mother. He offered her a seat, but she refused. They talked for a few moments about strategies to help Ernest. "They let him out. Are you going to let him back?" she asked.

"Of course, but only if we figure out how we are going to work together to help Ernest. It would be nice if you came by more often." The principal waited for a response.

"The bus goes right by here so I guess I can do that."

The principal spoke on Ernest's behalf at Ernest's hearing, and he was sentenced to probation. Over the next weeks, months, and years, Ernest's mother, the principal, and his teachers developed a better relationship, and Ernest managed to attend school, do his work, and, for the most part, stay out of significant trouble.

Four years later, Ernest graduated from high school. Four years after that, Ernest graduated from college, the first to do so in his entire family. Ernest invited the principal to his college graduation party held in the basement of the local church. There were few people there to celebrate Ernest's success. Present were one brother, the few distant relatives who could make the trip, and a few church volunteers. Ernest's mother approached the principal.

"What do you want?" said Ernest's mother, exactly as she had several years earlier. The principal became nervous, thinking that the animosity that had dominated their early relationship was still very much real. Ernest's mother turned her stare to a smile, laughed, and grabbed a hand of the principal between both of hers. "Thank you for saving my baby," she said, with tears forming in her eyes.

"*I* didn't save him," responded the principal. "*We* did."

Questions for Reflection

1. How does the story make you feel about what you do?

2. What made the principal visit Ernest in jail?

3. What made the principal visit Ernest's mother?

4. The outcome of this story is a positive one. What key actions played a role in the positive outcome?

5. What belief system did Ernest possess? What belief system did his mother have? What about the principal? How did their beliefs change over time?

6. What do you think is a key ingredient that made the outcome of this story a positive one?

7. Had the principal never visited Ernest's mother, what do you think the outcome would have been?

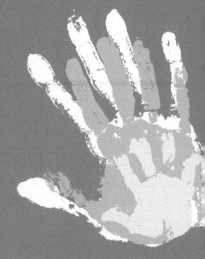

CHAPTER 4

Engaging Every Family in Middle and High School

At the high school level, I don't know that teachers need any more parental involvement other than more parental involvement at home. I guess the high school level teachers would just appreciate the support at home for what they do; making sure the work gets done, making sure they have a phone number that they can [use to] reach a parent if there is a problem at school.

—Wilkerson and Kim (2010)

Of all the questions, comments, and conversations I have as I travel the country working with educators, one of the most often-repeated questions is this: How do we get families to engage at the high school? I can't recall a visit to a school, district, or conference where this question didn't come up—so much so that it motivated me to add this chapter.

By now, you understand a few important concepts regarding family engagement:

1. It is a process (not an event or a series of events).

2. It must become part of the culture of the school.

3. The components of the Five Simple Principles are universal, meaning they apply to all schools and all levels.

The beginning of the answer to the question of secondary school family engagement is knowing that the system and process you have already learned applies to middle schools and high schools as much as it applies to elementary schools and preschools. The difference is in the nuance and execution of family engagement so that it complements secondary school experiences and enhances student experiences and engagement in and out of school. It's not that we should scale back engagement or simply not do it; rather, it is how we do family engagement at the secondary level that has the most impact on student success.

What is important in designing family engagement processes for high school is that we have a clear understanding of why families are engaged at lower levels. Knowing the answer to that question will help shape a potential process to engage every family at the middle school and high school level. Every middle school and high school wants to improve. Every middle school and high school has students who, for a variety of reasons, are not meeting with success. Middle schools and high schools report more issues with absences, less student engagement, an increase in student behaviors that require intervention and support, and a need to meet both the academic and social-emotional needs of students. When focused on academic improvements, however, high schools (and, to a lesser extent, middle schools) focus their efforts on improved student outcomes by centering strategies on the student (Lehr, Hansen, Sinclair, & Christenson, 2003). This is a mistake that no school can afford. Even though research has proven that family engagement has a positive impact on many aspects of students' experiences in secondary schools, reform efforts rarely include them. Family engagement should be a cornerstone of school improvement at the secondary school level and is always an ingredient in high-performing schools (National Association of Secondary School Principals, 2004, 2006; National Middle School Association/Association for Middle Level Education, 2010).

Why are there so many families eager and willing to participate in multiple ways at the elementary school, but as their children move through secondary classrooms, the engagement of families significantly diminishes (Simon, 2004; Spera, 2005)? There is no question that a steep decline in family engagement is a reality. Understanding the underpinnings of the problem will help to craft the kinds of processes necessary to support meaningful and relevant family engagement at the secondary school level. The decline in family engagement at the high school level is less about students growing up and moving into higher grades (thus making less engagement inevitable) and more about the relationship between teacher outreach and the level of decline in family engagement.

> The decline in family engagement at the high school level is . . . more about the relationship between teacher outreach and the level of decline in family engagement.

WHY DO FAMILIES DISENGAGE FROM SECONDARY SCHOOLS?

It may be human nature to assume that when someone is not engaged in something, even after being invited or encouraged, the reason is either apathy or the placing of little value on the proposed engagement. Wallace (2013) shares an important point: There is danger in assuming that families who are not routinely engaged in their child's education place little or no value on their children's school experiences and success.

From the onset, the premise of this book has been clear: Educators alone cannot ensure that every student meets with success. Schools are expected to engage families throughout high school and must consider federal mandates to do so (e.g., Every Student Succeeds Act, Individuals with Disabilities Education Act). To suggest that at the middle school and high school level, families are no longer critical to student success is an ill-advised assumption. As middle schools and high schools work to improve the learning outcomes for all students, it is imperative that families be part of the equation. In short, to help make families effective partners in learning, families need to know what is happening in school and what is expected of them at home (Seitsinger, 2019). They will need guidance as to how to create home learning opportunities and support the good work that is done in classrooms each day. But there are barriers to engaging families at the secondary school level that are not as pervasive at the elementary school level.

Barriers to Engaging Families

The Flamboyan Foundation (2019), an organization that is dedicated to school–family engagement, lists five significant barriers to engaging families at the high school level:

1. Educator mindsets: Often, educators do not place a great deal of value on family engagement or do not associate family engagement with learning outcomes for students. Biases and assumptions limit relationships between school and home.

2. Unwelcoming environments: How families feel when they enter the building and how they are greeted feed the degree to which they feel welcomed and valued.

3. Common definition of family engagement: Family engagement means

many things to many people. It can mean anything from volunteering to ensuring that homework agenda books are checked. Multiple definitions and expectations are compounded by the numbers of teachers, classes, and so on.

4. Complex structures: Secondary schools are far larger and more complicated than most elementary schools. What seems navigable to those of us accustomed to high schools can be very foreign to families.

5. Educator capacity: Because little time, energy, and resources are given to the topic of family engagement, teachers and other staff members do not have the support and knowledge to engage families in meaningful ways.

The culture of secondary schools tends to be one rooted in tradition, and, as such, most schools encourage passive support (Wallace, 2013). School staff often provide checklists and documents to families as to their responsibilities or the responsibilities that their children need to meet. Families are most often welcomed to very structured, predetermined events at the school. These strategies are not seen by many families as a desire to promote a true relationship or partnership. Teachers tend to use methods of communication that are institutional in nature (e.g., the school email system or parent portal component of the school information system). Families prefer more personal, individualized invitations for their engagement. As a result, this mismatch in communication delivery and desire create discouragement between teachers and families and can lead to inaccurate perceptions on both sides (Halsey, 2005). When teachers reach out, build relationships, and communicate important information that promotes the efficacy of the family, student academic prowess is significantly improved (Seitsinger, 2019).

> Structured, predetermined school events are not seen by many families as a desire to promote a true relationship or partnership.

Family engagement strategies are underutilized at the secondary school level. There seem to be barriers that exist at the secondary level that do not exist at the elementary level. Two of those barriers are ideological differences and cultural biases related to socioeconomically disadvantaged families. For example, Wilkerson and Kim (2010) report that urban teachers find families less competent if they are of a lower socioeconomic status. There seems to be a history behind teacher attitudes and perceptions toward high school family engagement; this history has led to a creation of a culture that tends to operate in an effort to minimize family engagement with the creation of rules, policies, procedures, and practices that make engagement more difficult and create an arena for potential conflicts with families.

The very nature of secondary schools—the culture, if you will—does not lend itself to relationships between families and school staff. For example, families of middle school students tend to provide more structure for learning at home: supervising homework or creating dedicated spaces for children to learn (Hill & Tyson, 2009; McGill, Hughes, Alicea, & Way, 2012). While these activities support student learning and improvement, they do little to help families and teachers form the necessary relationships for supportive family engagement. The number of teachers and the less welcoming environments of secondary schools both act as a deterrent to engaging every family (Hill & Tyson, 2009). In Grades 7 through 9, one of the strongest predictors of home-based engagement were invitations for engagement from students themselves.

High school families, taking cues from their adolescents' developmental needs and the schools' parameters for inclusion of families, engage in less-direct types of school-related activities. This type of engagement often leads families to communicate more frequently with teachers. The nature and amount of this communication, given different styles and expectations as noted above, can lead to more prevalent disengagement. However, teachers may not see parents as having a role in the education of their child at the high school, preferring to believe that independence and autonomy are most important (Wilkerson & Kim, 2010). What appears to be more important at the high school level are more indirect forms of engagement. Families report more conversations about school values and holding high educational expectations. These, coupled with a more authoritative parenting style, were strong predictors of improved academic achievement (Jensen & Minke, 2017).

What is interesting and seemingly counterintuitive to traditional thinking about family engagement at the high school is that homework help, at best, shows mixed results with regard to student achievement. Yet, most of the "engagement" demonstrated by high schools is just that: directing families to ensure that homework is completed and turned in on time. High schools also create events for families to attend. Open houses, back-to-school nights, financial aid nights, and other controlled opportunities again show mixed results with regard to engagement and student productivity (Jensen & Minke, 2017).

Family engagement with conferences diminishes from middle school to high school (Bhargava & Witherspoon, 2015). Families find less relevance in attending and often have the perception that there is no role for them in the high school years other than monitoring progress from afar. Families believe they need to provide their children with more autonomy and, as a result, reduce involvement in those activities that may be seen as obtrusive by their children (Wang, Hill, & Hofkens, 2014). This diminished role of families can bring about frustrations for both school staff and families. However, a clear and simple pathway forward is to understand that at the secondary school level, especially at the high school, family engagement shifts from school-based involvement to home-based involvement.

ACADEMIC SOCIALIZATION AND HOME-BASED ENGAGEMENT

Promoting family efficacy and the notion of invisible engagement are two foundational ideas for encouraging family engagement at the high school level. The need for autonomy by adolescents, the advanced level of curriculum and learning, and the intimidating nature of large schools are all reasons why promoting home-based involvement is a far better option than trying to increase the number of events at school or lure families into the school with other types of activities. Efforts that teachers make to promote family efficacy at the high school level translate into more parental satisfaction with their child's school (Seitsinger & Brand, 2012). In diverse communities, school staff tend to limit family engagement to those events that happen at school or are school related instead of focusing on the power of collaboration with families. Engaging these families as equals shows significant positive results as well (Auerbach, 2010; Doucet, 2011). Certain families for whom English is not a main language find school-based activities inaccessible, which again argues for the need for collaboration and school academic socialization (Crozier & Davies, 2007).

For reasons that are not completely clear, both families and educators at the high school level very often think (and behave) in a way that

A QUICK WORD ABOUT PARENT EVENTS

Many schools spend a great deal of time, energy, and resources on hosting events at school (nonathletic or arts events), only to be disappointed at family turnout. Schools go to great lengths providing support for family attendance—food, childcare, and, in some cases, transportation. However, these efforts could be for naught if families perceive that teachers do not see them as playing an important role (Wilkerson & Kim, 2010).

suggests that family engagement is somehow not as important or is less essential at the high school level. Nothing could be further from the truth—family engagement is proven to support the academic prowess of high school–aged students (Bean, Bush, McKenry, & Wilson, 2003; Voydanoff, 2004). Middle school teachers report meeting and interacting with families twice as often as high school teachers (Seitsinger, 2019). These challenges further support the idea that home-based engagement is a better vehicle to deliver family efficacy, engagement, and, ultimately, student success.

In order for the home-based engagement to be fruitful, families should engage in academic socialization. In Chapter 3, it was suggested that a culture of academic socialization improves student learning. Families, armed with a keen knowledge of what is happening in school, can socialize their child to the importance of learning and thus assist in improving student outcomes. Academic socialization becomes increasingly important as children get older and advance through school and is the most developmentally appropriate strategy for high school families (Hill & Tyson, 2009). Academic socialization allows families to retain engagement with their children's learning while continuing to support student autonomy and decision making.

Academic socialization is not about selecting courses or poring over weekly grade reports. These activities have been found to discourage home-based engagement. Volunteerism and teacher communication both suffer as families disengage; however, families do welcome the opportunity to participate in activities that promote academic socialization (Bhargava & Witherspoon, 2015). It's possible, then, that family engagement has not declined as much as we think; perhaps it is merely different and invisible to us. And maybe that's not a bad idea!

How Families Can Engage Children in Academic Socialization

- Communicating specific information about the importance of education and tying that to career exploration and post–high school planning

- Having frank and open conversations with children about academic expectations and educational attainment

- Engaging with present and upcoming learning to support children at home, understand better home learning needs, and reinforce the need for a focus on school

Promoting and Sustaining Home-Based Engagement and Family Academic Socialization

Home-Based Engagement	• Communicate frequently and provide updates on student progress to parents.
	• Provide parents with thorough examples of how to complete homework assignments (e.g., brief demonstrations streamed through the class website or personal demonstrations, homework guides).
	• Send links to websites that provide support for families.
	• Provide materials and detailed examples of homework in the family's home language.
	• Suggest ways for structuring the home environment to promote homework completion (e.g., designated workspace, materials).
	• Offer ideas and resources to promote high-quality student engagement at home (e.g., age-appropriate and high-quality literature, web resources).
Academic Socialization	• Ask parents open-ended questions about their goals for their child and their child's goals.
	• Suggest strategies for parents to use in discussing academic aspirations with their child.
	• Develop assignments that require students to investigate a possible career, develop future plans, and share those with their parents.
	• Provide resources for parents (e.g., on the school website, in the school library, or in the school parent center) that facilitate knowledge of and discussion around the student's career, postsecondary education, and independent living options.
	• Make time available for parents and their child to meet with school guidance counselors or vocational counselors.

Source: DeSpain, Conderman, and Gerzel-Short (2018, p. 237).

DESIGNING FAMILY ENGAGEMENT AT THE SECONDARY SCHOOL LEVEL

Hopefully, you now see that family engagement at the secondary level is as important as the engagement of families in the primary and elementary years. Family engagement at the secondary level looks different than family engagement at the elementary school level. Rather than relying on a continuous flow of information (usually communicated one-way from school to home), conferences, grade reporting, and school events, secondary teachers would be much better served to build collaborative relationships with the families of the students who are not meeting their potential, promote the efficacy of those families through collaborative relationships and equal partnerships, and promote the concepts of home-based engagement and family academic socialization.

Promote the efficacy of families through collaborative relationships and equal partnerships.

Mac Iver, Sheldon, Epstein, Rice, Mac Iver, and Simmons (2018) suggest that to improve the outcomes of incoming ninth-grade students, schools should give more systematic attention to families by providing information and support that are focused on learning. In order to accomplish that with the maximum return in student achievement, the authors also suggest a theory of change for secondary schools.

What the Administration Can Do

1. Promote professional development for staff in the area of family engagement.

2. Create a family engagement plan and institute practices that are well planned and lead to improved outreach to all families.

3. Increase support for and promote family efficacy. Improve teacher–parent and student–parent interaction, which will lead to improved attendance and homework completion.

4. Better attendance and learning will increase course passing rates and on-time graduation rates. This also benefits higher passing rates in the ninth-grade year.

Other Strategies for Enhancing Family Engagement

1. Cultivate relationships with all families so that positive communication forms the basis of school–family relationships. Don't wait for an issue to arise before contacting a family.

2. Provide families with multiple means of contacting school personnel. Not everyone communicates in the same manner. Phone calls, emails, texts, and social media are all ways in which families can communicate. Make it simple for them to reach you.

3. Create updated calendars and share them with all families.

4. Greet families on the telephone or in-person in welcoming, inviting ways. This will go a long way toward establishing trusting relationships.

5. Create a family resource library.

6. Create conditions so that families are comfortable sharing their thoughts on specific topics.

7. Determine how families best communicate, then use that method to establish a good two-way communication protocol.

8. Reach out to new families through home visits or other community opportunities.

Source: DeSpain, Conderman, and Gerzel-Short (2018).

If family engagement at the secondary school level were simple, more schools would be successful in engaging the disengaged and positively affecting the learning outcomes of all students. We've already covered the barriers and other obstacles to creating meaningful family engagement at the secondary school level. Table 5.1 is an adaptation of the information found in DeSpain, Conderman, and Gerzel-Short (2018, p. 239) with regard to issues and solutions in family engagement. Solutions have been augmented with additional information and ideas regarding both school-based and home-based engagement.

As is the case when reviewing and understanding the Five Simple Principles, educators must begin any attempt in engaging families of secondary school students with a few nonnegotiable ideas. First, we must believe and understand the importance of engaging families at the secondary school level. Second, we must understand that the barriers to family engagement at the secondary level are different; thus, the solutions will look different. Third, we must understand that all families, regardless of their station in life, wish for their children to exceed them in their quality of life and are very much interested in their children's school experiences, especially at the high school level. Lastly, in addition to hosting school-based activities, we must promote home-based engagement and academic socialization among secondary school families to positively impact the learning outcomes of all secondary school students.

Table 4.1

Issues and Solutions in Family Engagement

Logistical Issue in Family Engagement	Potential Solution
Relationships with all families	• Make positive personal phone calls home to learn about the family and to share information. • Send regular updates on student progress and class happenings. • Be available during the week for parent drop-ins (e.g., in-person at school, electronically). • Create a parent survey to understand their wants, needs, and availability. Update the survey at least twice during the school year. • Create a class website to share information and encourage communication between parents and the teacher (e.g., a blog). • Use a home–school communication system. • Invite parents to share their knowledge of their child (e.g., what motivates their child, what works at home).
Language barriers	• Determine the preferred home language of family members. • Invite translators to every school event. • Have the child invite their parents to a school event with a letter, email, or text. • Ensure that all communication and school signage represent languages spoken by families.
Scheduling	• Determine the best times for meeting for each family. • Offer alternative times for events, including weekends. • Offer alternative forms of engagement (e.g., in-person, Skype, teleconference, video chat, etc.). • Respect special days associated with family culture.
Transportation	• Offer help at neutral sites in the neighborhood with copies of textbooks at such locations. • Offer free transportation to the school site. • Make some prescheduled and mutually agreed-upon home visits. • Hold events at a convenient neutral site (e.g., the library, YMCA, community building). • Provide public transportation passes or taxi vouchers.
Childcare (for school-based events)	• Offer free childcare during school events. • Encourage and invite extended family members to attend school events. • Connect with and use local childcare agencies (e.g., YMCA, home- or center-based childcare centers). • Connect with and use services of local high school or college student organizations (e.g., Future Teachers of America).

Incentives for attending school-based events	• Provide a stipend for a student or professional development course at a local community college or university (e.g., computer course, math course).
	• Provide gift cards for food/gas.
	• Offer passes to local children's museums.
	• Provide a bag of books or school supplies.
	• Enter the parent's name into a raffle or prize drawing.
	• Provide a small meal during the event/activity.

CHAPTER 5

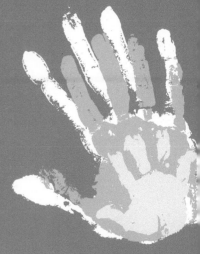

An Introduction to the Five Simple Principles

WHERE TO START

One of the most often-asked questions by educators who desire to improve family engagement is where to start. We tend to initially gravitate to those few strategies that might seem to further our engagement efforts (e.g., welcome signs, greeters, communications technology, etc.). However, helping to define a starting point with regard to attitudes and perceptions about family engagement is essential to developing a measurable process for improvement.

Essential to the practice of increasing family engagement is understanding that it truly can be assessed and measured. As is the case with all of the outcomes we desire for our students, it is important to have a starting point to determine where we are so goals can be set for where we want to be.

The following questions are by no means comprehensive in assessing the degree to which your school is successful in engaging every family. They are designed to give you a snapshot, a starting point on your journey to improve the learning outcomes of every student through positive and supportive relationships and engagement with every family.

ACTIVITY
Where You Are

Directions

For each of the ten questions below, rate your answer on a scale of 1 (strongly disagree) to 4 (strongly agree). If you don't know or are unsure of an answer, select the *don't know* category.

Read each question carefully. Think about your answer and select a response that mirrors what you know to be true today. Remember, 1 (strongly disagree), 2 (disagree), 3 (agree), 4 (strongly agree), and 5 (don't know).

	1 (Strongly disagree)	2	3	4 (Strongly agree)	5 (Don't know)
Every family feels welcome in our school.					
Our stated core values clearly speak to the importance of family engagement.					
I regularly provide tools and resources to families to support learning at home.					
Our school ensures that families have the opportunity to provide feedback before new policies or procedures are created.					
We have few families that seem apathetic toward our school and their children's education.					

(Continued)

(Continued)

I encourage feedback and dialogue from the family of every student I serve.					
We value the participation of community members in our school.					
I can easily communicate with families for whom English is not a first language.					
Our school's shared decision-making model is inclusive of every family.					
We have strong business and civic partnerships that support our school.					

This survey, with directions and scoring, is available for download at **http://www .drsteveconstantino.com**

Calculating Your Score

Each response carries a point value:

Strongly disagree	1 point
Disagree	2 points
Agree	3 points
Strongly agree	4 points
Don't know	0 points

Add together the score for each question and total that number. For example, if you answered every question *strongly disagree*, you would give yourself 1 point for each answer for a total of 10 points (10 questions, 1 point each). For every *don't know* answer, add 0 (zero). Answers in the *don't know* category carry no points.

Use the scale below to determine where your answers fell on a rubric for successfully engaging every family:

Engaging Every Family Response Interval Scale

0–11: Not Evident

Responses that fall within this range indicate little or no evidence that a process for promoting the ongoing engagement of every family is in place or that the culture of the school embraces family engagement as a pathway to improved student outcomes. A significant effort should be employed to build the capacity of staff to understand and implement practices that engage every family.

12–24: Basic

Responses that fall within this range indicate a basic understanding of the importance of family engagement and some evidence that strategies and ideas have been implemented. There may be evidence of culture change to promote family engagement, but it is sporadic at best. A continued commitment to family engagement as a professional learning strand coupled with measurable goals and objectives as a component of the school improvement plan will increase the likelihood of continuous improvement.

25–34: Emerging

Responses that fall within this range suggest that the school is well along in creating systems and processes that consistently engage every family and that the culture is accepting of this practice. Many staff members are engaging with families and consider this engagement essential to student success. Determine, through survey or other means of data collection, the degree to which all staff are consistent in the application of family engagement principles and create action plans for continued improvement. Look at student learning data to determine where family engagement practice can support growth.

35–40: Proficient

Responses in this category suggest that the school is proficient at engaging every family and has the data to prove it. Everyone agrees that the culture of the school is conducive to engaging every family. All staff believe in the importance of engaging families, and data collected from families support their perception that the school welcomes their engagement. There is clear, consistent, and compelling evidence that family engagement is a significant portion of the school culture and leads to improved learning outcomes for all students.

Suggestions for This Simple Assessment

There are many ways to use this simple assessment. It is a quick way to determine where you are with regard to engaging every family. Even though it is not meant to be comprehensive, the assessment does provide a snapshot of attitudes, actions, and evidence with regard to family engagement. Here are some ideas for use:

- If you are reading this book by yourself, ask your immediate teammates or subject colleagues to take the survey.
- If you are using this book for a study, have everyone in the study group take the survey and create a comparison of responses.
- Have the leadership team of your school take the survey.
- Provide a copy of the survey to every staff member.
- After completing the book and implementing some ideas, come back to the survey and take it again. How did things change? If they did not change at all, why do you think that is?
- Visit http://www.drsteveconstantino.com for copies of the assessment that you can download as many times as you want!

INTRODUCING THE FIVE SIMPLE PRINCIPLES

Since the original development and inception of the Five Simple Principles in 2010, feedback, program evaluations, and additional action research and learning have helped to improve the model. The model has been updated to reflect the process and outcomes of the Five Simple Principles more clearly, thus bringing about a systemic and more consistent implementation of school family engagement practices. The principles are meant to help educators build the capacity to formulate necessary partnerships with every family to promote improved student learning.

For as many years as there has been research in the field of family engagement, there has existed the frustration that successful engagement practices—those that can be directly connected to student achievement—are sporadic at best. Within school districts, there might be a handful of schools that embrace the concept of family engagement and, within a school, perhaps only a handful of teachers doing the same.

The Five Simple Principles are a systemic process that can be overlaid onto schools or school districts so that measurable and tangible results can be recorded and celebrated.

THE LOGIC MODEL

The term *logic model* has its roots in the field of evaluation. As the term suggests, logic models represent the thinking behind a program and its rationale. A logic model's purpose is to communicate an underlying theory, assumption, or hypothesis about why the program will work or why it is a good solution to an identified problem. Logic models are typically diagrams, flow sheets, or some other type of visual schematic that conveys relationships between contextual factors and programmatic inputs, processes, and outcomes (Parsons & Schmitz, 1999).

Figure 4.1 represents a logic model for *Engage Every Family: Five Simple Principles*. The logic model is designed to place the principles by which true family engagement and the ultimate development and nurturing of family efficacy can be implemented and measured into a hierarchal order. The model supports the notion that there is a process to successful family engagement practice.

Each of the principles (within which additional statements are written to support the main idea) falls into a logical sequence of action. In other words, schools and districts wishing to bring about systemic reform in family engagement should begin at the beginning (Principle 1) and follow the model clockwise around the circle.

Figure 5.1 **The Logic Model for *Engage Every Family: Five Simple Principles***

The following discussion is intended to share the rationale as to why the model is constructed in the manner it is. Subsequent chapters will expand more specifically on the importance of the principles, their placement within the model, and most importantly, how the ideas of the principles can be implemented and sustained.

Principle #1
A Culture That Engages Every Family

> Creating a culture and climate for family engagement is the first and most important step in a process to bring about systemic reform in family engagement.

The model clearly delineates creating a culture and climate for family engagement as the first and most important step in a process to bring about systemic reform in family engagement. If the collective beliefs, values, assumptions, actions, attitudes, and rituals within an organization are not supportive of engaging every family, then there is little hope that the subsequent strategies will have any lasting effect.

More often than not, desired change in an organization that is temporary, sporadic, or fleeting has at its root the idea that the change never permeates and alters the culture of the organization. Therefore, the notion of culture as the leading standard is essential for long-term success and growth.

Principle #2
Communicate Effectively and Develop Relationships

When an accepting culture is established and fosters the engagement of every family, it seems logical that the necessary relationships with families are developed. Developing relationships with every family, especially those that are disengaged, is essential in supporting improved student learning. Within the framework of relationships and the trust that ensues lies the important notion of communication. Research supports clear and consistent two-way communication as an important pillar in family engagement practice.

Relationships and trust are rooted in distinct, meaningful, and thoughtful systems of two-way communication that display a value in reaching out and connecting with every family, which indicates the importance of listening and feedback. Communication, for purposes of this principle, also includes the important concept of welcoming environments in schools.

Principle #3

Build Family Efficacy

Building family efficacy encourages and improves learning at home. In simple terms, *efficacy* is the power of one (or some) to produce an effect. In the Five Simple Principles logic model, the principle of efficacy takes family engagement to a new level and begins to allow a school or district to put into place a tangible and concrete approach to implementing processes and collecting data that link family engagement to student achievement.

Establishing instructional and curricular processes that are inclusive of families allows families to become immersed in school learning and to enhance and support learning at home. If the culture of the district is not accepting of the idea to engage every family and the communication is poor, thus eroding trusting relationships between families and the school, the results will likely produce little in the way of family efficacy.

Principle #4

Engage Every Family in Decision Making

Improvement plans, strategic plans, comprehensive plans, and the idea of school improvement planning have changed over the years, certainly since the advent of the Every Student Succeeds Act of 2015. For many years, schools have sought to include families in decision making at the local school level. Common in many school districts are school board–appointed ad hoc committees or task forces of families and citizens charged with reviewing issues and making sound recommendations to the board. Inherent in all of this is the concept of engaging every family in school-related decision making. On the surface, this can seem to be a daunting and impossible task.

The arguments set forth in a later chapter identify key reasons why every family needs a voice in certain school decisions, and school leaders must put mechanisms into place to ensure that every voice will be heard. Returning to the logic model, after a culture of engagement is established and a foundation of relationships and efficacy has been built, creating mechanisms for family engagement in decision making enhances and ensures that policies, procedures, and practices have a support mechanism for engaging every family at their core.

Principle #5

Engage the Greater Community

Many family engagement models include the involvement and engagement of the greater community as a conduit to improving schools. The key to effective community engagement is to first conceptualize what that engagement should look like with a clear delineation of desired outcomes. There are rich and deep resources in most communities; however, many schools and districts struggle in leveraging those resources.

Without the logic model in place and the sequential building of family engagement, the engagement of the greater community makes little sense. Business, civic, and community leaders who cannot determine a specific role for their engagement simply will not become involved or immerse themselves in the school or district. Setting the stage with the first four standards is an essential pathway to creating strong and meaningful community engagement.

THE FIVE SIMPLE PRINCIPLES FURTHER DEFINED

The key to the Five Simple Principles is the ability to remember them in the correct order and, to the degree possible, implement and evaluate your efforts and success with the same logic model that is prescribed. *Culture, relationships, efficacy, decision making, and community*—five simple ideas that all educators and families can relate to and that all can remember.

As cultural underpinnings of your school, these five principles can bring about lasting and effective change in the ability to engage every family. Of course, there is some danger in trying to oversimplify the principles. That could lead to understanding the concept without the ability to truly drill down to the salient points, thus rendering the principles ineffective.

Below is a description of each of the principles. For each of the principles listed, there are clarifying statements to support the principle presented. Later, each of the principles and their clarifying statements will be discussed in more detail.

Principle #1

A Culture That Engages Every Family

Description: The collective beliefs, attitudes, norms, values, actions, and assumptions of the school organization explicitly embrace and are committed to the notion of families as a foundational core component to improvement and

(Continued)

(*Continued*)

greater student learning and performance. The culture is reflected in the actions of those in the organization, in the artifacts, and in the organizational practices.

1.1 The school has created and sustained a culture that is conducive to family engagement through explicit beliefs, actions, norms, values, and assumptions made about the value of families being engaged with their children's school experiences.

1.2 A culture of family engagement exists within the school such that policies, programs, practices, and procedures specifically connect families with student learning to support increased achievement and enhance student learning and performance.

1.3 A culture of family engagement exists within the school and community that directly and positively impacts the social and emotional growth of all students.

Principle #2

Communicate Effectively and Develop Relationships

Effective communication and relationship development create environments in the schools that are welcoming, respectful, and conducive to family engagement.

Description: There is consistent evidence that effective communication and relationship development create environments in the schools that are welcoming, respectful, and conducive to family engagement. The school places an emphasis on effective two-way communication with every family and stakeholder within the learning community and seeks to develop relationships based on mutual trust.

2.1 The school creates and maintains a welcoming and respectful environment that is inviting, supportive, and encouraging to every family.

2.2 The school employs strategies that extend opportunities to develop relationships beyond the school walls so that every family can substantially contribute to the education of their children.

2.3 The school ensures that healthy, two-way communication is consistently maintained. A sense of caring to truly collaborate with every family exists, as evidenced by numerous mechanisms to allow families to communicate easily and directly with the school.

Principle #3
Build Family Efficacy

Description: Families are recognized as essential members of the learning team for each student—their participation is welcomed, valued, and encouraged by the school. The school understands that families are important and influential resources because they know their children best.

3.1 The school makes a conscious effort to educate families in how to play a proactive role in the learning life of their child throughout their child's school career.

3.2 The school is committed to the academic socialization of families and, to that end, develops and deploys strategies that encourage and support family engagement with specific learning in all classrooms.

3.3 Families participate in the development of the student's learning plan, help monitor and assess progress, and provide support for their child's learning.

3.4 Families suggest learning strategies and experiential possibilities and use their local knowledge, personal skills, assets, and networks in ways that support the school's program.

Principle #4

Engage Every Family in Decision Making

Description: The school recognizes the entitlement of families to be consulted and participate in decisions concerning their own children. The school is genuinely inclusive in its approach to decision making. It recognizes that this type of process creates a sense of shared responsibility among families, students, community members, educators, and administrators.

4.1 The school creates opportunities for families to lead and participate in school learning, consultative, planning, social, and community events.

4.2 The school ensures that families and students have representation on the school's governing body and in relevant decision-making groups.

Principle #5

Engage the Greater Community

Description: The school places a strong focus on building and creating partnerships external to the school. The school recognizes the strengths and talents that exist in its community that influence student learning and development and seeks to use these to strengthen and support the school, students, and their families.

The principle also recognizes that the school can be a focal point for communities to come together and engage in capacity building and renewal. The school views itself as an important community asset and has community representatives on the school's governing body. There is a clear recognition from the school that the greater community plays an integral role in the educational success of the school.

5.1 Partnerships are made with individuals and organizations in work and community places to take on mentoring roles within student internship and work placement programs. The partnerships also have a role to play within other activities, such as community-based learning projects, guest speaker programs, job shadowing opportunities, apprenticeship opportunities, and tutoring services.

5.2 Partnerships are made with other learning institutions—other schools, technical colleges, universities, and other training providers in order for students to pursue learning opportunities, build their skills, and achieve learning credentials.

5.3 Opportunities evolve from the school for creating and implementing adult learning and community development courses to be run within the school building.

What will follow is a more in-depth discussion of each of the principles and descriptions of best practices, allowing every school to determine their present level of performance and set goals with metrics for improvement.

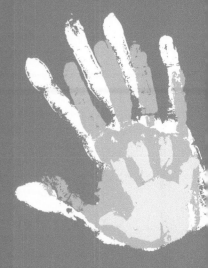

CHAPTER 6

Principle #1
A Culture That Engages Every Family

A culture will be strong or weak depending on the interactions between people in the organization. In a strong culture, there are many overlapping and cohesive interactions, so that knowledge about the organization's distinctive character—and what it takes to thrive in it—is widely spread.

—Ebony Bridwell-Mitchell (Shafer, 2018)

CULTURE DRIVES EVERYTHING

In most organizations, culture is not among the daily thoughts of its members. We don't normally dwell on or think about it. We pass through each day in normal and established routines and barely give notice to how the culture, which is all around us, is shaping everything we do. Nor do we notice our role in defining and shaping the culture within which we work.

70

Principle #1

A Culture That Engages Every Family

Description: The collective beliefs, attitudes, norms, values, actions, and assumptions of the school organization explicitly embrace and are committed to the notion of families as a foundational core component to improvement and greater student learning and performance. The culture is reflected in the actions of those in the organization, in the artifacts, and in the organizational practices.

1.1 The school has created and sustained a culture that is conducive to family engagement through explicit beliefs, actions, norms, values, and assumptions made about the value of families being engaged with their children's school experiences.

1.2 A culture of family engagement exists within the school such that policies, programs, practices, and procedures specifically connect families with student learning to support increased achievement and enhance student learning and performance.

1.3 A culture of family engagement exists within the school and community that directly and positively impacts the social and emotional growth of all students.

Upon a cursory glance, organizational culture can be deceiving. In the case of engaging families, it is easy to make a quick assumption that we are doing a good job. But when we stop and take a close look and examine the culture carefully, we may very well see something completely different. We now see things that have always been there but have gone undetected. We make assumptions about the culture and often, the culture, like an illusionary illustration, can deceive us. Sometimes the culture that we work in deceives us as well.

Every organization, including schools, has a culture of its own. In most cases, the culture has evolved over time. Sadly, in many instances, school culture is not inclusive of every family. For whatever reasons—and there are many varied ones—cultures that embrace the notion of truly engaging every family are not the norm. Without a culture that embraces family engagement, success for every student will undoubtedly remain yet another illusion.

CULTURES AND SUBCULTURES

Inside any school organization, subunits such as departments, teams, groups, hierarchical levels, and so forth reflect their own unique cultures. Difficulties in coordinating and integrating processes or organizational activities, for example, are often a result of culture clashes among different subunits.

Interestingly, families are also subunits of schools. They bring their own unique attitudes, beliefs, and culture, and their behavior can be dictated by the behaviors and attitudes of the employees within the school.

Deal and Peterson (1999) provide a simple sentence that speaks volumes about the notion of the importance of sustained positive culture: "The culture of an enterprise plays the dominant role in exemplary performance" (p. 1).

Numerous authors, thinkers, and researchers have put their stamp on school culture. In 1932, Willard Waller wrote the following:

> Schools have a culture that is definitely their own. There are, in the school, complex rituals of personal relationships, a set of folkways, mores and irrational sanctions, [and] a moral code based upon them. There are games, which are sublimated wars, teams, and an elaborate set of ceremonies concerning them. There are traditions, and traditionalists waging their world-old battle against innovators. (as cited in Sims and Sims, 2004, p. 141)

Another description of school culture emanates from Boyd (1992), who defines *culture* as the encompassing attitudes and beliefs of those both inside and outside the school. Also included are the cultural norms of the school and the relationships among persons in the school. Attitudes and beliefs are core issues in the success of any school. Relationships involve actions and interactions of people. These actions are based on attitudes and beliefs, which can also be defined as *values*.

Culture permeates everything:

- The way people act
- How they dress
- What they talk about or avoid talking about
- Whether or not they seek out colleagues for help
- How teachers feel about their work, their students, and the families of those students

Schein (2010) proposes that culture can be "analyzed at several different levels, with the term *level* meaning the degree to which the cultural phenomenon is visible to the observer" (p. 23). Discussed are three levels of culture: the surface level or artifacts, the intermediary level or espoused beliefs and values, and the final level containing all underlying assumptions within the organization.

There is no question that we are at a crossroads in education. There is the potential to positively reshape and reaffirm the basic tenets of education so that all students benefit from it. Successful schools have a rich and positive school culture at their core. As has been clearly shared, there is no real reform without a permanent shift in culture, and part of that shift must be family engagement.

> We are at a crossroads in education. There is the potential to positively reshape and reaffirm the basic tenets of education so that all students benefit from it.

Research continues to support the notion that creating a demanding culture that includes relational trust and a positive school climate for students and their families is essential for continuous improvement (Bryk & Schneider, 2002; Fullan, 2001; Gonder, 1994). Some attempts at improving schools are failing because little attention is being paid to improving the culture of schools. Re-culturing is essential to school change and improvement. Baars, Shaw, Mulcahy, and Menzies (2018) found that school culture varies more by school performance than by the actual location of the school. Cutting across the high-performing schools in their study, the engagement of families was a consistent variable.

School personnel who can apply a panoramic or holistic view to their schools will better understand the concept of culture and how it applies a context for understanding the complexities and problems that affect schools, especially the delicate relationships that are necessary to move the organization forward. We must hold ourselves accountable for assessing the quality of our own school culture, especially as it relates to family engagement.

POINTS TO PONDER

Take this opportunity to record your thoughts regarding the three levels of culture in your organization and how the culture relates to engaging every family:

1. What artifacts within your organization speak to the culture in your school and its acceptance of family engagement?

2. What espoused beliefs and values do you think are predominant in your organization with regard to family engagement?

3. What basic underlying assumptions does your organization hold that shape its present culture with regard to family engagement?

CULTURAL CHALLENGES

Schools that do not include the fundamental changes to culture necessary to allow families to fully engage with their children are doomed to implement endless strategies that have shortened lifespans and ultimately produce no long-lasting results.

For as many years as researchers have been writing about family engagement and its importance to overall student achievement and school improvement, schools have been desperately trying to engage every family with less-than-stellar results. Researchers have offered numerous strategies for schools to implement so that more families, especially those that are traditionally disengaged with their children's education, can become engaged and attached to the school so that their child's learning improves.

While there is no argument that progress has been made with regard to understanding the importance of family engagement and attaining the empirical evidence that it is indeed important, to suggest that real family engagement is ingrained in the culture of every school is an overstatement.

Why then have we had so much trouble with successfully infusing family engagement practices with schools? The answer lies in one word: culture.

BREAKING THE CYCLE

Most educators quietly acknowledge that over the years, numerous ideas have been implemented to help students learn better and achieve more. Every year, school and district leaders stand before the collective body and announce the ideas that will be initiated that year. Many, especially those who have been in education for a long period of time, instinctively know that by the year's end, most if not all of the initiatives will be gone or, at best, will show little result for the effort and cost.

It is at this juncture that an important question needs to be asked: Why? The answer is simple: Initiatives do not last because the culture of organizations never changes to embrace and sustain the idea. Ideas, objectives, initiatives, and strategies that represent a fundamental antithesis toward the existing culture will always succumb to the existing culture unless significant work is done to augment, expand, and shift the culture to embrace the desired change. Courageous leadership is needed to permanently change a culture. Culture can eat change for lunch.

In order to allow family engagement to be the important component to school reform that research has proven it must be, changing the culture of the school to be accepting and inclusive of family engagement is critical.

These simple questions help to get to the core of beliefs about family engagement. More often than not, educators create opinions and perceptions of family engagement based on prior experiences. If the majority of interactions that teachers and other school staff have with families are negative, then it stands to reason that teachers and school staff, over time, will develop negative perceptions of families or at least those that are traditionally disengaged. Worse yet, these experiences can cause teachers and school staff to resign themselves to operating in a culture that does not engage families because the task seems ominous or has little return value for the effort.

How many times has a principal of a school started the school year by asking all teachers to make five positive phone calls a week? And how many of those phone calls were really made after the first week or two of school? In order to create a culture for families, a thorough understanding that our actions within the organization impact the organization is critical. Then—and only then—can an organization move forward to create a culture that is truly reflective of valuing the partnership and empowerment of all families.

Think back to a story shared at the beginning of this book—the discussion between an educator and his friend about the move from a public school to a charter school. The simple notion of caring was the root of the parent making a fairly dramatic decision. The actions of the people within the organization could have prevented the move from ever occurring.

If we truly desire families to be engaged with schools and in the academic lives of their children, then we must work to change the culture of schools so that the process of educating children is more humanized. If we are to succeed, we have to be responsive to the individual, regardless of their background.

This change, however, requires that those involved understand and desire the need for the change itself and take ownership in the process. An educational setting that can measure and assess progress with shared goals, shared power, respect for human dignity, and cooperation is well on its way to reshaping the culture forever.

> An educational setting that can measure and assess progress with shared goals, shared power, respect for human dignity, and cooperation is well on its way to reshaping the culture forever.

SCHOOL CULTURE DEFINED

Theorists, scholars, researchers, and authors have argued about the meaning of culture for hundreds of years. According to famed anthropologist Clifford Geertz (1973), culture represents a historically transmitted pattern of meaning. Culture is passed on from generation to generation primarily by parents and educational systems of particular societies (Haviland, 1975). This process is often referred to as *enculturation*.

Schein (2010) defines *culture* as the shared assumptions and ideologies of an organization, with the basic assumption being that everyone is responsible for the future of children. Culture is interchanged with the words *climate*, *ethos*, and *saga* (Deal, 1993). The definition of culture must also include deep patterns of values, beliefs, and traditions that have been formed over the course of the school's history (Deal & Peterson, 1990).

The beliefs of teachers, students, and principals transcend the business of creating an efficient learning environment to focus more on the core values needed to teach students. The distinctive identity of an organization is derived directly from its culture (Schein, 2010). Successful school cultures have strong leadership, competent staff, robust support in building staff capacity, and strong ties to families and the community (Bryk, 2010).

Considering these ideas, one definition of school culture has at its core the historically transmitted patterns of meaning that include norms, values, beliefs, ceremonies, rituals, traditions, and myths and how well these ideas are understood or ingrained in the members of the organization (Stolp & Smith, 1994). Simply put, culture shapes what people think and how they act and is shaped by the very same. School culture can be summarized as follows:

- School culture affects the behavior and achievement of elementary and secondary school students.
- School culture does not fall from the sky; it is created and thus can be manipulated by people within the school.
- School cultures are unique; no two are exactly alike.
- School culture becomes the cohesion that bonds the school together.
- Culture can be counterproductive and an obstacle to success; culture can also be oppressive for various subgroups.
- Lasting change requires a change in the school culture, which is a slow process. (Patterson, Purkey, & Parker, 1986)

Wagner (2004/2005) cites three major indicators of improved school culture: collaboration, collegiality, and efficacy, all of which are represented throughout the Five Simple Principles. Central themes include the degree to which people work together and share information, the sense of belonging to an organization, and how members of the organization view themselves within the organization.

These ideas can be easily translated to family engagement: the degree to which schools and families work together, the sense of belonging to the school held by families, and how families view their role within the school organization. When determining how to engage every family, collaborative cultures should be inclusive of the important and trusting relationships between school staff and families, which promotes the important ideas of collegiality and efficacy. However, the process to attain this collaborative culture must be real and organic and not contrived.

Focusing on engaging every family is much more prevalent at the school level than it is at the district level. In larger districts, it is quite common for some schools to embrace family engagement and others to not. In many school districts, there tends to be more attention to families at the primary level and less at the secondary level. All of these situations detract from creating cultures that support the engagement of every family.

SCHOOL DISTRICT INCONSISTENCY WITH FAMILIES

As an example, let's take the fictitious Marshall family. The Marshalls are a fairly engaged family. They have one child in school, Joseph. Joseph's teacher, Mrs. Knight, supports the notion of engaging every family. She makes building relationships with families a priority.

The Marshalls feel comfortable with Mrs. Knight; as a result, Joseph is doing quite well. Mrs. Knight is communicative, creates opportunities for parents to engage with their children's schoolwork, helps parents preview upcoming work, and makes numerous telephone calls and home visits to all families. The Marshalls and Joseph have a wonderful year in Mrs. Knight's class.

The following year, Joseph is assigned to Mr. Bradford. Mr. Bradford is an excellent teacher but does not subscribe to the mentality of engaging every family. The Marshalls do not have the access or relationship with Mr. Bradford that they did with Mrs. Knight. Mr. Bradford does not make phone calls unless a problem occurs in school and sends home only work that has been completed with no preview of upcoming work. He does not make home visits.

Even though Mr. Bradford is a fine teacher, the Marshalls do not believe he is as effective as Mrs. Knight. The Marshalls become increasingly frustrated, and the relationship between the Marshalls and Mr. Bradford grows tense because the Marshalls expected to have the same experience they had with Mrs. Knight.

While this story is fictitious and designed to illustrate a point, the lack of *systemic* attention to family engagement effectively undoes any work by individual schools or teachers who are promoting the idea of engaging every family. The answer to this inconsistent pattern is for the school district to adopt policies, procedures, and practices that support the notion of engaging every family to enhance student achievement.

A Culture of Family Academic Socialization

Academic socialization encompasses the variety of parental beliefs and behaviors that influence children's school-related development. Parents are considered to be the primary agents of child socialization with the school. High levels of parent academic socialization can be found as early as elementary school (Inoa, 2017). Children's academic attitudes are shaped by their families. The more the family is invested in and knowledgeable about their children's learning, the more likely it is that children will improve academically. Over time, parents reduce home- and school-based involvement but consistently engage in academic socialization (Bhargava & Witherspoon, 2015). The relationship between parent satisfaction and student motivation is directly impacted by the academic socialization, or the degree to which parents understand the importance of achievement and translate that message to their children's socialization with schooling (Suizzo et al., 2016).

It stands to reason, then, that those families that are disengaged or marginally engaged lack the academic socialization necessary to help shape their children's views and attitudes toward school. Without specific ongoing knowledge of what is taking place in school, families cannot socialize to the school, which results in their inability or unwillingness to socialize their children to important learning goals. For example, Cross, Marchand, Medina, Villafuerte, and Rivas-Drake (2019) found a positive correlation between the academic socialization of Latino parents and their children's academic self-efficacy.

An Example: Looking at Chronic Absenteeism Through the Lens of Academic Socialization

As a result of the implementation of the Every Student Succeeds Act (ESSA), many school districts around the country are now focused on chronic absenteeism, with a majority of states requiring data to monitor improvement. A great debate begins when absenteeism is the topic to determine who is actually responsible for student absence from school. Educators are often quick to suggest that schools cannot control student attendance, leaving the responsibility squarely in the lap of families. Conversely, families believe that aspects of the school's culture and climate are reasons why students do not place more value on consistent school attendance. Perhaps the answer to this great debate lies somewhere in the middle.

Children who hold positive attitudes toward school were less likely to be chronically absent than those who did not. The more parents are engaged with current school activity and expectation, the lower the odds of absenteeism (Gottfried & Gee, 2017). Schools that were well organized and were more successful with family engagement showed lowered rates of absenteeism (Lenhoff & Pogodzinski, 2018). But with this said, there are reasons that parents give for the absence of their children.

Challenges related to children's mental health, a lack of parent activities, negative interactions with other children at school, and transportation were all factors in understanding parent viewpoints of chronic absenteeism. Parents feel that in order to improve their child's attendance, schools should increase communication, express more compassion about why children are absent, and provide alternative settings for children to be successful (Wallace, 2017).

What does all of this mean? It seems the more we can devote ourselves to a culture that promotes the academic socialization of families, the more likely we will be successful in meeting the academic and social-emotional needs of children. In order to better position schools and families to support all children, policies addressing family engagement need to be explicit and supportive of promoting the capacity of schools to embrace family engagement as a means toward better school outcomes.

START WITH POLICY

Today, family engagement is an integral part of school reform and improved student achievement. For many years, family engagement was a relatively low priority among the nation's school districts. As of late, that is all changing (Mapp & Kuttner, 2013). Meaningful and actionable policy at the district level can bring about the levels of family engagement that have often eluded and frustrated schools and districts, especially when trying to engage all types of families. Educators report initiatives in family engagement as among their most challenging work (Markow, Macia, & Lee, 2013).

It is imperative that thoughtful, meaningful, and collaborative family engagement policy is created in all school districts. Unlike most policies, family engagement policy is created in a dual-capacity manner, where the school district recognizes a shared responsibility with families and enacts policies that are both developed and implemented by the school district and the families that it serves (Mapp & Kutner, 2013).

Mapp and Kutner (2013) proposed that in order to effectively develop policy in a shared manner, challenges must be overcome. First,

> Family engagement policy is created in a dual-capacity manner, where the school district recognizes a shared responsibility with families and enacts policies that are both developed and implemented by the school district and the families that it serves.

educators need training and capacity building in the area of family engagement. Families who are traditionally disengaged with schools are a focus of the capacity building such that policy development truly represents the voices of the school district and their families.

The National Association for Family, School, and Community Engagement (NAFSCE) is an organization dedicated to bringing a deeper awareness of the importance of family engagement by promoting meaningful policy that ultimately impacts the improved learning and social-emotional outcomes for all students.

NAFSCE provides a very sound rationale for the development of appropriate policy in the arena of family engagement:

> Family engagement is more than an education issue; for many families, it is a civil rights issue. Often, low-income families don't have access or opportunity to becoming engaged in their child's education. It is typically misunderstood as a parent's lack of desire, and that is mistaken. While many of the common barriers to engagement are certainly not the fault of schools, without an intentional and strategic approach to culturally respond to, welcome and engage low-income families, these children are at a distinct disadvantage to achieve. It is time to significantly increase our investment in high-impact family engagement, thereby maximizing the opportunity for families to become learning partners, so that we can close the achievement gap, turn around failing schools, and ensure that all children have the resources and support to realize their dreams. Family engagement is NOT about good public relations. It is about leveraging a parent or caregiver's expertise about their child in ways that improve instruction, support improved student behavior and increased engagement, ultimately resulting in improved achievement and graduation rates. (NAFSCE, 2019)

With ESSA in full implementation, it is incumbent upon school districts to understand the policy necessary to meet the requirements spelled out in ESSA. Unlike its predecessor legislation, No Child Left Behind (NCLB), ESSA requires multiple measures (such as improvement planning, roles for families, consulting with families, and demonstrating a clear foundation of family engagement) in which school districts demonstrate their commitment and successes with regard to family engagement.

Districts can establish robust practice in family engagement through the development of targeted and far-reaching policy. "Sound district-level parent and family engagement policies aligned with government policy yield sound school-level policies that set the expectation of welcoming, family-friendly environments that boost parent and family engagement and, ultimately, student achievement" (Scholastic FACE, n.d., p. 5).

The District Family Engagement Policy Toolkit (Scholastic FACE, n.d.) shares the following as components of an effective district-level family engagement policy:

1. Involve parents/families in the development.

2. Build the capacity of parents/families.

3. Empower parents/families, particularly in matters of decision making.

4. Coordinate strategies with parents/families in other programs.

5. Conduct annual evaluations of the effectiveness of parent and family engagement efforts.

6. Design strategies for school improvement from annual evaluations.

7. Annually revise the district policy.

8. Involve families in school activities.

ACTIVITY
School-Family Culture Inventory

Earlier in the book, a short survey to gauge your school's efforts with family engagement was introduced. This culture inventory takes data collecting a step further to understand the beliefs and attitudes of staff members. Distribute this survey to staff, either on paper or online, and average the responses for each statement.

For each of the statements below, rate your answer by circling the appropriate number on a scale from I (strongly disagree) to 5 (strongly agree). Calculate your final score by averaging the cumulative scores. (Add the total of the scale numbers and divide by I0.) This quick inventory can be taken by one person or everyone on your staff. It is designed to give you a snapshot of the present culture of your school with regard to the beliefs, values, and attitudes surrounding family engagement.

(Continued)

(Continued)

An average score of between 1–2 is considered below standard. A score of 4–5 is considered at or above standard.

1. The core values of my school are inclusive of strong family engagement in learning.
   Strongly Disagree   1   2   3   4   5   Strongly Agree

2. I believe that every family wants to be engaged with their children's school experiences.
   Strongly Disagree   1   2   3   4   5   Strongly Agree

3. I believe that I am the primary catalyst for building relationships with families.
   Strongly Disagree   1   2   3   4   5   Strongly Agree

4. Family engagement is a priority at my school.
   Strongly Disagree   1   2   3   4   5   Strongly Agree

5. I believe that student ability to learn is ultimately derived from their family background.
   Strongly Disagree   1   2   3   4   5   Strongly Agree

6. I believe that families value my efforts to successfully teach their children.
   Strongly Disagree   1   2   3   4   5   Strongly Agree

7. I believe that family engagement is valued by all school staff.
   Strongly Disagree   1   2   3   4   5   Strongly Agree

8. I believe that it is the desire of every family that their children be successful.
   Strongly Disagree   1   2   3   4   5   Strongly Agree

9. Decision making at my school is collaborative and inclusive of student and family voice.
   Strongly Disagree   1   2   3   4   5   Strongly Agree

10. I believe that family apathy toward learning is minimal or nonexistent.
    Strongly Disagree   1   2   3   4   5   Strongly Agree

Scoring Rubric for the School–Family Culture Inventory

Scoring Rubric

The following rubric is designed to help you determine the present culture of your school as it relates to family engagement. First, determine your score by adding the scores for each of the ten questions together.

1.	6.
2.	7.
3.	8.
4.	9.
5.	10.

Total (add together scores for each of the 10 statements): _____

Divide the total above by 10: _____

Take the final score from the step above and plot it on the scoring line below:

| 1 | 1.5 | 2.0 | **2.5** | 3 | 3.5 | 4 | 4.5 | 5 |

Interpreting Your Score

1–2.5

If your score falls within this range, there is much work to do on creating a culture to engage every family. Scores in this range suggest that there is little or no organizational focus or importance placed on engaging every family in the academic lives of their children and that there is no evidence of a concerted effort to focus on those families that are disengaged and disenfranchised from the school or their child's experiences and learning in school. The perceptions, assumptions, and attitudes about families incorporate doubt that families wish to be engaged or care deeply about the learning success of their children. It is possible that negative attitudes toward families or certain families drive a culture of mistrust and, potentially, fear. A score in this range is evidence that there is a strong need to strengthen relationships between school staff and families as well as build the capacity of staff in understanding the relationships of family engagement and successful student learning. A score in this range also is an indication of procedures and practices within the school that are not conducive to engaging every family. There is little evidence that the culture is able to sustain family engagement in such a way as to impact student learning in a positive fashion.

2.5–4

If your score falls within this range, there is evidence that attention is being paid to the importance of engaging every family in the academic lives of their children. Emerging within the school culture may be core beliefs, values, and goals that are inclusive of family engagement. School staff may be inconsistent in their knowledge and approach to family engagement, but generally speaking, they desire that all families be engaged with learning and school experiences. There is evidence that perceptions and assumptions about families may be more positive than negative and that there is a growing desire to be inclusive of family engagement in the overall improvement process of the school. There is some emerging evidence that suggests the school is moving toward engaging families and promoting their efficacy.

4–5

If your score falls within this range, it suggests that family engagement is a strong component of the school's core beliefs, mission, and vision. At this level, school staff

(Continued)

(Continued)

most likely understand and welcome the engagement of families and perceptions about families; their desires and beliefs are generally positive and accurate. School staff see the efforts as strategic to the overall effort to promote continuous improvement in the school. Perceptions of families and their contributions to learning are generally positive. With a positive culture of family engagement, the likelihood of promoting or being able to promote family efficacy is quite high.

CULTURE CASE STUDY: THE SCIENCE PROJECT

The case study below is designed to promote conversation and dialogue about the ideas presented in this chapter. At the conclusion of the case study, several questions for discussion are listed.

Mary teaches middle school science. She has assigned her students the long-term project of picking one of the planets in the solar system and preparing a display and report to be shared with the class and exhibited at the school's open house. Mary spends considerable time each year on this project. The displays are always well received, and the principal always comments about how the project puts the school in a very positive light with the community. The students use their library and writing skills, research skills, and presentation skills, and they coordinate their creativity and ability to conceptualize and apply their knowledge. By all accounts, it is an excellent project.

Some parents have contacted Mary to ask questions about specific aspects of the assignment, trying to determine what Mary's expectation is with regard to the display portion of the project. Mary has become quite used to parent calls and skillfully answers each question to the satisfaction of parents. One parent, Mrs. Smith, explains to Mary that she is on a fixed income and cannot afford the art materials necessary for her child to fully participate in the project. She fears not only a bad grade but that her child will be embarrassed at the open house if the display is not up to the standards of the displays of other students. Mary tries to assure Mrs. Smith that whatever her child produces will be acceptable, provided that the guidelines of the assignment are followed.

Mary indicates that the project should be driven by the child, not the parent, and that Mrs. Smith should support her child but not worry about the amount of money spent or the "glitz factor" of the final project. Presentation boards and construction paper will be supplied by the school.

Even though the conversation was pleasant, Mary sensed that Mrs. Smith was not completely comfortable with her responses. Mary mentioned to the principal that there is a chance he might hear from Mrs. Smith. She explained the situation to the principal and the principal thanked her for the heads up. No further conversation took place.

Mrs. Smith was not convinced that this assignment was fair and takes her concern to the principal. The principal listens to Mrs. Smith and assures her that there will be no repercussion if significant money is not spent nor will there be preferential treatment for different displays of creativity within the project. Feeling that she can do nothing more, she leaves the principal's office calm but frustrated.

Mrs. Smith supports and works with her child for several weeks to help create the best display and report possible. The Smith family does not have a home computer or printer. The family car is taken to work by Mr. Smith, who works the 3–11PM shift at the local warehouse; therefore, driving to the library is not possible. Mrs. Smith asked if her daughter could use a computer at school and was told yes, but the school could not allow the students to print their reports, since the school had a limited paper and ink budget for the computers. Mrs. Smith, remembering that writing was an important aspect of the assignment, encouraged her child to use her best penmanship and write the assignment by hand on notebook paper. Mrs. Smith directed her daughter to write neatly and legibly or the process would begin again.

Mrs. Smith's child turned in the project on time. Her child receives a grade of 85 on the project.

When Mrs. Smith came to the open house, she quickly saw that many of the projects were indeed elaborate—a paper-mache model of Mars, complete with canyons and craters, color photographs, and a report done on a computer and printed in color. There were planets spinning on battery-powered spindles representing an axis and one that was able to form the gaseous clouds of the planet's atmosphere because of a parent's expertise in atmospheric engineering.

Mrs. Smith noticed that her child's project was not among the others. When she asked Mary, Mary indicated that there was not enough room in the hallway for all of the projects and that some were displayed in the classroom. Upon entering the classroom, Mrs. Smith noticed that the three projects in the classroom, including her child's project, had no special effects and the reports were handwritten. While they met the spirit of the assignment, they were obviously not as elaborate as the others on display in the hallway.

Mrs. Smith was angry at the situation and made no effort to conceal her emotions toward Mary and the principal. Her child, embarrassed by the entire situation, left the school building and waited outside until Mrs. Smith was finished yelling at the teacher and the principal. The principal asked Mrs. Smith and Mary to step into his office. He told Mrs. Smith that her child received a good grade and that her behavior toward Mary and him was inappropriate.

Mary was in tears, and Mrs. Smith was close to tears. The principal told Mrs. Smith that there was nothing wrong with the display configuration and that Mary was an excellent teacher who had prepared these assignments successfully for many years. He believed the entire incident should not have happened and told Mrs. Smith that all she had accomplished was to undermine the relationship between herself and Mary and embarrass her child. Mrs. Smith was unable to express her feelings of inadequacy about the incident, the project, and the fact that what happened was exactly what she feared, given similar situations in past years.

Feeling outnumbered and outmatched, Mrs. Smith left the principal's office, found her child, and went home. Her child was absent from school the next day.

Source: Used with permission from Dr. Joni Samples, Family Friendly Schools.

Questions for Reflection

1. Given what you have learned about the culture, how would you characterize the culture of this school? (Consider the beliefs, values, assumptions, actions, and attitudes of all.)

2. Based on your opinions and answers with regard to the above question, what specific information in the story led you to the conclusions you made? Be specific.

3. The story depicts a school project that, for at least one family, went horribly wrong. What steps could have been taken to prevent what happened in the story?

4. What specific changes in culture do you see that are necessary to provide a different outcome to this situation?

5. If you had to surmise the attitudes of the principal and teacher toward family engagement, what would you think their attitudes were?

6. Do you think the principal supports family engagement in the school?

7. What was the purpose of the project? Why did it exist?

8. Given what you have read and discussed, could this situation happen in your school? Why or why not?

CREATING A CULTURE TO ENGAGE EVERY FAMILY

Each of the Five Simple Principles has clarifying statements designed to further assist schools with implementation. Subsequent to each one of the statements is a description of best practice with regard to the ideas in the statements. Subsequent to that description are a number of ideas and suggestions on how to go about creating the environment as described.

PRINCIPLE #1

Where We Are

Description

The collective beliefs, attitudes, norms, values, actions, and assumptions of the school organization explicitly embrace and are committed to the notion of families as a foundational core component to improvement and greater student learning and performance. The culture is reflected in the actions of those within the organization, in the artifacts, and in the organizational practices.

Based on the description, discuss and record where you think your school is today as it relates to the principle description.

1.1 The school has created and sustained a culture that is conducive to family engagement through explicit beliefs, actions, norms, values, and assumptions made about the value of families being engaged with their children's school experiences.

Principle 1.1 Assessment

Use this chart to determine your organization's present level of performance.

Practice/Attribute/ Condition	Discuss/Reflect/Record the Present Status in Your School
Everyone at our school desires to engage with every family, regardless of difficulty.	

(Continued)

(Continued)

Our leadership has set high, clear expectations for engaging every family.	
Our core beliefs include the importance of engaging with every family.	
We can measure the degree to which we are successful in engaging families with our school (beyond attendance to events).	
All staff promote an active role for families to engage with learning in the school.	
Our school believes that family engagement is important to our continued improvement.	
Our families feel a strong sense of belonging in our school.	

Use the clarifying statement and the best practice description to help you shape your future culture.

Best Practice Description

The culture at the school consistently provides support for and embraces the notion of engaging every parent and family member rather than settling for those families that are already engaged or those families that are traditionally easier to engage. School leadership has set high standards for the engagement of every family and, in tandem with staff, lives by culture statements that reflect the organization's beliefs about the benefits of engaging every family.

Measurable objectives with regard to family engagement are clear. The beliefs of all teaching and support staff sustain the notion that families should be engaged and empowered to have an active role in the education of their children as is evidenced by their consistent actions, attitudes, and assumptions.

The norms and values of the organization support the principle of family engagement as an effective and necessary component to overall school improvement, and there is tangible and credible evidence of every family being engaged with all aspects of their children's learning and the operation of the school. Every family feels a strong sense of belonging to the school.

Practices to Be Implemented

1.2 A culture of family engagement exists within the school such that policies, programs, practices, and procedures specifically connect families with student learning to support increased achievement and enhance student learning and performance.

Principle 1.2 Assessment

Use this chart to determine your organization's present level of performance.

Practice/Attribute/Condition	Discuss/Reflect/Record the Present Status in Your School
We have tangible evidence that our school staff are committed to engaging every family.	
We encourage families to become engaged with learning on an ongoing and continuous basis.	
Our school procedures and practices are designed to encourage family engagement.	
We believe that families are the first and most influential teachers of children.	
We not only inform families of what has occurred but we also communicate and engage families in upcoming learning.	

(Continued)

(Continued)

We value and support learning that takes place outside of school and the role that families play in that learning.	
Professional development for teachers and staff includes capacity building in family engagement.	

Use the clarifying statement and the best practice description to help you shape your future culture.

Best Practice Description

There is consistent, tangible, credible, and measurable evidence that the school culture believes in and values the engagement of every family in support of student learning. The school has devised structures and supports to improve student learning and performance outcomes for all students, especially those in traditional subgroups that struggle to attain acceptable achievement levels.

School staff embrace a culture in which families are encouraged to become and supported as partners in the learning lives of their children, and there is consistent and tangible evidence of such policies and practices. School staff believe in and embrace the idea of a seamless learning process between school and home. The culture of the school clearly denotes families as the first and most influential teachers of children and has designed or redesigned its systems and processes to support this concept.

Teachers and other school staff have formative mechanisms in place to help every family understand what their child is learning in school and how that learning can be supported in the home. Rather than reducing family engagement to event attendance, the school has embraced the notion that engagement with learning outside of the school has the most significant impact on student outcomes.

The school provides ongoing training and support for families in understanding and becoming immersed in the academic requirements of their children because they believe and value the concept. Professional learning for teachers consistently contains a family engagement strand or component.

Practices to Be Implemented

1.3 A culture of family engagement exists within the school and community that directly and positively impacts the social and emotional growth of all students.

Principle 1.3 Assessment

Use this chart to determine your organization's present level of performance.

Practice/Attribute/Condition	Discuss/Reflect/Record the Present Status in Your School
Community partners take an active role in the growth and development of students.	
Community partners provide resources that help build successful relationships between families and school staff.	
Our school believes in and subscribes to the concept of the need to educate the whole child.	
The climate of the school reinforces a commitment to engaging every family.	
All staff participate in capacity-building professional development focused on improving family engagement.	

Use the clarifying statement and the best practice description to help you shape your future culture.

(*Continued*)

(Continued)

Best Practice Description

The culture of the school includes families, community agencies, and noneducational partners in the relational growth and development as well as the sense of belonging for all students in the school and within the community. With the help of identified resources in the community, clear and consistent support and practices nurture positive and productive relationships between school staff and every family so that all students are cared for and are learning in the appropriate environments.

The culture of school, family, and community relationships has a unified support of the development of the whole child at its core. The climate and practices of the school continually reinforce the growth of families as teachers and supporters of education. The school provides opportunities for parents to develop their skills so that the emotional and social growth of children can extend from school to home.

The school has made a significant commitment to professional learning for all staff that helps teachers understand the social and emotional growth of children and how family and community relationships enhance the efforts to help all children learn.

Practices to Be Implemented

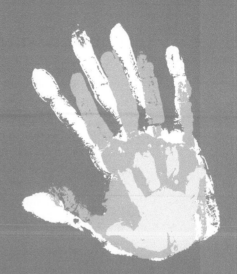

CHAPTER 7

Principle #2
Communicate Effectively and Develop Relationships

They expect me to go to school so they can tell me my kid is stupid or crazy. They've been telling me that for three years, so why should I go and hear it again? They don't do anything. They just tell me my kid is bad.

—A father (from Finders & Lewis, 1994)

Let's start out with some easy ideas that promote Principle #2!

Communicate
Effectively
and Develop
Relationships

2

- Professional development for staff on the importance of family involvement (This book is a great start!)
- Community outreach meetings
- Training for parents and family leaders
- Include families in school-based trainings
- Honor a family of the month
- Create a family hall of fame

93

- Celebrate family week
- Celebrate the community
- Map the assets of the community
- Create a family center
- Provide family parking
- Post welcome signs
- Dedicate a marquee
- Support relationships via email
- Provide family resources on the school website
- Send out welcoming and informative voicemails
- Use social media (Twitter, Facebook, blogs, wikis, etc.) to communicate
- Ask parents to be cultural translators
- Provide professional development for promoting parent leadership and capacity building
- Parents as interpretive vehicles: Encourage parents and teachers to pick up each other's vocabulary

Source: Used with permission from Dr. Joni Samples of Family Friendly Schools.

Principle #2

Communicate Effectively and Develop Relationships

Description

There is consistent evidence that effective communication and relationship development create environments in the schools that are welcoming, respectful, and conducive to family engagement. The school places an emphasis on effective two-way communication with every family and stakeholder within the learning community and seeks to develop relationships based on mutual trust.

2.1 The school creates and maintains a welcoming and respectful environment that is inviting, supportive, and encouraging to every family.

2.2 The school employs strategies that extend opportunities to develop relationships beyond the school walls so that every family can substantially contribute to the education of their children.

2.3 The school ensures that healthy, two-way communication is consistently maintained. A sense of caring to truly collaborate with every family exists, as evidenced by numerous mechanisms to allow families to communicate easily and directly with the school.

Within Principle #2, Communicate Effectively and Develop Relationships, there are three core ideas that are essential in developing the principles:

1. Developing effective relationships and building trust with every family

2. Communicating effectively with every family

3. Creating welcoming environments in schools to promote active family engagement

A significant number of strategies and practices focus on the welcoming environment of a school and/or the need to effectively communicate with families and ensure that the communication is two-way. Principle #2 takes those concepts a step further, suggesting that both of these ideas flourish with better and more trusting relationships with families. For that reason, these three ideas form the basis for the principle. To have a meaningful conversation about two-way communication, technology and social media environments must be considered in the area of relationships and communication.

ACTIVITY
What Role Do Communication and Relationships Play in the Success of Your Students?

This short activity is designed to get you thinking about communication and relationships with families and their effects on student learning. Follow the instructions below.

In the first column of boxes below, list the five highest-performing students that you presently teach or, if you are not presently teaching, the five highest-performing students you have taught at some point in your career. Next to each student's name and in the second set of boxes to the right of the student's name, think about your relationship and communication with their family. Consider the following questions:

- Did the family respond to requests for information?

- Did they call you? Did you call them?

(Continued)

(Continued)

- Did they attend conferences and school activities?

- Did you communicate regularly or as needed?

- Did you feel positive about the relationships you had with the families of these students that you listed?

- Would you consider these families engaged?

These are just a few questions to get you thinking. Jot down any notes or ideas attached to the communication and relationship you have/had with each student's families.

Names of Five Highest-Performing Students	Notes on Communication/ Relationships With Families of Those Students
1.	
2.	
3.	
4.	
5.	

On the next chart, start by listing the five lowest-performing students you teach or have taught. Next to each one of those names, use the same process that you used above to determine the communication and relationships you have/had with the families of this set of students.

Names of Five Lowest-Performing Students	Notes on Communication/ Relationships With Families of Those Students
1.	
2.	
3.	
4.	
5.	

Now that you have completed both charts, compare the notes and ideas you have on the communication and relationships with families. Here are a couple of discussion questions to help you reflect:

1. What similarities and differences are there between the interactions with each set of families?

2. If there are differences, why do you think those differences exist?

3. Do you think there is a correlation between the learning outcomes of each set of students and the communication and relationships you had with each of their families?

The key to engaging every family is to believe that every family cares about their children and strongly desires that their children exceed them in their quality of life. An understanding of the disengaged is essential to effectively create systems and processes for effectively and efficiently engaging every family. In Chapter 3, we learned about disengagement and how it occurs. Below are more specific ideas and information about family disengagement with schools.

Charts are available for download at http://www.drsteveconstantino.com

IT'S THE LITTLE THINGS

From time to time, I have the good fortune to stay in a very posh, upscale hotel. The services these hotels provide are simply over the top. These high-end hotels are focused on one thing: your comfort while there as a guest and the hope that you will return soon.

When I open the closet door in my room, I sometimes see elegant bathrobes hanging on fancy, padded hangers. I always notice a little tag hanging from the robe and hanger and it usually says something like this: "We are pleased to provide this robe for your use while a guest in our hotel. If you would like to purchase the robe, they are available in our gift shop."

What does that sentence mean? Exactly. Don't steal the robe! But the message is sent in a very subtle and classy way. Now, let's think about the messages we send to those who visit our schools.

> Warning! Trespassers Will Be Prosecuted
>
> No Skateboarding; No Running; No Motorcycles
>
> All Visitors Must Report to the Main Office
>
> This Parking Lot Is for Faculty/Staff Only
>
> Your Presence Is Being Recorded

When we think about the welcoming environment of our schools, we must think about the messages that our visitors receive the minute they come onto our property and then enter our schools.

Not so subtle. When we think about the welcoming environment of our schools, we must think about the messages that our visitors receive the minute they come onto our property and then enter our schools. Make sure the words *welcome*, *please*, and *thank you* are visible:

> Welcome to our school! We are glad you are here! Please sign in at our main office. This way [arrow or directions].
>
> Thank you for being here today. We appreciate it. Come back soon! [Sign over the door as people exit.]

While we may think that these small gestures are not worth our trouble, we must consider why, then, businesses and retailers all over the globe go out of their way to welcome us and to ensure that our experience is a positive one.

And while we are on the subject, is there a difference between a visitor and a guest? Disney seems to think so. Guests are those that have an open invitation and for whose arrival and visit we plan for in order to ensure a positive experience. A visitor is someone we do not invite or for whom we do not plan with the hope that they won't stay long.

CASE STUDY: I KNOW WHAT THEY THINK OF ME

The following short case study is designed to act as a catalyst for discussion regarding relationships with parents. At the conclusion of the case study are questions for discussion.

An urban school district wished to analyze its present commitment to family engagement and then set about trying to improve. The vast majority of families served were economically disadvantaged and represented a myriad of cultures and ethnicities. The teachers were embracing the new commitment to family engagement but, understandably, were skeptical of the outcomes and frustrated with yet another new initiative.

A group of elementary teachers at one of the schools located in a relatively impoverished neighborhood were in a reporting meeting regarding their initial efforts to engage families. They had gone through the first training modules and were reporting on their experiences thus far. These teachers were frustrated, indicating they had tried everything to engage families and that their success rate was minimal. At one point, a frustrated teacher exclaimed, "We did everything that was suggested. We made home visits, we sent personal invitations, we made the work we were doing relevant to the parents and families, we had food, we had childcare and tutoring, and we even arranged for transportation. After all of that, three parents participated in our workshop. We can't do any more."

The session the teachers were having was with a coach/consultant. The consultant said, "Well then, it looks like we are going to have to figure out why this isn't working. We need to find out why parents and families are not responding to your efforts."

"How will we do that?" the teachers asked.

"We—you and I—are going to go ask them." Three teachers and the consultant made their way to the home of a parent who had not attended the event as planned. The home was located in a housing project within walking distance of the school. The group arrived at the apartment door and the teachers looked nervously at the consultant.

"Now what?" they asked rather nervously.

"How about we knock on the door?" the consultant answered.

A woman, dressed in a housecoat with curlers in her hair, came to the door and opened it as far as the door chain would allow. When she saw the teachers, she opened the door and invited the group in, looking rather cautiously at the consultant. It was noted that the apartment was barely inhabitable, with a broken window, a space heater, and a family of five living in what amounted to two rooms. After a bit of small talk, the consultant took the lead, explaining to the parent why the group had visited her. She was asked if the teachers had told her about the event—they did. She was asked if she knew how the event would eventually help her child—she did. She was asked if she had received personal invitations and reminders—she indicated that she had. She also knew there was childcare, knew there was food, and knew there was transportation if she needed it. She also freely admitted that she told the teachers she would attend.

"But you didn't attend?" the consultant asked.

"That's right," said the parent.

"May I ask why?"

"Because I know what they all think of me over there."

Questions for Discussion

1. What do you think is lacking in the relationship between the parent and the teachers in the story?

2. What perceived value of building a relationship do the teachers hold? What about the parent? Do you think the perceived value is the same in both cases? Why or why not?

3. What do you think the teachers can do to improve this situation? What would you do if you were one of the teachers? What would you do if you were the parent?

4. How did the story make you feel about family engagement with socioeconomically disadvantaged families?

5. Do you see value in working toward a better relationship with this parent? Why or why not?

UNDERSTANDING THE IMPORTANCE OF RELATIONSHIPS WITH FAMILIES

Relationships between families and the schools that their children attend are complex. Often, there is great ambiguity with regard to the differing interests of families and policies, procedures, and practices, and this ambiguity has an effect on the health of the relationship (Cullingford & Morrison, 1999). It is impossible to think that teachers can cultivate strong relationships with the students they teach yet not create the very same strong relationships with their students' families.

However, when schools understand and nurture effective relationships with all families, tremendous dividends are paid in the form of achievement for every student. Mapp (2003) summarizes it best:

> According to the parents, when school personnel initiate and engage in practices that welcome parents to the school, honor their contributions, and connect them to the school community through an emphasis on the children, these practices then cultivate and sustain respectful, caring, and meaningful relationships between parents and school staff. (p. 36)

Perceived value plays a huge role in whether or not relationships to support students will be fruitful.

No matter to what lengths we go to to improve family engagement, without a real relationship built on trust and honesty, the efforts will probably fall short. If you do not honor all families and convey true appreciation for what they can bring to the partnership, regardless of their station in life, then those families will see your efforts to engage them through a lens of skepticism.

Actions, attitudes, assumptions, beliefs, and values must all work together in order to build engagement with every family. And most importantly, when working with the disengaged, you must consider it really as working with one family at a time. Daunting? Yes. Impossible? No.

> Actions, attitudes, assumptions, beliefs, and values must all work together in order to build engagement with every family.

We cannot fix socioeconomic disparities, but we can convince every family, regardless of their station in life, that they have value and are truly needed to complete the circle of people that will successfully educate their children.

In a study conducted by Crozier and Davies (2007), the authors found that while parents were disengaged, they were by no means difficult, obstructive, or indifferent. Instead of labeling parents as hard to reach, conclusions were that the schools themselves inhibited accessibility of these parents. It is common for schools to set policies and procedures that actually work against fostering relationships with all parents and then complain that parents and families are hard to reach.

One could argue that it is a classic self-fulfilling prophecy. Relationships between schools and families are dependent on policies that have nothing to do with family engagement (Hallgarten, 2000). If family engagement is truly a priority for schools, then building successful relationships with all families should be embedded into the procedures and practices of a school or district rather than implied, or worse yet, ignored.

Procedures, Practices, and Policies

Every school (or organization, for that matter) develops and operates by a set of procedures, practices, and policies. These "three *P*s" are designed to bring continuity in process to the organization, remain focus on stated goals or outcomes, and guide daily operation. First, let's look at some simple definitions of the three words:

> **Procedures:** An established or official way of doing something
>
> **Practices:** The customary, habitual, or expected procedure or way of doing something
>
> **Policies:** A course or principle of action adopted or proposed by a government, party, or business

In public schools governed by local school boards, it is the school board that sets policies for the district. No other entity in a school or school district has the ability to create official policies—only the school board can do that. But the word *policy* appears quite a bit in schools: dress policy, attendance policy, grading policy, and so on. I would argue that in these cases, the word *policy* is being misused. Schools create procedures and practices that implement the policies adapted by the school board. Look again at the definitions above. I would argue that schools are actually developing procedures and then aligning their practices to those procedures. It is important to keep a clear distinction between each of these words because it is within this realm of procedures, practices, and policies that family engagement can be enhanced or stymied.

School Board Policy

It is the job of the school board to steer the school district toward success by creating goals; creating and submitting budget requests to governing bodies or the locality; ensuring that laws are being enforced; and, most importantly, creating, evaluating, and revising school district policy. There are almost as many variations of policies as there are school districts, and the same holds true for family engagement policy. Below is an example of a policy statement regarding family engagement in a school district:

> The [name] district supports and encourages the active participation of parents and members of the community. The involvement of parents, volunteers, and others in the community is a fundamentally important component of successful school programs. The school principal or designee of each school will approve the activities of parents, volunteers, and other community resources at the building level.

Here is another policy statement:

> A school board shall provide opportunities for parental and community involvement in every school in the school district.

Both of these policy statements, which can likely be found in whole or in part in board policy documents, are short and vague. Some would argue that policy should be vague and allowed to be left to interpretation. I would agree with that statement in most cases, but not when it comes to family engagement. Policies such as the examples above leave a wide berth of interpretation by the schools within the district. There is nothing in the policy that governs the consistency or continuity of policy implementation, nor is there any sort of mandate for families to become partners in learning.

Take a look at the school policies in your district or surrounding districts. You will see plenty of variation. Some policies are short and to the point (similar to the example); some are longer and articulate the role of families in more detail. Some districts only have parent involvement/family engagement policies for their Title I schools, as this is required by federal law. In all of these variations of policy, there is a common thread—the *how*. How families can be engaged with the school is most often left up to the procedures and practices developed in the individual school.

Look back at the first sample policy wording above. You will note the last statement: *The school principal or designee of each school will approve the activities of parents, volunteers, and other community resources at the building level.* In the second policy statement, responsibility for implementation is even more vague and undefined.

From building to building within a district, different procedures and practices can be developed and implemented. In many schools, these procedures are informal, created by school staff or groups of staff members to create clarity with regard to expectations. It is this inconsistency that hinders family engagement. If, for example, a parent is welcome to visit one school at any time of their choosing but at another the parent must give 24 hours' notice, what message does the parent receive?

Here are some actual procedures and practices implemented in schools around the country:

1. Each parent of a student shall sign and return to the school a statement acknowledging the receipt of the school board's standards of student conduct.

2. Any teacher assigning a grade of *D* or *F* must contact the parent before issuing the grade.

3. It is important for teachers to maintain an effective working relationship with the administration and all coworkers, including other teachers and support staff.

4. Each teacher is to contact every parent in their homeroom within the first school days. Please document contacts in a parent contact log. The contact log should be available upon request by administration and will be collected at the end of each school year.

5. It is essential that students who are at risk for being retained be brought to the Student Assistance Team. Parent contact should be made prior to the last grading period, with procedures as determined by the committee being completed and documented by the last week of school.

6. Parent/teacher conferences are scheduled when necessary by the parent or the teacher.

7. If the student's conduct is not satisfactory, the first responsibility for correcting the misbehavior shall be with the teacher. If additional assistance is needed, contact should be made with the parents, counselor, and/or administration.

8. As teachers near the end of a grading period and have students who are in danger of failing a class, teachers are required to send a warning letter home to the parent, informing them that their child is in danger of failing the class and the specific steps that may be taken to avoid failure.

9. Conferences may be arranged with parents by sending a note, emailing, or calling home. Such conferences may be arranged during periods when instruction is not scheduled for the teacher.

10. If any problem arises that has the potential to become serious (or is at the first instance), contact parents/guardians.

What patterns emerge from the statements listed above? How do each of these statements help or hinder positive relationships with families or the engagement of families in the academic lives of their children?

In most cases, the procedures and practices that are implemented as a result of school board policy are often punitive in nature and not inclusive of family voice, even though the vast majority of procedures and practices are implemented with children. Procedures and practices rarely devote major sections to engagement expectations with families or promote understanding of procedures rather than evidence that procedure has been received. In some cases, procedures are created based on the needs and parameters of the district or school, with no account taken for families within the community. Every school (or organization, for that matter) develops procedures, practices, and policies to allow the organization to stay focused on its goals and also to guide daily operation.

ACTIVITY
Practices, Procedures, and Policies—Looking Through a Different Lens

How are relationships between your school and families helped or hindered by the procedures, practices, and policies that are implemented in your school and district? Look through the lens of every family and conduct a thorough inventory of procedures, practices, and policies to better understand how family engagement practices are interpreted in your school.

Conduct a review of each category:

1. Find your school district family engagement/parent involvement policy. What does it say? How is your school interpreting the school board policy?

2. Look at your district teacher policy manual. What does it say specifically about family engagement and the expectations of staff?

3. Look at your school or teacher handbook. What speaks directly to enhancing family engagement? What might inhibit the engagement of every family?

4. Look at the school/teacher/classroom procedures and practices and determine if your practices and procedures are consistent and engaging to every family. Are there schoolwide practices that hinder the ability of families to be engaged? Procedures and practices usually exist with everything from communication to homework to classroom visits to volunteerism.

5. With a group of colleagues, review the district family engagement/parent involvement policy, then brainstorm a list of everything you can think of that can be considered a procedure or practice associated with your classrooms or school.

6. Once you have finished compiling a master list, group the items into different categories and label them.

7. As a staff, look at the categories and lists through the lens of families and consider how practices or policies could be changed or improved to engage every family.

Karen Mapp has conducted extensive research in parent involvement and is the architect of "The Joining Process." Dr. Mapp is also one of the authors of *Beyond the Bake Sale: The Essential Guide to Family–School Partnerships* (Henderson, Mapp, Johnson, & Davies, 2007). In the three-part Joining Process, the school community

1. welcomes parents into the school,

2. honors their participation, and

3. connects with parents through a focus on the children and their learning.

Dr. Mapp and her colleagues provide ideas as catalysts for changes in practice and behavior by giving us items and ideas that support the concept of the joining process as well as items and ideas that may prevent the concept from taking shape in a school that wishes to engage every family. Here are some examples (Henderson et al., 2007):

Do More	Do Less
Hello! Welcome to our school. How may I help you?	Who are you? What do you want?
Hang welcome signs with the name of the school and principals	NO TRESPASSING signs
Parent meetings that break into small discussion groups, each picking a leader	Parent meetings dominated by a few officers

It is clear that how we communicate and engage with families can either help or hinder our efforts to create a culture that welcomes and joins with every family. From the way families are greeted by our employees and signage; how and when we schedule, organize, and conduct meetings; how we value the contributions families make to our school; or how we go about engaging them in new curriculum or instructional methodology, our approaches and attitudes will have a lot to do with our ultimate success.

There are many categories for us to consider when desiring to engage every family. A few have already been mentioned (communication, signage, meeting times and structures, and so forth). What ideas do you have? Create your own "do more" chart of items that you know will assist you in your efforts to engage every family.

	Do More
How do you welcome families?	
What welcoming signage have you posted?	
How do you encourage participation?	
How do you solicit input and opinions?	
How do families learn of new programs and curricular initiatives?	
How do you promote parent/ family leadership?	
How do you honor the role of families in the educational lives of their children?	
How do you celebrate achievement?	

The Difference Between Communication and Engagement

In most schools around the country, communication is the number-one job. School personnel are constantly looking for ways to inform families about school information, student progress, events, and so on. For the most part, schools do a good job with communication. There are numerous ways to communicate with families, from face-to-face conversations to newsletters and websites to social media and texts. But there is a fundamental question that needs to be asked by each of us: Am I communicating or engaging? Informing families is not engagement. Reporting information is not engagement. Sharing information is not engagement. All of these communication processes are necessary, but they are *not* engagement.

I won't argue that there are many times when communication is appropriate and necessary. But there are so many things we can do to move the needle from simple communication to engagement. Consider the following definitions of the two words:

Communication: The imparting or exchanging of information or news

Engagement: The act of engaging; the state of being engaged; emotional involvement and commitment

At a minimum, effective engagement practices have two-way communication that enhances the efficacy of families at their core (more on efficacy in Chapter 8). Communicating about what is happening in school and what is going to happen tends to move us in a direction of engagement as opposed to communicating what has already occurred.

The simple lesson is this: Communication is not engagement.

WORKING WITH THE "HARD TO REACH"

I am reminded of my time both as a principal and as a superintendent when seemingly hard-to-reach families wanted to speak directly with me. Regardless of the hard-to-reach label and the lamenting of staff about being unable to reach the family, they reached me. Quite easily, I might add. It occurred to me that if they can reach me, I can reach them.

For a moment, let's ponder the label of the "hard-to-reach" family. Did these families label themselves? Did they arrive to our schools and announce that they are hard to reach so we should not bother to try? Perhaps there are a handful of families who indicate that they cannot be reached or prefer not to be reached, but clearly, they are a microscopic minority. The fact is that we have labeled families *hard to reach* when they don't seem to conform to our perceptions of our standard communication protocols. However, they can be reached. It just takes knowing how and the willingness to make the necessary changes.

> We have labeled families *hard to reach* when they don't seem to conform to our perceptions of our standard communication protocols. However, they can be reached. It just takes knowing how and the willingness to make the necessary changes.

Often, educators request strategies and ideas to communicate with these types of families. The first strategy is really not a strategy at all but harkens back to Principle #1: A Culture That Engages Every Family. The first and most important strategy is for us to believe that reaching out to these families has value and is worth our time and effort. If we don't believe that this effort has any benefit, then it is highly unlikely that we will see any results.

A second strategy is to embody the ethic of caring. In many cases, families who are disengaged or disenfranchised are often facing significant challenges in their personal lives. Stress from finances, work, and family take their toll on just about everyone but have a greater impact on those who may be less fortunate.

We should not judge these families or make assumptions about their support of their child's education. We need to understand the life situations that these families often find themselves in and let them know that all will be well and, more importantly, that partnering with them and building a relationship is something we welcome. We can convince them that regardless of their circumstances, together, we can improve the outcomes for their children.

Thousands of studies have been written about the ability of socioeconomically disadvantaged students to learn, and those studies all indicate that while there are obstacles, the students in this category are able to learn at rather impressive levels. Most of us are witness to numerous success stories of children with disadvantages rising up and beating the educational odds. In most cases, we shed preconceived notions and stereotypes about the children, their families, and their ability to learn. This is a third important strategy when looking to engage the hard-to-reach family. Keep an open mind about the family, regardless of who they are and where they live.

Ron Edmonds, the late researcher and father of the Effective Schools Movement, is credited with coining the phrase *all children can learn*. A cornerstone idea in the Effective Schools Movement is the setting of high expectations for all students. Many have argued that leaving this one concept out of the equation has supported the achievement gaps that still plague education today. The fourth strategy in working with hard-to-reach families is to set high expectations for the relationship. Believe that the family cares about their child. Believe that they have the capacity to support learning at home, and believe that they really want to engage with the school.

Lastly, be sensitive to the needs of families. Provide plenty of advance notice of meetings and multiple reminders. Everyone leads a busy life. One communication about a meeting is likely to get lost in a sea of other information. When offering important events, offer them more than once, on various days, and at various times. Give families more than one option for participation. Provide information for those who cannot attend and look for alternative meeting sites, especially those that are not in the school.

ACTIVITY
Event Location Planner

In many schools, there seems to be an unwritten law demanding that every meeting take place in the school library or cafeteria. This activity is designed to open the door

(Continued)

to hosting school-related meetings at nonschool locations. Use the following chart to determine how events and activities at your school can subscribe to the notion of family outreach.

In the first column, list all of the activities, events, meetings, conferences, and so forth that are presently hosted at your school. Include *everything*. If you think you should not add something—add it! In the second column, determine if the activity can be moved from the school to another venue (i.e., does the Parent–Teacher Association [PTA] meeting have to be in the library?). If you determine that there is an opportunity to move the activity/event, then determine possible locations within your community. An example is given to stimulate your thinking.

Event/Activity/ Meeting/ Conference	Can It Be Moved From the School?	If So, What are Some Potential Locations?
Parent conferences	Yes	Local library/apartment complex meeting room; community conference room at Walmart

Source: Used with permission of Dr. Joni Samples, Family Friendly Schools.

HOME VISITS

In many workshops, I ask veteran teachers if they remember a time when home visits were part of the established routine for teachers. Every time I ask, the answer is the same: Yes. Teachers who have been around for a while remember home visits and even admit that they used to do them. My next question, though, rarely gets answered: Why did you stop?

The phrase *home visits* often strikes fear in the hearts of teachers. We cannot imagine that we have the time in our day to visit the homes of students and their families. Furthermore, teachers point to the safety and risk factors of home visits as another reason for avoiding this outreach strategy. However, as we have already learned earlier, there is an old adage that frames engaging the disengaged: "Before they will come to you, you must go to them." Home visits, when implemented comprehensively and with fidelity to a relational home visit model, deliver strong, measurable results.

Programs that provide time and funding for teachers to visit students and families on their own turf are a way for teachers to learn more about their students, get families more involved in their children's education, and bridge cultural gaps that may be in place between student and teacher. Teachers who participate in home visits report them having a lasting effect on their own attitudes and biases, the child, the family, and parent–teacher communication.

Teachers' visits to students' homes can take many forms. The visitation approach might vary from school to school and from teacher to teacher. The approach might also depend on the funding source. In some schools, teachers prefer to travel in pairs to their visits; they feel more comfortable that way, and sometimes teachers need a translator in order to communicate with a child's parents. Pairing up also gives teachers the opportunity to reflect together on what they learned from the experience and how they can apply that learning in the classroom. Other teachers visit one-on-one with parents. Some interact with the child and the parents. They bring along learning activities for the child that also involve a parent's participation. Visits can last anywhere from thirty to ninety minutes, depending on the teacher and the activities. In any case, the visit should be focused on developing and deepening the relationship between teachers, families, and children.

Arranging the visits can require some creative scheduling. Teachers report that sometimes it can be a challenge to find a mutually agreeable time for a home visit. Some teachers go to the workplace of the parent if the parent is not able to be home during the day or early evening. Providing teachers with tools that prepare them to call families to make the first contact can be a way to support and encourage more teachers to take this first step. Many teachers who have started home visits report that they are actually surprised that families are more willing and interested in connecting outside of school than they first expected.

Some teachers report they were uncomfortable at first with the idea of visiting their students' homes, but most of those discomforts seem to dissipate once the actual visits begin. Teachers find that parents are typically very warm and enthusiastic about welcoming them into their homes. If parents are uncomfortable with the idea of a home visit, they are invited to meet the teacher at school or at another location. Enabling parents to become more involved in their child's education by opening their homes to teacher visits has brought positive results to many schools and teachers who have tried it.

One note of caution: While teachers who participate in home visits love them, it is wise to set them up for success with the proper professional development. Home visits benefit from skill and knowledge on the part of the teacher and the administration to implement a successful program. Effective programs prepare teachers to form a relationship, bring what they've learned back to the classroom, and apply it to the child's academic progress. Strategies for getting started with home visits, from making the first call to families to debriefing and incorporating the learning into professional practice, are important professional development opportunities for teachers and schools.

Parent Teacher Home Visits (PTHV) is one of the most successful training models for teachers to prepare for effective home visits. This model is a departure from typical assessment or disciplinary home visit programs and is specifically designed for teachers and parents to come together as equal partners, building trust, accountability, and cultural respect. PTHV was founded as a way to fundamentally shift relationships between families and teachers from mutual blame to mutual trust. These relationships allow both teachers and parents to discover and challenge their assumptions about each other, promote equity, and honor the wisdom and assets that each brings to educating children.

This isn't merely a feel-good model. A rigorous study across a variety of social and geographic contexts demonstrated the measurable impacts that the PTHV model has had on students, families, and teachers. This research, conducted by RTI International (McKnight, Venkateswaran, Laird, Robles, & Shalev, 2017) and Johns Hopkins University (Sheldon & Jung, 2018) found that

- families become more confident in communicating with educators about students' needs,
- educators shift from deficit-based to asset-based beliefs and actions toward families and students,
- the PTHV model aligns with research-backed strategies to reduce implicit bias among both teachers and parents, and that
- schoolwide odds of students scoring proficient on English Language Arts (ELA) tests increased by 35 percent and students' likelihood of being chronically absent decreased

by 22 percent—*whether individual students received a home visit or not* (for schools that implemented the PTHV model with at least 10 percent of their student population).

PTHV's 3-hour introductory home visit training module prepares teachers and other educators to put the PTHV model into practice in their schools and classrooms. Facilitated by teams that include both parents and teachers, the training reviews the core elements of the PTHV model, allows educators to practice some of the steps to start home visits, and helps teachers identify and troubleshoot potential barriers to doing home visits.

QUICK TIP
Professional Development for Home Visits

The Parent Teacher Home Visit Project website has resources regarding effective home visits and contact information for its affiliates in over 17 states. Visit its site at http://www.pthvp.org

WORKING WITH FAMILIES WITH LIMITED ENGLISH PROFICIENCY

Questions about engaging the hard-to-reach family can quickly turn to the challenges associated with families with limited English proficiency. The basic strategies listed above are universal and can be applied with any category of disengaged family. However, there are factors to consider and specific strategies to employ to improve relationships with families with limited English proficiency. Creativity in engaging these families can produce rewarding results (Mapp, Carver, & Lander, 2017).

Family engagement in the United States is vastly different than family engagement in other countries. In some countries, the concept is completely foreign. The school is an extension of the state government, and parents play no role in the education of their children. Upon arrival to the United States, these families are suddenly faced with our family engagement expectations, which they simply do not understand. Often, when families stay away and do not respond to schools, they are doing what they believe to be correct and expected. Educators must exercise patience when establishing these relationships.

Even though we all desire to communicate and connect with families who do not speak English or do not speak or understand it well, it can be a daunting proposition due to lack of fluency in English as well as families' lack of understanding of expectations, which can cause disengagement from the onset (Grant & Ray, 2019). As was discussed in Chapter 3, fear is a tremendous motivator for disengagement, and families for whom English is a second language have fears about misunderstanding, losing face with the school, or the delivery of bad news.

It should come as no surprise that the first principle to apply in working with these families has its roots in culture. Exploring, learning, and valuing family beliefs are important foundations when working with families with limited English proficiency. The more we can learn about and value the customs of particular cultures, the greater the likelihood that we can create relationships built on respect and trust. It is also important to note that families for whom English is not a first language may be very interested in engaging with their children's school experiences (Zacarian, 2011). Using antibias or prodiversity approaches to review all documents, correspondences, and communications can go a long way to building trusting relationships with families (Gonzalez-Mena, 2014).

Often, schools run up against families' expectation barriers based on a number of factors. For example, families may feel judged by their occupation, economic status, and social group. Their self-esteem may be low because of assimilation issues with regard to their new culture. Their children adapt to American customs far faster than their families. Understand that many first-generation immigrant families are experiencing a kind of culture shock upon which schooling adds another dimension.

Communication is a key factor in working with families with limited English proficiency. Understand the differences between formal and informal communication and the differences in perception of face-to-face conversations and telephone conversations of the cultures with which you are working. In most cases, community leaders can help educators understand the nuances of culture and custom and how to apply the best communication methods available. Adopting a process for bilingual volunteers, usually a parent or community member, can enhance communication by having a liaison that can explain practices, establish phone chains for same-language families, help with registration of new students, and build teacher capacity for understanding cultural nuances of different families (Grant & Ray, 2019).

Families will feel more comfortable in connecting with a school if orientation sessions in native languages are provided for families. Allowing families to form parent groups based on culture and language may seem antithetical to our inclusive philosophy; however, research shows that these groups actually help families acclimate to the culture of the school and make the transition to established school groups smoother and more successful.

Strategies for Working With Non-English or Limited-English-Speaking Families

- Learn a few phrases in the major languages.
- When calling home, find a translator to assist you.
- Believe that families wish to be engaged with their children's education.
- Conduct home visits. Learn about a family's culture first. Take an interest in them, their customs, their dreams, and their desires.
- Build relationships with parents and use them as translators.
- Locate community organizations that can help with translation or connecting with families (churches, community agencies, etc.).
- Use simultaneous translation equipment for school events.
- Schedule events for specific families. Make presentations in their native language.
- Look for technology/social media tools that can translate to and from different languages.

ENGAGING WITH FAMILIES OF CHILDREN WITH SPECIAL NEEDS

Most of the time, we desire tangible evidence of family engagement. We want to know that families participate in events we host or that they have reviewed information we send to them. The evidence produced from these kinds of interactions helps us to know that our efforts are assisting with improved communication and, perhaps more importantly, the self-efficacy of families.

Families of children with special needs often devote a great deal more time to ensuring the success of their children, both in and out of school. Engaging the families of children with special needs provides a unique set of challenges. Between individualized education program (IEP) meetings, required accommodations to student learning plans, the requirement to inform families of their due process rights, and so forth, there is a significant amount of engagement already inherent in the relationship. Or is there?

Interestingly, with all of these opportunities for interaction, families of students with special needs report less interaction with schools because of the perceived barriers in engagement (Rodriguez, Blatz, & Elbaum, 2014). Even though there is often more established contact between families of students with special needs and schools, levels of family engagement, when compared to general education students, remained about the same (Derubetis & Yanok, 1989). Deslandes and colleagues (1999) suggest that families with children with special needs may hold the perception that they are less likely, capable, or able to have an impact on their child's academic life and, as such, tend to be less engaged.

Different Degrees of Family Engagement for Families of Children With Special Needs

In their study, Rodriguez, Blatz, and Elbaum (2014) discovered themes within the context of the engagement of families of children with special needs. For example, families that spoke positively about the school's ability and desire to collaborate frequently mentioned the accessibility of teachers and, more importantly, that teachers and families could openly disagree without being disagreeable. Families who spoke unfavorably about this theme pointed to the rigidity of staff members and the need to go higher up the chain of command to resolve issues.

Families of children with special needs are very much in tune with the academic progress of their children and the extent to which the school provides the necessary support for success. Properly trained teachers, competency, and choice were all ideas presented by families who spoke favorably about their child's school and the progress their child was making. The death knell, it seems, is the perception of families that some teachers were "unfamiliar with their children's IEP" (Rodriguez et al., 2014, p. 87).

Families of students with special needs believe that it is important for them to be persistent with regard to the services their children need. Families of children with special needs will take initiative and action regardless or in spite of a school's failure to engage them. These families desire the school to facilitate their engagement in the education of their children (Rodriguez et al., 2014).

Families of children with special needs identify three characteristics of communications they deem positive: (1) communication that occurs regularly, (2) communication that is focused on the child's progress, and (3) communication that allows a variety of methods of interaction (Rodriguez et al., 2014). Families often speak of differences from year to year with regard to changes in personnel at school. The inconsistency from teacher to teacher translates into parental concern on the part of the school to care for their children. Family views of schools' efforts to engage them are directly connected to their views of the quality of the education and services that are provided to their children.

Consider this scenario: A parent or family member arrives at an IEP meeting. She walks into the meeting and sees numerous people seated around a table—a teacher, the special education teacher, a counselor, a psychologist, an administrator, and, depending on the specific plan, other types of support staff. The parent is told what will occur, and then, after everyone speaks at her, she is asked to sign a form about the IEP for her child. If she disagrees with the IEP or refuses to sign it, a sheet of paper with her rights is handed to her.

Perhaps this example is exaggerated; perhaps it is not. The processes associated with students with special needs can be daunting to families. It's no wonder that the level of family engagement seems to be somewhat extreme—either extremely involved with advocates and lawyers or extremely disengaged with educational processes designed to improve student learning. Brinckerhoff and Vincent (1986) suggested in their research that IEP processes were not good examples of two-way communication.

Families of children with special needs support and work with their children every moment the children are not in school. Depending on the disability, it can be both daunting and exhausting for these families. More often than not, when contacted by the school, they receive negative information and rarely perceive that they are treated as equal partners in the education of their children. All of this mixed together spells disaster for engaging all of these families.

The answers to these issues are many and perhaps could be a book by themselves. In the quest to keep it simple, let's look at some high-return ideas to improve the engagement of families of children with special needs:

- Provide parent/staff training in writing developmental assessments: When assessing a child's developmental level, it will be beneficial to have parents understand how these processes occur.
- Promote professional development for teachers in how to participate in a meeting and how to establish priorities.
- Create welcoming physical environments in meeting rooms and special education areas.
- Assign a parent liaison to meet and greet families, understand their needs and expectations, explain to families what to expect, and reinforce to families that the school is interested in their views.

CASE STUDY: JONATHAN AND THE SELF-CONTAINED ENGLISH CLASS

Elizabeth Wood is a seasoned special education teacher and, by all accounts, one of the finest teachers at R. D. Lynch High School. Both the administration and her colleagues respect the work that she does and the knowledge that she brings to educating children with special needs. Elizabeth embraces students with disabilities and is the one who always offers to take on the most challenging teaching assignments. Her success rate in student learning is unmatched.

Jonathan Downey has been assigned to Elizabeth's self-contained English 9 class. There are nine students in the classroom and all of them are challenged with various behavioral disorders. Jonathan has a history of school failure and a pattern of disruptive behavior in school. His school experiences have been negative almost since the day he entered kindergarten. Jonathan's mother, Valerie, is committed to Jonathan's success and has been an engaged parent and a champion for her son, despite her own adverse experiences in school. She has experienced her share of setbacks and issues with Jonathan and is adept at navigating school bureaucracy to advocate for her son.

Prior to the first day of class, Elizabeth contacted the families of each of the nine students in her self-contained classroom. She introduced herself and had the simple goal of establishing a positive relationship with the families of the students in her classes. Skeptical of the call, Valerie quizzed Elizabeth about classroom procedures and expectations. Elizabeth skillfully answered the questions but kept the focus on the need to build a trusting relationship between school and home.

Jonathan arrived to class on the first day exhibiting the behaviors that had caused him issues for most of his education. He behaved immaturely and was unable to control his outbursts in class. He was not a danger to his classmates but was clearly disruptive to the learning environment for himself and others. Elizabeth's first assignment was for each of the students to create an autobiographical collage to share with the class. Elizabeth faced a significant challenge in getting Jonathan to focus on the assignment; however, she was able to learn from the pictures he chose that Jonathan was an avid basketball fan and enjoyed computers.

After a few days of disruptive behavior, Elizabeth called Valerie again. In the conversation, Elizabeth did not mention the poor classroom behaviors exhibited by Jonathan but rather focused on what she had learned about Jonathan's learning style and the environment in which she believed he would flourish. Elizabeth shared with Valerie the things she would do to support Jonathan in class. Valerie waited for the negative comments about her son, but they never came.

Each week, the calls were the same. Elizabeth reached out to Valerie to inform her of the progress Jonathan was making, even though his behaviors and outbursts were continuing. Jonathan would arrive home and his mother would inform him that Ms. Wood called her. Fearing the worst, Jonathan would begin to defend himself only to find out that Ms. Wood had nothing but praise for the progress Jonathan was making.

After five weeks of school, Jonathan's behavior in class markedly improved. He was attentive and significantly less disruptive. He started to emerge as a class leader and even learned to raise his hand instead of blurting out answers or off-task comments. Elizabeth never wrote a referral for Jonathan's behavior. She simply continued to keep lines of communication open with Jonathan's mother and continued to reward and praise the behavior that was expected in her classroom.

During a conference at the end of the nine-week grading period, Valerie commented to Elizabeth that for the first time in her experience with the school system, Jonathan was not being disciplined or suspended from class. She shared that Jonathan still seemed to have problems in other classes that resulted in disciplinary interventions and loss of instructional time that would never be recovered. Elizabeth worked with Valerie on strategies to help Jonathan be as successful in other classrooms as he was in English 9. Valerie ended the conversation by saying, "Jonathan just adores you . . . and so do I. Thank you for believing in my son."

Questions for Discussion

1. Can you think of situations that you have been in where students similar to Jonathan have created a difficult classroom environment? How did you react?

2. Why do you think that Elizabeth never mentioned the difficulties she was experiencing in class with regard to Jonathan's behaviors?

3. What do you think Elizabeth deems most important when working with a student like Jonathan?

4. What was Elizabeth's goal in reaching out to Valerie?

5. Why do you think Jonathan's behaviors improved in Elizabeth's class but did not improve in other classes?

6. Thinking about the Five Simple Principles, which were at work to help Jonathan be successful?

Family Engagement Advisory Councils

Family engagement advisory councils are a great way to garner input and ensure family voice in school planning and effective engagement. These groups can be effective at the building, district, regional, and even state level.

Kirsten Baesler, North Dakota State Superintendent of Public Instruction, recognized the need to improve the ability of all schools to engage families. As part of a multiyear, multifaceted plan, Baesler created the Family Engagement Cabinet and invited families from all regions of the state to participate in the cabinet. The Family Engagement Cabinet provides an outlet for family members to share experiences in education and advocate for changes they'd like to see be made. The Family Engagement Cabinet assists the department in facilitating partnerships and collaboration with families and schools.

To learn more about the North Dakota Family Engagement Cabinet, visit the State Department of Public Instruction website at www.nd.gov/dpi

THE ROLE OF FEAR AND TRUST IN RELATIONSHIPS WITH FAMILIES

There can be no relationship without trust. Often, disengaged families are distrusting of the school system (see Chapter 3). Either their children have had negative experiences or they hearken back to their own school experiences that planted the seeds of mistrust years before their own children attended school.

Whether or not there was ever a time when families unconditionally trusted teachers and educators is hard to say. What is easier to say is that there is a need in today's society to work toward building trust between home and school. We simply live in a different world, a world that is dominated by anonymity and insecurity. Building trusting relationships with every family will go a long way to negate the ills we face.

What actions promote distrust between schools and families? The following lists are by no means exclusive. The items below represent common actions that promote distrust between schools and families.

School Actions That Can Promote Mistrust

- Inaccurate information, out-of-date information, or lack of information on school websites or in other forms of communication.

- Teacher websites that are unused or not updated. Many schools have added teacher websites as another means to promote communication. Unfortunately, with inconsistent use, these items work almost in the opposite fashion than intended.
- Lack of follow-through (promises not kept, mistakes in grading left unattended, important information not corrected, etc.).
- Practices and procedures that are limiting to families (no-visit policies, no volunteers needed, etc.).
- Discipline issues. A lack of understanding, perceived unfairness, or disagreement with discipline can play a significant role in parental mistrust of schools.
- Lack of involvement in decisions. School districts, schools, and classrooms often make decisions without involving or engaging stakeholders in the process.

Parental Actions That Promote Mistrust

- Sporadic attendance patterns of children. Educators become skeptical and suspicious of families where there are attendance issues. Educators tend to believe it is the parents' responsibility for the child to attend school.
- Defensive posture toward school actions. Some parents continuously defend the actions of their children and hold the school accountable for all situations.
- Lack of response to school-initiated communication. School personnel quickly become skeptical of parents when letters or emails go unanswered or phone calls are not returned.
- Defensive or threatening responses to school communication.
- Nonattendance to school functions designed for parents and families. Many families do not attend school functions or conferences, leaving a great deal of doubt in the minds of educators as to their commitment to their children's learning.
- Aggressive actions toward the school. Whether storming the main office and demanding an audience with the principal, public displays of aggression in meetings or assemblies, or sending tersely worded emails, aggressive behavior by parents often leads to distrustful relationships.

Questions for Discussion

1. Have any of the items in the lists above ever happened in your school?

2. Can you think of other actions or behaviors that promote mistrust?

3. What strategies can we employ to reduce these issues and thus build more trusting relationships with every family?

CASE STUDIES: WHAT COULD HAVE BEEN DONE DIFFERENTLY?

Each of these three case studies is a short vignette designed to help you think through the process of building relationships and trust with every family. The purpose of reading the studies and reflecting on the questions is not to determine right or wrong but to determine a different process that may lead to a different outcome—hopefully one that builds trusting relationships. For each of the case studies, answer the following questions:

1. What could the school personnel have done to help this situation end better for all involved?

2. What could the parent(s) have done to help this situation end better for all involved?

3. What kind of relationship do you think the parents had with the school before the issue? What do you think will happen to the relationship now that the issue has occurred?

4. Why did the circumstances happen the way they did? What insights do you have into the culture of the school in each of the studies?

5. What role does trust play in the case study?

Case Study #1: The Project

A middle school teacher designed a four-week project for students to complete. The project had a deadline, and the teacher made it clear to students there would be no negotiation: Late or missing assignments would be treated with a significantly reduced grade. On the day of the assignment, a student, Susan, turned it in as instructed. She vividly recalls handing the assignment to the teacher. Susan is an excellent student with good grades and no behavior issues at school.

The next day, the teacher asked Susan where her assignment was. Susan indicated she had handed it in. The teacher refuted Susan's claim and told her, "If you handed it in, I would have it." Susan went home upset and explained the issue to her parents. Both of her parents escorted her to school the next morning in hopes that they could speak to the teacher and sort it out.

Susan's parents were told the teacher was unavailable, and they were going to have to speak to the principal. They agreed. After waiting about fifteen minutes, they were ushered into the principal's office. They explained the situation to the principal. The principal indicated that he was not going to step into the situation. The teacher had made the rules clear and the rules were not followed. He then indicated that it was common for students who did not finish assignments to say they had handed them in. The conversation became heated, and Susan's parents left very upset, vowing to call the superintendent's office.

Case Study #2: The Fight

Joey and his friend Alan had a falling out. The next day during lunch, Joey and Alan met up again. This time, Joey pushed Alan and Alan fell to the ground. Joey tried to punch Alan, but another student intervened. Alan did not strike Joey but did antagonize him, causing Joey to become angry.

The assistant principal suspended both boys from school for three days for fighting. Joey's parents did not contest the discipline. Alan's parents, however, believed that because Alan did not strike Joey back or hit Joey first, Alan should be spared the suspension. The school cited their student discipline code and indicated that Alan provoked the fight with his words. Further, the assistant principal indicated that there was no time to "sort out who did what to whom"; thus, the suspension stood. Alan's parents were upset and headed to their attorney's office.

Case Study #3: The School Visit

John was an elementary school student. John's mother speaks little English and, even though she attends all of his conferences and meetings, she does not clearly understand all that is being presented to her. Because she came to this country to do the best she could for her children, she is always compliant and never argues with or questions the school. In her country, one does not question the school.

John began to decline academically and behaviorally. John's mother understood that her son was having problems in school but didn't know what to do to help him. John also became more problematic at home. John's mother, being a single parent and raising three children, was at her wit's end with John and decided to go to the school for help.

When she arrived, she found the doors of the school locked. The sign with the instructions to get into the school was in English, and she could not understand how to enter the school. She banged on the door until someone passing by let her into the school. She asked for help in her native language, but the person opening the door shrugged his shoulders in an "I do not know" gesture and continued to walk toward his destination.

John's mother walked into the first office she saw, which happened to be the security office. There, she tried to explain her situation to a woman behind the desk. The woman indicated that she did not understand and motioned John's mother to follow her. The woman led her to the main office and motioned for her to sit down. She told the office secretary that she didn't understand what John's mother's problem was, and it would be better if someone in the main office talked with her. The secretary and the woman from security talked for a few more minutes about unrelated matters while John's mother waited in her seat.

About twenty minutes went by, and the principal approached John's mother and extended his hand to greet her. She said, "Hello." The principal only spoke English and could only say in his second language that he did not speak the second language. John's mother tried to share her concerns about John, but the communication between the principal and John's mother was poor. John's mother began to cry. The principal indicated that John was a good boy and was doing fine in school. John's mother thanked the principal for his time and left the school. She cried uncontrollably after exiting the school.

IDEAS TO PROMOTE TRUSTING RELATIONSHIPS BETWEEN SCHOOLS AND EVERY FAMILY

Henderson and colleagues (2007) make the following point about school–family relationships: "When school staff construct caring and trustful relationships with parents, treating parents as partners in their children's education, parents are far more likely to become involved and stay involved" (p. 47). Educators instinctively know that relationships are important but struggle to figure out ways to actually make these relationships work.

Much of the information on building relationships centers on making schools welcoming to families. Later in this chapter, we'll explore the ideas of welcoming environments more closely. First, let's test what you believe about engaging every family.

Determine Whether or Not You Concur With the Following Statements	Agree or Disagree?
1. Every family, regardless of their station in life, can make a contribution toward their children's education.	

2. Parents should have a voice in the education of their children.

3. Parents should have a voice in selecting teachers for their children.

4. It is important to include difficult parents in school decisions.

5. Respecting parental points of view is essential to successfully educating their children.

6. It is important to build a relationship with every family.

7. I fear talking with some families.

8. Parents should be allowed to visit classrooms anytime they wish.

9. Helping parents guide their children's learning is as important as teaching the children.

10. Every family has value.

Each of the statements above reflects a value statement that supports the ideas presented in Principle #2 regarding the importance of building relationships. There is no sliding scale to determine where your attitude is regarding effectively building relationships with families. For those statements with which you disagree, spend some time reflecting on why. Discuss these ideas with colleagues. Remember, what we believe and value shapes our attitudes and assumptions. As our actions and thoughts change, so does the culture of our organization.

Patterson, Grenny, McMillan, and Switzler (2012) indicate that a crucial conversation is one that can best be described as any day-to-day conversation in which the outcome is critical or crucial to long-term success. A key ingredient in building relationships with families is understanding the importance of communication and conversations that are open, honest, and a true exchange of ideas. One-sided conversations, talking without listening, talking down to parents, or simply putting everything in an email are surefire ways either to destroy relationships or never build them in the first place.

A significant challenge to building relationships is one-way communication flow. Schools that send things home and do not invite return information, comments, or engagement chip away at the very foundation of needed relationships. (The ideas presented in "The Weekly Folder" section in Chapter 8 combat this problem too!)

Teachers often report a fear of building relationships with every family. Most of the time, this fear is built upon experiences. If a teacher's interactions with families are largely negative, then it stands to reason that their opinions of building relationships and engaging with families will also be negative.

The solution lies in devoting some professional development time to working effectively with families and communication training. In order to do so, however, we must see the connection between engaging every family and student learning outcomes. We must value relationships with families as an express conduit to improved academic performance in all children.

We often mistake silence for acceptance and negative responses or dialogue as a sign of disagreement. Actually, the reverse is also true. Silence could very well speak to an individual's frustration with a system and their loss of hope in terms of believing they can effect any positive change. A disagreeable person who is questioning or arguing does not necessarily mean the person disagrees but rather is seeking clarification the best way they know how. Dialogue promotes understanding and support.

THE WELCOMING ENVIRONMENT OF SCHOOLS

One does not have to look far to find a large amount of literature devoted to the notion of a welcoming environment in schools. Often, this concept is the easiest for schools to check off their to-do lists: placing welcome signs, directional signs, and so forth. While these efforts are certainly important to the welcoming environment of schools, it is the attitude of the personnel within the school that will either support a welcoming environment or clearly send messages to parents that welcoming signs are merely window dressing.

A common complaint among families is a lack of a welcoming environment of their child's school. They report feeling as if they are imposing or interrupting when they visit the school. Because of the need for increased security, they often are buzzed into the school and questioned about the reason for their visit. In larger, more complex schools, finding the correct door (usually only one is unlocked, if any) and finding their way once inside the building can be daunting. Even though they appreciate the attention to safety and security, once inside, they are somewhat intimidated not only by the complexity of an environment that seems foreign to them but also by a less-than-warm reception from school employees.

ACTIVITY
Getting to the Destination

Here is a simple activity that not only can underscore the experiences families have when arriving to our schools but can actually begin to create an inventory of needs to make the school more welcoming.

Go outside and move to the edge of the school property. Pretend that you have never been to the school before. Ask yourself: Can I get where I want to go? Are the entrances clearly marked? Are there signs directing me to the office or guest area? Are there people who can assist? As a guest who has never been to the school before, can I find my way to my destination?

Now, repeat the process above, only this time, in addition to pretending that you have never been to the school before, also pretend that you neither speak nor understand English. Now, ask yourself the same question again: Can I get to where I want to go?

Taking a few minutes to participate in this activity can completely change your perceptions of the welcoming environment of your school and help you begin to change those systems that will ultimately help to engage every family.

CUSTOMER SERVICE

Like it or not, public education is quickly becoming a commodity. For a very long time, maybe since the inception of public schools, educators have not seen themselves as having to convince customers of the quality of their product. Today, that has all changed. With the rise of alternatives to the public school setting, the way we think, behave, market, and conduct our business will define our future success.

Consider for a moment the rapid development of online learning platforms. In the last few years, the use of online learning has skyrocketed. An increasing number of states now require students to have at least one online learning experience as a component of successful graduation, and online high schools are here now. Online learning uses resources and teachers very differently and is already significantly altering everything from school scheduling to teacher contracts. There are many who note that the advent of online learning can save money traditionally devoted to teacher salaries. In effect, it could put us out of business, if some get their way.

Every business in the private sector understands the basic tenets of doing business: customer requirements. Find out what the needs of the customer are and then provide the product or solution to meet the customer's needs. The better the company and product, the more likely the sale. Educators would be well served to adopt this philosophy of thinking.

As important as customer requirements are, so is customer service. The service that we provide before, during, and after the "sale" of our product will be strategic in our efforts to maintain a healthy market share. There are some basic principles of customer service that are important to understand and incorporate into all we do.

First and foremost, we must be good at what we do. Greeting people warmly and with a genuine smile and caring attitude is important, but being good at what we do is essential, otherwise we are not providing the kind of service expected by our customer. We must model excellence, always.

Follow-through and trustworthiness are essential to quality services. We need to do what we say we will do and always try to exceed the expectations of our customers. Simple things, such as making and returning phone calls in a timely fashion, pay huge dividends with families. Scheduling meetings at a convenient time for families and ensuring that we are in attendance may seem like a small token, but the message these efforts send is a resounding "We care."

Our students and their families must always feel respected and well cared for. Each family, regardless of their background or preconceived notion, must instinctively sense our desire to make an important personal connection with them, to value their role in the educational partnership, and to support the notion that they are important.

> If all families truly had a choice in the schools to which they would send their children, would they choose yours?

Let's ask this important question again: If all families truly had a choice in the schools to which they would send their children, would they choose yours? In other words, what differentiates your school from other schools and options that are and increasingly will be open to families? Could placing a high value on family relationships set you apart from your competition? How far beyond common expectations are you willing to go in order to gain and keep customers?

Every day, we have problems and challenges in our business. We are a people business, and most of what we do centers on the interaction of humans. We cannot avoid the daily challenges that come with educating children. However, how we interact with our customer, how we handle and respond to the challenges we face, and the consistency with which we develop relationships with families will ultimately dictate our success.

Basic Customer Service Tips to Get You Started

Creating and sustaining a welcoming environment in your school is probably the lowest-hanging fruit with regard to engaging every family. It is simple, doesn't cost any money, and the implementation can begin tomorrow. Following are a couple of ideas to get you going.

The Ten-Second Rule. When someone enters your school or office, do not let him or her wait for more than ten seconds before they are acknowledged. Even a "Thank you for coming today. Please be patient, I'll be with you in a few minutes," is better than nothing or a stiff "Just a minute."

The Telephone Answer. Yes, there is most definitely something important in how the telephone is consistently answered in your school. Create a greeting to which everyone will subscribe. "It's a great day at [School Name]. My name is _____. How can I help you?" Try it. It works. The attitude people have toward your organization will improve.

The Warm Transfer. There is nothing more annoying to any of us than calling an organization, explaining our question or concern, and then being transferred to another person, only to start our story over again. The warm transfer is an old business technique that requires the caller to explain their concern, question, or problem once. If the person answering the phone cannot help, they keep the caller on the line, secure the person who can help, then put the caller and the new person together on the line. The dialogue can be as simple as this: "Mr. Jones, I have John on the line and I have explained your concern to him. He is going to take it from here, because he is the person who can help you. Is there anything else I can do for you today? Thank you for calling." This little technique pays huge dividends to organizations wishing to improve perception and customer loyalty.

Administrator Check-Ins. Every day, schools get calls from families with concerns or questions. Keep a log of those calls. At the end of a week, the administrator should pick two or three of those calls and call the parent or family member who originally called with a concern. The administrator can simply ask if the problem was resolved or not and reinforce to the parent the school or district commitment to resolving conflicts. A follow-up call from the head of the organization will leave a lasting, positive impression, regardless of the outcome of the original concern.

A Simple Thank You. As education becomes more and more of a commodity, try this idea. It could very well alter the trajectory of your success. Have every member of the organization make a phone call to a parent or family member for no other reason than to say this: "I wanted to call today to let you know how much I enjoy having your son/daughter in my classroom. We value your child and you. Thank you for choosing to attend [school/district]." The purpose of the call is nothing more than to reinforce that you do not take a parent's choice for granted. Start this. It will make a difference.

A Simple and Effective Welcome. More and more businesses are providing staff members to greet and welcome customers. From saying hello, handing you a shopping cart, or providing you with a list of the daily specials, the use of greeters is seen as an effective way to make customers feel welcome. Different companies have different techniques, from the simple to the attention grabbing. One of the most notable is the greeting one gets upon arriving to Moe's Southwestern Grill. When the door opens, every employee behind the counter stops whatever they are doing and yells, "Welcome to Moe's!" They are consistent from customer to customer and restaurant to restaurant. Everyone who goes to Moe's knows of this famous welcoming greeting. The next time you find yourself near a Moe's, try stopping by! How do you welcome guests to your school?

WELCOMING EVERY FAMILY

The chart below offers you an opportunity to consider those items known to increase the welcoming environments of schools. The chart acts as an action plan of sorts to determine what is in place and what needs to be improved. Get a group of colleagues together to review the chart. Then, ask families and students their opinions as well. Sometimes our perceptions as educators are very different from those of the families and students we serve.

How Can We Increase the Welcoming Environment of Our School?

Questions for Consideration	Present Conditions	Necessary or Desired Outcomes	Things to Be Done to Achieve Desired Outcomes	Notes, Questions, etc.
Do your school entrances welcome every family?				

Are entrances clearly marked and understandable by all?				
Are security measures clearly posted and communicated to all families?				
Are your faculty, student, and community parking spots well marked and recognized by all?				
Is handicapped parking clearly marked?				
Are handicapped entrances accessible and clearly marked?				
Are the parking lots and entrances well lit?				
If graffiti appears at your school, is it promptly removed?				
Is the interior of your school clean and well kept?				
Do families perceive your school as being safe?				
Does your school have a standing school beautification committee?				
Does your school building contain understandable directional signs?				

(Continued)

(Continued)

Questions for Consideration	Present Conditions	Necessary or Desired Outcomes	Things to Be Done to Achieve Desired Outcomes	Notes, Questions, etc.
Is there a comfortable reception area for families?				
Does your school have a parent/family center?				
Is your school administration approachable for all families?				
Does your school provide translation services for families who do not speak English?				
Must families ask for translation or is the service evident upon arrival?				
Does your school minimize the use of educational jargon?				
Do staff members treat families courteously?				
Does your school have an engaging website?				
Does your school use social media tools to communicate and welcome families?				

Source: Used with permission of Dr. Joni Samples, Family Friendly Schools. The chart is available for download at **http://www.drsteveconstantino.com**

QUICK TIP
Helping Everyone Feel Welcome

For guests who do not speak English, it is often cumbersome and embarrassing to ask for translation. In many cases, the need to ask for translation deters non-English-speaking guests from coming to school. There are two easy solutions to this: (1) Find volunteers who speak the native language(s) in your school and make them a button that says "I speak [language]" in the native language. Upon entering, a non-English-speaking guest is put at ease. (2) If volunteers are not available, place a decal or placard in the window or door of the entrances to the schools with the same message as above. Guests will know that someone speaks their language. These are two simple tips that go a long way toward establishing welcoming environments for everyone!

ISSUES AND SOLUTIONS IN COMMUNICATING WITH FAMILIES

Very little professional development time, if any at all, is devoted to helping teachers communicate with every family. The following section is designed to take issues and challenges in communicating with every family and provide practical solutions that can be implemented in a very simple fashion.

Issues in communication seem to be the ones that can anger both teachers and families and create tension, which hinders positive relationship building. Here are some tips and ideas to improve communication in relationships:

1. *Don't make major changes.* Don't make major instructional or curricular changes without either family input or notice. Changes to calendars, meetings, planned activities, and so forth without sufficient notice or involvement lead to mistrust and animosity.

2. *Share information in a timely fashion.* The more quickly and thoroughly information is shared with families, the less likely families will be angry, rumors will swirl, and misconceptions will form.

3. *No surprises.* We don't like surprises. Neither do families.

4. *Don't make promises you can't keep.* If you indicate to a parent you will do something, then do it. Often, we indicate we will do something or promise to do something and, for a host of reasons, do not follow through. This only breeds mistrust.

5. *Keep in mind the letter of the law and the spirit of the law.* Use common sense with issues that surround children and families. Don't overreach your authority to prove a point or hold your ground on a particular issue. Know the difference between policy and common sense.

6. *Don't label.* Never label parents by marital status, religious affiliation or beliefs, ethnicity, or socioeconomic status.

7. *Don't get defensive.* Remember that most of the messages parents have received over time are perceived to protect teachers and schools without regard to students and their families. Whether true or fair, the perception exists. Defensiveness is natural but unwise and is almost always perceived as guilt.

8. *Consider parents when setting up meetings.* Give parents a say in meeting calendars. Setting dates with no input and without checking for parent availability is unwise.

9. *Identify meeting purposes.* One of the most damaging things we can do to relationships with families is to set meetings with them and not let them know the purpose of the meeting.

10. *Identify physical and verbal barriers.* Using furniture, tables, or room setup to keep parents and school employees separated reinforces the notion that we do not value relationships with every family. Using sarcasm or belligerent or demeaning words or actions is never a good idea, regardless of the situation.

11. *Hold meeting participants to a minimum.* Parents are often overwhelmed when they come to meetings and the room is filled with specialists and support personnel. If it is critical for these people to be at the meeting, contact the parent and let them know who will be at the meeting and their purpose for attending. Put them at ease by assuring them that the meeting will be productive.

12. *Show up.* If you have a scheduled conference or meeting, attend. Don't send an email or a grade sheet in your place.

13. *Don't blame others.* When things don't go exactly right, don't point fingers and blame students, parents, the school,

the administration, or other entities. Describe the challenge and work together to find solutions. It doesn't really matter how the problem started or who started it.

14. *Be trustworthy*. You cannot make people trust you, but you can earn the trust of anyone. Personal and professional behavior that withstands scrutiny and invites confidence goes a long way toward establishing healthy relationships with every family.

15. *Keep an open mind*. Don't prematurely judge people you do not know based on rumors or the comments made by others.

16. *Keep calm*. There are difficult people on the earth. Always remain calm. Remember the old saying, "To change a difficult person, you must first change yourself."

17. *If you are wrong or make a mistake, admit it, apologize for it, and move on*. Trying to avoid responsibility will not end well—for anyone.

18. *Do your homework*. When confronted with a meeting with a difficult or angry parent, find a piece of positive information about the parent, family, or student and use it to ease the tension.

19. *Think about responses*. If you are angered by a parent, use the "wait 24 hours" rule before responding. Never use email and TYPE IN ALL CAPITALS. I call that "e-yelling."

20. *Have a strategy for demands*. When a parent makes a demand that you cannot meet, do not say, "I cannot do that." Simply reiterate the things that you can do. After a few minutes, the strategy will have a calming effect and allow you an opportunity to enlist the parent's help in problem solving.

21. *Remember that anger is a mask for fear.*

22. *Don't do certain things*. Don't do the following: Interrupt. Think about what you are going to say while the parent is talking. Change the subject. Focus on things that cannot be changed. Complain about your own agenda or situation. Embark in silent combat (stare down). Rehearse your answers before you have heard the question. Give advice unless you are asked. Persuade everyone that you are right and they are wrong. Try so hard to be neutral that you show no empathy. Compulsively talk and overexplain. Lie. Let yourself get abused or bullied when sincerely trying to communicate.

CONNECTING COMMUNICATION AND RELATIONSHIPS WITH TECHNOLOGY

Employing strategies that extend relationship-building opportunities beyond the school walls so that every family can substantially contribute to the education of their child is critical to long-term success in engaging every family. While not a replacement for human engagement, technology and the growing impact of social media can play an important role in extending the efforts of school personnel to connect with all families.

Technology is pervasive in American homes and has impacted daily life in a manner that many could not imagine just a few short years ago. Over 95 percent of families report cell phones in their household; 84 percent of children ages use the Internet; and seven in ten Americans use social media to connect with one another, engage with news content, share information, and entertain themselves (Pew Research Center, 2019). And most astonishing, 100 percent of people ages 18–29 own a cell phone. Ninety-eight percent of adults age 30–49 own a cell phone; of those, 89 percent are a smartphone.

In order to use technology carefully and to be considerate of family needs and privacy, there are three distinct attributes that schools should look for when deciding on how to incorporate technology into their family engagement processes (Livingtree, Inc., 2019):

1. The technology should have secure, two-way communication. Private networks and password-protected areas are absolutely essential in ensuring the privacy of students and families when communicating via technology or social media.

2. Mobile access of the technology is essential. With so many people using their cell phone as the first line of communication, any platform that doesn't conform easily to a mobile device is already obsolete.

3. Any platform used to engage with families should have the ability to comprehensively translate into multiple languages. *Comprehensive translation* in this context means that the system can translate from English and then back to English if the family chooses their native language to communicate.

It is advised that a school or district come together and adapt one method or one piece of technology to communicate with families. If there is limited direction from the school or district as to what technology can and should be used, teachers are left to fend for themselves and often will download or use apps and technology that is free to them. This could result in multiple platforms being used in the same district or school, which results in increasing frustration on the part of families trying to find current information. In many cases, families give up; thus, technology becomes a deterrent to engagement.

I cannot begin to list all of the apps and technology platforms that exist and are available to teachers, schools, and districts; nor can I provide a comprehensive comparison and assessment of all of that technology. What is important, however, is that the technology allows for effective engagement rather than merely one-way communication of events, information, or past student performance.

Consider this question: How do you engage someone with something that has already occurred? The simple answer is, you don't. More often than not, school districts have implemented elaborate student information systems that have a family component to them. This family component is often a window or portal for families to stay abreast of their children's grades, behavior, and school attendance, all of which are usually data from the past.

As was already stated in this chapter, a fundamental component of engagement is robust, two-way communication. Families must have the same opportunities to communicate directly with teachers as teachers do with families. Two-way communication promotes trust and that trust can enhance the use of technology as an engaging proposition. Technology that allows school personnel to promote family engagement is far superior to simple communication tools. Platforms that allow teachers to share upcoming learning and include families in the process or promote their active engagement can quickly move a school or district far beyond information sharing.

There is no question that there is and will continue to be a cultural shift with the use of technology. Districts and schools that embrace it in a uniform and systemic manner will find greater impact on student learning due to the inclusion of families in the learning process.

COMMUNICATE EFFECTIVELY AND BUILD RELATIONSHIPS

Description. There is consistent evidence that effective communication and relationship development create environments in the schools that are welcoming, respectful, and conducive to family engagement. The school places an emphasis on effective two-way communication with every family and stakeholder within the learning community and seeks to develop relationships based on mutual trust.

PRINCIPLE #2

Where We Are

Based on the description, discuss and record where you think your school is today as it relates to the principle description.

2.1 The school creates and maintains a welcoming and respectful environment that is inviting, supportive, and encouraging to every family.

Principle 2.1 Assessment

Use this chart to determine your organization's present level of performance.

Practice/Attribute/Condition	Discuss/Reflect/Record the Present Status in Your School
Families are consistently consulted as to the improvement of the environment of the school.	
Leadership has focused personnel and resources on the welcoming aspects of the school.	
New families are welcomed and oriented to the school.	
All families are welcome, and their safety, security, and needs are incorporated into the school environment.	
The school dedicates space for a family center or family-oriented area.	

Professional development focuses on
creating strong relationships between
families and school staff.

Continuous feedback and two-way
communication are hallmarks of the
school.

Use the clarifying statement and the best practice description to help you shape your future
communication and relationships.

Best Practice Description

Families are surveyed annually to determine ways to maintain and improve
the welcoming environment of the building. A standing committee
is in place that continuously monitors and improves the welcoming
environment of the school. Friendly and welcoming signs in multiple
languages are posted at all intersections and points where families and
guests must make a decision about direction.

The safety and security of all families and guests are evident, and
accommodations for guests with disabilities exist. The history and
culture of the school are celebrated with artifacts on display. Greeters
(either staff or volunteers) welcome all families and guests, and
translation is advertised and readily available. A family-oriented and
family-operated program is in place to welcome and orient all new
families to the school.

The school creates a comfortable area for families, such as a family
resource center stocked with books, computers, Internet access, parenting
tips, homework, and curricular information, and offers classes to families
on a multitude of academic topics suggested by families and student
achievement data. Student work adorns all offices and public areas of the
school with explanations of standards and assessments and is rotated
regularly. Pictures of students and staff adorn all areas, giving the school a
sense of home and community. School events celebrate the culture of the
community and are often cross-curricular in nature.

(Continued)

(Continued)

Relationships between teachers and family are evident through collaboration with and encouragement from school staff to be engaged with the school and learning. Professional development is available to further improve interactions between families and teachers. Above all, school staff value the importance of building relationships with all families, regardless of background. The school implements a process to garner continuous feedback on family engagement efforts.

Practices to Be Implemented

2.2 The school employs strategies that extend opportunities to develop relationships beyond the school walls so that every family can substantially contribute to the education of their children.

Principle 2.2 Assessment

Use this chart to determine your organization's present level of performance.

Practice/Attribute/Condition	Discuss/Reflect/Record the Present Status in Your School
Core values and belief statements of the school include the importance of family engagement.	
Numerous and varied opportunities are available and encouraged for families and school staff to come together.	

There is a regular and recurring program of home visits to families.	
The school allows venues for families to share concerns, ideas, and suggestions in a nonthreatening manner.	
Data support the idea that all families feel valued and maintain a sense of belonging at the school.	

Use the clarifying statement and the best practice description to help you shape your future communication and relationships.

Best Practice Description

The school moves beyond traditional satisfaction data to understand patterns of engagement. Data show that families feel a sense of belonging to the school. All relationships with families are child centered. The school has developed a culture or belief statement(s) that supports the notion of building strong relationships with every family. Welcoming behaviors are consistent throughout the school staff.

Customer service goals are established and monitored. To garner a sense of caring, the school has multiple smaller gatherings for classrooms/grade levels to make time between families and staff more meaningful and intimate. Families are recognized and embraced for their contributions, however large or small, and the majority of families feel their efforts are acknowledged and validated.

School personnel accept all families at their station in life and do not hold expectations or build relationships with them based on school-driven ideas. Families feel comfortable expressing their ideas and concerns and are treated in a respectful manner, regardless of the circumstances.

All school staff are committed to home visitations, and the school regularly schedules meetings and events outside of the school, promoting a commitment to continuous outreach. Technology, including the extensive use of social media and other means, allows families access to staff and information; however, the commitment by the school for face-to-face

(Continued)

(Continued)

interactions enhances family confidence in their child's school. Technology does not replace face-to-face contact and the important relationships that result from that direct contact.

Practices to Be Implemented

2.3 The school ensures that healthy, two-way communication is consistently maintained. A sense of caring to truly collaborate with every family exists, as evidenced by numerous mechanisms to allow families to communicate easily and directly with the school.

Principle 2.3 Assessment

Use this chart to determine your organization's present level of performance.

Practice/Attribute/Condition	Discuss/Reflect/Record the Present Status in Your School
Two-way communication is consistent and pervasive among all school staff and every family. Efforts are continually measured and improved.	
Families for whom English is not a first language are included wholly in the school.	

Upcoming learning information as well as details, dates, and activities are shared with every family.

Conferences are attended by a majority of families and are student centered.

Feedback supports the idea that the majority of families give the school high marks in engagement and communication.

Use the clarifying statement and the best practice description to help you shape your future communication and relationships.

Best Practice Description

All staff in the school believe that two-way communication with all families is essential in the learning process. School staff create multiple avenues for two-way communication of learning goals and the ongoing assessment of those goals. Families are equally comfortable in contacting school staff about how they might better support learning goals at home.

Two-way communication is regular, and child-centered strategies for home learning and evidence of success are routinely shared. The school has a mechanism in place to allow teachers to regularly communicate with families for whom English is not a first language. All communication is easily understood and free of educational jargon. Families are routinely given examples and ideas of learning activities that can be accomplished at home that support the standards being taught.

Families have timely access to current grades, assignments, standards, and other academic information that help them support their child(ren). Teachers publish calendars of activities far enough in advance to allow families time to plan. Teachers regularly use telephone, email, texting, teacher web pages, and blogs to share information with families and communicate what is being taught in the classroom. Conferences are inclusive of students when appropriate, are scheduled at mutually

(Continued)

(Continued)

convenient times, and focus on enhancing learning rather than deficit behaviors.

Conferences are student centered, with the student participating. Home visits by all staff reinforce the school's commitment to families and learning and reinforce family confidence in their child's progress. The school solicits information on the best ways to communicate and uses those data to improve all forms of two-way communication. Families consistently report high satisfaction with the communication with their child's teacher, the school, and the school district. The school uses the feedback data to set new targets and improve systems.

Practices to Be Implemented

CHAPTER 8

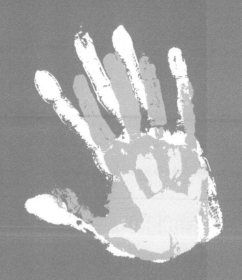

Principle #3
Build Family Efficacy

Self-belief does not necessarily ensure success, but self-disbelief assuredly spawns failure.

—Albert Bandura (1997, p. 77)

Families that believe they can make a positive difference in their children's educational lives are said to have a high level of efficacy.

Build Family Efficacy

3

Parental efficacy simply means that one possesses skills, abilities, and resources to parent effectively and to improve the family's school and community or they are empowered to produce a positive effect on their child's educational outcomes. Families with strong efficacy see challenges as opportunities rather than roadblocks and hold high expectations for their children. They maintain a positive outlook on their child's ability to learn and be successful in school. Families with strong efficacy

145

are more likely to be engaged with their children's educational experiences in a variety of ways, all of which support a healthy learning environment in school.

Principle #3

Build Family Efficacy

Description: Families are recognized as essential members of the learning team for each student—their participation is welcomed, valued, and encouraged by the school. The school understands that families are important and influential resources because they know their children best.

3.1 The school makes a conscious effort to educate families in how to play a proactive role in the learning life of their child throughout their child's school career.

3.2 The school is committed to the academic socialization of families and, to that end, develops and deploys strategies that encourage and support family engagement with specific learning in all classrooms.

3.3 Families participate in the development of the student's learning plan, help monitor and assess progress, and provide support for their child's learning.

3.4 Families suggest learning strategies and experiential possibilities and use their local knowledge, personal skills, assets, and networks in ways that support the school's program.

WHAT IS EFFICACY?

The idea of self-efficacy is simple: It refers to the belief that one has the ability or capability to act in ways that will produce whatever outcomes are desired (Bandura, 1997). One can argue that it is human nature to consider potential outcomes of an action before one decides to take the action. The same holds true for family engagement and efficacy. In other words, if we don't see our engagement with something as producing any desirable or different results, the likelihood of our engagement is significantly diminished. The key to effective engagement is to make experiences for families both meaningful and relevant. *Meaningful* and *relevant* are two very important words when engaging every family.

> The key to effective engagement is to make experiences for families both meaningful and relevant.

I can hear your argument: "We offer a lot of things for parents, but they simply don't show up." We have already learned that there are many challenges facing families that either limit their engagement or that have created circumstances for them to be disengaged. Sending a flyer home about an important meeting may or may not resonate with a family. They may not understand how this meeting is relevant to them or their children. But when we take a different approach and personalize activities and explain how the activity will positively impact their child or why this activity is essential to their child's development, we have promoted their efficacy and, over time, their attendance or participation levels will improve.

Efficacy is not about possessing specific skills or knowledge. For example, family engagement with homework in secondary schools tends to wane largely because the parent or family member does not believe they possess the knowledge to assist their child. Efficacy is focused on how the family member approaches a problem or task and accesses needed support, not what knowledge they possess. The sense of efficacy for helping children succeed in school is an important contributor to how and why parents decide to be involved and engaged with their children's learning (Hoover-Dempsey, Walker, & Sandler, 2005).

A parent whose efficacy is supported and developed by the school, for example, is more likely to participate in a workshop so she can help her child with math homework or language skills. The same parent may take a series of classes on understanding the Internet or how to help children find resources on the Internet. Efficacy provides a parent with the belief that her involvement makes a difference to her child and the ultimate learning outcomes of that child. If she doesn't know something or some way to help her child, she will seek out what she needs from the school or some other community service.

Families make decisions about their involvement and engagement in part by thinking about the potential outcomes of that involvement (Hoover-Dempsey et al., 2005). I'm sure all of us can think of an experience that encapsulates the idea stated above. Family members who believe they can make a difference in their children's lives, including their learning life, are important resources for schools. They cannot make a difference if we do not assist them in seeing their value.

Dialogue about school in many homes usually centers on two questions:

1. What did you do in school today?

2. Do you have any homework?

Of course, the answer to the first question is "nothing" and the answer to the second question is "no." Interestingly, when I ask educator audiences if they have asked their own children these two questions, they indicate in the affirmative. If these are the best questions that we as educators can ask our children, what hope do families have that don't know what we know?

What if the process of promoting family efficacy were as simple as ensuring that these two questions were never asked again in any home? What if we could develop a system by which we could leverage the efficacy of families such that they would be true partners in the learning life of their children? Helping families to engage with their children about school on a meaningful and relevant level accomplishes two things: Family efficacy is developed, and families are empowered to engage in the educational lives of their children. In other words, supply them with information that allows them to ask better questions. If we change the questions families ask, we have immediately empowered them to have a role in the education of their children. Empowerment is efficacy. Efficacy is empowerment. However, families cannot ask their children better questions if we do not assist them in understanding what happens in school every day. Telling them what happened last week or last month isn't very helpful in promoting true empowerment.

What if a child walks through the door after school and a parent asks, "What is the order of operations?" or "Show me the quiz that you took in science today" or "Explain longitude and latitude to me." If we could figure out mechanisms to share this type of information with families, conversations between parents and children would change substantially and efficacy would take root. So, how can we do it?

Here is what I know to be true: As educators, we are really good at sending stuff home. We have mastered the art of one-way communication. As is highlighted in the section devoted to changing the weekly folder, sending home information about things that already have occurred will most likely not inspire a great deal of efficacy. However, sending things home that are interactive in nature, meaning they require a conversation between the student and their parent and some sort of response that will be returned to the teacher, will alter conversations and go a long way toward engaging every family, regardless of who they are or their station in life.

THE WEEKLY FOLDER

For as long as anyone can remember, elementary students have carried home a weekly folder. One day of the week is designated as "folder day." The students are given their folders and instructed to bring them home to share with their families. Students are told that the folder must come back to school the following day and a signature from a parent must be included.

Presumably, the parent signature is needed to ensure safe delivery of the information. Students clearly understand that they will only get one folder for the year and dire consequences could exist if the folder doesn't come back the next day!

Folders usually contain examples of work that has been done in school by the student as well as information for parents. The purpose of the weekly folder is noble: to communicate what is happening in school to parents and to give them examples of progress in learning as well as keep parents informed of school happenings.

Teachers spend a great deal of time preparing information for the weekly folder and rely on this method of communication to keep school information flowing to the home. But does the folder meet the expected objectives? (We can debate using youngsters as conduits of communication at a later time!)

Let's look more closely at the folder and, more importantly, look at ways in which the folder could be improved with no additional monies, effort, or time. Remember, family engagement is not about doing more, it's about doing things differently. One of the first salient questions is about engagement. How do we expect families to engage with things that have *already* happened? A folder full of information of what has already occurred leaves little or no opportunity for families to engage in learning.

The required signature is largely so that the teacher knows the families have received the information she wished to communicate and that an adult caregiver viewed the information. In many cases, required signatures become a method of establishing proof of communication when families raise questions. Again, we need to ask a simple question: Does a signature mean that a parent has received the information or received and *understood* the information? Big difference.

In most cases, the signature cannot prove to the teacher that the information was clearly communicated and understood. Is there a way to change the weekly folder without adding any extra time or work for a teacher but to significantly increase its use and understanding by parents? The answer is simple: Yes.

Instead of using the folder to communicate what has occurred, change the focus to what *will* occur. What is happening in school tomorrow or next week, and how can parents support the teacher and their child's learning? Fill the folder with examples of what will be learned and how parents can extend the learning into the home. If a teacher feels strongly that examples of completed work are essential, then divide the folder in half. On the left side, put a few examples of completed work, and on the right side, place items that will be covered in the coming week.

Lastly, instead of a signature, why not pose a question instead? Let's say, for example, that students are studying dinosaurs as part of a science unit. Instead of a required signature, pose this question: "This week, we studied dinosaurs and covered a lot of information. Ask your child what they have learned about dinosaurs and write down what they say here. Thank you."

Let's take an inventory of what we can accomplish with the same folder, the same resources, and the same amount of time but with a different focus:

1. Family support for home learning

2. Family understanding of concepts covered in school

3. Classroom learning extended into the home

4. Family efficacy for learning

5. The teacher's ability to check for conceptual understanding

No additional time. No additional resources. Just a change in what we do and how we do it. This simple change is but one of a number of examples of school practice and procedure that, when slightly altered, produce very different results.

It's important to note that in some schools, the weekly folder has been replaced by a modern-day e-version. Whether information is shared on paper or on a web page or via email, the goals are the same: to help families engage in the upcoming learning and to provide evidence of understanding of what has been shared.

CREATING THE TRANSPARENT SCHOOL

A pioneer in family engagement research (and a great friend) was Dr. Jerold Bauch, professor emeritus at Vanderbilt University. I credit Jerry with exposing me to the whole notion of family engagement and setting me on the journey that I still travel today. Sadly, since the first edition of this book, Dr. Bauch has passed away.

Jerry was a man ahead of his time. In 1989, he created "The Transparent School Model," a system by which computer-assisted telephone technology could be used to connect parents and teachers every day to support the home learning of students (Bauch, 1989).

It's important to remember that in 1989, there was no Internet or cell phones and no Twitter, Snapchat, Instagram, Voxer, or Facebook. We had a telephone. (At least it had buttons instead of a rotary dial!)

Ninety-five percent of American adults today have a cell phone, with 58 percent of adults having a smartphone (Pew Research Center, 2019). Interestingly, 67 percent of us check our cell phones for calls, texts, and alerts even if they are not ringing or vibrating! Consider for a moment the sheer magnitude of differences in communication between 1989 and 2019.

Take the seemingly antiquated technology of the home phone and 1980s voicemail out of the equation and focus on the concept: a method using technology that allowed for robust two-way communication between teachers and families, every day if they wished, about school activities so that parents could have a more meaningful conversation with their children and ask them better questions. In those days, teachers would take a simple voicemail system and, instead of parents leaving messages for teachers to contact them, teachers would leave messages, less than a minute long, about what happened in school (or in class at the high school level). Read the following paragraph and time yourself. How long does it take you to read it?

> Hello. My name is Tom Smith, and today is January 1, 2015. I am your child's third period algebra teacher. All this week, we will be studying the order of operations: multiplication, division, addition, and subtraction. It is important that your child understand the order of operations because all of our work in algebra is built on this important concept. What you could do for me this week is ask your child to share the order of operations and make sure they say "multiplication, division, addition, and subtraction." You can remember the order yourself by saying the phrase *My Dear Aunt Sally*. We are having a quiz on this information on Friday, so attendance this week is very important. When you call again next Monday, I will tell you how the quiz went and the next exciting thing we are doing in algebra. And, as always, if there is anything I need to know about your child, please press the pound sign and leave me a message.

How long did it take you to read that passage? (It took me 43 seconds.) If you are an average reader, it should have taken you under a minute. By leaving this message, you have shared specific information with parents about how they can interact with their children about school in a much better manner, and you have increased support for home learning, which translates into better class participation and better grades. You have promoted the efficacy of parents in the educational lives of their children, and you have given families a meaningful process by which to establish two-way communication and better relationships. And it only took you a minute!

Here's the Question to Ask Yourself

Is less than a minute of my time worth better student achievement for every child? Today's technology has far surpassed the 1989 telephone, but the concept of The Transparent School Model is as relevant today as it was when conceived by Dr. Bauch in 1989.

Today, technology allows instant communication and access to a world of information. Rather than use technology to communicate, we want to use technology to engage (see Chapter 7). To do so means to structure our messages to families in such a way as it promotes their efficacy and invites feedback from them as to their experiences. Let's take the telephone message above and reformat it into a message that could be sent using modern technology or social media platforms:

> Dear families,
>
> All this week, we will be studying the order of operations: multiplication, division, addition, and subtraction. It is important that your child understand the order of operations because all of our work in algebra is built on this important concept. What you could do for me this week is ask your child to share the order of operations and make sure they say "multiplication, division, addition, and subtraction." You can remember the order yourself by saying the phrase *My Dear Aunt Sally*. We are having a quiz on this information on Friday, so attendance this week is very important. Please reply to this message and let me know if your child had any trouble remembering the order of operations! Thank you.

It still was less than a minute for me to type the modern version of The Transparent School Model message. Whatever technology, apps, or platforms you use can now support engagement as opposed to only communication. Easy!

Now you try it!

Think about a concept that you teach. Consider how you can engage families in your efforts. Remember, the point of efficacy is not to teach families but rather to give them information that improves the conversations and interactions with their own children. The components to the message are simple:

1. What is being studied? What needs to be learned?

2. How can families easily support learning at home? (The key word is *easily*.)

3. How can families provide feedback regarding their interactions with their children?

CASE STUDY: CLASS ISN'T THE SAME WITHOUT YOU

Jessica Mulhaney teaches geometry at the local high school. Jessica is a very popular teacher, and there are always more students and families requesting Jessica as a teacher than can be accommodated by the school. She is friendly and supportive of students, builds strong relationships with families, and simultaneously holds high standards in place for all of her students. She has the highest pass rate on the state geometry test of all the teachers in her school district.

Several years ago, Jessica went through The Transparent School Model training. She immediately saw applications for her class and began to use the voicemail system as taught in the professional development class. As part of that training and process implementation, Jessica encourages families to leave her messages about what is happening outside of school that could cause an interference with learning. She learned long ago that teenagers' emotions run the gamut and when behaviors are odd, there is usually something provoking them.

On a very typical Thursday morning, her first-period geometry students began to wander into the classroom—some energetic, some still wiping cobwebs from their eyes. A few students were downing their last sips of coffee and soda as well as the last bites of their breakfasts. Suddenly, Jason entered the room in a manner she had never seen before. He threw his book bag to the floor and himself onto his desk. He immediately covered his head with his arms. When a classmate asked what was wrong, Jason became angry and yelled for the classmate to mind their own business. Another classmate, feeling Jason was being unreasonable, scolded him for his behavior. This action made Jason even more angry. He jumped from his seat and postured as if he was going to fight the other student.

Jessica tried to intervene, and Jason ignored her. Once again, he angrily sat down, covered his head with his arms, and told Jessica to get lost. Under normal circumstances, Jason most likely would have been removed from class and sent to the assistant principal's office for discipline. But Jessica didn't take that action. She knew something and that something had changed the course of her interaction with Jason.

Upon her arrival to school that morning, Jessica had listened to her messages. There was one message, and it was from Jason's mother. She explained that the family had been through a traumatic ordeal the evening before; the beloved family dog had passed away. Jason's mother went on to explain that the dog had been there since Jason was a small child and that he and his sister were taking the death of the dog quite hard. Jason didn't sleep at all during the night. His mother ended the message by saying, "If he is not doing well, please let me know. I am happy to come and get him. I told him not to go to school today, but he insisted he had to go."

Jessica calmly walked over to Jason, whose head was still buried under his arms. She spoke in a whisper: "Jason, I am very sorry about what happened to your dog. I cannot imagine how you must feel today. Please know that I truly do understand." Jason didn't move. "I am not going to bother you today. However, if and when you are ready and you want to participate, I welcome your involvement. You know, Jason, class is never the same without you." With that, Jessica left Jason and started class.

About fifteen minutes into class, Jason raised his head, opened his book, and joined the class.

Questions for Discussion

1. What do you think would have occurred if Jessica did not have the opportunity to listen to the message Jason's mother left?

2. What actions did Jessica take that made this situation work out the way it did?

3. How did Jessica's action promote efficacy and trust in the relationships among the student, the parent, and herself?

4. Has something similar ever happened to you as a teacher? If so, how did you handle the situation?

5. What can we learn from this case study that we can apply to real-world situations?

FAMILY-STUDENT-TEACHER CONFERENCES

In 2017, the *Phi Delta Kappan* published an article titled "Why I'm Not Involved: Parental Involvement from a Parent's Perspective." In that article, author Jung-ah Choi wrote about her conference experiences with her son:

> I left the conference feeling disappointed, humiliated, and dumbfounded. I had expected something fundamentally different. I expected to have a conversation with the teacher. I expected the teacher to ask questions about Michael's family life. I expected a true parent–teacher partnership for the benefit of his education. I expected the teacher to take an interest in my approach to raising Michael. But all I heard

from his teachers—that year and the next—was information about where he stood on the spectrum from struggling to smart and where he stood on the obedience spectrum (from disruptive to respectful).

While this excerpt and accompanying article are the views of one person, there have been countless parents and families (including me) who have expressed similar views about the point of conferences and whether the return on investment was worth the time. In order to ensure engagement, we must make sure that all experiences for families are both meaningful and relevant. For example, if families rely on an hourly wage, careful consideration will be made as to whether or not there is enough value in attending a conference to offset the salary that is lost.

Conferences can be a very powerful way to promote family efficacy in their children's learning. However, many schools report low attendance rates to conferences, and in some cases, conferences are only held if a parent requests one. Given the amount of technology that allows parents access to all of the information about their children that once was the center of conferences, it seems the time is right to shift the focus and purpose of the traditional parent–teacher conference and replace it with a more efficacy-based family–student–teacher conference.

To engage families and to build their efficacy, we need to create opportunities for them that provide information that is meaningful and relevant. Their lives are busy and complicated. Sending a flyer home and indicating that the annual conferences are coming up will solicit responses from those families that are already engaged. To improve the attendance of families who are traditionally disengaged or for whatever reason do not attend conferences and meetings, consider a student-led model. When students are part of the equation, the experience instantly becomes much more meaningful and relevant to families.

> To improve the attendance of families who are traditionally disengaged . . . consider a student-led model. When students are part of the equation, the experience instantly becomes much more meaningful and relevant to families.

The idea of student-led conferences has been around for a while but continues to grow in popularity, especially at the secondary level. Individual student-led conferences at the high school level, for example, are far more productive in helping families understand the successes and challenges their own children face and are more likely to build the efficacy necessary to support improved achievement.

If conferences do not address the questions and issues that parents have for their children's education, then they are no longer meaningful or relevant. To successfully alter the course of conferences and to improve attendance and impact, families could be asked prior to the conference what they want to glean from the meeting. What information do they desire about their children? What do they want to know? Given that most parents have the capability to monitor attendance and grades on the Internet without creating meaningful dialogue in a conference, there is little incentive for parents to attend. Seeing no real opportunity for efficacy building, the participation stops. It shouldn't be surprising to us.

Try This

The next time there is a conference scheduled, reach out to the family by phone or in-person and use the following dialogue:

> We are very happy to have the opportunity to talk with you about [the student's] progress in school. As we prepare, what questions do you have? What would you like to know as a result of our conference? How can we make this a meaningful experience for you?

Hoover-Dempsey and Sandler (1997) are influential researchers in the area of family efficacy. They found that parents' sense of efficacy, meaning their view of their own ability to help their children with school-related work, primarily focused on the extent that parents believed that through their engagement, they could exert positive influence on the child's educational outcomes. Parents clearly make choices as to the level of their involvement with their child's education. Those choices are often directly connected to their own perceptions of their ability to help their child.

A major factor in parents making positive decisions with regard to their role in education is determined by their perception of a parental role in general or, more specifically, what they believe they should and should not be doing as parents (Hoover-Dempsey & Sandler, 1997). Roles in any organization inclusive of parents and school personnel are characterized by the interaction between the members of the group over time.

Thus, if school personnel interact with every family, then every family understands that supporting and extending learning is a basic function of the parental role. Conclusively, school personnel can shape the role parents and families perceive they should play with regard to engagement in school-related activities and the academic lives of their own children. Schools that discourage, limit, or simply place little value on engaging families are helping to shape parental role perceptions that will continue to plague the culture of the school.

Empowering every family, then, is the notion that parents and families can help to produce positive educational outcomes with their child. Traditional avenues of parent involvement do not take building the capacity—the efficacy—of parents to transfer knowledge from school to their children into consideration.

Generally speaking, practices that promote parental efficacy

1. are grounded in student achievement and parent perceptional data;

2. are action oriented, meaning parents learn by doing, then transfer the knowledge to their children;

3. take parental levels of education into consideration;

4. work around barriers to successful family engagement;

5. meet parent and family needs; and

6. are part of a larger process to promote family engagement.

QUICK TIP
Designing Opportunities for Families

Most teachers design workshops and other experiences for parents and families to better help them understand student learning expectations. More often than not, however, teachers design these events. The contents of the events are decided upon and controlled by teachers. To help the experience be more meaningful and relevant to families, solicit their input on their needs. Ask them what they need to know or want to know. Design opportunities based on family feedback. Attendance will start to climb, and support will start to improve!

Stilwell and Ferguson (n.d.) published a report that shares four ways for schools to assist families to increase their sense of efficacy; it is reprinted here with permission.

Promote Successful Personal Experiences for Family Members

Anytime family members feel welcome and effective in school when talking with school personnel or when working with their children, they are developing belief in their ability to make a difference. Schools that have volunteers who greet families, help them feel comfortable, and [help them] accomplish their reasons for coming to school create a successful experience.

Teachers who ask and listen to families—trying to understand their values and preferences in order to tailor learning and curriculum for students—help family members feel like they are an important part of schooling. Building positive associations with parent involvement helps enhance the parent's sense

(Continued)

(Continued)

of efficacy—he believes his participation has a positive impact on his child's learning—and increases the likelihood of continued future involvement.

Help Family Members Learn from Each Other

Helping family members have successful experiences can also be indirect. When school personnel connect families that might have experiences to share, they expand feelings of success. Hearing about other students' experiences, learning from teachers who are successful with students, and sharing with other families in similar and different family situations all build confidence, knowledge, and efficacy.

Teachers could model efficacious behavior to parents ("When I run across something I don't know, this is how I search for the answer") or design workshops where parents can witness good responses to various situations.

Always Offer Encouragement

School personnel don't always agree with families' choices or perspectives. Sometimes these differences are fleeting and easily resolved with more complete communication. Sometimes the differences are deeper reflections of culture, values, and history. Nevertheless, school professionals are in positions of power with respect to many families. Many parents feel that teachers' opinions and ideas hold more weight than their own. Families' ideas and feelings can easily be crushed by a busy teacher, and their feelings of efficacy diminished.

A good solution is for school personnel to always take an encouraging stance with family members, even when they don't completely understand their position or might even disagree. Encouragement coming from someone with more currency and power can ensure ongoing communication instead of inadvertently shutting it down. After a parent volunteers on a project, sending a thank-you note that comments on a job well done helps her feel that her contribution makes a difference. Persuasion is another way of offering encouragement. Persuading the parent that her involvement is appreciated and has a positive effect increases her sense of efficacy.

Focus on Emotional Well-Being and Stress Reduction

Stress poses a big threat to parental efficacy. Anything the school can do to foster calm and reduce tension will help increase families' ability to make a difference. This might mean providing specific tools or community resources to parents so that they can feel more in control of their lives. If lack of food is stressing a family out, hook them up with food banks. If it's lack of health care that's the problem, brainstorm options with the family and make referrals. Sometimes the act of listening itself can help reduce stress.

DO WE NEED TO INTERACT WITH EVERY FAMILY?

The question posed above may seem antithetical to the whole premise of this book. The question, however, is an important one and may hold the key to unlocking more potential to promoting family efficacy and improving learning outcomes for all children.

Family social class also plays a role in the degree to which families believe in their own efficacy with their children's education. Social class influences parent decision making in shaping home support roles (Lareau, 1987). Many parents and families that are deemed socioeconomically disadvantaged suffer the additional burdens of having less education and low income. They view their own abilities as significantly lower than those of their economically advantaged counterparts and, as such often send their children to school and simply hope for the best (Eccles & Harold, 1994).

Consider, for a moment, the desire to host math night for all parents in a particular grade level or subject. An evening meeting dedicated to assisting families usually begins with planning. Teachers plan a meeting that includes information and possibly activities to help families understand what their children are learning in school. A great deal of effort goes into designing a meeting that is both informative and engaging.

A letter is sent to all of the families announcing the special meeting and encouraging all families to attend. The letter is usually sent home with students or sometimes attached to the weekly newsletter published by the school or a parent organization. Either way, time, energy, resources, and talent are invested in communicating about this important evening. Teachers and school staff usually arrange for light snacks and, in some cases, babysitting services for younger children, understanding that the only way families can attend is to bring children along.

Generally speaking, when the meeting night arrives, one of two scenarios emerges. The first scenario includes more teachers present than parents. The second scenario seems on the surface a bit more successful: a full complement of parents and family members eager to learn. Upon closer examination, the roomful of parents usually comprises those parents of students who are thoroughly engaged with school and whose children are usually successful: This is often described as *engaging the already engaged*. Parents who attend have usually garnered significant self-efficacy and are engaged with the school and their children's education at many levels. I often ask teachers in workshops, "If you have a roomful of parents, are they the parents who needed to be there?" The answer is almost always "No."

Schools that wish to engage those that are traditionally not engaged or less engaged understand that at the core of family efficacy is the use of student data to target and focus on a subset of families whose children could benefit from their understanding of and engagement with schoolwork.

More importantly, the notion of learning at home seems to be a more stringent predictor in family engagement practices that supports student learning. Whether at home or at school, motivating parents and families to become engaged is the first step to promoting better success for every student and family.

WHAT MOTIVATES FAMILIES?

The Hoover-Dempsey, Walker, and Sandler model (2005) includes three motivational sources of parental engagement with learning. The first centers on parents' motivational beliefs, including the construction of the role of the parent and parental beliefs about parents' self-efficacy to support their children while in school. The second is the degree to which parents and families believe that the school values their participation and the genuine nature of the invitation to become engaged, and the third is the contexts of parents' personal lives and how those inform their own perception of whether or not it is feasible for them to be engaged and the degree to which they believe their own skill, time, and energy are conducive to their engagement.

The salient question for discussion is this: Do families really believe that through their efforts to become engaged in the school/learning lives of their children they can exercise a more positive outcome in their children's school performance? Families will set preconceived goals for their involvement with school. These goals run along a continuum of low to high and are directly related to a parent's belief in their own efficacy (Hoover-Dempsey & Sandler, 1997). It stands to reason, then, that schools would be well served to interact with families and support parent and family knowledge. By doing so, families' views of their own efficacy will rise and, ultimately, so will their engagement with their child.

INTERACTIVE HOMEWORK DESIGN: INVISIBLE ENGAGEMENT

An excellent idea for promoting the efficacy of families is to design homework assignments that engage families or interact with them. Rather than simply ask, "Did you do your homework?" families can have a role in the homework and lesson. With the advent of the use of technology, there are even more opportunities to engage families outside of the school.

We often consider *family engagement* as activities that happen at school, activities that we can see. Consider for a moment that promoting the efficacy of families relies on those types of activities that we inspire but may not see. It is more likely that these types of activities will happen in the home and not at school. While we don't see the actual engagement, we can clearly see the results of that engagement. I refer to this as *invisible engagement*: engagement we don't necessarily see but of which we see the results.

Generally speaking, interactive homework

- promotes parent–child interactions and meaningful conversations about learning (more than assigning vocabulary or multiplication table memorization);
- promotes family interest, which in turn facilitates and bolsters student interest;
- promotes activities that encourage families and children to reason through tasks, fosters critical thinking, and entices families to engage; and
- should use constructivist techniques, which are techniques that encourage children to construct their own understandings through interactions with their environments, especially with significant adult figures such as parents and teachers

> We often consider family engagement as activities that happen at school. . . . Consider for a moment that promoting the efficacy of families relies on those types of activities that we inspire but may not see.

SHARING DATA WITH FAMILIES

It is nearly impossible to have a thorough discussion of promoting family efficacy without including the ideas of data sharing. With data driving everything from daily instruction to school district evaluation, it is imperative that we learn how to share appropriate and relevant data with families. There are great benefits to student learning when families understand data and what they can do to promote better learning at home.

Approaching data sharing with families is best done in the context of the whole child. Families need reassurances in our high-stakes testing environment that their children's future does not depend on one test score and that we make evaluations on student progress through multiple measures, such as attendance, classroom observations, and so forth (Harvard Family Research Project, 2013).

Teachers can work together to determine how to present data to families. In some cases, it is important to remember cultural backgrounds and communication protocols for different cultures. Finding appropriate ways of communicating data (privacy), sharing a range of data to show the whole child, and giving families a voice in the conversation all lead to better family understanding of student progress (Harvard Family Research Project, 2013).

Lastly, teachers are best served to avoid the use of jargon and acronyms, focus data conversations on areas of growth and improvement that can be supported by families, and provide families with potential resources that can be used with children outside of school (Harvard Family Research Project, 2013).

What Ideas Do You Have?

Promoting efficacy among families is allowing families to have a hand in the education of their children. It does not transfer the responsibility solely to families but allows them to be part of the equation in a way that is meaningful and relevant to them. Some ideas have already been presented in this chapter. Considering what you have learned about promoting family efficacy, what additional ideas do you have? Jot them down here and come back later to work on an implementation plan.

CASE STUDY: TRYING TO TALK TO THE MATH TEACHER

Mr. and Mrs. Jones were very engaged in their children's education. Their older daughter seemed to sail through school effortlessly, but their middle son, Bobby, struggled. Bobby always ended up passing classes, but the Joneses were always concerned that he was teetering on the edge of academic disaster and feared what would occur as he transitioned to middle school and high school.

It was during his eighth-grade year that the Joneses' fears started to materialize. They received an interim report card indicating that Bobby was failing Algebra I. Not wanting too much time to go by, Mr. Jones contacted Bobby's guidance counselor to set up a meeting with the math teacher. The Joneses were interested in what more they could do at home to increase Bobby's success in math.

The guidance counselor was very pleasant with Mr. Jones and empathized with his concern. She also commended Mr. Jones for being proactive and asking for the meeting. Mr. Jones told the counselor that he realized the teachers were busy and he would change his schedule, regardless of what he had to do, to accommodate the math teacher's schedule and needs. The counselor indicated that the best time for the teacher was 12:30 p.m. They set a date.

"So, let me confirm what we said," started Mr. Jones. "My wife and I will be meeting with the math teacher on Thursday at 12:30 p.m., correct?"

"Oh, Mr. Jones, the meeting will be with the entire team, not just the math teacher," responded the counselor. Until this point, there had been no mention that the meeting would include Bobby's other teachers.

"I must not have been clear; I apologize," said Mr. Jones. "We really only need to talk with the math teacher. He seems to be doing pretty well everywhere else."

"Mr. Jones, our policy is that when a parent requests a meeting with a teacher, the entire team comes to the meeting. That is the way we do it here."

"I don't really need to waste the time of the other teachers," Mr. Jones said as he started to get agitated with the conversation. "We are really wanting to focus on math."

"I realize what you want to focus on, Mr. Jones. But the teachers are the experts, and they can tell you what to focus on. The other team members may have suggestions for you and your wife." The counselor sensed that Mr. Jones was becoming irritated.

"Look," snapped Mr. Jones, "I don't *want* to meet with the other teachers, and I don't *need* to meet with the other teachers. I simply want a meeting with my son's math teacher. Are you going to set that up or not?"

"Mr. Jones, there is no need to become cross with me—"

Mr. Jones cut her off. "Lady, listen. I don't know what kind of policies you have at that school, but I think I have the right to meet with whomever I want to meet with, and in this instance, I want to meet with the math teacher." Mr. Jones was now angry.

"Mr. Jones, here is what you need to understand. If you want to have a meeting on Thursday at 12:30 p.m. to talk about your son's math problems, you will meet with the entire team or there will be no meeting. I'm sorry you disagree with our practice, but we find that it is quite effective in dealing with our youngsters and their parents." The counselor was firm and final in her tone.

"Fine!" yelled Mr. Jones. "I'll meet with the whole darn team just to talk to one person. I've never heard of anything so stupid in all my life." With that, he slammed down the phone.

At the meeting, the five teachers on the team sat in a row behind student desks. Two chairs with no desks were set up in front of the teachers. The assistant principal, who was not scheduled to be there, arrived at the meeting and began it. The Joneses had no idea that the assistant principal would be present at the meeting.

"Mr. Jones, I know you are upset with the school, and your tone with the guidance counselor was uncalled for. I think your anger is a bit displaced. We are here to talk about your son and his failure to comply with his teacher's requirements, which are now resulting in his failure. I am quite sure we can have a meeting today that is professional and calm. If not, then I will end the meeting abruptly, and it will continue with just me in my office. Is that understood?"

The meeting was scheduled to last twenty minutes. Each teacher took three to five minutes to share information about Bobby's grades, assignments, tests, and abilities. The math teacher reported that Bobby did not do his homework, and if he applied himself, he would do better in math. The Joneses never asked a question and never spoke a word.

The Joneses left the meeting and withdrew Bobby from the school that day.

Questions for Discussion

1. What are your thoughts about the policy of meeting the entire team of teachers when a conference with one is requested?

2. How did the policy promote family efficacy? Why?

3. Why do you think the team meeting philosophy is in place at this school?

4. How could this conference have provided a better outcome for all involved?

CASE STUDY: TEACHING RESPONSIBILITY?

David Smith was a high school senior and was facing a comprehensive test in math. If David failed the test, he would not be allowed to graduate. David had failed the test one time before. David's parents noticed that he seemed very stressed and withdrawn. Usually talkative, David was now quiet, choosing to sit in his room rather than be with the rest of his family and the family dog, whom David had loved since getting him as a puppy in fifth grade.

"I'm going to fail again; I just know it!" yelled David when his mother tried to talk with him about his sullen mood.

"Maybe I can talk with your teacher. She might be able to help me understand what we can do to get you through this test. You know, I was pretty good at math in my day," David's mother said lovingly.

"Do what you want, Mom, it won't make any difference. I am not going to graduate with my friends because of this stupid test. Let's just face it." David stormed away from his mother.

The following day, David's mother made an appointment to see the teacher. David's two older siblings had had the same teacher for math, so she felt as though she knew the teacher and had a rapport that might help her better understand how to help her son.

"Thank you for meeting with me on such short notice," said Mrs. Smith.

"No problem at all," responded the math teacher. "I am happy to answer any questions you might have."

"As you probably know, David is frantic over this math test and feels defeated. He is already predicting he will fail and that he will not graduate with his class. This test is the only thing that is standing in his way. I thought perhaps you could give me some materials or guidance as to how my husband and I might help David at home. He still has a week before the test. If I knew what areas he was weak in, we could work with him."

"Mrs. Smith," began the teacher, "I applaud you for wanting to help your son; I really do. But he is seventeen years old. Don't you think it's time that he took responsibility for himself? His parents won't always be there to bail him out of trouble."

"We are not looking to bail David out of trouble. We were hoping that there were some problems or worksheets or other materials that you could point us to so that we could work with him at home to prepare for the test. If we knew what areas he was struggling with, we could emphasize that." Mrs. Smith's tone remained calm and reasonable.

"David has been given everything he needs to be successful on that test. I do not have the time to create individual support packets for every student who decides now, in their senior year, to take their education seriously. You should be asking David for this information, not me. At some point, we need to teach our young people to take responsibility. I teach responsibility to my students. It is my job. It is not my job to ensure that every student passes the test. I provide the materials to the students. I show them how to solve the problems. The rest is up to them. They have to have some skin in the game."

The math teacher agreed to give Mrs. Smith the same study packet that she had given to David. She also mentioned that the study packet was to have been completed and turned in for a grade. David did not turn his in and received two zeros, since the assignment was given double weight. He failed the course as a result.

David did not pass the comprehensive test and did not graduate. He chose not to attend summer school and got a job at the local supermarket instead.

Questions for Discussion

1. Was the request of David's mother reasonable? Why or why not?

2. What are your thoughts on the teacher's handling of this conference?

3. How did this exchange improve or impede family efficacy?

4. How could this situation be altered to improve the likelihood of family efficacy?

QUICK TIP
Confronting the "We Already Tried That" Syndrome

Honestly, there may not be very many strategies left to engage families that haven't been thought up and tried by educators. Unfortunately, more often than not, the strategies were quickly abandoned when they did not provide the expected outcomes. Later, when the strategy is revived, a chorus of "we tried that already and it didn't work" rises up to meet the new (old) idea. In most cases, the strategies were good ones. The reason for their failure or poor outcomes had little to do with the strategy and more to do with the lack of developing empowering practices for success. On a separate page, use the column headings suggested below to list those things that you have already tried, and then apply the concepts of family efficacy to them. When you try them again, you will see an improved outcome!

Things we have tried	Looking through a new lens of efficacy: What can we do differently?

Questions to Ponder

1. How often do you provide families with information about their children's academic progress?

2. How do you encourage family involvement by creating enhanced home learning environments and activities?

3. Are your school planning and curriculum documents available to families?

4. Does your school require conferences with families of all students?

Available for download at **http://www.drsteveconstantino.com**

A CRITICAL COMPONENT OF INVITING FAMILY PARTICIPATION

So far, we know that to engage families in the learning lives of their children, we must change our approach. We don't have to add more time or spend more money to do so, we simply need to look at our present practice and modify it based on the Five Simple Principles. Let's take a look at a common practice and how to improve it so that more families are engaged.

This entire chapter is about promoting the efficacy of parents, empowering them to have a positive effect on the education and learning of their children. We spend a great deal of time creating experiences for families to participate in meetings, events, and workshops designed to help them support their children and understand better what is being learned in school and why. Educators spend a great deal of time encouraging families to participate. Over and over, we stress the importance of their engagement and involvement with whatever it is we deem valuable.

We encourage, demand, and even guilt families into participation in these events. Even then, there are still those who, for reasons we have learned, do not participate. After planning and executing the event, what is it we then do with those parents who did not attend? The answer: Nothing. Usually, we shrug our shoulders, assume they don't care, and move on.

Consider this: If someone repeatedly told you that taking a specific action was important to your well-being, hammering the idea that the action is absolutely necessary and essential, then said nothing more to you after you didn't take the action, what would you think?

The logical conclusion is that the action must not have been that important. This is exactly the idea we reinforce in parents who do not participate in the events we plan. We do nothing and reinforce to them that it wasn't important after all.

There is a simple remedy to this. For each of the parents that do not participate, call them immediately and say, with an even and nonjudgmental tone, "I am sorry that you could not participate in our event. I still think this information is important. How can I get it to you?" This simple communication can alter the course of family engagement and efficacy in the child's education by communicating the importance of the parents' participation. Do this a few times and watch the changes occur.

BUILDING SUCCESSFUL RELATIONSHIPS THAT PROMOTE FAMILY EFFICACY

Any teacher can incorporate family engagement principles so that children's classroom learning engages families and provides the support at home that teachers are desperate to attain. The following ten practices are designed to help every teacher build better relationships with all families, with an emphasis on building relationships with those families that are disengaged from their child's learning.

1. Relationships Are the Key

Disengaged families have lost trust in the educational system. Many families who create disingenuous relationships with teachers do so because of past experiences. Every teacher has a wonderful opportunity to rekindle a strong and healthy relationship with all families, which is the first step in rebuilding trust:

- Make your first contact with families a positive one, with no agenda except to say hello and begin a dialogue.
- Use language that families can understand. Many disengaged families may have weak educational skills and may be reluctant to get into conversations with teachers.
- Ask parents to share their concerns and opinions about school and then address those concerns.
- Work within your professional learning community to accommodate parents' work schedules.

2. Make Learning Meaningful and Relevant

Making learning meaningful and relevant to parents and families by providing families with information on current and upcoming classroom activities so that parents and families can ask their children better questions. When learning becomes more meaningful and relevant to parents and families, they are more engaged in supporting learning outcomes at home. Provide specific information to parents so that the questions they ask contain the attributes of the ones below:

- Tell me about (the order of operations, the book report draft that is due tomorrow, etc.)
- Show me (the story you have to read tonight, the book chapter that you are going to be tested on this Friday, etc.)
- Teach me (multiplication tables, Spanish, etc.)

3. Communicate What Is Coming, Not What Has Passed

Teachers spend a significant amount of time trying to communicate with families, only to feel frustrated at the relatively low response levels from the homes of their students. In many cases, the communication from schools (such as grade reports or weekly folders) communicate what has already taken place.

Change the premise of communication to upcoming learning instead of learning that has passed. Send a weekly folder home that contains information about what is going to happen in class over the next week as opposed to what has already happened. Many teachers use a variety of apps to share information with parents and families about what occurred in school today and what will occur tomorrow. Consistently communicating upcoming learning will begin to engage more families because learning is now meaningful and relevant to families and they now have information so that they can support classroom learning at home.

4. Share Hopes and Concerns and Make a Plan

Parents and families desire the opportunity to dialogue about the hopes and dreams they have for their children. All families, regardless of their ethnicity or socioeconomic status, want what is best for their children so that each child can prosper and exceed them in their quality of life (Constantino, 2003).

Teachers should seek avenues to have these types of discussions with the parents and families of their children. To enhance the traditional parent–teacher conference, take some time to understand the hopes and dreams of families. Listen to their concerns and fears about their children. Practices that honor the contributions of families help strengthen relationships (Mapp, 2003). Use the commonality of the desire of success for your students to create goals and plans with parents and families that not only help children achieve at higher levels but send a clear and powerful message to families that teachers do care a great deal.

5. Link Communication to Learning

Many schools instinctively believe that the school newsletter is read by very few parents and families. How we communicate learning goals with families becomes a centerpiece of engaging them in the educational lives of their children; we understand that the goal in engaging families is to make their child's learning meaningful and relevant.

Classroom newsletters that are short (one page) and more frequent (weekly) are read more often and by more parents than a longer monthly newsletter that is distributed by the school. Whether sent home in a backpack or posted online, newsletters are meaningful and relevant to families because they are linked to their own child's learning. The classroom newsletter can be linked to learning in class that week. For example, share the state standard that is being met by the lessons that week. Choose one or two subject areas.

Share what is being taught and provide families with an activity that can be done at home or provide information that families can ask their children to reinforce learning. For example, at the bottom of the weekly classroom newsletter, the teacher may write: *Ask your child about dinosaurs. Write down what they tell you and send this back to class tomorrow.* If there is a television program to be broadcast that will enhance learning that week, remind families of the program. Most importantly, provide an area for families to give you feedback. Ask them to share their experiences or record the results of an activity. The engagement of families and students will begin to improve when communication is linked to learning.

In many of today's classrooms, the classroom newsletter has morphed into texts and tweets. However information is shared, it should inspire family empowerment in learning outside of the school.

6. Use Social Media or Other Technology

The use of apps and social media has increased in popularity. Keep in mind the following information when working with technology:

- Determine the percentage of families that have access to the Internet. If everyone does not have access, then using technology may not result in increased efficacy or engagement.
- Be current and consistent with information. The greatest detriment to technology use is the failure to keep information current. Once information is being pushed out through social media more often, families will come to expect information on some sort of schedule. As a rule, always let families know when you will provide new information via technology.
- Use the technology to reinforce your classroom learning and activities. Post a PowerPoint or video online, if possible. Allow families to download information that was presented in class. Give them access to free information online that will support your efforts.
- Invite feedback from families about your technology use. Work toward increased responses from families as a signal that their efficacy is improving.

7. Integrate Families Into Lesson Planning

Create a lesson that engages families. Design a lesson over a day or two or, better yet, over a weekend that requires the student to engage their family in the material. Keeping family engagement in learning simple will encourage the disengaged to participate and build their confidence. Family integration into lesson planning does not have to occur every day or every week. Initially, set a goal to create four or five family lessons a year. The components of an integrated lesson are exactly the same as any lesson you would plan. The significant differences are (a) the lesson requires family participation and (b) there is a mechanism for families to record and send back their experiences to the teacher. Call a few of the parents or families you feel might be reluctant to participate and encourage them. Let them know that their contributions are essential elements in the learning life of their child.

8. Support the Knowledge and Skills of Every Family

Having parents and families share their expertise is not a new concept in education. Unfortunately, there is less and less of this type of experiential learning because of limited time and the need to meet mastery objectives.

Determine knowledge and expertise held by the parents and families of students. Record that information for future use. Parents who work within the home can provide valuable resources to teachers. For example, skills such as cooking can be incorporated into math lessons. A parent who is a house painter can support a geometry lesson by bringing a ladder to school and allowing the class to help determine the correct angle and placement of the ladder for its safe use. With the need to develop a twenty-first-century workforce, engaging family knowledge has never been more critical.

Often, schools and classrooms gravitate to those parents who have interesting and exciting jobs. Remember, though, every parent has value. Find that value and use it to support the learning that is taking place in the classroom.

9. Develop the Efficacy of Families

Family efficacy is the notion that parents can help to produce positive educational outcomes with their child. Traditional avenues of parent involvement do not take into consideration building the capacity—the efficacy of parents—to transfer knowledge from school to their children. The most common place to improve family efficacy is to start with those activities already in place that are designed to promote learning outside of the classroom. Math nights, reading nights, and so forth all have value in helping families understand not only what their child needs to learn and master but, more importantly, how they can participate in their child's learning.

Even with the very best intentions of educators, attendance to these types of events is often sporadic. At times, only a handful of parents attend. Schools report that when they do fill a room with parents, the parents of those students who are struggling are usually absent. To understand why this happens is to understand the role of family efficacy.

The improvements sought in these evening events are not to increase attendance but to make sure that the parents of the children who need the support are in attendance or are getting the support they need. Incorporate the following ideas into planned learning events for every family to improve the event and build efficacy in all parents and families:

- Use student work as a basis for parent learning.
- Engage families in learning that they can then transfer to their children at home.
- Take parental levels of education into consideration.
- Incorporate the needs of families, such as translation services and childcare, into the meeting or workshop.

- Consistently provide materials to families who could not attend.

Parents and families need to know that they can play an important role in producing an effect with regard to their children's upbringing and education.

10. Believe That Family Engagement Is Essential

Believing in family engagement speaks directly to the culture of the classroom and the school. Consider the following two statements made by a teacher and a parent:

> **Teacher**: Parents who want to be involved are involved. Those who don't are not. I can't spend any more time chasing ghosts. Many parents simply don't care enough to do the right thing, or they just check out. My job is to teach children, not their parents. We talk about this all the time at lunch and my colleagues agree with me. We can't handle one more thing.

> **Parent**: At some point, you just give up. I want to know what my son is doing, but I don't get any information. I get the report card, but by then, it's too late. I want to help him, but I don't know how. I have asked and asked for help and now, . . . well, they just think I am a troublemaker. You can only bang your head against the wall for so long, you know? The last time I went there, I could see it on their faces that they didn't want me meddling in their school. I wanted a conference and they said OK, but half the teachers didn't come. I haven't been back since. I guess I will just pray that everything comes out all right.

The statements above reflect what two people believe about the education of the same child. It is clear to the reader what each person believes and how they came to believe it. New actions that beget new results is an effective strategy to modify one's beliefs about issues and challenges.

All parents and families care about their children. On any given day, they may not express it in the manner we would wish nor do they respond in ways that help their children learn. However, parents and families are the first and most influential teachers of children. Believing that they choose to be disengaged will only serve to ensure that the struggles we face in successfully teaching all children will remain with us forever.

PRINCIPLE #3

Where We Are

Description

Families are recognized as essential members of the learning team for each student—their participation is welcomed, valued, and encouraged by the school. The school understands that families are important and influential resources because they know their children best.

Based on the description, discuss and record where you think your school is today as it relates to the principle description.

3.1 The school makes a conscious effort to educate families in how to play a proactive role in the learning life of their child throughout their child's school career.

Principle #3.1 Assessment

Use this chart to determine your organization's present level of performance.

Practice/Attribute/ Condition	Discuss/Reflect/Record the Present Status in Your School
Families are included in ongoing and upcoming learning in school.	
Feedback from families strongly suggests they maintain a healthy efficacy toward their child's learning.	
School staff interact with families about learning on an ongoing and regular basis.	
School staff remove barriers so that every family can engage and build efficacy.	
A family mentoring program is in place, which allows families to be trained in assisting other families.	

Use the clarifying statement and the best practice description to help you shape your efforts to build family efficacy.

est Practice Description

s the school system and its component schools improve quality and
erformance, they also improve the neighborhoods and surrounding areas
s better places for families to grow. All families have the tools necessary
 assist their children with schoolwork and understand what their child
eeds to know in order to make continuous progress and meet high
andards for achievement. Regardless of race, color, creed, or economic
atus, families feel a sense of efficacy toward helping their children and, in
urn, a strong sense of loyalty to the school.

ll school staff believe that families are integral to student performance
nd success and, as such, design student instruction with families in mind.
ritten communication about student learning is augmented with frequent
onversations and strong relationships between teachers and families.
gnificant professional learning is devoted to empowering parents and families
nd leveraging family efficacy as a conduit to improved student achievement.

chool staff work directly with families to ensure that there are clear policies
nd procedures so that every family can participate and voice opinions
nd concerns. Metrics are established to determine the effectiveness of
mily efficacy programs, and evaluation processes are in place to promote
ontinuous improvement. The district and its component schools have in
lace a family mentoring program, supported with a budget and training so
hat families can directly assist other families in advocating for their child.

Practices to Be Implemented

(Continued)

(Continued)

3.2 The school is committed to the academic socialization of families and, to that end, develops and deploys strategies that encourage and support family engagement with specific learning in all classrooms.

Principle #3.2 Assessment

Use this chart to determine your organization's present level of performance.

Practice/Attribute/ Condition	Discuss/Reflect/Record the Present Status in Your School
All teachers and appropriate school staff understand that families are the primary agents of child socialization with the school.	
All teachers and appropriate staff collaborate on a consistent and continuing basis with every family.	
Evidence obtained by the school indicates that families are invested and knowledgeable about present and upcoming learning.	
The school measures the impact of family engagement not by attendance to events but by the degree to which family efficacy is improved and socialization of families is evident.	

Use the clarifying statement and the best practice description to help you shape your efforts to build family efficacy.

Best Practice Description

School personnel clearly understand that children's academic attitudes are shaped primarily by their families. Collaborative cultures exist with every family and are inclusive of the important and trusting relationships between school staff and families. This partnership promotes the important ideas of collegiality and efficacy among families, as families are considered to be the primary agents of child socialization with school.

Families are invested and knowledgeable about their children's learning. Teachers and appropriate school staff supply ongoing information about learning in the school, providing families with specific knowledge about classroom learning and expectations. As the efficacy of families is promoted, so is their academic socialization of their child's experiences, which ultimately improves the self-efficacy of students and produces better and more consistent learning outcomes. The school does not measure the degree of engagement by attendance to school events but rather gauges efficacy of families and its power to socialize them toward their children's education.

Practices to Be Implemented

3.3 Families participate in the development of the student's learning plan, help monitor and assess progress, and provide support for their child's learning.

Principle #3.3 Assessment

Use this chart to determine your organization's present level of performance.

Practice/Attribute/Condition	Discuss/Reflect/Record the Present Status in Your School
A variety of school and community resources are used to assist families in understanding academic expectations and goals.	

(Continued)

(Continued)

Communication regarding student progress is continuous, with an emphasis on promoting efficacy among all families.	
School personnel promote a commitment to family engagement and efficacy through various engagement strategies, including a regular home visit program.	
All families are aware of and have access to extended learning opportunities for their children.	
The school's efforts are supported by various community entities and agencies that assist in engaging every family with their children's educational experiences.	

Use the clarifying statement and the best practice description to help you shape your efforts to build family efficacy.

Best Practice Description

The school system and its component schools use a variety of school and community resources to ensure that every family understands what is expected academically from every child. Continuous communication of academic progress is available via verbal conversation, through written communication, and with the use of technology.

Family efficacy is promoted through a schoolwide commitment to outreach that includes the building of civic capacity, community engagement, home visits to families, and opportunities for parent leadership and advocacy development within the community. Outreach and extended learning activities are consistent and routine among all school staff. School strategic goals are written to measure the effectiveness and success of outreach activities designed to enhance school improvement.

The school is a critical partner with community agencies that foster a support mechanism for all families. Collaboration to provide parent training to support student learning is implemented and funded. Parent and family leaders, liaisons, and outreach staff continuously work to encourage engaged families to support the learning outcomes of all children.

Practices to Be Implemented

3.4 Families suggest learning strategies and experiential possibilities and use their local knowledge, personal skills, assets, and networks in ways that support the school's program.

Principle #3.4 Assessment

Use this chart to determine your organization's present level of performance.

Practice/Attribute/ Condition	Discuss/Reflect/Record the Present Status in Your School
Teacher professional development includes capacity building in extending learning into the home (beyond assigning homework) and promoting family efficacy.	
Teachers consistently use interactive lesson designs to be inclusive of families in ongoing learning.	
Teachers balance academic communication to families with evidence of past learning and engagement in future learning.	
Professional development activities are designed for or inclusive of families.	
Evidence supports the reengagement of families that are traditionally disengaged from their children's learning.	

Use the clarifying statement and the best practice description to help you shape your efforts to build family efficacy.

(Continued)

(Continued)

Best Practice Description

School staff are keenly aware that learning does not start and stop during the school day or at the school door. Learning extended into the home is an expected and critical component in the construction and design of instructional methodology for all students, in all classrooms, by all teachers. All teachers successfully complete training to promote parental efficacy with outreach strategies and interactive lessons designed to engage parents in student learning.

Academic communication to parents and families includes a balance of student work that has been completed (with a foreshadowing of the learning to take place) and the work yet to be done so that all families can engage with future learning. All families have adequate information and understanding of the standards that their children are expected to meet.

All school personnel are inclusive of families in designing lessons and further promote the efficacy of families by enhancing their belief in their ability to assist their child with academic work. Workshops, meetings, and other opportunities for families are designed to promote their understanding of what their children are to accomplish in school and provide specific resources, tools, support, and processes to encourage better and deeper learning outside of school.

All parents and families participate, and the school makes an extra effort to successfully include families that are or have been traditionally disengaged. There is tangible evidence that the engagement of these families and the promotion of their own efficacy produce better academic outcomes for their children. Families report high levels of satisfaction with their children's progress.

Practices to Be Implemented

CHAPTER 9

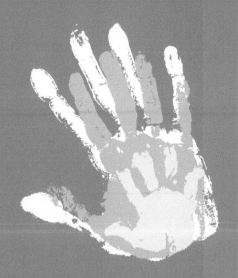

Principle #4
Engage Every Family in Decision Making

Public schools have become increasingly distant from the families of the children they serve, increasingly impersonal agents of a larger society.

—James Coleman (1985, p. 26)

Progressive transformation of schools must include constituents in decision-making processes. Schools that regularly include families in decision making understand that the varying perspectives strengthen the impact of the school and learning (Meador, 2018). Having a substantial and meaningful voice not only in what happens in school but also how it happens helps the organization create a culture of fairness and inclusivity (Shapiro & Stefkovish, 2016).

4 **Engage Every Family in Decision Making**

There is a great deal written on the importance of family engagement in governance and advocacy within the schools. Studies show that children of parents who are engaged in some aspects of school decision making have high levels of student achievement as well as a more supportive community and public at large (Epstein et al., 2002; National PTA, 2000).

Many schools, however, limit family engagement opportunities to ways in which the families can assist teachers and the school. Encouraging home–school association membership, volunteering in the classroom, volunteering for chaperoning field trips, and assisting with special activities or projects are just a few examples of how schools are inclusive of families (University of Washington, 2017).

While these are perfectly acceptable ways to engage families, there is a danger. These traditional methods of engagement can support a top-down power structure or, as Anne Henderson put it, the "come if we call you school" (Henderson, Mapp, Johnson, & Davies, 2007). Often, these opportunities limit the participation of families to those that are more privileged and, in many schools, are seen as catering to white, privileged families, which marginalizes low-income families and supports feelings of institutional racism. Partnering with families differently and giving them a greater voice in decision making can deconstruct the race or power-based structures (University of Washington, 2019).

> Traditional methods of engagement can support issues of a top-down power structure, or as Anne Henderson put it, the "come if we call you school."

Dr. Joyce Epstein is unquestionably one of the nation's most prolific and most often-cited researchers in the field of family engagement. Dr. Epstein is the architect of the Six Types of Family Involvement and heads the National Network of Partnership Schools.

Principle #4

Engage Every Family in Decision Making

Description: The school recognizes the entitlement of families to be consulted and participate in decisions concerning their own children. The school is genuinely inclusive in its approach to decision making. It recognizes that this type of process creates a sense of shared responsibility among families, students, community members, educators, and administrators.

4.1 The school creates opportunities for families to lead and participate in school learning, consultative, planning, social, and community events.

4.2 The school ensures that families and students have representation on the school's governing body and in relevant decision-making groups.

Of the Six Types of Family Involvement, decision making is number five. Below is the language used by Dr. Epstein with regard to this particular type of involvement:

> Decision Making—Type 5. The fifth type of parental involvement is decision making. Parents' voices must be heard when it comes to decision making at the school. This enables families to participate in decisions about the school's programs and activities that will impact their own and other children's educational experiences. All parents must be given opportunities to offer ideas and suggestions on ways to improve their schools. Having families as true stakeholders in the school creates feelings of ownership of the school's programs and activities. (National Network of Partnership Schools, n.d.)

Sample Activities

Examples of activities schools could conduct to promote decision making include but are not limited to

- encouraging parents to attend school improvement team meetings;
- assigning staff members to help parents address concerns or complaints;
- engaging families in surveys or focus groups to garner feedback;
- inviting staff and parent groups to meet collaboratively and providing space and time for them to do so;
- helping families advocate for each other; and
- involving families in planning orientation programs for new families, developing parenting skills programs, and hiring staff members.

PROBLEMS AND SOLUTIONS

Schools and districts should not only be aware of the input they receive from families but should also send the clear message that the input is welcomed and valued. It is essential that the opinions and ideas reflect the diversity of a school population. Student opinions are also important at the secondary level. Schools are encouraged to promote student and family representation in the decision-making process. The thoughts and ideas of all those participating must be trusted, respected, and heard.

Engaging families in real decision making and school governance, in many cases, warrants a huge shift in the norms of school cultures. Family engagement in decision making can be varied and can come in the form of community meetings, surveys, open houses, workshops, polling, school site councils, and other forms of engagement. This shift includes a redefinition of roles, a changed belief system with regard to relationships for all, and a redistribution of power (Bauch & Goldring, 1995). Families with students who are intellectually or developmentally disabled report that schools regularly exclude them from decision making (Love, Zagona, Kurth, & Miller, 2017).

These changing roles of parents and families can have a significantly positive impact on the educational outcomes of all students (Wehlage, Smith, & Lipman, 1992). The roles of parents are expanding into new arenas; most notably, parents are now taking on the role of customer or consumer because of the rise in choices for their children's education. With these new roles, parents begin to assume a greater voice in school governance and decision making.

Parents providing input into their children's education and exercising influence are the basic components of participation and empowerment, respectively (Bauch & Goldring, 1995). The involvement of families in the educational lives of their children has taken various turns and has been redefined over the years.

At the turn of the twentieth century, schools became more bureaucratic, espousing a "we know best" attitude and portraying educators as experts. This fundamental change in education began to significantly limit community influence over the school and limited further the influence of parents, especially those who were poor or those who were immigrants to the United States. The site-based management movement in education stressed a governance role of families to provide the best possible conditions for educating children (Havinghurst, 1972).

But changing the role that families have historically held continues to be problematic. *School councils, school improvement teams, and school correlate teams* are different terms used to describe groups of people—usually administrators, teachers, parents, students, and at times, members of the community—that direct the strategic operation and improvement of a school.

When these groups were established, families involved in these types of committees rarely gave input on the important components of school success: the budget, personnel, and programs (Bauch & Goldring, 1995). It seems that the reluctance of families to fully participate is directly related to their lack of understanding and information about school activities and school operations (Malen & Ogawa, 1988). Furthermore, Malen and Ogawa (1988) cite parental discomfort in questioning professionals and the manner in which parents are invited or appointed to participate on the council.

When school administration selects families to participate, it is engaging in a not-so-subtle form of control that manifests itself as a search for families who will be unlikely to rock the boat. It stands to reason that the problematic nature of engaging families in school decision making is unquestionably related directly to their reluctance to disturb or, worse yet, violate the established cultural norms of the school. Until this barrier is removed, it is unlikely that family engagement with governance and decision making will move far beyond token opportunities that provide few tangible results.

The inclusion of families in school decision making is an essential element for any school or district wishing to engage every family. To implement changes successfully, it is critical that all stakeholders have the opportunity to share in decisions about why changes are needed and how they are to be made (Kotter & Cohen, 2002). Research has found that changes that have involved or been led by families have resulted in significant achievements (Harris, 2009).

DeLaney (1997) has found that family involvement in school decision making must result in an overall satisfying experience or else schools will risk alienating the public and undermining their ongoing support for change.

Questions to Determine Effective Parent-Family Roles in School Decision Making

1. Does your school/district truly value the input of all families?

2. Do you offer parent leadership training to build the capacity and efficacy for family engagement in decision making?

3. In what decisions do you (will you) engage families? Why? What decisions will not include families? Why?

4. How will you ensure that engagement in decision making is representative of all the families that your school serves?

WHERE WE ARE TODAY

In many cases, we have made great strides in understanding the importance of family engagement, empowerment, and advocacy. Organizations such as Project Appleseed and the Governor's

Commonwealth Institute for Parent Leadership (GCIPL) have created standards for parental involvement and include decision making as one of those important standards (Pritchard Committee for Academic Excellence, 2015). The goal for parental involvement in decision making is to include parents in school decisions as well as to develop parent leaders and representatives.

In their report, *The Missing Piece of the Proficiency Puzzle*, the Kentucky Commissioner's Parent Advisory Council (2007) suggested that Kentucky become the first state in the nation to set standards for family and community engagement. Setting this standard involved creating six overarching objectives: (1) relationship building, (2) communications, (3) decision making, (4) advocacy, (5) learning opportunities, and (6) community partnerships. Within the objective devoted to decision making, the report encourages school staff to support and expect parents to be involved in school improvement decisions and to monitor and assist with school improvement.

These are the very notions upon which the Five Simple Principles are built. The National PTA (2000), developing its own set of parent involvement standards, clearly delineates the importance of parents as full partners in the decisions that affect all children and families.

LET EVERY FAMILY HAVE A SAY

Parent involvement in school governance is a significant pillar in the site-based or school-based infrastructure. Whether through empowerment, advocacy, or participation, parents and families having a say in the operation of their children's school and, more importantly, in their own child's education is a critical component in any listing of family engagement objectives for schools.

Whether through advocacy committees, traditional organizations (such as Parent–Teacher Associations [PTAs] and other groups), or school councils designed to lead the school through strategic planning and school improvement, family engagement with decision making and governance cannot be overlooked when designing a comprehensive set of standards to implement and measure the effectiveness of family participation in education.

Regardless if families volunteer, are appointed, or are elected, their involvement and, more importantly, their engagement with the strategic direction of the school are essential not only for school improvement but also for the improvement of the learning outcomes for all children.

A WORKING DEFINITION

A new standard definition incorporating family engagement in decision making, advocacy, and governance should encompass the simple concept of family engagement with the strategic (macro) direction of the school and the development, implementation, and evaluation of programs, policies, and practices (micro) within the school that impact the education of students. From this definition, the standards can be developed.

It is important for families to know that their children attend a school that has adopted the philosophy of continuous improvement. Engaging families with strategic planning and goal setting is critical to this process. School leaders should make ample time to share pertinent data and information about student achievement in a format that all families can understand. For those parents who will have a direct responsibility for assisting with the strategic goal setting, training should be made available so that parents are equal partners when the time comes to review and analyze data and make recommendations for advancement.

> It is important for families to know that their children attend a school that has adopted the philosophy of continuous improvement. Engaging families with strategic planning and goal setting is critical to this process.

The school council or school improvement team is essential to family engagement with governance. However, having only one committee limits the degree to which parents are engaged with school governance and strategic planning. School leaders and members of the council should expand the work of the main council by forming subgroups around the data, goals, and objectives of the strategic plan. These subgroups, similar in construction to the main council, act as an extension of the council, looking deeper into data, following implementation strategies closely, and looking for evidence of success to be reported to the larger community.

HOW TO SELECT FAMILIES

Probably one of the most difficult challenges to engaging families in this type of governance is finding enough parents willing to give of their time and then ensuring that the parents doing the work are representative of the entire community. Further, you may find yourself trying to convince a family that their participation and opinions are indeed valued and necessary. While many family engagement standards are inclusive of the notion that a wide variety of parents and families must be involved, there is little guidance as to how to create a representative pool of parents. Failure to implement a system that ensures that all parents are represented runs the risk of a certain type or class of parents being involved in all aspects. This actually moves to further disengage those parents who are already disengaged from the school.

Geographic Representation

The first option open to school leaders and councils is to study the geography and population of the school attendance area. Most district offices can provide an analysis of where families live and the concentration of families within neighborhoods and regions. Often, transportation maps and student pick-up plans can provide great data to determine where families live. Knowing this information helps to balance the representation, much like the census does in establishing senate and congressional districts. The fictitious example below represents this approach to engaging parents in governance:

Anytown Elementary School

Student population: 800

Number of parents/families needed to fill council/committee positions: 30

Neighborhood	Number of Families	Percentage of Whole*	Number of Representatives
Barron Estates	150	19	6
West Village	200	25	8
East Village	50	6.2	2
City Apartments	260	32.4	9
Mount Pleasant	50	6.2	2
Amberton Valley, Links Estates, Rural Families	90	11.2	3
Total	800	100	30

*Percentages rounded and adjusted.

When looking for parents and families to participate in various school governance councils, this simple chart can guide recruiting efforts. Representatives can go to homeowner associations, apartment complex committees, and so forth to share why the school needs the assistance and how the engagement of families from this particular area will be proportionally representative of the families that the school serves.

For cities and rural areas, maps can be drawn and divided by quadrants or other ways to garner representative support. Local high school math classes might welcome the real-life math problem to help their own school or neighboring schools.

Ethnic Representation

The very same process as identified above can also work if schools wish to divide parent participation by ethnicity and race in those schools that are significantly diverse. A stratification of the above two charts can even provide a more pinpointed approach to parent engagement by not only determining the neighborhood or area but also using the multicultural aspects of the areas to ensure that parents are geographically represented, as are their ethnicity, nationality, and race.

These representatives then can become ambassadors for their neighborhoods and areas. The school frequently publishes (with consent) the names, addresses, and contact information of family participants so that any family that may have a question, concern, or idea understands that there is a representative just for them. These ambassadors can also hold neighborhood meetings, parent coffees, and so forth to help all families understand the information being created with regard to the strategic plan and vision of the school.

GETTING BACK TO THE TIP OF THE SPEAR

Consistent adherence to this type of process changes culture. Over time, as the expectations, beliefs, and values of all stakeholders change, the processes will get easier, largely because they become ingrained into the fabric of the school. Regardless of leadership or committee changes, the process will be intact for years to come.

School administrators spend a great deal of time working with families who raise concerns and objections to issues that occur within the context of the school day. From academic issues ("Why did my son get a zero?") to behavioral issues ("Why was my son suspended for three days?") to school climate issues ("I think my daughter's clothes are appropriate and are not suggestive!"), administrators spend an inordinate amount of time helping families through the maze of policies, procedures, and practices within the school.

This time away from the "tip of the spear" of school leadership—the focus on student performance and school improvement—is a symptom of a larger problem. Administrators often lament that the time to focus on instructional issues is significantly reduced because of these other noninstructional issues. Developing customer understanding and loyalty toward the policies that govern the school and the procedures and practices that allow the school to function each day is rooted in the degree to which parents and families are engaged from the beginning or, better yet, before the beginning.

> Developing customer understanding and loyalty toward the policies that govern the school and the procedures and practices that allow the school to function each day is rooted in the degree to which parents and families are engaged from the beginning or, better yet, before the beginning.

When processes that cultivate family understanding and loyalty are touted as a conduit to success, school personnel have the same reaction: We have no time to do that. As the late Stephen R. Covey taught us, we have the choice to focus on what is urgent or what is important. It seems reasonable that spending the time to cultivate understanding and loyalty to a school and its procedures will save a great deal of time that would be devoted to problem solving, family distress, and negative catalysts that ultimately cause school–family relationships to be severely limited or, worse yet, destroyed.

By using effective communication for family feedback (surveys, focus groups, websites, flyers, parent organizations, etc.), school personnel can engage a significant portion of the population. Below is an example of how to engage and build understanding and loyalty toward a school policy, procedure, or practice.

AN EXAMPLE OF FAMILY GOVERNANCE IN ACTION

The Anytown High School Tardy Policy

Data from Anytown High School suggest a growing problem with the number of students either late to school or arriving late to classes throughout the day. Five-year data indicate a 25 percent increase in the number of students tardy to school or class.

The data have been disaggregated further to show that the problem is more pronounced with students in the ninth grade and the rate of tardiness among minority students outpaces that of majority students. The principal of Anytown High School has decided to take the issue to the school council to develop a new, more stringent tardy policy.

The scenario above is fairly common among schools. By analyzing data, the administration discovers a problem; the school leadership, along with the council, wishes to resolve the problem. In most cases, there will be discussion in the council of how the tardy policy can be strengthened so that the problem is diminished or resolved.

The administration develops a new plan, brings it to the council for approval, and, once approved, the policy is implemented the following school year. While this process seems sound, it does not engage enough families in the policies, procedures, and practices of the school and, as such, when the policy is enacted, the administration is in for a large contingent of angry students and families who will be caught off-guard by the change.

A better, more productive way is to elicit information from students and families in a meaningful way so that the new policy is truly representative of the thoughts and ideas of the entire community. Steps toward this enhanced process might include the following:

- Parent ambassadors host community (neighborhood) meetings to share the information.
- Information is shared via homeowner or neighborhood email lists.
- Focus groups conducted by representatives of the school council are implemented to garner information and opinions.
- Students who have been offenders of the policy are interviewed to determine the root causes of the tardiness.
- The information that has been collected is collated and reviewed by the committee to determine if it is policy that needs to be changed or if there are practices that can be changed that would resolve the problem.
- The results are effectively communicated through numerous vehicles long before the policy, procedure, or practice is put into effect.
- The council and subcommittees put into place mechanisms to monitor and provide feedback during the initial inception of the new policy to determine its effectiveness.

Research and practice agree that there are a number of tangible strategies that, when employed with fidelity, increase family engagement with school decision making and allow every family to have a voice in the education of their children.

Attention to how families are invited to participate in school governance and decision-making activities is critical. Attention to ethnic, social, and economic diversity is important when setting the stage to allow every family to have a voice. Professional learning that includes families, families who mentor or adopt other families, and varied measures of collecting information all lend themselves well to creating a culture that demonstrates a strong commitment to reaching beyond the few families that are traditionally engaged.

Most important is the clear idea that parents and families are welcomed and valued as part of the school decision-making process. Building the capacity of families in decision making ensures that in time, every family will have a voice.

CASE STUDY: THE UNIFORM POLICY

David Marks was the new principal at River Crest Middle School. David was new to the school and new to the school district, having worked as an assistant principal in a district over 200 miles from his new school. At David's former school, a strict uniform policy was in place that all students were required to comply with. Students had their choice of a few colors of shirts and were required to wear khaki pants or, for girls, knee-length skirts. There was assistance available in acquiring uniforms for families in need.

David's first order of business at River Crest was to garner support for a uniform policy. He knew that uniforms reduced misbehavior rates in school and had a profound effect on homework completion rates and test scores. He also had data to prove his assertions. He wanted to be sure that the same level of success could be generated at River Crest as at his previous school.

River Crest student achievement had been declining in recent years. The school had seen enrollment growth beyond its functional capacity and a significant shift in the demographics of the student population. River Crest had been in the process of being identified as a Title I school when its previous principal decided to retire. David knew that he had his work cut out for him and also believed that getting the uniform policy in place was a key ingredient in his plan for success.

During the first days of summer, David gathered the school improvement team for a meeting. The team consisted of a few teachers who were team leaders at the school, the assistant principal, the guidance counselor, and three parents. One of the parents was the president of the PTA, and the other two parents were recruited to serve on the committee by the previous principal. Decisions regarding school processes, policies, and procedures were first discussed at the School Improvement Team meetings and then, if agreement existed, taken to the faculty and the PTA for feedback.

David did an excellent job of pitching his idea of school uniforms. The School Improvement Team was actually excited about the idea and pledged its full support. David wondered aloud to the group if the policy could start in the fall. No one saw why not. There was plenty of time left in the summer to communicate the policy to families and for families to prepare.

The teachers on the School Improvement Team sent a survey to all staff to gather input on the new uniform policy. Concurrently, the PTA president sent an email to all members of the PTA who had given their email addresses. The remaining parents vowed to share the information with other parents as well. The incoming class of sixth-grade students and their families were not on any email lists. David promised to send a letter to all of those parents explaining the process of developing this new policy.

Within a week or so, David received excellent news: Over 85 percent of the school staff were in favor of the new uniform policy. The PTA president reported that the overwhelming majority of people who responded to her email were also in favor of the new policy. The two parents on the committee in addition to the PTA president reported, "Everyone that we talked to loved the idea." David was thrilled. His first goal had been completed. At the beginning of the next week, with over eight weeks left of the summer before school started, David sent out a letter introducing himself as the new principal and outlining the expectations for the new uniform policy that was to take effect when school started in the upcoming fall.

As David's letters started arriving at homes and were read by parents, the River Crest phones went on overload. The secretaries could not keep up with the calls coming in to complain about the new uniform policy. Parents were angry, and some were somewhat hostile on the phone with staff. Within a few hours, David had over 100 phone messages to return. At the same time, numerous parents took to Facebook, and the comments were not positive or supportive. David watched in disbelief as the number of "likes" for the comment "Get rid of the new principal and the uniforms" added up right in front of his eyes. An anti-uniform campaign had already been organized and was being disseminated through Facebook and Twitter. Hundreds of parents were attaching their support to ensure that this policy never materialized.

At the summer school board meeting, over fifty River Crest parents were in attendance. Many spoke to the school board about the unfairness of the policy and being "blindsided" by the new principal. Parents demanded the superintendent and/or school board members step in and, in the words of one parent, "stop this madness." The superintendent contacted David the next morning to discuss the matter.

David was dumbfounded. He explained that he understood the process for policy changes at the school and had followed it precisely. A survey was sent to faculty and parents and all the information came back supportive. The superintendent indicated that the district communications office had now confirmed that opposition to the policy far outweighed support. David was told to put a hold on his policy until he could demonstrate support in the community for it.

David's happiness was short-lived. He had been the principal for barely one month, but he had already created a problem that had landed at the doorstep of the school board and superintendent. His School Improvement Team members tried to cheer David up and let him know that they would help him get the support he needed.

David was privately thinking that he had made a terrible mistake in accepting this new job.

Questions for Discussion

1. David followed the school process for new policies. Why did things go wrong?

2. With all of the initial feedback coming back so positive and supportive, how did David miss the overwhelming negative reaction?

3. Why did so many families react negatively? What were they negative about?

4. How could David have better understood his community before launching his new policy?

5. Given what you have learned about family engagement in governance and decision making, what could have been done differently to avoid the confrontation?

PRINCIPLE #4

Where We Are

Description

The school recognizes the entitlement of families to be consulted and participate in decisions concerning their own children. The school is genuinely inclusive in its approach to decision making. It recognizes that this type of process creates a sense of shared responsibility among families, students, community members, educators, and administrators.

Based on the description, discuss and record where you think your school is today as it relates to the principle description.

4.1 The school creates opportunities for families to lead and participate in school learning, consultative, planning, social, and community events.

Principle #4.1 Assessment

Use this chart to determine your organization's present level of performance.

Practice/Attribute/ Condition	Discuss/Reflect/Record the Present Status in Your School
Multiple opportunities and venues for family engagement in decision making exist in the school.	
Families are regularly invited and encouraged to attend professional development sessions that are important for the school's continued improvement.	
Every family is represented in the strategic planning and evaluation of the school.	
The school has a systemic process for family feedback prior to significant decisions or policy revisions.	
The school subscribes to the notion that it is a community learning center and, as such, is inclusive of families in aspects of governance and operation that directly affect them or their children.	

Use the clarifying statement and the best practice description to help you shape your efforts to engage families in decision making.

Best Practice Description

The school has developed, implemented, and evaluated an extensive network of opportunities for families to learn and be engaged with their children's learning as well as decisions that affect their children and has an effective public relations plan to ensure that every family understands the opportunities open to them. Families are invited to participate in training and professional learning programs for teachers and other staff and have specific professional learning programs designed for them.

(Continued)

(Continued)

There are systems in place for participation in strategic planning and rules and procedures development, and data show a significantly high level of family engagement. The school creates mechanisms for feedback prior to implementing programs or practices that will affect children and their families. The school is dedicated to a system of strategic communication that frames issues and ideas for families and thoughtfully engages them to solicit feedback, ideas, and opinions.

The school understands its role as a community learning center; the school works in tandem with families to ensure that school goals and environments are reflective of family input and opinion. The school/district hosts social and community events in different parts of the district and is inclusive of all families in the events, with detailed attention toward language, culture, and demographic issues. Data collected by the school indicate a high satisfaction and engagement rate among all families regarding their ability to become involved and immersed in learning, planning, and events.

Practices to Be Implemented

4.2 The school ensures that families and students have representation on the school's governing body and in relevant decision-making groups.

Principle #4.2 Assessment

Use this chart to determine your organization's present level of performance.

Practice/Attribute/ Condition	Discuss/Reflect/Record the Present Status in Your School
Leadership is committed to providing avenues for all families to engage in shared decision making.	
Policies, procedures, and practices governing family engagement in decision making are evident and supported by all school staff.	
The selection of families for representative decision making is done in a manner that ensures inclusivity of all families and neighborhoods.	
Schools have councils or committees established to guide school improvement, and families have a representative seat on this council/ committee.	
Evidence that is collected supports that family engagement in school decision making is authentic and that families feel valued as a result of the process.	

Use the clarifying statement and the best practice description to help you shape your efforts to engage families in decision making.

Best Practice Description

The leadership and staff of the school and district believe that a platform of shared decision making is critical to creating an environment of continuous improvement and, as such, allows for numerous vehicles by which every family can have a say in the decisions made within the individual schools and at the district level. Not only have policies and procedures been put into place at the system level, but monies are budgeted to ensure that sufficient training supports quality processes.

(Continued)

(Continued)

The culture of the organization has shifted and has redefined the roles of families; created a changed belief system with regard to building and maintaining effective relationships to promote shared decision making; and redistributed power to allow for families to partner in the governance of the schools, including budget and school improvement issues. The district understands the role of families as customer and consumer and has in place systems and metrics to determine the needs of its customers and involve its customers in decisions that affect the overall operation and governance of the school.

Every school within the district has a council on which family representatives participate. Schools have ensured through a well-defined process that all neighborhoods and geographical areas within the attendance zone are represented on the council and that there is a mechanism in place to establish how parents and families will be appointed and for what length of time they will serve. Interpreters and materials translated into native languages are available.

Whether the council is advisory in nature or has voting and operational rights/control, at the center is the belief of the school system and its employees that families have a voice in decision making and governance. Mechanisms are also in place to garner the opinions of families or the community when decisions are being discussed and considered.

Families participating on decision-making councils report that their participation is authentic; they feel that there is significant value in the process and report to a wide range of families on the work of the council. A mechanism of family mentorship is in place to ensure that quality participation is continually maintained.

Practices to Be Implemented

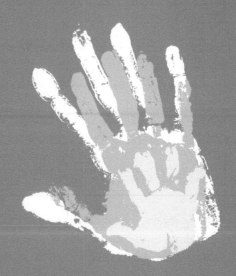

CHAPTER 10

Principle #5
Engage the Greater Community

THE POWER OF COMMUNITY

5

Engage the Greater Community

Today, schools find themselves in an era of increased accountability, standard-based reforms, and shifting federal and state law to support the continuous improvement of schools. Savvy school leaders recognize the importance of community engagement and partnership. Community partners have a positive impact on schools, especially urban schools. These important relationships can improve schools, combat economic barriers, and meet the increasing accountability demands (Cummings & Olsen, 2019).

199

Principle #5

Engage the Greater Community

Description: The school places a strong focus on building and creating partnerships external to the school. The school recognizes the strengths and talents that exist in the community that influence student learning and development and seeks to use these to strengthen and support the school, students, and their families. The principle also recognizes that the school can be a focal point for communities to come together and engage in capacity building and renewal. The school views itself as an important community asset and has community representatives on the school's governing body. There is a clear recognition from the school that the greater community plays an integral role in the educational success of the school.

5.1 Partnerships are made with individuals and organizations in work and community places to take on mentoring roles within student internship and work placement programs. The partnerships also have a role to play within other activities, such as community-based learning projects, guest speaker programs, job shadowing opportunities, apprenticeship opportunities, and tutoring services.

5.2 Partnerships are made with other learning institutions—other schools, technical colleges, universities, and other training providers in order for students to pursue learning opportunities, build their skills, and achieve learning credentials.

5.3 Opportunities evolve from the school for creating and implementing adult learning and community development courses to be run within the school building.

The quality of connections between children's education and the community that surrounds that education is a significant component in the successful education of every child (Christenson & Sheridan, 2001). For those community partnerships to be effective, there must exist a keen understanding of the cultural, socioeconomic, health, social, and recreational needs and interests of each school's families. Family literacy programs, health services, English as a second language programs, and vocational training programs are all examples of community-based programs that support families, which in turn support the education of children (Espinosa, 1995).

School and community partnerships can lead a school toward more effective school reform and improvement. The traditional notion of community partnerships is now expanded to include the social, emotional, and health aspects of student experiences in school. This interagency approach broadens the educational mission of the school and assists in supporting all students and families (Valli, Stefanski, & Reuben, 2018). When school leaders adopt a community-based approach to leadership, relationships with families improve and families are connected to important and needed resources. As a result of this focus, families and schools come together to recognize assets and problem-solve school and community issues. In other words, there is universal benefit in social capital approaches to school leadership (DeMatthews, 2018).

> The traditional notion of community partnerships is now expanded to include the social, emotional, and health aspects of student experiences in school.

Experts and researchers in the field of community engagement provide advice on building partnerships between schools and community groups and agencies. Experts agree that conceptualizing the role of the partnership and then planning for it are essential first steps, with the planning phase often cited as the most important step.

POINTS TO PONDER

1. How do you presently engage the community in your classroom/ school/ district?

2. How does that engagement translate into student learning?

3. How can you enhance community engagement to support learning for all students?

4. How can community support assist with the social, emotional, and health aspects of your students' lives?

The school principal and the community need to work together on establishing goals, assessing needs, developing a vision, and deciding management issues. Evaluating the effectiveness as well as the outcomes of the partnerships are also essential if partnerships are to succeed and persevere (Gretz, 2003).

SOCIAL CAPITAL AND MODERN SCHOOL-COMMUNITY PARTNERSHIPS

The networks of relationships among people who live and work in a particular society, which enables that society to function more effectively, is a definition of social capital theory. While there are varied definitions of the constructs of social capital theory, all of them generally focus on the social relationships that have productive benefits (Claridge, 2004).

With a great deal of attention focused on preparing high school students for what comes after graduation, schools everywhere are turning to business and industry partnerships as a way to improve the quality and relevance of education to students (Ehlen, van der Klink, & Boshuizen, 2015). Outreach to community partners is not limited simply to providing more authentic learning environments for students. A growing number of schools recognize the increased social and emotional needs of students and thus are coordinating efforts with various community partners and agencies. The idea behind the concept of a "community of practice" suggests that the social capital theory involved brings together the necessary supports to improve opportunities for children with these needs (Botha & Kourkoutas, 2015).

COMMUNITY SCHOOLS AND ASSET MAPPING

A community school is both a set of partnerships and a place where an integrated focus on academics, services, supports, and opportunities leads to improved student learning, stronger families, and healthier communities. Using public schools as a hub, community schools knit together inventive, enduring relationships among educators, families, community volunteers, and community partners—businesses, family support groups, health and social service agencies, youth development organizations, community organizations, and other organizations—committed to children. They act in concert to transform traditional schools—permanently—into partnerships for excellence. Because individual schools and the school system join forces with community agencies and organizations to operate community schools, schools are not left to work alone (Blank, Melaville, & Shah, 2003).

Community schools can vary in offerings or the ways they operate. Many schools either sustain or partner with programs to increase student achievement and school quality through

- integrated student supports,
- expanded learning time and opportunities,
- family and community engagement, and
- collaborative leadership and practice.

Community schools lead to improved outcomes when their programs are well implemented and contribute to the needs of all students, with emphasis on those students that are low achieving or attend high-poverty schools (Learning Policy Institute, 2017).

THE ADVANTAGES OF COMMUNITY SCHOOLS

Supporters of community education understand the advantages of community-based educational opportunities and the social capital that is created with partnerships between schools and the communities they serve. Being able to build a better and stronger capacity for helping students achieve at their highest levels is at the core of why educators need to embrace the concept of community schools. Involving communities provides access to additional resources and opportunities for school environments and programs that meet the needs of all students, not only some students. Developing students in an academic venue has been a core process of public education from its inception.

A community school not only develops academic proficiencies but inspires students to learn and grow in nonacademic venues as well. This marriage produces the landscape within which all students can learn at high levels. Lastly, the idea of social capital, reinforced and enhanced by connecting students to the community, is now a source of learning and exploration.

As presented by Kretzmann and McKnight (1993), community asset mapping is a capacity-focused way of redeveloping communities. This positive approach is proposed as a substitute for the traditional focus on deficits when examining a community's needs and problems. Using problems to formulate human service interventions, the authors maintain, targets resources to service providers rather than residents, fragments efforts to provide solutions, places reliance on outside resources and outside experts, and leads to a maintenance and survival mentality rather than to community development.

> Community asset mapping is a capacity-focused way of redeveloping communities. This positive approach is proposed as a substitute for the traditional focus on deficits when examining a community's needs and problems.

Instead, the authors propose the development of policies and activities based on an understanding or map of the community's resources— individual capacities and abilities and organizational resources with the potential for promoting personal and community development (Kretzmann & McKnight, 1993). This mapping is designed to promote connections or relationships between individuals, between individuals and organizations, and between organizations and organizations.

The asset-based approach, the authors maintain, does not remove the need for outside resources but makes their use more effective. The community assets approach

- starts with what is present in the community;
- concentrates on the agenda-building and problem-solving capacity of the residents; and
- stresses local determination, investment, creativity, and control.

In this context, spatial mapping may or may not be used. Within any given neighborhood or community, most assets as defined by Kretzmann and McKnight (1993) do not have a spatial quality. Community asset mapping has very little to do with spatial mapping and much more to do with a community survey and the mobilizing of individuals and organizations to make connections and build capacity.

The information obtained through the survey process must be organized and accessed in an inventory format. It can be computerized as a database inventory. Computerized mapping can be used, showing the location of assets on a geographic map as well as the attributes attached to each asset.

The community asset mapping process is intended to initiate a process that will fully mobilize a community to use its assets around a vision and a plan to solve its own problems. Their guidebook provides considerable detail about how this might be accomplished, with numerous examples of the types of connections that can be developed.

Assets Map: Possible Components

An asset map can include all or any portion of the ideas presented below, depending on the needs of the school or school district. Map, collect, and discuss your findings.

Geographic representation (may look more like a map)

- Geographic features (rivers, mountains, etc.)

- Demographics (population density areas)

- Features (highways, businesses)

- Other

Broad categories (create lists)

- Resources (services, businesses, faith groups, clubs)

- Attributes (geographic, people power, etc.)

- Opportunities (coming soon, could be, and what ifs)

- Needs/concerns (problems, gaps, etc.)

- Other

Social capital resources (list or matrix name, service/product, consumer population)

- Health and human services organizations

- Public and private organizations

- Cultural groups (library, museum, etc.)

- Foundations

- Faith-based organizations

- Service clubs

- Social and fraternal groups

- Schools

- Recreation programs

- Businesses

- Manufacturers, retailers (large and small)

- Other

School district (may be lists and graphs)

- Assets

- Concerns

- Demographics

- Population of municipalities in the district

- Racial/cultural breakdown

- Predominant languages

- Student proficiency levels/test scores

- Community support

- Other

How can this information garner community support for your school? This information is available for download at **http://www.drsteveconstantino.com**

ACTIVITY
Community Asset Mapping Made Simple

Step One

Put together your focus team. (I like the word *team* rather than *group* because it translates into teamwork.) The team should include an administrator, teacher, community representative, parent, student, parent from the Parent–Teacher Association, businessperson, park and recreation representative, and so forth. Provide as much diversity as possible when forming your asset mapping team.

Step Two

Supply the team with a three-by-five foot or enlarged attendance area map, laminated and (if possible) framed onto corkboard. Provide each team member with color-coded pushpins and some round label tags (like you use on a key ring).

Step Three

Ask your team to define assets and then brainstorm assets in your community. Assets can include but are not limited to things such as parks, health clinics and hospitals, skate parks, community services or agencies, potential partners, or anything the group sees as an asset for their community. Once the team identifies all of the potential assets within the school community, the team can partner up and canvass a portion of the attendance area, interview someone from the facility, get a flyer, and write a short statement about what is offered at that facility.

Step Four

Color code the asset map. (For example: Blue is for health clinics. Take a blue pushpin and number the facility.)

Step Five

Construct a small write-up about that facility—hours, services, and so forth.

Step Six

Translate the write-ups into the languages of the school and put them in an online database that can be shared and updated as necessary. If possible, create an e-version of your map and hyperlink it to the color-coded assets in your community. Of course, there is always the tried-and-true, old-fashioned way of putting everything into a notebook!

This information is available for download at **http://www.drsteveconstantino.com**

THE START OF AN ASSET MAP

Below is a depiction of what the start of an asset map might look like:

Community Asset Map

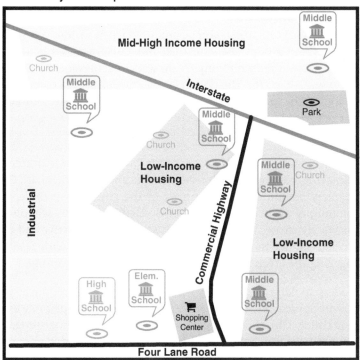

This map, which can be considerably more detailed, notes the following:

- The location of schools
- The location of churches, parks, and shopping centers
- The location of types of neighborhoods
- The location of roads, main thoroughfares, and highways
- The location of nonresidential areas

Here are a few questions that the asset map might help answer. Remember to consider the nonspatial applications of assets:

- What challenges may be inherent to this district?
- What challenges may be inherent to the individual schools?
- What kinds of engagement challenges do you think the schools have?
- What community resources are available and how could they be used to support the schools?

- What other information might be good to know that should be added to this map? In other words, what don't you know that you probably need to know?

THE IDEA OF COLLECTIVE IMPACT

A new type of capital can also be produced when various community agencies and groups abandon their individual agendas in favor of "a collective approach to improving student achievement" (Kania & Kramer, 2011, p. 36). The notion of *collective impact* is a commitment of a group of specific actors from various sectors of the community to work together in creating a common agenda or solving a specific social problem.

The successful example of this process is Project Strive, which seems to be making a difference with regard to education in Cincinnati, Ohio. In many communities, the impact of the engagement of separate community agencies brings about isolated impacts to schools and thus rarely creates the change that is sought. Project Strive and other projects similar to it are said to be turning the tide with regard to engaging the greater community to support student learning.

Leaders looking to make a true difference for education adapt a holistic approach to reform, realizing that trying to repair one aspect of a child's educational experience, such as after-school programs, will not have the desired long-term effect unless all of the necessary components improve simultaneously (Kania & Kramer, 2011). The textbook definition for *collective impact* is, "the commitment of a group of important actors from different sectors to a common agenda for solving a specific social problem" (p. 36).

HOW COMMUNITY CONNECTIONS CAN HELP

Minority students now make up 42 percent of public-school enrollment (Kena et al., 2014). In the vast majority of schools that have seen a rise in minority students, many because of the surge of Latino and Hispanic students, the students themselves often lag behind. According to the National Assessment of Educational Progress (NAEP), low-achieving youngsters accounted for 37.6 percent of students scoring in the lowest quintile (Flanagan & Grissmer, 2002). Price (2008) suggests there are a number of challenges with which community engagement can help, such as closing the gap of what students know and need to know, drop-out rates, student disengagement, and the gap in higher education attainment.

With all of this evidence, why is it that community engagement with schools is overlooked by educators as a primary strategy by which to combat low student achievement? Some would argue that most teachers and administrators are educated to think of themselves as individual leaders of classrooms, schools, or districts, with little attention paid to the importance of teamwork and collaborations with parents, community partners, and others interested in students' success in school.

Colleges and universities have been slow to change required curricula to incorporate the preparation of teacher and leadership candidates to work with families, and communities have been slow to respond as well (McBride, 1991). Epstein and Sanders (2006) surveyed 161 colleges and universities and found that while some progress has been made with regard to this issue, much work needed to be done to ensure that educators emerging from preparation programs could act as catalysts and effectively foster collaborative partnerships that supported all children.

THE NECESSARY INGREDIENTS FOR SUCCESSFUL COMMUNITY ENGAGEMENT

In order for partnerships to be effective, four factors need to be present to allow schools to build successful linkages and relationships with community groups and agencies that result in improved learning for all students (Sanders & Harvey, 2002). The school's commitment to learning, the principal's support and vision for community involvement, the school's receptivity and openness to community involvement, and the school's willingness to engage in two-way communication are all important ingredients.

Today, the term *professional learning community* is well established in U.S. schools. Epstein and Salinas (2004) offer a new term, the *school learning community*, as a stronger alternative. The authors make the following comparison between professional learning communities and school learning communities:

> A professional learning community emphasizes the teamwork of principals, teachers, and staff to identify school goals, improve curriculum and instruction, reduce teachers' isolation, assess student progress, and increase the effectiveness of school programs. Professional teamwork is important and can greatly improve teaching, instruction, and professional relationships in a school, but it falls short of producing a true community of learners. In contrast, a school learning community includes educators, students, parents, and community partners who

work together to improve the school and enhance students' learning opportunities. (p. 12)

As is the case with other authors and researchers, Epstein and Salinas (2004) suggest action teams made up of the internal and external constituents listed above and well-crafted action plans to design, implement, and evaluate successful school learning communities. Organizationally, educators, parents, and other partners work together to strengthen and maintain their community involvement programs over time. These partners also recognize that they all have roles to play in helping students succeed in school.

THE BENEFITS OF ENGAGING THE COMMUNITY

Schools continue to struggle with issues that act as barriers to allowing all students to be successful in school. Engaging and connecting with the greater community and developing strong, measurable partnerships with them provide successful academic dividends to all children.

Attendance

Epstein and Sheldon (2002) found that schools are more likely to improve student attendance and reduce chronic absenteeism with three broad strategies: (1) taking a comprehensive approach to attendance with activities that involve students, families, and the community; (2) using more positive involvement activities than negative or punishing activities; and (3) sustaining a focus on improving attendance over time. Schools that conduct a variety of activities that involve students, parents, and community partners see increases in favorable attendance.

Supporting Language-Minority Students

Language-minority students suffer a mismatch between the language and culture of their schools and those they experience at home and in their community (Adger & Locke, 2000). The more schools establish programs with community-based organizations, the more likely language-minority students will prosper and learn in their local schools. Adger and Locke (2000) suggest that a few partnerships have made radical changes in elementary schooling and at the secondary school level; partnerships often use traditional methods of assisting students academically, such as tutoring students in the academic areas, supporting English language development, and organizing programs to promote students' leadership skills and higher education goals.

But they also address social factors that may interfere with students' achievement. For example, the Filipino Youth Empowerment program directly targets gang participation as a risk factor. This partnership also offers innovative services, such as bridging gaps between immigrant parents and their Americanized children. In secondary schools, partnerships are apt to work with existing school structures without altering them significantly, although this is not always the case.

Several recommendations are made to foster these important collaborations, including commitment by both parties and the need to start small and build the partnership. Research summaries clearly show that language-minority students benefit from school and community-based partnerships.

After-School Programs

It is important that the after-school program staff understand and link their efforts to the school curriculum. Henderson, Mapp, Johnson, and Davies (2007) share steps to ensure the proper curricular alignment between after-school programs and schools (p. 107):

- Encourage after-school program staff and teachers to observe each other at work and share ideas and information about the students.
- Invite program staff to attend professional development sessions to update and build their teaching skills.
- Inform program staff about the school's curriculum and learning programs (especially math and reading).
- Exchange textbooks, assignments, and learning materials.
- Share the school's data on student achievement and other outcomes.

Authors and researchers repeatedly underscore the need to link student learning to programs and activities that support in-school learning. This type of work also leads to building a more successful and broader base of engagement for families by connecting them to others in the community.

Successful partnerships can emanate from just about anywhere: committed leadership, teachers, and community supporters and/ or activists. The challenge to all administrators is not to carve up responsibilities among a shrinking roll of educators but to look to their communities for the resources necessary and reconceptualize the role of schools and their relationships to communities so that the education of every child is enhanced. The relationship between a community and its public schools must be strengthened if the schools wish to have lasting success for every child.

ADDITIONAL BENEFITS OF SCHOOL-COMMUNITY PARTNERSHIPS

In addition to the return on investment already discussed, there are other benefits from exploring and building partnerships with community groups, agencies, and businesses. Partnerships increase the likelihood that community members become more knowledgeable and aware of school environment and performance and can give better input and support as a result of this knowledge. Community members gain a better appreciation and understanding of the larger social, economic, and cultural demands placed on the schools, students, and their families.

In an era of decreasing revenue and increased scrutiny of the expenditure of taxpayer funds, community partnerships help those outside of the schools to see the wise and efficient expenditure of funds and garner a better understanding of how and why money is spent.

Community partnerships provide students with firsthand engagement with positive role models, increasing the odds for student success in school. Providing mentorships and working directly with schools offer community members the intrinsic satisfaction of knowing the positive differences they have made in the lives of children.

Business partners can be a valuable source of information and opportunity for students and staff. Providing real-world experiences—such as internships, apprenticeships, and a better understanding of career and job opportunities—is invaluable to schools as they work with students on future plans. Educators gain important insights into the world and workforce demands, and students gain a better appreciation for the opportunities that may exist after high school graduation. In some cases, schools receive financial support for program implementation, student counseling, and career development.

> Community partnerships provide students with firsthand engagement with positive role models, increasing the odds for student success in school. Providing mentorships and working directly with schools offer community members the intrinsic satisfaction of knowing the positive differences they have made in the lives of children.

DESIGNING COMMUNITY ENGAGEMENT

One of the most significant challenges to community engagement with schools is the ability for those within the school or district to conceptualize exactly what the engagement looks like and, more importantly, what will occur as a result of the engagement. Often, educators instinctively know that community engagement can have a positive impact on their school and rush to garner that engagement, only to find that it is short-lived. The biggest barrier to successful engagement is the lack of conceptualizing what it actually is.

Recently, I was introduced to a concept that I found very exciting: *design thinking*. While I had heard this term before, it was only after a few presentations that I fully understood the power of the design thinking process. Design thinking has been used successfully in industry and business to develop innovative solutions to complex problems. Design thinking emerged out of the work of designers in the fields of product design and engineering.

Design, in its most effective form, is really a process or an action minus a result. Design thinking is an operational title or definition to a process for designing solutions to ambiguous problems or, in other words, a problem-solving protocol. Often, conceptualizing and creating pathways for community engagement can be ambiguous and daunting. The process, similar to other improvement processes, allows for a group to work through the various steps in order to create a desired result. Following are the steps in the design thinking process:

Discovery: Discovery allows participants to gain insights into the needs and the problem being addressed.

Define the problem: The define step is a way to ensure we really understand the problem. By refining and acquiring feedback, the problem can be either refined or revised based on the input.

Create and consider many options: This is the fun, creative part of the design thinking process. This step allows participants to start with a blank slate and create a volume of ideas in both words and pictures.

Refine and evaluate: Any good process for discovery of improved outcomes has an evaluation component. Participants often ask themselves what they like about the ideas created or what they don't like about the ideas. This is also an opportunity to ask questions and seek clarification and suggestions on the work already accomplished. Once this step is finished, go back and begin to refine the solution(s) to the problem. Evaluation without refinement usually ends up killing good ideas.

Note that the steps above may need to be repeated until such time that the correct answers become obvious.

Solve (execute): At some point, however, the group is satisfied that they have created a solution to their problem. Pick the best idea and execute it!

The next page gives you an opportunity to try out the design thinking process for yourself. Think about a challenge in your school that community engagement and support could help alleviate. Maybe it's reading levels or discipline issues. Use the data and improvement plans that exist within your school to determine a challenge that could be enhanced through thoughtful community engagement and use the design thinking model to create an idea that can be implemented.

Discovery: Discuss, interview, research, dig, and find information about the reason a change is needed and why or how community engagement will play a role.

Define the problem: What is the problem to be solved? Define it; get feedback on it; revise it.

Create and consider many options. Generate solutions to the problem. Get creative!

Refine and evaluate: Clarify, refine, and hone in on the solution.

Solve and execute: State the process to be implemented that allows community engagement to address a challenge.

PRINCIPLE #5

Where We Are

Description

The school places a strong focus on building and creating partnerships external to the school. The school recognizes the strengths and talents that exist in its community that influence student learning and development and seeks to use these to strengthen and support the school, students, and their families. The principle also recognizes that the school can be a focal point for communities to come together and engage in capacity building and renewal. The school views itself as an important community asset and has community representatives on the school's governing body. There is a clear recognition from the school that the greater community plays an integral role in the educational success of the school.

Based on the description, discuss and record where you think your school is today as it relates to the principle description.

5.1 Partnerships are made with individuals and organizations in work and community places to take on mentoring roles within student internship and work placement programs. The partnerships also have a role to play within other activities, such as community-based learning projects, guest speaker programs, job shadowing opportunities, apprenticeship opportunities, and tutoring services.

Principle #5.1 Assessment

Use this chart to determine your organization's present level of performance.

Practice/Attribute/ Condition	Discuss/Reflect/Record the Present Status in Your School
Evidence exists of strong, two-way partnerships with business and civic organizations that positively impact student learning.	
A significant community volunteer program is evident in the school.	
The community understands the role it plays in supporting the local school.	
Partnerships have been created and deployed to respond to the unique needs of the students at the school.	

Use the clarifying statement and the best practice description to help you shape your efforts to engage the larger community.

Best Practice Description

The school system as well as the individual schools have developed strong two-way and effective partnerships with numerous business and civic organizations to support the learning needs and outcomes of all students within the district and individual schools. Schools are encouraged to and have developed similar meaningful partnerships that are designed to specifically support their unique or individual needs.

(Continued)

(Continued)

The district and its component schools value the participation of adult community members in the education of its students, and as a result, numerous opportunities to connect learning to the community are evident. Individual needs, such as tutoring, learning and service projects, job shadowing, apprenticeships, guest speaker programs, and other community-based programs are evident in schools.

The district, along with community partners, has focused on the needs of students and can track and measure the results of the efforts. The district and its partners have also developed and implemented an effective process of ensuring the community's understanding of the opportunities available for partnership and the support of student learning outcomes.

Practices to Be Implemented

5.2 Partnerships are made with other learning institutions—other schools, technical colleges, universities, and other training providers in order for students to pursue learning opportunities, build their skills, and achieve learning credentials.

Principle #5.2 Assessment

Use this chart to determine your organization's present level of performance.

Practice/Attribute/Condition	Discuss/Reflect/Record the Present Status in Your School
Effective partnerships with other learning institutions in the community are evident and positively impact student experiences in the school.	

Student experiential learning is supported by strategic business and industry partnerships.

Data and evidence are available to support continued efforts in community partnerships and engagement.

Use the clarifying statement and the best practice description to help you shape your efforts to engage the larger community.

Best Practice Description

The school system and its component schools have created numerous effective partnerships with other learning institutions to support the learning outcomes of all students. Universities, colleges, technical colleges, trade schools, employment training entities, and other institutions partner with the system and its component schools to help in the education of its students.

The district and its component schools value the participation of other learning and training institutions in the education of its students, and as a result, numerous opportunities to connect learning to the community are evident. The district and its partners have focused on the needs of students and can track and measure the results of the efforts.

The district and its partners have also developed and implemented an effective process for ensuring that the community understands the opportunities available for partnership and supports student learning outcomes. The school system has developed a mechanism of continuous data reporting (e.g., dashboards) to allow the community to access the latest data regarding student achievement and system operations.

Practices to Be Implemented

(Continued)

(Continued)

    5.3 Opportunities evolve from the school for creating and implementing adult learning and community development courses to be run within the school building.

Use this chart to determine your organization's present level of performance.

Practice/Attribute/Condition	Discuss/Reflect/Record the Present Status in Your School
Adult learning is part of the core mission of the district and its component schools.	
Adult literacy is supported by the school with assistance from community partners.	
Adult learning opportunities are robust within the school community.	

Use the clarifying statement and the best practice description to help you shape your efforts to engage the larger community.

Best Practice Description

Adult learning is valued in the school system and individual schools and is seen as a part of the core mission of the district. The leadership of the school system, together with community and business partners, seeks adult participation in educational programs with a specific eye toward parents and families of students and has created substantial opportunities for adult learning through community partnerships. The education of parents and families is seen as a direct conduit to improved academic achievement of students.

The school district, its component schools, and partners develop and maintain services to families that support the learning needs and outcomes of all students. School and community-based learning opportunities for adults are valued and are a core component of the school and community culture. The school system and partners have also reached beyond programs to support adult learning to focus on language acquisition and adult literacy among those for whom English is not a first language.

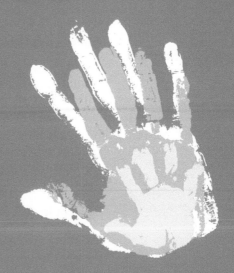

CHAPTER 11

Taking Action and Measuring Success

Congratulations on making it this far! By now, you should have a thorough and working understanding of *Engage Every Family: Five Simple Principles*. But we are not yet finished. At this point, there is a very important question that needs to be asked: So, given this information, what do we do?

What gets measured gets done. This simple sentence summarizes the profound implications of engaging every family; by following the Five Simple Principles, you have evidence that your efforts have made a difference in the learning lives of students and the degree to which families positively impact that learning.

All of us who have dedicated our lives to educating children have a fundamental understanding of this phrase. We know that if there is measurement, the likelihood of our following through is much greater than if we perceive there to be no measurement or expectation of improvement. Educators have been party to countless initiatives in education that seemingly dissipate into thin air, largely because there was never a real performance expectation or way to measure the improvement. Remember, culture eats change for lunch.

> If family engagement is to become a force that improves the learning outcomes of all students, then the degree to which we can plan, execute, and measure our efforts becomes essential.

If family engagement is to become a force that improves the learning outcomes of all students, then the degree to which we can plan, execute, and measure our efforts becomes essential. Short of that, we simply have another idea that sounds good—perhaps even looks good on paper—and has the philosophical support of many, but in the final analysis provides little in shaping more positive outcomes for students.

Let's not let that happen.

Executing strategies that engage every family and have an impact on the learning outcomes of students should be approached with no less attention or vitality than those goals and objectives that are written to produce better results with all students. In a nutshell, family engagement is measurable. Goals and objectives that engage families in the learning lives of their children will produce results if they are well conceived, executed, and measured.

START WITH DATA

> To ensure that our efforts in family engagement result in improved learning outcomes for students, we should first look at the data we generate to determine where our finite amount of time, energy, and resources will provide us with the best results.

Many well-intentioned educators set lofty goals for family engagement. Goals that indicate *more family engagement* or *increased family engagement* may produce little with regard to student achievement. To ensure that our efforts in family engagement result in improved learning outcomes for students, we should first look at the data we generate to determine where our finite amount of time, energy, and resources will provide us with the best results.

Schools have data—in most cases, more data than they can handle. Most of the time the focus is on data that show learning trends. Benchmark testing and formative or collaborative assessments usually lead to a high-stakes test upon which principals, teachers, and schools are judged.

It is impossible to list the data that are available in every school. What can be shared here are categories of data. The following chart is an example of the kind of data available in most schools. It is by no means meant to be an all-inclusive list. Feel free to remove those items that are not germane to your school and add those that are.

Let's get started. The list below is an example of certain kinds of data in schools. It is not comprehensive and may or may not be reflective of the data used in your school. You are encouraged to create a chart that reflects the specific data that are used in your school to promote growth and continuous improvement.

There is no doubt that educators could easily fill this chart, probably more, with the data that are used to promote student achievement and continuous improvement.

General Student Performance Data	College or Career	Formative	Diagnostic	Summative
Attendance data	SAT	Common formative assessments	Reading diagnostic	Certain types of benchmarks
Absenteeism	ACT	Unit tests	Math diagnostics	Simulated state tests for practice
Discipline data	Career certifications	Spelling/ vocabulary tests	Language acquisition diagnostic	Required state test
Disproportionality data	Military testing (ASVAB)	Benchmark tests		Any summative test that is required
RTI data	Training completer certificates	Assessments derived from purchased programs that help track growth		
Physical fitness tests	National Assessment of Educational Progress (NAEP)	Project-based learning assignments		
Graduation rates				
Dropout rates				
Retention rates				
Credit accrual data				

To effectively engage every family, it will be important to start with the data that are most important to your school or district. Take the time to complete this chart so that it accurately reflects what is important to your school.

GOAL STATEMENTS

The broader a goal, the less likely it will be met. The more grandiose a goal, the less likely it will be effective. Here is an example of a goal that might be considered a bit broad and slightly grandiose:

- Every student in the United States will graduate from high school and go to college.

There is no argument that this goal is necessary, but given its broad and grandiose nature, the likelihood of achieving it is fairly slim. (No Child Left Behind might be an example of another goal that simply proved to be impossible to meet.) The same holds true for family engagement. We tend to compartmentalize family engagement goals separately from learning and school improvement goals. It is common to see family engagement goals that look like this:

- Increase family engagement in our school/district
- Improve parent satisfaction rates with our school/district
- Increase membership in our Parent–Teacher Association (PTA)
- Increase attendance of parents to back-to-school night

What do you think of these goals? Are they manageable? Do you think you will see the results of your labors if you try to implement these goals? Most importantly, how will these goals directly address student performance improvements?

I don't believe that there is a single educator alive who has not heard of or does not understand the premise of SMART goals. Most everyone in education has become adept at writing SMART goals. However, on the off chance that you have never heard this term, a SMART goal is one that contains a statement that is *specific, measurable, attainable, result oriented,* and *time bound.* There are other versions of the SMART goal, but in essence, this is it. The idea is to ensure that whatever goal we write is specific in its desire to improve, and it is attainable (at least in our lifetime), measurable, and has a finite end. Quite simple, really.

Let's start by going back to our data chart. For the purposes of this illustration, we'll pick discipline data. (You should choose whatever data are relevant to your situation.) As we drill through these data, we start to see patterns emerging. Perhaps it is the number and types of students who repeat poor choices and behaviors. Perhaps there are grade-level patterns of discipline issues or maybe a higher rate of disciplinary issues in those grades that are transitions (first year of middle school, etc.).

Whatever the case, review and analyze the data that are available. To further illustrate this example, we'll assume the following is true in the discipline data that we have reviewed.

We can glean the following from the data presented above:

- Bullying seems to be an issue in our district middle school(s).
- Bullying escalates as students get older.
- Bullying is a significant problem in Grade 8.

Grade Level	Infraction	Number of Instances
4th grade	Bullying	0
5th grade	Bullying	I
6th grade	Bullying	9
7th grade	Bullying	I7
8th grade	Bullying	29

Of course, real data would most likely tell us more regarding gender, race, economic status, and so forth. At this point, educators will usually begin to look at strategies and solutions to improve the challenge. Perhaps more aggressive disciplinary procedures, student awareness programs, or a campaign to promote an anti-bullying atmosphere might all be considered or implemented.

Now is the time to think about families. What strategies could be employed that would engage families in the issues as well? The first step is to determine where among the Five Simple Principles to look for help, ideas, and goals associated with this issue.

Looking through the lens of the Five Simple Principles, we now can see some different kinds of options for goal statements or action statements that will help move the organization toward the desired improvement.

Assuming the school would like to tackle the problem where it is most acute, designing goal and action statements for bullying in the eighth grade seems in order. Following are some examples:

Principle	Rationale
#1 Create a culture that engages every family.	A problem such as bullying in school can affect any family at any time. Engaging every family is essential to long-term or permanent success.
#2 Communicate effectively and build relationships.	Effectively communicating the behavioral expectations of students in the school is important when faced with a disciplinary problem such as bullying.
#3 Empower every family.	Creating information to help educate families on appropriate behavior or to assist families in working with their children regarding an anti-bullying message will be essential to success.

(Continued)

(Continued)

Principle	Rationale
#4 Engage every family in decision making.	As the school looks for options to deal with bullying or change its disciplinary procedures, family input throughout the process will be critical in shaping policies and procedures. A survey of family knowledge or attitudes about bullying could prove useful.
#5 Engage the greater community.	A plan to use community-based resources to assist with the problem could result in more widespread information dissemination.

Goal Statement: By [month, year], [school name] will decrease instances of bullying in the eighth grade by [specific percentage] through various strategies, including family engagement.

Let's check to see if the goal statement is a SMART goal. The goal statement is

- **s**pecific (bullying decreases)
- **m**easurable (decreased by a specific percentage)
- **a**ttainable (assumes the percentage is reasonable)
- **r**esults oriented (better behaviors, fewer bullying issues)
- **t**ime bound (by a specific month and year)

It meets the criteria for a SMART goal! Now, how can families be inserted into the process? The answer lies in the action steps. Undoubtedly, any school can determine numerous action steps that will help curb this particular problem. With that said, let's focus on those action statements that could engage every family in the solution as well:

Action Step #1: Distribute information and discuss the importance of bullying prevention and maintaining a safe and secure school environment with families. Engaging every family in the topic begins to share the focus of the school and the desire of the school to work with all families to resolve issues and promote healthy, safe school environments (create a culture that engages every family, Principle #1).

Action Step #2: Design recurring communication to families that supports them in discussing the topic of bullying prevention with their children and shares the goals the school has established to reduce the occurrences of bullying. Recurring communication will help to keep the topic in front of families and encourage them to ask questions, respond, and participate in a supportive and trusting manner (communicate effectively and develop relationships, Principle #2).

Action Step #3: Design and implement a series of workshops for families on bullying prevention. Workshops can be created to educate parents in the areas needed and as a way to help the school distribute information about bullying prevention strategies. Workshops can also be designed to help families have crucial conversations with their children about the topic (build family efficacy, Principle #3).

Action Step #4: Once the initial strategies are implemented, survey all eighth-grade parents to determine the effectiveness of the strategies and collect information on what more the school can/should do to reduce instances of bullying. Questions about policies and practices can be asked to garner family feedback. You can also set up a disciplinary committee with families to hear cases of alleged bullying in the school (engage every family in decision making, Principle #4).

Action Step #5: Engage with local civic groups to enhance the anti-bullying message shared with students and their families. Community groups are always looking for ways to support schools. Conceptualize which groups can help and what that help might look like. By doing so, you are engaging the community and sharing accurate information about your school (engage the greater community, Principle #5).

The action steps above take into consideration the logic model that guides the Five Simple Principles. For example, engaging the community first will probably not provide a great deal of benefit, since little has been done to frame the issue for families. In addition to action steps that focus on students, discipline programs, and so forth, these sample family engagement action steps can produce data that will support the school's success with regard to reducing bullying infractions in the eighth grade.

NOW IT'S YOUR TURN

Use the following templates to generate a meaningful family engagement goal. Refer back to the data chart you created at the beginning of this chapter. Choose a data area for focused improvement and follow the process outlined above.

Data selected: _____

Goal statement: _____

Information on disaggregated data: _____

Goal Statement: Is It SMART?

S:

M:

A:

R:

T:

Principle	Rationale
#1 Create a culture that engages every family.	

#2 Communicate effectively and develop relationships.

#3 Build family efficacy.

#4 Engage every family in decision making.

#5 Engage the greater community.

Action steps: Record each of the action steps necessary to achieve the goal.

Action Step I (Principle #I)

Action Step 2 (Principle #2)

Action Step 3 (Principle #3)

Action Step 4 (Principle #4)

Action Step 5 (Principle #5)

At the end of this chapter, there is a sample goal statement and action-planning chart that will help you examine your data to create SMART goals and action steps to provide measurement to achieve your goals. Use whatever data are important to your school and follow the process outlined in this chapter to connect your improvement goals with family engagement.

It's that simple!

ENGAGE EVERY FAMILY: FIVE SIMPLE PRINCIPLES

School/District Principles Implementation Format Plan

Principle (check one)

_____ **A Culture That Engages Every Family**

_____ **Communicate Effectively and Build Relationships**

_____ **Build Family Efficacy**

_____ **Engage Every Family in Decision Making**

_____ **Engage the Greater Community**

Specific standard to be addressed:

Goal statement:

Strategy to be Employed	Who Is Responsible?	What Resources Are Needed?	What Budget Considerations Are There?	Evidence That the Strategy was Successful (Outcome)

Epilogue
Exceeding Expectations

The moment of critical mass, the threshold, the boiling point.

—Malcolm Gladwell (2000, p. 12)

At the onset of this book, I challenged you to take one simple step and begin to embrace the concept of engaging every family in the academic lives of young people. Hopefully, as you worked your way through this book, you have taken numerous steps to engage every family in order to bring about better learning for their children. If you got this far and you are still enthused or at least intrigued, then now is the time to make the changes necessary to engage every family in your school or district. You will not be sorry.

Consider for a moment that there exists a family somewhere in your school district that very much cares about the success of their children, especially as it relates to school. They want what is best for their child and, as we have learned, they seek the opportunity for their children to exceed them in their quality of life. For generations, parents have desired this simple goal, and for many generations, it has come true.

Our society and economy are changing dramatically. For the first time in anyone's memory, our children may not (and in some cases, cannot) exceed us in their quality of life. It is this very notion that strikes fear in many families, and it is because of this notion that we must engage every family.

Family engagement is not optional. It is not an idea that can sit on a shelf until we determine we have the time or interest. It should not be relegated to the end of the list of important reforms we must enact. We are spending a great deal of time, energy, and resources on learning all we can about twenty-first century instruction. We spend millions of professional development dollars searching for those ideas that will bring us success with every student—a success that still eludes us. In all of this, the notion of family engagement, empowering the first and most influential teachers of children, somehow seems to get lost. We simply cannot let that continue to happen.

And so, you have a decision to make. Will you consider the ideas in this book? Will you truthfully examine your beliefs and values and determine what you think about this whole idea of family engagement? Will you

> Family engagement is not optional.

work toward a permanent change in the culture of your school, a change that has at its nucleus the belief that families can be a powerful force in helping us succeed with our students? Will you confront whatever fears you may have about families and work to eliminate them? Will you embrace the simple idea that in order to be successful with every student, we must engage every family? Will you help others to do the same?

> Will you work toward a permanent change in the culture of your school, a change that has at its nucleus the belief that families can be a powerful force in helping us succeed with our students?

TWO HUGE QUESTIONS

While you are thinking about the questions above, let me try and put it another way. Let's limit the questions to two—but two really big, really important questions.

In just about every workshop, I get to a point where I try to support and justify the importance of family engagement and what it will take to be successful with every family. You will recall that in Chapter 1, I told the story of *Yagottawanna*. The premise of *Yagottawanna* is simple: Your personal desire to make a difficult change (or choice or decision) starts with the very simple notion that the change (choice, decision) is something you desire. If it isn't, then the likelihood of success isn't very high.

So, to encapsulate this idea, let me now ask you two very important questions. The questions might seem simple, but after a few moments of consideration, they could easily become more daunting. There is space below to provide answers or to jot notes about your answers to each question.

Question 1: What Do You Want?

For purposes of this exercise, limit your thinking to your professional career as an educator or, if you are still in school or just starting out, think about what a satisfying career in education would look like. What do you want as an educator?

_____

_____

_____

_____

_____

_____

(Continued)

(Continued)

What did you write? Did you write about your personal and professional satisfaction? Did you write about being happy in your chosen field? Did you list specific items, such as "all children will be successful in my classroom"? Did you state your responses in the form of what you did not want—"I don't want students who misbehave"? The beauty of this question is that there are no wrong answers. Whatever you think is exactly right. Now let's move to Question 2.

Question 2: Considering Your Response(s) to Question 1, What Are You Willing to Do to Get What You Want?

Regardless of what you wrote as responses to Question 1, you now have to determine what you are willing to do to get what you said you wanted. What are you willing to do either personally or professionally to attain what you believe is important to you?

Only you can answer these questions. But here is what I know: Every educator I have had the privilege of coming into contact with wants to be successful. They gravitate toward those ideas that are proven to be successful, and they work incredibly hard at helping every one of their students learn. I see evidence of this every day. It is this belief that encourages me to be hopeful that more and more educators will embrace the important concept of family engagement.

If you follow the processes outlined in this book, embrace the philosophy, believe that every family desperately wants to be engaged but may not know how or have the opportunity to do so, and believe that family engagement leads to student success, then you will hit the critical mass—the tipping point of family engagement.

What did we do in school today? We learned that the power of family engagement will change the trajectory of school improvement. We learned that with an examination of our values and beliefs and a simple process, we can truly begin to engage every family and leverage success for every student . . . *every* student.

And yes, there is homework.

References

Adger, C., & Locke, J. (2000). *Broadening the base: School/community partnerships serving language minority students at risk.* (Educational Practice Rep. No. 6). Santa Cruz, CA: Center for Research on Education, Diversity and Excellence.

Auerbach, S. (2010). Beyond coffee with the principal: Toward leadership for authentic school–family partnerships. *Journal of School Leadership, 20*(6), 728–757.

Baars, S., Shaw, B., Mulcahy, E., & Menzies, L. (2018). *School cultures and practices: Supporting the attainment of disadvantaged pupils.* Research Report. Social Science in Government. Department of Education. Retrieved December 21, 2019 from https://www.researchgate.net/profile/Loic_Menzies/publication/330812071_School_cultures_and_practices_supporting_the_attainment_of_disadvantaged_pupils_A_qualitative_comparison_of_London_and_non London_schools_Research_Report/links/5c54d2ea92851c22a3a25d20/School-cultures-and-practices-supporting-the-attainment-of-disadvantaged-pupils-A-qualitative-comparison-of-London-and-non-London-schools-Research-Report.pdf

Baker, A. J. (2000). Making the promise of parent involvement a reality. *The High School Magazine, 7*(15), 15–17.

Bandura, A. (1997). *Self-efficacy: The exercise of control.* New York, NY: Freeman.

Bauch, J. P. (1989). The transparent school model. *Educational Leadership, 47*(2), 32–34.

Bauch, P. A., & Goldring, E. B. (1995). Parent involvement and school responsiveness: Facilitating the home–school connection in schools of choice. *Educational Evaluation and Policy Analysis, 17*(1), 1–21.

Bean, R. A., Bush, K. R., McKenry, P. C., & Wilson, S. M. (2003). The impact of parental support, behavioral control and psychological control on the academic achievement and self-esteem of African American and European American adolescents. *Journal of Adolescent Research, 18*(5), 523–541.

Bhargava, S., & Witherspoon, D. (2015). Parental involvement across middle and high school: Exploring contributions of individual and neighborhood characteristics. *Journal of Youth and Adolescence, 44*(9), 1702–1719.

Blank, M., Melaville, A., & Shah, B. P. (2003). *Making the difference: Research and practice in community schools.* Washington, DC: Coalition for Community Schools. Retrieved from http://www.communityschools.org/CCSFullReport.pdf

Bolman, L. G., & Deal, T. E. (2002). *Reframing the path to school leadership.* Thousand Oaks, CA: Corwin.

Botha, J., & Kourkoutas, E. (2015). A community of practice as an inclusive model to support children with social, emotional and behavioural difficulties in school contexts. *International Journal of Inclusive Education, 20*(7), 784–799.

Bouffard, S. M., Westmoreland, H., O'Carroll, K., & Little, P. M. (2011). Engaging families in out-of-school time programs. In H. Kreider & H. Westmoreland (Eds.), *Promising practices for family engagement in out-of-school time* (pp. 3–19). Charlotte, NC: Information Age Publishing.

Boyd, V. (1992). *School context: Bridge or barrier to change?* Austin, TX: Southwest Educational Development Laboratory.

Brinckerhoff, J., & Vincent, L. (1986). Increasing parental decision-making at their child's individualized educational program meeting. *Journal of the Division for Early Childhood, 11*(1), 46–58.

Bryk, A. S. (2010). Organizing schools for improvement. *Phi Delta Kappan, 91*(7), 23–30. https://doi.org/10.1177/003172171009100705

Bryk, A. S., & Schneider, B. (2002). *Trust in schools: A core resource for improvement.* New York, NY: Russell Sage Foundation.

Caplan, J. G. (2000). *Building strong family–school partnerships to support high student achievement.* Arlington, VA: Educational Research Service.

Chavkin, N. F. (2017). *Family engagement with schools.* New York, NY: Oxford University.

Cherng, H-Y. S. (2016). Is all classroom conduct equal? Teacher contact with parents of racial/ethnic minority and immigrant adolescents. *Teachers College Record, 118*(11), 1–32.

Christenson, S. L., & Sheridan, S. M. (2001). *School and families: Creating essential connections for learning.* New York, NY: The Guilford Press.

Claridge, T. (2004). *Social capital and natural resource management: An important role for social capital?* Unpublished Thesis, University of Queensland, Brisbane, Australia.

Clark-Loque, A. R., Lindsey, R. B., Quezada, R. L., & Jew, C. L. (2020). *Equity partnerships: A culturally proficient guide to family, school and community engagement.* Thousand Oaks, CA: Corwin.

Coleman, J. S. (1985). Schools and the communities they serve. *Phi Delta Kappan, 66*, 527–532.

Commissioner's Parent Advisory Council. (2007). *The missing piece of the proficiency puzzle.* Final Report to the Kentucky Department of Education. Pritchard Committee for Academic Excellence.

Constantino, S. M. (2003). *Engaging all families: Creating a positive school culture by putting research into practice.* Lanham, MD: Rowman and Littlefield.

Cross, F. L, Marchand, A. D., Medina, M., Villafuerte, A., & Rivas-Drake, D. (2019). Academic socialization, parental educational expectations, and academic self-efficacy among Latino adolescents. *Psychology in the Schools, 56*(4), 483–496.

Crozier, G., & Davies, J. (2007). Hard to reach parents or hard to reach schools? A discussion of home–school relations, with particular reference to Bangladeshi and Pakistani parents. *British Educational Research Journal, 33*(3), 295–313.

Cullingford, C., & Morrison, M. (1999). Relationships between parents and schools: A case study. *Educational Review, 51*(3), 1, 253–262.

Deal, T. E. (1993). The culture of schools. In M. Sashkin & H. J. Walberg (Eds.), *Educational leadership and school culture*. Berkeley, CA: McCutchan Publishing.

Deal, T. E., & Peterson, K. D. (1990). *The principal's role in shaping school culture*. Washington, DC: Office of Educational Research and Improvement.

Deal, T. E., & Peterson, K. D. (1999). *Shaping school culture: The heart of leadership*. San Francisco, CA: Jossey-Bass.

DeLaney, R. (1997, March). *Parent participation in educational decision making: A high stakes procedure*. Paper presented at the annual meeting of the American Educational Research Association, Chicago, IL.

DeMatthews, D. (2018). School leadership, social capital, and community engagement: A case study of an elementary school in Ciudad Juarez, Mexico. *School Community Journal, 28*(1), 167–194.

Derubetis, D., & Yanok, J. (1989). Comparative study of parental participation in regular and special education programs. *Exceptional Children, 56*, 195–200.

Deslandes, R., Royer, E., Potvisn, P., & Leclere, D. (1999). Patterns of home and school partnership for general and special education students at the secondary level. *Exceptional Children, 65*, 496–506.

DeSpain, S. N., Conderman, G., & Gerzel-Short, L. (2018). Fostering family engagement in middle and secondary schools. *The Clearing House, 91*(6), 236–242.

Doucet, F. (2011). Parent involvement as a ritual system. *Anthropology and Education Quarterly, 42*(4), 404–421.

Drake, D. D. (2000). Parents and families as partners in the education process: Collaboration for the success of students in public schools. *ERS Spectrum*, 34–35.

Eccles, J. S., & Harold, R. D. (1994, November). Family involvement in children's and adolescents' schooling. In *Family–school links: How do they affect educational outcomes?* Symposium conducted at Pennsylvania State University.

Ehlen, C. G. J. M., van der Klink, M. R., & Boshuizen, H. P. A. (2015). Unravelling the social dynamics of an industry–school partnership: Social capital as perspective for co-creation. *Studies in Continuing Education, 38*(1), 61–85. doi: 10.1080/0158037X.2015.1030610

Epstein, J. L., & Becker, H. J. (1982). Teacher practices of parent involvement: Problems and possibilities. *Elementary School Journal, 83*, 103–113.

Epstein, J. L., & Salinas, K. C. (2004). Partnering with families and communities. *Educational Leadership, 61*(8), 12–18.

Epstein, J. L., & Sanders, M. G. (2006). Prospects for change: Preparing educators for school, family, and community partnerships. *Peabody Journal of Education, 81*(2), 81–120.

Epstein, J. L., Sanders, M. G., Sheldon, S. B., Simon, B. S., Salinas, K. C., Jansorn, N. R., . . . Williams, K. J. (2009). *School, family, and community partnerships: Your handbook for action* (3rd ed.). Thousand Oaks, CA: Corwin.

Epstein, J., Sanders, M., Simon, B., Salinas, K., Jansorn, N., & Voorhis, F. (2002). *School, family and community partnerships: Your handbook for action.* Thousand Oaks, CA: Corwin.

Epstein, J. L., & Sheldon, S. B. (2002). Present and accounted for: Improving student attendance through family and community involvement. *Journal of Educational Research, 95*, 308–318.

Espinosa, L. M. (1995). *Hispanic parent involvement in early childhood programs.* ERIC Clearinghouse on Elementary and Early Childhood Education. Retrieved from ERICDigests.org (ED382412).

Finders, M., & Lewis, C. (1994). Why some parents don't come to school. *Educating for Diversity, 51*(8), 50–54. Available at http://www.ascd.org/publications/educational-leadership/may94/vol51/num08/Why-Some-Parents-Don%27t-Come-to-School.aspx

Flamboyan Foundation. (2019). *HS series: 5 barriers to family engagement in high school.* http://flamboyanfoundation.org/ourstories/barriers-to-family-engagement-in-high-school/

Flanagan, A., & Grissmer, D. (2002). The role of federal resources in closing the achievement gap. In J. E. Chubb & T. Loveless (Eds.), *Bridging the achievement gap* (pp. 199–225). Washington, DC: Brookings Institute.

Fullan, M. (2001). *Leading in a culture of change.* San Francisco, CA: Jossey-Bass.

Gaitan, C. D. (2012). Culture, literacy, and power in family–community–school relationships. *Theory into Practice, 51*(4), 305–311.

Garcia, J. (2019). Sustaining indigenous family and community engagement. In S. B. Sheldon and T. A. Turner-Vorbeck (Eds.), *Family, school, and community relationships in education* (pp. 71–90). Hoboken, NJ: John Wiley and Sons.

Geertz, C. (1973). *The interpretation of cultures.* New York, NY: Basic Books.

Gladwell, M. (2000). *The tipping point.* New York, NY: Little, Brown.

Glenn, H. S., & Nelsen, J. (1988). *Raising self-reliant children in a self-indulgent world.* Roseville, CA: Prima Publishing.

Gonder, P. O. (1994). Improving school climate & culture. In D. L. Hymes (Ed.), *AASA critical issues series.* Retrieved from http://files.eric.ed.gov/fulltext/ED371485.pdf

Gonzalez-Mena, J. (2014). *50 strategies for communicating and working with diverse families* (3rd ed.). Boston, MA: Pearson.

Gottfried, M. A., & Gee, K. A. (2017). Identifying the determinants of chronic absenteeism: A bioecological systems approach. *Teachers College Record, 119*(7).

Grant, K. B., & Ray, J. A. (2019). *Home, school, and community collaboration: Culturally responsive family engagement* (4th ed.). Thousand Oaks, CA: SAGE.

Gretz, P. (2003). School and community partnerships: Cultivating friends (High school ed.). *Principal Leadership, 3*, 32–40.

Hallgarten, J. (2000). *Parents exist, ok!?* Norfolk, UK: Biddles.

Halsey, P. A. (2005). Parent involvement in junior high schools: A failure to communicate. *American Secondary Education, 34*(1), 57–69.

Harris, A. (2009). *Distributed leadership: Different perspectives.* Amsterdam, the Netherlands: Springer.

Harvard Family Research Project. (2013). *Tips for administrators, teachers, and families: How to share data effectively.* Cambridge, MA: Harvard Family Research Project. Retrieved from http://www.hfrp.org/publications-resources/browse-our-publications/tips-for-administrators-teachers-and-families-how-to-share-data-effectively

Haviland, W. A. (1975). *Cultural anthropology* (3rd. ed.). New York, NY: Holt, Rhinehart & Winston.

Havinghurst, R. J. (1972). *Developmental tasks and education.* New York, NY: McKay.

Henderson, A. T., Mapp, K. L., Johnson, V. R., & Davies, D. (2007). *Beyond the bake sale: The essential guide to family–school partnerships.* New York, NY: The New Press.

Hill, N. E., & Tyson, D. F. (2009). Parental involvement in middle school: A meta-analytic assessment of the strategies that promote achievement. *Developmental Psychology, 45*(3), 740–763. doi: 10.1037/a/0015362

Hoover-Dempsey, K. V., & Sandler, H. (1997). Why do parents become involved in their children's education? *Review of Educational Research, 67*(1), 3–42.

Hoover-Dempsey, K. V., Walker, J. M. T., & Sandler, H. M. (2005). Parents' motivations for involvement in their children's education. In E. N. Patrikakou, R. P. Weisberg, S. Redding, & H. J. Walberg (Eds.), *School–family partnerships for children's success* (pp. 40–56). New York, NY: Teachers College Press.

Hornby, G. (2011). Barriers to parent involvement in education: An exploratory model. *Educational Review, 63*(1), 37–52.

Inoa, R. (2017). Parental involvement among middle-income Latino parents living in a middle-class community. *Hispanic Journal of Behavioral Sciences, 39*(3), 316–335. Available at https://doi.org/10.1177/0739986317714200

Jensen, K. L., & Minke, K. M. (2017). Engaging families at the secondary level: An underused resource for student success. *School Community Journal, 27*(2), 167–191.

Kania, J., & Kramer, M. (2011, Winter). Collective impact. *Stanford Social Innovation Review.* Retrieved from https://ssir.org/articles/entry/collective_impact

Kena, G., Aud, S., Johnson, F., Wang, X., Zhang, J., Rathbun, A., . . . Kristapovich, P. (2014). *The condition of education 2014* (NCES 2014-083). Washington, DC: U.S. Department of Education, National Center for Education Statistics. Retrieved from http://nces.ed.gov/pubsearch

Kirwan Institute for the Study of Race and Ethnicity. (2019). *Understanding implicit bias.* Retrieved from http://kirwaninstitute.osu.edu/research/understanding-implicit-bias/

Kotter, J. P., & Cohen, D. S. (2002). *The heart of change.* Boston, MA: Harvard Business School Press.

Kretzmann, J. P., & McKnight, J. L. (1993). *Building communities from the inside out: A path toward finding and mobilizing a community's assets.* Evanston, IL: Institute for Policy Research.

Lake Forest College. (2010). *History of the effective schools movement.* Retrieved from https://www .lakeforest.edu/library/archives/effective-schools/HistoryofEffectiveSchools.php

Lareau, A. (1987). Social class differences in family–school relationships: The importance of cultural capital. *Sociology of Education, 60,* 73–85.

Learning Policy Institute. (2017). *Community schools as an effective school improvement strategy: A review of the evidence.* Retrieved from https://learningpolicyinstitute.org/product/ community-schools-effective-school-improvement-brief

Lehr, C. A., Hansen, A., Sinclair, M. F., & Christenson, L. L. (2003). Moving beyond dropout towards school completion: An integrative review of data-based interventions. *School Psychology Review, 32*(3), 342–364.

Lenhoff, S. W., & Pogodzinski, B. (2018). School organizational effectiveness and chronic absenteeism: Implications for accountability. *Journal of Education for Students Placed at Risk, 23*(1–2), 153–169.

Liontos, L. (1992). *At-risk families and schools becoming partners.* ERIC Clearinghouse of Educational Management. Retrieved from EricDIGEST (ED242055).

Livingtree, Inc. (2019). *Can technology improve family engagement?* Retrieved from http://learn .livingtree.com/can-technology-improve-family-engagement/

Love, H. R., Zagona, A. L., Kurth, J. A., & Miller, A. L. (2017). Parents' experiences in educational decision making for children and youth with disabilities. *Inclusion, 5*(3), 158–172.

Mac Iver, M. A., Sheldon, S., Epstein, J., Rice, E., Mac Iver, D., & Simmons, A. (2018). Engaging families in the high school transition: Initial findings from a continuous improvement initiative. *School Community Journal, 28*(1), 37–66.

Malen, B., & Ogawa, R. T. (1988). Professional–patron influence on site-based governance councils: A confounding case study. *Educational Evaluation and Policy Analysis, 10,* 251–270.

Mapp, K. L. (2003). Having their say: Parents describe why and how they are engaged in their children's learning. *The School Community Journal, 13*(1), 35–64.

Mapp, K. L., Carver, I., & Lander, J. (2017). *Powerful partnerships: A teacher's guide to engaging families for student success.* New York, NY: Scholastic.

Mapp, K. L., & Kuttner, P. J. (2013). *Partners in education: A dual capacity-building framework for building family school partnerships.* Austin, TX: SEDL.

Markow, D., Macia, L., & Lee, H. (2013). *The Metlife survey of the American teacher: Challenges for school leaders.* New York, NY: Metlife.

McBride, B. (1991). Preservice teachers' attitudes toward parental involvement. *Teacher Education Quarterly, 18,* 59–67.

McGill, R. K., Hughes, D., Alicea, S., & Way, N. (2012). Academic adjustment across middle school: The role of public regard and parenting. *Developmental Psychology, 48*(4), 1003–1018. doi: 10.1037/a0026006

McKnight, K., Venkateswaran, N., Laird, J., Robles, J., & Shalev, T. (2017). Mindset shifts and parent teacher home visits. *RTI International*. Retrieved from http://www.pthvp.org/wp-content/uploads/2018/12/171030-MindsetShiftsandPTHVReportFINAL.pdf

Meador, D. (2018). Transform your school with collaborative decision making. *ThoughtCo*. Retrieved from thoughtco.com/transforming-your-school-collaborative-decision-making-4063907

National Assessment of Educational Progress (NAEP). (2019). *Results from the 2019 mathematics and reading assessments*. Retrieved from https://www.nationsreportcard.gov/mathematics/supportive_files/2019_infographic.pdf

National Association for Family, School, and Community Engagement (NAFSCE). (2019). *NAFSCE's policy agenda*. Retrieved from https://nafsce.org/page/PolicyAgenda

National Association of Secondary School Principals. (2004). *Breaking ranks II: Strategies for leading high school reform*. Reston, VA: Author.

National Association of Secondary School Principals. (2006). *Breaking ranks in the middle*. Reston, VA: Author.

National Equity Project. (2019). *Core beliefs*. Retrieved from https://nationalequityproject.org/about/core-beliefs

National Middle School Association/Association for Middle Level Education. (2010). *This we believe: Keys to educating young adolescents*. Columbus, OH: Author.

National Network of Partnership Schools. (n.d.). *Epstein's six types of parent involvement*. Retrieved from http://www.csos.jhu.edu/p2000/sixtypes.htm

National PTA. (2000). *Building successful partnerships*. Bloomington, IN: National Education Service.

Parsons, B. A., & Schmitz, C. C. (1999). *Everything you wanted to know about logic models but were afraid to ask*. Paper presented at the annual meeting of the American Evaluation Association, Orlando, FL.

Patterson, J. L., Purkey, S. C., & Parker, J. V. (1986). *Productive school systems for a nonrational world*. Alexandria, VA: Association for Supervision and Curriculum Development.

Patterson, K., Grenny, J., McMillan, R., & Switzler, A. (2012). *Crucial conversations: Tools for talking when stakes are high* (2nd ed.). New York, NY: McGraw-Hill.

Pew Research Center. (2019). *Technology adoption*. Retrieved from https://www.pewresearch.org/topics/technology-adoption/

Phi Delta Kappa. (2014, September). *Kappan*. Available at https://pdkpoll.org/assets/downloads/2014pdkpoll46.pdf

Phi Delta Kappa International. (2019). *PDK poll of the public's attitudes toward the public schools*. Retrieved from https://pdkpoll.org/results

Phi Delta Kappan. (2017). *Why I'm not involved: Parental involvement from a parent's perspective*. Retrieved from https://kappanonline.org/choi-why-im-not-involved-parental-involvement-parents-perspective/

Pink, D. (2009). *Drive: The surprising truth about what motivates us*. New York, NY: Riverhead.

Price, H. B. (2008). *Mobilizing the community to help students succeed*. Alexandria, VA: ASCD.

Pritchard Committee for Academic Excellence. (2015). *About the Governor's Commonwealth Institute for Parent Leadership*. Retrieved from https://www.americaspromise.org/resource/commonwealth-institute-parent-leadership

Rodriguez, R. J., Blatz, E. T., & Elbaum B. (2014). Parents' views of schools' involvement efforts. *Exceptional Children, 81*(1), 79–95.

Sanders, M. G., & Harvey, A. (2002). Beyond the school walls: A case study of principal leadership for school–community collaboration. *Teachers College Record, 104*(7), 1345–1368.

Schein, E. H. (2010). *Organizational culture and leadership* (4th ed.). San Francisco, CA: Jossey-Bass.

Scholastic FACE (n.d.). *District family engagement policy toolkit*. New York, NY: Scholastic.

Seitsinger, A. M. (2019). Examining the effect of family engagement on middle and high school students' academic achievement and adjustment. In S. B. Sheldon & T. A. Turner-Vorbeck (Eds.), *Family, school, and community relationships in education* (pp. 163–182). Hoboken, NJ: John Wiley & Sons.

Seitsinger, A. M., & Brand, S. (2012). The school–family context for adolescent development during high school. In T. Patelis (Ed.), *Research studies, literature reviews and perspectives in psychological science* (pp. 49–56). Athens, Greece: Athens Institute for Education and Research.

Shafer, L. (2018, July 23). What makes a good school culture? *Harvard Graduate School of Education*. Retrieved from https://www.gse.harvard.edu/news/uk/18/07/what-makes-good-school-culture

Shapiro, J. P., & Stefkovish, J. A. (2016). *Ethical leadership and decision making in education*. New York, NY: Routledge. https://doi.org/10.4324/9781315773339

Sheldon, S. B., & Jung, S. B. (2018, November). Student outcomes and parent teacher home visits. *Johns Hopkins School of Education*. Retrieved from http://www.pthvp.org/wp-content/uploads/2018/12/18-11-30-Student-Outcomes-and-PTHV-Report-FINAL.pdf

Simon, B. S. (2004). High school outreach and family involvement. *Social Psychology of Education, 7*, 185–209.

Sims, S. J., & Sims, R. R. (2004). *Managing school system change: Charting a course for renewal*. Greenwich, CT: Information Age Publishing.

Smrekar, C., & Cohen-Vogel, L. (2001). The voices of parents: Rethinking the intersection of family and school. *Peabody Journal of Education, 76*(2), 75–100.

Spera, C. (2005). A review of the relationship among parenting practices, parenting styles, and adolescent school achievement. *Educational Psychology Review, 17*(2), 125–146.

Stilwell, A., & Ferguson, D. (n.d.). [*Did you know . . .*] *About four ways to increase parental efficacy?* National Institute for Urban School Improvement. Retrieved from http://www.niusi.org/pdf/parent_efficacy.pdf?v_document_name=Increase%20Parental%20Efficacy

Stolp, S., & Smith, S. C. (1994, January). School culture and climate: The role of the leader. *OSSC Bulletin*. Eugene: Oregon School Study Council.

Suizzo, M. A., Jackson, K. M., Pahlke, E., McClain, S., Marroquin, Y. Blondeau, L. A., & Hong, K. J. (2016). Parents' school satisfaction and academic socialization predict adolescents' autonomous motivation. *Journal of Adolescent Research, 31*(3), 343–374.

University of Washington. (2017, July 24). From volunteer to decision-maker: How parents can play a greater role in schools. *ScienceDaily*. Retrieved from http://www.sciencedaily.com/releases/2017/07/170724162124.htm

Valli, L., Stefanski, A., & Jacobson, R. (2018). School–community partnership models: Implication for leadership. *International Journal of Leadership in Education, 21*(1), 31–49.

Voydanoff, P. (2004). Work, community, and parenting resources as predictors of adolescent problems and grades. *Journal of Adolescent Relations, 12*(2), 155–173.

Wallace, C. (2017). *Parent/guardian perspectives on chronic absenteeism and the factors that influence decisions to send their children to school*. Unpublished Doctoral Dissertation, University of Pittsburgh.

Wallace, M. (2013). High school teachers and African American parents: A (not so) collaborative effort to increase student success. *The High School Journal, 96*, 195–208.

Waller, W. (1932). *The sociology of teaching*. New York, NY: Wiley.

Wang, M., Hill, N. E., & Hofkens, T. (2014). Parental involvement and African American and European American adolescents' academic, behavioral, and emotional development in secondary school. *Child Development, 85*(6), 2151–2168. doi: 10.1111/cdev.12284

Wehlage, G., Smith, G., & Lipman, P. (1992, Spring). Restructuring urban schools: The new futures experience. *American Educational Research Journal, 29*(1), 51–93.

Wilkerson, D., & Kim, H-W. (2010). "We have a lot of sleeping parents": Comparing inner-city and suburban high school teachers' experiences with parent involvement. *Advances in Social Work, 11*(2), 144–157.

Zacarian, D. (2011). *Transforming schools for English learners: A comprehensive framework for school leaders*. Thousand Oaks, CA: Corwin.

Index

Leadership That Makes an Impact

MICHAEL FULLAN & MARY JEAN GALLAGHER

With the goal of transforming the culture of learning to develop greater equity, excellence, and student well-being, this book will help you liberate the system and maintain focus.

PETER M. DEWITT

This step-by-step how-to guide presents the six driving forces of instructional leadership within a multistage model for implementation, delivering lasting improvement through small collaborative changes.

BRYAN GOODWIN

If you've ever wondered anything, really—just out of curiosity—then you have what it takes to lead your school to restored curiosity and your students to well-being and success.

JOHN HATTIE & RAYMOND L. SMITH

Based on the most current Visible Learning® research with contributions from educational thought leaders around the world, this book includes practical ideas for leaders to implement high-impact strategies to strengthen entire school cultures and advocate for all students.

DAVIS CAMPBELL & MICHAEL FULLAN

The model outlined in this book develops a systems approach to governing local schools collaboratively to become exemplars of highly effective decision-making, leadership, and action.

MICHAEL FULLAN, JOANNE QUINN, & JOANNE MCEACHEN

The comprehensive strategy of deep learning incorporates practical tools and processes to engage educational stakeholders in new partnerships, mobilize whole-system change, and transform learning for all students.

JOANNE QUINN, JOANNE MCEACHEN, MICHAEL FULLAN, MAG GARDNER, & MAX DRUMMY

Dive into deep learning with this hands-on guide to creating learning experiences that give purpose, unleash student potential, and transform not only learning, but life itself.

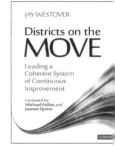

JAY WESTOVER

The transformative framework outlined in this book creates a districtwide approach for changing the culture of learning and creating a coherent system of continuous improvement.

To order your copies, visit **corwin.com/leadership**

**ANTHONY KIM,
EARA MASCARENAZ,
& KAWAI LAI**

This guide provides battle-tested practices to help leaders build better habits for team learning, meetings, and projects, to achieve a more responsive, innovative organization.

EVAN ROBB

Build the foundations of effective leadership despite daily distractions. Learn how to intentionally use ten-minute opportunities to consider and execute your vision.

**AMY TEPPER &
PATRICK FLYNN**

Nineteen strategies help leaders, coaches, and teachers improve their ability to identify desired outcomes, recognize learning in action, collect relevant evidence, and develop effective feedback.

JULIE M. WILSON

Learn to make sense of challenging change journeys and accelerate implementation with this practical framework that includes human-centered tools, resources, and mini case studies.

GRANT LICHTMAN

Our rapidly evolving world is dramatically impacting how we view schools. Thrive shows educators how they can help their schools not only survive but thrive during rapid change.

ERIC SHENINGER

The future-forward framework in this book prepares leaders to harness the power of innovative ideas and digital strategies to create relevant, engaging, and intuitive school cultures.

**CHRISTINE MASON,
PAUL LIABENOW, &
MELISSA PATSCHKE**

Envision and enact transformative change with an iterative visioning process, thought-provoking vignettes, case studies from exemplary schools, key strategies and tools, and practical implementation ideas.

**KIRSTEN RICHERT,
JEFFREY IKLER, &
MARGARET ZACCHEI**

Shifting empowers educational change leaders to proactively and coherently navigate complex, unprecedented change in schools and establish a school culture in which changemakers can thrive.